CONTENTS

CHAPTER 3: **Narration: Telling Stories of Culture and Customs**   **59**

CHAPTER 4: Description: Showing Details of People, Places, and Things   113

CHAPTER 5: Exemplification: Discovering Culture Through Examples   179

CHAPTER 6: **Comparison and Contrast:
Exploring Similarities and Differences Across Cultures** **241**

CHAPTER 7: Process Analysis: Cultural Rituals   297

CHAPTER 8: Classification and Division: Categorizing and Analyzing Cultural Features   361

CHAPTER 9: Cause and Effect: Exploring Causal Connections in Society and Culture   429

CHAPTER 10: Definition: Identifying Meanings in Different Cultures   491

CHAPTER 13: Using Combined Patterns 707

An up-to-the-minute report from the Arctic underscores
the seriousness of irreversible climate changes resulting from
the buildup of carbon dioxide in the earth's atmosphere.

Cultures past and present differ greatly in their ideas about
what is edible.

Her reconstructive surgery prompts this writer to explore her attitudes about
"beauty" as well as others' intolerance toward those who look different.

The founder of Planned Parenthood describes how she became an advocate
for providing birth control to women.

The author assumes the guise of a social planner to pose a shocking
solution to his country's widespread poverty.

THEMATIC CONTENTS

Because each reading generally addresses more than one single theme, certain selections are listed under more than one thematic topic.

Family Ties

Perspectives on Language

Issues Past and Present

Ethical Problems

PREFACE

 ## HOW IS *PATTERNS ACROSS CULTURES* DIFFERENT?

Our world is getting smaller, while our classrooms are becoming increasingly diverse. An understanding of other cultures and countries has never been more important. As authors of nearly thirty texts, we have witnessed these trends and considered their implications for college education. We saw a need for a text that does not merely touch on multiculturalism, but immerses the reader in it; that encourages students to actively engage with cultural issues and discover commonalities between their own experiences and those of others who may initially seem radically different; and that examines not only the cultures of other countries but also the diverse perspectives within American culture. In addition, we have listened carefully to the many requests from composition instructors for a text with fresh, new readings—and other forms of rhetoric, especially visuals—that would not only complement their rhetorical instruction but also excite and challenge their students in the process. *Patterns Across Cultures* is that text.

FEATURES OF *PATTERNS ACROSS CULTURES*

- **Eighty selections representing thirty-one countries, numerous ethnic groups, and a blend of new and familiar voices.** The selections were carefully chosen to provide both broad cultural perspectives and clear models of the rhetorical patterns. Students will read classic authors (including Frederick Douglass, George Orwell, Jessica Mitford, Simone de Beauvoir, and Martin Luther King, Jr.) alongside well-known contemporary writers (such as Amy Tan, Frank McCourt, Maya Angelou, Judith Ortiz Cofer, N. Scott Momaday, Jamaica Kincaid, and Lucy Grealy) and writers they are not likely to have encountered before (Tepilit Ole Saitoti, Natsume Soseki, Luisa Valenzuela, Machado de Assis, Fatima Mernissi, Gloria Anzaldúa, Immaculée Ilibagiza, and Nawal El Saadawi, among others), some of whom are making their first-ever appearance in a college text.
- **Emphasis on visual rhetoric.** Forty-five visual texts related to the essay topics and the rhetorical patterns allow students to hone their visual-literacy skills while gaining new perspectives on how to use rhetorical strategies. An overview in Chapter 1 provides guidance on interpreting and evaluating images, along

with brief sample analyses of a photo and a cartoon from the text that demonstrate how to put these concepts into practice. Students can then sharpen their visual-literacy skills by reviewing twenty-four full-color images (divided into three portfolios) and twenty-one black-and-white images embedded within particular selections. Accompanying prompts invite students to consider how these visuals illuminate the readings.

- **Organization based on the rhetorical patterns.** Chapters 3–12 explain and illustrate the basic rhetorical patterns that students will need to master in college writing: *narration, description, exemplification, comparison and contrast, process analysis, classification and division, cause and effect, definition,* and *argument.* An *Other Patterns* prompt for each selection in the text asks students to consider how the author used additional patterns to support the primary one, while the ways authors combine patterns to achieve specific purposes is the focus of Chapter 13. Chapters 5, 8, and 11 also feature real-life applications of patterns in the form of a job application letter, a résumé, and a letter of complaint.

- **Sample student essays for all rhetorical patterns.** Twelve student essays, one in each pattern chapter, model writing in that particular pattern. Accompanying *Strategies for Writing* detail key aspects of the essays that students may apply to their own writing.

- **Variety of genres.** Among the professional selections are eight short works of fiction and one poem, which enable students to consider the rhetorical patterns at work in different contexts.

- **Introductory chapter with detailed coverage of the reading and writing processes.** Chapter 1 introduces the skills students need to be successful college writers, including critical reading and writing; annotating and summarizing a text; keeping a journal; and analyzing an author's meaning, technique, and style. This chapter also includes step-by-step instructions on the writing process, including prewriting and planning strategies, invention techniques, crafting the thesis statement, outlining, drafting, and revising.

- **Early chapter on research and documentation skills.** Chapter 2 covers important research skills, including finding, using, and documenting print and Internet sources; note taking; integrating source material; and avoiding plagiarism. A discussion of MLA documentation is illustrated with a sample MLA-format student research paper.

- **Innovative chapter on problem solving.** Chapter 11 presents a collection of essays in which the featured authors grapple with a variety of social, cultural, and personal dilemmas, showing how "problem solving" can be used as a rhetorical strategy.

- **Argument chapter that examines timely issues.** Chapter 12 presents opposing sides of three contentious contemporary issues—the use of animals in genetics research, the use of torture in fighting terrorism, and the presence of steroids in sports—via paired reading selections.

- **Extensive pedagogy to support the selections.** Pedagogy for all selections in the text helps students understand the rhetorical strategies that good writers use.

All of the pattern chapters open with a detailed introduction containing examples that illustrate how the pattern may be used. Each selection is introduced with a headnote that provides context for the selection and a thought-provoking *Before You Read* prompt. After each selection, three sets of questions—*Meaning, Technique,* and *Language*—and *Suggestions for Writing* prompts emphasize critical writing, research assignments, and thematic links to other selections.

- **Help with grammar.** Key grammar tips to specifically consider when writing in a particular pattern are provided near the end of each pattern chapter.

- **Practical guidance on writing.** The rhetorical chapters conclude with pattern-specific writing *Guidelines*, a revision *Checklist*, and numerous *Additional Writing Assignments and Activities*, including suggestions for collaborative activities.

- **Additional support.** A *Geographical Index*, located on the inside front cover, lends geographic context to the selections, outlining the countries of origin for the authors of some selections and the countries where other selections are situated. A *Thematic Contents* arranges the selections under eleven broad themes, allowing *Patterns Across Cultures* to serve a variety of teaching and learning objectives. Finally, a *Glossary of Rhetorical Terms* provides short definitions of terms student writers need to know.

 ## SUPPLEMENTAL RESOURCES FOR STUDENTS AND INSTRUCTORS

HM WriteSPACE™ is Houghton Mifflin's comprehensive location for extensive interactive online products and services to accompany composition texts. Students and instructors can access HM WriteSPACE™ content through text-specific student and instructor websites; via Eduspace®, Houghton Mifflin's online course management system; and through other course management systems, including Blackboard and WebCT. For a demonstration of WriteSPACE or to discuss special packaging options available for this text, please consult your local Houghton Mifflin representative (locatable through *college.hmco.com*).

HM WriteSPACE™ Instructor Website (college.hmco.com/pic/hirschberg)

Instructors can access HM WriteSPACE™ content at any time via the Internet. Resources include links to HM Interactives and PowerPoint slides for HM NewsNow powered by the Associated Press and a passkey-protected *Instructor's Resource Manual* with a concise overview of the text's chapters and visuals; sample syllabi; suggestions for how to approach each selection in the text; answers to the post-reading Meaning, Technique, and Language questions; and a pronunciation guide for assistance with the many unfamiliar names in the text.

HM WriteSPACE™ Student Website (college.hmco.com/pic/hirschberg)

Accessible to students via the Internet, HM WriteSPACE™ content for this text includes links to websites related to the authors, topics, and themes in the text; guidance on documentation, including a comparison of MLA and APA documentation styles; links to HM Interactives and HM NewsNow powered by the Associated Press; links to hundreds of e-Exercises for practicing grammar and writing skills; and access to the numerous anti-plagiarism resources available in Houghton Mifflin's Plagiarism Prevention Zone. Some content may be passkey-protected.

HM WriteSPACE™ with Eduspace®

Eduspace®, Houghton Mifflin's course management system, offers instructors a flexible and interactive online platform for communicating with students, organizing course material, evaluating student work, and tracking results in a powerful gradebook. In addition to HM WriteSPACE™ resources, students and instructors using Eduspace benefit from course management tools, including a gradebook; practice and homework exercises; HM Assess; and an online handbook, *Digital Keys for Writers*.

HM Interactives powered by the Associated Press

HM Interactives are multimedia news presentations prepared by the Associated Press that feature videos, audio clips, graphs, charts, maps, and other media content. Each Interactive is accompanied by critical-thinking questions, content-based and rhetorical questions, and writing prompts that instructors can assign for in-class work or homework. Students can even use the Interactives as the basis for researching full-length papers. HM Interactives also provide students with practice in analyzing non-print formats, which is especially beneficial for auditory and visual learners, and teach them to apply critical reasoning to multimedia content so that they are better able to evaluate what they see and hear on TV, online, and in other media. HM Interactives are available through either HM WriteSPACE™ or HM WriteSPACE™ with Eduspace®.

HM NewsNow powered by the Associated Press

Houghton Mifflin's partnership with the Associated Press lets instructors bring the most current news into the classroom in order to spark discussion, engage students' interest, and help them learn how to analyze media content. Our content experts scour Associated Press headlines for the most thought-provoking and relevant news stories of the week, then place articles, videos, and photos into PowerPoint® slides that instructors can download to their own computers from our passkey-protected HM WriteSPACE™ Instructor Website. Instructors can use the slides to start classroom discussions and can assign the accompanying prompts for in-class, journal, or essay writing. Students have access to the same multimedia news content on the HM WriteSPACE™ Student Website, so instructors have the option of asking them to read the material before class.

■■■ ACKNOWLEDGMENTS

We are especially grateful for the many helpful suggestions offered by our reviewers:

Diane S. Baird, Palm Beach Community College
Martin Behr, College of Southern Nevada
S. Griffith Brownlee, University of Mississippi
Vicki Byard, Northeastern Illinois University
Juliana F. Cardenas, Grossmont College
Lucia Cherciu, Dutchess Community College
Nancy Cox, Arkansas Tech University
Melia B. Gagliardo, Gadsden State Community College
Hank Galmish, Green River Community College
Iris Rose Hart, Santa Fe Community College
Elizabeth F. Heath, Florida Gulf Coast University
L. Miller Jackson, Southwest Tennessee Community College
Robert Jakubovic, Cincinnati State Technical and Community College
William M. Northcutt, Dyersburg State Community College
Sherry Rosenthal, College of Southern Nevada
Rosie M. Soy, Hudson County Community College
Greg Stone, Tulsa Community College
Tricia Swoope, Tidewater Community College
Basak Tarkan-Blanco, Miami Dade College—Kendall Campus
Amy Towne, Florida Gulf Coast University
Carol S. Warren, Georgia Perimeter College

We would also like to thank the following individuals at Houghton Mifflin Company: Development Editor Amy Gibbons, for her patience, good humor, and invaluable help in making this book as good as it could be, and Senior Sponsoring Editor Lisa Kimball, for overseeing this project. Our appreciation also goes to Suzanne Phelps Weir for signing us on; Anne Seitz and Samantha Ross for doing such an excellent job with the production; Barbara Willette for her fine copyediting; and Mary Dalton-Hoffman for obtaining the permissions. A special note of thanks goes to all of the students whose essays are included in this text.

Stuart Hirschberg
Terry Hirschberg

CRITICAL
THINKING,
READING, AND
WRITING

WHAT IS READING CRITICALLY?

You have probably had the experience of receiving an e-mail forward from a friend recounting a supposedly true story that struck you as difficult to believe. Your skepticism might have led you to do an Internet search to find out whether or not it really happened, and perhaps, in doing so, you discovered that it was nothing more than an urban legend, a modern tall tale that is presented and circulated as fact. By questioning (and then investigating) the truth of the story, you employed **critical thinking,** the process of analyzing and evaluating information. When you think critically, you consider such factors as the source of the information, the perspective or bias of the source, the purpose the information serves (such as to inform, entertain, or persuade), and any evidence that supports or contradicts it. In the case of the urban legend, for example, you might have decided to research the story online because the source—a mass e-mail originally written by a complete stranger—did not seem very reliable or because the details of the story did not seem to fit with something you already knew. The need to think critically is very important because it allows you to sift through the enormous amount of information that you encounter every day that is designed to influence your beliefs and actions without naively taking that information at face value.

    Critical reading is the process of applying critical thinking to written texts—in other words, the process of analyzing and evaluating what you read. When you read critically, you "read between the lines" and look beyond the immediately observable features of the text (such as the topic and length) to gain a deeper understanding. Some ways to engage in critical reading are to:

- consider what you already know about the topic,
- identify the author's purpose for writing,
- assess the author's credibility,
- determine the audience for whom the text is intended,
- locate the main ideas in the text and any evidence that supports or contradicts these ideas,
- examine the techniques, strategies, and language the author uses to communicate his or her ideas, and
- evaluate how well the author presents his or her ideas and achieves his or her purpose.

It is very difficult to appreciate all of these factors on a first reading, when you are just getting acquainted with a text. Therefore, when reading critically, it is very important to read selections a second and sometimes even a third time.

By taking such an active role in the reading process, you enter into a dialogue with the text. As in other conversations, you can pose questions, ask for clarification, and respond. You can agree or disagree or even argue with the author. Drawing on any prior knowledge you may have of the subject matter, you can question discrepancies between what you read and what you already believe. Sometimes, as in the case of the urban legend, what you read might be inaccurate or outright false. On the other hand, critical reading can also alert you to your own preconceptions, expectations, biases, and mistaken beliefs and may even cause you to change your views.

Critical reading also requires you to evaluate the relative strengths and weaknesses of the author's presentation and to distinguish facts from opinions. Facts (such as the repair records of various models of cars) can be verified by checking reliable sources, whereas opinions (such as "it's a girl (or guy) car") require a well-supported argument to be persuasive. Critical reading sometimes also involves comparing what one writer says with the observations and claims of other writers.

THE PROCESS OF READING CRITICALLY

As you have seen, critical reading involves much more than just comprehending the words on the page. The process of critical reading has three parts: gaining an overview of the text, reading it, and then rereading and actively analyzing it. As you read, you can annotate the text or record your observations in a reading journal. Both techniques are described later in this chapter.

Preview the Text

When you look over the text, there are several places you should check first to gain a clear idea of what you are going to read. These include (1) the first and last paragraphs, (2) subheadings that divide the text into sections, and, of course, (3) the title.

Also, as with the selections in this reader, there are often biographical sketches or headnotes that tell you about the author and where the reading was originally published. These clues, taken together, will give you a good initial overview of what the selection is about and the way in which the author approaches the topic.

Scan the Text for Key Ideas and Organization   As you are gaining an overview of an unfamiliar selection, it is important to identify the author's main idea and the way in which the organization of the piece develops this idea. The kind of organization the writer uses reflects his or her purpose, whether it is to explain something, describe how something works, solve a problem, tell a story, or argue for a particular point of view. The way in which the reading is organized reflects how the writer uses particular kinds of rhetorical strategies.

Consider the Author's Strategies   As was discussed earlier in this chapter, what distinguishes critical reading from "regular" reading is that in critical reading, you consider many unstated factors to develop a deeper understanding of how the piece "works." A key factor to consider is how the author uses rhetorical strategies to relate to the audience. Specifically, you should take into account:

1. The author's background, knowledge about the subject, and feelings about it—as far as you can determine from the language he or she uses.
2. The intended readers, what they might already know or feel about the subject, and the kind of language the author uses to connect to them.
3. What the writer wants to achieve, as mentioned above. Most pieces of writing blend different objectives of providing information, sharing feelings, telling an interesting story, or getting the readers to agree with them. But there is usually a dominant rhetorical strategy that controls the way in which the reading is developed. For example, in the sample annotated essay that follows, Octavio Paz explains why fiestas are so important in Mexico by focusing on the powerful feelings that fiestas evoke.
4. The context in which the reading was first published and who the audience was. Perhaps the writer's reasons can be found in the headnote preceding the selection.
5. Anything you already know about the subject or any strong feelings or opinions you have about it. If it is unfamiliar or seems difficult, do you want to spend the time necessary to better understand it?

Reading the Text Critically

One of the most useful skills to develop as you are reading an unfamiliar selection is taking notes to keep track of your reactions as you read. Your notes can go right on the pages of the text, as annotations, or they can go in a reading journal. You will find these notes invaluable later, when you write your own essay.

Application 1.1

For the following essays and short stories in this book, think about what you already know about the topic, whether or not you would be interested in the subject, and whether you would be likely to find the selection easy or difficult.

1. "The Paradox of St. Mark's"
2. "The Initiation of a Maasi Warrior"
3. "That Lean and Hungry Look"
4. "An Island Passover"
5. "The Real Vampire"
6. "Circumcision of Girls"
7. "Social Time: The Heartbeat of Culture"
8. "The Mbuti Pygmies"
9. "Big Mac and the Tropical Forests"
10. "The Unfashionable Human Body"
11. "The Case for Torture"
12. "I Am A Cat"

Text Annotations   When you react to what you are reading with observations and notes, you are creating a conversation with the writer. Some of the kinds of things on which you might want to comment include:

1. whether you agree or disagree with the author's views;
2. the meaning of the ideas expressed in the title and at the beginning and at the end of the essay;
3. the main or controlling idea the reading develops (the thesis), whether explicitly stated or what you assume it to be from clues provided in the text (you might wish to note what this thesis is in your own words, as in the following annotated essay);
4. how the writer uses evidence such as vivid examples, compelling statistics, expert opinions, and graphs, charts, and tables to support or illustrate important ideas;
5. words you need to look up and write definitions for in the margins; and
6. how the writer connects different sections with transitional words and/or phrases that express particular relationships (such as *now* and *then* for time, *because* for cause and effect, *moreover* for added information, or *although* or *however* for qualifying information).

You can see how this process works in the sample annotation of Octavio Paz's essay "Fiesta" that follows.

OCTAVIO PAZ

Fiesta

The Nobel Prize–winning poet and writer Octavio Paz (1914–1998) was born in Mexico City and served the Mexican government in many different capacities, including posts to France and Japan and as Ambassador to India. Both his fiction and nonfiction are characterized by a depth of knowledge of Mexican culture and a graceful style in which he communicates profound psychological insights. Best known among his poetry are the volumes *Sun Stone* (1958) and *The Monkey Grammarian* (1981). Collections of his essays include *The Other Mexico* (1972) and *The Labyrinth of Solitude* (1961), in which the following selection first appeared. In it, Paz investigates the reasons why fiestas are so deeply rooted in the Mexican culture and psyche.

BEFORE YOU READ

What qualities do you associate with Mexican fiestas?

■ ■ ▨

1 The solitary Mexican loves fiestas and public gatherings. Any occasion for getting together will serve, any pretext to stop the flow of time and commemorate men and events with festivals and ceremonies. We are a ritual people, and this characteristic enriches both our imaginations and our sensibilities, which are equally sharp and alert. The art of the fiesta has been debased almost everywhere else, but not in Mexico. There are few places in the world where it is possible to take part in a spectacle like our great religious fiestas with their violent primary colors, their bizarre costumes and dances, their fireworks and ceremonies and their inexhaustible welter of surprises: the fruit, candy, toys and other objects sold on these days in the plazas and open-air markets.

2 Our calendar is crowded with fiestas. There are certain days when the whole country, from the most remote villages to the largest cities, prays, shouts, feasts, gets drunk and kills, in honor of the Virgin of Guadalupe or Benito Juaréz. Each year on the fifteenth of September, at eleven o'clock at night, we celebrate the fiesta of the *Grito*[1] in all the plazas of the Republic, and the excited crowds actually shout for a whole hour . . . the better, perhaps, to remain silent for the rest of the year. During the days before and after the twelfth of

Paz explains why fiestas are so important in Mexican culture.

---

[1] Padre Hildalgo's call-to-arms against Spain, 1810.—*Tr.*

December,[2] time comes to a full stop, and instead of pushing us toward a deceptive tomorrow that is always beyond our reach, offers us a complete and perfect today of dancing and revelry, of communion with the most ancient and secret Mexico. Time is no longer succession, and becomes what it originally was and is: the present, in which past and future are reconciled.

Fiestas offer a release from the pressures of ordinary life.

3   But the fiestas which the Church and State provide for the country as a whole are not enough. The life of every city and village is ruled by a patron saint whose blessing is celebrated with devout regularity. Neighborhoods and trades also have their annual fiestas, their ceremonies and fairs. And each one of us—atheist, Catholic, or merely indifferent—has his own saint's day, which he observes every year. It is impossible to calculate how many fiestas we have and how much time and money we spend on them. I remember asking the mayor of a village near Mitla, several years ago, "What is the income of the village government?" "About 3,000 pesos a year. We are very poor. But the Governor and the Federal Government always help us to meet our expenses." "And how are the 3,000 pesos spent?" "Mostly on fiestas, señor. We are a small village, but we have two patron saints."

Towns spend more on fiestas than they can afford.

4   This reply is not surprising. Our poverty can be measured by the frequency and luxuriousness of our holidays. Wealthy countries have very few: there is neither the time nor the desire for them, and they are not necessary. The people have other things to do, and when they amuse themselves they do so in small groups. The modern masses are agglomerations of solitary individuals. On great occasions in Paris or New York, when the populace gathers in the squares or stadiums, the absence of people, in the sense of *a* people, is remarkable: there are couples and small groups, but they never form a living community in which the individual is at once dissolved and redeemed. But how could a poor Mexican live without the two or three annual fiestas that make up for his poverty and misery? Fiestas are our only luxury. They replace, and are perhaps better than, the theater and vacations, Anglo-Saxon weekends and cocktail parties, the bourgeois reception, the Mediterranean café.

Fiestas offer an escape from poverty.

5   In all of these ceremonies—national or local, trade or family—the Mexican opens out. They all give him a chance to reveal himself and to converse with God, country, friends

Paz captures the exuberance of fiestas.

---

[2] Fiesta of the Virgin of Guadalupe.—*Tr.*

or relations. During these days the silent Mexican whistles, shouts, sings, shoots off fireworks, discharges his pistol into the air. He discharges his soul. And his shout, like the rockets we love so much, ascends to the heavens, explodes into green, red, blue, and white lights, and falls dizzily to earth with a trail of golden sparks. This is the night when friends who have not exchanged more than the prescribed courtesies for months get drunk together, trade confidences, weep over the same troubles, discover that they are brothers, and sometimes, to prove it, kill each other. The night is full of songs and loud cries. The lover wakes up his sweetheart with an orchestra. There are jokes and conversations from balcony to balcony, sidewalk to sidewalk. Nobody talks quietly. Hats fly in the air. Laughter and curses ring like silver pesos. Guitars are brought out. Now and then, it is true, the happiness ends badly, in quarrels, insults, pistol shots, stabbings. But these too are part of the fiesta, for the Mexican does not seek amusement: he seeks to escape from himself, to leap over the wall of solitude that confines him during the rest of the year. All are possessed by violence and frenzy. Their souls explode like the colors and voices and emotions. Do they forget themselves and show their true faces? Nobody knows. The important thing is to go out, open a way, get drunk on noise, people, colors. Mexico is celebrating a fiesta. And this fiesta, shot through with lightning and delirium, is the brilliant reverse to our silence and apathy, our reticence and gloom.

> Everyday roles are put aside during fiestas.

6   According to the interpretation of French sociologists, the fiesta is an excess, an expense. By means of this squandering the community protects itself against the envy of the gods or of men. Sacrifices and offerings placate or buy off the gods and the patron saints. Wasting money and expending energy affirms the community's wealth in both. This luxury is a proof of health, a show of abundance and power. Or a magic trap. For squandering is an effort to attract abundance by contagion. Money calls to money. When life is thrown away it increases; the orgy, which is sexual expenditure, is also a ceremony of regeneration; waste gives strength. New Year celebrations, in every culture, signify something beyond the mere observance of a date on the calendar. The day is a pause: time is stopped, is actually annihilated. The rites that celebrate its death are intended to provoke its rebirth, because they mark not only the end of an old year but also the beginning of a new. Everything attracts its opposite. The fiesta's function, then, is more utilitarian than we think: waste attracts or promotes wealth, and is an investment

> Sociologists believe that excess serves as a ritual sacrifice.

> The squandering of wealth produces abundance.

like any other, except that the returns on it cannot be measured or counted. What is sought is potency, life, health. In this sense the fiesta, like the gift and the offering, is one of the most ancient of economic forms.

7   This interpretation has always seemed to me to be incomplete. The fiesta is by nature sacred, literally or figuratively, and above all it is the advent of the unusual. It is governed by its own special rules, that set it apart from other days, and it has a logic, an ethic and even an economy that are often in conflict with everyday norms. It all occurs in an enchanted world: time is transformed to a mythical past or a total present; space, the scene of the fiesta, is turned into a gaily decorated world of its own; and the persons taking part cast off all human or social rank and become, for the moment, living images. And everything takes place as if it were not so, as if it were a dream. But whatever happens, our actions have a greater lightness, a different gravity. They take on other meanings and with them we contract new obligations. We throw down our burdens of time and reason.

Ordinary time is suspended during fiestas.

8   In certain fiestas the very notion of order disappears. Chaos comes back and license rules. Anything is permitted: the customary hierarchies vanish, along with all social, sex, caste, and trade distinctions. Men disguise themselves as women, gentlemen as slaves, the poor as the rich. The army, the clergy, and the law are ridiculed. Obligatory sacrilege, ritual profanation is committed. Love becomes promiscuity. Sometimes the fiesta becomes a Black Mass. Regulations, habits and customs are violated. Respectable people put away the dignified expressions and conservative clothes that isolate them, dress up in gaudy colors, hide behind a mask, and escape from themselves.

Barriers drop between the sexes and social classes.

9   Therefore the fiesta is not only an excess, a ritual squandering of the goods painfully accumulated during the rest of the year; it is also a revolt, a sudden immersion in the formless, in pure being. By means of the fiesta society frees itself from the norms it has established. It ridicules its gods, its principles, and its laws: it denies its own self.

10   The fiesta is a revolution in the most literal sense of the word. In the confusion that it generates, society is dissolved, is drowned, insofar as it is an organism ruled according to certain laws and principles. But it drowns in itself, in its own original chaos or liberty. Everything is united: good and evil, day and night, the sacred and the profane. Everything merges, loses shape and individuality and returns to the primordial mass. The fiesta is a cosmic experiment, an experiment in disorder,

reuniting contradictory elements and principles in order to bring about a renascence of life. Ritual death promotes a rebirth; vomiting increases the appetite; the orgy, sterile in itself, renews the fertility of the mother or of the earth. The fiesta is a return to a remote and undifferentiated state, prenatal or presocial. It is a return that is also a beginning, in accordance with the dialectic that is inherent in social processes.

11　　The group emerges purified and strengthened from this plunge into chaos. It has immersed itself in its own origins, in the womb from which it came. To express it in another way, the fiesta denies society as an organic system of differentiated forms and principles, but affirms it as a source of creative energy. It is a true "re-creation," the opposite of the "recreation" characterizing modern vacations, which do not entail any rites or ceremonies whatever and are as individualistic and sterile as the world that invented them.

12　　Society communes with itself during the fiesta. Its members return to original chaos and freedom. Social structures break down and new relationships, unexpected rules, capricious hierarchies are created. In the general disorder everybody forgets himself and enters into otherwise forbidden situations and places. The bounds between audience and actors, officials and servants, are erased. Everybody takes part in the fiesta, everybody is caught up in its whirlwind. Whatever its mood, its character, its meaning, the fiesta is participation, and this trait distinguishes it from all other ceremonies and social phenomena. Lay or religious, orgy or saturnalia, the fiesta is a social act based on the full participation of all its celebrants.

13　　Thanks to the fiesta the Mexican opens out, participates, communes with his fellows and with the values that give meaning to his religious or political existence. And it is significant that a country as sorrowful as ours should have so many and such joyous fiestas. Their frequency, their brilliance and excitement, the enthusiasm with which we take part, all suggest that without them we would explode. They free us, if only momentarily, from the thwarted impulses, the inflammable desires that we carry within us. But the Mexican fiesta is not merely a return to an original state of formless and normless liberty: the Mexican is not seeking to return, but to escape from himself, to exceed himself. Our fiestas are explosions. Life and death, joy and sorrow, music and mere noise are united, not to re-create or recognize themselves, but to swallow each other up. There is nothing so joyous as a Mexican fiesta, but there is also nothing so sorrowful. Fiesta night is also a night of mourning.

> Fiestas are an important outlet for normally reserved Mexicans.

14　　　If we hide within ourselves in our daily lives, we discharge ourselves in the whirlwind of the fiesta. It is more than an opening out: we rend ourselves open. Everything—music, love, friendship—ends in tumult and violence. The frenzy of our festivals shows the extent to which our solitude closes us

How does this picture of feast day fireworks at San Miguel de Allende capture the qualities of a Mexican fiesta as described by Octavio Paz?

off from communication with the world. We are familiar with delirium, with songs and shouts, with the monologue . . . but not with the dialogue. Our fiestas, like our confidences, our loves, our attempts to reorder our society, are violent breaks with the old or the established. Each time we try to express ourselves we have to break with ourselves. And the fiesta is only one example, perhaps the most typical, of this violent break. It is not difficult to name others, equally revealing: our games, which are always a going to extremes, often mortal; our profligate spending, the reverse of our timid investments and business enterprises; our confessions. The somber Mexican, closed up in himself, suddenly explodes, tears open his breast and reveals himself, though not without a certain complacency, and not without a stopping place in the shameful or terrible mazes of his intimacy. We are not frank, but our sincerity can reach extremes that horrify a European. The explosive, dramatic, sometimes even suicidal manner in which we strip ourselves, surrender ourselves, is evidence that something inhibits and suffocates us. Something impedes us from being. And since we cannot or dare not confront our own selves, we resort to the fiesta. It fires us into the void; it is a drunken rapture that burns itself out, a pistol shot in the air, a skyrocket.

Thesis: Fiestas in Mexico release people from ordinary existence and lead to a rebirth of spirit.

■ ■ ▨

The Reading Journal   In addition to annotating the text, you can jot down your thoughts, questions, and impressions in a reading journal. For example, you could use your journal to list the facets of the essay you are analyzing. You can also use your journal to record short summaries of pieces you read (for hints, see "Summarizing What You Read"). A reading journal can serve as a storehouse from which to draw for your own writing. In fact, some instructors may require you to hand in your reading journal with your drafts and final paper.

If a reading journal is part of the required work for your class, the instructor may specify particular topics for the entries. If not, here are some suggestions for journal entries about reading selections:

- Take notes during the class discussion. Afterward, respond to a comment by your instructor or another student.
- Write about a question you had while you were reading the text. Explain the reasons for your questions, and discuss whether a rereading of the text answered it.
- Write about why you agree or disagree with a point the author made.
- Explain why you can or cannot identify with a particular character or situation in the reading selection.

- Write a letter to the author asking questions or making comments about the work.
- Copy a phrase or a sentence from the reading selection that seems particularly memorable or particularly puzzling, and discuss your response to it.

Summarizing What You Read   A summary condenses the original source, restating its main ideas and distinguishing them from the supporting details. You can summarize at any time, but it is most effective to do it after a full and careful reading.

Begin your summary by writing one or two sentences that capture the main idea of each paragraph or group of related paragraphs. Then edit this list to avoid duplicate expressions of the same idea. After this, create a single sentence that expresses the overall point that is made in the essay. Draft a rough summary by combining this statement with the key ideas you have noted and only the most crucial supporting details. Edit this rough summary against the original to make sure you have touched on the key ideas. Finally, double-check to make sure that you have not inadvertently put in your own views and opinions. For example, notice that the sample summary below starts with a sentence that identifies the title and author of the work being summarized and the main idea of the essay.

Does this summary accurately and fairly express the main ideas of the original without injecting personal opinions? Why or why not?

Analyzing What You Read

After you have read and annotated Octavio Paz's "Fiesta," you might wish to compare your answers to the following end-of-selection questions with our sample student answers. These questions follow the same pattern as the end-of-selection questions after each of the readings:

- The first set, "Meaning," ask you to think critically about the content, meaning, and purpose of the selection.

Sample Summary of Octavio Paz's "Fiesta"

In "Fiesta," Octavio Paz explains that fiestas are so popular in Mexican society because they provide an escape from the normal restrictions of social class and the emotional isolation that is characteristic of everyday life. Fiestas are enjoyed by every social class and stratum in Mexican society, and many towns spend more money than they have for these celebrations. Fiestas are communal and joyous and offer a new beginning that is achieved by plunging the community into a chaotic atmosphere of noise, gaiety, fireworks, and crossing lines of social class. In these celebrations, which often bankrupt communities, the people do not worry about the past or the future but lose themselves in the exuberance of the moment.

- The questions under "Technique" ask you to evaluate the author's use of the specific rhetorical strategy and any other patterns.
- The questions in "Language" focus on the voice the author projects in relation to his or her audience and on his or her use of word choice and style.

MEANING

1. What factors contribute to the popularity of fiestas in Mexico, as described by Paz?

Fiestas are enjoyed by every social class and stratum in Mexican society but seem to mean the most to those who have the least. The popularity of the fiesta can be understood, says Octavio Paz in his essay "Fiesta," if we realize that the Mexicans are "a ritual people." Although they are demonstrative and exhibit an openness that is foreign to other nationalities, this openness is a facade, a personality that Mexicans adopt in order to function in society while their true selves are normally reserved and solitary. For this reason, fiestas provide an outlet to purge pent-up emotion and as a release from the depression of poverty. Paz comments that fiestas are so popular throughout the country that even the ones that are decreed by the church or state are not sufficient, and every city and village has its own fiesta to celebrate its patron saints.

2. In what way do people experience time differently during the fiesta than they do during the rest of the year?

Although time simply passes during the year, when fiestas occur, fiesta time is defined as the present. People do not worry about the consequences of tomorrow or the problems of the past but lose themselves in the exuberance of the moment. In this sense, fiestas can be seen in their role as a much needed time-out from the solitude of everyday life and from pervasive poverty.

TECHNIQUE

1. How does Paz use objective descriptions to draw the reader into the exuberant spectacle of the fiesta?

Paz's descriptions communicate the chaotic mood of these celebrations. He projects the kaleidoscope of noise, gaiety, fireworks, sexual promiscuity, and ridicule of the powers that be and re-creates a carnival night of liberty in which everything that is normally denied is permitted.

2. How does Paz use subjective descriptions to offer insight into the inner nature of Mexican life and explain why fiestas are so important?

His description of the importance fiestas have in Mexican society starts from the assumption that everyday life tends to separate people according to their social class; keeps them emotionally restrained; and promotes values of sobriety, thrift, and a kind of saturnine fatalism. By contrast, fiestas allow Mexicans to be profligate and to disencumber themselves from restrictions of social class that prove so crushing at all other times.

3. **Other Patterns.** How do Paz's comparisons between Mexican attitudes toward celebrations, life, and death with those of Europeans and North Americans make it easier for his readers to understand his thesis?

In contrast to the tepid pastimes of going to the theater, taking vacations, or attending cocktail parties, which are said to be the preferred amusements of Europeans and North Americans, fiestas are communal and joyous. They achieve a new beginning by plunging the community into a chaotic ferment. Even people who are poor can enjoy a temporary illusion of wealth and carelessness. Paz also uses comparisons when he connects fiestas to the timeless world of Mayan ancestors, although they are enacted in the guise of a Christian holiday.

LANGUAGE

1. In what sense does a fiesta provide an opportunity for the solitary individual to be "at once resolved and redeemed"? What do you think Paz means by this?

Paz says that the mask of composure and propriety in which individual Mexicans disguise themselves is discarded during the extravagance of fiestas. All inhibitions and constraints that are part of normal Mexican life are shed at the inception of a fiesta and resumed once it is over. It is the time, says Paz, when age, the barriers between social classes, and constraints in the relationships between sexes are ritually disgarded, and people can express their suppressed identities.

2. How does the citation of "about 3,000 pesos a year" underscore how much fiestas mean to impoverished villages?

During fiestas, towns whose economies border on bankruptcy think nothing of indulging all their income for an evening's celebration. Clearly, no culture, says Paz, would spend so much time and money on events that were not integrally vital to its psychological and cultural well-being. The fiesta is an event apart from normal economic considerations. Money is spent as though it is in ample supply, although the Mexican economy is not healthy. In fact, several towns attribute their economic misery to the fact that because they have several patron saints, they must have several fiestas each year and spend more money than they can ever accumulate in any one year.

All selections also include "Suggestions for Writing" that invite you to extend your thinking through assignments that apply the pattern for that chapter, provide opportunities to make connections between selections within the chapter, develop research on the author and/or issue using outside sources, and create a paper using combined patterns.

For example, the sample student essay at the end of this chapter was written in response to the following question:

> How do comparable celebrations in America (such as lavish weddings, quinceañeras, proms, *and* Mardi Gras) allow for emotional release, the crossing of social classes, and the enjoyment of temporary luxuries? Describe one of these that you have attended (or would like to attend), and include a full range of illustrative details.

WHAT IS WRITING CRITICALLY?

Critical writing is based on critical thinking and critical reading. You have to ask questions, analyze one or more sources about a topic, and draw conclusions. In college, critical writing assignments usually entail analyzing a single source or analyzing and then synthesizing two or more sources.

In an analytical essay (the kind you will write for the exercises at the end of each reading), you will evaluate the text according to a set of standards, which may be general (such as use of evidence, clarity of presentation, or absence of bias or preconceived opinion) or specific to a particular field of study or discipline (such as history, economics, political science, women's studies, anthropology, or biology). When you write an analytical essay, you move beyond your personal reactions and base your writing on the information you have gained from a critical reading of the source. Once you have identified the thesis, supporting points, types of evidence, chain of reasoning, overall organization, and style, you are ready to begin to form conclusions about the text. An analytical essay can address such topics such as:

1. the organization (the order in which ideas, topics, and issues are discussed),
2. the style (sentence structure, word choice, use of figurative language),
3. the author's attitude toward the topic (the tone adopted), and
4. the validity and objectivity (lack of bias) of the evidence and supporting materials.

An essay that is based on two or more sources (the kind you will write for the "Thematic Links" exercises at the end of each selection) needs to consider some additional questions, such as these:

1. Does one reading or source reinforce or contradict another?
2. Do the readings represent entirely different points of view without opposing each other?
3. What additional insight might a third source or even a fourth add to the analysis?

THE PROCESS OF WRITING CRITICALLY

Writing critically requires planning, organizing, rethinking, reorganizing (sometimes), and polishing. It is very different from sending off a quick e-mail, and the result is very different too. We will consider the four parts of the process—prewriting and

Basic Questions Before You Begin to Write

To spend your time more efficiently on a writing project, no matter what kind it is, you need to start thinking about its *context*, or the rhetorical situation (which we explored from the reader's perspective in the discussion of critical reading):

1. What is the assigned topic, if there is one? What is the assigned length? How much time do you have to complete the paper?
2. What do you already know about the topic? What more do you need to find out? What sources might you use?
3. Who is the audience? In college courses, it may be the instructor, other students, or an unspecified general audience. How much does the audience know about your topic? How much background information will you need to provide? For example, if not everyone in your audience has read the source you are analyzing, you might have to describe it in more detail than you would if everyone was familiar with it.
4. What is your purpose? The most basic purposes of writing are to convey information (expository writing), to argue for the acceptance of an idea or interpretation (persuasive writing), or to express personal feelings or to entertain (expressive writing). Many of the selections in this book combine all three purposes, but most of your writing for college classes will be expository or persuasive—or a combination of the two.

planning, drafting, revising, and proofreading—one by one, but you might need to return to some parts more than once. For example, as you draft your paper, you might discover that you have taken on too big a topic, so you need to revisit your invention strategies and see how you can narrow the topic. Or as you are revising, you might see that your introductory paragraph no longer works, so you need to redraft it. After we describe the four basic elements of the critical writing process, we will discuss how to use sources for critical writing.

Prewriting and Planning

Prewriting is a little like batting practice before stepping up to the plate. It is the process of finding your thesis and exploring how best to support it.

Invention Strategies   Invention, or prewriting, strategies help you to discover ideas and explore them in an informal way. (These strategies can also help you at any point in the writing process when you feel that you have run into a dead end.) We describe three of the most common strategies here: freewriting, the five W's, and mapping (or clustering). These strategies are more than simple lists of ideas; they can help you to discover connections between ideas.

Freewriting is setting down whatever occurs to you on a topic within a few minutes. There are no restrictions on what you can or cannot put down. Do not worry about using complete sentences or about spelling, punctuation, or grammar. Write without stopping to edit or correct. You will find that you are more creative when you simply free-associate without stopping to censor, evaluate, or edit your thoughts.

As an example, here is a student's freewriting based on Paz's essay "Fiesta":

During fiestas people lose themselves in the music, spectacle, and freedom from everyday restrictions on behavior. A person who lives in modest circumstances may enjoy a temporary illusion of wealth and carelessness. Rules governing ordinary life are forgotten (temporarily). The average person can externalize desires and act on them without consequences. If the everyday Mexican is solitary and morose, then fiestas are communal and joyous.

Write down your topic, and then ask yourself the questions that journalists often use to find out about a subject, known as "*the Five W's*":

1. Who is involved?
2. What is it?
3. Where did it happen?
4. When did it happen?
5. Why did it happen?

Although these questions are not useful for every topic, they can sometimes reveal new information or a new perspective.

Mapping (also called clustering) is a prewriting strategy that allows you to visually perceive the relationship between ideas. Begin by writing the word or phrase that represents the starting point (as the phrase "Why are fiestas so popular in Mexico?" does in Figure 1.1) in the center of the page and drawing a circle around it. Jot down related ideas, topics, or details around this main idea, and connect them to the main idea and to one another with lines to represent the relationships between them. When you group ideas in this way, you discover a map, or cluster, of ideas and patterns that will help you to decide which ideas are central and which are subordinate. This strategy can help you to narrow your topic and see details and examples that you can use to support your thesis.

In the map shown in Figure 1.1, the student began with the central idea of the popularity of fiestas in Mexico and discovered the more specific topic of "cross-cultural similarities."

Identifying Your Thesis   When you investigate and explore different avenues of your topic using the invention strategies previously discussed, you may hit upon an idea that is so compelling that it can serve as a thesis for your paper. The thesis should contain your own unique approach to the topic and suggest how you intend to develop your essay. Keep in mind that you can change it at any point once you have started writing. The thesis alerts your readers to your purpose in writing the paper and is a kind of promise that they will expect you to fulfill. For example, the

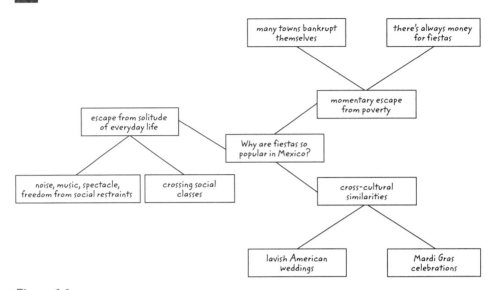

Figure 1.1
An example of mapping.

following is a thesis a student composed for the rough draft of her paper on the reading annotated earlier in this chapter:

In "Fiesta," Octavio Paz refutes the common notion that fiestas are a superfluous pastime by showing how they offer a release from solitude and regenerate social, economic, and sexual aspects of Mexican life.

Notice how this preliminary thesis includes the title of the reading, the author's name, and the points her paper will develop, presented as a single sentence. On the basis of this thesis, readers would expect the writer to:

- describe Mexican fiestas and explain why Paz finds them so important,
- show in detail specifically how fiestas offer a release from isolation, and
- show how fiestas renew vital aspects of Mexican life

These three points would then be explored in separate paragraphs or sections of the paper. You might wish to compose an informal outline to help you see in greater depth how each of these ideas could be developed and think about how you would use supporting evidence.

Outlining to Support Your Thesis   Once you have drafted a trial thesis (which you can always change as you are writing your paper), you need to evaluate the kinds of supporting evidence that would illustrate, clarify, or document your assertion. An informal outline can help you do this before you put in the effort of writing a rough draft. It can give you a schematic overview of what each section of your paper will look like. You can notice either flaws in the structure of the essay or places where you need more evidence. For example, here is an informal outline a student, Samantha Clarke, created for her paper on the legal and ethical issues stemming from the ability to spot genetic flaws:

I.   New capabilities created by genetic research—supported by evidence in the form of expert opinions as to how defective genes can be fixed

II. The need to keep genetic information private—supported by evidence in the form of personal testimony, interviews, and surveys as to potential discrimination by employers or insurance companies

III. The release of genetic information could infringe on entire families—supported by evidence from scientists and legal experts showing that genetic information applies to the person's relatives and future offspring

IV. The need to map out legal and ethical parameters for the release of genetic information—supported by evidence from philosophers, ethicists, and legal scholars to ensure a fair assessment and scrupulous oversight for those who are found to have genetic flaws

An outline such as this would prove quite helpful in giving Samantha an overview of the territory her paper would cover. She should also check her rough draft against this outline to make sure she has covered all the important points.

Drafting

The process of writing more than one draft is at the heart of what writers do. It is how they explore, develop, and refine the ideas they generate during prewriting and planning.

The main purpose of your first draft is to get all your ideas down on paper. To start your first draft, review your purpose, your audience, and your topic; look through your reading journal and your annotations; and think about what your thesis might be. Then begin writing as quickly as you can, without worrying about diction or spelling (which are concerns for the revision and proofreading stages, discussed later in this chapter). You do not necessarily have to write the paragraphs in order; if some paragraphs or ideas come more readily than others, write those first and come back to the others later. A draft is not carved in stone and can be changed many times.

While you read through your first draft, try to see how it might look to a reader. If you did not already know what you meant, would you be able to understand your ideas from the words on the page? (A peer review of your writing at this point can be helpful.) If some of the ideas are not clear, would a change in the order of presentation make them clearer? Which of the ideas needs additional explanation or more supporting evidence?

In your next draft, you can try out different organizational arrangements and, if necessary, use invention strategies to think of additional supporting evidence.

It can also be helpful to review each paragraph (or section) of the draft to see whether it supports your thesis. You might discover that information you assumed was essential is in fact extraneous, or you might see discarded ideas in a new light.

Writing the Introduction The introduction is the first opportunity you have to engage the readers' interest and tell them your views on the subject (in a thesis) and how you intend to approach the issue. You might not be able to write the introduction when you begin your paper, but you can go back to compose it later after the form of the paper begins to take shape.

If you are arguing for a particular point, include your thesis at the beginning. If you are analyzing a subject or exploring a question, you can wait until the final paragraphs and present your thesis as a conclusion. The writers in this anthology use many different ways of introducing their essays. You can adapt one of these strategies for your introduction. Some are:

- a relevant story, as in Austin Bunn's "The Bittersweet Science" (Chapter 11, "Problem Solving");
- a brief description of a key figure, place, or event, as in Paul Barber's "The Real Vampire" (Chapter 9, "Cause and Effect");
- a summary of an issue that divides people, as in Thomas H. Murray's "The Coercive Power of Drugs in Sports" (Chapter 12, "Argument");
- the political, historical, or social background, as in Simone de Beauvoir's "The Married Woman" (Chapter 10, "Definition");
- an attention-getting question, as in Elizabeth W. Fernea and Robert A. Fernea's "A Look Behind the Veil" (Chapter 10, "Definition"); and
- a thought-provoking quotation, as in Mimi Sheraton's "We Eat What We Are" (Chapter 8, "Classification and Division").

Application 1.2

What methods would you want to use to develop an essay on any of the following topics?

profiling
arranged marriages
global warming
obesity
eating disorders
socialized medicine
gangs
deceptive advertising
fashion
organic foods

Whether you use one of these methods or another method, make sure that the introduction is not just interesting for its own sake, but also engages your reader and relates to the topic.

Developing and Organizing the Body of the Essay   The organizational choices that are open to you when you write the middle portion, or body, of your essay depend on the best way to support your thesis. For example, if the thesis reads, "Office computers are being used in ways that infringe on the privacy of employees," then the middle portion of the essay might demonstrate how new software can monitor various aspects of employees' behavior (including productivity, contents of their files, e-mail, and Internet surfing). In this case, the body of the essay would demonstrate the causal relationship (the impact of office computers on privacy) implied in the thesis.

Different strategies, or methods of development, are particularly suited to different purposes. These organizational patterns (traditionally referred to as *rhetorical modes*) include narration, description, illustration (or exemplification), comparison and contrast, process analysis, classification/division, causal analysis, definition, and argument.

Narration (Chapter 3) is the recounting of events to explain, entertain, or persuade. A narrative can be brief, such as the various anecdotes Fatima Mernissi recounts in her essay on how privacy was hard to obtain in the Moroccan harem of her childhood. Or an entire essay can be in the form of a narrative. For example, Frederick Douglass alludes to the history and background of slavery in telling the story of his attempt to learn to become literate. Effective narration usually focuses on a single action. Narratives can dramatize an idea or event that is important to the writer.

Descriptions (Chapter 4) are powerful because they can evoke an image in readers' minds and create an emotional response. Effective descriptions use specific language, carefully chosen details, and an orderly sequence. For example, Gordon Parks describes the central figure of his essay with evocative details that enlist the reader's sympathy for one of the multitudes of poor living in *favelas* (urban slums) in the outskirts of Rio de Janeiro, Brazil. Objects and places can be described spatially (top to bottom, right to left, near to far) as Mary McCarthy does when she describes the appearance of the façades and architecture of St. Mark's Square in Venice. Events and places can also be described chronologically, as Jamaica Kincaid does when we see Antigua from the perspective of newly arrived tourists.

When you use *illustration* or *exemplification* (Chapter 5), you provide one or more examples that document or substantiate the idea you wish to clarify. Well-chosen examples are useful for showing the nature and character of a whole group through individual cases. One instance can represent many others in the same category. Exemplification is especially useful as a technique for explaining abstract concepts. Examples drawn from personal experience can help to support an assertion, although several examples are more effective in supporting a generalization. For instance, Robert Levine and Ellen Wolff give examples from various countries to support their claim that every culture has its own concept of what being on time means.

Comparison and contrast (Chapter 6) are useful techniques for helping audiences to understand basic differences and for pointing out unsuspected similarities or differences between two or more subjects. For example, Suzanne Britt builds her essay around contrasts between thin people and overweight people and their attitudes toward setting goals for themselves; William Bryant Logan compares and contrasts the aesthetic meanings and practical uses of oak trees and the Eiffel Tower.

Comparative essays may be arranged in one of two ways. In the subject-by-subject method, the writer first discusses all the relevant features of one subject (such as the characterization, setting, costumes, and plot of a movie) and then retraces the same points as they apply to a second subject (such as another movie). The second method of organization is point by point, which alternates between the features of the two subjects (by comparing, for example, the characterizations of two movies, then their settings, then their costumes, and then their plots).

When you use *process analysis* (Chapter 7), you provide a detailed set of instructions on how to do something or a step-by-step analysis of how something works. Process analysis aims at showing readers how to reach a desired result and includes signposts or milestones to measure their progress. For example, Rigoberta Menchu uses this technique to help her readers understand the rituals the Quiché Indians of Guatemala use to introduce a newborn infant into the community.

Writers use *classification/division* (Chapter 8) to sort or group ideas, issues, topics, themes, and arguments into categories based on one or more criteria. In an effective classification, a writer identifies significant features in a systematic way, divides phenomena into at least two different classes on the basis of these criteria, and presents the results in a logical and consistent manner. For example, George Orwell uses this technique to help readers understand the unsuspected importance of ordinary objects for soldiers during the Spanish Civil War.

Causal analysis (Chapter 9) is a technique that is often used in persuasive essays. Its purpose is to determine whether a cause-and-effect relationship exists. As Vaughn M. Bryant, Jr., and Sylvia Grider do in their investigation into why people kiss under the mistletoe at Christmas, writers may work backward from the effect to seek the cause or chain of causes that could have produced the observed effect; they may also explore potential effects from a known cause, as Joseph K. Skinner does in his analysis of how fast-food chains are responsible for the destruction of tropical forests.

Definition (Chapter 10) is a useful method for specifying the basic nature of any phenomenon, idea, or condition. A definition can be a sentence that gives the exact meaning of a word or key term (to eliminate ambiguity), or it might extend several paragraphs or even become a complete essay. For example, the definition of the word *purdah* (or seclusion) is central to Elizabeth W. Fernea and Robert A. Fernea's essay exploring the role of veiling in Middle Eastern cultures.

Arguments (Chapter 12) are used by writers who attempt to change readers' thinking or to get them to take a new course of action. The basic structure of an argument is (1) the statement of an opinion and (2) the presentation of reasons and evidence to support that opinion. Arguments are more persuasive when they try to take into account readers' prior knowledge, beliefs, and values and their probable reactions to the argument. For example, in arguing against the use of torture, Henry Porter assumes that his readers have prior knowledge and strong opinions on this current issue. If the argument suggests a course of action, it should be objective about other possible solutions to the problem.

The most persuasive arguments use various combinations of *logical* appeals, *ethical* appeals, and *emotional* appeals to win over the audience. An appeal to logic is based on sound evidence and reasoning. For example, Alan T. Durning uses statistics to argue against the disproportionate use of resources by industrialized nations. Sometimes the chain of reasoning in an argument is explicitly stated, but at other times, unstated assumptions form the links in that chain, and readers need to fill those gaps.

An ethical appeal is based on the writer's (or spokesperson's) expertise or reputation. In addition, value judgments (that something is good or bad according to a specified standard) should be supported with clearly defined ethical or moral criteria. For example, Thomas H. Murray argues against the use of steroids in sports on the principle that they introduce an unequal competitive advantage. If an emotional appeal is the only type of appeal an argument uses, however, it becomes a faulty argument.

Writing the Conclusion   The ideas that are developed in your essay can be pulled together in the conclusion in ways that readers will find satisfying. As with the introduction, several strategies you may want to consider are:

- summing up the major points developed in your essay, as does Stephen Chapman in "The Prisoner's Dilemma" (Chapter 6, "Comparison and Contrast");
- reminding readers of the main point or thesis your essay addressed or echoing the language of the introduction, as do Robert Levine and Ellen Wolff in "Social Time: the Heartbeat of Culture" (Chapter 5, "Exemplification");
- emphasizing how you feel about the subject, as does N. Scott Momaday in "The Way to Rainy Mountain" (Chapter 4, "Description"); and
- touching on implications that readers can think about beyond the issue at hand, as does Maya Angelou in "Champion of the World" (Chapter 3, "Narration").

Revising

As the term "re-vision" implies, the process of improving your rough draft involves seeing it as if for the first time. Try to see your paper as a reader would, that is, as someone who did not know in advance the ideas you wanted to present. Reading your essay aloud can help you see what you actually wrote, rather than what you intended to write. You might hear mistakes in grammar or syntax as well as repeated words or phrases that you had not been been aware of as you were writing. You also might make an appointment at the campus writing center and take advantage of the services they provide.

It is best to do revision in stages. Look first at the entire paper, then at sections and paragraphs, and last at individual sentences.

Looking at the Entire Paper   Consider the entire paper from your audience's point of view. Would a reader want to continue further after the introduction? Does your paper present major points in the most effective sequence? If not, try changing the order of the sections. Have you supplied enough examples to support your analysis? Can your readers understand how different sections relate to each other? If not, add transitional words or phrases to guide them from one section to the next.

Looking at Paragraphs   At the paragraph level, consider whether each paragraph develops a single idea or has an explicit topic sentence. Do the sentences in the paragraph clarify, illustrate, or explain this main idea? Do the sentences follow in a logical order within the paragraph, or would some other order be better? Are any of your paragraphs too long or too short to adequately develop the idea at the heart of the paragraph?

Looking at Sentences   At the sentence level, are most of your sentences written in the active rather than the passive voice? If not, rephrase those that are in the passive voice to add force. Can you substitute single words for roundabout phrases (such as *because* for *due to the fact that, after* for *at the conclusion of, if* for *in the event that*)? Can you find unambiguous ways to express technical terms (jargon), trite phrases (clichés), and unclear figurative language (confusing metaphors and similes)? Finally, try to identify mistakes that you usually make in grammar, usage, punctuation, or spelling, and correct them.

Editing on a Computer   Writing and editing on a computer allows great flexibility when you are drafting multiple versions of your essay. Some software programs create an outline for what you are writing, which you can then check against the informal one you made up. Editing on a computer will not relieve you of the responsibility of spotting and correcting mistakes, but some software programs can help you to identify areas in grammar, punctuation, and spelling. What an editing program cannot do is spot grammatical errors that are spelled correctly, such as the incorrect use of the past tense. Also, these programs cannot spot errors if the word is spelled correctly but is the wrong word for the context, such as "then" for "than," "there" for "their," or "affect" for "effect." Computers have no way of grasping your intentions or understanding the context in which a statement occurs.

What editing programs *can* do is flag sentences that are too long, since error rates tend to go up with sentence length. They can also identify when you use the passive voice and enable you to change it to the more acceptable active voice. Many programs also make backup copies of the material as you work in case you accidently delete something. If not, keep a copy of your original text as a separate document in case you need to retrieve the original. Style programs have become quite sophisticated and can even flag sexist and other discriminatory kinds of language as well as clichés and frequently misused words. Some are also linked to a thesaurus and allow you to introduce variety and substitute synonyms to make your writing more interesting. These programs do not substitute for the need to carefully review

Application 1.3

What do the following titles from the essays and stories in this book suggest about the author's approach?

"Misguided Guide" (narration)
"The Paradox of St. Mark's" (description)
"Advertisements for Oneself" (exemplification)
"Eiffel and Oak" (comparison and contrast)
"Birth Ceremonies" (process analysis)
"Polite Lies" (classification)
"Why I Quit the Klan" (cause and effect)
"The Stolen Party" (definition)
"The Role of Religion in Modern Society" (problem solving)
"The Case for Torture" (argument)

what you have written; for example, they cannot tell you if a word is missing, but they can alert you to the kinds of errors you will want to eliminate.

Choosing the Title   The title that you select should reflect your essay's subject or your thesis, that is, your position on the issue or your attitude toward the subject. Stay away from single-word titles (such as "Genetics") and breezy but uninformative ones (such as "You and Your DNA") that do not provide useful clues about your purpose in writing the piece. If possible, the title should suggest the dominant rhetorical strategy your paper develops. For example, C. P. Ellis's title "Why I Quit the Klan" (in Chapter 9, "Cause and Effect") leads readers to anticipate an analysis of the causes leading to Ellis's decision.

Proofreading

Proofreading means focusing on spelling, punctuation, repeated words, spacing, margins, and anything else that would impair the look and accuracy of the final paper. You might find it easier and more accurate to proofread on paper than onscreen. You might also wish to read what you have written aloud to pick up errors your eye might miss. It is generally best to wait a bit after editing to start proofreading so that you can look at what you have written with fresh eyes. Carefully examine each word you have written for small, seemingly insignificant typos; transposed letters; errors in spelling; punctuation such as commas outside closing quotation marks; and words, phrases, or titles that need to be underlined. Strategies to help you focus on every word and line include moving a sheet of paper down the page except for the line you are proofreading and reading your paper from end to beginning, so that you do not get caught up in the ideas but simply look at the words, lines, and sentences you have written.

Basic Formatting Guidelines for Your Paper

- Use good-quality 8-1/2 × 11 inch paper.
- Keep 1-inch margins on each side and at the top and bottom.
- Double-space the paper throughout, including any list of works cited.
- Put the list of works cited on a separate page at the end of the paper.
- Use a standard 10- to 12-point font throughout.
- Include one space after periods, question marks, and exclamation points unless your instructor requires two spaces.
- Number the pages in the top right margin (putting your last name before the page number in MLA style).
- Indent paragraphs five spaces or 1/2 inch from the left margin.
- On the first page (or on a separate page if your instructor requires one), include the title of the paper, your name, the course, the section, the instructor's name, and the date.

Formatting

Now that you have drafted, revised, edited, and proofread your essay, you need to prepare it according to certain guidelines. English courses usually require that you follow the guidelines of the Modern Language Association (MLA), discussed in Chapter 2. Other instructors may require the *Chicago Manual of Style* (CMS) format. In other disciplines, you will be asked to follow the guidelines of the American Psychological Association (APA) or the Council of Science Editors (CSE).

SAMPLE STUDENT ESSAY

Starting the Process

After reading Octavio Paz's "Fiesta," Joanna Richmond, a first-year composition student, was asked to write an essay using description. She decided to answer the question about comparable American celebrations (p. 15). She began by generating notes using some of the invention strategies she had learned in class. These notes offered several promising leads that would enable her to write a first draft based on her experience attending her cousin's lavish wedding. Here are the notes she put in her journal:

- What would Paz think of a lavish and costly American wedding?
- Could my cousin's wedding be an example of this?
- I could describe how being hockey fans permeated my cousin's entire wedding.
- List details of the ceremony, reception, and dinner.

- Describe how the color scheme of red for the Devils and orange for the Ducks was reflected in the flowers, outfits, candles, table settings, and gifts.
- My Aunt Irene loved the idea too.
- I wondered about the high cost and whether they were getting into debt for a long time to pay this off.
- I thought it was worth it and can now understand why fiestas are so important.
- The little details were the most amazing (arch of hockey sticks, cake topper, center-pieces with Devils and Ducks, "Hey Song" played).
- Try to remember details of the dinner.
- Should I mention John, whom I met at the wedding?

After several attempts to organize her notes, Joanna created the following informal outline from which she could write a rough draft:

1. Begin with story of my cousin and her fiancé's plans for a hockey-themed wedding.
2. Give examples of the hockey theme in colors and unusual arch.
3. Describe the costly wedding gown and the attire of groom and attendants.
4. Give examples of the hockey theme reflected in candle ceremony, DJ outfits, and music played.
5. Describe the color scheme of the table settings and favors.
6. Describe the lavish dinner, custom-made wedding cake, and overall expense (parallel to expenses of fiestas).
7. Describe gifts reflecting hockey theme for attendants and how I met John.

Continuing the Process

After submitting her rough draft for peer review, Joanna had a better idea of what she needed to do to strengthen subsequent drafts. For example, here is an early draft of the next to the last paragraph:

The dinner included tasty appetizers, a clear soup, salad, and a choice of a main course. At the end everyone had dessert and coffee. Holding hockey sticks, the custom-made cake topper continued the sports theme with figures of the bride and groom dressed in their team's colors which were decorated with red and orange flowers. I wondered how much this cost, how long it would take to pay off, and if it was worth it.

As she revised her rough draft, she made the following notes to herself on how to improve it:

- Provide many more specific descriptive details of exactly what was served at each course of the dinner.

- Move misplaced modifier starting the third sentence, which is unintentionally funny.
- Be more specific about the custom-made cake topper.
- State how I really feel about the expenses for this wedding and that it was worth it.

We have annotated Joanna's essay to show how she used description as a primary pattern and supported it with narration, exemplification, and cause and effect. You can see the changes she made in the next-to-last paragraph.

Richmond 1

My Cousin's Wedding
Joanna Richmond

1   When my cousin, Katie Johnson, an avid New Jersey Devils fan, was a freshman at Rutgers University, she met a fellow student, Mark Heller, far from his home in Riverside, California. He was a staunch Anaheim Ducks fan. They dated and discovered that despite their different team allegiances, they were highly compatible. In March 2005, Mark proposed, and they scheduled their wedding for Saturday, December 30, 2006, at the Brooklake Country Club in Florham Park, New Jersey. Because of their mutual love of hockey, they wanted their wedding ceremony and reception to reflect this. My Aunt Irene, Katie's mother, was also a big hockey fan and was enthusiastic about their plans.

Introduction sets up Joanna's description using narration and cause and effect.

2   At the wedding, everything you saw was decorated in the team colors of red, for the Devils, and orange, representing the Ducks. The couple exchanged vows under an arch formed of logo-bearing hockey sticks, decorated with floral arrangements of red and white roses and red, orange, and white carnations.

Examples illustrate hockey theme.

3   When I went with Katie to choose a wedding gown, we both fell in love with a white satin floor-length gown with red trim and a veil with a crown of red flowers. She really looked beautiful, and during the wedding she carried a bouquet of red, orange, and white roses. She had been concerned that she was already blowing the budget, as the gown cost $2,500. The other three bridesmaids and I wore lipstick-red taffeta scoop-necked, short-sleeved, ankle-length gowns. Mark was dressed in a black tuxedo with an orange-and-white striped vest and tie. His groomsmen wore black tuxedos with solid orange vests and matching ties.

Descriptive details connect with the underlying issue of cost.

4   In the unity-candle ceremony, symbolizing the joining of the two families, Katie and Mark's parents came forward to light the side tapers of red and orange, and these were then used to light the center white candle. Both Katie and Mark each presented their mothers with a rose in the color of the other's team. After the ceremony, at the reception, the DJ wore the Devils jersey to start with and then put on an orange one later to please Mark's family and friends who were also Ducks fans. As the wedding party was introduced, the DJ played the popular sports anthem known as the "Hey Song," which you hear at the Continental Airlines Arena, the Devils' home ice, and at the Honda Center, where the Ducks play.

Describes sights and sounds that illustrate hockey theme.

5   The color scheme for the affair was also reflected in the elaborate table settings of orange and red tablecloths; floral centerpieces with little red devils and white and orange ducks; crystal glasses for champagne, red wine, white wine, and water; bone china; and silverware for five courses—for 150 guests. The wedding favors for each guest included mini-hockey-stick drink stirrers along with red and orange M&Ms.

Examples of team colors and hockey motif.

6   The dinner started with tomato and avocado halves stuffed with crabmeat, consommé, and endive salad and included a choice of prime rib, filet of salmon, or Cornish game hen, accompanied by winter vegetables. At the end of the meal, everyone went to the dessert and coffee stations, where every imaginable sweet was available, along with fruit and cheese platters. Their wedding cake was special too, decorated with red and orange flowers and an unusual custom-made cake topper with the bride wearing a Devils cap and veil, the groom wearing a Ducks cap, and both of them wielding hockey sticks. I began to wonder how much all of this was going to cost and whether Katie and Mark and their parents were putting themselves into debt for a really long time. On the other hand, this was a really special day, and some celebrations are more important than money.

Revised detailed description of dinner is arranged chronologically.

Joanna gives her conclusion regarding cost.

7   All of the attendants received a hockey jersey personalized with the wedding date. Katie's side received Devils home red, and Mark's side (since this was an "away" game) was given the Ducks

Richmond 3

white. One of Mark's attendants, his new friend from Rutgers, John, was a really cute guy who sat next to me at dinner. We got into a conversation about sports, and it turns out that he is a Nets fan and I am a Knicks fan. Stay tuned!

> Description concludes with additional examples of hockey theme and a personal anecdote.

WORDS CREATE IMAGES; IMAGES CONVEY IDEAS

As this student's essay illustrates, the ability to create compelling images in picturesque language is an important element in communicating the writer's thoughts, feelings, and experiences. Also, the way in which a writer chooses to describe something expresses an opinion that is capable of persuading an audience. Increasingly, the information that reaches us combines texts with visual elements. And while you acquire skills in reading, analyzing, interpreting, and creating your own texts, you also need to understand the way in which visual texts interweave words with images in the form of tables, charts, photographs, and other graphic elements. Most often, visuals are used to illustrate a point, but they can just as easily communicate values, portray conflicts, and shape the audience's response to an issue. Before we look at the basic ways in which images serve as tools of communication, ask yourself: What categories of images do you see everyday, and what purpose do they serve (for example, brand logos)?

Throughout this text, there are many visual images that connect with the issues and ideas in the chapters. In some cases, they illustrate the rhetorical patterns that are presented in the chapter. These images can be studied or read much as you would a written text and can be analyzed to discover how they use many of the rhetorical strategies you observe in written texts. You are already familiar with many of these kinds of images, since you encounter hundreds of them everyday on television; in films; on the Internet; and in newspapers, magazines, and books. Some, like magazine ads, billboards, CD covers, store windows, and photographs, are purely static visual images. Others, such as webpages, films, and ads on TV, have the added layers of sound and movement.

Cultural Meanings in Images

Visual images can also tell us a lot about our world. The people they show, the activities in which the people are engaged, and the backgrounds and settings against which these activities take place all say something about the intangible values and aspirations that the images point to and illustrate. The form of the image is important too. Photographs are assumed to be realistic and lifelike. Fine art pieces carry the distinctive stamp of the artist. Cartoons are meant to offer social perspective and ironic insight. And, of course, advertisements try to shape our behavior and convince us to purchase a product or service.

Therefore, for each visual image we see, we should first try to gauge the purpose for which it was designed and the potential audience for which it was intended. To do this, you should try to determine who created the image—a business or a non-profit organization, an artist, a website designer—and when it was created. Is the image in color or in black and white, and is it accompanied by any headings or words?

For example, the picture in photo insert A (p. A-1) of an elderly woman being embraced by a younger man on the border of Kashmir appears, at first glance, to show the emotions of relief and joy. We do not know the exact relationship between the two of them (mother and son? nephew and aunt?), but if we checked the picture credit, we would see that it was taken by a photographer for the Reuters News Service on November 17, 2005, the day after Pakistan and India relaxed restrictions on the Kashmir border and permitted family members to be reunited.

When we look more closely at the image, we notice that it is *balanced*, with the left and right sides mirroring each other, and *dynamic*, or suggestive of motion, since the overall composition emphasizes diagonal lines. Moreover, the figures in the picture are emphasized to a much greater degree than is the background. This use of *proportion*, or relative size of the elements in the image, puts the viewer in a direct, intimate connection with the subjects. Also, notice the use of *contrast* in the different color tones of the figures and their apparel.

Translated into visual terms, the rhetorical patterns displayed in the photo are *narration* (the picture tells a story), *description* (through a wealth of details), *exemplification* (an example of a reunited family), and *comparison and contrast* (between the two figures, expressed through differences in age, gender, and what they are wearing). The images throughout this text embody a similar blend of cultural themes and rhetorical techniques translated into visual terms, and you can analyze any of them in much the same way.

If you then analyzed what the image suggests about the photographer's intentions, you might surmise that he wanted to give a powerful human impact to an abstract news report. It might be his way of saying that the border should be left open so that people could be reunited with their loved ones in the future. If you were to evaluate this image for publication in a worldwide press release, would you say that it was successful in communicating what the photographer intended?

Is the Image Real?

No visual analysis would be complete without consideration of whether the image is real or has been digitally manipulated. Just as written texts can be edited to reflect a particular point of view or facts can be selected or quoted out of context to mislead an audience, images can be edited or cropped. They may actually be composites of two or more images combined in ways that are hard to detect. Models who appear on magazine covers might have been digitally slenderized. Advertisers spend considerable money, time, and effort in creating ads that are designed to foster favorable perceptions of their products. Pictures sometimes do lie, and seeing is *not* always believing.

Evaluating an Image in Context

We can look more deeply into these images if we become aware of the themes they embody and the larger cultural contexts that operate just out of sight to imbue them with meaning.

Just how this works can be seen by analyzing a "Family Circus" cartoon by Jeff and Bil Keane (see color insert A-7). Like many cartoons, this one has the dual purpose of entertaining readers and persuading them to adopt the attitude of, or at least empathize with, the characters. The cartoon shows four scenes of a young boy meeting his favorite fictional characters: the Cat in the Hat, Harry Potter, Huck Finn, and a knight in armor on a horse (perhaps Lancelot). The titles of the books are blurred so that the readers at a subliminal level will supply the titles of their own favorite books.

The strip ends with a much larger image of the boy relaxing in bed reading one of the many books scattered around him. The words that accompany this last panel contain the boy's conclusion that reading allows him to travel to different worlds of fantasy and history while being "warm and cozy here in my own bed."

The cartoon's creators seem to assume that readers will have read these books themselves and be able to identify the characters the boy is meeting for the first time. The persuasive message that is implicit in the cartoon might have been crafted to counter the deluge of electronic entertainment and show their readers what children today might be missing.

As we can see from this cartoon, images are really another form of text that tell stories about ourselves, our culture, and our world.

Finding Themes in Images

As you look at the images in this text and prepare to discuss or write about them, you might wish to use the following questions as guidelines:

- What idea or concept does the image communicate?
- What incident or occasion motivates the creation of the image?
- What conflict or issue portrayed in the image addresses an important social theme?
- What aspects of a particular culture does the image communicate?
- What cultural assumptions or values underlie the way in which the subject is portrayed?
- Does the image focus on the advantages or disadvantages of being male or female in a particular culture?
- How would you characterize the artist's tone and his or her attitude toward the person, place, event, or idea?
- Is one type of image (e.g., photograph, painting, cartoon) especially effective in communicating the ideas involved?
- Does the image suggest an unrealistic or overly sentimental view of the subject?
- Does the image examine the issue in terms of forces that shape history?

FINDING, USING, AND DOCUMENTING SOURCES

S ome assignments may require you to do additional research using books and other resources from your library or information found on the Internet. This chapter will introduce you to the methods by which you can pursue your inquiry and document your results.

The steps involved in this process are choosing and limiting a topic, finding sources, evaluating the usefulness of sources, taking worthwhile notes, drafting a thesis statement, organizing the information, writing your paper, and documenting your sources.

LIMITING YOUR TOPIC

The best research papers are written on subjects that are interesting to the writer. However, in choosing your topic, you must also consider the amount of time you have to write your paper and the kind of resources that your library can provide.

If you have not been assigned a topic in class, you can speed up your search for an interesting subject by paying attention to (1) controversial issues reported in the news, (2) subjects about which you and your friends have heated discussions, and (3) topics that seemed interesting when they were discussed in your other courses. At this stage, you can consider almost anything as a potential topic for your paper, but we suggest drawing up a list of topics phrased as questions and looking carefully at each topic to see what would be involved. For example, if you were interested in the new frontiers of genetic engineering and drew up a list of questions about topics on which you would like to become better informed and able to express a well-supported opinion, your list might read as follows:

1. How do certain defective genes cause diseases in humans?

2. How do scientists identify the location of defective genes?

3. How do scientists replace defective genes with healthy ones?

4. Who should decide which genes should be altered?

5. How can we keep genetically "flawed" individuals from being discriminated against in the workplace, by insurance companies, and by society?

6. Who decides whether genetic information about a person is shared with the rest of their family?

7. How should the line between fixing "defective" genes and enhancing "normal" genes be drawn?

8. Will genetic engineering lead to a return to eugenics?

The next step is to scan your list of topics and decide which ones to rule out because they would be too difficult to develop. For example, questions 1, 2, and 3 might be too technical. Questions 4, 5, and 8 would be too general and clearly beyond the scope of your paper, and question 6 would probably be hard to find information on. This leaves you with question 7 as a possible topic for your investigation.

You are now ready to immerse yourself in the print and electronic sources of information available to you in the library, assess which ones would be useful to you, and start taking notes.

▓▓▓ USING AND EVALUATING PRINT SOURCES

Your library contains a vast store of information: books, magazine and newspaper articles, government documents, handbooks, dictionaries, encyclopedias, dissertations, and even multimedia items such as DVDs, videotapes, and filmstrips. The gateways to locating these resources are your library's online card catalog and periodical indexes and other databases.

Your Library's Online Catalog

The computerized card catalog in your library lists all the books in the library along with other holdings. It might also tell you when materials have been checked out and when they are due. These materials are listed by author, title, subject, and location, along with complete publication information, and might even tell you whether the same material is available at other regional libraries. Catalog systems differ, but they all have terminals (some with printers attached that permit you to print what you are looking at on the screen). You conduct searches by typing in key terms that reflect the way in which the book is categorized by author, title, and subject according to the Library of Congress system. This system classifies books and other materials according to alphabetical codes that use numbers for further subdivisions.

Locating Relevant Reference Works

The range of resources available in the library includes general reference works with entries written by experts in specific fields that will give you a comprehensive, balanced overview. If you need more specialized information, there are encyclopedias, handbooks, dictionaries, and biographical volumes that provide more in-depth treatment of particular subjects, define unfamiliar terms, and provide information on prominent people. You might wish to check how the same topic is discussed in more than one reference work, since different aspects are emphasized in each one. Bibliographies that follow these articles can lead you to other sources.

Useful General Reference Works

Encyclopedias

Chambers Encyclopedia
Colliers Encyclopedia (as of 1998, Encarta)
Encyclopedia Americana
Encyclopedia Britannica
Merriam Webster's Collegiate Encyclopedia

Encyclopedias usually contain a separate index in the last volume that will provide all the cross-references to your topic.

Dictionaries

Webster's Collegiate Dictionary
The Oxford English Dictionary (in twenty volumes)

Dictionaries will give you information on the origins, meanings, usage, and status of terms. More specialized dictionaries also include technical terms that are not found in general dictionaries.

Biographical Resources

Dictionary of National Biography
Dictionary of American Biography
Current Biography
Who's Who in America
Contemporary Authors
Who Was Who in America (for historical figures)

These works will give you a brief outline of the person's life. In addition, there are more specialized biographies that focus on professions, gender, ethnicity, and nationality.

Application 2.1

What kinds of reference sources would you most likely consult for information on the following topics? For which topics would you need to consult a more specialized reference work?

1. The history of a U.S. Supreme Court decision
2. How a word in current use evolved from its original meaning
3. Writers who specialize in war stories
4. What menus on the *Titanic* can tell us about social class
5. How the terms *salsa* or *masala* have broadened their meanings
6. The symbolism of outfits worn by clowns or mimes
7. Gender messages in fairy tales
8. The blogosphere
9. Athletes as role models
10. Films about boxing
11. Inventions that improve everyday life

Other Print Sources

In addition to general and specialized reference works and books listed in the online catalog, your library has periodical indexes that will point you toward articles in newspapers and magazines as well as more specialized journals in which recent research results are published. These indexes alphabetically list subjects and authors in a range of periodicals. Periodicals are works that appear regularly in print and have the exact same title for successive issues. They can be newspapers; popular magazines, such as *Newsweek* or *Sports Illustrated*; or professional journals, such as the *American Journal of Psychology*, published for people in a specific field. The best procedure is to start with a general periodical index such as *The Reader's Guide to Periodical Literature*, which covers numerous general magazines and journals. From there, you can further narrow your search by consulting specialized indexes such as *The Social Sciences Index* or *The Humanities Index*.

Another type of valuable print source is abstracts that contain brief summaries of articles in different subject areas, such as *Psychological Abstracts, Dissertation Abstracts International*, and *Abstracts of English Studies*. An abstract has the same information as an index and is used in the same way to locate articles in periodicals but has the advantage of being both an index and a source of concise summaries of original articles.

If your topic is something that is newsworthy, you might consult one of the newspaper indexes, such as *The New York Times Index*, which summarizes news stories alphabetically under specific subject headings. Indexes are also available for the *Los Angeles Times*, the *Wall Street Journal*, and the *Christian Science Monitor*.

Using Database Indexes

Other valuable resources to consult in your search are the numerous database indexes that allow you to locate articles in journals, magazines, and newspapers. It is best to start with general coverage databases such as InfoTrac and EBSCOhost (covering business, academic, and general circulation periodicals) and then go to more specialized databases such as ERIC (Education Resource Information Center) and Lexis-Nexis (legal information, news, and public affairs). The search terms that you use, either alone or in combination, can yield a wealth of information—or even too much information—on your topic. To be efficient, you should combine broad search terms (such as "genetic") with a more specific term (such as "screening") connected by the word AND or a + sign. These databases can generally be accessed either online or on a CD-ROM or DVD-ROM. The advantage of accessing online databases is that most of them are updated daily. However, in order for you to be able to use them, your library needs to subscribe to the service.

Evaluating Print Sources

The sheer number of books, articles, and other print-based resources that you can find makes it all the more important that you screen the information in terms of what will be most useful to you. Some of the questions to ask are as follows:

- Is it immediately obvious how this source is related to the question you want to answer (for example, "How should the line between fixing defective genes and enhancing normal genes be drawn?")?
- What special knowledge, background, or training does the author possess in this area?
- Is the source timely and relevant to the knowledge you have accumulated on this subject?
- Does the author have an agenda that could bias the results or conclusions that he or she presents?

Application 2.2

What key terms could you use to search online catalogs, periodical indexes, abstracts, or databases to create a potentially useful list of sources for the following key terms?

- The influence of the Civil War in fiction by twentieth-century southern writers
- The need to restrict global arms sales
- The effectiveness of group prayer
- The failure of crop substitution programs
- Irresponsible marketing practices geared toward children
- Limits on malpractice suits
- The role of dark energy in the universe

There is no magic number of sources that you will need, but for a ten-page paper between four and twelve sources would most likely provide you appropriate coverage and depth, as long as each source was relevant to your topic.

Creating a Log of Print Sources

As you read and identify a source that might be useful, be sure to record all the information you will later need to cite in your bibliography or list of works cited. You can put this information in a computer file or on notecards, using a separate card for each source (4" × 6" is best, since that gives you room enough and is still easy to carry). For books, you will need to record the call number; the author's name as well as any editors or translators; the title and subtitle; the edition, if other than the first; and complete publication data, including the city, the publisher's name, and the date. For articles in periodicals, record any and all authors; the title and subtitle of the article; the complete title of the journal, magazine, or newspaper; the volume number and issue number, if given; and the date it was published, as well as the page numbers of the entire article.

USING AND EVALUATING INTERNET SOURCES

You can assess the quality and usefulness of Internet sources using many of the same criteria that you would apply to print sources. But there are some important differences as well. Moreover, Internet sources should be used in conjunction with, not as a replacement for, print sources. Some important guidelines to consider are as follows:

- Is the source relevant to the question you want to answer?
- Can you corroborate the information from the Internet source with printed sources?
- Is the information up to date, unless the nature of your topic allows you to use older material that pertains to a settled issue?
- On the basis of who the author of the website is (an individual, organization, or company), do you have any reason to believe that the information has been selected to support an agenda? The domain name suffix will give you a clue to who hosts the website: .com (commercial), .edu (educational institution), .gov (government), .mil (military), .net (network provider), or .org (nonprofit organization). Countries outside the United States have different suffixes, such as .de for Germany, .ca for Canada, .uk for Great Britain, and .nz for New Zealand.
- What kind of expertise does the author bring to the issue?
- Does the site have useful links to other sites that are actively maintained and updated? Is it user-friendly (takes few clicks to find what you want) and free of errors in grammar and spelling?

Using Search Directories

Search engines such as Yahoo! include directories that categorize websites according to subjects. These are especially useful when you have a general issue that you want to investigate, but you do not have a sense of what would be involved in locating resources on a specific topic. Yahoo!'s homepage has a link to a "directory" section that shows multiple categories of subjects. For example, if you were searching for information on genetics, you would click on the category of "science," which would then bring you through a directory on biology to one on genetics. If you then clicked on "genetics," you could follow this line of inquiry until you got to gene therapy, which has its own directory of relevant websites that would allow you to investigate your research question on the ethical issues arising from genetic engineering. You could then use these sites to supplement and corroborate your print sources.

Searching with Key Words

As an alternative to searching from general to specific through subject directories, you can also use search engines to retrieve information if your topic is very specific and well defined, but your search must use highly specific key words, either alone or in combination, to yield a manageable number of "hits," or matches. In other words, add modifiers such as "ethical issues and genetic engineering" to a basic term ("genetics") to narrow your topic.

Creating a Log of Internet Sources

It is important to keep track of information about each Internet source you consult, just as you would for a printed text. You will need the following:

- The name of the author, host, or sponsoring agency
- The title and subtitle of the document
- The date when the document was posted or last modified
- The date when you accessed the information
- The publication information for the print version (if applicable)
- The web address of the site (the URL)

▨▨▨ DEVELOPING A THESIS STATEMENT

In the process of becoming familiar with available sources of information on your issue or research question, you have become informed enough to spot contradictions between sources, have developed a sense of what sources are reliable, and have reached the point at which you can make a claim about your topic and back it up with evidence. You now can acknowledge views that are different from your own and respond to them. In essence, you have become something of an expert on the aspect of the subject that most interested you when you first started.

At this point, you are ready to develop a preliminary thesis that can always be revised later. Your thesis statement will help you when you start to take notes from your sources, although what you discover might encourage you to change it. If you look carefully at the way your thesis is worded, you will notice that it can clarify the relationship between the evidence you find and suggest which rhetorical mode will be most useful to you when you start to arrange and present your results. For example, if your thesis were "fixing defective genes for medical reasons causes far fewer problems than using gene therapy to enhance intelligence, beauty, or strength," the body of your paper could use a comparison-and-contrast organization supported by a cause-and-effect analysis. Or on the basis of the results of your research, your thesis might read "the way insurance companies classify risks and charge premiums is weighted against those with a family history of genetic defects." A paper that was organized around this statement would use classification and division and definition (as to what constitutes a risk) as the organizational patterns.

Remember that a research paper can simply explain something and does not have to offer an opinion, evaluation, or interpretation, and it certainly does not need to be an argument.

NOTE-TAKING PROCEDURES

Note taking is an essential part of the research process, since the quality of your result depends to a great degree on the evidence you accumulate from your sources. More notes do not necessarily lead to a better paper. It is the quality and usefulness of the information you record, rather than sheer volume, that will permit you to enter into the discussion with your own ideas. Some people prefer to take notes on legal pads or index cards; others prefer to use a computer. Software is available that will help you not only to keep track of your sources, but also to organize your notes into related idea clusters. If you use index cards, put only one source of information on each card, and be sure to record the title and page number of the source.

To help you later when you are putting your paper together, include a few words or a phrase with each source that will remind you of the aspect of your research to which the source relates. Later, these key phrases will help you to spot recurring themes that can be consolidated in major sections of your paper. They can even be used to create a working outline that will tell you whether each section is equally developed.

Your notes can take the form of (1) summaries that give an overview of the original source (discussed in Chapter 1), (2) quotations of exact words used at one point in the source, and (3) paraphrases that restate ideas and information from a source in your own words.

Quoting

Direct quotations of a source should include all the original punctuation, reproducing *exactly*, word for word, what is in the original. Quote sparingly and only when ideas are stated so vividly that a summary or paraphrase would fail to do justice to them. You quote when you want your readers to hear the voices of authorities or experts and when you want to convey a strong sense of the original passage. When you are integrating quotes into your paper, you *must* include a phrase that puts the quote in context and identifies the source. Otherwise, you are committing *plagiarism*, that is, using someone else's words as if they were your own (discussed later in this chapter).

Quotes of fewer than four lines are run into the text and enclosed in double quotation marks. In MLA style, the citation style that is commonly used in the humanities, a parenthetical citation for the page number(s) of the source precedes the punctuation mark at the end of the sentence. For example:

According to Weil and Rosen, "People who never take drugs also seek out highs" (15).

If this quotation was longer than four lines, it would be indented ten spaces from the left margin, double-spaced without an extra space above or below, reproduced without quotation marks, and introduced by a lead-in phrase (followed by a comma) or sentence (followed by a colon). Unlike in a quote that is run into the text, in a block quote the parenthetical citation appears *after* the period that ends the quote, separated by one space.

If you change the original quote in any way, you must signal this to your reader. For example, if you omit part of a quote, place three spaced periods (an ellipsis mark) to indicate this:

According to Weil and Rosen, "Highs are states of consciousness marked by feelings of . . . self-transcendence, concentration, and energy" (15).

Be careful of what you delete; the deletion should not change the meaning of the original quotation.

Paraphrasing

Much of the material you want to use from sources will require you to restate in your own words (or *paraphrase*) the original. By restating the thoughts, ideas, and opinions of the source in this way, you demonstrate that you truly have grasped the meaning of what you have read. Unlike concise summaries, paraphrases are the same length as or slightly shorter than the original. The thoughts and ideas are those of the authors, but the language is yours. Paraphrases should be not merely a copy of the original with a few words changed, but rather a restatement of the key ideas in a new way that reflects your own understanding. You might wish to place the original to one side and write down the points that you remember, thinking the idea through thoroughly and using language that is natural to you. Then check the original to see whether you have inadvertently used the exact phrases or left out an important point.

Paraphrasing is a perfectly acceptable way of drawing on an original source and requires documentation just as summaries and quotations do. But the paraphrase itself must *completely* translate the original into your own words. Not to do so would make you guilty of plagiarism.

For example, here is an original passage from Andrew Weil and Winifred Rosen's *Chocolate to Morphine* (Boston: Houghton Mifflin, 1983, p. 15):

> Many drug users talk about getting high. Highs are states of consciousness marked by feelings of euphoria, lightness, self-transcendence, concentration, and energy. People who never take drugs also seek out highs. In fact, having high experiences from time to time may be necessary to our physical and mental health, just as dreaming at night seems to be vital to our well-being. Perhaps that is why a desire to alter normal consciousness exists in everyone and why people pursue the experiences even though there are sometimes uncomfortable side effects.

You would commit plagiarism if you duplicated the language or even the sentence structure of the original or substituted synonyms for the original words.

In addition, you must introduce paraphrased material with a signal phrase that names the authors or the source and conclude your paraphrase with a parenthetical page citation. For example, the following *unacceptable* paraphrase is too close to the sentence structure of the original and simply provides synonyms. It also does not include a signal phrase or a page citation.

Drug takers mention experiencing feelings of floating, altered states and ego-enhancement. Non drug-users also search for these feelings. Actually, feeling high occasionally is probably required for the health of our minds and bodies, much as having dreams is key to overall health. Maybe the need to change everyday awareness is shared by one and all and explains why people pursue these experiences despite the unpleasant side effects.

This uses the ideas, the sentence structure, and even some phrases of the original without giving credit to the authors.

Here is an *acceptable* paraphrase, along with the required signal phrase and page citation.

Weil and Rosen note that drugs allow the user to experience a feeling of vitality, excitement, loss of ego, and a heightened sense of well-being. Since people all over the world engage in non-drug-taking activities to produce this state, we might conclude that human beings have an innate need to "alter consciousness" that is so strong that it will make people overlook possible bad reactions produced by the drugs (<u>Chocolate to Morphine</u> 15).

As in this example, you can use exact words from the original as long as you enclose them in quotation marks.

Notice how paraphrasing makes the writer think carefully about the ideas in order to express them in different words. Paraphrasing is a way of thinking through the subject by taking into account what others have had to say about it. Remember that because you are using someone else's ideas, facts, and research as a basis for your own paper, you must always provide a reference that indicates your source.

AVOIDING PLAGIARISM

As we pointed out in the discussion of paraphrasing, you must always document the words and ideas of others. This includes word-for-word quotations from print or electronic sources, summaries or paraphrases of original sources restated in your own words, and factual or statistical references in whatever form they are presented, including visual formats. To avoid accidental plagiarism, take accurate notes on any source you plan to use. Carefully compare the information in your notes (or on your note cards) with the original sources to check that you have put sets of double quotation marks around quotations. For summarized or paraphrased material, be sure that you have not unintentionally used the phrasing, words, or overall structure or form of the original. As we saw with paraphrasing and quoting, you must include an introductory phrase that identifies the author of the original material and a page reference.

A double standard appears to exist between crediting print sources and Internet sources because many students believe that downloading and incorporating material from websites does not require documentation of thoughts, ideas, words, phrases, and statistics, as material from print sources would. This belief is incorrect. The collaborative nature of the Internet might delude you into thinking that you do not have to provide signal phrases, citations, or even quotation marks around original words or phrases. But you do. You will be commiting plagiarism if you do not. Aside from the severe penalties that many colleges impose on students who plagiarize, consider all the money, time, and effort you have devoted to your education and the way you would be shortchanging yourself by simply copying someone else's work without doing the research yourself and framing your conclusions in your own words and style.

The only exception is information that is considered **common knowledge**, that is, ideas, facts, and terms that an educated person could be expected to know. Information that is available in multiple sources and concepts that are widely used in specific fields of study do not require documentation. Commonly used quotes (for example, "After three days, fish and guests stink," attributed to John Lily 1554?–1606) also fit into this category and can be used without documentation. However, you should use the "common knowledge exception" with great caution. If there is any doubt about whether or not you need to provide a reference for something, you should always document it.

For more information on avoiding plagiarism, visit the website for this book at **college.hmco.com/pic/hirschberg.**

For students from other countries (such as Russia, China, Japan, Korea, and India), the issue of plagiarism may be difficult to grasp, since their cultures prize collaborative effort rather than individual performance. It might even be considered impolite or egotistical to assert the value of one's own work. These students should take care to be aware of the importance of acknowledging the use of information that in those cultures might be regarded as being in the public domain. The work of others should *always* be documented.

USING MLA STYLE TO DOCUMENT YOUR SOURCES

The recommended method for documenting sources in the humanities is that developed by the Modern Language Association (MLA) (www.mla.org). This style consists of a brief parenthetical citation in the text that corresponds to an entry in the list of works cited at the end of the paper. It has the advantage of providing the author's name and a page reference in the text that directs the reader to the full information on the source in the list of works cited.

For example, here is a parenthetical text citation from a student paper:

The debate of technological haves and have-nots, known as the "Digital Divide," is a major problem that our educational system faces today (Attewell 252).

The corresponding entry in the list of works cited gives full information on this source:

Attewell, Paul. "The First and Second Digital Divides." Sociology of Education 74 (2001): 252–59.

In-Text Citations

The form your citation takes depends on how much information you have already provided and the nature of the source. You can either introduce the author's name in your own sentence and cite the page number in parentheses, or identify both the author and the page within the parentheses, as in the example above. Notice that the documentation is placed before the punctuation in the sentence. In addition to a work by one author, the most common forms are as follows:

A Work with Two or Three Authors

Wearing the veil has come to symbolize a political stance as well as a cultural and religious imperative (Fernea and Fernea 70).

For more information on MLA style, visit the website for this book at **college.hmco.com/pic/hirschberg.**

A Work with More Than Three Authors

Use only the first author's last name followed by "et al." (meaning "and others").

The concept of land reform created a revolution in rural societies (Burke et al. 77).

Electronic Source

Electronic sources are cited like print sources by using the author's name or the title if the author is not known. If paragraph numbers are supplied in the source use the abbreviation "par." or "pars." in the citation.

In Japanese culture, maintaining one's personal space is of the utmost importance (Caesar, pars. 2–3).

Multivolume Work

Separate the volume number and page number with a colon:

According to Toynbee, respect for ancestors provides a stabilizing force in primitive cultures (7: 114).

Two or More Works by the Same Author

When you cite one of several works by the same author, include the work's title and shorten it to the key word(s). The complete title for this citation is *The Man That Corrupted Hadleyburg.*

In his later years, Twain's cautionary fables concentrate on greed among other things (Hadleyburg 377).

Indirect Source

When quoting someone else, use "qtd. in" followed by the last name of the author in which you find the reference and the page number.

Lykken asserts that "more of these unique characteristics than we previously thought may be determined by a particular combination of genes" (qtd. in Holden 35).

Be sure to list the indirect source in the list of works cited.

Work Without a Listed Author

Use the complete or abbreviated version of the title.

A recent editorial analyzes the reasons for the failure to achieve peace in the Middle East ("Building Mideast Peace" 26).

More Than One Work in a Citation

There is intense debate over such basic definitional questions as to whether the most serious manifestations of alcohol disorders should be treated as "diseases" (Keller 76; Robinson 72).

Literary Works

Since works of fiction, poetry, and drama appear in different editions, you need to provide more specific information in your citation. For a novel, give the chapter or section number in addition to the page number in the edition you used.

> Anne Tyler, in <u>Saint Maybe</u>, describes her main character, Ian, as "handsome and easy-going" (2; ch. 1).

For a poem, provide line numbers, not page numbers. You can include up to three lines of poetry in your text separated by a slash (/) with a space on each side.

> In "The Orange," Diane Wakowski describes the speaker's sense of freedom in an unusual way: "driving through the desert at night in summer / can be / like peeling an orange" (lines 1–3).

For a play that has parts, acts, or scenes, cite them as follows (in the example below, Act 1, line 140).

> In Dario Fo's <u>We Won't Pay! We Won't Pay!</u>, Giovanni learns some surprising news: "You mean she's pregnant?" (1.140).

List of Works Cited in MLA Style

The works cited list includes only those works to which you refer in the text of your paper. The works cited page should begin on a new numbered page at the end and should be titled "Works Cited" (without quotation marks). Double-space the entire list and list works alphabetically by the author's last name. Works without named authors are alphabetized by the first main word in the title (not "a," "the," or "an"). Start the first line at the left margin, and indent subsequent lines of each entry one-half inch or five spaces.

Citing Books in MLA Style

Book by One Author

Put the last name first for a single author followed by a comma and the first name. Give the full title including any subtitles, and underline it. Include the city of publication, the publisher, and date of publication. Use periods to separate these items of information as follows:

> McCarthy, Mary. <u>Venice Observed</u>. New York: Harper, 1966.

In this context, "New York" refers to the city, not the state.

Book by Two or Three Authors

List the second and third author (if any) in normal order as they appear on the book's title page.

Ward, Peter D., and Donald Brownlee. <u>Rare Earth</u>. New York: Copernicus, 2000.

(Note that only the first author's name is reversed.)

Book by Three or More Authors

You can list all the authors or only the first author followed by "et al." (meaning "and others"). If you use "et al." in your list of works cited, use the same form in your parenthetical citations.

Burke, Martin, Brian Mahoney, William White, and Eben Simon. <u>Peasant Revolutions</u>.
New York: Random, 1999.

Burke, Martin, et al. <u>Peasant Revolutions</u>. New York: Random, 1999.

Two or More Works by the Same Author

Provide the author's name for the first work only. For subsequent works, provide the title, preceded by three unspaced hyphens and a period.

Peters, Fritz. <u>Finistere</u>. New York: Farrar, 1951.

---. <u>Gurdjieff Remembered</u>. New York: Samuel Weiser, 1971.

Book with an Author and an Editor

Nanda, Serena. <u>The Naked Anthropologist</u>. Ed. Philip R. deVita. Belmont: Wadsworth, 1992.

Translation

Paz, Octavio. <u>The Labyrinth of Solitude</u>. Trans. Lysander Kemp. New York: Grove, 1961.

Revised Edition

Vilar, Esther. <u>The Manipulated Man</u>. 2nd ed. New York: Farrar, 1998.

Anthology

Lopate, Phillip, ed. <u>The Art of the Personal Essay: An Anthology from the Classical Era to
the Present</u>. New York: Doubleday, 1994.

Selection in an Anthology

Page numbers for the entire selection appear at the end of the entry.

Didion, Joan. "Goodbye to All That." <u>The Art of the Personal Essay: An Anthology from the
Classical Era to the Present</u>. Ed. Phillip Lopate. New York: Doubleday, 1994. 681–88.

More Than One Selection from the Same Anthology

When the anthology is listed separately under the editor's name, all entries within that anthology need to include only a cross reference to the anthology entry.

Dillard, Annie. "Seeing." Lopate 693–706.

Chapter or Section in a Book

Carver, Raymond. "Why Don't You Dance?" <u>Where I'm Calling From: New and Selected Stories</u>. New York: Random, 1989. 155–61.

Foreword, Preface, Introduction, or Afterword

Trilling, Lionel. Introduction. <u>Homage to Catalonia</u>. By George Orwell. New York: Harcourt, 1980. v–xxiii.

Article in a Reference Work

"Faberge, Peter Carl." <u>The Concise Columbia Encyclopedia</u>. 2nd ed. 1989.

Citing Periodicals: Journals, Magazines, and Newspapers

Article in a Journal with Continuous Pagination Throughout an Annual Volume

Some journals, especially scholarly ones, are numbered continuously throughout all the issues within a year. For these, give the title of the journal followed by volume number, the year of publication in parenthesis followed by a colon, and the page numbers of the article.

Rockas, Leo. "A Dialogue on Dialogue." <u>College English</u> 41 (1980): 570–80.

Article in a Journal with Separate Pagination in Each Issue

For journals that begin each issue with page 1, give the issue number after the volume number, followed by the date, a colon, and the page numbers.

Hellman, Leo. "The Psychology of Adolescence." <u>Cognitive Studies</u> 19.7 (2000): 15–22.

Monthly Magazine

Gibbs, W. Wayt. "How Should We Set Priorities?" <u>Scientific American</u> Sept. 2005: 108–15.

(Note: In MLA style, all months are abbreviated except May, June, and July. If an article does not appear on consecutive pages, include only the first page followed by a + sign.)

Weekly Magazine

Sylvester, David. "Genius of Michelangelo by Moore." <u>New York Times Magazine</u> 8 Mar. 1964: 24–29.

Article in a Newspaper

If the article is printed on nonconsecutive pages, list the first page, including the section and pages numbers or letters followed by a + sign. Do not include an introductory article (*Wall Street Journal*, not *The Wall Street Journal*).

> Petzinger, Thomas J., Gary Putka, and Stephen J. Sansweet. "High Flyers." Wall Street
> Journal 12 Sept. 1983, sec. 1: 1+.

Citing Electronic Sources

CD-ROMS and Other Portable Databases: Periodically Published Databases

> Stewart, Amy. "Reasons for the Rising Rates of Autism." New York Times 17 June
> 2002, late ed.: B1. New York Times Ondisc. CD-ROM. UMI-Proquest. Nov. 2002.

Citations in this form should consist of the following items: author, "title" of article and publication data, *title* of the database, publication medium (CD-ROM), vendor (distributor), date of publication (release date, as shown on the title screen or above the menu of the database).

CD-ROMS and Other Portable Databases: Nonperiodically Published Databases

> The Oxford English Dictionary. 2nd ed. CD-ROM, Oxford: Oxford UP, 1992.

CD-ROM publications in this form are not continually revised but are issued a single time. The work is cited as you would a book, but add a description of the medium of publication.

Publication on Magnetic Tape or Diskette

> "Kansas State University." Peterson's College Database. Magnetic tape. Princeton:
> Peterson's, 1994.
> "Hughes, Ted." Vers. 1.1 Disclit: World Authors. Diskette. Dublin: Hall and
> OCLC, 1994.

A magnetic tape publication or a diskette is also cited as you would a book but includes the medium and any edition or version after the title.

Citing Online Sources When you cite sources obtained on the Internet, you follow the same procedure as you do for print sources, but you also supply some additional items of information: (1) the date when your source was published electronically (if given), (2) the date you accessed the source, and (3) the source's electronic address, or URL, in angle brackets. Moreover, the form for citing different kinds of sources on the Internet requires different kinds of information, as shown in following examples. (Note: When creating a citation for an Internet source, the MLA style requires that you break URLs only after a slash.)

An Entire Website (Scholarly Project, Information Database, Journal, or Professional Website)

If you are citing an entire site or project rather than a short work within it, begin your entry with the site's title (underlined) followed by the editor or person responsible for maintaining the site. Then include the date when the site was last updated (if known), the name of the sponsoring institution or organization (if known), the date you accessed the site, and the URL in angle brackets. End with a period.

> MLA: Modern Language Association. 9 May 2003. Mod. Lang. Assn. of Amer. 9 Nov. 2003 <http://www.mla.org>.
>
> Perseus Digital Library. Ed. Gregory Crane. Updated daily. Tufts U. 9 Sept. 2003 <http://www.perseus.tufts.edu>.

An Entire Online Book

> London, Jack. The Iron Heel. New York: Macmillan, 1908. The Jack London Collection. 10 Dec. 1999. Berkeley Digital Lib. SunSITE. 22 Dec. 2006 <http://sunsite.berkeley.edu/London/Writing/IronHeel/>.

Part of an Online Book

> Muir, John. "The City of the Saints." Steep Trails. 1918. 17 July 2006 <http:// encyclopediaindex.com/b/sttr110.htm>.

Article in an Online Journal

> Walters, Julie. "In and Out of Elevators in Japan." Journal of Mundane Behavior 1.1 (2000): 6 pars. 12 Mar. 2000 <http://www.mundanebehavior.org/issues/v1n1/ walters.htm>.

If the pages or paragraphs are numbered, include that information. The abbreviation for pages is pp., and the abbreviation for paragraphs is pars.

Article in an Online Magazine

> Ollivier, Debra S. "Mothers Who Think: Les birds et les bees." Salon 12 May 1998. 19 June 2004 <http://www.salon.com/mwt/feature/1998/05/12feature2.html>.

Article in an Online Reference Book

"Barthes, Roland." <u>Encyclopaedia Britanica Online</u>. Vers. 99.1 1994–2000.

    Encyclopaedia Britanica. 19 June 2000 <http://search.eb.com/bol/

    topic?eu=13685&sctn=1&pm=1>.

E-mail

Reichel, Ruth. "Lemon Cake." E-mail to the author. 2 Dec. 2006.

Article from a Library Subscription Service

For library subscription services that are available online, including EBSCOhost, Lexis-Nexis, ProQuest, and InfoTrac, first provide information about the print sources appropriate to the kind of document, whether book, magazine, article from a newspaper, or other item. Give the name of the database, the name of the service, the name of the library or library subscription system, and the date of access. Give the URL; if it is too long, give the URL of the search page or homepage. If the service provides only the starting page, cite it followed by a hyphen, a space and a period, for example: 148- .

    Gray, Katti. "The Whistle Blower." <u>Essence</u> Feb. 2001: 148- . <u>Academic Search Premier</u>.

        EBSCO. Millburn Free Public Lib. 12 Dec. 2006 <http://searchepnet.com/direct/

        asp?an=4011390&db=aph>.

Article from an Online Newspaper

Smith, Dinitia. "Critic at the Mercy of His Own Kind." <u>New York Times on the Web</u>.

    24 May 2003. 25 May 2003 <http://www.nytimes.com/2003/05/24/books/

    24WOOD.html>.

Online Posting

Provide the author's name, the title of the document as posted on the subject line, the label "Online posting," and the date of posting and the name of the forum (without underlining or quotion marks). Follow this with the date of access and URL or address of the discussion list.

    Palmer, Megan. "Global Warming." Online posting. May 15, 2001. Environmental

        Science Bulletin Board. 18 July 2001 <http://www.escribe.com/science/es/bb/

        index.html?bID=29>.

Personal or Home Webpage

Kingsolver, Barbara. Home page. 28 Feb. 2004. 28 June 2004 <http://

    www.kingsolver.com>.

Citing Other Nonprint Sources

Television or Radio Program

The Mahabharata. "The Game of Dice." Dir. Peter Brook. PBS. WNET, New York.
    28 Feb. 1989.

Cartoon

Assay, Chuck. "Whose rights should legislators protect?" Cartoon. Colorado Springs
    Gazette Telegraph 12 Dec. 1993: 11.

Personal or Phone Interview

Ruesch, Hans. Phone interview. 17 Mar. 2006.

Film, Recording, Videotape, or DVD

Give the author or composer (if appropriate), the title (underlined), the director,
conductor, and/or performer, and year of release.

The Messenger: The Story of Joan of Arc. Dir. Luc Bresson. Perf. Milla Jovovich. DVD.
    Columbia, 2000.

A BRIEF NOTE ON THE APA STYLE OF DOCUMENTATION

Although most humanities courses require students to use MLA style, other disciplines in the social sciences (for example, anthropology, education, business,
economics, political science, law, psychology, and sociology) use the documentation style of the American Psychological Association (www.apastyle.org), known as
APA style. In this system, sometimes called the name-and-date style, sources used
are listed alphabetically by the author's last name double-spaced on a separate
page titled "References" or "Reference List" following the final page of the text.

   In-text citations of sources present the author's name and date of publication
in parenthetical references throughout the paper, not just at the end of the line
as in MLA style. For example:

A study of interactions between doctors and nurses (Stewart, 1992) concludes . . .

This style emphasizes the publication date so that newer studies can immediately
be distinguished from older ones.

For more information on APA style, visit the website for this book at
college.hmco.com/pic/hirschberg.

SAMPLE STUDENT RESEARCH PAPER
IN MLA STYLE

The following student essay uses the MLA style of documentation. We have included marginal comments that point out how Megan combines her own ideas with paraphrases and quotations from her sources.

Hanel 1

Megan Hanel
Professor Ainsworth
English 010
November 17, 2006

Mediocre Media

Do you know where Reese Witherspoon bought her daughter's rain boots? Do you know which restaurant is the trendiest restaurant in New York City?

Attention-getting opener

If you turn on any TV station, open any newspaper or magazine, log onto the Internet, or even listen to the radio, chances are you know these answers. This is because the line between what constitutes entertainment and news has become distorted in American journalism. At the local CVS pharmacy, I counted 36 different magazines devoted to subjects such as celebrity lives or home improvement ideas. On Google, searching for "Tabloid News" brings in 1.9 million results. Even in newspapers, the entertainment section is expanding.

Thesis statement

In fact, the amount of "fluff" reported as news has increased from fifteen percent to forty-three percent in the past thirty years (Hickey 28). This fluff, also known as soft news, is now so prevalent that it is hard to distinguish between what is news and what is entertainment. While the consumers are partly to blame for the blur between news and entertainment because of their insatiable demand for entertainment, the media are largely at fault because of their vested interest in profits. The rise of media conglomerates such as News Corporation and Viacom has led to an intense focus on profits achieved by substituting cheap journalism such as entertainment fluff for hard news. Finally, the line between news and entertainment is further blurred by the conglomerates' ability to promote across various kinds of media.

Paragraph combines Megan's ideas with a paraphrase and statistics from the Hickey article.

Hanel 2

Although only partially responsible, consumers are at fault for entertainment being reported as news. Today's society is obsessed with wealth, fame, and beauty. On the front page of newspapers and on TV, celebrities embody the ideal person: a person who has the money to spend on several homes, the beauty to appear on magazines, and the fame to get the person whatever he or she wants. People idolize celebrities not because "they are beyond the ordinary person but instead because they are extraordinary people who reflect what we have the potential to become" (Drucker and Cathcart 37). What better way to facilitate this obsession than in the news? The demand for entertainment in the news was first recognized in the late 1970s. To determine why newspapers were losing readership, the American Society of Newspaper Editors and the Newspaper Advertising Bureau hired researcher Ruth Clark to conduct a survey for probable causes. After surveying two thousand people nationwide via telephone calls and house visits, she concluded that readers were simply not interested in what was being reported (Koch 1122). At the time, foreign issues such as the OPEC crisis and the Cold War dominated the front pages of newspapers and the headlines of the nightly news. However, readers not only wanted more "news you could use" (Koch 1127) but also wanted to feel connected to what they were reading (Drucker and Cathcart 24). Because of Clark's findings, which showed that audiences were more interested in entertainment than news, the media began to report more entertainment stories and less hard news in order to increase readership.

> Paragraph combines Megan's ideas, a paraphrase and a quotation from Drucker and Cathcart, and a paraphrase and quote from Koch.

While it is the consumer who demanded an increase in entertainment news, it is the media, not the consumer, who bear the most blame for the lack of hard news because of the media conglomerates' ever-increasing focus on profits. Prior to 1975, most media companies were privately owned by one person or one family. However, during an 18-month period between 1984 and 1986, nonjournalistic corporations, such as GE, purchased each of the three major U.S. broadcast networks (Hickey 29). Today, only

> Paragraph combines Megan's ideas with a paraphrase from the Hickey article and a paraphrase from the Hatch article.

five media powerhouses—Time Warner, Disney, General Electric, News Corp, and Viacom—control up to 80 percent of America's prime-time TV programming. These large corporations took an interest in growth business models such as media in order to create more revenues (Hatch 847). For example, GE's primary business specialties, appliances and electricity, are fairly steady businesses. By buying into media such as cable and movie studios, GE was able to capture a source of expanding revenue.

With these mergers and acquisitions, the corporations could become more efficient than a privately held company. By owning several media outlets, news could be produced at one location and then shared with other related companies. As the competition among news companies grew, the focus shifted from high-quality journalism to growing revenue and increased profits, which attract public investors. Shareholders require higher stock prices and want high dividends in order to make a profit on their investments. To achieve this, media companies look for ways to continually improve profits. One of the most logical ways is to reduce the costs of production. For example, Reader's Digest demanded that costs be decreased up to ten percent annually, year after year, to achieve a higher profit (Hickey 32). Eventually, companies looked directly to the news divisions in order to improve profitability. News divisions had "sprawling, highly paid staffs, lavish operating budgets, and perishable product and ratings that would prevent ad sales from ever covering costs reliably" and thus were a great place to cut costs (Hickey 33). For instance, by eliminating just one U.S. correspondent stationed in a city such as Hong Kong, Paris, or Moscow, the company is able to save $500,000 a year by eliminating pay, perks, and living expenses. Thus, parent companies began to decrease the number of journalists and camera operators employed and the amount of money spent on research for each story (Greenblatt 856).

> Paragraph uses material from the Hickey and Greenblatt articles to support Megan's conclusion.

However, by eliminating high-quality journalists, they were also eliminating high-quality, in-depth stories. Yet the need for news forced companies to look for cheaper news. The prime source for this cheap news is entertainment (Greenblatt 854). First,

> Paragraph combines Megan's ideas with a paraphrase from the Greenblatt article.

Hanel 4

instead of having to employ a photojournalist who requires a yearly salary, benefits and insurance, media companies are able to hire freelance photographers, also known as paparazzi, on a day-to-day basis. Thus, the companies are not required to provide a yearly salary or insurance, which decreases overall costs.

Not only does entertainment news not require expensive professional photojournalists, it also does not require in-depth research. Whereas a report on Myanmar's repressive government restrictions on electricity usage would require extensive research and time which equates to money, a report on Britney Spears' eating habits takes very little time and money. A writer must just contact Britney's personal representative, asking for the details. The PR rep will then issue a statement on behalf of Britney. The whole process can be done over the phone or Internet, making costs almost nonexistent.

> Paragraph develops Megan's ideas.

Finally, entertainment is useful for low-cost news because it does not involve controversial topics. While controversial, cutting-edge issues used to be at the forefront of journalism, today controversy is shied away from. By reporting on the tensions in the Middle East or the oppressive actions of North Korean President Kim Il Sung, journalists are more likely to offend not only the readers, but also their advertisers and their corporate parents (Koch 1138). For instance, Al Neuharth, chairman of <u>USA Today</u>, insisted that the paper would contain "no downers," such as the Middle East conflict, because they eliminate potential readers (Thomas). Entertainment, however, is rarely as controversial as political tensions. Thus, when faced with the choice between politics and fluff, it is more beneficial for the journalists to publish the entertainment stories.

> Paragraph combines Megan's ideas with a paraphrase from the Koch article and a quotation from the Thomas article.

Overall, the rise of conglomerates and their focus on profits has led to the increase in cheaply produced entertainment news. Entertainment has become a large part of what passes for news not only because its low cost of production but also because of the parent companies' ability to advertise its programming across multiple forms of media at a relatively low cost.

Increased promotion not only raises the profit for the entertainment being promoted but also captures a wider viewing audience for the program on which the advertising appears. Cross-promotion increases profits by decreasing advertising costs. Today advertising is a very expensive business. However, it is considerably cheaper for a movie studio to advertise in another medium such as television when the channel is owned by the same parent company. As a result, the parent companies flood their markets with advertisements. For instance, on GE's website, in the right lower corner, a small trailer for the movie Man of the Year can be watched. It just so happens that the movie is produced by Universal Studios, a subsidiary of GE.

Another example of cross-promotion is seen on news shows. Recently, Fox News aired a segment about the television show The Simpsons. Although it does not constitute news, but rather entertainment, The Simpsons appeared on the Fox News Network because both Fox News and The Simpsons are owned by News Corporation. By airing a segment on The Simpsons, News Corporation was able to raise profits in two ways. First, it was able to bring in a wider audience to the Fox News program. The demographic for cable news programs is an older, more mature crowd. However, by airing a story on a program watched mostly by teenagers, Fox News was able to attract these viewers. In the process of increasing viewership for Fox News, News Corporation is also advertising for The Simpsons. Therefore, because cross-promotion increases profits in two ways simultaneously, parent companies are making news programs more like entertainment shows.

But how can journalism shift back to the coverage of hard news when entertainment as news satisfies both consumers' and producers' needs? Perhaps the answer lies with Jon Stewart and Steven Colbert. Although theirs are mock news programs, Stewart's show had more male viewers aged 18 to 34 than any of the network evening news shows ("Young America"). Perhaps it is because Jon Stewart pokes fun at the stories he is reporting. On the promotions for the evening news, the tag lines always

Paragraph uses statistics from the CNN article to support Megan's conclusions.

Hanel 6

sound like life or death. I have heard countless times that if I did not tune in, I could be missing information that "could save my life." However, Jon Stewart advertises using humor. He pokes fun at serious issues yet still gives the facts. By making the actual news more entertaining instead of making it actual entertainment, I think that journalism can still retain its authority while captivating an audience.

> In your paper, the Works Cited would begin a new page.

Works Cited

> Heading centered

Drucker, Susan J., and Robert S. Cathcart, eds. <u>American Heroes in a Media Age</u>. Cresskill: Hampton, 1994.

> An anthology

Greenblatt, Alan. "Media Bias." <u>CQ Researcher</u> 14.36 (2004): 853–76. 27 Nov. 2006 <http://library.cqpress.com/cqresearcher/cqresrre2004101500>.

> Online journal articles

Hatch, David. "Media Ownership." <u>CQ Researcher</u> 13.35 (2003): 845–68. 27 Nov. 2006 <http://library.cqpress.com/cqresearcher/cqresrre2003101000>.

Hickey, Neil. "Money Lust: How Pressure for Profit Is Perverting Journalism." <u>Columbia Journalism Review</u> July/Aug. 1998: 28–36.

Koch, Kathy. "Journalism Under Fire." <u>CQ Researcher</u> 8.48 (1998): 1121–44. 27 Nov. 2006 <http://library.cqpress.com/cqresearcher/cqresrre1998122500>.

Thomas, Bill. "Finding Truth in the Age of 'Infotainment.'" <u>Editorial Research Reports</u>. 1990. <u>CQ Researcher Online</u> 27 Nov. 2006. Document ID: cqresrre1990011900.

"Young America's News Source: Jon Stewart." <u>CNN.com</u> 2 Mar. 2004. 29 Nov. 2006 <http://www.cnn.com/2004/SHOWBIZ/TV/03/02/apontv.stewarts.stature.ap/>.

> Online television program

NARRATION

3

Telling Stories of Culture and Customs

Narration is an essential technique that is used by writers across a wide range of cultures. An African American poet recreating an account of a memorable incident from radio broadcasts and eyewitness reports, a boy in Ireland writing to share his experiences, a girl in Morocco reporting on her family's experiences in a harem, and a Russian writer who creates an amusing story to portray first love are all using narration, albeit for different purposes. The events related through narrative can entertain, inform, dramatize an important moment, or clarify a complex idea, as we shall see in the selections that follow.

Effective narration focuses on a single significant action that dramatically changes the relationship of the writer (or main character) to his family, friends, or environment. A significant experience may be defined as a situation in which something important to the writer, or to the people he or she is writing about, is at stake.

Narratives can entertain or amuse or be written to dramatize an idea or event that is important to the writer. For example, Frederick Douglass's "Learning to Read and Write" recounts the crucial incident that showed him how he might learn to read and write and thus escape slavery:

> The idea as to how I might learn to write was suggested to me by being in Durgin and Bailey's ship-yard, and frequently seeing the ship carpenters, after hewing, and getting a piece of timber ready for use, write on the timber the name of that part of the ship for which it was intended. When a piece of timber was intended for the larboard side, it would be marked thus—"L." When a piece was for the starboard side, it would be marked thus—"S." . . . I soon learned the names of these letters, and for what they were intended when placed upon a piece of timber in the shipyard. I immediately commenced copying them, and in a short time was able to make the . . . letters named.

In the full narrative reprinted in this chapter, Douglass begins his story just before the key episode and relates the details ("I wished to learn how to write, as I might have occasion to write my own pass") that permit his readers to understand what being a slave meant and to share Douglass's resolve to escape from an intolerable situation. His story has the elements of a good narrative: the high drama of an event that permanently changes Douglass's life combined with invaluable insights into a turbulent period in America's past.

Narration can appear in the form of a public account such as Douglass's historical recollections or as private diaries, journals, or memoirs. For example, the account of Fatima Mernissi was written as a record of the experiences that she and her family faced living in a communal harem in Morocco under French occupation. Mernissi's memoir is especially poignant because it relates a time when private family life was nearly impossible. One incident in particular sheds light on the need to create a moment of privacy:

> We would be transplanted to the terrace, like nomads, with mattresses, tables, trays, and my little brother's cradle, which would be set down right in the middle of everything. Mother would be absolutely out of her mind with joy. No one else from the courtyard dared to show up, because they understood all too well that Mother was fleeing from the crowd.

Mernissi's narrative expresses her personal feelings toward the institution of the harem and shows how something as ordinary as a private dinner could symbolize her mother's rebellion against communal life.

Whereas each of the narratives described above was written by using the first-person point of view, events can also be related through the more intimate second-person ("you") or objective third-person ("he," "she," "they") point of view.

The use of dialogue is invaluable in creating a sense of dramatic immediacy through its ability to provide insight into the speaker's state of mind. For example, Evgeny Zamyatin, in his story "The Lion," creates a narrative in which the two main characters have the following conversation:

> "Er, are you, that is, are policewomen allowed to get married like in the course of duty? I mean, not in the course of duty, but in general, seeing as your work is sort of military . . . ?"
>
> "Married?" said policewoman Katya, leaning on her rifle. "We're like men now: if we take a fancy to someone, we have him."

The dialogue in this scene is important in creating the impression of two personalities: a bashful young man and a self-possessed policewoman.

Often, narration is presented in the past tense, whereas dialogue is set in the present (as if the dialogue is spoken at the moment it is read). This alternation between background narrative (past tense) and foreground dialogue (present tense) allows writers to summarize, explain, or interpret events using narration and to dramatize important moments through dialogue.

"Chopsticks," Guanlong Cao's recollection of his days as a student in an automotive institute in China, alternates between past and present tenses to heighten the ironic nature of the effort one student spent in making chopsticks and the few times they were used to eat real food:

> He cherished the chopsticks as sacred objects, not intended for daily use. He employed them only on special occasions or festival days when excitement rippled through the student body:
>
> "Today we are going to eat meat!"
>
> Only then would he take his chopsticks from his trunk. Applying a thin layer of beeswax, he would polish them for at least ten minutes with a piece of suede. Then they were ready to be brought into the dining room.

The contrast between the value of the handmade chopsticks and the scarcity of food is underscored by the movement between background narration in the past tense and foreground dialogue in the present tense.

Narratives offer writers means by which they can discover the truth of their experiences through the process of writing about them. When the writer is torn by conflicting desires and learns the truth about himself or herself only by telling the story, the resulting account can be intensely dramatic.

In "Misguided 'Guide,'" R. K. Narayan, the noted Indian writer, relates his experience of having his successful novel made into a movie that became more unlike his original than he had foreseen:

> I began to realize that monologue is the privilege of the film maker, and that it was futile to try butting in with my own observations. But for some obscure reason, they seemed to need my presence, though not my voice. I must be seen and not heard.

Narayan relates his experiences through a multitude of revealing details. He ultimately realizes that he has become nothing more than a token presence without a say in how his novel should be filmed.

Autobiographical narratives offer a way to gain insight into the meaning of our experiences. For example, in "Irish Step Dancing," Frank McCourt tells us about a time when his parents paid for him to take dance lessons to teach him the value of Irish culture. Because of his decision to spend the money on movies instead, he was chastised by his parents and priest. By telling when the story happened, who was involved, and how the events appeared from a first-person point of view, McCourt provides his readers with a coherent framework within which to interpret the events of the story:

> He tells me I'm a bad boy, he's ashamed of me that I went to the pictures instead of learning Ireland's national dances, the jig, the reel, the dances that men and women fought and died for down those sad centuries. He says there's many a young man that was hanged and now moldering in a lime pit that would be glad to rise up and dance the Irish dance.

McCourt's narrative is shaped to reveal the connection between his childhood experiences and his later quest for independence when he left Ireland for America. Most important, the process of writing itself allows McCourt to move toward a deeper understanding of his relationship to his own past.

Just as individuals can discover the meaning of their own past experiences through the process of writing about them, some writers use narration to focus on important moments of collective self-revelation. Maya Angelou, a distinguished poet and novelist, employs a full spectrum of narrative techniques in "Champion of the World" to recreate the moment in the segregated South of the 1930s when Joe Louis's victory over a white contender galvanized the black community:

> It would take an hour or more before people would leave the Store and head home. Those who lived too far had made arrangements to stay in town. It wouldn't do for a Black man and his family to be caught on a lonely country road on a night when Joe Louis had proved that we were the strongest people in the world.

Angelou draws on records, her own memory, and accounts from that time for specific details that are important in recreating the scene for her readers, summarizing the necessary background information in order to set the stage for this dramatic historic moment. Angelou is faithful to the actual facts, yet her account is compelling and memorable because of her extraordinary skill as a writer.

Narratives, as shown in the works of Douglass, Mernissi, and Zamyatin, are effective ways of sharing experiences. In the work of Cao, narration is used to clarify an abstract idea. Narration is also a writing strategy that Narayan and McCourt use in their autobiographies to gain insight into their own lives. Writers such as Angelou rely on this pattern as well to investigate and preserve important historical events.

These are the kinds of applications in which writers have found narration useful. You will doubtless discover your own unique way of using narratives in your own writing.

FREDERICK DOUGLASS

Learning to Read and Write

The inspiring story of Frederick Douglass (1818–1895) begins in Maryland, where he was born as a slave. The harsh conditions that he endured and his longing for freedom led him to undertake a secret plan to become literate. He repeatedly attempted to escape and finally succeeded in going to New York with documents of a freed black sailor. He took the name of Douglass; lived in New Bedford, Massachusetts; and spoke out against slavery. As an activist, he became editor of the *North Star*, an abolitionist paper from 1847 to 1860. He was instrumental in influencing Lincoln's Emancipation Proclamation. In the following section from his autobiography, *The Narrative of Frederick Douglass, an American Slave* (1845), he leads us through the crucial series of events that culminated in his quest to break the invisible shackles of illiteracy as a first step in gaining his freedom.

BEFORE YOU READ

Why would it have been an advantage for slaveholders to deny slaves the opportunity to become literate?

■ ■ ▨

1   I lived in Master Hugh's family about seven years. During this time, I succeeded in learning to read and write. In accomplishing this, I was compelled to resort to various stratagems. I had no regular teacher. My mistress, who had kindly commenced to instruct me, had, in compliance with the advice and direction of her husband, not only ceased to instruct, but had set her face against my being instructed by any one else. It is due, however, to my mistress to say of her, that she did not adopt this course of treatment immediately. She at first lacked the depravity indispensable to shutting me up in mental darkness. It was at least necessary for her to have some training in the exercise of irresponsible power, to make her equal to the task of treating me as though I were a brute.

2   My mistress was, as I have said, a kind and tender-hearted woman; and in the simplicity of her soul she commenced, when I first went to live with her, to treat me as she supposed one human being ought to treat another. In entering upon the duties of a slaveholder, she did not seem to perceive that I sustained to her the relation of a mere chattel, and that for her to treat me as a human being was not only wrong, but dangerously so. Slavery proved as injurious to her as it did to me. When I went there, she was a pious, warm, and tender-hearted woman. There was no sorrow or suffering for which she had not a tear. She had bread for the hungry, clothes for the naked, and comfort for every mourner that came within her reach. Slavery soon proved its ability to divest her of these heavenly qualities. Under its influence, the tender heart became stone, and the lamb-like disposition gave way to one of tiger-like fierceness. The first step in her downward course was in her ceasing to instruct me. She now commenced to practice her husband's precepts. She finally became

even more violent in her opposition than her husband himself. She was not satisfied with simply doing as well as he had commanded; she seemed anxious to do better. Nothing seemed to make her more angry than to see me with a newspaper. She seemed to think that here lay the danger. I have had her rush at me with a face made all up of fury, and snatch from me a newspaper, in a manner that fully revealed her apprehension. She was an apt woman; and a little experience soon demonstrated, to her satisfaction, that education and slavery were incompatible with each other.

3   From this time I was most narrowly watched. If I was in a separate room any considerable length of time, I was sure to be suspected of having a book, and was at once called to give an account of myself. All this, however, was too late. The first step had been taken. Mistress, in teaching me the alphabet, had given me the *inch*, and no precaution could prevent me from taking the *ell*.[1]

4   The plan which I adopted, and the one by which I was most successful, was that of making friends of all the little white boys whom I met in the street. As many of these as I could, I converted into teachers. With their kindly aid, obtained at different times and in different places, I finally succeeded in learning to read. When I was sent on errands, I always took my book with me, and by doing one part of my errand quickly, I found time to get a lesson before my return. I used also to carry bread with me, enough of which was always in the house, and to which I was always welcome; for I was much better off in this regard than many of the poor white children in our neighborhood. This bread I used to bestow upon the hungry little urchins, who, in return, would give me that more valuable bread of knowledge. I am strongly tempted to give the names of two or three of those little boys, as a testimonial of the gratitude and affection I bear them; but prudence forbids;—not that it would injure me, but it might embarrass them; for it is almost an unpardonable offence to teach slaves to read in this Christian country. It is enough to say of the dear little fellows, that they lived on Philpot Street, very near Durgin and Bailey's ship-yard. I used to talk this matter of slavery over with them. I would sometimes say to them, I wished I could be as free as they would be when they got to be men. "You will be free as soon as you are twenty-one, *but I am a slave for life!* Have not I as good a right to be free as you have?" These words used to trouble them; they would express for me the liveliest sympathy, and console me with the hope that something would occur by which I might be free.

5   I was now about twelve years old, and the thought of being *a slave for life* began to bear heavily upon my heart. Just about this time, I got hold of a book entitled "The Columbian Orator."[2] Every opportunity I got, I used to read this book. Among much of other interesting matter, I found in it a dialogue between a master and his slave. The slave was represented as having run away from his

---

[1] An ell is equal to 1.14 meters.

[2] *The Columbian Orator* (1797): Written by Caleb Bingham: it was one of the first readers used in New England schools.

master three times. The dialogue represented the conversation which took place between them, when the slave was retaken the third time. In this dialogue, the whole argument in behalf of slavery was brought forward by the master, all of which was disposed of by the slave. The slave was made to say some very smart as well as impressive things in reply to his master—things which had the desired though unexpected effect; for the conversation resulted in the voluntary emancipation of the slave on the part of the master.

6   In the same book, I met with one of Sheridan's mighty speeches on and in behalf of Catholic emancipation. These were choice documents to me. I read them over and over again with unabated interest. They gave tongue to interesting thoughts of my own soul, which had frequently flashed through my mind, and died away for want of utterance. The moral which I gained from the dialogue was the power of truth over the conscience of even a slaveholder. What I got from Sheridan was a bold denunciation of slavery, and a powerful vindication of human rights. The reading of these documents enabled me to utter my thoughts, and to meet the arguments brought forward to sustain slavery; but while they relieved me of one difficulty, they brought on another even more painful than the one of which I was relieved. The more I read, the more I was led to abhor and detest my enslavers. I could regard them in no other light than a band of successful robbers, who had left their homes, and gone to Africa, and stolen us from our homes, and in a strange land reduced us to slavery. I loathed them as being the meanest as well as the most wicked of men. As I read and contemplated the subject, behold! that very discontentment which Master Hugh had predicted would follow my learning to read had already come, to torment and sting my soul to unutterable anguish. As I writhed under it, I would at times feel that learning to read had been a curse rather than a blessing. It had given me a view of my wretched condition, without the remedy. It opened my eyes to the horrible pit, but to no ladder upon which to get out. In moments of agony, I envied my fellow-slaves for their stupidity. I have often wished myself a beast. I preferred the condition of the meanest reptile to my own. Any thing, no matter what, to get rid of thinking! It was this everlasting thinking of my condition that tormented me. There was no getting rid of it. It was pressed upon me by every object within sight or hearing, animate or inanimate. The silver trump of freedom had roused my soul to eternal wakefulness. Freedom now appeared, to disappear no more forever. It was heard in every sound, and seen in every thing. It was ever present to torment me with a sense of my wretched condition. I saw nothing without seeing it, I heard nothing without hearing it, and felt nothing without feeling it. It looked from every star, it smiled in every calm, breathed in every wind, and moved in every storm.

7   I often found myself regretting my own existence, and wishing myself dead; and but for the hope of being free, I have no doubt but that I should have killed myself, or done something for which I should have been killed. While in this state of mind, I was eager to hear any one speak of slavery. I was a ready listener. Every little while, I could hear something about the abolitionists. It was some time before I found what the word meant. It was always used in such connections

as to make it an interesting word to me. If a slave ran away and succeeded in getting clear, or if a slave killed his master, set fire to a barn, or did any thing very wrong in the mind of a slaveholder, it was spoken of as the fruit of *abolition*. Hearing the word in this connection very often, I set about learning what it meant. The dictionary afforded me little or no help. I found it was "the act of abolishing," but then I did not know what was to be abolished. Here I was perplexed. I did not dare to ask any one about its meaning, for I was satisfied that it was something they wanted me to know very little about. After a patient waiting, I got one of our city papers, containing an account of the number of petitions from the north, praying for the abolition of slavery in the District of Columbia, and of the slave trade between the States. From this time I understood the words *abolition* and *abolitionist,* and always drew near when that word was spoken, expecting to hear something of importance to myself and fellow-slaves. The light broke in upon me by degrees. I went one day down on the wharf of Mr. Waters; and seeing two Irishmen unloading a scow of stone. I went, unasked, and helped them. When we had finished, one of them came to me and asked me if I were a slave. I told him I was. He asked, "Are ye a slave for life?" I told him that I was. The good Irishman seemed to be deeply affected by the statement. He said to the other that it was a pity so fine a little fellow as myself should be a slave for life. He said it was a shame to hold me. They both advised me to run away to the north; that I should find friends there, and that I should be free, I pretended not to be interested in what they said, and treated them as if I did not understand them; for I feared they might be treacherous. White men have been known to encourage slaves to escape, and then, to get the reward, catch them and return them to their masters. I was afraid that these seemingly good men might use me so; but I nevertheless remembered their advice, and from that time I resolved to run away. I looked forward to a time at which it would be safe for me to escape. I was too young to think of doing so immediately; besides, I wished to learn how to write, as I might have occasion to write my own pass. I consoled myself with the hope that I should one day find a good chance. Meanwhile, I would learn to write.

8   The idea as to how I might learn to write was suggested to me by being in Durgin and Bailey's ship-yard, and frequently seeing the ship carpenters, after hewing, and getting a piece of timber ready for use, write on the timber the name of that part of the ship for which it was intended. When a piece of timber was intended for the larboard side, it would be marked thus—"L." When a piece was for the starboard side, it would be marked thus—"S." A piece for the larboard side forward, would be marked thus—"L. F." When a piece was for starboard side forward, it would be marked thus—"S. F." For larboard aft, it would be marked thus—"L. A." For starboard aft, it would be marked thus—"S. A." I soon learned the names of these letters, and for what they were intended when placed upon a piece of timber in the ship-yard. I immediately commenced copying them, and in a short time was able to make the four letters named. After that, when I met with any boy who I knew could write, I would tell him I could write as well as he. The next word would be, "I don't believe you. Let me see you try it." I would

then make the letters which I had been so fortunate as to learn, and ask him to beat that. In this way I got a good many lessons in writing, which it is quite possible I should never have gotten in any other way. During this time, my copy-book was the board fence, brick wall, and pavement; my pen and ink was a lump of chalk. With these, I learned mainly how to write. I then commenced and continued copying the Italics in Webster's Spelling Book, until I could make them all without looking on the book. By this time, my little Master Thomas had gone to school, and learned how to write, and had written over a number of copy-books. These had been brought home, and shown to some of our near neighbors, and then laid aside. My mistress used to go to class meeting at the Wilk Street meetinghouse every Monday afternoon, and leave me to take care of the house. When left thus, I used to spend the time in writing in the spaces left in Master Thomas's copy book, copying what he had written. I continued to do this until I could write a hand very similar to that of Master Thomas. Thus, after a long, tedious effort for years, I finally succeeded in learning how to write.

■ ■ ▨

Meaning

1. What cultural barriers blocked Douglass from becoming literate? How did he become aware of the invisible shackles that were more difficult to break than the physical ones that might have bound him?

2. Why was Douglass's relationship with the mistress of the household, Sophia Auld, made more difficult when she became aware of how earnestly he wished to learn to read and write?

3. What reading materials motivated Douglass to throw off the shackles of slavery and want to become literate?

4. What ingenious methods did Douglass use to learn how to read and write? What insight do you get into his motivation to do so?

Technique

1. How does Douglass structure his narrative by identifying important milestones in his struggle to learn to read and write?

2. In what way does Douglass's desire to write his own transit pass serve as the key element in his account?

3. In what way does Douglass situate his account of an event that changed his life in a social context that gives readers insights into this period of America's past?

4. **Other Patterns.** How does Douglass's **description** of Sophia Auld offer a human dimension of a slaveholder that is both insightful and objective?

Language

1. In what context did Douglass become acquainted with the concept of *abolition*, and how did it influence his quest to become literate?

2. How did the specific terms used for identifying pieces of timber in the shipyard where Douglass worked provide a key for his self-education?

3. If you don't know the meanings of the following words, look them up: *depravity* (1), *emancipation* (5), *loathed* (6), *wretched* (6), *abolition* (7).

SUGGESTIONS FOR WRITING

1. **Critical Writing.** Douglass observes that "education and slavery were incompatible with each other." How does this account illustrate his belief?

2. What importance is given to this episode in biographies about Douglass such as Dickson Preston's *Young Frederick Douglass* (1980) or Waldo Martin, Jr.'s *The Mind of Frederick Douglass* (1984) or in critical assessments such as *Critical Essays on Frederick Douglass*, edited by William L. Andrews (1991)? Read one of these, and write an essay about the importance of this episode in light of what you discover.

3. List important stages or milestones in your own education. Choose one of these, and freewrite for a short period. Expand on this stage by describing the events, associations, and significance that made it so important.

4. What would your life be like if you could not read or write? **Describe** a day in your life, providing specific **examples** that would dramatize being illiterate.

5. **Thematic Links.** How does the struggle against culturally imposed restrictions play an important role in the narratives of Douglass and of Maya Angelou in "Champion of the World"?

MAYA ANGELOU

Champion of the World

The poet, novelist, and playwright Maya Angelou was born in St. Louis in 1928. Her personal triumph over a turbulent childhood is described in her uncompromisingly honest and inspiring six-volume autobiography beginning with *I Know Why the Caged Bird Sings* (1970), from which the following recollection is drawn. In it, she describes the momentous impact of Joe Louis's victory over a white contender to retain his world heavyweight championship during the 1930s. His achievement represented much more than a boxing match, and his victory carried the aspirations of an entire race. Angelou's accomplishments include being awarded the Presidential Medal of Freedom. Her recent works are *Mother: A Cradle to Hold Me* and *Celebrations: Rituals of Peace and Prayer*, both published in 2006.

BEFORE YOU READ

What sports figure today has taken on a larger-than-life quality, as Joe Louis did in his day?

■ ■ ▨

1   The last inch of space was filled, yet people continued to wedge themselves along the walls of the Store. Uncle Willie had turned the radio up to its last notch so that youngsters on the porch wouldn't miss a word. Women sat on kitchen chairs, dining-room chairs, stools, and upturned wooden boxes. Small children and babies perched on every lap available and men leaned on the shelves or on each other.

2   The apprehensive mood was shot through with shafts of gaiety, as a black sky is streaked with lightning.

3   "I ain't worried 'bout this fight. Joe's gonna whip that cracker like it's open season."

4   "He gone whip him till that white boy call him Momma."

5   At last the talking finished and the string-along songs about razor blades were over and the fight began.

6   "A quick jab to the head." In the Store the crowd grunted. "A left to the head and a right and another left." One of the listeners cackled like a hen and was quieted.

7   "They're in a clinch, Louis is trying to fight his way out."

8   Some bitter comedian on the porch said, "That white man don't mind hugging that niggah now, I betcha."

9   "The referee is moving in to break them up, but Louis finally pushed the contender away and it's an uppercut to the chin. The contender is hanging on, now he's backing away. Louis catches him with a short left to the jaw."

10   A tide of murmuring assent poured out the door and into the yard.

11   "Another left and another left. Louis is saving that mighty right ..." The mutter in the Store had grown into a baby roar and it was pierced by the clang

of a bell and the announcer's "That's the bell for round three, ladies and gentlemen."

12   As I pushed my way into the Store I wondered if the announcer gave any thought to the fact that he was addressing as "ladies and gentlemen" all the Negroes around the world who sat sweating and praying, glued to their "Master's voice."

13   There were only a few calls for RC Colas, Dr. Peppers, and Hires root beer. The real festivities would begin after the fight. Then even the old Christian ladies who taught their children and tried themselves to practice turning the other cheek would buy soft drinks, and if the Brown Bomber's victory was a particularly bloody one they would order peanut patties and Baby Ruths, also.

14   Bailey and I laid coins on top of the cash register. Uncle Willie didn't allow us to ring up sales during a fight. It was too noisy and might shake up the atmosphere. When the gong rang for the next round we pushed through the near-sacred quiet to the herd of children outside.

15   "He's got Louis against the ropes and now it's a left to the body and a right to the ribs. Another right to the body, it looks like it was low . . . Yes, ladies and gentlemen, the referee is signaling but the contender keeps raining the blows on Louis. It's another to the body, and it looks like Louis is going down."

16   My race groaned. It was our people falling. It was another lynching, yet another Black man hanging on a tree. One more woman ambushed and raped. A Black boy whipped and maimed. It was hounds on the trail of a man running through slimy swamps. It was a white woman slapping her maid for being forgetful.

17   The men in the Store stood away from the walls and at attention. Women greedily clutched the babes on their laps while on the porch the shufflings and smiles, flirtings and pinching of a few minutes before were gone. This might be the end of the world. If Joe lost we were back in slavery and beyond help. It would all be true, the accusations that we were lower types of human beings. Only a little higher than apes. True that we were stupid and ugly and lazy and dirty and, unlucky and worst of all, that God Himself hated us and ordained us to be hewers of wood and drawers of water, forever, and ever, world without end.

18   We didn't breathe. We didn't hope. We waited.

19   "He's off the ropes, ladies and gentlemen. He's moving towards the center of the ring." There was no time to be relieved. The worst might still happen.

20   "And now it looks like Joe is mad. He's caught Carnera with a left hook to the head and a right to the head. It's a left jab to the body and another left to the head. There's a left cross and a right to the head. The contender's right eye is bleeding and he can't seem to keep his block up. Louis is penetrating every block. The referee is moving in, but Louis sends a left to the body and it's an uppercut to the chin and the contender is dropping. He's on the canvas, ladies and gentlemen."

21   Babies slid to the floor as women stood up and men leaned toward the radio.

22   "Here's the referee. He's counting. One, two, three, four, five, six, seven . . . Is the contender trying to get up again?"

23   All the men in the store shouted, "NO."

How does this picture of Joe Louis with his son add another perspective to Angelou's description of Joe Louis?

24   "—eight, nine, ten." There were a few sounds from the audience, but they seemed to be holding themselves in against tremendous pressure.

25   "The fight is all over, ladies and gentlemen. Let's get the microphone over to the referee . . . Here he is. He's got the Brown Bomber's hand, he's holding it up . . . Here he is . . ."

26   Then the voice, husky and familiar, came to wash over us—"The winnah, and still heavyweight champeen of the world . . . Joe Louis."

27   Champion of the world. A Black boy. Some Black mother's son.

28   He was the strongest man in the world. People drank Coca-Colas like ambrosia and ate candy bars like Christmas. Some of the men went behind the Store and poured white lightning in their soft-drink bottles, and a few of the bigger boys followed them. Those who were not chased away came back blowing their breath in front of themselves like proud smokers.

29   It would take an hour or more before people would leave the Store and head home. Those who lived too far had made arrangements to stay in town. It wouldn't do for a Black man and his family to be caught on a lonely country road on a night when Joe Louis had proved that we were the strongest people in the world.

■ ■ ▨

MEANING

1. In what sense was the sporting event Angelou describes about much more than who would win a boxing match?
2. What can you infer about the state of race relations in the segregated South in the 1930s from Angelou's narrative?
3. What insight does Angelou offer into why Joe Louis became an icon in popular culture?
4. To what extent did Angelou share the feelings of the people listening to the fight?

TECHNIQUE

1. Angelou was quite young when this event occurred. How does she combine an adult's sophisticated knowledge of the past with her childhood memories?
2. How does Angelou integrate many speaking voices into her narrative to dramatize the urgency with which African Americans at the time viewed Louis's victory?
3. How does Angelou draw on figurative and literal images in paragraphs 16 and 17 to suggest the powerful, even desperate, identification the community felt with Joe Louis?
4. **Other Patterns.** How does Angelou use **description** to give the reader a strong sense of the physical setting in which this momentous event occurred?

LANGUAGE

1. What details help to put the reader into the scene and convey the shifting mood of the crowd as the match proceeds?
2. Identify phrases in this narrative that a child would never use, such as "my race groaned," that makes clear the way in which Angelou overlays her memories with an adult's perspective.
3. How does Angelou use colloquial speech and picturesque metaphors to convey the flavor of the listeners' conversations and comments?
4. If you don't know the meanings of the following words, look them up: *maimed* (16), *ambrosia* (28).

SUGGESTIONS FOR WRITING

1. **Critical Writing.** The black athlete has always borne the additional burden (as Angelou points out) of being a standard bearer for collective achievement. How has this expectation influenced the way in which the media covers athletes of color?

2. For a history and analysis of boxing, you might read Joyce Carol Oates's *On Boxing* (1994). Read this book, and in an essay, compare Oates's analysis of Mike Tyson with Angelou's portrayal of Joe Louis.

3. In films about boxing such as *Rocky* (1976), *Raging Bull* (1980), and *Cinderella Man* (2005), boxing becomes a metaphor for the individual's struggle against society. In a short essay, discuss how any of these or other boxing films can be understood as social criticism.

4. Describe an incident from your childhood in which an athlete (or other public figure) took on larger-than-life importance because of his or her cultural meaning.

5. What criteria could be used to evaluate whether a great fighter of one era is equal to or better than one of another era? In a few paragraphs, **compare** the relative strengths of Joe Louis with any other fighter such as Jack Johnson, "Sugar" Ray Robinson, Muhammad Ali, or any contemporary boxer.

6. ***Thematic Links.*** What insights into the segregated South are offered by Angelou and by C. P. Ellis in "Why I Quit the Klan" in Chapter 9, "Cause and Effect"?

FRANK MCCOURT

Irish Step Dancing

A Pulitzer Prize–winning author, Frank McCourt was born in Brooklyn in 1931, but his family moved back to Limerick, Ireland, when he was only four years old. McCourt returned to America when he was nineteen and held a variety of jobs, including being a high school teacher in Staten Island. His acclaimed autobiography *Angela's Ashes* (1996), from which the following excerpt is drawn, was later made into a film (1999). McCourt's brief stint taking Irish step dancing lessons at his parents' insistence is humorous and poignant. Recently, he has written *Teacher Man: A Memoir* (2005) and *Angela and the Baby Jesus* (2007).

BEFORE YOU READ

How might dance lessons serve as a means to connect you to a culture?

■ ■ ▨

1 On a Saturday morning Mam finishes her tea and says, You're going to dance.

2   Dance? Why?

3   You're seven years old, you made your First Communion, and now 'tis time for the dancing. I'm taking you down to Catherine Street to Mrs. O'Connor's Irish dancing classes. You'll go there every Saturday morning and that'll keep you off the streets. That'll keep you from wandering around Limerick with hooligans.

4   She tells me wash my face not forgetting ears and neck, comb my hair, blow my nose, take the look off my face, what look? never mind, just take it off, put on my stockings and my First Communion shoes which, she says, are destroyed because I can't pass a canister or a rock without kicking it. She's worn out standing in the queue at the St. Vincent de Paul Society begging for boots for me and Malachy so that we can wear out the toes with the kicking. Your father says it's never too early to learn the songs and dances of your ancestors.

5   What's ancestors?

6   Never mind, she says, you're going to dance.

7   I wonder how I can die for Ireland if I have to sing and dance for Ireland, too. I wonder why they never say, You can eat sweets and stay home from school and go swimming for Ireland.

8   Mam says, Don't get smart or I'll warm your ear.

9   Cyril Benson dances. He has medals hanging from his shoulders to his kneecaps. He wins contests all over Ireland and he looks lovely in his saffron kilt. He's a credit to his mother and he gets his name in the paper all the time and you can be sure he brings home the odd few pounds. You don't see him roaming the streets kicking everything in sight till the toes hang out of his boots, oh, no, he's a good boy, dancing for his poor mother.

10   Mam wets an old towel and scrubs my face till it stings, she wraps the towel around her finger and sticks it in my ears and claims there's enough wax there to grow potatoes, she wets my hair to make it lie down, she tells me shut up and stop the whinging, that these dancing lessons will cost her sixpence every Saturday, which I could have earned bringing Bill Galvin his dinner and God knows she can barely afford it. I try to tell her, Ah, Mam, sure you don't have to send me to dancing school when you could be smoking a nice Woodbine and having a cup of tea, but she says, Oh, aren't you clever. You're going to dance if I have to give up the fags forever.

11   If my pals see my mother dragging me through the streets to an Irish dancing class I'll be disgraced entirely. They think it's all right to dance and pretend you're Fred Astaire because you can jump all over the screen with Ginger Rogers. There is no Ginger Rogers in Irish dancing and you can't jump all over. You stand straight up and down and keep your arms against yourself and kick your legs up and around and never smile. My uncle Pa Keating said Irish dancers look like they have steel rods up their arses, but I can't say that to Mam, she'd kill me.

12   There's a gramophone in Mrs. O'Connor's playing an Irish jig or a reel and boys and girls are dancing around kicking their legs out and keeping their hands to their sides. Mrs. O'Connor is a great fat woman and when she stops the record to show the steps all the fat from her chin to her ankles jiggles and I wonder how she can teach the dancing. She comes over to my mother and says, So, this is little Frankie? I think we have the makings of a dancer here. Boys and girls, do we have the makings of a dancer here?

13   We do, Mrs. O'Connor.

14   Mam says, I have the sixpence, Mrs. O'Connor.

15   Ah, yes, Mrs. McCourt, hold on a minute.

16   She waddles to a table and brings back the head of a black boy with kinky hair, big eyes, huge red lips and an open mouth. She tells me put the sixpence in the mouth and take my hand out before the black boy bites me. All the boys and girls watch and they have little smiles. I drop in the sixpence and pull my hand back before the mouth snaps shut. Everyone laughs and I know they wanted to see my hand caught in the mouth. Mrs. O'Connor gasps and laughs and says to my mother, Isn't that a howl, now? Mam says it's a howl. She tells me behave myself and come home dancing.

17   I don't want to stay in this place where Mrs. O'Connor can't take the sixpence herself instead of letting me nearly lose my hand in the black boy's mouth. I don't want to stay in this place where you have to stand in line with boys and girls, straighten your back, hands by your sides, look ahead, don't look down, move your feet, move your feet, look at Cyril, look at Cyril, and there goes Cyril, all dressed up in his saffron kilt and the medals jingling, medals for this and medals for that and the girls love Cyril and Mrs. O'Connor loves Cyril for didn't he bring her fame and didn't she teach him every step he knows, oh, dance, Cyril, dance, oh, Jesus, he floats around the room, he's an angel out of heaven and stop the frowning, Frankie McCourt, or you'll have a puss on you like a pound of tripe, dance, Frankie,

dance, pick up your feet for the love o'Jesus, onetwothreefourfivesixseven one-twothree and a onetwothree, Maura, will you help that Frankie McCourt before he ties his two feet around his poll entirely, help him, Maura.

18   Maura is a big girl about ten. She dances up to me with her white teeth and her dancer's dress with all the gold and yellow and green figures that are sup-posed to come from olden times and she says, Give me your hand, little boy, and she wheels me around the room till I'm dizzy and making a pure eejit of myself and blushing and foolish till I want to cry but I'm saved when the record stops and the gramophone goes hoosh hoosh.

19   Mrs. O'Connor says, Oh, thank you, Maura, and next week, Cyril, you can show Frankie a few of the steps that made you famous. Next week, boys and girls, and don't forget the sixpence for the little black boy.

20   Boys and girls leave together. I make my own way down the stairs and out the door hoping my pals won't see me with boys who wear kilts and girls with white teeth and fancy dresses from olden times.

21   Mam is having tea with Bridey Hannon, her friend from next door. Mam says, What did you learn? and makes me dance around the kitchen, onetwothree-fourfivesixseven onetwothree and a onetwothree. She has a good laugh with Bridey. That's not too bad for your first time. In a month you'll be like a regular Cyril Benson.

22   I don't want to be Cyril Benson. I want to be Fred Astaire.

23   They turn hysterical, laughing and squirting tea out of their mouths, Jesus love him, says Bridey. Doesn't he have a great notion of himself. Fred Astaire how are you.

24   Mam says Fred Astaire went to his lessons every Saturday and didn't go around kicking the toes out of his boots and if I wanted to be like him I'd have to go to Mrs. O'Connor's every week.

25   The fourth Saturday morning Billy Campbell knocks at our door. Mrs. McCourt, can Frankie come out and play? Mam tells him, No, Billy. Frankie is going to his dancing lesson.

26   He waits for me at the bottom of Barrack Hill. He wants to know why I'm dancing, that everyone knows dancing is a sissy thing and I'll wind up like Cyril Benson wearing a kilt and medals and dancing all over with girls. He says next thing I'll be sitting in the kitchen knitting socks. He says dancing will destroy me and I won't be fit to play any kind of football, soccer, rugby or Gaelic foot-ball itself because the dancing teaches you to run like a sissy and everyone will laugh.

27   I tell him I'm finished with the dancing, that I have sixpence in my pocket for Mrs. O'Connor that's supposed to go into the black boy's mouth, that I'm going to the Lyric Cinema instead. Sixpence will get the two of us in with tup-pence left over for two squares of Cleeves' toffee, and we have a great time look-ing at *Riders of the Purple Sage.*

28   Dad is sitting by the fire with Mam and they want to know what steps I learned today and what they're called. I already did "The Siege of Ennis" and "The Walls of Limerick," which are real dances. Now I have to make up names

and dances. Mam says she never heard of a dance called "The Siege of Dingle" but if that's what I learned go ahead, dance it, and I dance around the kitchen with my hands down by my sides making my own music, diddley eye di eye di eye diddley eye do you do you, Dad and Mam clapping in time with my feet. Dad says, Och, that's a fine dance and you'll be a powerful Irish dancer and a credit to the men who died for their country. Mam says, That wasn't much for a sixpence.

29   Next week it's a George Raft film and the week after that a cowboy film with George O'Brien. Then it's James Cagney and I can't take Billy because I want to get a bar of chocolate to go with my Cleeves' toffee and I'm having a great time till there's a terrible pain in my jaw and it's a tooth out of my gum stuck in my toffee and the pain is killing me. Still, I can't waste the toffee so I pull out the tooth and put it in my pocket and chew the toffee on the other side of my mouth blood and all. There's pain on one side and delicious toffee on the other and I remember what my uncle Pa Keating would say, There are times when you wouldn't know whether to shit or go blind.

30   I have to go home now and worry because you can't go through the world short a tooth without your mother knowing. Mothers know everything and she's always looking into our mouths to see if there's any class of disease. She's there by the fire and Dad is there and they're asking me the same old questions, the dance and the name of the dance. I tell them I learned "The Walls of Cork" and I dance around the kitchen trying to hum a made-up tune and dying with the pain of my tooth. Mam says, "Walls o' Cork," my eye, there's no such dance, and Dad says, Come over here. Stand there before me. Tell us the truth, Did you go to your dancing classes today?

31   I can't tell a lie anymore because my gum is killing me and there's blood in my mouth. Besides, I know they know everything and that's what they're telling me now. Some snake of a boy from the dancing school saw me going to the Lyric Cinema and told and Mrs. O'Connor sent a note to say she hadn't seen me in ages and was I all right because I had great promise and could follow in the footsteps of the great Cyril Benson.

32   Dad doesn't care about my tooth or anything. He says I'm going to confession and drags me over to the Redemptorist church because it's Saturday and confessions go on all day. He tells me I'm a bad boy, he's ashamed of me that I went to the pictures instead of learning Ireland's national dances, the jig, the reel, the dances that men and women fought and died for down those sad centuries. He says there's many a young man that was hanged and now moldering in a lime pit that would be glad to rise up and dance the Irish dance.

33   The priest is old and I have to yell my sins at him and he tells me I'm a hooligan for going to the pictures instead of my dancing lessons although he thinks himself that dancing is a dangerous thing almost as bad as the films, that it stirs up thoughts sinful in themselves, but even if dancing is an abomination I sinned by taking my mother's sixpence and lying and there's a hot place in hell for the likes of me, say a decade of the rosary and ask God's forgiveness for you're dancing at the gates of hell itself, child.

How does this image of a Irish dance competition suggest why it was so important to McCourt's parents that he take lessons?

MEANING

1. What does Irish step dancing mean to McCourt's parents, and why is he less than enthusiastic about taking lessons?

2. How does McCourt's decision to skip dance classes and go to the movies lead to a public confession?

3. How would you describe McCourt's relationship with his parents, especially his mother?

4. Why do McCourt's parents see Irish step dancing as a patriotic act rather than simply a hobby?

TECHNIQUE

1. How does McCourt's uncanny knack for evoking a scene through dialogue make his account more realistic?

2. How does McCourt draw the reader into the scene so that we anticipate what his parents will say when they find out and at the same time feel sorry for him?

3. How does McCourt use a first-person point of view to provide a coherent framework in which to interpret the events in his account?

4. *Other Patterns.* How do the **descriptive** details with which McCourt enlivens his narrative add humor and irony?

LANGUAGE

1. What colloquial expressions that are unique to Irish culture does McCourt include, and how do they depend on hyperbole ("you'll have a puss on you like a pound of tripe")?

2. How does leaving out the quotation marks on what we know is dialogue give the account a stream-of-consciousness flavor?

3. Why is the name of the dance "The Walls of Cork" funny in the context of the account?

4. If you don't know the meaning of the following words, look them up: *hooligans* (3), *saffron* (9), *kilt* (9), *Woodbine* (10), *whinging* (10), *gramophone* (12), *sixpence* (14), *moldering* (32).

SUGGESTIONS FOR WRITING

1. **Critical Writing.** What insight does McCourt provide into the role of religion in Irish culture?

2. In your opinion, what elements or characteristics of McCourt's novel *Angela's Ashes* (1996) have been translated effectively into the 1999 film by the same name?

3. When you were six or seven years old, would you have chosen going to the movies or taking dance lessons? Explain your answer, and give **examples** that illustrate your choice.

4. How do dance lessons provide a bridge to learning about other cultures?

5. **Thematic Links.** How do both McCourt and Fatima Mernissi's mother in "Moonlit Nights of Laughter" rebel against the imposed expectations of their respective communities?

GUANLONG CAO

Chopsticks

The Chinese-born writer Guanlong Cao saw his family evicted from their home by the ruling Communists and wrote about these experiences in *The Attic: Memoirs of a Chinese Landlord's Son* (1996), from which the following chapter is taken. In it, he tells how he and the other students at a trade school found ways to pass the time by making chopsticks with bamboo they had stolen. Cao came to America in 1987 and, after receiving degrees from Middlebury College and Tufts University, has pursued a career as an artist and sculptor.

BEFORE YOU READ

If you have ever used chopsticks, how does your attitude toward food change when you use them?

■ ■ ▨

1   I always think chopsticks are an invention unique to Asian culture. Its historical and cognitive significance is no less than that of the Great Wall, the compass, gunpowder, and paper.

2   The greatest wisdom appears to be foolishness. Complexity ultimately ends in simplicity. Maybe it is because chopsticks are so simple that, just as air's weight was long ignored and white light was mislabeled as colorless, in thousands of years no one has ever scientifically or conscientiously researched them. A sensitive probe for examining the characteristics of Asian culture has been ignored. In my four years at the automotive school, I witnessed and experienced a splendid chopsticks civilization. I record it here for the benefit of future researchers.

3   In those days almost every male student carried an elongated pouch hanging from his belt. It was fashioned from canvas, leather, or leatherette. Like a warrior's dagger, it dangled all day from the student's waist.

4   Female students didn't wear belts, so the slim bags usually hung from a cord around their necks. Their materials were more delicate: nylon, silk, or linen. Embroidery was often added as an embellishment.

5   Within these bags were chopsticks.

6   Because the rationed food offered insufficient calories, oxygen-intensive activities were not encouraged. Chess, card games, and calligraphy were the officially recommended pastimes. But the most popular activity was making chopsticks.

7   The number of students at the school increased each year, and new dormitories were constantly being built. Owing to limited funds, the dormitory roofs were constructed out of tar paper, straw, and bamboo. That bamboo became the primary source of chopstick lumber.

8   The selection of material was critical. Segments close to the plant's roots were too short. The meat between the skin and hollow core of the segments close to the top was too thin. A bamboo tree about one inch thick provided only a few middle segments that could be used to make quality chopsticks.

9   The bamboo poles were covered with a tarp and stored on the construction site. In the evenings, taking advantage of the absence of the construction workers, we started looting.

10   If only a few trees were missing, nobody would have noticed. But when an idea becomes a fad, things can easily get out of hand. There were hundreds of students. A newly delivered pile of bamboo would be half gone the morning after an all-out moonlit operation.

11   The superintendent of the construction site was furious and demanded that the student dormitories be searched. We got scared and threw our booty out the windows. The superintendent called a meeting of the school leaders to deal with the problem. He arrived with both arms laden with cut segments of bamboo. With a crash, he slammed the sticks down on the meeting table. The leaders, gathered around the table, looked like diners at an exotic feast.

12   The next day, a large notice was posted listing the price of the transgression: one bamboo tree = one big demerit. But the punishment was never really put into effect. After the immediate storm passed, the bamboo continued to go missing, but not in the same flagrant quantities.

13   After a bamboo segment was split open, it had to be dried in the shade for about a week. Experienced students put their bamboo strips on the mosquito netting over their beds. Their rising body heat helped evaporate the moisture.

14   Although the bamboo's skin is hard, it must be stripped away. If left on, the different densities of the inner and outer materials cause the chopsticks to warp. The best part comes from the quarter inch of meat just inside the skin. There the texture is even and dense, and the split will go precisely where the knife directs it.

15   The student-made chopsticks usually had a round cross-section. Round chopsticks require little skill to make. Wrap sandpaper around the strip of bamboo and sand for an hour or two, and a round cross-section is the result.

16   Only experts dared to make square cross-sectioned chopsticks. To make the four sided straight and symmetrical from tail to tip required real expertise. Sandpaper could not be used, because it would wear away the sharp edges you were trying to create.

17   To begin the procedure, you have to soak a fine-grained brick in water for a couple of days, and then grind it flat on a concrete floor. Laying the roughed-out chopstick on the brick, with one finger applying pressure to the tail and another to the top, you slowly ground the stick on the brick. Water was dripped on the brick to ensure fine grinding. Only by this painstaking process could chopsticks be formed with clear edges and smooth surfaces.

18   A boy student unprecedently produced a pair of five-sided chopsticks, which created a sensation on campus. The boy dedicated his efforts to a girl on whom he had a crush. Unfortunately, his gift was spurned and, desolate, he broke the chopsticks in front of his peers. This became the classic tragedy of the school year.

19   In addition to varying cross-sections, the top two or three inches were another place to show off your skill. The usual decoration was a few carved lines with inlaid color. Some students borrowed techniques from seal carving and sculpted miniature cats, turtles, and dragons out of the upper portions of the sticks. One student, who was good at calligraphy, carved two lines of a Song dynasty poem on his chopsticks:

> "Vinegar fish from the West Lake," read one of them.
> "Cinnamon meat from East Hill," read the other.

20   He cherished the chopsticks as sacred objects, not intended for daily use. He employed them only on special occasions or festival days when excitement rippled through the student body:

> "Today we are going to eat meat!"

21   Only then would he take his chopsticks from his trunk. Applying a thin layer of beeswax, he would polish them for at least ten minutes with a piece of suede. Then they were ready to be brought into the dining room.

22   Following the epochal five-sided masterpiece, chopsticks became a popular gift for boys to give to girls. If the girl liked the boy, she would accept his present and later give a gift to her admirer—a sleeve for chopsticks. The painstaking needle-work expressed her sentimental attachment. We had never heard about Freud, but with our raw wisdom we subconsciously felt that there was some symbolic mean-ing, which could hardly be expressed in words, in this exchange, in the coming and going of the chopsticks and the sleeves. But school regulations clearly stated:

NO DATING ON CAMPUS

23   I think the regulation was well supported by science. Dating belonged to the category of oxygen-intensive activities. Before you could open your mouth, your heart started jumping and your cheeks were burning, clearly indicating a rapid consumption of valuable calories.

MEANING

1. What is the relationship between scarcity of food at the automotive school and the time and effort students spent making their own chopsticks?
2. How did the making of chopsticks become a means by which students could rebel against the regimentation and also serve as gifts of courtship?
3. Why was making chopsticks such a popular pastime for students at the automotive school?
4. How did making chopsticks become an artistic competition?

TECHNIQUE

1. How does Cao's analysis of the process by which chopsticks were made enhance the reader's comprehension of the ritual aspects of chopstick making?

2. What details emphasize the lengths to which some students would go to make their chopsticks into art objects?

3. How does Cao's account alternate between past and present tenses to emphasize the irony of the great effort put into making chopsticks as compared with the rare occasions the students could use them?

4. **Other Patterns.** In what sense might Cao's essay be considered an extended **definition** of chopsticks?

LANGUAGE

1. How does Cao's use of irony convey his attitude toward the authorities and his feelings about his experiences?

2. How does the reference to Sigmund Freud's theory emphasize the students' naiveté toward their first feelings of love and sexuality?

3. If you don't know the meanings of the following words, look them up: *cognitive* (1), *conscientiously* (2), *flagrant* (12), *epochal* (23).

SUGGESTIONS FOR WRITING

1. Cao describes how the making of chopsticks took over student life and what it meant to them as individuals and as a group. What campuswide activities or projects have galvanized the student population at your school?

2. How does the type of utensil used, such as chopsticks, change your attitude toward the food you eat, what it should look like, how it should be served, and how it should be eaten?

3. **Critical Writing.** What are some of the **differences** between eating a meal in a Chinese restaurant and in a typical American restaurant? In a few paragraphs, discuss the implications of the way in which food appears, how it is prepared, and how it is served.

4. **Thematic Links.** What complementary perspectives are provided by Cao and by Margaret Visser in "Fingers" in Chapter 8, "Classification"?

FATIMA MERNISSI

Moonlit Nights of Laughter

Noted author and scholar Fatima Mernissi (b. 1940), grew up in Fez, Morocco, within the restricted communal environment of a harem. Her work explores the plight of women in these circumstances in books such as *Dreams of Trespass: Tales of a Harem Girlhood* (1994), from which this selection is drawn, and, more recently, *Scheherazade Goes West: Different Cultures, Different Harems* (2001) and *The Forgotten Queens of Islam* (2003).

BEFORE YOU READ

How might the lack of privacy be a problem if you lived in a harem?

■ ■ ▨

1   On Yasmina's farm, we never knew when we would eat. Sometimes, Yasmina only remembered at the last minute that she had to feed me, and then she would convince me that a few olives and a piece of her good bread, which she had baked at dawn, would be enough. But dining in our harem in Fez was an entirely different story. We ate at strictly set hours and never between meals.

2   To eat in Fez, we had to sit at our prescribed places at one of the four communal tables. The first table was for the men, the second for the important women, and the third for the children and less important women, which made us happy, because that meant that Aunt Habiba could eat with us. The last table was reserved for the domestics and anyone who had come in late, regardless of age, rank, or sex. That table was often overcrowded, and was the last chance to get anything to eat at all for those who had made the mistake of not being on time.

3   Eating at fixed hours was what Mother hated most about communal life. She would nag Father constantly about the possibility of breaking loose and taking our immediate family to live apart. The nationalists advocated the end of seclusion and the veil, but they did not say a word about a couple's right to split off from their larger family. In fact, most of the leaders still lived with their parents. The male nationalist movement supported the liberation of women, but had not come to grips with the idea of the elderly living by themselves, nor with couples splitting off into separate households. Neither idea seemed right, or elegant.

4   Mother especially disliked the idea of a fixed lunch hour. She always was the last to wake up, and liked to have a late, lavish breakfast which she prepared herself with a lot of flamboyant defiance, beneath the disapproving stare of Grandmother Lalla Mani. She would make herself scrambled eggs and *baghrir*, or fine crêpes, topped with pure honey and fresh butter, and, of course, plenty of tea. She usually ate at exactly eleven, just as Lalla Mani was about to begin her purification ritual for the noon prayer. And after that, two hours later at the communal table, Mother was often absolutely unable to eat lunch. Sometimes, she would skip it altogether, especially when she wanted to annoy

Father, because to skip a meal was considered terribly rude and too openly individualistic.

5   Mother dreamed of living alone with Father and us kids. "Whoever heard of ten birds living together squashed into a single nest?" she would say. "It is not natural to live in a large group, unless your objective is to make people feel miserable." Although Father said that he was not really sure how the birds lived, he still sympathized with Mother, and felt torn between his duty towards the traditional family and his desire to make her happy. He felt guilty about breaking up the family solidarity, knowing only too well that big families in general, and harem life in particular, were fast becoming relics of the past. He even prophesied that in the next few decades, we would become like the Christians, who hardly ever visited their old parents. In fact, most of my uncles who had already broken away from the big house barely found the time to visit their mother, Lalla Mani, on Fridays after prayer anymore. "Their kids do not kiss hands either," ran the constant refrain. To make matters worse, until very recently, all my uncles had lived in our house, and had only split away when their wives' opposition to communal life had become unbearable. That is what gave Mother hope.

6   The first to leave the big family was Uncle Karim, Cousin Malika's father. His wife loved music and liked to sing while being accompanied by Uncle Karim, who played the lute beautifully. But he would rarely give in to his wife's desire to spend an evening singing in their salon, because his older brother Uncle Ali thought it unbecoming for a man to sing or play a musical instrument. Finally, one day, Uncle Karim's wife just took her children and went back to her father's house, saying that she had no intention of living in the communal house ever again. Uncle Karim, a cheerful fellow who had himself often felt constrained by the discipline of harem life, saw an opportunity to leave and took it, excusing his actions by saying that he preferred to give in to his wife's wishes rather than forfeit his marriage. Not long after that, all my other uncles moved out, one after the other, until only Uncle Ali and Father were left. So Father's departure would have meant the death of our large family. "As long as [my] Mother lives," he often said, "I wouldn't betray the tradition."

7   Yet Father loved his wife so much that he felt miserable about not giving in to her wishes and never stopped proposing compromises. One was to stock an entire cupboardful of food for her, in case she wanted to discreetly eat sometimes, apart from the rest of the family. For one of the problems in the communal house was that you could not just open a refrigerator when you were hungry and grab something to eat. In the first place, there were no refrigerators back then. More importantly, the entire idea behind the harem was that you lived according to the group's rhythm. You could not just eat when you felt like it. Lalla Radia, my uncle's wife, had the key to the pantry, and although she always asked after dinner what people wanted to eat the next day, you still had to eat whatever the group—after lengthy discussion—decided upon. If the group settled on couscous with chick-peas and raisins, then that is what you got. If you happened to hate chick-peas and raisins, you had no choice but to shut up and settle for a frugal dinner composed of a few olives and a great deal of discretion.

8   "What a waste of time," Mother would say. "These endless discussions about meals! Arabs would be much better off if they let each individual decide what he or she wanted to swallow. Forcing everyone to share three meals a day just complicates things. And for what sacred purpose? None of course." From there, she would go on to say that her whole life was an absurdity, that nothing made sense, while Father would say that he could not just break away. If he did, tradition would vanish: "We live in difficult times, the country is occupied by foreign armies, our culture is threatened. All we have left is these traditions." This reasoning would drive Mother nuts: "Do you think that by sticking together in this big, absurd house, we will gain the strength we need to throw the foreign armies out? And what is more important anyway, tradition or people's happiness?" That would put an abrupt end to the conversation. Father would try to caress her hand but she would take it away. "This tradition is choking me," she would whisper, tears in her eyes.

9   So Father kept offering compromises. He not only arranged for Mother to have her own food stock, but also brought her things he knew she liked, such as dates, nuts, almonds, honey, flour, and fancy oils. She could make all the desserts and cookies she wanted, but she was not supposed to prepare a meat dish or a major meal. That would have meant the beginning of the end of the communal arrangement. Her flamboyantly prepared individual breakfasts were enough of a slap in the face to the rest of the family. Every once in a long while, Mother *did* get away with preparing a complete lunch or a dinner, but she had to not only be discreet about it but also give it some sort of exotic overtone. Her most common ploy was to camouflage the meal as a nighttime picnic on the terrace.

10   These occasional tête-à-tête dinners on the terrace during moonlit summer nights were another peace offering that Father made to help satisfy Mother's yearning for privacy. We would be transplanted to the terrace, like nomads, with mattresses, tables, trays, and my little brother's cradle, which would be set down right in the middle of everything. Mother would be absolutely out of her mind with joy. No one else from the courtyard dared to show up, because they understood all too well that Mother was fleeing from the crowd. What she most enjoyed was trying to get Father to depart from his conventional self-controlled pose. Before long, she would start acting foolishly, like a young girl, and soon, Father would chase her all around the terrace, when she challenged him. "You can't run anymore, you have grown too old! All you're good for now is to sit and watch your son's cradle." Father, who had been smiling up to that point, would look at her at first as if what she had just said had not affected him at all. But then his smile would vanish, and he would start chasing her all over the terrace, jumping over tea-trays and sofas. Sometimes both of them made up games which included my sister and Samir (who was the only one of the rest of the family allowed to attend our moonlit gatherings) and myself. More often, they completely forgot about the rest of the world, and we children would be sneezing all the next day because they had forgotten to put blankets on us when we had gone to sleep that night.

11   After these blissful evenings, Mother would be in an unusually soft and quiet mood for a whole week. Then she would tell me that whatever else I did with my

life, I had to take her revenge. "I want my daughters' lives to be exciting," she would say, "very exciting and filled with one hundred percent happiness, nothing more, nothing less." I would raise my head, look at her earnestly, and ask what one hundred percent happiness meant, because I wanted her to know that I intended to do my best to achieve it. Happiness, she would explain, was when a person felt good, light, creative, content, loving and loved, and free. An unhappy person felt as if there were barriers crushing her desires and the talents she had inside. A happy woman was one who could exercise all kinds of rights, from the right to move to the right to create, compete, and challenge, and at the same time could feel loved for doing so. Part of happiness was to be loved by a man who enjoyed your strength and was proud of your talents. Happiness was also about the right to privacy, the right to retreat from the company of others and plunge into contemplative solitude. Or to sit by yourself doing nothing for a whole day, and not give excuses or feel guilty about it either. Happiness was to be with loved ones, and yet still feel that you existed as a separate being, that you were not there just to make them happy. Happiness was when there was a balance between what you gave and what you took. I then asked her how much happiness she had in her life, just to get an idea, and she said that it varied according to the days. Some days she had only five percent; others, like the evenings we spent with Father on the terrace, she had full-blown one hundred percent happiness.

12   Aiming at one hundred percent happiness seemed a bit overwhelming to me, as a young girl, especially since I could see how much Mother labored to sculpt her moments of happiness. How much time and energy she put into creating those wonderful moonlit evenings sitting close to Father, talking softly in his ear, her head on his shoulder! It seemed quite an accomplishment to me because she had to start working on him days ahead of time, and then she had to take care of all the logistics, like the cooking and the moving of the furniture. To invest so much stubborn effort just to achieve a few hours of happiness was impressive, and at least I knew it could be done. But how, I wondered, was I going to create such a high level of excitement for an entire lifetime? Well, if Mother thought it was possible, I should certainly give it a try.

13   "Times are going to get better for women now, my daughter," she would say to me. "You and your sister will get a good education, and you'll walk freely in the streets and discover the world. I want you to become independent, independent and happy. I want you to shine like moons. I want your lives to be a cascade of serene delights. One hundred percent happiness. Nothing more, nothing less." But when I asked her for more details about how to create that happiness, Mother would grow very impatient. "You have to work at it. One develops the muscles for happiness, just like for walking and breathing."

14   So every morning, I would sit on our threshold, contemplating the deserted courtyard and dreaming about my beautiful future, a cascade of serene delights. Hanging on to the romantic moonlit terrace evenings, challenging your beloved man to forget about his social duties, relax and act foolish and gaze at the stars while holding your hand, I thought, could be one way to go about developing

muscles for happiness. Sculpting soft nights, when the sound of laughter blends with the spring breezes, could be another.

15   But those magical evenings were rare, or so they seemed. During the days, life took a much more rigid and disciplined turn. Officially, there was no jumping around or foolishness allowed in the Mernissi household—all that was confined to clandestine times and spaces, such as late afternoons in the courtyard when the men were out, or evenings on the deserted terraces.

■ ■ ■

MEANING

1. What features of communal life in the harem did Mernissi's mother find most restrictive?
2. What compromises did Mernissi's mother invent to offset these limitations?
3. Why was skipping a meal considered rude and individualistic?
4. What did Mernissi's mother want for her daughters that they could not achieve living in the harem?

TECHNIQUE

1. How does Mernissi focus her account on her mother's reaction to the governing principle in the harem that "you lived according to the group's rhythm. You could not just eat when you felt like it"?
2. How do the episodes in which the family could enjoy a private dinner on the terrace come to symbolize her mother's rebellion against the system?
3. **Other Patterns.** In what way is Mernissi's account imbued with a **comparison and contrast** between the rights of men and those of women in this culture?

LANGUAGE

1. In light of Mernissi's mother's experiences, discuss the wishes or desires she projected onto her daughter. What do you think she meant by the phrase "one hundred percent happiness"?
2. How do Mernissi's word choices express her personal feelings toward the institution of the harem?
3. If you don't know the meanings of the following words, look them up; *flamboyant* (4), *prophesied* (5), *lute* (6), *discretion* (7), *camouflage* (9).

SUGGESTIONS FOR WRITING

1. Imagine living in a communal setting of the kind described by Mernissi. How do you think you would react to the lack of privacy at mealtimes and the need to arrange your schedule to conform to that of the group? What positive features might offset these disadvantages?

2. **Critical Writing.** How are harems depicted in fairy tales, in films, and on television? What assumptions about the Hollywood image of the harem are absent from Mernissi's account?

3. To what extent has privacy become an increasingly rare luxury in modern culture? In a few paragraphs, explore the reasons for this.

4. **Argue** for or against the proposition that preserving the culture's distinctive customs was all the more important because Morocco at that time was occupied by the French.

5. **Thematic Links.** What contrasting cultural expectations for women can you discover in Mernissi's account and in Marilyn Yalom's analysis in "The Wife Today" in Chapter 10, "Definition"?

R.K.NARAYAN

Misguided "Guide"

The acclaimed Indian novelist R. K. Narayan (1906–2001) is best known for his imaginative re-creation of a fictional village, Malgudi, in the south of India (in his novels *A Tiger for Malgudi*, 1983; *Talkative Man*, 1986; and *The World of Nagaraj*, 1990). The following selection describes what happened when film producers wanted to transform his popular novel *The Guide* (1958) into a Hollywood-style film—with hilarious results.

BEFORE YOU READ

What qualities do you associate with Indian-made "Bollywood" films or with "Hollywood" films?

■ ■ ▨

1   The letter came by airmail from Los Angeles. "I am a producer and actor from Bombay," it read. "I don't know if my name is familiar to you."

2   He was too modest. Millions of young men copied his screen image, walking as he did, slinging a folded coat over the shoulder carelessly, buffing up a lock of hair over the right temple, and assuming that the total effect would make the girls sigh with hopeless longing. My young nephews at home were thrilled at the sight of the handwriting of Dev Anand.

3   The letter went on to say, "I was in London and came across your novel *The Guide*. I am anxious to make it into a film. I can promise you that I will keep to the spirit and quality of your writing. My plans are to make both a Hindi and an English film of this story." He explained how he had arranged with an American film producer for collaboration. He also described how he had flown from London to New York in search of me, since someone had told him I lived there, and then across the whole continent before he could discover my address. He was ready to come to Mysore if I should indicate the slightest willingness to consider his proposal.

4   I cabled him an invitation, already catching the fever of hurry characteristic of the film world. He flew from Los Angeles to Bombay to Bangalore, and motored down a hundred miles without losing a moment.

5   A small crowd of autograph-hunters had gathered at the gate of my house in Yadava Giri. He expertly eluded the inquisitive crowd, and we were soon closeted in the dining room, breakfasting on *idli, dosai,* and other South Indian delicacies, my nephews attending on the star in a state of elation. The talk was all about *The Guide* and its cinematic merits. Within an hour we had become so friendly that he could ask without embarrassment, "What price will you demand for your story?" The checkbook was out and the pen was poised over it. I had the

---

For a visual to accompany this selection, see color insert photo A-2.

impression that if I had suggested that the entire face of the check be covered with closely knit figures, he would have obliged me. But I hemmed and hawed, suggested a slight advance, and told him to go ahead. I was sure that if the picture turned out to be a success he would share with me the glory and the profits. "Oh, certainly," he affirmed, "if the picture, by God's grace, turns out to be a success, we will be on top of the world, and the sky will be the limit!"

6   The following months were filled with a sense of importance: Long Distance Calls, Urgent Telegrams, Express Letters, sudden arrivals and departures by plane and car. I received constant summonses to be present here or there. "PLEASE COME TO DELHI. SUIT RESERVED AT IMPERIALL HOTEL. URGENTLY NEED YOUR PRESENCE."

7   Locking away my novel-in-progress, I fly to Delhi. There is the press conference, with introductions, speeches and overflowing conviviality. The American director explains the unique nature of their present effort: for the first time in the history of Indian movie-making, they are going to bring out a hundred-percent-Indian story, with a hundred-percent-Indian cast, and a hundred-per-cent-Indian setting, for an international audience. And mark this: actually in colour-and-wide-screen-first-time-in-the-history-of-this-country.

8   A distinguished group of Americans, headed by the Nobel Prize winner Pearl Buck, would produce the film. Again and again I heard the phrase: "Sky is the limit," and the repeated assurances: "We will make the picture just as Narayan has written it, with his co-operation at every stage." Reporters pressed me for a statement. It was impossible to say anything but the pleasantest things in such an atmosphere of overwhelming optimism and good fellowship.

9   Soon we were assembled in Mysore. They wanted to see the exact spots which had inspired me to write *The Guide*. Could I show them the locations? A photographer, and some others whose business with us I never quite understood, were in the party. We started out in two cars. The American director, Tad Danielewski, explained that he would direct the English version first. He kept discussing with me the finer points of my novel. "I guess your hero is a man of impulsive plans? Self-made, given to daydreaming?" he would ask, and add, before I could muster an answer, "Am I not right?" Of course he had to be right. Once or twice when I attempted to mitigate his impressions, he brushed aside my comments and went on with his own explanation as to what I must have had in mind when I created such-and-such a character.

10   I began to realize that monologue is the privilege of the film maker, and that it was futile to try butting in with my own observations. But for some obscure reason, they seemed to need my presence, though not my voice. I must be seen and not heard.

11   We drove about 300 miles that day, during the course of which I showed them the river steps and a little shrine overshadowed by a banyan on the banks of the Kaveri, which was the actual spot around which I wrote *The Guide*. As I had recalled, nothing more needed to be done than put the actors there and start the camera. They uttered little cries of joy at finding a "set" so readily available. In the summer, when the river dried up, they could shoot the drought scenes with equal ease. Then

I took them to the tiny town of Nanjangud, with its little streets, its shops selling sweets and toys and ribbons, and a pilgrim crowd bathing in the holy waters of the Kabini, which flowed through the town. The crowd was colourful and lively around the temple, and in a few weeks it would increase a hundredfold when people from the surrounding villages arrived to participate in the annual festival—the sort of crowd described in the last pages of my novel. If the film makers made a note of the date and sent down a cameraman at that time, they could secure the last scene of my novel in an authentic manner and absolutely free of cost.

12   The producer at once passed an order to his assistant to arrange for an out-door unit to arrive here at the right time. Then we all posed at the portals of the ancient temple, with arms encircling each other's necks and smiling. This was but the first of innumerable similar scenes in which I found myself posing with the starry folk, crushed in the friendliest embrace.

13   From Nanjangud we drove up mountains and the forests and photographed our radiant smiles against every possible background. It was a fatiguing business on the whole, but the American director claimed that it was nothing to what he was used to. He generally went 5,000 miles in search of locations, exposing hundreds of rolls of film on the way.

14   After inspecting jungles, mountains, village streets, hamlets and huts, we reached the base of Gopalaswami Hill in the afternoon, and drove up the five-mile mud track; the cars had to be pushed up the steep hill after encroaching vegetation had been cleared from the path. This was a part of the forest country where at any bend of the road one could anticipate a tiger or a herd of elephants; but, luckily for us, they were out of view today.

15   At the summit I showed them the original of the "Peak House" in my novel, a bungalow built 50 years ago, with glassed-in verandas affording a view of the wildlife at night, and a 2,000-foot drop to a valley beyond. A hundred yards off, a foot-track wound through the undergrowth, leading on to an ancient temple whose walls were crumbling and whose immense timber doors moved on rusty hinges with a groan. Once again I felt that here everything was ready-made for the film. They could shoot in the bright sunlight, and for the indoor scenes they assured me that it would be a simple matter to haul up a generator and lights.

16   Sitting under a banyan tree and consuming sandwiches and lemonade, we discussed and settled the practical aspects of the expedition: where to locate the base camp and where the advance units consisting of engineers, mechanics, and truck drivers, in charge of the generator and lights. All through the journey back the talk involved schedules and arrangements for shooting the scenes in this part of the country. I was impressed with the ease they displayed in accepting such mighty logistical tasks. Film executives, it seemed to me, could solve mankind's problems on a global scale with the casual confidence of demigods, if only they could take time off their illusory pursuits and notice the serious aspects of existence.

17   Then came total silence, for many weeks. Finally I discovered that they were busy searching for their locations in Northern India.

18   This was a shock. I had never visualized my story in that part of India, where costumes, human types and details of daily life are different. They had settled

upon Jaipur and Udaipur in Rajaputana, a thousand miles away from my location for the story.

19   Our next meeting was in Bombay, and I wasted no time in speaking of this problem. "My story takes place in south India, in Malgudi, an imaginary town known to thousands of my readers all over the world," I explained. "It is South India in costume, tone and contents. Although the whole country is one, there are diversities, and one has to be faithful in delineating them. You have to stick to my geography and sociology. Although it is a world of fiction there are certain inner veracities."

20   One of them replied: "We feel it a privilege to be doing your story." This sounded irrelevant as an answer to my statement.

21   We were sitting under a gaudy umbrella beside a blue swimming pool on Juhu Beach, where the American party was housed in princely suites in a modern hotel. It was hard to believe that we were in India. Most of our discussions took place somewhat amphibiously, on the edge of the swimming pool, in which the director spent a great deal of his time.

22   This particular discussion was interrupted as a bulky European tourist in swimming briefs fell off the diving plank, hit the bottom and had to be hauled out and rendered first aid. After the atmosphere had cleared, I resumed my speech. They listened with a mixture of respect and condescension, evidently willing to make allowances for an author's whims.

23   "Please remember," one of them tried to explain, "that we are shooting, for the first time in India, in wide screen and Eastman Colour, and we must shoot where there is spectacle. Hence Jaipur."

24   "In that case," I had to ask, "Why all that strenuous motoring near my home? Why my story at all, if what you need is a picturesque spectacle?"

25   I was taken aback when their reply came! "How do you know that Malgudi is where you think it is?"

26   Somewhat bewildered, I said, with what I hoped was proper humility, "I suppose I know because I have imagined it, created it and have been writing novel after novel set in the area for the last 30 years."

27   "We are out to expand the notion of Malgudi," one of them explained. "Malgudi will be where we place it, in Kashmir, Rajasthan, Bombay, Delhi, even Ceylon."

28   I could not share the flexibility of their outlook or the expanse of their vision. It seemed to me that for their purpose a focal point was unnecessary. They appeared to be striving to achieve mere optical effects.

29   I recalled a talk with Satyajit Ray, the great director, some years earlier, when I met him in Calcutta. He expressed his admiration for *The Guide* but also his doubts as to whether he could ever capture the tone and atmosphere of its background. He had said, "Its roots are so deep in the soil of your part of our country that I doubt if I could do justice to your book, being unfamiliar with its milieu. . . ." Such misgivings did not bother the American director. I noticed that though he was visiting India for the first time, he never paused to ask what was what in this bewildering country.

30   Finally he solved the whole problem by declaring, "Why should we mention where the story takes place? We will avoid the name 'Malgudi.'" Thereafter the director not only avoided the word Malgudi but fell foul of anyone who uttered that sound.

31   My brother, an artist who has illustrated my stories for 25 years, tried to expound his view. At a dinner in his home in Bombay, he mentioned the forbidden word to the director. Malgudi, he explained, meant a little town, not so picturesque as Jaipur, of a neutral shade, with characters wearing dhoti and jibba when they were not barebodied. The Guide himself was a man of charm, creating history and archeology out of thin air for his clients, and to provide him with solid, concrete monuments to talk about would go against the grain of the tale. The director listened and firmly said, "There is no Malgudi, and that is all there is to it."

32   But my brother persisted. I became concerned that the controversy threatened to spoil our dinner. The director replied, in a sad tone, that they could as well have planned a picture for black and white and narrow screen if all one wanted was what he contemptuously termed a "Festival Film," while he was planning a million-dollar spectacle to open simultaneously in 2,000 theaters in America. I was getting used to arguments every day over details. My story is about a dancer in a small town, an exponent of the strictly classical tradition of South Indian *Bharat Natyam*. The film makers felt this was inadequate. They therefore engaged an expensive, popular dance director with a troupe of a hundred or more dancers, and converted my heroine's performances into an extravaganza in delirious, fruity colours and costumes. Their dancer was constantly traveling hither and thither in an Air India Boeing no matter how short the distance to be covered. The moviegoer, too, I began to realize, would be whisked all over India. Although he would see none of the countryside in which the novel was set, he would see the latest U.S. Embassy building in New Delhi, Parliament House, the Ashoka Hotel, the Lake Palace, Elephanta Caves and whatnot. Unity of place seemed an unknown concept for a film maker. (Later Mrs. Indira Gandhi, whom I met after she had seen a special showing of the film, asked, "Why should they have dragged the story all over as if it were a travelogue, instead of confining themselves to the simple background of your book?" She added as an afterthought, and in what seemed to me an understatement: "Perhaps they have other considerations.")

33   The co-operation of many persons was needed in the course of the film making, and anyone whose help was requested had to be given a copy of *The Guide*. Thus there occurred a shortage, and an inevitable black market, in copies of the book. A production executive searched the bookshops in Bombay, and cornered all available copies at any price. He could usually be seen going about like a scholar with a bundle of books under his arm. I was also intrigued by the intense study and pencil-marking that the director was making on his copy of the book; it was as if he were studying it for a doctoral thesis. Not until I had a chance to read his "treatment" did I understand what all his penciling meant: he had been marking off passages and portions that were to be avoided in the film.

34   When the script came, I read through it with mixed feelings. The director answered my complaints with "I have only exteriorized what you have expressed. It is all in your book."

35   "In which part of my book," I would ask without any hope of an answer.

36   Or he would say, "I could give you two hundred reasons why this change should be so." I did not feel up to hearing them all. If I still proved truculent he would explain away, "This is only a first draft. We could make any change you want in the final screenplay."

37   The screenplay was finally presented to me with a great flourish and expressions of fraternal sentiments at a hotel in Bangalore. But I learned at this time that they had already started shooting and had even completed a number of scenes. Whenever I expressed my views, the answer would be either, "Oh, it will all be rectified in the editing," or, "We will deal with it when we decide about the retakes. But please wait until we have a chance to see the rushes." By now a bewildering number of hands were behind the scenes, at laboratories, workshops, carpentries, editing rooms and so forth. It was impossible to keep track of what was going on, or get hold of anyone with a final say. Soon I trained myself to give up all attempts to connect the film with the book of which I happened to be the author.

38   But I was not sufficiently braced for the shock that came the day when the director insisted upon the production of two tigers to fight and destroy each other over a spotted deer. He wished to establish the destructive animality of two men clashing over one woman: my heroine's husband and lover fighting over her. The director intended a tiger fight to portray the depths of symbolism. It struck me as obvious. Moreover it was not in the story. But he asserted that it was; evidently I had intended the scene without realizing it.

39   The Indian producer, who was financing the project, groaned at the thought of the tigers. He begged me privately, "Please do something about it. We have no time for tigers; and it will cost a hell of a lot to hire them, just for a passing fancy." I spoke to the director again, but he was insistent. No tiger, no film, and two tigers or none.

40   Scouts were sent out through the length and breadth of India to explore the tiger possibilities. They returned to report that only one tiger was available. It belonged to a circus and the circus owner would under no circumstances consent to have the tiger injured or killed. The director decreed, "I want the beast to die, otherwise the scene will have no meaning." They finally found a man in Madras, living in the heart of the city with a full-grown Bengal tiger which he occasionally lent for jungle pictures, after sewing its lips and pulling out its claws.

41   The director examined a photograph of the tiger, in order to satisfy himself that they were not trying to palm off a pi-dog in tiger clothing, and signed it up. Since a second tiger was not available, he had to settle for its fighting a leopard. It was an easier matter to find a deer for the sacrifice. What they termed a "second unit" was dispatched to Madras to shoot the sequence. Ten days later the unit returned, looking forlorn.

42   The tiger had shrunk at the sight of the leopard, and the leopard had shown no inclination to maul the deer, whose cries of fright had been so heartrending

that they had paralyzed the technicians. By prodding, kicking and irritating the animals, they had succeeded in producing a spectacle gory enough to make them retch. "The deer was actually lifted and fed into the jaws of the other two," said an assistant cameraman. (This shot passes on the screen, in the finished film, in the winking of an eye as a bloody smudge, to the accompaniment of a lot of wild uproar.)

43   Presently another crisis developed. The director wanted the hero to kiss the heroine, who of course rejected the suggestion as unbecoming an Indian woman. The director was distraught. The hero, for his part, was willing to obey the director, but he was helpless, since kissing is a co-operative effort. The American director realized that it is against Indian custom to kiss in public; but he insisted that the public in his country would boo if they missed the kiss. I am told that the heroine replied; "There is enough kissing in your country at all times and places, off and on the screen, and your public, I am sure, will flock to a picture where, for a change, no kissing is shown." She stood firm. Finally, the required situation was apparently faked by trick editing.

44   Next: trouble at the governmental level. A representation was made to the Ministry dealing with the films, by an influential group, that *The Guide* glorified adultery, and hence was not fit to be presented as a film, since it might degrade Indian womanhood. The dancer in my story, to hear their arguments, has no justification for preferring Raju the Guide to her legally wedded husband. The Ministry summoned the movie principals to Delhi and asked them to explain how they proposed to meet the situation. They promised to revise the film script to the Ministry's satisfaction.

45   In my story the dancer's husband is a preoccupied archaeologist who has no time or inclination for a marital life and is not interested in her artistic aspirations. Raju the Guide exploits the situation and weans her away from her husband. That is all there is to it—in my story. But now a justification had to be found for adultery.

46   So the archaeological husband was converted into a drunkard and womanizer who kicks out his wife when he discovers that another man has watched her dance in her room and has spoken encouragingly to her. I knew nothing about this drastic change of my characters until I saw the "rushes" some months later. This was the point at which I lamented most over my naiveté: the contract that I had signed in blind faith, in the intoxication of cheques, bonhomie, and backslapping, empowered them to do whatever they pleased with my story, and I had no recourse.

47   Near the end of the project I made another discovery: the extent to which movie producers will go to publicize a film. The excessive affability to pressmen, the entertaining of V.I.P.s., the button-holding of ministers and officials in authority, the extravagant advertising campaigns, seem to me to drain off money, energy and ingenuity that might be reserved for the creation of an honest and sensible product.

48   On one occasion Lord Mountbatten was passing through India, and someone was seized with the sudden idea that he could help make a success of the picture. A banquet was held at Raj Bhavan in his honor, and the Governor of Bombay,

Mrs. Vijayalaxmi Pandit, was kind enough to invite us to it. I was home in Mysore as Operation Mountbatten was launched, so telegrams and long-distance telephone calls poured in on me to urge me to come to Bombay at once. I flew in just in time to dress and reach Raj Bhavan. It was red-carpeted, crowded and gorgeous. When dinner was over, leaving the guests aside, our hostess managed to isolate his Lordship and the "Guide"-makers on a side veranda of this noble building. His Lordship sat on a sofa surrounded by us; close to him sat Pearl Buck, who was one of the producers and who, by virtue of her seniority and standing, was to speak for us. As she opened the theme with a brief explanation of the epoch-making effort that was being made in India, in colour and wide-screen, with a hundred-percent-Indian cast, story and background, his Lordship displayed no special emotion. Then came the practical demand: in order that this grand, stupendous achievement might bear fruit, would Lord Mountbatten influence Queen Elizabeth to preside at the world premiere of the film in London in due course?

49   Lord Mountbatten responded promptly, "I don't think it is possible. Anyway what is the story?"

50   There was dead silence for a moment, as each looked at the other wondering who was to begin. I was fully aware that they ruled me out; they feared that I might take 80,000 words to narrate the story, as I had in the book. The obvious alternative was Pearl Buck, who was supposed to have written the screenplay.

51   Time was running out and his Lordship had others to talk to. Pearl Buck began.

52   "It is the story of a man called Raju. He was a tourist guide. . . ."

53   "Where does it take place?"

54   I wanted to shout, "Malgudi, of course," But they were explaining, "We have taken the story through many interesting locations—Jaipur, Udaipur."

55   "Let me hear the story."

56   "Raju was a guide," began Pearl Buck again.

57   "In Jaipur?" asked his Lordship.

58   "Well, no. Anyway he did not remain a guide because when Rosie came . . ."

59   "Who is Rosie?"

60   "A dancer . . . but she changed her name when she became a . . . a . . . dancer. . . ."

61   "But the guide? What happened to him?"

62   "I am coming to it. Rosie's husband . . ."

63   "Rosie is the dancer?"

64   "Yes, of course . . ." Pearl Buck struggled on, but I was in no mood to extricate her.

65   Within several minutes Lord Mountbatten said, "Most interesting." His deep bass voice was a delight to the ear, but it also had a ring of finality and discouraged further talk. "Elizabeth's appointments are complicated these days. Anyway her private secretary Lord — must know more about it than I do. I am rather out of touch now. Anyway, perhaps I could ask Philip." He summoned an aide and said, "William, please remind me when we get to London. . . ." Our Producers went home feeling that a definite step had been taken to establish the film in proper quarters. As for myself, I was not so sure.

66   Elaborate efforts were made to shoot the last scene of the story, in which the saint fasts on the dry river's edge, in hopes of bringing rain, and a huge crowd turns up to witness the spectacle. For this scene the director selected a site at a village called Okla, outside Delhi on the bank of the Jamuna river, which was dry and provided enormous stretches of sand. He had, of course, ruled out the spot we had visited near Mysore, explaining that two coconut trees were visible a mile away on the horizon and might spoil the appearance of unrelieved desert which he wanted. Thirty truckloads of property, carpenters, lumber, painters, artisans and art department personnel arrived at Okla to erect a two-dimensional temple beside a dry river, at a cost of 80,000 rupees. As the director kept demanding, "I must have 100,000 people for a helicopter shot," I thought of the cost: five rupees per head for extras, while both the festival crowd at Nanjangud and the little temple on the river would cost nothing.

67   The crowd had been mobilized, the sets readied and lights mounted, and all other preparations completed for shooting the scene next morning when, at midnight, news was brought to the chiefs relaxing at the Ashoka Hotel that the Jamuna was rising dangerously as a result of unexpected rains in Simla. All hands were mobilized and they rushed desperately to the location to save the equipment. Wading in knee-deep water, they salvaged a few things. But I believe the two-dimensional temple was carried off in the floods.

68   Like a colony of ants laboriously building up again, the carpenters and artisans rebuilt, this time at a place in Western India called Limdi, which was reputed to have an annual rainfall of a few droplets. Within one week the last scene was completed, the hero collapsing in harrowing fashion as a result of his penance. The director and technicians paid off the huge crowd and packed up their cameras and sound equipment, and were just leaving the scene when a storm broke—an unknown phenomenon in that part of the country—uprooting and tearing off everything that stood. Those who had lingered had to make their exit with dispatch.

69   This seemed to me an appropriate conclusion for my story, which, after all, was concerned with the subject of rain, and in which Nature, rather than film makers, acted in consonance with the subject. I remembered that years ago when I was in New York City on my way to sign the contract, before writing *The Guide*, a sudden downpour caught me on Madison Avenue and I entered the Viking Press offices dripping wet. I still treasure a letter from Keith Jennison, who was then my editor. "Somehow I will always, from now on," he wrote, "associate the rainiest days in New York with you. The afternoon we officially became your publishers was wet enough to have made me feel like a fish ever since."

■ ■ ▰

MEANING

1. How did Narayan's attitude toward the filming of his novel change over the course of the project?

2. Why do you think the American producers changed the locations, story line, and characters of Narayan's novel?

3. What was Malgudi like as Narayan envisioned it originally?

4. Why did the producers introduce elements of jealousy, revenge, animal fights, and other unrelated incidents into the film?

TECHNIQUE

1. What key stages or incidents can you discover that led to Narayan's change of perspective?

2. What incidents does Narayan choose to dramatize (or explore through dialogue), and how do these enhance his narrative account?

3. How do the episodes involving lavish sets washed away by torrential rains and banquets given for uninterested royalty accentuate Narayan's satire?

4. **Other Patterns** How is the humor of Narayan's account based on the **comparison and contrast** between the story he wrote and that of the filmmakers?

LANGUAGE

1. What linguistic clues alert the reader that Narayan does not spare himself in this satirical look at Hollywood-style filmmaking in India?

2. How does the term "Bollywood" suggest that the Bombay (now called Mumbai) film industry is attempting to emulate Hollywood? How is this connected to the issue of authenticity in Narayan's account?

3. If you don't know the meanings of any of the following words, look them up: *collaboration* (3), *conviviality* (7), *banyan* (11), *portals* (12), *amphibiously* (21), *picturesque* (24), *milieu* (29), *distraught* (43).

SUGGESTIONS FOR WRITING

1. **Critical Writing.** In a short essay, discuss some of the ways in which a Bollywood movie differs from a Hollywood film in terms of the cultural values of each society.

2. Would a film that adhered to Narayan's novel been necessarily better than the version that was made? Why or why not?

3. **Describe** films that you have seen that were based on novels or short stories. Analyze one of these in terms of the transformation from fiction into film.

4. **Thematic Links.** **Compare** the different cultural values that are implicit in movies made in India and those of the Marx Brothers as discussed by Ivan Karp in "Good Marx for the Anthropologist" (Chapter 6, "Comparison and Contrast").

EVGENY ZAMYATIN

The Lion

A satirist who is best known for his imaginative futurist fiction, Evgeny Zamyatin (1884–1937) grew up in Tsarist Russia and later under Soviet rule. His acclaimed novel *We* (1920) has been compared with the work of H. G. Wells and Aldous Huxley in its depiction of a dehumanized future society. The following short story reveals a lighter, more whimsical side of Zamyatin in its portrayal of Petya, a young student who is willing to make a fool of himself to win the attentions of Katya, a young policewoman.

BEFORE YOU READ

What is the stupidest thing you have ever done to get the attention of someone who was the object of your romantic fantasies?

■ ■ ▨

1 It all began with a most bizarre incident: the lion, great king of the beasts, was found hopelessly drunk. He kept tripping over all four paws and rolling onto his side. It was an utter catastrophe.

2 The lion was a student at Leningrad University and at the same time worked as an extra in the theatre. In that day's performance, dressed in a lionskin, he was to have stood on a rock, waiting to be struck down by a spear hurled at him by the heroine of the ballet; thereupon he was to fall onto a mattress in the wings. At rehearsals everything had gone off splendidly, but now suddenly, only half an hour before the curtain was due to go up for the première, the lion had taken it into his head to behave like a pig. No spare extras were available, but the performance couldn't be postponed since a cabinet minister from Moscow was expected to be there. An emergency conference was in session in the office of the theatre's Red director.

3 There was a knock on the door and the theatre fireman, Petya Zherebyakin, came in. The Red director (now he really was red—with anger) rounded on him.

4 "Well, what is it? What do you want? I've no time. Get out!"

5 "I . . . I . . . I've come about the lion, Comrade Director," said the fireman.

6 "Well, what about the lion?"

7 "Seeing, I mean, as our lion is drunk, that is, I'd like to play the lion, Comrade Director."

8 I don't know if bears ever have blue eyes and freckles but, if they do, then the enormous Zherebyakin in his iron-soled boots was much more like a bear than a lion. But suppose by some miracle they could make a lion out of him? He swore that they could: he had watched all the rehearsals from backstage, and when he was in the army he had taken part in *Tsar Maximillian*. So, to spite the producer,

who was grinning sarcastically, the director ordered Zherebyakin to put the costume on and have a try.

9   A few minutes later the orchestra was already playing, *con sordini*, the "March of the Lion" and Petya Zherebyakin was performing in his lion costume as if he had been born in the Libyan desert rather than in a village near Ryazan. But at the last moment, when he was supposed to fall off the rock, he glanced down and hesitated.

10   "Fall, damn you, fall!" whispered the producer fiercely.

11   The lion obediently plumped down, landed heavily on his back and lay there, unable to get up. Surely he was going to get up? Surely there was not to be another catastrophe at the last moment?

12   He was helped to his feet. He got out of the costume and stood there, pale, holding his back and giving an embarrassed smile. One of his upper front teeth was missing and this made the smile somewhat rueful and childlike (incidentally, there is always something rather childlike about bears, isn't there?).

13   Fortunately he appeared not to be seriously hurt. He asked for a glass of water, but the director insisted that a cup of tea be brought from his own office. Once Petya had drunk the tea the director began to chivvy him.

14   "Well, Comrade, you've appointed yourself lion, you'd better get into the costume. Come on, come on, lad, we'll soon be starting!"

15   Someone obligingly sprang forward with the costume, but the lion refused to put it on. He declared that he had to slip out of the theatre for a moment. What this unforeseen exigency was he wouldn't explain; he simply gave his embarrassed smile. The director flared up. He tried to order Zherebyakin to stay and reminded him that he was a candidate-member of the Party and a shockworker, but the shockworker-lion obstinately stood his ground. They had to give in, and with a radiant, gap-toothed smile Zherebyakin hurried off out of the theatre.

16   "Where the devil's he off to?" asked the director, red with anger again. "And what are all these secrets of his?"

17   Nobody could answer the Red director. The secret was known only to Petya Zherebyakin—and of course to the author of this story. And, as Zherebyakin runs through the autumnal St Petersburg rain, we can move for a while to that July night when his secret was born.

18   There was no night that night: it was the day lightly dozing off for a second, like a marching soldier who keeps in step but cannot distinguish dream from reality. In the rosy glass of the canals doze inverted trees, windows and columns— St Petersburg. Then suddenly, at the lightest of breezes, St Petersburg disappears and in its place is Leningrad. A red flag on the Winter Palace stirs in the wind; and by the railings of the Alexandrovsky Park stands a policeman armed with a rifle.

19   The policeman is surrounded by a tight group of night tramworkers. Over their shoulders Petya Zherebyakin can see only the policeman's face, round as a Ryazan honey-apple. Then a very strange thing happens: somebody seizes the policeman's hands and shoulders, and one of the workers, thrusting his lips forward in the shape of a trumpet, plants an affectionate smacking kiss on his cheek.

The policeman turns crimson and blows a loud blast on his whistle; the workers run away. Zherebyakin is left face to face with the policeman—and the policeman disappears, just as suddenly as the reflection of St Petersburg in the canal, puffed away by the breeze: in front of Zherebyakin stands a girl in a policeman's cap and tunic—the first policewoman to be stationed by the Revolution on Nevsky Prospekt. Her dark eyebrows met angrily over the bridge of her nose and her eyes flashed fire.

20   "You ought to be ashamed of yourself, Comrade," was all she said—but it was the way she said it! Zherebyakin became confused and muttered guiltily:

21   "But it wasn't me, honestly. I was just walking home."

22   "Come off it, and you a worker too!" The policewoman looked at him—but what a look!

23   If there had been a trapdoor in the roadway, as there is in the theatre, Zherebyakin would have fallen straight through it and been saved; but he had to walk away slowly, feeling her eyes burning into his back.

24   The next day brought another white night, and again Comrade Zherebyakin was walking home after his duty-turn in the theatre, and again the policewoman was standing by the railings of the Alexandrovsky Park. Zherebyakin wanted to slip past, but he noticed she was looking at him, so he gave a guilty, embarrassed nod. She nodded back. The twilight glinted on the glossy black steel of her rifle, turning it pink; and in the face of this pink rifle Zherebyakin felt more cowardly than before all the rifles which for five years had been fired at him on various fronts.

25   Not until a week later did he risk starting up a conversation with the policewoman. It turned out that she too was from Ryazan, just like Zherebyakin, and moreover she too remembered their Ryazan honey-apples—you know, the sweet ones with a slightly bitter taste; you can't get them here . . .

26   Every day on his way home Zherebyakin would stop by the Alexandrovsky Park. The white nights had gone quite mad: the green, pink and copper-coloured sky did not grow dark for a single second. The courting couples in the park had to look for shady spots to hide in just as if it were daytime.

27   One such night Zherebyakin, with bear-like awkwardness, suddenly asked the policewoman:

28   "Er, are you, that is, are policewomen allowed to get married like in the course of duty? I mean, not in the course of duty, but in general, seeing as your work is sort of military . . .?"

29   "Married?" said policewoman Katya, leaning on her rifle. "We're like men now: if we take a fancy to someone, we have him."

30   Her rifle shone pink. The policewoman lifted her face towards the feverishly blazing sky and then looked past Zherebyakin into the distance and completed her thought:

31   "If there was a man who wrote poetry like . . . or perhaps an actor who came out onto the stage and the whole audience started clapping . . ."

32   It was like the honey-apple—sweet and yet bitter at the same time. Petya Zherebyakin saw that he'd better be off and not come back there again, his cause was done for . . .

33   But no! Wonders haven't ceased! When there occurred that bizarre incident of the lion, thank the Lord, drinking himself silly, an idea flashed into Petya Zherebyakin's head and he flew into the director's room . . .

34   However, that is all in the past. Now he was hurrying through the autumn rain to Glinka Street. Luckily it wasn't far from the theatre and luckily he found policewoman Katya at home. She wasn't a policewoman now, but simply Katya. With her sleeves rolled up, she was washing a white blouse in a basin. Dewdrops hung on her nose and forehead. She had never looked sweeter than like this, in her domestic setting.

35   When Zherebyakin placed a free ticket in front of her and told her he had a part in the ballet that evening she didn't believe him at first; then she grew interested; then for some reason she became embarrassed and rolled her sleeves down; finally she looked at him (but what a look!) and said she would definitely come.

36   The bells were already ringing in the theatre smoking-room, in the corridors and in the foyer. The bald cabinet minister was in his box, squinting through a pince-nez. On the stage behind the curtain, which was still down, the ballerinas were smoothing their skirts with the movement swans use to clean their wings under the water. Behind the rock the producer and the director were both fussing round Zherebyakin.

37   "Don't forget, you're a shockworker. Mind you don't ruin everything!" whispered the director into the lion's ear.

38   The curtain rose, and behind the bright line of the footlights the lion suddenly saw the dark auditorium, packed to the roof with white faces. Long ago, when he was simply Zherebyakin, and had to climb out of trenches with grenades exploding in front of him, he used to shudder and automatically cross himself, but still run forward. Now, however, he felt unable to take a single step, but the producer gave him a shove and, somehow moving arms and legs which seemed not to belong to him, he slowly climbed up onto the rock.

39   On top of the rock, the lion raised his head and saw, right next to him, policewoman Katya, leaning over the front barrier of one of the second-row boxes. She was looking straight at him. The leonine heart thumped once, twice, and then stopped. He was trembling all over. His fate was about to be decided. Already the spear was flying towards him . . . Ouch!—it struck him in the side. Now he had to fall. But suppose he again fell the wrong way and ruined everything? He had never felt so terrified in all his life—it was far worse than when he used to climb out of the trenches . . .

40   The audience had already noticed that something wasn't right: the mortally wounded lion was standing stock-still on top of the rock and gazing down. The front rows heard the producer's terrible whisper:

41   "Fall, damn you, fall!"

42   Then they all saw a most bizarre thing: the lion raised its right paw, quickly crossed itself, and plumped down off the rock like a stone . . .

43   There was a moment of numbed silence, then a roar of laughter exploded in the auditorium like a grenade. Policewoman Katya was laughing so hard that she was in tears. The slain lion buried its muzzle in its paws and sobbed.

MEANING

1. What circumstances bring Petya into the theater to audition for the part of the lion?
2. What is ironic about the initial encounter between Petya and Katya?
3. How would you characterize Petya? What sort of a person does he seem to be?
4. How does the contrast between Petya's experiences in the military and job as a fireman and his paralyzing shyness with women make the readers sympathetic toward him?

TECHNIQUE

1. What early details foreshadow the outcome?
2. How would you characterize the omniscient narrator and the way in which he comments on the events in the story?
3. How does Zamyatin use dialogue to convey impressions about the main characters?
4. **Other Patterns.** How does Zamyatin use **description** to evoke the atmosphere of the theater, the appearance of his main characters, and the climactic scene?

LANGUAGE

1. How would you **describe** the tone of the story (e.g., approving, judgmental)?
2. How does the simplicity of the language and Zamyatin's gentle irony suit the characters and subject of the story?
3. If you don't know the meanings of any of the following words, look them up: *rueful* (12), *chivvy* (13), *exigency* (15), *bizarre* (33), *pince-nez* (36).

SUGGESTIONS FOR WRITING

1. **Critical Writing.** Start at the point where the story ends, and describe what you think happens next between Petya and Katya.
2. What actions and reactions serve as indicators of being in love?
3. If you ever acted in a play, how would you **define** the condition of stage fright?
4. **Thematic Links.** **Compare** the different customs of courtship in their respective cultures in Zamyatin's story and Guanlong Cao's essay "Chopsticks."

▓▓▓ STUDENT ESSAY: NARRATION

The following essay by Melissa Roberts relates her experiences as a runner and is typical of the kind of narrative writing that students are asked to do in composition classes. As you are reading Melissa's essay, notice the way in which she employs different narrative techniques. We have annotated her paper and provided an assessment ("Strategies") to help you understand narration.

A New Horizon

Melissa Roberts

1   There is a place in this world where you can feel the thunderheads rolling in before you can see or hear them. There's a subtle but electrifying energy in the ground, a vibration that only a runner can sense. As 83rd Street rushes by under my sneakers, I can feel myself getting closer to this place where the concept of unity with nature is a reality. In this place your past is closer to the present than you could ever believe and your future is yours to catch. This place is my truly my home.

> Introduction creates the context: a runner's journey past memorable landmarks.

> Thesis statement or narrative point

2   They call it "The Bottoms." Why? I'm not entirely sure. It's low-lying, flat land; but then again, I've seen lower, flatter land than this. Last season's corn and soybean crops stretch out in neat rows, and the landscape is marred only by a rotting barn and County Route 34. The road forms a solitary and serpentine black shape in front of me and behind me. Were I to turn around, I'd see the line of trees that borders the Bottoms from the town.

3   But I never turn around, it's against a runner's instincts. My teammates and I used to joke on our Monday long runs about how we had trouble looking over our shoulders to check a blind spot while driving. It's the race mentality that prevents it. When you race, the world runs on your time. You have control of every situation, and your strengths and weaknesses dictate how it all plays out in the end. To glance back over your shoulder would be unheard of. It means that you're worried about the runner behind you. It means that you think they might be catching up. It means that you've stopped racing.

> Narrative is told in the present tense from a first-person point of view.

4   As I continue, the little pocket of civilization where I live fades from memory and consciousness, and I continue into the known and the unknown all at once. I've run this way more times than I can count. I recognize every crack in the sidewalk, every solid yellow line, and every telephone pole. I can run this road in the dark, in the snow, in ice, in rain so torrential you can hardly see. This is my road.

> Narrative relates events in a chronological order.

5   Even though this is my road, and the cracks in the pavement never move, it changes daily. Each run is completely different because each run brings a new set of challenges to confront and overcome. Pain is the worst of them, but a lack of motivation can plague a runner as well. It helps when the team runs together, but today I run alone. It was fun while it lasted, but everyone has since gone off to separate colleges, and each is lacing up their running shoes in a different location across the state.

> Details reveal writer's state of mind.

6   The line of trees that separates this place from town wasn't always there. When the Great Depression hit in the 1930s, Kansas was already in the midst of the Dustbowl. Topsoil erosion and lack of crop rotation led to the worst dust storms of the century. At least, that's what I was told in American History class. The WPA sent workers out to the plains of Kansas and Oklahoma to plant lines of trees across the barren landscape, and this is one of those tree lines.

> Past events that make the present more meaningful

7   The Bottoms used to house the sand plant, but now all that remains of that enterprise is a burned out foundation and the dunes. The dunes meld into the graying fields, and those continue on as far as the eye can see. They, in turn, meld into the horizon. You can barely make out that line of infinity, because the sky is that same shade of gray, not really a color but lack thereof.

8   The only part of the landscape that stands out is the "Tree of Life." The Hispanics in the town call it La Montana. I call it the four mile turnaround. But today, I'm going a little farther into the distance. I sense a storm brewing in the distance, and I'll try to catch the horizon before the thunderheads overtake me. I continue out into nothingness.

> Key or transforming experience is introduced.

9   I start to hear phantom footsteps around me, and I am a senior in high school, surrounded by my best friends and teammates. As we jog through the Bottoms, we talk about everything and nothing all at once. Boys, friends, unfair parents, life, death, politics, science, anything. There was a time at which we started telling the same stories to each other over again, because we had simply shared everything about ourselves that there was to know. Then the time came when all of our stories began with "Hey, do you

> Analysis of the key experience

Roberts 3

remember that time that . . ." because we had been together any time worth remembering. But today I hear only echoes; I know it will never be the same again, and yet it will never leave me.

10   Finally, the distant claps of thunder are audible over my staggered breathing and the hypnotizing rhythm of my Nikes on the pavement. They get louder as the miles fly under me. The sky slowly fades from the un-gray to a glowing yellow color and I know that the storm is almost here. I shift gears and begin to wind up for my kick like a giant rubber band; each step is a twist that tenses me and prepares me for the final, sprinting release. My pace quickens, my breath quickens, my instinctual fear kicks in, and I'm no longer running to escape civilization, but to escape this natural beast that I know is in pursuit and threatens to swallow me whole.

11   Then I hear it. Softly at first, then louder and closer. The pitter patter of a million little footsteps that start in the distance and speed up. I can hear them coming up behind me, and I begin a full out sprint. But I can't run from nature, and the sheet of rain catches me from behind. The raindrops that were so threatening a moment before now cool me and comfort me. I stop and stand there a moment, utterly exhausted and exhilarated as I feel the rain beat down on my shoulders and the sting of the sweat that has been washed into my eyes.

> Sentence structure enhances the tension and drama of her experience.

12   The tornado siren from the town over the hill brings me back to reality, and I know that it's time to turn around and head back. My family and friends will be waiting, worried that I've gone running in tornado weather again. I guess the horizon will have to wait. I tear myself from the scene, slowly turn, and begin the run back into town. But just before I round the final bend that will take me into town, I stop one more time. I look back at the tree, the rain-streaked sky, my home. This is the place where I chase infinity, a better understanding of the past, and perhaps a glimpse of my future. A strange sadness passes over me, but it only lasts a moment. I know that this place will be the same when I return. It may be tomorrow, it may not be for years. And yet, despite its continuity, it will be completely different, a road, a new run, and a new horizon.

> Conclusion makes connection to title.

Strategies for Writing Essays in Narration

1. Identifying the Conflict or Dilemma

As the title of her essay suggests, Melissa has chosen to focus on the way running over a familiar stretch of ground can be a transforming experience. Her introduction arouses the reader's interest by building suspense as to what this location is and why it means so much to her.

2. Narrative Point or Thesis

Melissa's thesis statement—"in this place your past is closer to the present than you could ever believe and your future is yours to catch"—tells us that she will juxtapose past memories to her present run and accept whatever changes the future may bring as she leaves her high school experience behind.

3. Narrative Sequence

Melissa's narrative is organized chronologically from early in her run to the moment she hears the tornado siren from the town and decides to head back. Each section introduces a different aspect of her experience along with background information on the history of the area in which she is running. The moment of truth for her is the realization that her days of running with friends and teammates in high school are over but will always be a part of her. The concluding portion of the essay reinforces the meaning of the title and communicates her newfound insight. Throughout her essay, Melissa uses time markers and transitions ("as I continue," "I start to hear," "finally,") to guide her readers from section to section.

4. Details that Advance the Narrative

Melissa's narrative provides a multitude of details that enable her readers to see, hear, and feel what she experiences. We can feel the ground underneath her feet; see the sinuous shape of the road, the lines of trees behind her, and the landmark tree; hear the echoes of footsteps, claps of thunder, and the siren warning of a tornado; and feel the pelting rain. The only time she uses dialogue is in a flashback about how her teammates exchanged stories.

5. Point of View and Verb Tense

Melissa uses a first-person point of view consistently throughout her narrative and stays within the present tense except when she gives the historical background of "the Bottoms" and in her brief flashback about previous runs with her high-school teammates.

6. Suggestions for Revision

One aspect of Melissa's essay that needs to be made clearer is the way she shifts the meaning of horizon from a physical location to a psychological state and back again. Some readers might see her historical account of the "the Bottoms" as a digression that does not advance her narrative. She also seems to have injected a bit too much drama in personifying the advancing rainstorm as a "beast."

Guidelines for Writing an Essay in Narration

- If your assignment requires you to create a narrative, locate the issue or dilemma that your essay will explore. Have you clearly communicated the significance of the event in your thesis?

- Have you provided sufficient details to allow the reader to understand what happened and why it was important without unnecessary commentary and explanations?

- Have you communicated key events in a narrative sequence (usually chronological)? You can use flashbacks to illuminate crucial events. End in such a way as to wrap up the narrative.

- Do the sections of your narrative divide into paragraphs, each with a clear focus and linked to each other by effective time signals or transitions?

- Vary the sentence structure, and use dialogue to allow the reader to hear what people said to each other in the situation. Use specific sensory details about people, places, and events.

- Remember that narratives may tell the story in the past tense but use the present tense for dialogue. Stick to a consistent point of view, either first-person singular or third-person.

RHYMES WITH ORANGE   **BY HILARY B. PRICE**

How does Hilary B. Price's cartoon personalize aspects of grammar?

Grammar Tips for Narration

Because narratives are really stories, one way to make them lively and effective is to make sure your verbs are active rather than passive, strong instead of weak, and consistent in tense throughout the entire narrative.

1. Active: When given a choice, always choose verbs in the active voice that emphasize who is performing the action rather than the object that is acted upon. For example:

Active: John drove the truck.
Passive: The truck was driven by John.

2. Strong: Strong verbs appeal to specific senses rather than giving vague and general impressions. For example:

Strong: The rain splashed against the door and pelted the windowpanes.
Weak: The rain was heavy and made a lot of noise.

3. Consistent in Tense: When relating a series of events occurring at the same time, whether in the past or present, stay with one tense and avoid shifting tenses in closely linked sentences. For example:

Consistent Tense: Judy explains that some of the rides at the theme park are not suitable for children. She says that parents should check the age and height requirements before buying a ticket.

Inconsistent Tenses: Judy explains that some of the rides at the theme park are not suitable for children. She said that parents should check the age and height requirements before buying a ticket.

Checklist for Revising Narrative Essays

- Have you identified the turning point your essay will explore?
- Have you clearly stated the meaning of this event in your thesis statement?
- Have you supplied sufficient details for readers to grasp the context?
- Have you communicated key events in a clear way?
- Have you told the story from a consistent viewpoint and effectively used dialogue?
- Do your transitional words and phrases guide the reader through the sequence of events?

ADDITIONAL WRITING ASSIGNMENTS AND ACTIVITIES

COMMUNICATING WITH DIFFERENT AUDIENCES

1. Write a letter to a mail-order catalog company about an item that you ordered with which you were satisfied or unsatisfied.

2. Write a letter to a television show explaining why you would make a good contestant (e.g., dance contests or shows like *American Idol, Jeopardy,* or *Survivor*).

3. You are in charge of sending a newsletter to contributors asking for donations based on the good work your organization has done (e.g., the time when the organization sent food and medical supplies to people who were devastated by a natural disaster such as a hurricane or fire).

WRITING FOR A NEWSPAPER

Write a letter about a building that you believe should be demolished and replaced with one whose structure and appearance are better suited to the location.

NARRATIVE ESSAYS

1. What name or combination of six letters and/or numbers would you choose for a personalized license plate, and what would it say about you?

2. Write a narrative about the purchase of a piece of jewelry, a watch, or a costly personal ornament.

3. Is there something you bought years ago that you would not consider buying now? What caused you to change your attitude toward this item?

4. What incident reveals your attitude about taking care of something you borrowed that was accidentally damaged?

5. What stories, fables, or parables illustrate the downside of owning a lot of things? Do you agree or disagree with the message?

6. Do people suspend good judgment and frugality at key turning points such as weddings, funerals, births, or anniversaries?

7. Imagine a day in your life without the use of any electronic gadgets. What would it be like?

8. Invent a food-related nickname for yourself or one of your friends, and explain why it would be appropriate.

9. Write a short narrative about a ceremony or ritual in which food reflecting an ethnic heritage played a key role.

10. Narrate an experience you have had at a store during a big sale.

11. Narrate an experience you have had of returning an item of clothing to a store that gave you a hard time.

12. Tell about a recent or memorable instance of flirting, including the circumstances, dialogue, gestures, and outcome.

13. Tell about a time when you were stereotyped because of the way you looked, what you were wearing, and the dynamics of the situation.

14. Tell about instances in which you received expectations from parents, relatives, or peers as to what being a girl or boy meant in your community.

15. What are the sure signs of being in love that you have experienced or witnessed?

16. Relate a story that involved the ethnic or cultural origins of your first or last name.

17. Recreate or imagine a conversation in which the participants speak in dialect or use colloquial language that communicates who they are.

18. Tell about the time when you made an effort to learn another language and whether and when it proved useful.

19. Write about the time you visited a circus or carnival and the memorable incidents that occurred.

20. What moment or hour or day would you choose to relive throughout eternity?

21. Tell about a time you won a prize or contest, the circumstances, and how it made you feel.

22. Tell a secret about your town, family, or campus that you can share without incriminating anyone.

23. Tell about the time you had to say goodbye to a friend and what you said, what you felt, and the circumstances, and include flashbacks to your relationship.

24. Imagine that you have arrived at a party and have been asked to introduce yourself. On impulse, you invent a wild story about who you are to impress the other guests. What would you say?

RESEARCH SUGGESTIONS

1. Research the history of different garments worn in different professions such as medicine, the law, or academia.

2. Research the history of a sport in which animals have played a part (e.g., horse or dog racing, bearbaiting in the Renaissance).

COLLABORATIVE ACTIVITIES

1. What are the distinctive features of episodes of cooking shows or cooking competitions that have become so popular?

2. Compare experiences of bringing home to meet your family a date who was perhaps from another culture or race and not necessarily of the opposite sex.

DESCRIPTION

4

Showing Details of People, Places, and Things

Writers in different disciplines use description for a variety of purposes related to the goals of their particular fields of study. In the sciences, objective descriptions recreate the appearance of objects, events, or scenes. In the liberal arts, subjective description permits readers to empathize with the writer's feelings and reactions toward scenes, objects, or events. In both the liberal arts and the social and political sciences, we often encounter combinations of objective and subjective description.

N. Scott Momaday's evocation of a wilderness landscape in "The Way to Rainy Mountain" illustrates how powerfully description can work in the hands of an artist to re-create the sensory nature of a place through precise images:

> Descending eastward, the highland meadows are a stairway to the plain. In July the inland slope of the Rockies is luxuriant with flax and buckwheat, stonecrop, and larkspur. The earth unfolds and the limit of the land recedes. Clusters of trees and animals grazing far in the distance cause the vision to reach away and wonder to build upon the mind.

Momaday recreates the harmony and compatibility of the natural world. We can see, feel and almost touch the scene as if we were actually there, experiencing the landscape through Momaday's description.

Subjective description is useful for communicating the writer's personal feelings and reactions to the idea, event, or person being described. As such, it is well suited to portray a person so that the reader not only knows how the subject looked, but also gains insight into the person's unique qualities, character traits, and nature. Jamaica Kincaid accomplishes this in her description of tourists who visit her home island of Antigua without noticing that features that they find so pleasant (the scorching sun and lack of rain) are hardships for native Antiguans:

> and since you are on your holiday, since you are a tourist, the thought of what it must be like for someone who had to live day in, day out in a place that suffers constantly from drought, and so has to watch carefully every drop of fresh water used . . . , must never cross your mind.

We learn that tourists apply different standards (is it picturesque and quaint? is it always sunny?) to places they visit on vacation than they do at home.

The ability of description to accurately convey physical characteristics (height, shape, dimensions, appearance) makes description an especially effective writing strategy for anthropologists, social scientists, and historians. Writing in these disciplines requires close observation and documentation of social, political, and cultural phenomena. In "The Paradox of St. Mark's," Mary McCarthy describes the appearance of St. Mark's and the paradox that something so jumbled and garish should be known as the epitome of beauty:

> St. Mark's as a whole, unless seen from a distance or at twilight, is not beautiful. The modern mosaics (seventeeth century) are generally admitted to be extremely ugly, and I myself do not care for most of the Gothic statuary of the pinnacles. The horses, the colored marble veneers, the Byzantine Madonna of the front, the old mosaic on the left, the marble columns of the portal, the gold encrustations of the top, the five grey domes with their strange ornaments, like children's jacks—these are the details that captivate. As for the rest, it is better not to look too closely, or the whole will begin to seem tawdry, a hodge-podge, as so many critics have said.

McCarthy appeals to the sense of sight when she describes the incongruous juxtaposition of mosaics, statuary, gold decorations, and the five gray domes. The less than inspiring effect of the scene for McCarthy heightens the paradox that the facade of St. Mark's should be associated with beauty and enchantment.

Perhaps the most useful method of arranging details within a description is the technique of focusing on an impression that dominates the entire scene. This main impression can center on a prominent physical feature, such as a tower or church steeple, or a significant psychological trait, such as the tourist's self-centeredness and indifference to the reality of the way in which people live on the islands the tourists visit.

A skillful writer will often arrange his or her description around this central impression, in much the same way that a good photographer will locate a focal point for pictures. Natsume Soseki, in his story "I Am A Cat," uses this technique in his description of how a young cat reacted to being picked up:

> What impressed me as being most strange still remains deeply imbedded in my mind: the face which should have been covered with hair was a slippery thing similar to what I now know to be a teakettle. I have since come across many other cats but none of them are such freaks. Moreover, the center of the Student's face protruded to a great extent, and from the two holes located there, he would often emit smoke. I was extremely

annoyed by being choked by this. That was what they term as tobacco, I came to know only recently.

A series of specific descriptive details create the scene from the cat's perspective. Yet the primary impression is of the cat's naive surprise at seeing a human face for the first time.

In "The Initiation of a Maasai Warrior," Tepilit Ole Saitoti, a native of Kenya, finds description indispensable to document the unique way in which circumcision rituals are viewed within his culture. Saitoti describes the painful and frightening ritual he had to endure to become a Maasai warrior—and its aftermath:

> I laid on my own bed and bled profusely. The blood must be retained within the bed, for according to Maasai tradition, it must not spill to the ground. I was drenched in my own blood. I stopped bleeding after about half an hour but soon was in intolerable pain.

Through Saitoti's evocative details, we can "see" the scene and feel his anguish before he recovers enough to walk outside.

Description is most effective when the writer arranges details so as to produce a certain effect on the audience. For example, in "Flavio's Home," Gordon Parks organizes the details of his description to give his readers insight into the cramped quarters and conditions of hardship in which hundreds of thousands of people live in the *favelas*, or slums, on the outskirts of Rio de Janeiro.

> The shack was about six by ten feet. Its grimy walls were a patchwork of misshapen boards with large gaps between them, revealing other shacks below stilted against the slopes. The floor, rotting under layers of grease and dirt, caught shafts of light slanting down through spaces in the roof. A large hole in the corner served as a toilet. Beneath that hole was the sloping mountainside.

Notice how Parks arranges his description so that his readers "follow him" inside the shack and gradually discover what it would be like to be a *favelado*. Whatever principle of order a writer chooses (from top to bottom, left to right, far to near, or any variations on these), the presentation of details must seem natural. Parks organizes his description in order to lead his readers through the scene in a way that evokes the experiences of the slum dwellers.

Another effective way of organizing a description is to select and present details in order to create a feeling of suspense. Mark Salzman uses this technique in "Lessons" to recreate the tension he felt while witnessing his teacher, Pan, practice a combat routine in which either student or teacher could be gravely injured:

> Without warming up at all, Pan ordered the woman with the spear to get ready, and to move fast when the time came. His body looked as though electricity had suddenly passed through it, and the huge blade flashed toward her. Once, twice the dadao flew beneath her feet, then swung around in a terrible arc and rode her back with flawless precision. The third time he added a little twist at the end, so that the

blade grazed up her neck and sent a little decoration stuck in her pigtails flying across the room.

Salzman introduces one detail after another to heighten suspense as to whether Pan can guide the heavy spear well enough to show his students the correct routine without harming the girl. The description is arranged to transport the readers into the scene so that they see what Salzman saw on that day: a martial arts master making something incredibly hard look effortless.

Thus, description, as it is used by writers in many cultures, is an indispensable tool for conveying the external appearance of people, places, and things and a means by which writers can relate their emotional reaction to the subjects they describe.

You will find description useful in writing tasks, whether in college or at work, that require you to provide specific details that evoke people, places, objects, and even your feelings.

The Paradox of St. Mark's

Mary McCarthy (1912–1989) was an American novelist, short story writer, essayist, and critic. She was born in Seattle and attended a convent, an Episcopal school, and Vassar College, after which she settled in Paris. The qualities of intellectual virtuosity and satiric insights are on display in this piece, which is an acute appraisal of the city of Venice that originally appeared in *Venice Observed* (1966). In it, McCarthy emphasizes the commercial and materialistic aspects of the city and the clash between the reality and its fairy-tale image. Among her well-known works are *The Group* (1963), which became a popular film three years later, and her posthumous autobiography *Intellectual Memoirs: New York, 1936–1938* (1992).

BEFORE YOU READ

What associations do you have with Venice or any other European city?

■ ■ ▨

1   It was from Byzantium that the taste for refinement and sensuous luxury came to Venice. *"Artificiosa voluptate se mulcebat,"*[1] a chronicler wrote of the Greek wife of an early doge. Her scents and perfumes, her baths of dew, her sweet-smelling gloves and dresses, the fork she used at table scandalized her subjects, plain Italian pioneer folk. The husband of this effeminate woman had Greek tastes also. He began, says the chronicler, "to work in mosaic," importing mosaic workers— and marbles and precious stones—to adorn his private chapel, St. Mark's, in the Eastern style that soon became second nature to the Venetians.

2   The Byzantine[2] mode, in Venice, lost something of its theological awesomeness. The stern, solemn figure of the Pantocrator[3] who dominates the Greek churches with his frowning brows and upraised hand does not appear in St. Mark's in His arresting majesty. In a Greek church, you feel that the Eye of God is on you from the moment you step in the door; you are utterly encompassed by this all-embracing gaze, which in peasant chapels is often represented by an eye over the door. The fixity of this divine gaze is not punitive; it merely calls you to attention and reminds you of the eternal, the Law of the universe arching over time and circumstance. The Pantocrator of the Greeks has traits of the old Nemesis,[4]

---

[1] "She indulged herself in artificial desire." The doge was the chief magistrate of the republic of Venice.

[2] *Byzantine:* pertains to a method of construction in the Byzantine Empire with round arches, low domes, a highly formal structure, and the use of rich color.

[3] Christ as "Ruler of All."

[4] An ancient goddess who dealt out retributive justice.

For a visual to accompany this selection, see color insert photo A-3.

sweetened and purified by the Redemption. He is also a Platonic idea, the End of the chain of speculation.

3   The Venetians were not speculators or philosophers, and the theological assertion is absent from St. Mark's mosaics, which seek rather to tell a Biblical story than to convey an abstraction. The *clothing* of the story assumes, in Venice, an adventitious interest, as in the fluffy furs worn by Salome in the Baptistery. . . .

4   St. Mark's, in the Ravenna style, was begun in 829, but it was twice destroyed, burned down once by the people in rebellion against a tyrannous doge, restored, and torn down again by an eleventh-century doge who wanted his chapel in the fashionable Byzantine style. (It was his successor, Doge Selvo, that married the Greek wife.) The present St. Mark's in the shape of a Greek cross with five domes and modeled, some think, on the church of the Twelve Apostles in Constantinople, is the result of his initiative. . . .

5   From the outside, as is often observed, St. Mark's looks like an Oriental pavilion—half pleasure-house, half war-tent, belonging to some great satrap. Inside, glittering with jewels and gold, faced with precious Eastern marbles, jasper and alabastar, prophyry and verdantique, sustained by Byzantine columns in the same materials, of varying sizes and epochs, scarcely a pair alike, this dark cruciform cave has the look of a robber's den. In the chapel of the Crucifix, with a pyramidal marble roof topped by a huge piece of Oriental agate and supported by six Byzantine columns in black and white African marble, stands a painted crucifix, of special holiness, taken from Constantinople. In the atrium, flanking St. Clement's door, are two pairs of black and white marble columns, with wonderful lion's and eagle's heads in yellowish ivory; tradition says they came from the Temple of Solomon in Jerusalem. From Tyre came the huge block of Mountain Tabor granite on the altar in the Baptistery—said to be the stone on which Christ was wont to pray. In the Zen chapel, the wall is lined with onion marbles and verdantique, reputedly the gravestones of the Byzantine Emperors.

6   In the chapel of St. Isidore sleeps the saint stolen from Chios; he was hidden for two centuries for fear of confiscation. St. Theodore, stolen from Byzantium, was moved to San Salvatore. St. Mark himself was lost for a considerable period, after the fire in 976, which destroyed most of the early church; he revealed his presence by thrusting forth his arm. He was not the original saint of Venice, but, so to speak, a usurper, displacing St. Theodore. Thus, he himself, the patron, was a kind of thieving cuckoo bird, and his church, which was only the Doge's private chapel, imitated him by usurping the functions of San Pietro in Castello, the seat of the Patriarch and the real Cathedral (until very recent times) of Venice. In the same style, the early doges had themselves buried, in St. Mark's porch, in sarcophagi that did not belong to them, displacing the bones of old pagans and paleo-Christians.

7   Venice, unlike Rome or Ravenna or nearby Verona, had nothing of its own to start with. Venice, as a city, was a foundling, floating upon the waters like Moses in his basket among the bulrushes. It was therefore obliged to be inventive, to steal and improvise. Cleverness and adaptivity were imposed by the original situation, and the get-up-and-go of the early Venetian business men was typical of a self-made

society. St. Mark's church is a (literally) shining example of this spirit of initiative, this gift for improvisation, for turning everything to account. It is made of bricks, like most Venetian churches, since brick was the easiest material to come by. Its external beauty comes from the thin marble veneers with which the brick surface is coated, just as though it were a piece of furniture. These marbles, for the most part, like the columns and facing inside, were the spoils of war, and they were put on almost haphazardly, green against gray, against red or rose or white with red veining, without any general principle of design beyond the immediate pleasure of the eye. On the Piazzetta side, this gives the effect of a gay abstract painting. Parvenu art, more like painting than architecture . . . , and yet it "worked." The marble veneers of St. Mark's sides, especially when washed by the rain so that they look like oiled silk, are among the most beautiful things in Venice. And it is their very thinness, the sense they give of being a mere lustrous coating, a film, that makes them beautiful. A palace of solid marble, rainwashed, simply looks bedraggled.

8   St. Mark's as a whole, unless seen from a distance or at twilight, is not beautiful. The modern mosaics (seventeenth century) are generally admitted to be extremely ugly, and I myself do not care for most of the Gothic statuary of the pinnacles. The horses, the colored marble veneers, the Byzantine Madonna of the front, the old mosaic on the left, the marble columns of the portal, the gold encrustations of the top, the five grey domes with their strange ornaments, like children's jacks—these are the details that captivate. As for the rest, it is better not to look too closely, or the whole will begin to seem tawdry, a hodge-podge, as so many critics have said. The whole is not beautiful, and yet again it is. It depends on the light and the time of day or on whether you narrow your eyes, to make it look flat, a painted surface. And it can take you unawares, looking beautiful or horribly ugly, at a time you least expect. Venice, Henry James said, is as changeable as a nervous woman, and this is particularly true of St. Mark's façade.

9   But why should it be beautiful at all? Why should Venice, aside from its situation, be a place of enchantment? One appears to be confronted with a paradox. A commercial people who lived solely for gain—how could they create a city of fantasy, lovely as a dream or a fairy-tale? This is the central puzzle of Venice, the stumbling-block that one keeps coming up against if one tries to *think* about her history, to put the facts of her history together with the visual fact that is there before one's eyes. It cannot be that Venice is a happy accident or a trick of light. I have thought about this a long time, but now it occurs to me that, as with most puzzles, the clue to the answer lies in the way the question is framed. "Lovely as a dream or a fairy tale. . . ." There is no contradiction, once you stop to think what images of beauty arise from fairy tales. They are images of money. Gold, caskets of gold, caskets of silver, the miller's daughter spinning gold all night long, thanks to Rumplestiltskin, the cave of Ali Baba stored with stolen gold and silver, the underground garden in which Aladdin found jewels growing on trees, so that he could gather them in his hands, rubies and diamonds and emeralds, the Queen's lovely daughter whose hair is black as ebony and lips are red as rubies, treasure buried in the forest, treasure guarded by dogs with eyes as big as carbuncles, treasure guarded by a Beast—this is the spirit of the enchantment under which Venice

lies, pearly and roseate, like the Sleeping Beauty, changeless throughout the centuries, arrested, while the concrete forest of the modern world grows up around her.

10 A wholly materialist city is nothing but a dream incarnate. Venice is the world's unconscious: a miser's glittering hoard, guarded by a Beast whose eyes are made of white agate, and by a saint who is really a prince who has just slain a dragon.

11 A list of the goods in which the early Venetian merchants trafficked arouses a sense of pure wonder: wine and grain from Apulia, gems and drugs from Asia, metal-work, silk, and cloth of gold from Byzantium and Greece. These are the gifts of the Magi, in the words of the English hymn: "Pearls from the ocean and gems from the mountain; myrrh from the forest and gold from the mine." During the Middle Ages, as a part of his rightful revenue, the doge had his share in the apples of Lombardy and the crayfish and cherries of Treviso—the Venetian mind, interested only in the immediate and the solid, leaves behind it, for our minds, clear, dawn-fresh images out of fairy tales.

■ ■ ▨

MEANING

1. What is the paradox to which McCarthy refers in the title?
2. How does the history of St. Mark's help to explain this incongruity?
3. How does the fact that Venice, unlike other cities in Italy, "had nothing of its own to start with" help explain its improvised architecture?
4. In what sense have the mercenary aspects of Venice been concealed by a facade of glamor?

TECHNIQUE

1. How does McCarthy's description underscore the contrast between the tawdry aspects of Venice and the glamorous romantic image with which it is commonly associated?
2. How does McCarthy's account allow us to see Venice as beautiful only when seen at a distance and as more garish as we get closer?
3. **Other Patterns.** Where does McCarthy use **comparison and contrast** to stress how unlike other cities in Italy Venice is and how garish it appears when viewed up close and at certain angles?

LANGUAGE

1. How does the phrase a "robber's den" provide a metaphor with which to understand how the commercial and materialistic aspects of Venice strike the visitor? How does the sentence structure of paragraph 5 reinforce this impression?
2. What does McCarthy mean by calling Venice the "world's unconscious"?
3. If you don't know the meanings of the following words, look them up: *effeminate* (1), *Platonic* (2), *adventitious* (3), *satrap* (5), *epochs* (5), *verdantique* (5), *veneers* (8), *tawdry* (8), *carbuncles* (9).

Suggestions for Writing

1. **Critical Writing.** How does McCarthy's depiction of Venice differ from the way it is usually represented in films and travel books?

2. After reading Thomas Mann's short novel *Death in Venice* (1913), discuss how the city serves as a backdrop.

3. How does the film *Casanova* (2005) use Venice as a setting to enhance the mood of the story?

4. Write a short **narrative** in order to change someone else's perception of a place, event, or person.

5. **Thematic Links.** **Compare** McCarthy's description of Venice with R. K. Narayan's account of the filmmaking process in "The Misguided 'Guide' " (Chapter 3, "Narration") as a hodgepodge of disparate elements.

TEPILIT OLE SAITOTI

The Initiation of a Maasai Warrior

Although the tall, elegant Maasai of Kenya and Tanzania are familiar from images of East Africa, it is rare to read a firsthand account of the rituals by which one becomes accepted as a warrior in this culture. Tepilit Ole Saitoti does this in the following essay, which was first published in his autobiography, *The Worlds of a Maasai Warrior* (1986). He has studied in the United States and was the subject of a National Geographic Society documentary, *Man of Serengeti* (1971). Saitoti is currently politically active in Kenya on issues of land redistribution within Maasai territory.

Before You Read

How might circumcision serve as a rite of passage?

■ ■ ▨

1 "Tepilit, circumcision means a sharp knife cutting into the skin of the most sensitive part of your body. You must not budge; don't move a muscle or even blink. You can face only one direction until the operation is completed. The slightest movement on your part will mean you are a coward, incompetent and unworthy to be a Maasai man. Ours has always been a proud family, and we would like to keep it that way. We will not tolerate unnecessary embarrassment, so you had better be ready. If you are not, tell us now so that we will not proceed. Imagine yourself alone remaining uncircumcised like the water youth [white people]. I hear they are not circumcised. Such a thing is not known in Maasailand; therefore, circumcision will have to take place even if it means holding you down until it is completed."

2   My father continued to speak and every one of us kept quiet. "The pain you will feel is symbolic. There is a deeper meaning in all this. Circumcision means a break between childhood and adulthood. For the first time in your life, you are regarded as a grownup, a complete man or woman. You will be expected to give and not just to receive. To protect the family always, not just to be protected yourself. And your wise judgment will for the first time be taken into consideration. No family affairs will be discussed without your being consulted. If you are ready for all these responsibilities, tell us now. Coming into manhood is not simply a matter of growth and maturity. It is a heavy load on your shoulders and especially a burden on the mind. Too much of this—I am done. I have said all I wanted to say. Fellows, if you have anything to add, go ahead and tell your brother, because I am through. I have spoken."

For a visual to accompany this selection, see color insert photo A-4.

3   After a prolonged silence, one of my half-brothers said awkwardly, "Face it, man . . . it's painful. I won't lie about it, but it is not the end. We all went through it, after all. Only blood will flow, not milk." There was laughter and my father left.

4   My brother Lellia said, "Men, there are many things we must acquire and preparations we must make before the ceremony, and we will need the cooperation and help of all of you. Ostrich feathers for the crown and wax for the arrows must be collected."

5   "Are you *orkirekenyi?*" one of my brothers asked. I quickly replied no, and there was laughter. *Orkirekenyi* is a person who has transgressed sexually. For you must not have sexual intercourse with any circumcised woman before you yourself are circumcised. You must wait until you are circumcised. If you have not waited, you will be fined. Your father, mother, and the circumciser will take a cow from you as punishment.

6   Just before we departed, one of my closest friends said, "If you kick the knife, you will be in trouble." There was laughter. "By the way, if you have decided to kick the circumciser, do it well. Silence him once and for all." "Do it the way you kick a football in school." "That will fix him," another added, and we all laughed our heads off again as we departed.

7   The following month was a month of preparation. I and others collected wax, ostrich feathers, honey to be made into honey beer for the elders to drink on the day of circumcision, and all the other required articles.

8   Three days before the ceremony my head was shaved and I discarded all my belongings, such as my necklaces, garments, spear, and sword. I even had to shave my pubic hair. Circumcision in many ways is similar to Christian baptism. You must put all the sins you have committed during childhood behind and embark as a new person with a different outlook on a new life.

9   The circumciser came the following day and handed the ritual knives to me. He left drinking a calabash of beer. I stared at the knives uneasily. It was hard to accept that he was going to use them on my organ. I was to sharpen them and protect them from people of ill will who might try to blunt them, thus rendering them inefficient during the ritual and thereby bringing shame on our family. The knives threw a chill down my spine; I was not sure I was sharpening them properly, so I took them to my closest brother for him to check out, and he assured me that the knives were all right. I hid them well and waited.

10   Tension started building between me and my relatives, most of whom worried that I wouldn't make it through the ceremony valiantly. Some even snarled at me, which was their way of encouraging me. Others threw insults and abusive words my way. My sister Loiyan in particular was more troubled by the whole affair than anyone in the whole family. She had to assume my mother's role during the circumcision. Were I to fail my initiation, she would have to face the consequences. She would be spat upon and even beaten for representing the mother of an unworthy son. The same fate would befall my father, but he seemed unconcerned. He had this weird belief that because I was not particularly handsome, I must be brave. He kept saying, "God is not so bad as to have made him ugly and a coward at the same time."

11   Failure to be brave during circumcision would have other unfortunate consequences: the herd of cattle belonging to the family still in the compound would be beaten until they stampeded; the slaughtered oxen and honey beer prepared during the month before the ritual would go to waste; the initiate's food would be spat upon and he would have to eat it or else get a severe beating. Everyone would call him Olkasiodoi, the knife kicker.

12   Kicking the knife of the circumciser would not help you anyway. If you struggle and try to get away during the ritual, you will be held down until the operation is completed. Such failure of nerve would haunt you in the future. For example, no one will choose a person who kicked the knife for a position of leadership. However, there have been instances in which a person who failed to go through circumcision successfully became very brave afterwards because he was filled with anger over the incident; no one dares to scold him or remind him of it. His agemates, particularly the warriors, will act as if nothing had happened.

13   During the circumcision of a woman, on the other hand, she is allowed to cry as long as she does not hinder the operation. It is common to see a woman crying and kicking during circumcision. Warriors are usually summoned to help hold her down.

14   For women, circumcision means an end to the company of Maasai warriors. After they recuperate, they soon get married, and often to men twice their age.

15   The closer it came to the hour of truth, the more I was hated, particularly by those closest to me. I was deeply troubled by the withdrawal of all the support I needed. My annoyance turned into anger and resolve. I decided not to budge or blink, even if I were to see my intestines flowing before me. My resolve was hardened when newly circumcised warriors came to sing for me. Their songs were utterly insulting, intended to annoy me further. They tucked their wax arrows under my crotch and rubbed them on my nose. They repeatedly called me names.

16   By the end of the singing, I was fuming. Crying would have meant I was a coward. After midnight they left me alone and I went into the house and tried to sleep but could not. I was exhausted and numb but remained awake all night.

17   At dawn I was summoned once again by the newly circumcised warriors. They piled more and more insults on me. They sang their weird songs with even more vigor and excitement than before. The songs praised warriorhood and encouraged one to achieve it at all costs. The songs continued until the sun shone on the cattle horns clearly. I was summoned to the main cattle gate, in my hand a ritual cowhide from a cow that had been properly slaughtered during my naming ceremony. I went past Loiyan, who was milking a cow, and she muttered something. She was shaking all over. There was so much tension that people could hardly breathe.

18   I laid the hide down and a boy was ordered to pour ice-cold water, known as *engare entolu* (ax water), over my head. It dripped all over my naked body and I shook furiously. In a matter of seconds I was summoned to sit down. A large crowd of boys and men formed a semicircle in front of me; women are not allowed to watch male circumcision and vice versa. That was the last thing I saw clearly. As soon as I sat down, the circumciser appeared, his knives at the ready. He spread

my legs and said, "One cut," a pronouncement necessary to prevent an initiate from claiming that he had been taken by surprise. He splashed a white liquid, a ceremonial paint called *enturoto*, across my face. Almost immediately I felt a spark of pain under my belly as the knife cut through my penis' foreskin. I happened to choose to look in the direction of the operation. I continued to observe the circumciser's fingers working mechanically. The pain became numbness and my lower body felt heavy, as if I were weighed down by a heavy burden. After fifteen minutes or so, a man who had been supporting from behind pointed at something, as if to assist the circumciser. I came to learn later that the circumciser's eyesight had been failing him and that my brothers had been mad at him because the operation had taken longer than was usually necessary. All the same, I remained pinned down until the operation was over. I heard a call for milk to wash the knives, which signaled the end, and soon the ceremony was over.

19   With words of praise, I was told to wake up, but I remained seated. I waited for the customary presents in appreciation of my bravery. My father gave me a cow and so did my brother Lellia. The man who had supported my back and my brother-in-law gave me a heifer. In all I had eight animals given to me. I was carried inside the house to my own bed to recuperate as activities intensified to celebrate my bravery.

20   I laid on my own bed and bled profusely. The blood must be retained within the bed, for according to Maasai tradition, it must not spill to the ground. I was drenched in my own blood. I stopped bleeding after about half an hour but soon was in intolerable pain. I was supposed to squeeze my organ and force blood to flow out of the wound, but no one had told me, so the blood coagulated and caused unbearable pain. The circumciser was brought to my aid and showed me what to do, and soon the pain subsided.

21   The following morning, I was escorted by a small boy to a nearby valley to walk and relax, allowing my wound to drain. This was common for everyone who had been circumcised, as well as for women who had just given birth. Having lost a lot of blood, I was extremely weak. I walked very slowly, but in spite of my caution I fainted. I tried to hang on to bushes and shrubs, but I fell, irritating my wound. I came out of unconsciousness quickly, and the boy who was escorting me never realized what had happened. I was so scared that I told him to lead me back home. I could have died without there being anyone around who could have helped me. From that day on, I was selective of my company while I was feeble.

22   In two weeks I was able to walk and was taken to join other newly circumcised boys far away from our settlement. By tradition Maasai initiates are required to decorate their headdresses with all kinds of colorful birds they have killed. On our way to the settlement, we hunted birds and teased girls by shooting them with our wax blunt arrows. We danced and ate and were well treated wherever we went. We were protected from the cold and rain during the healing period. We were not allowed to touch food, as we were regarded as unclean, so whenever we ate we had to use specially prepared sticks instead. We remained in this pampered state until our wounds healed and our headdresses were removed. Our heads

were shaved, we discarded our black cloaks and bird headdresses and embarked as newly shaven warriors, Irkeleani.

23 As long as I live I will never forget the day my head was shaved and I emerged a man, a Maasai warrior. I felt a sense of control over my destiny so great that no words can accurately describe it. I now stood with confidence, pride, and happiness of being, for all around me I was desired and loved by beautiful, sensuous Maasai maidens. I could now interact with women and even have sex with them, which I had not been allowed before. I was now regarded as a responsible person.

24 In the old days, warriors were like gods, and women and men wanted only to be the parent of a warrior. Everything else would be taken care of as a result. When a poor family had a warrior, they ceased to be poor. The warrior would go on raids and bring cattle back. The warrior would defend the family against all odds. When a society respects the individual and displays confidence in him the way the Maasai do their warriors, the individual can grow to his fullest potential. Whenever there was a task requiring physical strength or bravery, the Maasai would call upon their warriors. They hardly ever fall short of what is demanded of them and so are characterized by pride, confidence, and an extreme sense of freedom. But there is an old saying in Maasai: "You are never a free man until your father dies." In other words, your father is paramount while he is alive and you are obligated to respect him. My father took advantage of this principle and held a tight grip on all his warriors, including myself. He always wanted to know where we all were at any given time. We fought against his restrictions, but without success. I, being the youngest of my father's five warriors, tried even harder to get loose repeatedly, but each time I was punished severely.

25 Roaming the plains with other warriors in pursuit of girls and adventure was a warrior's pastime. We would wander from one settlement to another, singing, wrestling, hunting, and just playing. Often I was ready to risk my father's punishment for this wonderful freedom.

26 One clear day my father sent me to take sick children and one of his wives to the dispensary in the Korongoro Highlands. We rode in the L.S.B. Leakey lorry. We ascended the highlands and were soon attended to in the local hospital. Near the conservation offices I met several acquaintances, and one of them told me of an unusual circumcision that was about to take place in a day or two. All the local warriors and girls were preparing to attend it.

27 The highlands were a lush green from the seasonal rains and the sky was a purple-blue with no clouds in sight. The land was overflowing with milk, and the warriors felt and looked their best, as they always did when there was plenty to eat and drink. Everyone was at ease. The demands the community usually made on warriors during the dry season when water was scarce and wells had to be dug were now not necessary. Herds and flocks were entrusted to youths to look after. The warriors had all the time for themselves. But my father was so strict that even at times like these he still insisted on overworking us in one way or another. He believed that by keeping us busy, he would keep us out of trouble.

28 When I heard about the impending ceremony, I decided to remain behind in the Korongoro Highlands and attend it now that the children had been treated.

I knew very well that I would have to make up a story for my father upon my return, but I would worry about that later. I had left my spear at home when I boarded the bus, thinking that I would be coming back that very day. I felt lighter but now regretted having left it behind; I was so used to carrying it wherever I went. In gales of laughter resulting from our continuous teasing of each other, we made our way toward a distant kraal. We walked at a leisurely pace and reveled in the breeze. As usual we talked about the women we desired, among other things.

29   The following day we were joined by a long line of colorfully dressed girls and warriors from the kraal and the neighborhood where we had spent the night, and we left the highland and headed to Ingorienito to the rolling hills on the lower slopes to attend the circumcision ceremony. From there one could see Oldopai Gorge, where my parents lived, and the Inaapi hills in the middle of the Serengeti Plain.

30   Three girls and a boy were to be initiated on the same day, an unusual occasion. Four oxen were to be slaughtered, and many people would therefore attend. As we descended, we saw the kraal where the ceremony would take place. All those people dressed in red seemed from a distance like flamingos standing in a lake. We could see lines of other guests heading to the settlements. Warriors made gallant cries of happiness known as *enkiseer*. Our line of warriors and girls responded to their cries even more gallantly.

31   In serpentine fashion, we entered the gates of the settlement. Holding spears in our left hands, we warriors walked proudly, taking small steps, swaying like palm trees, impressing our girls, who walked parallel to us in another line, and of course the spectators, who gazed at us approvingly.

32   We stopped in the center of the kraal and waited to be greeted. Women and children welcomed us. We put our hands on the children's heads, which is how children are commonly saluted. After the greetings were completed, we started dancing.

33   Our singing echoed off the kraal fence and nearby trees. Another line of warriors came up the hill and entered the compound, also singing and moving slowly toward us. Our singing grew in intensity. Both lines of warriors moved parallel to each other, and our feet pounded the ground with style. We stamped vigorously, as if to tell the next line and the spectators that we were the best.

34   The singing continued until the hot sun was overhead. We recessed and ate food already prepared for us by other warriors. Roasted meat was for those who were to eat meat, and milk for the others. By our tradition, meat and milk must not be consumed at the same time, for this would be a betrayal of the animal. It was regarded as cruel to consume a product of the animal that could be obtained while it was alive, such as milk, and meat, which was only available after the animal had been killed.

35   After eating we resumed singing, and I spotted a tall, beautiful *esiankiki* (young maiden) of Masiaya whose family was one of the largest and richest in our area. She stood very erect and seemed taller than the rest.

36   One of her breasts could be seen just above her dress, which was knotted at the shoulder. While I was supposed to dance generally to please all the spectators,

I took it upon myself to please her especially. I stared at and flirted with her, and she and I danced in unison at times. We complemented each other very well.

37   During a break, I introduced myself to the *esiankiki* and told her I would like to see her after the dance. "Won't you need a warrior to escort you home later when the evening threatens?" I said. She replied, "Perhaps, but the evening is still far away."

38   I waited patiently. When the dance ended, I saw her departing with a group of other women her age. She gave me a sidelong glance, and I took that to mean come later and not now. With so many others around, I would not have been able to confer with her as I would have liked anyway.

39   With another warrior, I wandered around the kraal killing time until the herds returned from pasture. Before the sun dropped out of sight, we departed. As the kraal of the *esiankiki* was in the lowlands, a place called Enkoloa, we descended leisurely, our spears resting on our shoulders.

40   We arrived at the woman's kraal and found that cows were now being milked. One could hear the women trying to appease the cows by singing to them. Singing calms cows down, making it easier to milk them. There were no warriors in the whole kraal except for the two of us. Girls went around into warriors' houses as usual and collected milk for us. I was so eager to go and meet my *esiankiki* that I could hardly wait for nightfall. The warriors' girls were trying hard to be sociable, but my mind was not with them. I found them to be childish, loud, bothersome, and boring.

41   As the only warriors present, we had to keep them company and sing for them, at least for a while, as required by custom. I told the other warrior to sing while I tried to figure out how to approach my *esiankiki*. Still a novice warrior, I was not experienced with women and was in fact still afraid of them. I could flirt from a distance, of course. But sitting down with a woman and trying to seduce her was another matter. I had already tried twice to approach women soon after my circumcision and had failed. I got as far as the door of one woman's house and felt my heart beating like a Congolese drum; breathing became difficult and I had to turn back. Another time I managed to get in the house and succeeded in sitting on the bed, but then I started trembling until the whole bed was shaking, and conversation became difficult. I left the house and the woman, amazed and speechless, and never went back to her again.

42   Tonight I promised myself I would be brave and would not make any silly, ridiculous moves. "I must be mature and not afraid," I kept reminding myself, as I remembered an incident involving one of my relatives when he was still very young and, like me, afraid of women. He went to a woman's house and sat on a stool for a whole hour; he was afraid to awaken her, as his heart was pounding and he was having difficulty breathing.

43   When he finally calmed down, he woke her up, and their conversation went something like this:

44   "Woman, wake up."

45 "Why should I?"

46 "To light the fire."

47 "For what?"

48 "So you can see me."

49 "I already know who you are. Why don't *you* light the fire, as you're nearer to it than me?"

50 "It's your house and it's only proper that you light it yourself."

51 "I don't feel like it."

52 "At least wake up so we can talk, as I have something to tell you."

53 "Say it."

54 "I need you."

55 "I do not need one-eyed types like yourself."

56 "One-eyed people are people too."

57 "That might be so, but they are not to my taste."

58 They continued talking for quite some time, and the more they spoke, the braver he became. He did not sleep with her that night, but later on he persisted until he won her over. I doubted whether I was as strong-willed as he, but the fact that he had met with success encouraged me. I told my warrior friend where to find me should he need me, and then I departed.

59 When I entered the house of my *esiankiki*, I called for the woman of the house, and as luck would have it, my lady responded. She was waiting for me. I felt better, and I proceeded to talk to her like a professional. After much talking back and forth, I joined her in bed.

60 The night was calm, tender, and loving, like most nights after initiation ceremonies as big as this one. There must have been a lot of courting and lovemaking.

61 Maasai women can be very hard to deal with sometimes. They can simply reject a man outright and refuse to change their minds. Some play hard to get, but in reality are testing the man to see whether he is worth their while. Once a friend of mine while still young was powerfully attracted to a woman nearly his mother's age. He put a bold move on her. At first the woman could not believe his intention, or rather was amazed by his courage. The name of the warrior was Ngengeiya, or Drizzle.

62 "Drizzle, what do you want?"

63 The warrior stared her right in the eye and said, "You."

64 "For what?"

65 "To make love to you."

66 "I am your mother's age."

67 "The choice was either her or you."

68 This remark took the woman by surprise. She had underestimated the saying "There is no such thing as a young warrior." When you are a warrior, you are expected to perform bravely in any situation. Your age and size are immaterial.

69 "You mean you could really love me like a grownup man?"

70 "Try me, woman."

71   He moved in on her. Soon the woman started moaning with excitement, calling out his name. "Honey Drizzle, Honey Drizzle, you *are* a man." In a breathy, stammering voice, she said, "A real man."

72   Her attractiveness made Honey Drizzle ignore her relative old age. The Maasai believe that if an older and a younger person have intercourse, it is the older person who stands to gain. For instance, it is believed that an older woman having an affair with a young man starts to appear younger and healthier, while the young man grows older and unhealthy.

73   The following day when the initiation rites had ended, I decided to return home. I had offended my father by staying away from home without his consent, so I prepared myself for whatever punishment he might inflict on me. I walked home alone.

■ ■ ▨

MEANING

1. How is the warrior candidate's destiny dependent on the bravery he shows during the ceremony? What consequences would his family suffer if he were to flinch or shudder?

2. What responsibilities does Saitoti assume, and what privileges is he allowed upon successful completion of the ceremony?

3. What is the significance of Saitoti's throwing away his possessions and having his head shaved three days before the ceremony?

4. What customs reveal the symbiotic relationship the Maasai have with the natural world? For example, why is Saitoti careful to prevent blood from his wound spilling onto the ground?

TECHNIQUE

1. How is Saitoti's account shaped to explore not only the sequence of events, but also the profound transformation in status that it produces for him personally?

2. How does Saitoti's account emphasize the interval during which he recovers from his wound and the important lessons that he learns?

3. **Other Patterns.** How does Saitoti use a **narrative** framework to create suspense as to how he will react to the operation?

LANGUAGE

1. What is the function of the relentless taunting by warriors and those who were newly circumcized?

2. What terms and images reveal the symbiotic relationship between the Maasai and their environment?

3. How does the language Saitoti uses to describe his feelings after the ceremony reflect the idea that he has been reborn into the community?

4. If you do not know the meanings of the following words, look them up: *circumcision* (1), *calabash* (9), *paramount* (24), *kraal* (28), *unison* (36).

SUGGESTIONS FOR WRITING

1. What initiation rituals have you witnessed or undergone that had the effect of serving as a rite of passage, for example, a bat or bar mitzvah, a confirmation ceremony, or any other ritual that unites the candidate with his or her community?

2. How would you characterize Saitoti's attitude toward his father? What assumptions about his son's responsibilities explain how the father treats Saitoti?

3. **Critical Writing.** What similarities can you discover between Saitoti's initiation and the training that recruits receive to transform them into Marines? You might focus on the head shaving, the role played by songs, what is expected of each as a warrior, and the weapons displayed and worn. How are these ceremonies designed to deepen the bond between the initiate and his tribe?

4. Despite the differences between the Maasai and contemporary Americans, Saitoti's relationships with his friends and the opposite sex are those of a typical teenage boy. In a short essay, explore these similarities using **illustrative narratives**.

5. **Thematic Links. Compare** the rituals Rigoberta Menchu describes in "Birth Ceremonies" (Chapter 7, "Process Analysis") with ones described by Saitoti as the way in which identity within the community is affirmed.

MARK SALZMAN

Lessons

Mark Salzman (b. 1959) graduated with honors in 1982 from Yale, where he special-ized in Chinese literature and language. After graduating, he lived in Hunan, China, where he taught English at the local medical school and began training in the martial art of *wushu* with a legendary master, Pan Quingfu. It was unheard of at the time for a *wushu* master to take a Westerner as a student, and Salzman benefited greatly from this experience. He shares his discoveries and insights in the following essay, from *Iron and Silk* (1986). He has also written novels, including, most recently, *True Notebooks* (2003).

BEFORE YOU READ

Is there a skill you have that you could exchange for lessons in something you wish to learn?

■　■　▨

1   I was to meet Pan at the training hall four nights a week, to receive private instruction after the athletes finished their evening workout. Waving and wish-ing me good night, they politely filed out and closed the wooden doors, leaving Pan and me alone in the room. First he explained that I must start from scratch. He meant it, too, for beginning that night, and for many nights thereafter, I learned how to stand at attention. He stood inches away from me and screamed, "Stand straight!" then bored into me with his terrifying gaze. He insisted that I maintain eye contact for as long as he stood in front of me, and that I meet his gaze with one of equal intensity. After as long as a minute of this silent torture, he would shout "At ease!" and I could relax a bit, but not smile or take my eyes away from his. We repeated this exercise countless times, and I was expected to practice it four to six hours a day. At the time, I wondered what those staring contests had to do with wushu, but I came to realize that everything he was to teach me later was really contained in those first few weeks when we stared at each other. His art drew strength from his eyes; this was his way of passing it on.

2   After several weeks I came to enjoy staring at him. I would break into a sweat and feel a kind of heat rushing up through the floor into my legs and up into my brain. He told me that when standing like that, I must at all times be pre-pared to duel, that at any moment he might attack, and I should be ready to defend myself. It exhilarated me to face off with him, to feel his power and taste the fear and anticipation of the blow. Days and weeks passed, but the blow did not come.

3   One night he broke the lesson off early, telling me that tonight was special. I followed him out of the training hall, and we bicycled a short distance to his apartment. He lived with his wife and two sons on the fifth floor of a large, anonymous cement building. Like all the urban housing going up in China

today, the building was indistinguishable from its neighbors, mercilessly practical and depressing in appearance. Pan's apartment had three rooms and a small kitchen. A private bathroom and painted, as opposed to raw, cement walls in all the rooms identified it as the home of an important family. The only decoration in the apartment consisted of some silk banners, awards and photographs from Pan's years as the national wushu champion and from the set of *Shaolin Temple.* Pan's wife, a doctor, greeted me with all sorts of homemade snacks and sat me down at a table set for two. Pan sat across from me and poured two glasses of baijiu. He called to his sons, both in their teens, and they appeared from the bedroom instantly. They stood in complete silence until Pan asked them to greet me, which they did, very politely, but so softly I could barely hear them. They were handsome boys, and the elder, at about fourteen, was taller than me and had a moustache. I tried asking them questions to put them at ease, but they answered only by nodding. They apparently had no idea how to behave toward something like me and did not want to make any mistakes in front of their father. Pan told them to say good night, and they, along with his wife, disappeared into the bedroom. Pan raised his glass and proposed that the evening begin.

4 　　He told me stories that made my hair stand on end, with such gusto that I thought the building would shake apart. When he came to the parts where he vanquished his enemies, he brought his terrible hand down on the table or against the wall with a crash, sending our snacks jumping out of their serving bowls. His imitations of cowards and bullies were so funny I could hardly breathe for laughing. He had me spellbound for three solid hours; then his wife came in to see if we needed any more food or baijiu. I took the opportunity to ask her if she had ever been afraid for her husband's safety when, for example, he went off alone to bust up a gang of hoodlums in Shenyang. She laughed and touched his right hand. "Sometimes I figured he'd be late for dinner." A look of tremendous satisfaction came over Pan's face, and he got up to use the bathroom. She sat down in his chair and looked at me. "Every day he receives tens of letters from all over China, all from people asking to become his student. Since he made the movie, it's been almost impossible for him to go out during the day." She refilled our cups, then looked at me again. "He has trained professionals for more than twenty-five years now, but in all that time he has accepted only one private student." After a long pause, she gestured at me with her chin. "You." Just then Pan came back into the room, returned to his seat and started a new story. This one was about a spear:

5 　　While still a young man training for the national wushu competition, Pan overheard a debate among some of his fellow athletes about the credibility of an old story. The story described a famous warrior as being able to execute a thousand spear-thrusts without stopping to rest. Some of the athletes felt this to be impossible: after fifty, one's shoulders ache, and by one hundred the skin on the left hand, which guides the spear as the right hands thrusts, twists and returns it, begins to blister. Pan had argued that surely this particular warrior would not have been intimidated by aching shoulders and blisters, and soon a challenge was raised. The next day Pan went out into a field with a spear, and as the other

athletes watched, executed one thousand and seven thrusts without stopping to rest. Certain details of the story as Pan told it—that the bones of his left hand were exposed, and so forth—might be called into question, but the number of thrusts I am sure is accurate, and the scar tissue on his left palm indicates that it was not easy for him.

6   One evening later in the year, when I felt discouraged with my progress in a form of Northern Shaolin boxing called "Changquan," or "Long Fist," I asked Pan if he thought I should discontinue the training. He frowned, the only time he ever seemed genuinely angry with me, and said quietly, "When I say I will do something, I do it, exactly as I said I would. In my whole life I have never started something without finishing it. I said that in the time we have, I would make your wushu better than you could imagine, and I will. Your only responsibility to me is to practice and to learn. My responsibility to you is much greater! Every time you think your task is great, think how much greater mine is. Just keep this in mind: if you fail"—here he paused to make sure I understood—"I will lose face."

7   Though my responsibility to him was merely to practice and to learn, he had one request that he vigorously encouraged me to fulfill—to teach him English. I felt relieved to have something to offer him, so I quickly prepared some beginning materials and rode over to his house for the first lesson. When I got there, he had a tape recorder set up on a small table, along with a pile of over-sized paper and a few felt-tip pens from a coloring set. He showed no interest at all in my books, but sat me down next to the recorder and pointed at the pile of paper. On each sheet he had written out in Chinese dozens of phrases, such as "We'll need a spotlight over there," "These mats aren't springy enough," and "Don't worry—it's just a shoulder dislocation." He asked me to write down the English translation next to each phrase, which took a little over two and a half hours. When I was finished, I asked him if he could read my handwriting, and he smiled, saying that he was sure my handwriting was fine. After a series of delicate questions, I determined that he was as yet unfamiliar with the alphabet, so I encouraged him to have a look at my beginning materials. "That's too slow for me," he said. He asked me to repeat each of the phrases I'd written down five times into the recorder, leaving enough time after each repetition for him to say it aloud after me. "The first time should be very slow—one word at a time, with a pause after each word so I can repeat it. The second time should be the same. The third time you should pause after every other word. The fourth time read it through slowly. The fifth time you can read it fast." I looked at the pile of phrase sheets, calculated how much time this would take, and asked if we could do half today and half tomorrow, as dinner was only three hours away. "Don't worry!" he said, beaming. "I've prepared some food for you here. Just tell me when you get hungry." He sat next to me, turned on the machine, then turned it off again. "How do you say, 'And now, Mark will teach me English'?" I told him how and he repeated it, at first slowly, then more quickly, twenty or twenty-one times. He turned the machine on. "And now, Mark will teach me English." I read the first phrase, five times as he had requested, and he pushed a little note across the table. "Better read it six times," it read, "and a little slower."

8   After several weeks during which we nearly exhausted the phrasal possibilities of our two languages, Pan announced that the time had come to do something new. "Now I want to learn routines." I didn't understand. "Routines?" "Yes. Everything, including language, is like wushu. First you learn the basic moves, or words, then you string them together into routines." He produced from his bedroom a huge sheet of paper made up of smaller pieces taped together. He wanted me to write a story on it. The story he had in mind was a famous Chinese folk tale, "How Yu Gong Moved the Mountain." The story tells of an old man who realized that, if he only had fields where a mountain stood instead, he would have enough arable land to support his family comfortably. So he went out to the mountain with a shovel and a bucket and started to take the mountain down. All his neighbors made fun of him, calling it an impossible task, but Yu Gong disagreed: it would just take a long time, and after several tens of generations had passed, the mountain would at last become a field and his family would live comfortably. Pan had me write this story in big letters, so that he could paste it up on his bedroom wall, listen to the tape I was to make and read along as he lay in bed.

9   Not only did I repeat this story into the tape recorder several dozen times—at first one word at a time, and so on—but Pan invited Bill, Bob and Marcy over for dinner one night and had them read it a few times for variety. After they had finished, Pan said that he would like to recite a few phrases for them to evaluate and correct. He chose some of his favorite sentences and repeated each seven or eight times without a pause. He belted them out with such fierce concentration we were all afraid to move lest it disturb him. At last he finished and looked at me, asking quietly if it was all right. I nodded and he seemed overcome with relief. He smiled, pointed at me and said to my friends, "I was very nervous just then. I didn't want him to lose face."

10   While Pan struggled to recite English routines from memory, he began teaching me how to use traditional weapons. He would teach me a single move, then have me practice it in front of him until I could do it ten times in a row without a mistake. He always stood about five feel away from me, with his arms folded, grinding his teeth, and the only time he took his eyes off me was to blink. One night in the late spring I was having a particularly hard time learning a move with the staff. I was sweating heavily and my right hand was bleeding, so the staff had become slippery and hard to control. Several of the athletes stayed on after their workout to watch and to enjoy the breeze that sometimes passed through the training hall. Pan stopped me and indicated that I wasn't working hard enough. "Imagine," he said, "that you are participating in the national competition, and those athletes are your competitors. Look as if you know what you are doing! Frighten them with your strength and confidence." I mustered all the confidence I could, under the circumstances, and flung myself into the move. I lost control of the staff, and it whirled straight into my forehead. As if in a dream, the floor raised up several feet to support my behind, and I sat staring up at Pan while blood ran down across my nose and a fleshy knob grew between my eyebrows. The athletes sprang forward to help me up. They seemed nervous, never

having had a foreigner knock himself out in their training hall before, but Pan, after asking if I felt all right, seemed positively inspired. "Sweating and bleeding. Good."

11 Every once in a while, Pan felt it necessary to give his students something to think about, to spur them on to greater efforts. During one morning workout two women practiced a combat routine, one armed with a spear, the other with a *dadao*, or halberd. The dadao stands about six feet high and consists of a broadsword attached to a thick wooden pole, with an angry-looking spike at the far end. It is heavy and difficult to wield even for a strong man, so it surprised me to see this young woman, who could not weigh more than one hundred pounds, using it so effectively. At one point in their battle the woman with the dadao swept it toward the other woman's feet, as if to cut them off, but the other woman jumped up in time to avoid the blow. The first woman, without letting the blade of the dadao stop, brought it around in another sweep, as if to cut the other woman in half at the waist. The other woman, without an instant to spare, bent straight from the hips so that the dadao slashed over her back and head, barely an inch away. This combination was to be repeated three times in rapid succession before moving on to the next exchange. The women practiced this move several times, none of which satisfied Pan. "Too slow, and the weapon is too far away from her. It should graze her back as it goes by." They tried again, but still Pan growled angrily. Suddenly he got up and took the dadao from the first woman. The entire training hall went silent and still. Without warming up at all, Pan ordered the woman with the spear to get ready, and to move fast when the time came. His body looked as though electricity had suddenly passed through it, and the huge blade flashed toward her. Once, twice the dadao flew beneath her feet, then swung around in a terrible arc and rode her back with flawless precision. The third time he added a little twist at the end, so that the blade grazed up her neck and sent a little decoration stuck in her pigtails flying across the room.

12 I had to sit down for a moment to ponder the difficulty of sending an object roughly the shape of an oversized shovel, only heavier, across a girl's back and through her pigtails, without guide ropes or even a safety helmet. Not long before, I had spoken with a former troupe member who, when practicing with this instrument, had suddenly found himself on his knees. The blade, unsharpened, had twirled a bit too close to him and passed through his Achilles' tendon without a sound. Pan handed the dadao back to the woman and walked over to me. "What if you had made a mistake?" I asked. "I never make mistakes," he said, without looking at me.

■ ■ ▨

MEANING

1. What aspects of Chinese culture has Salzman come to appreciate when he trades English lessons for martial arts instruction?

2. What factors might explain why Pan chooses Salzman to be the only private student (American or Chinese) he has ever had?

How does this photo of a student practicing *wushu* at the famed Shi Cha Hai sports school in Beijing in 2006 enhance Salzman's description of the demanding nature of his lessons with Pan?

3. Why is Pan's performance with a heavy spear so impressive?

4. Why is the exercise of standing at attention so important in developing Salzman's martial arts abilities?

TECHNIQUE

1. What is the relevance of the Chinese folk tale "How Yu Gong Moved the Mountain" to Salzman's apprenticeship?

2. How does Salzman emphasize similarities between the way in which Pan learns English and Pan's methods for teaching martial arts?

3. *Other Patterns.* What **examples** does Salzman offer that illustrate how demanding and how inspiring Pan is as a teacher?

LANGUAGE

1. How does the idea of "routines" help the reader to understand the way in which Pan approaches learning English?

2. What part does the concept of "losing face" play in Chinese culture, and what values are expressed through this term? What evidence can you cite to show that Pan applies the same standard to Salzman as he does to himself?

3. If you don't know the meanings of the following words, look them up: *anonymous* (3), *wushu* (3), *baijiu* (3), *Achilles' tendon* (12).

SUGGESTIONS FOR WRITING

1. In your opinion, who learns more from the other, Pan from Salzman or Salzman from Pan, and why?

2. **Critical Writing.** In an essay, discuss the use of martial arts as a background for *Crouching Tiger, Hidden Dragon* (2000), the Academy Award–winning martial arts love story set in nineteenth-century China.

2. If you could master anything you wished, what would it be, and who would you want to be your teacher? Would you want to learn from someone like Pan? Why or why not?

3. **Compare** Pan's standard of living as a champion of martial arts (whose wife is a physician) with that of a comparable sports figure in the United States. What conclusions can you draw from this comparison?

4. **Thematic Links.** How do the accounts by Salzman and Guanlong Cao (see "Chopsticks" in Chapter 3, "Narration") demonstrate the importance of doing things well and skillfully? Is this a Chinese cultural value? Explain your answer.

GORDON PARKS

Flavio's Home

Distinguished African American filmmaker, photographer, composer, and writer Gordon
Parks (1912–2006) grew up in Kansas and Minnesota. Photography was a lifelong passion for Parks, and both *Life* and *Vogue* magazines took the unusual step of hiring him
as their first black photographer. The following selection is drawn from his 1990 volume
Voices in the Mirror; in it, Parks takes us on a harrowing journey through the slums (*favelas*) of Rio de Janeiro to meet a courageous twelve-year-old boy who helps to support his
family. Parks's last works include *Eyes with Winged Thoughts* (2005) and *A Hungry
Heart: A Memoir* (2005).

BEFORE YOU READ

Why do advertisements for Rio de Janeiro as a tourist destination fail to mention the
endemic poverty surrounding the city?

■ ■ ▨

1   I've never lost my fierce grudge against poverty. It is the most savage of all human
afflictions, claiming victims who can't mobilize their efforts against it, who often
lack strength to digest what little food they scrounge up to survive. It keeps growing, multiplying, spreading like a cancer. In my wanderings I attack it wherever
I can—in barrios, slums and favelas.

2   Catacumba was the name of the favela[1] where I found Flavio da Silva. It was
wickedly hot. The noon sun baked the mud-rot of the wet mountainside. Garbage
and human excrement clogged the open sewers snaking down the slopes. José
Gallo, a *Life* reporter, and I rested in the shade of a jacaranda tree halfway up
Rio de Janeiro's most infamous deathtrap. Below and above us were a maze of
shacks, but in the distance alongside the beach stood the gleaming white homes
of the rich.

3   Breathing hard, balancing a tin of water on his head, a small boy climbed
toward us. He was miserably thin, naked but for filthy denim shorts. His legs
resembled sticks covered with skin and screwed into his feet. Death was all over
him, in his sunken eyes, cheeks and jaundiced coloring. He stopped for breath,
coughing, his chest heaving as water slopped over his bony shoulders. Then jerk-
ing sideways like a mechanical toy, he smiled a smile I will never forget. Turning,
he went on up the mountainside.

4   The detailed *Life* assignment in my back pocket was to find an impoverished
father with a family, to examine his earnings, political leanings, religion, friends,
dreams and frustrations. I had been sent to do an essay on poverty. This frail

---

[1]Slums on the outskirts of Rio de Janeiro, Brazil, inhabited by seven hundred thousand
people (editors' note).

boy bent under his load said more to me about poverty than a dozen poor fathers. I touched Gallo, and we got up and followed the boy to where he entered a shack near the top of the mountainside. It was a leaning crumpled place of old plankings with a rusted tin roof. From inside we heard the babblings of several children. José knocked. The door opened and the boy stood smiling with a bawling naked baby in his arms.

5   Still smiling, he whacked the baby's rump, invited us in and offered us a box to sit on. The only other recognizable furniture was a sagging bed and a broken baby's crib. Flavio was twelve, and with Gallo acting as interpreter, he introduced his younger brothers and sisters: "Mario, the bad one; Baptista, the good one; Albia, Isabel and the baby Zacarias." Two other girls burst into the shack, screaming and pounding on one another. Flavio jumped in and parted them. "Shut up, you two." He pointed at the older girl. "That's Maria, the nasty one." She spit in his face. He smacked her and pointed to the smaller sister. "That's Luzia. She thinks she's pretty."

6   Having finished the introductions, he went to build a fire under the stove— a rusted, bent top of an old gas range resting on several bricks. Beneath it was a piece of tin that caught the hot coals. The shack was about six by ten feet. Its grimy walls were a patchwork of misshapen boards with large gaps between them, revealing other shacks below stilted against the slopes. The floor, rotting under layers of grease and dirt, caught shafts of light slanting down through spaces in the roof. A large hole in the far corner served as a toilet. Beneath that hole was the sloping mountainside. Pockets of poverty in New York's Harlem, on Chicago's south side, in Puerto Rico's infamous El Fungito seemed pale by comparison. None of them had prepared me for this one in the favela of Catacumba.

7   Flavio washed rice in a large dishpan, then washed Zacarias's feet in the same water. But even that dirty water wasn't to be wasted. He tossed in a chunk of lye soap and ordered each child to wash up. When they were finished he splashed the water over the dirty floor, and, dropping to his knees, he scrubbed the planks until the black suds sank in. Just before sundown he put beans on the stove to warm, then left, saying he would be back shortly. "Don't let them burn," he cautioned Maria. "If they do and Poppa beats me, you'll get it later." Maria, happy to get at the licking spoon, switched over and began to stir the beans. Then slyly she dipped out a spoonful and swallowed them. Luzia eyed her. "I see you. I'm going to tell on you for stealing our supper."

8   Maria's eyes flashed anger. "You do and I'll beat you, you little bitch." Luzia threw a stick at Maria and fled out the door. Zacarias dropped off to sleep. Mario, the bad one, slouched in a corner and sucked his thumb. Isabel and Albia sat on the floor clinging to each other with a strange tenderness. Isabel held onto Albia's hair and Albia clutched at Isabel's neck. They appeared frozen in an act of quiet violence.

9   Flavio returned with wood, dumped it beside the stove and sat down to rest for a few minutes, then went down the mountain for more water. It was dark when he finally came back, his body sagging from exhaustion. No longer smiling, he suddenly had the look of an old man and by now we could see that he

kept the family going. In the closed torment of that pitiful shack, he was waging a hopeless battle against starvation. The da Silva children were living in a coffin.

10   When at last the parents came in, Gallo and I seemed to be part of the family. Flavio had already told them we were there. "Gordunn Americano!" Luzia said, pointing at me. José, the father, viewed us with skepticism. Nair, his pregnant wife, seemed tired beyond speaking. Hardly acknowledging our presence, she picked up Zacarias, placed him on her shoulder and gently patted his behind. Flavio scurried about like a frightened rat, his silence plainly expressing the fear he held of his father. Impatiently, José da Silva waited for Flavio to serve dinner. He sat in the center of the bed with his legs crossed beneath him, frowning, waiting. There were only three tin plates. Flavio filled them with black beans and rice, then placed them before his father. José da Silva tasted them, chewed for several moments, then nodded his approval for the others to start. Only he and Nair had spoons; the children ate with their fingers. Flavio ate off the top of a coffee can. Afraid to offer us food, he edged his rice and beans toward us, gesturing for us to take some. We refused. He smiled, knowing we understood.

11   Later, when we got down to the difficult business of obtaining permission from José da Silva to photograph his family, he hemmed and hawed, wallowing in the pleasant authority of the decision maker. He finally gave in, but his manner told us that he expected something in return. As we were saying good night Flavio began to cough violently. For a few moments his lungs seemed to be tearing apart. I wanted to get away as quickly as possible. It was cowardly of me, but the bluish cast of his skin beneath the sweat, the choking and spitting were suddenly unbearable.

12   Gallo and I moved cautiously down through the darkness trying not to appear as strangers. The Catacumba was no place for strangers after sundown. Desperate criminals hid out there. To hunt them out, the police came in packs, but only in daylight. Gallo cautioned me. "If you get caught up here after dark it's best to stay at the da Silvas' until morning." As we drove toward the city the large white buildings of the rich loomed up. The world behind us seemed like a bad dream. I had already decided to get the boy Flavio to a doctor, and as quickly as possible.

13   The plush lobby of my hotel on the Copacabana waterfront was crammed with people in formal attire. With the stink of the favela in my clothes, I hurried to the elevator hoping no passengers would be aboard. But as the door was closing a beautiful girl in a white lace gown stepped in. I moved as far away as possible. Her escort entered behind her, swept her into his arms and they indulged in a kiss that lasted until they exited on the next floor. Neither of them seemed to realize that I was there. The room I returned to seemed to be oversized; the da Silva shack would have fitted into one corner of it. The steak dinner I had would have fed the da Silvas for three days.

14   Billowing clouds blanketed Mount Corcovado as we approached the favela the following morning. Suddenly the sun burst through, silhouetting Cristo Redentor, the towering sculpture of Christ with arms extended, its back turned against the slopes of Catacumba. The square at the entrance to the favela bustled

with hundreds of favelados. Long lines waited at the sole water spigot. Others waited at the only toilet on the entire mountainside. Women, unable to pay for soap, beat dirt from their wash at laundry tubs. Men, burdened with lumber, picks and shovels and tools important to their existence threaded their way through the noisy throngs. Dogs snarled, barked and fought. Woodsmoke mixed with the stench of rotting things. In the mist curling over the higher paths, columns of favelados climbed like ants with wood and water cans on their heads.

15   We came upon Nair bent over her tub of wash. She wiped away sweat with her apron and managed a smile. We asked for her husband and she pointed to a tiny shack off to her right. This was José's store, where he sold kerosene and bleach. He was sitting on a box, dozing. Sensing our presence, he awoke and commenced complaining about his back. "It kills me. The doctors don't help because I have no money. Always talk and a little pink pill that does no good. Ah, what is to become of me?" A woman came to buy bleach. He filled her bottle. She dropped a few coins and as she walked away his eyes stayed on her backside until she was out of sight. Then he was complaining about his back again.

16   "How much do you earn a day?" Gallo asked.

17   "Seventy-five cents. On a good day maybe a dollar."

18   "Why aren't the kids in school?"

19   "I don't have money for the clothes they need to go to school."

20   "Has Flavio seen a doctor?"

21   He pointed to a one-story wooden building. "That's the clinic right there. They're mad because I built my store in front of their place. I won't tear it down so they won't help my kids. Talk, talk, talk and pink pills." We bid him good-bye and started climbing, following mud trails, jutting rock, slime-filled holes and shack after shack propped against the slopes on shaky pilings. We sidestepped a dead cat covered with maggots. I held my breath for an instant, only to inhale the stench of human excrement and garbage. Bare feet and legs with open sores climbed above us—evils of the terrible soil they trod every day, and there were seven hundred thousand or more afflicted people in favelas around Rio alone. Touching me, Gallo pointed to Flavio climbing ahead of us carrying firewood. He stopped to glance at a man descending with a small coffin on his shoulder. A woman and a small child followed him. When I lifted my camera, grumbling erupted from a group of men sharing beer beneath a tree.

22   "They're threatening," Gallo said, "Keep moving. They fear cameras. Think they're evil eyes bringing bad luck." Turning to watch the funeral procession, Flavio caught sight of us and waited. When we took the wood from him he protested, saying he was used to carrying it. He gave in when I hung my camera around his neck. Then, beaming, he climbed on ahead of us.

23   The fog had lifted and in the crisp morning light the shack looked more squalid. Inside the kids seemed even noisier. Flavio smiled and spoke above their racket. "Someday I want to live in a real house on a real street with good pots and pans and a bed with sheets." He lit the fire to warm leftovers from the night before. Stale rice and beans—for breakfast and supper. No lunch; midday eating was out of the question. Smoke rose and curled up through the ceiling's cracks.

An air current forced it back, filling the place and Flavio's lungs with fumes. A coughing spasm doubled him up, turned his skin blue under viscous sweat. I handed him a cup of water, but he waved it away. His stomach tightened as he dropped to his knees. His veins throbbed as if they would burst. Frustrated, we could only watch; there was nothing we could do to help. Strangely, none of his brothers or sisters appeared to notice. None of them stopped doing whatever they were doing. Perhaps they had seen it too often. After five interminable minutes it was over, and he got to his feet, smiling as though it had all been a joke. "Maria, it's time for Zacarias to be washed!"

24   "But there's rice in the pan!"

25   "Dump it in another pan—and don't spill water!"

26   Maria picked up Zacarias, who screamed, not wanting to be washed. Irritated, Maria gave him a solid smack on his bare bottom. Flavio stepped over and gave her the same, then a free-for-all started with Flavio, Maria and Mario slinging fists at one another. Mario got one in the eye and fled the shack calling Flavio a dirty son-of-a-bitch. Zacarias wound up on the floor sucking his thumb and escaping his washing. The black bean and rice breakfast helped to get things back to normal. Now it was time to get Flavio to the doctor.

27   The clinic was crowded with patients—mothers and children covered with open sores, a paralytic teenager, a man with an ear in a state of decay, an aged blind couple holding hands in doubled darkness. Throughout the place came wailings of hunger and hurt. Flavio sat nervously between Gallo and me. "What will the doctor do to me?" he kept asking.

28   "We'll see. We'll wait and see."

29   In all, there were over fifty people. Finally, after two hours, it was Flavio's turn and he broke out in a sweat, though he smiled at the nurse as he passed through the door to the doctor's office. The nurse ignored it; in this place of misery, smiles were unexpected.

30   The doctor, a large, beady-eyed man with a crew cut, had an air of impatience. Hardly acknowledging our presence, he began to examine the frightened Flavio. "Open your mouth. Say 'Ah.' Jump up and down. Breathe out. Take off those pants. Bend over. Stand up. Cough. Cough louder, Louder." He did it all with such cold efficiency. Then he spoke to us in English so Flavio wouldn't understand. "This little chap has just about had it." My heart sank. Flavio was smiling, happy to be over with the examination. He was handed a bottle of cough medicine and a small box of pink pills, then asked to step outside and wait.

31   "This the da Silva kid?"

32   "Yes."

33   "What's your interest in him?"

34   "We want to help in some way."

35   "I'm afraid you're too late. He's wasted with bronchial asthma, malnutrition and, I suspect, tuberculosis. His heart, lungs and teeth are all bad." He paused and wearily rubbed his forehead. "All that at the ripe old age of twelve. And these hills are packed with other kids just as bad off. Last year ten thousand died from dysentery alone. But what can we do? You saw what's waiting outside. It's

How does this photo of the *favela* or hillside shantytown in Rio de Janeiro capture the desperate circumstances in which Flavio and his family live?

like this every day. There's hardly enough money to buy aspirin. A few wealthy people who care help keep us going." He was quiet for a moment. "Maybe the right climate, the right diet, and constant medical care might . . ." He stopped and shook his head. "Naw. That poor lad's finished. He might last another year—maybe not." We thanked him and left.

36   "What did he say?" Flavio asked as we scaled the hill.

37   "Everything's going to be all right, Flav. There's nothing to worry about."

38   It had clouded over again by the time we reached the top. The rain swept in, clearing the mountain of Corcovado. The huge Christ figure loomed up again with clouds swirling around it. And to it I said a quick prayer for the boy walking beside us. He smiled as if he had read my thoughts. "Papa says 'El Cristo' has turned his back on the favela."

39   "You're going to be all right, Flavio."

40   "I'm not scared of death. It's my brothers and sisters I worry about. What would they do?"

41   "You'll be all right, Flavio."

■ ■ ⁄

MEANING

1. What series of events have resulted in Flavio's having to do so much of the work involved in looking after his family?

2. What impression does Parks communicate about the living conditions in the *favela*?

3. How do we know that food is scarce, and how does this help to explain Flavio's guests' refusal of the food he offers?

4. What sort of accommodations is Parks staying in while in Rio, and why does he include a description of it?

TECHNIQUE

1. How does Parks present a wealth of sensory details that allow the reader to understand how unique Flavio is, given his impoverished surroundings?

2. How does Parks's **description** of the hotel where he is staying provide an ironic counterpoint to where Flavio lives?

3. How does Parks arrange his description so that his readers literally follow him inside a *favela* and discover what it would be like to live there?

4. **Other Patterns.** How does Parks use **narrative** episodes to allow the reader to understand the daily struggle to survive that Flavio's family endures?

LANGUAGE

1. What words and phrases communicate in a tangible and graphic way the dreadful environment in which Flavio lives?

2. How does Parks use Flavio's quoted remarks to demonstrate the boy's aspirations for a better life?

3. How do the doctor's comments add to the irony of this piece?

4. If you don't know the meanings of the following words, look them up: *barrios* (1), *jacaranda* (2), *jaundiced* (3), *spigot* (14), *interminable* (23).

SUGGESTIONS FOR WRITING

1. **Describe** the living conditions in a region or neighborhood with which you are familiar, using a broad range of descriptive details (both objective and subjective) to communicate what it looks like from the outside and what it feels like to live there.

2. **Critical Writing.** Rent the Brazilian-made 1981 film *Pixote*, which tells the story of a boy not unlike Flavio who survives the streets of Sao Paulo, and write a short essay on the similarities between the movie and Parks's account.

3. Have you ever met anyone who was as courageous in a limiting environment as Flavio was in his? Create a **narrative** about this person and his or her circumstances.

4. ***Thematic Links.*** How do Parks and Robert Levine and Ellen Wolff in "Social Time: The Heartbeat of Culture" (Chapter 5, "Exemplification") present very different perpectives on Brazilian culture?

N. SCOTT MOMADAY

The Way to Rainy Mountain

The Pulitzer Prize–winning novelist, essayist, playwright, and short-story writer N. Scott Momaday was born in Oklahoma in 1934 and received advanced degrees, including a PhD from Stanford in 1963. The geography, history, and mythology of the Kiowa nation inform his works as exemplified in his novel *House Made of Dawn* (1968), *The Names: A Memoir* (1976), and, more recently, *Four Arrows and Magic: A Kiowa Story* (2006) and *Three Plays* (2007). The following essay, drawn from the introduction to *The Way to Rainy Mountain* (1969) evokes the unique landscapes of the plains of Oklahoma where Momaday grew up and the timeless figure of his grandmother who lives on in his memory.

BEFORE YOU READ

Describe a member of your family who you would say was heroic in some way.

■ ■ ▨

1   A single knoll rises out of the plain in Oklahoma, north and west of the Wichita Range. For my people, the Kiowas, it is an old landmark, and they gave it the name Rainy Mountain. The hardest weather in the world is there. Winter brings blizzards, hot tornadic winds arise in the spring, and in summer the prairie is an anvil's edge. The grass turns brittle and brown, and it cracks beneath your feet. There are green belts along the rivers and creeks, linear groves of hickory and pecan, willow and witch hazel. At a distance in July or August the steaming foliage seems almost to writhe in fire. Great green-and-yellow grasshoppers are everywhere in the tall grass, popping up like corn to sting the flesh, and tortoises crawl about on the red earth, going nowhere in plenty of time. Loneliness is an aspect of the land. All things in the plain are isolate; there is no confusion of objects in the eye, but *one* hill or *one* tree or *one* man. To look upon that landscape in the early morning, with the sun at your back, is to lose the sense of proportion. Your imagination comes to life, and this, you think, is where Creation was begun.

2   I returned to Rainy Mountain in July. My grandmother had died in the spring, and I wanted to be at her grave. She had lived to be very old and at last infirm. Her only living daughter was with her when she died, and I was told that in death her face was that of a child.

3   I like to think of her as a child. When she was born, the Kiowas were living that last great moment of their history. For more than a hundred years they had controlled the open range from the Smoky Hill River to the Red, from the headwaters of the Canadian to the fork of the Arkansas and Cimarron. In alliance with the Comanches, they had ruled the whole of the southern Plains. War was their sacred business, and they were among the finest horsemen the world has

even known. But warfare for the Kiowas was preeminently a matter of disposition rather than of survival, and they never understood the grim, unrelenting advance of the U.S. Cavalry. When at last, divided and ill-provisioned, they were driven onto the Staked Plains in the cold rains of autumn, they fell into panic. In Palo Duro Canyon they abandoned their crucial stores to pillage and had nothing then but their lives. In order to save themselves, they surrendered to the soldiers at Fort Sill and were imprisoned in the old stone corral that now stands as a military museum. My grandmother was spared the humiliation of those high gray walls by eight or ten years, but she must have known from birth the affliction of defeat, the dark brooding of old warriors.

4   Her name was Aho, and she belonged to the last culture to evolve in North America. Her forebears came down from the high country in western Montana nearly three centuries ago. They were a mountain people, a mysterious tribe of hunters whose language has never been positively classified in any major group. In the late seventeenth century they began a long migration to the south and east. It was a long journey toward the dawn, and it led to a golden age. Along the way the Kiowas were befriended by the Crows, who gave them the culture and religion of the Plains. They acquired horses, and their ancient nomadic spirit was suddenly free of the ground. They acquired Tai-me, the sacred Sun Dance doll, from that moment the object and symbol of their worship, and so shared in the divinity of the sun. Not least, they acquired the sense of destiny, therefore courage and pride. When they entered upon the southern Plains, they had been transformed. No longer were they slaves to the simple necessity of survival; they were a lordly and dangerous society of fighters and thieves, hunters and priests of the sun. According to their origin myth, they entered the world through a hollow log. From one point of view, their migration was the fruit of an old prophecy, for indeed they emerged from a sunless world.

5   Although my grandmother lived out her long life in the shadow of Rainy Mountain, the immense landscape of the continental interior lay like memory in her blood. She could tell of the Crows, whom she had never seen, and of the Black Hills, where she had never been. I wanted to see in reality what she had seen more perfectly in the mind's eye, and traveled fifteen hundred miles to begin my pilgrimage.

6   Yellowstone, it seemed to me, was the top of the world, a region of deep lakes and dark timber, canyons and waterfalls. But, beautiful as it is, one might have the sense of confinement there. The skyline in all directions is close at hand, the high wall of the woods and deep cleavages of shade. There is a perfect freedom in the mountains, but it belongs to the eagle and the elk, the badger and the bear. The Kiowas reckoned their stature by the distance they could see, and they were bent and blind in the wilderness.

7   Descending eastward, the highland meadows are a stairway to the plain. In July the inland slope of the Rockies is luxuriant with flax and buckwheat, stonecrop and larkspur. The earth unfolds and the limit of the land recedes. Clusters of trees and animals grazing far in the distance cause the vision to reach away and wonder to build upon the mind. The sun follows a longer course in

the day, and the sky is immense beyond all comparison. The great billowing clouds that sail upon it are shadows that move upon the grain like water, dividing light. Farther down, in the land of the Crows and Blackfeet, the plain is yellow. Sweet clover takes hold of the hills and bends upon itself to cover and seal the soil. There the Kiowas paused on their way; they had come to the place where they must change their lives. The sun is at home in the plains. Precisely there does it have the certain character of a god. When the Kiowas came to the land of the Crows, they could see the dark lees of the hills at dawn across the Bighorn River, the profusion of light on the grain shelves, the oldest deity ranging after the solstices. Not yet would they veer southward to the caldron of the land that lay below; they must wean their blood from the northern winter and hold the mountains a while longer in their view. They bore Tai-me in procession to the east.

8   A dark mist lay over the Black Hills, and the land was like iron. At the top of a ridge I caught sight of Devil's Tower upthrust against the gray sky as if in the birth of time the core of the earth had broken through its crust and the motion of the world was begun. There are things in nature that engender an awful quiet in the heart of man; Devil's Tower is one of them. Two centuries ago, because they could not do otherwise, the Kiowas made a legend at the base of the rock. My grandmother said:

> "Eight children were there at play, seven sisters and their brother. Suddenly the boy was struck dumb; he trembled and began to run upon his hands and feet. His fingers became claws, and his body was covered with fur. Directly there was a bear where the boy had been. The sisters were terrified; they ran, and the bear after them. They came to the stump of a great tree, and the tree spoke to them. It bade them climb upon it, and as they did so, it began to rise into the air. The bear came to kill them, but they were just beyond its reach. It reared against the tree and scored the bark all around with its claws. The seven sisters were borne into the sky, and they became the stars of the Big Dipper."

From that moment, and so long as the legend lives, the Kiowas have kinsmen in the night sky. Whatever they were in the mountains, they could be no more. However tenuous their well-being, however much they had suffered and would suffer again, they had found a way out of the wilderness.

9   My grandmother had a reverence for the sun, a holy regard that now is all but gone out of mankind. There was a wariness in her, and an ancient awe. She was a Christian in her later years, but she had come a long way about, and she never forgot her birthright. As a child she had been to the Sun Dances; she had taken part in those annual rites, and by them she had learned the restoration of her people in the presence of Tai-me. She was about seven when the last Kiowa Sun Dance was held in 1887 on the Washita River above Rainy Mountain Creek. The buffalo were gone. In order to consummate the ancient sacrifice—to impale the head of a buffalo bull upon the medicine tree—a delegation of old men journeyed into Texas, there to beg and barter for an animal from the Goodnight herd. She was

ten when the Kiowas came together for the last time as a living Sun Dance culture. They could find no buffalo; they had to hang an old hide from the sacred tree. Before the dance could begin, a company of soldiers rode out from Fort Sill under orders to disperse the tribe. Forbidden without cause the essential act of their faith, having seen the wild herds slaughtered and left to rot upon the ground, the Kiowas backed away forever from the medicine tree. That was July 20, 1890, at the great bend of the Washita. My grandmother was there. Without bitterness, and for as long as she lived, she bore a vision of deicide.

10   Now that I can have her only in memory, I see my grandmother in the several postures that were peculiar to her: standing at the wood stove on a winter morning and turning meat in a great iron skillet; sitting at the south window, bent above her beadwork, and afterwards, when her vision had failed, looking down for a long time into the fold of her hands; going out upon a cane, very slowly as she did when the weight of age came upon her; praying. I remember her most often at prayer. She made long, rambling prayers out of suffering and hope, having seen many things. I was never sure that I had the right to hear, so exclusive were they of all mere custom and company. The last time I saw her she prayed standing by the side of her bed at night, naked to the waist, the light of a kerosene lamp moving upon her dark skin. Her long, black hair, always drawn and braided in the day, lay upon her shoulders and against her breasts like a shawl. I do not speak Kiowa, and I never understood her prayers, but there was something inherently sad in the sound, some merest hesitation upon the syllables of sorrow. She began in a high and descending pitch, exhausting her breath to silence; then again and again—and always the same intensity of effort, of something that is, and is not, like urgency in the human voice. Transported so in the dancing light among the shadows of her room, she seemed beyond the reach of time. But that was illusion; I think I knew that I should not see her again.

■ ■ ▨

MEANING

1. What different facets of Momaday's grandmother emerge from this account?

2. In what way did Momaday's grandmother serve as an inspiration to him?

3. What motivated Momaday to journey to Rainy Mountain and how did this visit connect him with the heritage of his people, the Kiowa?

4. How did Momaday's grandmother's prayers communicate a heritage that was just beyond the author's reach?

TECHNIQUE

1. What descriptive details bring the landscape of Momaday's childhood and his grandmother's to life for his readers?

2. How does Momaday's **description** of the meeting of the Kiowa with the Crows enable the reader to understand the culture of the plains they adopted?

3. **Other Patterns.** How does Momaday's **narration** of his thoughts provide a subjective dimension to the objective description?

LANGUAGE

1. How does his grandmother's account of the legend connected with Devil's Tower communicate the mythic world in which she lived?
2. What do you think Momaday means by the title? What might be an alternative?
3. If you don't know the meaning of the following words, look them up: *nomadic* (4), *profusion* (7), *tenuous* (8), *consummate* (9), *impale* (9), *deicide* (9).

SUGGESTIONS FOR WRITING

1. To what extent do Momaday's experiences of feeling that his grandmother represented a link to the Kiowa culture emerge from this account?
2. **Critical Writing.** Momaday's sudden arrival to be at his grandmother's grave suggests that it served as a catalyst to his desire to see himself as a Kiowa. Discuss this theme in his essay.
3. Momaday's grandmother was influential in the way Momaday saw himself. Give an **example** of a grandparent or someone else who was influential in your life.
4. **Thematic Link.** Discuss the need to come to terms with one's heritage as discussed in Momaday's essay and in Gloria Anzaldúa's "How to Tame a Wild Tongue" (Chapter 7, "Process Analysis").

JAMAICA KINCAID

A Small Place

Jamaica Kincaid (b. 1949) was raised in St. John's, Antigua, an island in the West Indies. Her works of fiction and nonfiction are distinguished by her sensitivity, empathy, and insight as well as a keen, acerbic view of the world. She has written for *The New Yorker*, *Rolling Stone*, and *Paris Review*. Her firsthand knowledge of what it is like to grow up in the West Indies and begin a new life in the United States is reflected in a book of stories, *Annie John* (1985), and a novel, *Lucy* (1990). In "A Small Place" (1988), she takes up the issue of the double standard that exists in Antigua for locals who have to put up with corruption and inadequately staffed hospitals, among other ills, and the newly arrived tourists who want only good weather. She has recently written a travel book, *Among Flowers: A Walk in the Himalaya* (2005).

BEFORE YOU READ

How does a tourist's view of a vacation spot differ from the view of people who live there?

■ ■ ▨

1   If you go to Antigua as a tourist, this is what you will see. If you come by aeroplane, you will land at the V. C. Bird International Airport. Vere Cornwall (V. C.) Bird is the Prime Minister of Antigua. You may be the sort of tourist who would wonder why a Prime Minister would want an airport named after him—why not a school, why not a hospital, why not some great public monument? You are a tourist and you have not yet seen a school in Antigua, you have not yet seen the hospital in Antigua, you have not yet seen a public monument in Antigua. As your plane descends to land, you might say, What a beautiful island Antigua is— more beautiful than any of the other islands you have seen, and they were very beautiful, in their way, but they were much too green, much too lush with vegetation, which indicated to you, the tourist, that they got quite a bit of rainfall, and rain is the very thing that you, just now, do not want, for you are thinking of the hard and cold and dark and long days you spent working in North America (or, worse, Europe), earning some money so that you could stay in this place (Antigua) where the sun always shines and where the climate is deliciously hot and dry for the four to ten days you are going to be staying there; and since you are on your holiday, since you are a tourist, the thought of what it might be like for someone who had to live day in, day out in a place that suffers constantly from drought, and so has to watch carefully every drop of fresh water used (while at the same time surrounded by a sea and an ocean—the Caribbean Sea on one side, the Atlantic Ocean on the other), must never cross your mind.

For a visual to accompany this selection, see color insert photo A-5.

2   You disembark from your plane. You go through customs. Since you are a tourist, a North American or European—to be frank, white—and not an Antiguan black returning to Antigua from Europe or North America with cardboard boxes of much needed cheap clothes and food for relatives, you move through customs swiftly, you move through customs with ease. Your bags are not searched. You emerge from customs into the hot, clean air: immediately you feel cleansed, immediately you feel blessed (which is to say special); you feel free. You see a man, a taxi driver; you ask him to take you to your destination; he quotes you a price. You immediately think that the price is in the local currency, for you are a tourist and you are familiar with these things (rates of exchange) and you feel even more free, for things seem so cheap, but then your driver ends by saying, "In U.S. currency." You may say, "Hmmmm, do you have a formal sheet that lists official prices and destinations?" Your driver obeys the law and shows you the sheet, and he apologises for the incredible mistake he has made in quoting you a price off the top of his head which is so vastly different (favouring him) from the one listed. You are driven to your hotel by this taxi driver in his taxi, a brand-new Japanese-made vehicle. The road on which you are travelling is a very bad road, very much in need of repair. You are feeling wonderful, so you say, "Oh, what a marvellous change these bad roads are from the splendid highways I am used to in North America." (Or, worse, Europe.) Your driver is reckless; he is a dangerous man who drives in the middle of the road when he thinks no other cars are coming in the opposite direction, passes other cars on blind curves that run uphill, drives at sixty miles an hour on narrow, curving roads when the road sign, a rusting, beat-up thing left over from colonial days, says 40 MPH. This might frighten you (you are on your holiday; you are a tourist); this might excite you (you are on your holiday; you are a tourist), though if you are from New York and take taxis you are used to this style of driving: most of the taxi drivers in New York are from places in the world like this. You are looking out the window (because you want to get your money's worth); you notice that all the cars you see are brand-new, or almost brand-new, and that they are all Japanese-made. There are no American cars in Antigua— no new ones, at any rate; none that were manufactured in the last ten years. You continue to look at the cars and you say to yourself, Why, they look brand-new, but they have an awful sound, like an old car—a very old, dilapidated car. How to account for that? Well, possibly it's because they use leaded gasoline in these brand-new cars whose engines were built to use non-leaded gasoline, but you mustn't ask the person driving the car if this is so, because he or she has never heard of unleaded gasoline. You look closely at the car; you see that it's a model of a Japanese car that you might hesitate to buy; it's a model that's very expensive; it's a model that's quite impractical for a person who has to work as hard as you do and who watches every penny you earn so that you can afford this holiday you are on. How do they afford such a car? And do they live in a luxurious house to match such a car? Well, no. You will be surprised, then, to see that most likely the person driving this brand-new car filled with the wrong gas lives in a house that, in comparison, is far beneath the status of the car; and if you were

to ask why you would be told that the banks are encouraged by the government to make loans available for cars, but loans for houses not so easily available; and if you ask again why, you will be told that the two main car dealerships in Antigua are owned in part or outright by ministers in government. Oh, but you are on holiday and the sight of these brand-new cars driven by people who may or may not have really passed their driving test (there was once a scandal about driving licenses for sale) would not really stir up these thoughts in you. You pass a building sitting in a sea of dust and you think, It's some latrines for people just passing by, but when you look again you see the building has written on it PIGOTT'S SCHOOL. You pass the hospital, the Holberton Hospital, and how wrong you are not to think about this, for though you are a tourist on your holiday, what if your heart should miss a few beats? What if a blood vessel in your neck should break? What if one of those people driving those brand-new cars filled with the wrong gas fails to pass safely while going uphill on a curve and you are in the car going in the opposite direction? Will you be comforted to know that the hospital is staffed with doctors that no actual Antiguan trusts; that Antiguans always say about the doctors, "I don't want them near me"; that Antiguans refer to them not as doctors but as "the three men" (there are three of them); that when the Minister of Health himself doesn't feel well he takes the first plane to New York to see a real doctor; that if any one of the ministers in government needs medical care he flies to New York to get it?

3   It's a good thing that you brought your own books with you, for you couldn't just go to the library and borrow some. Antigua used to have a splendid library, but in The Earthquake (everyone talks about it that way—The Earthquake; we Antiguans, for I am one, have a great sense of things, and the more meaningful the thing, the more meaningless we make it) the library building was damaged. This was in 1974, and soon after that a sign was placed on the front of the building saying, THIS BUILDING WAS DAMAGED IN THE EARTHQUAKE OF 1974. REPAIRS ARE PENDING. The sign hangs there, and hangs there more than a decade later, with its unfulfilled promise of repair, and you might see this as a sort of quaintness on the part of these islanders, these people descended from slaves—what a strange, unusual perception of time they have. REPAIRS ARE PENDING, and here it is many years later, but perhaps in a world that is twelve miles long and nine miles wide (the size of Antigua) twelve years and twelve minutes and twelve days are all the same. The library is one of those splendid old buildings from colonial times, and the sign telling of the repairs is a splendid old sign from colonial times. Not very long after The Earthquake Antigua got its independence from Britain, making Antigua a state in its own right, and Antiguans are so proud of this that each year, to mark the day, they go to church and thank God, a British God, for this. But you should not think of the confusion that must lie in all that and you must not think of the damaged library. You have brought your own books with you, and among them is one of those new books about economic history, one of those books explaining how the West (meaning Europe and North America after its conquest and settlement by Europeans) got rich: the West got rich not from the free (free—in this case meaning got-for-nothing) and then undervalued

labour, for generations, of the people like me you see walking around you in Antigua but from the ingenuity of small shopkeepers in Sheffield and Yorkshire and Lancashire, or wherever; and what a great part the invention of the wristwatch played in it, for there was nothing noble-minded men could not do when they discovered they could slap time on their wrists just like that (isn't that the last straw; for not only did we have to suffer the unspeakableness of slavery, but the satisfaction to be had from "We made you bastards rich" is taken away, too), and so you needn't let that slightly funny feeling you have from time to time about exploitation, oppression, domination develop into full-fledged unease, discomfort; you could ruin your holiday. They are not responsible for what you have; you owe them nothing; in fact, you did them a big favour, and you can provide one hundred examples. For here you are now, passing by Government House. And here you are now, passing by the Prime Minister's Office and the Parliament Building, and overlooking these, with a splendid view of St. John's Harbour, the American Embassy. If it were not for you, they would not have Government House, and Prime Minister's Office, and Parliament Building and embassy of powerful country. Now you are passing a mansion, an extraordinary house painted the colour of old cow dung, with more aerials and antennas attached to it than you will see even at the American Embassy. The people who live in this house are a merchant family who came to Antigua from the Middle East less than twenty years ago. When this family first came to Antigua, they sold dry goods door to door from suitcases they carried on their backs. Now they own a lot of Antigua; they regularly lend money to the government, they build enormous (for Antigua), ugly (for Antigua), concrete buildings in Antigua's capital, St. John's, which the government then rents for huge sums of money; a member of their family is the Antiguan Ambassador to Syria; Antiguans hate them. Not far from this mansion is another mansion, the home of a drug smuggler. Everybody knows he's a drug smuggler, and if just as you were driving by he stepped out of his door your driver might point him out to you as the notorious person that he is, for this drug smuggler is so rich people say he buys cars in tens—ten of this one, ten of that one—and that he bought a house (another mansion) near Five Islands, contents included, with cash he carried in a suitcase: three hundred and fifty thousand American dollars, and, to the surprise of the seller of the house, lots of American dollars were left over. Overlooking the drug smuggler's mansion is yet another mansion, and leading up to it is the best paved road in all of Antigua—even better than the road that was paved for the Queen's visit in 1985 (when the Queen came, all the roads that she would travel on were paved anew, so that the Queen might have been left with the impression that riding in a car in Antigua was a pleasant experience). In this mansion lives a woman sophisticated people in Antigua call Evita. She is a notorious woman. She's young and beautiful and the girlfriend of somebody very high up in the government. Evita is notorious because her relationship with this high government official has made her the owner of boutiques and property and given her a say in cabinet meetings, and all sorts of other privileges such a relationship would bring a beautiful young woman.

4   Oh, but by now you are tired of all this looking, and you want to reach your destination—your hotel, your room. You long to refresh yourself; you long to eat some nice lobster, some nice local food. You take a bath, you brush your teeth. You get dressed again; as you get dressed, you look out the window. That water—have you ever seen anything like it? Far out, to the horizon, the colour of the water is navy-blue; nearer, the water is the colour of the North American sky. From there to the shore, the water is pale, silvery, clear, so clear that you can see its pinkish-white sand bottom. Oh, what beauty! Oh, what beauty! You have never seen anything like this. You are so excited. You breathe shallow. You breathe deep. You see a beautiful boy skimming the water, godlike, on a Windsurfer. You see an incredibly unattractive, fat, pastrylike-fleshed woman enjoying a walk on the beautiful sand, with a man, an incredibly unattractive, fat, pastrylike-fleshed man; you see the pleasure they're taking in their surroundings. Still standing, looking out the window, you see yourself lying on the beach, enjoying the amazing sun (a sun so powerful and yet so beautiful, the way it is always overhead as if on permanent guard, ready to stamp out any cloud that dares to darken and so empty rain on you and ruin your holiday; a sun that is your personal friend). You see yourself taking a walk on that beach, you see yourself meeting new people (only they are new in a very limited way, for they are people just like you). You see yourself eating some delicious, locally grown food. You see yourself, you see yourself . . . You must not wonder what exactly happened to the contents of your lavatory when you flushed it. You must not wonder where your bathwater went when you pulled out the stopper. You must not wonder what happened when you brushed your teeth. Oh, it might all end up in the water you are thinking of taking a swim in; the contents of your lavatory might, just might, graze gently against your ankle as you wade carefree in the water, for you see, in Antigua, there is no proper sewage-disposal system. But the Caribbean Sea is very big and the Atlantic Ocean is even bigger; it would amaze even you to know the number of black slaves this ocean has swallowed up. When you sit down to eat your delicious meal, it's better that you don't know that most of what you are eating came off a plane from Miami. And before it got on a place in Miami, who knows where it came from? A good guess is that it came from a place like Antigua first, where it was grown dirt-cheap, went to Miami, and came back. There is a world of something in this, but I can't go into it right now.

5   The thing you have always suspected about yourself the minute you become a tourist is true: A tourist is an ugly human being. You are not an ugly person all the time; you are not an ugly person ordinarily; you are not an ugly person day to day. From day to day, you are a nice person. From day to day, all the people who are supposed to love you on the whole do. From day to day, as you walk down a busy street in the large and modern and prosperous city in which you work and live, dismayed, puzzled (a cliché but only a cliché can explain you) at how alone you feel in this crowd, how awful it is to go unnoticed, how awful it is to go unloved, even as you are surrounded by more people than you could possibly get to know in a lifetime that lasted for millennia, and then out of the corner of your eye you see someone looking at you and absolute pleasure is

written all over that person's face, and then you realise that you are not as revolting a presence as you think you are (for that look just told you so). And so, ordinarily, you are a nice person, an attractive person, a person capable of drawing to yourself the affection of other people (people just like you), a person at home in your own skin (sort of; I mean, in a way; I mean, your dismay and puzzlement are natural to you, because people like you just seem to be like that, and so many of the things people like you find admirable about yourselves—the things you think about, the things you think really define you—seem rooted in these feelings): a person at home in your own house (and all its nice house things), with its nice back yard (and its nice back-yard things), at home on your street, your church, in community activities, your job, at home with your family, your relatives, your friends—you are a whole person. But one day, when you are sitting somewhere, alone in that crowd, and that awful feeling of displacedness comes over you, and really, as an ordinary person you are not well equipped to look too far inward and set yourself aright, because being ordinary is already so taxing, and being ordinary takes all you have out of you, and though the words "I must get away" do not actually pass across your lips, you make a leap from being that nice blob just sitting like a boob in your amniotic sac of the modern experience to being a person visiting heaps of death and ruin and feeling alive and inspired at the sight of it; to being a person lying on some faraway beach, your stilled body stinking and glistening in the sand, looking like something first forgotten, then remembered, then not important enough to go back for; to being a person marvelling at the harmony (ordinarily, what you would say is the backwardness) and the union these other people (and they are other people) have with nature. And you look at the things they can do with a piece of ordinary cloth, the things they fashion out of cheap, vulgarly colored (to you) twine, the way they squat down over a hole they have made in the ground, the hole itself is something to marvel at, and since you are being an ugly person this ugly but joyful thought will swell inside you: their ancestors were not clever in the way yours were and not ruthless in the way yours were, for then would it not be you who would be in harmony with nature and backwards in that charming way? An ugly thing, that is what you are when you become a tourist, an ugly, empty thing, a stupid thing, a piece of rubbish pausing here and there to gaze at this and taste that, and it will never occur to you that the people who inhabit the place in which you have just paused cannot stand you, that behind their closed doors they laugh at your strangeness (you do not look the way they look); the physical sight of you does not please them; you have bad manners (it is their custom to eat their food with their hands; you try eating their way, you look silly; you try eating the way you always eat, you look silly); they do not like the way you speak (you have an accent); they collapse helpless from laughter, mimicking the way they imagine you must look as you carry out some everyday bodily function. They do not like you. *They do not like me!* That thought never actually occurs to you. Still, you feel a little uneasy. Still, you feel a little foolish. Still, you feel a little out of place. But the banality of your own life is very real to you; it drove you to this extreme, spending your days and your nights in the company of people who despise you, people you do not like really, people you would not want to have as your actual neighbour. And so you must devote yourself to puzzling out how much of what you are told is really, really true (Is ground-up bottle glass in peanut sauce really a delicacy around here, or will it do just what you think ground-up bottle glass will do? Is this rare, multicoloured, snout-mouthed fish really an aphrodisiac, or will it cause you to fall asleep permanently?). Oh, the hard work all of this is, and is it any wonder, then, that on your return home you feel the need of a long rest, so that you can recover from your life as a tourist?

6   That the native does not like the tourist is not hard to explain. For every native of every place is a potential tourist, and every tourist is a native of somewhere. Every native everywhere lives a life of overwhelming and crushing banality and boredom and desperation and depression, and every deed, good and bad, is an attempt to forget this. Every native would like to find a way out, every native would like a rest, every native would like a tour. But some natives—most natives in the world—cannot go anywhere. They are too poor. They are too poor to go anywhere. They are too poor to escape the reality of their lives; and they are too poor to live properly in the place where they live, which is the very place you, the tourist, want to go—so when the natives see you, the tourist, they envy you, they envy your ability to leave your own banality and boredom, they envy your ability to turn their own banality and boredom into a source of pleasure for yourself.

■ ■ ▨

MEANING

1. How does the fact that tourists that do not know that the "local" food is imported from Miami illustrate the artifically created impression of Antigua they have?

2. What inferences might you draw about the government's attitude toward tourists (compared with their concern about Antiguans) from the sight of the dilapidated schools and hospital alongside brand-new cars and fine government buildings?

3. Why is it ironic that history books credit England's wealth to the ingenuity of British shopkeepers and fail to mention the role played by the labor of colonized peoples?

4. How are ordinarily pleasant people transformed when they become tourists?

TECHNIQUE

1. What details most effectively suggest the atmosphere in which tourists apply very different standards than they would if the same "exciting" events happened back home? How do their expectations differ from those of people who must live in these places all the time?

2. How does Kincaid use the episode of the Queen of England's visit to suggest the government's double standard?

3. **Other Patterns.** How does Kincaid use the **narrative** structure of what a newly arrived tourist might or might not notice to frame her analysis?

LANGUAGE

1. How would you characterize Kincaid's tone (e.g., satiric, ironic), and what terms and images best illustrate this?

2. How does Kincaid attempt to capture the thought processes of tourists who naively take in experiences and maintain an unrealistic view of their importance?

3. If you don't know the meaning of the following words, look them up: *aerials* (3), *notorious* (3), *cliché* (5), *millennia* (5), *banality* (5), *aphrodisiac* (5).

SUGGESTIONS FOR WRITING

1. ***Critical Writing.*** To what extent was your perception of yourself as a tourist changed by reading Kincaid's account? In an essay, describe how you would have appeared to the people who live where you took your last vacation.

2. Before traveling to a place, did you construct a mental picture of what it would be like? Did your actual visit match your expectation or not? Explain your answer.

3. Create a **counterargument** to Kincaid's essay from the perspective of an Antiguan who believes that tourism is beneficial for the island and its people.

4. ***Thematic Links.*** How does Kincaid's account and that of C. P. Ellis in "Why I Quit the Klan" (Chapter 9, "Cause and Effect") employ dramatic shifts in perspective and the interaction of race and class?

NATSUME SŌSEKI

I Am A Cat

A much beloved author (whose picture appears on the 1,000-yen note), Natsume Sōseki (1867–1916) was in the forefront of Japanese writers who made contact with the outside world. He served as editor of the *Asahi* newspaper and taught English at Tokyo University. His writing focuses on the daily tragedies and comedies of middle-class life in Japan. These qualities are immediately apparent in the following selection from his widely recognized masterpiece *I Am A Cat* (1905). This whimsical story takes us inside the home of a schoolteacher and his family, who are viewed through the eyes of a stray cat that has been given a home but, not yet a name.

BEFORE YOU READ

What names have you given pets, and what significance did these names have?

■ ■ ▨

1   I am a cat but as yet I have no name.

2   I haven't the faintest idea of where I was born. The first thing I do remember is that I was crying "meow, meow," somewhere in a gloomy damp place. It was there that I met a human being for the first time in my life. Though I found this all out at a later date, I learned that this human being was called a Student, one of the most ferocious of the human race. I also understand that these Students sometimes catch us, cook us and then take to eating us. But at that time, I did not have the slightest idea of all this so I wasn't frightened a bit. When this Student placed me on the palm of his hand and lifted me up lightly, I only had the feeling of floating around. After a while, I got used to this position and looked around. This was probably the first time I had a good look at a so-called human being. What impressed me as being most strange still remains deeply imbedded in my mind: the face which should have been covered with hair was a slippery thing similar to what I now know to be a teakettle. I have since come across many other cats but none of them are such freaks. Moreover, the center of the Student's face protruded to a great extent, and from the two holes located there, he would often emit smoke. I was extremely annoyed by being choked by this. That this was what they term as tobacco, I came to know only recently.

3   I was snuggled up comfortably in the palm of this Student's hand when, after a while, I started to travel around at a terrific speed. I was unable to find out if the Student was moving or if it was just myself that was in motion, but in any case I became terribly dizzy and a little sick. Just as I was thinking that I couldn't last much longer at this rate, I heard a thud and saw sparks. I remember

---

For a visual to accompany this selection, see color insert photo A-6.

everything up till that moment but think as hard as I can, I can't recall what took place immediately after this.

4   When I came to, I could not find the Student anywhere. Nor could I find the many cats that had been with me either. Moreover, my dear mother had also disappeared. And the extraordinary thing was that this place, when compared to where I had been before, was extremely bright—ever so bright. I could hardly keep my eyes open. This was because I had been removed from my straw bed and thrown into a bamboo bush.

5   Finally, mustering up my strength, I crawled out from this bamboo grove and found myself before a large pond. I sat on my haunches and tried to take in the situation. I didn't know what to do but suddenly I had an idea. If I could attract some attention by meowing, the Student might come back to me. I commenced but this was to no avail; nobody came.

6   By this time, the wind had picked up and came blowing across the pond. Night was falling. I sensed terrible pangs of hunger. Try as I would, my voice failed me and I felt as if all hope were lost. In any case, I resolved to get myself to a place where there was food and so, with this decision in mind, I commenced to circle the water by going around to the left.

7   This was very difficult but at any rate, I forced myself along and eventually came to a locality where I sensed Man. Finding a hole in a broken bamboo fence, I crawled through, having confidence that it was worth the try, and lo! I found myself within somebody's estate. Fate is strange; if that hole had not been there, I might have starved to death by the roadside. It is well said that every tree may offer shelter. For a long time afterwards, I often used this hole for my trips to call on Mi-ke, the tomcat living next door.

8   Having sneaked into the estate, I was at a loss as to what the next step should be. Darkness had come and my belly cried for food. The cold was bitter and it started to rain. I had no time to fool around any longer so I went in to a room that looked bright and cozy. Coming to think of it now, I had entered somebody's home for the first time. It was there that I was to confront other humans.

9   The first person I met was the maid Osan. This was a human much worse than the Student. As soon as she saw me, she grabbed me by the neck and threw me outdoors. I sensed I had no chance against her sudden action so I shut my eyes and let things take their course. But I couldn't endure the hunger and the cold any longer. I don't know how many times I was thrown out but because of this, I came to dislike Osan all through. That's one reason why I stole the fish the other day and why I felt so proud of myself.

10   When the maid was about to throw me out for the last time, the master of the house made his appearance and asked what all the row was about. The maid turned to him with me hanging limp from her hand, and told him that she had repeatedly tried throwing this stray cat out but that it always kept sneaking into the kitchen again—and that she didn't like it at all. The master, twisting his moustache, looked at me for a while and then told the maid to let me in. He then left the room. I took it that the master was a man of few words. The maid, still mad at me, threw me down on the kitchen floor. In such a way, I was able to establish this place as my home.

11   At first it was very seldom that I got to see my master. He seemed to be a schoolteacher. Coming home from school he'd shut himself up in his study and would hardly come out for the rest of the day. His family thought him to be very studious and my master also made out as if he were. But actually, he wasn't as hard working as they all believed him to be. I'd often sneak up and look into his study only to find him taking a nap. Sometimes I would find him drivelling on the book he had been reading before dozing off.

12   He was a man with a weak stomach so his skin was somewhat yellowish. He looked parched and inactive, yet he was a great consumer of food. After eating as much as he possibly could, he'd take a dose of Taka-diastase and then open a book. After reading a couple of pages, however, he'd become drowsy and again commence drooling. This was his daily routine. Though I am a cat myself, at times I think that schoolteachers are very fortunate. If I were to be reborn a man, I would, without doubt, become a teacher. If you can keep a job and still sleep as much as my master did, even cats could manage such a profession. But according to my master—and he makes it plain—there's nothing so hard as teaching. Especially when his friends come to visit him, he does a lot of complaining.

13   When I first came to this home, nobody but the master was nice to me. Wherever I went, they would kick me around and I was given no other consideration. The fact that they haven't given me a name even as of today goes to show how much they care for me. That's why I try to stay close to my master.

14   In the morning, when my master reads the papers, I always sit on his lap; and when he takes his nap, I perch on his back. This doesn't mean that he likes it, but then, on the other hand, it doesn't mean that he dislikes it—it has simply become a custom.

15   Experience taught me that it is best for me to sleep on the container for boiled rice in the mornings as it is warm, and on a charcoal-burning foot warmer in the evenings. I generally sleep on the veranda on fine days. But most of all, I like to crawl into the same bed with the children of the house at night. By children, I mean the girls who are five and three years old respectively. They sleep together in the same bed in their own room. In some way or other, I try to slip into their bed and crawl in between them. But if one of them wakes up, then it is terrible. The girls—especially the smaller one—raise an awful cry in the middle of the night and holler, "There's that cat in here again!" At this, my weak-stomached master wakes up and comes in to help them. It was only the other day that he gave me a terrible whipping with a ruler for indulging in this otherwise pleasant custom.

16   In coming to live with human beings, I have had the chance to observe them and the more I do the more I come to the conclusion that they are terribly spoiled, especially the children. When they feel like it, they hold you upside down or cover your head with a bag; and at times, they throw you around or try squeezing you into the cooking range. And on top of that, should you so much as bare a claw to try to stop them, the whole family is after you. The other day, for instance, I tried sharpening my claws just for a second on the straw mat of the living room when the Mrs. noticed me. She got furious and from then on, she won't let me in the sitting room. I can be cold and shivering in the kitchen but they never

take the trouble to bother about me. When I met Shiro across the street whom I respected, she kept telling me there was nothing as inconsiderate as humans.

17   Only the other day, four cute little kittens were born to Shiro. But the Student who lives with the family threw all four of them into a pond behind the house on the third day. Shiro told me all this in tears and said that in order for us cats to fulfil parental affection and to have a happy life, we will have to overthrow the human race. Yes, what she said was all very logical. Mi-ke, next door, was extremely furious when I told him about Shiro. He said that humans did not understand the right of possession of others. With us cats, however, the first one that finds the head of a dried sardine or the navel of a gray mullet gets the right to eat it. Should anyone try to violate this rule, we are allowed to use force in order to keep our find. But humans depend on their great strength to take what is legally ours away from us and think it right.

18   Shiro lives in the home of a soldier and Mi-ke in the home of a lawyer. I live in the home of a schoolteacher and, in comparison. I am far more optimistic about such affairs than either of them. I am satisfied only in trying to live peacefully day after day. I don't believe that the human race will prosper forever so all I have to do is to relax and wait for the time when cats will reign.

19   Coming to think of the way they act according to their whims—another word for selfishness—I'm going to tell you more about my master. To tell the truth, my master can't do anything well but he likes to stick his nose into everything. Going in for composing *haiku*,[1] he contributes his poems to the *Hototogisu* magazine, or writes some modern poetry for the *Myojo* magazine; or at times, he composes a piece in English, but all grammatically wrong. Then again, he finds himself engrossed in archery or tries singing lyrical plays; or maybe he tries a hand at playing discordant tunes on the violin. What is most disheartening is the fact that he cannot manage any of them well. Though he has a weak stomach, he does his best.

20   When he enters the toilet, he commences chanting so he is nicknamed "Mr. Mensroom" by his neighbors. Yet, he doesn't mind such things and continues his chanting: "This is Taira-no-Munemori. . . ." Everybody says, "There goes Munemori again," and then bursts out laughing. I don't know exactly what had come over him about a month after I first established myself at his place, but one pay day he came home all excited carrying with him a great big bundle. I couldn't help feeling curious about the contents.

21   The package happened to contain a set of water colors, brushes and drawing paper. It seems that he had given up lyrical plays and writing verses and was going in for painting. The following day, he shut himself up in his study and without even taking his daily nap, he drew pictures. This continued day after day. But what he drew remained a mystery because others could not even guess what they were. My master finally came to the conclusion that he wasn't as good a painter as he had thought himself to be. One day he came home with a man who considers himself an aesthetic and I heard them talking to each other.

---

[1] Haiku: a major form of Japanese verse written in 17 syllables, divided into three lines of 5, 7, and 5 syllables, employing evocative allusions and comparisons.

22   "It's funny but it's difficult to draw as well as you want. When a painting is done by others, it looks so simple. But when you do a work with a brush yourself, it's quite a different thing," said my master. Coming to think of it, he did have plenty of proof to back up his statement.

23   His friend, looking over his gold-rimmed glasses, said, "You can't expect to draw well right from the beginning. In the first place, you can't expect to draw anything just from imagination, and by shutting yourself up in a room at that. Once the famous Italian painter Andrea del Sarto[2] said that to draw, you have to interpret nature in its original form. The stars in the sky, the earth with flowers shining with dew, the flight of birds and the running animals, the ponds with their goldfish, and the black crow in a withered tree—nature is the one great panorama of the living world. How about it? If you want to draw something recognizable, why not do some sketching?"

24   "Did del Sarto really say all those things? I didn't know that. All right, just as you say," said my master with admiration. The eyes behind the gold-rimmed glasses shone, but with scorn.

25   The following day, as I was peacefully enjoying my daily nap on the veranda, my master came out from his study, something quite out of the ordinary, and sat down beside me. Wondering what he was up to, I slit my eyes open just a wee bit and took a look. I found him trying out Andrea del Sarto's theory on me. I could not suppress a smile. Having been encouraged by his friend, my master was using me as a model.

26   I tried to be patient and pretended to continue my nap. I wanted to yawn like anything but when I thought of my master trying his best to sketch me, I felt sorry for him, and so I killed it. He first drew my face in outline and then began to add colors. I'd like to make a confession here: as far as cats are concerned, I have to admit that I'm not one of those you'd call perfect or beautiful; my back, my fur or even my face cannot be considered superior in any way to those of other cats. Yet, even though I may be uncomely, I am hardly as ugly as what my master was painting. In the first place, he shaded my color all wrong. I am really somewhat like a Persian cat, a light gray with a shade of yellow with lacquer-like spots—as can be vouched by anyone. But according to my master's painting, my color was not yellow nor was it black. It wasn't gray or brown. It wasn't even a combination of these colors but something more like a smearing together of many tones. What was most strange about the drawing was that I had no eyes. Of course, I was being sketched while taking a nap so I won't complain too much, but you couldn't even find the location of where they should have been. You couldn't tell if I was a sleeping cat or a blind cat. I thought, way down inside me, that if this is what they called the Andrea del Sarto way of drawing pictures, it wasn't worth a sen.

27   But as to the enthusiasm of my master, I had to bow my head humbly. I couldn't disappoint him by moving but, if you'll excuse my saying so, I had wanted to go outside to relieve myself from a long while back. The muscles of my body

---

[2] Andrea del Sarto (1486–1531).

commenced fidgeting and I felt that I couldn't hold out much longer. So, trying to excuse myself, I stretched out my forelegs, gave my neck a little twist and indulged in a long slow yawn. Going this far, there was no need for me to stay still any longer because I had changed my pose. I then stepped outside to accomplish my object.

28   But my master, in disappointment and rage, shouted from within the room, "You fool!" My master, in abusing others, has the habit of using this expression. "You fool!" This is the best he can manage as he doesn't know any other way to swear. Even though he had not known how long I had endured the urgent call of nature, I still consider him uncivilized for this. If he had ever given me a smile or some other encouragement when I climbed onto his back, I could have forgiven him this time, but the fact is that he never considers my convenience. That he should holler, "You fool!" only because I was about to go and relieve myself was more than I could stand. In the first place, humans take too much for granted. If some power doesn't appear to control them better, there's no telling how far they will go in their excesses.

29   I could endure their being so self-willed but I've heard many other complaints regarding mankind's lack of virtue, and they are much worse.

30   Right in back of the house, there is a patch of tea plants. It isn't large but it is nice and sunny. When the children of the house are so noisy that I can't enjoy my naps peacefully or when, because of idleness, my digestion is bad, I usually go out to the tea patch to enjoy the magnanimous surroundings. One lovely autumn day about two o'clock in the afternoon, after taking my after-lunch nap, I took a stroll through this patch. I walked along, smelling each tea plant as I went, until I reached a cryptomeria hedge at the west end.

31   There I found a large cat sleeping soundly, using a withered chrysanthemum in lieu of a mat. It seemed as if he didn't notice me coming, for he kept snoring loudly. I was overwhelmed at his boldness;—after sneaking into somebody else's yard. He was a big black cat.

32   The sun, now past midday, cast its brilliant rays upon his body and reflected themselves to give the impression of flames bursting from his soft fur. He had such a big frame that he seemed fit to be called a king of the feline family. He was more than twice my size. Admiration and a feeling of curiosity made me forget the past and the future, and I could only stare at him.

33   The soft autumn breeze made the branches of the paulawnia above quiver lightly and a couple of leaves came fluttering down upon the thicket of dead chrysanthemums. Then the great "king" opened his eyes. I can still feel the thrill of that moment. The amber light in his eyes shone much brighter than the jewels man holds as precious. He did not move at all. The glance he shot at me concentrated on my small forehead, and he abruptly asked me who I was. The great king's directness betrayed his rudeness. Yet, there was a power in his voice that would have terrified dogs, and I found myself shaking with fear. But thinking it inadvisable not to pay my respects, I said, "I am a cat though, as yet, I don't have any name." I said this while pretending to be at ease but actually my heart was

beating away at a terrific speed. Despite my courteous reply, he said. "A cat? You don't say so! Where do you live?" He was extremely audacious.

34   "I live here in the schoolteacher's house."

35   "I thought so. You sure are skinny." Gathering from his rudeness I couldn't imagine him coming from a very good family. But, judging from his plump body, he seemed to be well fed and able to enjoy an easy life. As for myself, I couldn't refrain from asking. "And who are you?"

36   "Me? Huh—I'm Kuro, living at the rickshawman's place."

37   So this was the cat living at the rickshawman's house! He was known in the vicinity as being awfully unruly. Actually he was admired within the home of the rickshawman but, having no education, nobody else befriended him. He was a hoodlum from whom others shied. When I heard him tell me who he was, I felt somewhat uneasy and, at the same time, I felt slightly superior. With the intention of finding out how much learning he had, I asked him some more questions.

38   "I was just wondering which of the two is the greater—the rickshawman or the schoolteacher."

39   "What a question! The rickshawman, naturally. Just take a look at your teacher—he's all skin and bones," he snorted.

40   "You look extremely strong. Most probably, living at the rickshawman's house, you get plenty to eat."

41   "What? I don't go unfed anywhere! Stick with me for a while instead of going around in circles in the tea patch and you'll look better yourself in less than a month."

42   "Sure, some day, maybe. But to me, it seems as though the schoolteacher lives in a bigger house than the rickshawman," I purred.

43   "Huh! What if the house is big? That doesn't mean you get your belly full there, does it?"

44   He seemed extremely irritated and, twitching his pointed cars, he walked away without saying another word. This was my first encounter with Kuro of the house of the rickshawman, but not the last.

45   Since then, we've often talked together. Whenever we do, Kuro always commences bragging, as one living with a rickshawman would.

46   One day, we were lying in the tea patch and indulging in some small talk. As usual, he kept bragging about the adventures he had had, and then he got around to asking me, "By the way, how many rats have you killed?"

47   Intellectually I am much more developed than Kuro but when it comes to using strength and showing bravado, there is no comparison. I was prepared for something like this but when he actually asked me the question, I felt extremely embarrassed. But facts are facts; I could not lie to him: "To tell the truth, I have been wanting to catch one for a long time but the opportunity has never come."

48   Kuro twitched the whiskers which stood out straight from his muzzle and laughed hard. Kuro is conceited, as those who brag usually are, so when I find him being sarcastic I try to say something to appease him. In this way, I am able to manage him pretty well. Having learned this during our first meeting, I stayed calm when he laughed. I realized that it would be foolish to commit myself now

by giving unasked-for reasons. I figured it best, at this stage, to let him brag about his own adventures and so I purred quietly, "Being as old as you are, you've probably caught a lot of rats yourself." I was trying to get him to talk about himself. And, as I had expected, he took the bait.

49   "Well, can't say a lot—maybe about thirty or forty." He was very proud of this and continued, "I could handle one or two hundred rats alone but when it comes to weasels, they're not to my liking. A weasel once gave me a terrible time."

50   "So? And what happened?" I chimed in. Kuro blinked several times before be continued. "It was at the time of our annual housecleaning last summer. The master crawled under the veranda to put away a sack of lime, and—what do you think? He surprised a big weasel which came bouncing out."

51   "Oh?" I pretended to admire him.

52   "As you know, a weasel is only a little bigger than a rat. Thinking him to be just another big mouse, I cornered him in a ditch."

53   "You did?"

54   "Yeah. Just as I was going in for the *coup de grace*—can you imagine what he did? Well, it raised its tail and—ooph! You ought to have taken a whiff. Even now when I see a weasel I get giddy." So saying, he rubbed his nose with one of his paws as if he were still trying to stop the smell. I felt somewhat sorry for him so, with the thought of trying to liven him up a little, I said, "But when it comes to rats, I hardly believe they would have a chance against you. Being such a famous rat catcher, you probably cat nothing else and that's why you're so plump and glossy, I'm sure."

55   I had said this to get him into a better mood but actually it had the contrary effect. He let a big sigh escape and replied, "When you come to think of it, it's not all fun. Rats are interesting but, you know, there's nobody as crafty as humans in this world. They take all the rats I catch over to the police box. The policeman there doesn't know who actually catches them so he hands my master five sen per head. Because of me, my master has made a neat profit of one yen and fifty sen, but yet he doesn't give me any decent food. Do you know what humans are? Well, I'll tell you. They're men, yes, but thieves at heart."

56   Even Kuro, who was not any too bright, understood such logic and he bristled his back in anger. I felt somewhat uneasy so I murmured some excuse and went home. It was because of this conversation that I made up my mind never to catch rats. But, on the other hand, neither do I go around hunting for other food. Instead of eating an extravagant dinner, I simply go to sleep. A cat living with a schoolteacher gets to become, in nature, just like a teacher himself. If I'm not careful I might still become just as weak in the stomach as my master.

57   Speaking of my master the schoolteacher, it finally dawned upon him that he could not ever hope to get anywhere with water-color painting. He wrote the following entry in his diary, dated December 1:

> Met a man today at a party. It's said that he's a debauchee and he looked like one. Such individuals are liked by women, so it may be quite proper to say that such people cannot help becoming dissipated. His wife was formerly a geisha girl and I envy him. Most of the people who criticize debauchees

generally have no chance to become one themselves. Still, others who claim to be debauchees have no qualifications to become so worldly. They simply force themselves into that position. Just as in the case of my water-color painting, there was absolutely no fear of my making good. But indifferent to others, I might think that I was good at it. If some men are considered worldly only because they drink *sake* at restaurants, frequent geisha houses and stop over for the night, and go through all the necessary motions, then it stands to reason that I should be able to call myself a remarkable painter. But my water-color paintings will never be a success.

58   In regard to this theory, I cannot agree. That a schoolteacher should envy a man who has a wife who was once a geisha shows how foolish and inferior my master is. But his criticism of himself as a water-color painter is unquestionably true. Though my master understands many of his own shortcomings, he cannot get over being terribly conceited. On December 4, he wrote:

> Last night, I attempted another painting but I have finally come to understand that I have no talent. I dreamed that somebody had framed the pictures I have lying around, and had hung them on the wall. Upon seeing them framed, I suddenly thought that I was an excellent painter. I felt happy and kept looking but, when the day dawned, I awoke and again clearly realized that I am still a painter of no talent.

59   Even in his dreams, my master seemed to regret his having given up painting. This is characteristic of a learned man, a frustrated water-color painter and one who can never become a man of the world.

60   The day after my master had had his dream, his friend, the man of arts, came to see him again. The first question he asked my master was "How are the pictures getting along?"

61   My master calmly answered, "According to your advice I'm working hard at sketching. Just as you said, I am finding interesting shapes and detailed changes of colors which I had never noticed before. Due to the fact that artists in Western countries have persisted in sketching, they have reached the development we see today. Yes, all this must be due to Andrea del Sarto." He did not mention what he had written in his diary, but only continued to show his admiration for del Sarto.

62   The artist scratched his head and commenced to laugh, "That was all a joke, my friend."

63   "What's that?" My master didn't seem to understand.

64   "Andrea del Sarto is only a person of my own highly imaginative creation. I didn't think you'd take it so seriously. Ha, ha, ha." The artist was greatly enjoying himself.

65   Listening to all this from the veranda, I couldn't help wondering what my master would write in his diary about that conversation. This artist was a person who took great pleasure in fooling others. As if he did not realize how his joke about Andrea del Sarto hurt my master, he boasted more: "When playing jokes, some people take them so seriously that they reveal great comic beauty, and it's a lot of

fun. The other day I told a student that Nicholas Nickleby had advised Gibbon to translate his great story of the French Revolution from a French textbook and to have it published under his own name. This student has an extremely good memory and made a speech at the Japanese Literature Circle quoting everything I had told him. There were about a hundred people in the audience and they all listened very attentively. Then there's another time. One evening, at a gathering of writers, the conversation turned to Harrison's historical novel *Theophano*. I said that it was one of the best historical novels ever written, especially the part where the heroine dies. "That really gives you the creeps'—that's what I said. An author who was sitting opposite me was one of those types who cannot and will not say no to anything. He immediately voiced the opinion that that was a most famous passage. I knew right away that he had never read any more of the story than I had."

66   With wide eyes, my nervous and weak-stomached master asked, "What would you have done if the other man had really read the story?"

67   The artist did not show any excitement. He thought nothing of fooling other people. The only thing that counted was not to be caught in the act.

68   "All I would have had to do is to say that I had made a mistake in the title or something to that effect." He kept on laughing. Though this artist wore a pair of gold-rimmed glasses, he looked somewhat like Kuro of the rickshawman's.

69   My master blew a few smoke rings but he had an expression on his face that showed he wouldn't have the nerve to do such a thing. The artist, with a look in his eyes as if saying, "That's why you can't paint pictures," only continued. "Jokes are jokes but, getting down to facts, it's not easy to draw. They say that Leonardo da Vinci once told his pupils to copy a smear on a wall. That's good advice. Sometimes when you're gazing at water leaking along the wall in a privy, you see some good patterns. Copy them carefully and you're bound to get some good designs."

70   "You're only trying to fool me again."

71   "No, not this time. Don't you think it's a wonderful idea? Just what da Vinci himself would have suggested."

72   "Just as you say," replied my master, half surrendering. But he still hasn't made any sketches in the privy—at least not yet.

73   Kuro of the rickshawman's wasn't looking well. His glossy fur began to fade and fall out. His eyes, which I formerly compared to amber, began to collect mucus. What was especially noticeable was his lack of energy. When I met him in the tea patch, I asked him how he felt.

74   "I'm still disgusted with the weasel's stink and with the fisherman. The fish seller hit me with a pole again the other day."

75   The red leaves of the maple tree were beginning to show contrast to the green of the pines here and there. The maples shed their foliage like dreams of the past. The fluttering petals of red and white fell from the tea plants one after another until there were none remaining. The sun slanted its rays deeper and deeper into the southern veranda and seldom did a day pass that the late autumn wind didn't blow. I felt as though my napping hours were being shortened.

76   My master still went to school every day and, coming home, he'd still bottle himself up in his study. When he had visitors he'd continue to complain about his job. He hardly ever touched his water colors again. He had discontinued taking Taka-diastase for his indigestion, saying that it didn't do him any good. It was wonderful now that the little girls were attending kindergarten every day but returning home, they'd sing loudly and bounce balls and, at times, they'd still pick me up by the tail.

77   I still had nothing much to eat so I did not become very fat but I was healthy enough. I didn't become sick like Kuro and, as always, I took things as they came. I still didn't try to catch rats, and I still hated Osan, the maid. I still didn't have a name but you can't always have what you want. I resigned myself to continue living here at the home of this schoolteacher as a cat without a name.

■ ■ ◪

MEANING

1. How does the cat's view of the schoolmaster show the man as he really is compared with the way he sees himself?

2. What subtle or overt resemblances link each of the cats mentioned with its owner? For example, how is the narrator like the schoolmaster, Mi-ke similar to the lawyer, and Kuro like the rickshawman?

3. What assumptions underlie the cat's statement that "the fact that they haven't given me a name even as of today goes to show how much they care for me"?

4. How does the schoolmaster reveal his naiveté when he is taken in by the so-called historical facts concerning Andrea del Sarto?

TECHNIQUE

1. What features display Sōseki's ingenuity in creating a human personality for the cat?

2. In what way is the cat's viewpoint effective in providing a vantage point on life in this Japanese household?

3. What details in the story suggest that the schoolmaster identifies with the cat in the sense that he too feels like an outsider in his own household?

4. **Other Patterns.** Where does Sōseki use **comparison and contrast** to juxtapose the experiences of the unnamed cat with the environments in which the other cats live?

LANGUAGE

1. Why is it significant that the cat does not have a name? What would you name it and why?

2. How do the schoolmaster's diary entries provide an interior view that makes him a more sympathetic character?

3. If you don't know the meaning of the following words, look them up: parched (12), mullet (16), panorama (24), lacquer-like (26), rickshawman (36), coup de grace (54), geisha (57), debauchee (57).

SUGGESTIONS FOR WRITING

1. **Critical Writing.** How does a family's life change after the family acquires a pet?

2. To what extent do pets allow people to make comments to each other that they otherwise could not directly express?

3. What could your pet say about you that no one else knows? Write a short **narrative** account.

4. What actions did a pet of yours or a friend's pet take that you believe manifested consciousness, motivation, and intelligence?

5. **Thematic Links.** What picture do you get of Japanese society from this story and from Kyoko Mori's essay "Polite Lies" (Chapter 8, "Classification and Division")?

▬▬ STUDENT ESSAY: DESCRIPTION

The following essay by Peter Granderson offers an effective example of an objective description based on an assignment that asked students to describe a place that made a strong impression. The annotations on Granderson's paper and the follow-up commentary ("Strategies") are designed to help you understand the pattern of description.

Granderson 1

Iwakuni: Truly Unique

Peter Granderson

1   Glistening water trickles down a small stream overhung with bamboo and lined with drooping grass. A lady clatters by on a rickety bicycle, squealing the brakes with one hand while she presses a cell phone to her ear with the other as she chatters continuously in Japanese. She slowly winds down the road toward a cluster of tile-roofed houses nestled in the bottom of the valley. Iwakuni, Japan, is different in almost every way possible from what Americans are familiar with—wide streets, spacious yards, pick-up trucks, etc. But the city's uniqueness is what makes it a fascinating place to visit.

Introduction creates the context—a visit to Iwakuni, Japan

Thesis statement (dominant impression)

2   Iwakuni rests on the southern tip of the main island of Japan, just below Hiroshima. To the east is the glimmering Inland Sea, spotted along its horizon with tiny islands. On the west rise green-carpeted mountains. Stretched along the coast, Iwakuni has quick access to forest, lakes, rivers, and beaches.

Granderson 2

3   Iwakuni, while being a fairly large city, still maintains many

features of a quaint village. Along the outskirts, rice fields and

acreage of lotus plants blanket the valleys. Individual families

living in the city own most of the farms. Deeper within the city,

the small houses with their tiny yards are squeezed tightly

together, split only by narrow streets that wind between them.

Carefully pruned bushes wall in the yards, and vines stretch over

the gates. Cars, vans, and trucks, shrunk to a miniature scale,

weave their way along the streets like ants.

> Details convey a sense of place.

4   In downtown Iwakuni the streets are wider and are lined

with businesses, parking garages, movie theaters, and department

stores. Even familiar places such as McDonald's and 7-Eleven

are featured. Crowds of Japanese, sprinkled with an occasional

American, wander the covered sidewalks. Buses and taxis

continually stream by, dropping people off, and trains arrive

periodically to dump floods of people out of the station doors.

Food stands selling fried fish, Coca-Cola, and Ritz crackers pepper

any open area. Tucked between the stores are restaurants selling

a variety of pork, steak, and fish, which is often served raw.

Theaters downtown show a schedule of movies consisting mostly

of American films. Some sections of the streets are covered to

create a sort of mall. Clothing, electronic, and music stores spill out

onto the street, ready to sell their goods to anyone who passes by.

> Details emphasize sights and sounds.

5   There are enough scenic locations around Iwakuni to satisfy the

most demanding tourist. A few miles north is Myajima Island. The

island juts abruptly out of the ocean, reaching an altitude of several

thousand feet. Featuring an old traditional village complete with Torii

gate, Myajima is definitely an all-day event. To the west of Iwakuni

lies the Kintai Bridge. Made in the nineteenth century, the multi-arched

bridge is truly a study in culture and architecture. A steady stream of

people in bright traditional clothing drifts across the weather-worn

planks of the bridge that spans the rushing water. High on the tip of

a mountain nearby, an oriental castle sits overlooking the valley. A

cable car glides slowly up the face of the mountain, carrying a flock

of camera-toting tourists toward the castle.

> Description conveys sense of movement and includes spatial details.

Granderson 3

6   Iwakuni is both rich in history, having existed for hundreds of years, and rich in technology, being part of one of the most modern countries in the world. With its marvelous natural beauty and fascinating architecture, quaint shops, and huge department stores, Iwakuni is an incredible place to visit—truly unique.

> Conclusion echoes main idea or dominant impression in the introduction.

Strategies for Writing Essays in Description

1. Dominant Impression

Granderson's description of a place that has a special meaning for him focuses on the unique features of Iwakuni, a town on the southern tip of Japan that still has the appeal and feeling of a village while being a modern city.

2. Details That Support the Dominant Impression

Granderson uses details that make his readers aware of what he is seeing and feeling as he includes sharply etched memorable images of sights and sounds. He describes rice fields around the city; quaint neighborhoods with small, well-kept homes; a bustling, lively downtown; beautiful land-scapes; and traditional architecture that is popular with tourists.

3. Organization

Granderson's purpose in writing this essay is to allow his readers to share the experience of vis-iting a place that is important to him. He makes it easy for the reader to accompany him by using a straightforward structure, beginning with the way in which this particular town differs from cities that are familiar to Americans. His essay leads readers through the city, observing sights and sounds on the way, and culminates in a visit to scenic landscapes outside the city, including Myajima Island and the Kintai Bridge. Granderson concludes his essay by underscoring the traditional yet modern nature of Iwakuni that makes it unique.

4. Picturesque Language and Varying Sentence Structure

By describing Iwakuni and its environs using vivid images that appeal to the senses ("glistening water trickles down a small stream"; "a lady clatters by on a rickety bicycle, squealing the brakes with one hand"; "green-carpeted mountains") Granderson conveys the sense of being drawn into an ancient culture that thrives in the modern world. He also enhances the descriptive effect of his essay by varying the length and structure of his sentences.

5. Revision

Without realizing it, Granderson has slipped into a pattern of beginning paragraphs in the early part of his paper with "Iwakuni." This could become monotonous and could easily be corrected.

Guidelines for Writing an Essay in Description

- If your assignment requires you to describe something, does your essay focus on a dominant impression and communicate your thesis? If you are writing a subjective description, have you included imagery and sensory details that will help your reader to share your feelings? If you are writing an objective description, have you included informative details that will allow the reader to clearly picture what you are describing?

- Have you organized your details so as to communicate your dominant impression and support your thesis? Does each section or paragraph of your essay have a clear focus and transitional words or phrases that guide your reader? Paragraphs can be organized by using a spatial order (near to far, top to bottom), chronologically (over time), or dramatically (from least striking to most striking).

- Details that support the dominant impression should be vivid and concrete rather than vague and abstract. Have you varied your sentence structure from a predictable subject-verb pattern in interesting ways?

Grammar Tips for Description

To make your descriptions as effective as possible, you will want to use language that is specific, concrete, vivid, and imaginative and use modifiers that clearly refer to the words they describe. While abstractions are useful to generalize about experience, concrete language allows readers to experience what you are describing almost as if they were there with you.

Concrete language appeals to the senses of sight, sound, touch, taste, and smell; and specific details focus the audience's attention on the experience you wish to convey. For example:

Concrete

Stooped over under the weight of their enormous backpacks, the students could barely climb the steep narrow stairs.

Abstract

The encumbered students struggled to climb the stairs.

Modifiers (that is, words and phrases describing people, places, and things) should be placed directly next to the word they modify. For example:

Correctly Placed Modifiers

The young man in a blue suit was walking the dog.

Misplaced or Dangling Modifiers

The young man was walking the dog in a blue suit.

Checklist for Revising Descriptive Essays

- Have you provided a clear, dominant impression and communicated this in your thesis statement?
- Are you writing an objective description that conveys your subject through exact terms?
- Alternatively, are you writing a subjective description that uses figurative language to convey a state of mind?
- Do your descriptive details appeal to the senses?
- Are your details organized to support your dominant impression and your thesis?
- Do your transitional words and phrases make it easy for the reader to experience your description?

ADDITIONAL WRITING ASSIGNMENTS AND ACTIVITIES

COMMUNICATING WITH DIFFERENT AUDIENCES

1. Write a letter to a company proposing a new slogan, design, and ad copy for one of their products or services.
2. Write a letter to a network suggesting a television show that does not now exist that you would like to see.

WRITING FOR A NEWSPAPER

1. Write an editorial that would appear in a newspaper in which you describe things that you believe ruin the landscape, such as billboards.
2. Write a column for your college newspaper describing a memorable event, replete with details that help the reader to imagine the scene.

DESCRIPTIVE ESSAYS

1. Describe a recent item you purchased to replace one that has become obsolete or has gone out of style and the social pressures and marketing strategies that made you want to replace it.
2. Make up an imaginary shopping list of everything you would buy if money were no object. What are the items, and why would you buy them?

3. Describe the kitschiest (tackiest) object you have ever seen or owned.

4. Describe an interesting and effective window display in a store in a local mall.

5. Describe a vivid dream that you have had. Speculate on what this dream might mean.

6. Write your own restaurant review, using picturesque terms that capture the atmosphere, menu, and other details of the location.

7. Describe the first outfit you remember having worn for the first day of school or an important celebration or religious holiday.

8. Describe an outfit worn by a pet, yours or someone else's.

9. Describe items of clothing that are unintentionally funny according to the context in which they are worn—for example, bow ties.

10. Describe the distinctive features of clothing in different regions of the world as an expression of climate and culture—for example, saris in India, sarongs in Malaysia.

11. Describe a wedding you would plan for yourself or someone else, including all the details—wedding gown, bridesmaids' dresses, color schemes, food, and so on.

12. Describe your favorite outfit that really defines you.

13. If you were to prune shrubbery into a shape, describe what it would be.

14. If you could create a new species of animal, describe what it would look like and its habitat, mating habits, preferred food, and new name.

15. Describe your very favorite place in the whole world in such detail that your readers will feel as though they are there.

16. Describe a utopian culture in which you would like to live, including details about its environment and social customs.

17. If you created a blog with a unique name, describe it and its significance.

18. What electronic community are you part of—for example, MySpace.com—and what social relationships has it created for you?

19. What gestures, expressions, and tone of voice do you use to judge whether someone is lying?

20. Describe a local or regional team and the way in which the uniforms, insignias, and logos create a distinctive identity.

21. Describe a dog or cat show or 4-H event with full details that place your reader at the scene.

22. Create a profile of your favorite sports figure, and provide enough details to achieve a balanced portrait.

23. If your picture were to appear on the cover of a national magazine, what would this magazine be and for what are you famous?

24. Describe an object with which you associate your parents or grandparents.

25. Describe a person you associate with a particular place.

RESEARCH SUGGESTIONS

1. How do novels written in the eighteenth or nineteenth century use description of material goods to enhance their readers' middle-class aspirations—for example, *Tom Jones, Emma, Vanity Fair,* or *Great Expectations*?

2. Describe the masks and costumes that are worn during Mardi Gras and the legends, myths, and characters that are depicted.

3. Do some research, including at your local town hall or library, on the origin and significance of the name of a natural feature such as a river or mountain near where you live that reflects local history, patterns of settlement, and migration.

COLLABORATIVE ACTIVITY

Describe a commonplace object as if it were an unfamiliar cultural artifact that you had unearthed. Speculate about its function and what it tells you about the culture—for example, roller blades, refrigerator, toilet, or piano.

EXEMPLIFICATION

5

Discovering Culture Through Examples

Good examples are an essential part of effective writing. A single well-chosen example or range of illustrations, introduced by "for example" or "for instance," can provide clear cases that document, substantiate, or illustrate the writer's ideas.

Judith Ortiz Cofer, a poet and novelist, cites a number of examples in "The Myth of the Latin Woman" to illustrate the stereotypes to which Hispanic woman are subjected:

> Mixed cultural signals have perpetuated certain stereotypes—for example, that of the Hispanic woman as the "hot tamale" or sexual firebrand. It is a one-dimensional view that the media have found easy to promote. In their special vocabulary, advertisers have designated "sizzling" and "smoldering" as the adjectives of choice for describing not only the foods but also the women of Latin America.

Well-chosen examples are useful when writers wish to show the nature and character of a whole group through individual cases. In "Advertisements for Oneself," Lance Morrow uses examples of different types of acronyms and euphemisms to illustrate the shorthand that people use in personal ads to communicate a great deal of information about themselves in a few words:

> There are poetic conventions and clichés and codes in composing a personal ad. One specifies DWF (divorced white female), SBM (single black male), GWM (gay white male) and so on, to describe marital status, race, sex. Readers should understand the euphemisms. "Zaftig" or "Rubenesque," for example, usually means fat. "Unpretentious" is liable to mean boring. "Sensuous" means the party likes sex.

179

The messages quoted here represent thousands of personal ads that use similar means of communication. Throughout the essay, Morrow illustrates important points by using examples that clearly show how different kinds of personal ads are designed according to the particular needs of the writers.

Journalists and social scientists often use typical case histories to represent classes or groups of people. Daniela Deane uses this technique in her account of the effects of China's one-child policy in "The Little Emperors":

> Another mother wanted her 16-year-old to eat some fruit, but the teen-ager was engrossed in a video game. Not wanting him to get his fingers sticky or daring to interrupt, she peeled several grapes and popped one after another into his mouth. "Not so fast," he snapped. "Can't you see I have to spit out the seeds?"
>
> Stories like these are routinely published in China's newspapers, evidence that the government-imposed birth-control policy has produced an emerging generation of spoiled, lazy, selfish, self-centered and overweight children.

By selecting typical case histories to represent the new generation of only children in China, Deane brings a human dimension to a shift in values that otherwise might remain an abstraction. Exemplification is effective in allowing Deane's readers to generalize from the short profile she presents to what is characteristic of the "40 million only children in China."

Raymonde Carroll, a cultural anthropologist, frequently uses in-depth interviews as examples of contemporary French and American attitudes toward repairing or replacing loaned items that have been unintentionally damaged. In "Minor Accidents," Carroll elicited responses from a French friend, who broke a typewriter he borrowed from her, which typify the views of the French toward such incidences:

> B, from Paris, returns the typewriter he borrowed from me, and, wearing the mischievous smile of a naughty child who knows he will be excused, tells me, "You know, your typewriter was very mean to me, it must not like me very much because it was skipping letters constantly. . . . I had to be very careful as I typed."

We learn that the French, unlike Americans, treat minor accidents as being the fault of the owner of the item they damaged and react to these accidents with jokes that reproach the owner. Carroll shows us—through a wealth of details and insights into the reasoning behind the reactions of the French to minor accidents—that we do not have an accurate picture of this custom. In-depth interviews are a useful technique because results that are gained from one interview can be accepted as typical of most members in the group being studied.

Exemplification is especially useful as a technique for bringing abstract concepts into a form that can be clearly understood. Although the idea of "social time" might be difficult to grasp at first, Robert Levine and Ellen Wolff, the writers of "Social Time: The Heartbeat of Culture," use an extended example to illustrate how the concept of time as people actually experience it differs from culture to culture:

> My journey started shortly after I accepted an appointment as visiting professor of psychology at the federal university in Niterói, Brazil, a midsized city across the bay from

Rio de Janeiro. As I left home for my first day of class, I asked someone the time. It was 9:05 a.m., which allowed me time to relax and look around the campus before my 10 o'clock lecture. After what I judged to be half an hour, I glanced at a clock I was passing. It said 10:20! In panic, I broke for the classroom, followed by gentle calls of "Hola, professor" and "Tudo bem, professor?" from unhurried students, many of whom I later realized, were my own. I arrived breathless to find an empty room.

Frantically, I asked a passerby the time. "Nine forty-five" was the answer. No, that couldn't be. I asked someone else. "Nine fifty-five." Another said: "Exactly 9:43." The clock in a nearby office read 3:15. I had learned my first lesson about Brazilians: Their timepieces are consistently inaccurate. And nobody minds.

The basic idea is that a country's sense of time is not measured by objective "clock time" but by the commonly understood pace of life. This extended example makes it possible for readers to understand the writers' thesis.

Illustrations may take a variety of forms, including case histories; single, multiple, or extended examples; and interesting anecdotes that make a point. For example, Geeta Kothari in "If You Are What You Eat, Then What Am I?" creates seventeen vignettes that illustrate how interconnected food and culture are for her family, newly emigrated from India:

Although she has never been able to tolerate the smell of fish, my mother buys the tuna, hoping to satisfy my longing for American food.

Indians, of course, do not eat such things.

Luisa Valenzuela, in "The Censors," tells the story of an idealistic young man who gradually loses his humanity when he takes a job as a government censor ("he applied simply to intercept his own letter, a consoling albeit unoriginal idea"). This anecdote communicates the corrosive effects of power.

Personal observations, especially those made by professionals in different fields of study, can help to substantiate a hypothesis, although a single example is rarely sufficient to support a generalization. Strong examples do not merely supplement the exploration of an idea but demonstrate its relevance in ways that readers are likely to find convincing.

For an illustration of the way in which exemplification can be used in a real-life situation, see a sample job application letter later in this chapter (pp. 231–232).

LANCE MORROW

Advertisements for Oneself

Lance Morrow (b. 1939) is a long time staff writer for *Time* magazine who received his undergraduate degree from Harvard in 1963. Morrow is a prolific writer with diverse interests ranging from personal themes, in such works as *Fishing in the Tiber* (1989) and *Heart: A Memoir* (1995), to philosophical and political inquiries, as in *Evil: An Investigation* (2003), *The Best Years of Their Lives* (2005), and *Second Drafts of History* (2006). In the following essay, Morrow tackles a personal aspect of contemporary society: the ads that people place in newspapers and magazines (and now online) to attract prospective mates. As a skilled writer, Morrow is especially attuned to the subtle connotations that the language of these ads display.

BEFORE YOU READ

What would you put in a personal ad about yourself, either in print or online?

■ ■ ▨

1   It is an odd and compact art form, and somewhat unnatural. A person feels quite uncomfortable composing a little song of himself for the classifieds. The personal ad is like haiku of self-celebration, a brief solo played on one's own horn. Someone else should be saying these things. It is for others to pile up the extravagant adjectives ("sensitive, warm, witty, vibrant, successful, handsome, accomplished, incredibly beautiful, cerebral, and sultry") while we stand demurely by. But someone has to do it. One competes for attention. One must advertise. One must chum the waters and bait the hook, and go trolling for love and laughter, for caring and sharing, for long walks and quiet talks, for Bach and brie. Nonsmokers only. Photo a must.

2   There are poetic conventions and clichés and codes in composing a personal ad. One specifies DWF (divorced white female), SBM (single black male), GWM (gay white male) and so on, to describe marital status, race, sex. Readers should understand the euphemisms. "Zaftig" or "Rubenesque," for example, usually means fat. "Unpretentious" is liable to mean boring. "Sensuous" means the party likes sex.

3   Sometimes the ads are quirkily self-conscious. "Ahem," began one suitor in the *New York Review of Books*. "Decent, softspoken sort, sanely silly, philosophish, seeks similar." Then he started to hit his stride: "Central Jersey DM WASP professional, 38, 6'2", slow hands, student of movies and Marx, gnosis and news, craves womanish companionship. . . ."

4   The sociology of personals has changed in recent years. One reason that people still feel uncomfortable with the form is that during the sixties and early seventies personal ads had a slightly sleazy connotation. They showed up in the back of underground newspapers and sex magazines, the little billboards

through which wife swappers and odd sexual specialists communicated. In the past several years, however, personal ads have become a popular and reputable way of shopping for new relationships. The *Chicago Tribune* publishes them. So does the conservative *National Review*, although a note from the publisher advises, "*NR* extends maximum freedom in this column, but *NR*'s maximum freedom may be another man's straitjacket. *NR* reserves the right to reject any copy deemed unsuitable." *National Review* would likely have turned down a West Coast entreaty: "Kinky Boy Scout seeks Kinky Girl Scout to practice knots. Your rope or mine?" *National Review*'s personals are notably chaste, but so are those in most other magazines. The emphasis is on "traditional values," on "long-term relationships" and "nest building." The sexual revolution has cooled down to a domestic room temperature. The raciest item might call for a woman with "Dolly Parton-like figure." One ad in Los Angeles stated: "Branflake patent holder tired of money and what it can buy seeks intellectual stimulation from big-bosomed brunette. Photo please." The *Village Voice* rejected the language of a man who wanted a woman with a "big ass." A few days later the man returned with an ad saying he sought a "callipygian" woman.

5   Every week *New York* magazine publishes five or six pages of personals. The *New York Review of Books* publishes column after column of some of the most entertaining personals. Many of them are suffused with a soft-focus romanticism. Firelight plays over the fantasy. Everyone seems amazingly successful. The columns are populated by Ph.D.s. Sometimes one encounters a millionaire. Occasionally a satirical wit breaks the monotony: "I am DWM, wino, no teeth, smell bad, age 40—look 75. Live in good cardboard box in low-traffic alley. You are under 25, tall, sophisticated, beautiful, talented, financially secure, and want more out of life. Come fly with me."

6   Humor helps, especially in a form that usually gives off a flat glare of one-dimensional optimism. It is hard not to like the "well read, well shaped, well disposed widow, early sixties, not half bad in the dusk with the light behind me." She sought a "companionable, educated, professional man of wit and taste," and she probably deserved him. Her self-effacement is fairly rare in personals. The ads tend sometimes to be a little nervous and needing, and anxiously hyperbolic. Their rhetoric tends to get overheated and may produce unintended effects. A man's hair stands on end a bit when he encounters "Alarmingly articulate, incorrigibly witty, overeducated, but extremely attractive NYC woman." A female reader of *New York* magazine might enjoy a chuckling little shudder at this: "I am here! A caring, knowing, daffy, real, tough, vulnerable, and handsome brown-eyed psychoanalyst." One conjures up the patient on the couch and a Freudian in the shape of Daffy Duck shouting: "You're desPICable!"

7   The struggle in composing one's ad is to be distinctive and relentlessly self-confident. What woman could resist the "rugged rascal with masculine determined sensual viewpoint"? An ad should not overreach, however, like the woman who began: "WANTED: One Greek god of refined caliber."

8   Not all the ads are jaunty or dewy-eyed. One begins: "Have herpes?" Some are improbably specialized: "Fishing Jewish woman over 50 seeks single man to

share delights of angling." Or: "Literate snorkeler . . . have room in my life for one warm, secure, funny man."

9   Anyone composing a personal ad faces an inherent credibility problem. While we are accustomed to the self-promotions of politicians, say, we sense something bizarre when ordinary people erupt in small rhapsodies of self-celebration that are occasioned by loneliness and longing. One is haunted by almost piteous cries that come with post office-box number attached: "Is there anyone out there? Anyone out there for me?"

10   Composing an ad with oneself as the product is an interesting psychological exercise, and probably good training in self-assertion. Truth will endure a little decorative writing, perhaps. The personals are a form of courtship that is more efficient, and easier on the liver, than sitting in bars night after night, hoping for a luck encounter. Yet one feels sometimes a slightly disturbed and forlorn vibration in those columns of chirpy pleading. It is inorganic courtship. There is something severed, a lost connection. One may harbor a buried resentment that there are not parents and aunts and churches and cotillions to arrange the meetings in more seemly style.

11   That, of course, may be mere sentimentalism. Whatever works. Loneliness is the Great Satan. Jane Austen, who knew everything about courtship, would have understood the personals columns perfectly. Her novel *Emma*, in fact,

How does this billboard posted by a Shanghainese woman in Sydney in 2004 (for a cost of $3200) illustrate the personal ads discussed by Morrow?

begins, "Emma Woodhouse, handsome, happy, clever, and rich, with a comfortable home and happy disposition." The line might go right into the *New York Review of Books*.

■ ■ ▨

MEANING

1. What different kinds of personal ads does Morrow identify, and what needs underlie each category?
2. Because personal ads are so short, what stylistic strategies are necessary to communicate a lot of information in a few words?
3. What are the most important attributes of an effective personal ad?
4. Why does Morrow believe that "the sexual revolution has cooled down to a domestic room temperature"?

TECHNIQUE

1. Which of Morrow's examples did you find especially well suited to illustrate how people choose to market themselves in personal ads?
2. How does Morrow's analysis illustrate his claim that ads are forms of self-promotion and, as Morrow says, "small rhapsodies of self-celebration"?
3. **Other Patterns.** Where does Morrow emphasize the **narrative** aspects that make personal ads stories about the writer?

LANGUAGE

1. Why are connotations of words particularly important in terms of the signals being sent?
2. In what way is the language used in these ads different from the usual interchanges between men and women?
3. Which words indicate romantic interests, which suggest intellectual interests, and which suggest that the advertiser is looking for a friend or someone to talk to?
4. If you don't know the meanings of the following words, look them up: *haiku* (1), *euphemisms* (2), *quirkily* (3), *callipygian* (4), *incorrigibly* (6).

SUGGESTIONS FOR WRITING

1. What set of circumstances might lead you to put a personal ad in a newspaper or magazine or on an online service? What would the ad say?
2. **Critical Writing.** Write an essay exploring how this theme is dramatized in the 1998 film *You've Got Mail*.
3. For a group activity, compose an ad for yourself, switch ads among class members, and try to identify who wrote which particular ad.

4. If your parents were to write an ad for you in an attempt to get you married, what would it say and how would it differ from the ad you would compose? **Describe** each version and **compare** them to each other.

5. *Thematic Links.* If Simone de Beauvoir (see "The Married Woman" in Chapter 10, "Definition") were to create a personal ad, what would it say?

The Myth of the Latin Woman: I Just Met a Girl Named Maria

Judith Ortiz Cofer (b. 1952) is a popular poet, essayist, and novelist whose work reflects Hispanic and feminist themes. She was born in Puerto Rico and received her education in the United States and at Oxford University. Cofer is a prolific writer; her recent collections include *Woman in Front of the Sun: On Becoming a Writer* (2001), *The Meaning of Consuelo* (2003), *Call Me Maria: A Novel* (2004), and *A Love Story Beginning in Spanish: Poems* (2005). The following essay was first published in *The Latin Deli: Prose and Poetry* (1993). In it, she describes instances of ethnic stereotyping and explains the cultural gap between customs in Puerto Rico and the United States that triggers these misperceptions.

BEFORE YOU READ

Do people judge you according to your ethnicity before they get to know you?

■ ■ ▨

1   On a bus trip to London from Oxford University where I was earning some graduate credits one summer, a young man, obviously fresh from a pub, spotted me and as if struck by inspiration went down on his knees in the aisle. With both hands over his heart he broke into an Irish tenor's rendition of "Maria" from *West Side Story*.[1] My politely amused fellow passengers gave his lovely voice the round of gentle applause it deserved. Though I was not quite as amused, I managed my version of an English smile: no show of teeth, no extreme contortions of the facial muscles—I was at this time of my life practicing reserve and cool. Oh, that British control, how I coveted it. But "Maria" had followed me to London, reminding me of a prime fact of my life: you can leave the island, master the English language, and travel as far as you can, but if you are a Latina, especially one like me who so obviously belongs to Rita Moreno's gene pool, the island travels with you.

2   This is sometimes a very good thing—it may win you that extra minute of someone's attention. But with some people, the same things can make *you* an island—not a tropical paradise but an Alcatraz, a place nobody wants to visit. As a Puerto Rican girl living in the United States and wanting like most children to "belong," I resented the stereotype that my Hispanic appearance called forth from many people I met.

3   Growing up in a large urban center in New Jersey during the 1960s, I suffered from what I think of as "cultural schizophrenia." Our life was designed by my parents as a microcosm of their *casas* on the island. We spoke in Spanish,

---

[1] *West Side Story:* a musical (1957) by Leonard Bernstein and Arthur Laurents, which featured the song "I Just Met a Girl Named Maria."

ate Puerto Rican food bought at the *bodega*, and practiced strict Catholicism at a church that allotted us a one-hour slot each week for mass, performed in Spanish by a Chinese priest trained as a missionary for Latin America.

4   As a girl I was kept under strict surveillance by my parents, since my virtue and modesty were, by their cultural equation, the same as their honor. As a teenager I was lectured constantly on how to behave as a proper *señorita*. But it was a conflicting message I received, since the Puerto Rican mothers also encouraged their daughters to look and act like women and to dress in clothes our Anglo friends and their mothers found too "mature" and flashy. The difference was, and is, cultural; yet I often felt humiliated when I appeared at an American friend's party wearing a dress more suitable to a semi-formal than to a playroom birthday celebration. At Puerto Rican festivities, neither the music nor the colors we wore could be too loud.

5   I remember Career Day in our high school, when teachers told us to come dressed as if for a job interview. It quickly became obvious that to the Puerto Rican girls "dressing up" meant wearing their mother's ornate jewelry and clothing, more appropriate (by mainstream standards) for the company Christmas party than as daily office attire. That morning I had agonized in front of my closet, trying to figure out what a "career girl" would wear. I knew how to dress for school (at the Catholic school I attended, we all wore uniforms), I knew how to dress for Sunday mass, and I knew what dresses to wear for parties at my relatives' homes. Though I do not recall the precise details of my Career Day outfit, it must have been a composite of these choices. But I remember a comment my friend (an Italian American) made in later years that coalesced my impressions of that day. She said that at the business school she was attending, the Puerto Rican girls always stood out for wearing "everything at once." She meant, of course, too much jewelry, too many accessories. On that day at school we were simply made the negative models by the nuns, who were themselves not credible fashion experts to any of us. But it was painfully obvious to me that to the others, in their tailored skirts and silk blouses, we must have seemed "hopeless" and "vulgar." Though I now know that most adolescents feel out of step much of the time, I also know that for the Puerto Rican girls of my generation that sense was intensified. The way our teachers and classmates looked at us that day in school was just a taste of the cultural clash that awaited us in the real world, where prospective employers and men on the street would often misinterpret our tight skirts and jingling bracelets as a "come-on."

6   Mixed cultural signals have perpetuated certain stereotypes—for example, that of the Hispanic woman as the "hot tamale" or sexual firebrand. It is a one-dimensional view that the media have found easy to promote. In their special vocabulary, advertisers have designated "sizzling" and "smoldering" as the adjectives of choice for describing not only the foods but also the women of Latin America. From conversations in my house I recall hearing about the harassment that Puerto Rican women endured in factories where the "boss-men" talked to them as if sexual innuendo was all they understood, and worse, often gave them the choice of submitting to their advances or being fired.

7   It is custom, however, not chromosomes, that leads us to choose scarlet over pale pink. As young girls, it was our mothers who influenced our decisions about clothes and colors—mothers who had grown up on a tropical island where the natural environment was a riot of primary colors, where showing your skin was one way to keep cool as well as to look sexy. Most important of all, on the island, women perhaps felt freer to dress and move more provocatively since, in most cases, they were protected by the traditions, mores, and laws of a Spanish/ Catholic system of morality and machismo whose main rule was: *You may look at my sister, but if you touch her I will kill you.* The extended family and church structure could provide a young woman with a circle of safety in her small pueblo on the island; if a man "wronged" a girl, everyone would close in to save her family honor.

8   My mother has told me about dressing in her best party clothes on Saturday nights and going to the town's plaza to promenade with her girlfriends in front of the boys they liked. The males were thus given an opportunity to admire the women and to express their admiration in the form of *piropos:* erotically charged street poems they composed on the spot. (I have myself been subjected to a few *piropos* while visiting the island, and they can be outrageous, although custom dictates that they must never cross into obscenity.) This ritual, as I understand it, also entails a show of studied indifference on the woman's part; if she is "decent," she must not acknowledge the man's impassioned words. So I do understand how things can be lost in translation. When a Puerto Rican girl dressed in her idea of what is attractive meets a man from the mainstream culture who has been trained to react to certain types of clothing as a sexual signal, a clash is likely to take place. I remember the boy who took me to my first formal dance leaning over to plant a sloppy, over-eager kiss painfully on my mouth; when I didn't respond with sufficient passion, he remarked resentfully: "I thought you Latin girls were supposed to mature early," as if I were expected to *ripen* like a fruit or vegetable, not just grow into womanhood like other girls.

9   It is surprising to my professional friends that even today some people, including those who should know better, still put others "in their place." It happened to me most recently during a stay at a classy metropolitan hotel favored by young professional couples for weddings. Late one evening after the theater, as I walked toward my room with a colleague (a woman with whom I was coordinating an arts program), a middle-aged man in a tuxedo, with a young girl in satin and lace on his arm, stepped directly into our path. With his champagne glass extended toward me, he exclaimed "Evita!"[2]

10   Our way blocked, my companion and I listened as the man half-recited, half-bellowed "Don't Cry for Me, Argentina." When he finished, the young girl said: "How about a round of applause for my daddy?" We complied, hoping this would bring the silly spectacle to a close. I was becoming aware that our little group

---

[2] *Evita:* a musical about Eva Duarte de Perón, the former first lady of Argentina, opened on Broadway in 1979; "Don't Cry for Me, Argentina" is a song from the musical.

was attracting the attention of the other guests. "Daddy" must have perceived this too, and he once more barred the way as we tried to walk past him. He began to shout-sing a ditty to the tune of "La Bamba"—except the lyrics were about a girl named Maria whose exploits rhymed with her name and gonorrhea. The girl kept saying "Oh, Daddy" and looking at me with pleading eyes. She wanted me to laugh along with the others. My companion and I stood silently waiting for the man to end his offensive song. When he finished, I looked not at him but at his daughter. I advised her calmly never to ask her father what he had done in the army. Then I walked between them and to my room. My friend complimented me on my cool handling of the situation, but I confessed that I had really wanted to push the jerk into the swimming pool. This same man—probably a corporate executive, well-educated, even worldly by most standards—would not have been likely to regale an Anglo woman with a dirty song in public. He might have checked his impulse by assuming that she could be somebody's wife or mother, or at least *somebody* who might take offense. But, to him, I was just an Evita or a Maria: merely a character in his cartoon-populated universe.

11   Another facet of the myth of the Latin woman in the United States is the menial, the domestic—Maria the housemaid or countergirl. It's true that work as domestics, as waitresses, and in factories is all that's available to women with little English and few skills. But the myth of the Hispanic menial—the funny maid, mispronouncing words and cooking up a spicy storm in a shiny California kitchen—has been perpetuated by the media in the same way that "Mammy" from *Gone with the Wind* became America's idea of the black woman for generations. Since I do not wear my diplomas around my neck for all to see, I have on occasion been sent to that "kitchen" where some think I obviously belong.

12   One incident has stayed with me, though I recognize it as a minor offense. My first public poetry reading took place in Miami, at a restaurant where a luncheon was being held before the event. I was nervous and excited as I walked in with notebook in hand. An older woman motioned me to her table, and thinking (foolish me) that she wanted me to autograph a copy of my newly published slender volume of verse, I went over. She ordered a cup of coffee from me, assuming that I was the waitress. (Easy enough to mistake my poems for menus, I suppose.) I know it wasn't an intentional act of cruelty. Yet of all the good things that happened later, I remember that scene most clearly, because it reminded me of what I had to overcome before anyone would take me seriously. In retrospect I understand that my anger gave my reading fire. In fact, I have almost always taken any doubt in my abilities as a challenge, the result most often being the satisfaction of winning a convert, of seeing the cold, appraising eyes warm to my words, the body language change, the smile that indicates I have opened some avenue for communication. So that day as I read, I looked directly at that woman. Her lowered eyes told me she was embarrassed at her faux pas, and when I willed her to look up at me, she graciously allowed me to punish her with my full attention. We shook hands at the end of the reading

and I never saw her again. She has probably forgotten the entire incident, but maybe not.

13   Yet I am one of the lucky ones. There are thousands of Latinas without the privilege of an education or the entrees into society that I have. For them life is a constant struggle against the misconceptions perpetuated by the myth of the Latina. My goal is to try to replace the old stereotypes with a much more interesting set of realities. Every time I give a reading, I hope the stories I tell, the dreams and fears I examine in my work, can achieve some universal truth that will get my audience past the particulars of my skin color, my accent, or my clothes.

14   I once wrote a poem in which I called all Latinas "God's brown daughters." This poem is really a prayer of sorts, offered upward, but also, through the human-to-human channel of art, outward. It is a prayer for communication and for respect. In it, Latin women pray "in Spanish to an Anglo God / with a Jewish heritage," and they are "fervently hoping / that if not omnipotent, / at least He be bilingual."

MEANING

1. What characteristics define, from Cofer's perspective, the "Maria" stereotype in terms of style, clothes, and behavior?
2. How has this stereotype been a source of discomfort for Cofer personally?
3. Why was the episode of her first public poetry reading such a distressing one?
4. Why is it important to understand the cultural gap between what is considered permissible dress for girls growing up in Puerto Rico and in New Jersey?

TECHNIQUE

1. How do the instances of ethnic stereotyping described by Cofer illustrate her thesis and enable her readers to better understand what she condemns?
2. What aspects of Cofer's essay enable the reader to understand why behavior that is considered normal in one culture is considered provocative in another?
3. How are the instances in which she is serenaded on a bus in England and on another occasion treated to a rendition of "Don't Cry for Me, Argentina" indicative of how Cofer is stereotyped?
4. **Other Patterns.** How does Cofer frame her lifelong battle with the Latina stereotype as a personal **narrative**?

LANGUAGE

1. To what extent does the skill with which Cofer uses language and her self-deprecating wit disprove the "myth of the Latin woman"?

2. How would you characterize Cofer's tone in this essay (e.g., justifiably outraged, defensive)?

3. If you don't know the meaning of the following words, look them up: *Alcatraz* (2), *bodega* (3), *señorita* (4), *innuendo* (5).

SUGGESTIONS FOR WRITING

1. **Critical Writing.** In a short essay, discuss the psychological mechanisms that are involved in stereotyping. Why do stereotypes often magnify unflattering characteristics rather than positive ones?

2. Using Cofer's essay as a model, write a few paragraphs on the "Myth of the _____ Woman (or Man)."

3. Have you ever been stereotyped? If so, **describe** an instance, and tell what steps, if any, you took to correct this misimpression.

4. **Thematic Links.** Compare the messages Cofer received from her mother in Puerto Rico with those given to the daughter in Jamaica Kincaid's story "Girl," in Chapter 7, "Process Analysis."

RAYMONDE CARROLL

Minor Accidents

Raymonde Carroll is an anthropologist and scholar who specializes in cross-cultural mis-understandings. She was born in Tunisia, was educated in France and the United States, and conducted research in Micronesia, in the Pacific east of the Philippines, for an extended period. Carroll has taught at Oberlin College for many years. The following selection, drawn from her book *Cultural Misunderstandings: The French-American Experience* (1988), reveals a profound difference in cultural assumptions that come into play when damage to personal property occurs.

BEFORE YOU READ

How can material objects get in the way of friendships?

■ ■ ▨

1   A commercial on American television shows a mother and daughter (twelve or thirteen years old) trying to resolve the problem of a stain on a blouse. The daughter is frantic; her mother promises to do her best to help her. Thanks to a miracle detergent, the blouse is returned to its former beautiful state. In order to understand the depth of the crisis resolved by the detergent in question, one must know that the stained blouse does not belong to the girl on the screen but to her older sister, who lent it to her. The situation is serious enough for the mother to enter the picture, and for us to be relieved (and thankful for the magic detergent) when the blouse, unharmed, is put in its proper place just before the arrival of its owner, who, as it turns out, wants to wear it that very evening. The crisis has been averted; the heroines smile.

2   Things are not so rosy in the "Dear Abby" column, which millions of Americans read every day in the newspaper. The same problem often appears in many forms: "X borrowed my thingamajig, returned it damaged, and offered neither to replace it nor to repair it. What should I do?"

3   Are Americans frightened by their older siblings (the first case), or incapable of resolving the slightest problem (the second case)? The list of "adjectives" and of "explanations" can go on, according to one's tastes and culture. What interests me here is the fact that in both "cases" there was a "minor accident." In the first case, the "guilty" party knows what to do while in the second the "victim" does not know what to do, which indicates that an expectation was not met.

4   For a French person, it is likely that both cases would serve as additional proof of the "keen sense of proprietorship characteristic of Americans." But why lend one's property if one feels that way about it? It seems, here again, that the nature of the problem lies elsewhere. Before going any further, however, it would be useful to review a few French cases of "minor accidents." Some of these cases are taken from personal experience. They seemed completely "normal" to the

French woman in me but slightly "strange" to the anthropologist in me, who considered them with a voluntarily "foreign" eye.

5   F (a French woman), her husband, and her daughter, who are preparing to leave a party, are standing in the foyer saying goodbye. As she leaves, F has a "minor accident": while putting on her coat, her hand brushes against a small painting, which, dislodged by the movement, falls to the ground. The lacquered wooden frame breaks, but the damage is reparable. F says to her host, from whom she was just taking leave: "Oh, sorry, I had a little accident." Then, suddenly joking: "But what an idea to put a painting in such a place! My word, you must have done it on purpose!" Not knowing what to do with the little painting which she now has in her hands, she turns it over, probably to examine the damage, and cries out joyously, "Oh, you see, it must have already been broken, since it has been glued." Upon saying this, she points to a piece of sticky paper which appears to have nothing to do with the frame itself. Everyone present clearly sees this, but they all act as if they hadn't noticed, and the host (who is French) hurriedly takes the painting from her and says "Don't worry about it, it's nothing, I'll take care of it." As F attempts to joke some more about the accident, her husband drags her toward the door, saying, "Listen, if you keep this up you'll never be invited here again." Everyone laughs. Exeunt all.

6   Not once did F offer to have the frame repaired. Rather, it seemed as if all her efforts tended toward minimizing the gravity of the accident by making a joke of it. She thus started recounting another incident: her daughter, when she was still a baby in her mother's arms, had unhooked a signed (she insists) plate from the wall behind her mother, and threw it onto the floor. "Well that was a real catastrophe, I didn't know what to do with myself . . ." In other words, the "truly" serious incident, that of the valuable (signed) plate, was the fault of the baby (and at the same time not her fault, since she was a baby?). In comparison, the incident with the frame appears (or should appear?) negligible.

7   Does the comparison of these two incidents also imply that F is not responsible either? Like the baby? The fact that she did not offer to repair the frame (which would be a recognition of her responsibility) seems to indicate that this is a plausible interpretation of this comparison. Of course, we can say that F was so embarrassed that in the second case, as in the first, she "didn't know what to do with herself" and that joking was a way to hide her embarrassment. But one can just as easily be sorry or embarrassed, and joke around to relax the atmosphere, while at the same time offering to repair the damage.

8   While at a party at the home of friends of her friends, D, twenty-two years old, Parisian, spills red wine (a full glass) on the carpet. She grabs a small paper napkin to wipe it up. The friend who had invited her quickly returns from the kitchen with enough paper towels to really soak up the large quantity of wine; someone else brings salt. D, while her friend is cleaning, says, "My God, L (the host) is not going to be happy . . . but can you imagine. . . . That's the trouble with light-colored carpeting, it's so difficult to clean!" D made an effort, although insufficient, to repair the damage. But her commentary is strangely similar to that of F. The "victim"

seems to be transformed into the truly responsible party, that is, into the person who is ultimately responsible for the accident: if the painting hadn't been placed there . . . if the carpet hadn't been chosen in such a light color . . .

9 Monsieur T, while visiting his son in the United States, discovers the existence of window shades, which are placed between the window panes and the curtains in the great majority of American homes and which serve to block out the sun. These shades are spring-loaded, which allows one to lower or raise them to any degree at will and thereby to adjust the quantity of light let in. In order to do this, one must learn to accompany the shade with one's hand, or else it winds itself up suddenly with a snap. The son demonstrates this for Monsieur T, insisting particularly on the fact that he must never release the shade and "let it roll up by itself" (which the French in the United States are endlessly tempted to do, even if they have been living here for more than twenty years, as I have). The next day, the son briefly reminds him of his instructions and only succeeds in exasperating Monsieur T ("Do you think I am a fool?"). A few days later, the son hears a snap, which sounds like a shot, followed by an exclamation. He runs over and finds his father in front of the window; as soon as he sees him come in, his father says, "This is horrible, you'd think you were in the devil's den. My word! Can't have a weak heart at your place. . . . It's not surprising that Americans all go to psychiatrists. . . . That gave me a terrible fright, and yet I did exactly as you said, I don't understand what happened."

10 L, twenty-eight years old, from the Bordeaux region, shares an apartment with V, approximately the same age, from Normandy. L burns one of her good saucepans while V is out. Upon V's return, L confesses, apologizes, and, in the course of her explanation adds, "because, you know, for me, a good saucepan or a bad saucepan are the same, because I'm not at all materialistic, I don't get attached to objects." In other words, if this is considered an "accident," it is only because it is V's nature to regret the loss of a simple saucepan, a mere object.

11 M, from Midi, lends his projector to S, who returns it, jammed, with these words: "Your projector is strange, it makes a funny noise." S later discovers a slide which is part of M's collection wedged in the slide mechanism.

12 S, from the Basque coast, borrows R's car, brings it back the next day, and asks with a sly smile: "Are you sure your car works well? Because it stalled twice. Once, I was even stuck in the middle of the road because I was trying to turn, and I was afraid a car would hit me." R, who is S's friend, adds, upon relating to me this incident: "S is a very nice guy, but he can't drive to save his life."

13 B, from Paris, returns the typewriter he borrowed from me, and, wearing the mischievous smile of a naughty child who knows he will be excused, tells me, "You know, your typewriter was very mean to me, it must not like me very much because it was skipping letters constantly. . . . I had to be very careful as I typed."

14 The preceding examples seem to indicate that French people do not offer to repair things when there has been an accident. Yet this is not the case. Among the cases I collected, offers to repair the damage were just as common as those

mentioned above. Thus L, who had already burned V's saucepan, had also, at another time, accidentally broken a hand-crafted pitcher which V had brought back from France. In this case, L, who did indeed understand the sentimental value of pitchers if not the material value of saucepans, offered, or rather promised, to replace the broken object ("I'll buy you one exactly like that"). Over a year later, V tells me, the pitcher had not been replaced, or even mentioned.

15   This same V, G tells me, borrowed an electronic, programmable calculator to do "a few simple calculations." The calculations were apparently too simple for the delicate mechanism of the instrument because it became "mysteriously" blocked. V offered to share the cost of repairing it with G, thus implying that there must have been something wrong with the machine before she borrowed it (or else she would have offered to pay all the costs). According to G, the cost of repairing it turned out to be so astronomical that he preferred to buy another inexpensive calculator, "just in case." In the meantime, according to G, V never mentioned sharing the costs and never asked for news of the wounded calculator. The last I heard, G and V are still friends.

16   A variation on this case consists of saying what one would have liked to do, but did not do, to repair an accident. For instance, a white tablecloth which K borrowed from a friend for a holiday meal was irreparably stained. "I thought of buying a tablecloth to replace yours, but I didn't know what you'd like," says K, several years after the accident. The friend asserts that she has never been compensated and that it never put their friendship on the line.

17   Finally, there are certain cases in which the repair was made. Yet the comments differ depending on whether one talks to the person who caused the "minor accident" and repaired the damage or to the person who was the "victim." I have on occasion heard the former say things such as "I paid a great deal to have a worthless rug cleaned," whereas the latter, whose car was dented and repaired by the friends who had borrowed it made the following comment: "Of course, they paid for the repairs, but now the car is totally ruined."

18   We might conclude from the preceding examples that the French break everything and repair or replace nothing. Certain French people think so, and, as a result, "do not lend anything to anyone" and "do not ask anything of anyone," because "they never give it back in the state you lent it." As we know from having learned La Fontaine's fables, "Madame Ant is slow to lend / The last thing, this, she suffers from."[1] But there are obviously many French people who do not hold this attitude, as is proven by the accident cases cited earlier. How then can we interpret the various ways in which the actors treated these accidents? As we have seen, the reactions ranged from playful jokes to reproachful jokes, and from reproachful jokes to disguised accusations. Offers of repairs were not made, made but never followed up on, mentioned as something one had thought of, or else made and followed up on but to no one's satisfaction.

---

[1] From "The Ant and the Grasshopper," in *A Hundred Fables from La Fontaine,* trans. Philip Wayne (Doubleday).

19   In other words, when I have a "minor accident," it is not really my fault. It is because an object was in a bad place (I might almost say "in my way"), because a carpet was too light to hide stains, because a machine was too delicate to function normally, because to have shades in a house is aberrant, and so on. In fact, I acted in all innocence and nothing would have happened if the others had correctly played their parts. It becomes clear that by joking and "taking things lightly," I place responsibility where it belongs, on the person who committed the error of poorly placing his painting, of choosing an insane color for a carpet, of buying an overly complicated calculator . . . and who, most of all, made the mistake of not sufficiently protecting his possession if he cared about it so much.

20   By pushing this logic to its extreme, I would say that when entertaining me, X runs the risk of having his good crystal broken if he chooses to use it ("accidents can happen") and that when lending me an object, he should warn me of its fragility. In fact, he should not lend, or put within my reach, an object which is fragile, and certainly not an object about which he cares a great deal. If he does this, X is obviously the one who should assume ultimate responsibility for the accident. Similarly, if I offer to repair or to pay for the damage ("tell me how much I owe you"), I have done my part, I have fulfilled my duty; it is up to X to request the necessary sum when required since I told him I would give it to him. Thus, I force the other to take responsibility for some of my acts, and in doing so I propose or reaffirm a relationship. If X refuses this relationship, he will never again invite me to his house or lend me anything more. And this does happen. But if X accepts the relationship, he reinforces it by placing more value on it than on the damaged object, as valuable as that object may be. Hence the "leave it, it's not important," which erases the accident. And as we more or less tacitly honor the same code, we each have a chance to be both victim and perpetrator of an accident, thus becoming linked to one another and affirming, sometimes against our wishes, the importance of these bonds.

21   Needless to say, an American would be completely baffled by such conduct. It is, in fact, this type of behavior that provokes the "Dear Abby" letters mentioned at the beginning of this chapter.

22   An informant described to me the "American general rule" as follows: "If I lend X my car, the minimum I can expect is that, before returning it, he will fill it with more gas than he consumed. If I lend him my car for a fairly long period, he will make a point of returning it to me in a better state than when I lent it to him (washed, waxed, vacuumed, etc.). He will not do this in order to point out my negligence but, in a sense, to repay me for my generosity. He will take responsibility for any necessary repairs, and I will hold him to this (unless it is an old wreck, in which case I would refuse to lend it to him so as to spare him some very predictable, but difficult to attribute, expenses)." Let us then look at some American cases, such as they have been reported to me.

23   At an elegant dinner, J breaks a crystal glass. She asks the hostess to lend her a glass of the same set, so that she can find a perfect replacement. The hostess honors her request.

24   P, fourteen or fifteen years old, meets a group of friends at D's house. They go to play basketball at the school basketball court and return, tired from the game, to D's house, where his mother serves them lunch. P, drawn without knowing why to a carafe on the buffet, picks up the stopper, which slips from his hands, falls back on the carafe, and chips it. P, confused, apologizes to D's mother for his clumsiness, and without hesitating offers to replace the carafe. P is over forty today, yet he remembers this scene very clearly. He remembers that at the very moment when he offered to replace the carafe he knew that he did not have, but would have to find, the necessary sum, and he also remembers that D's mother left him an escape route ("I'll let you know when I find one"), but not without her having expressed concern and regret over the accident. That is to say, according to him, D's mother was willing to be generous, but without diminishing P's responsibility.

25   A dinner with friends. M spills a glass of wine. His wife quickly runs to the kitchen, returns with the necessary products, and sponges up the wine—in short, does everything to repair the accident. M thanks his wife with a look of gratitude and apologizes for his clumsiness. Note: in this case, M's wife has repaired his clumsiness because she forms a couple with him and therefore shares responsibility for the accident, takes responsibility for it as well. This does not preclude the possibility that some couples have "sexist" habits, but it gives the gesture a deeper meaning, as is shown by the fact that the inverse is just as possible: a woman spills some wine and her husband tries to repair the damage. . . .

26   An informal evening. Guests are seated on the carpet, their drinks by their sides. An accident quickly occurs: N spills a glass of tomato juice. The same efforts to clean it, as well and as quickly as possible, are made. N asks if his hosts have a carpet cleaning foam. They respond in the negative. N offers to pay the cost of the cleaning. "Thanks, but don't worry, we'll take care of it, no problem." The difficulty seems to be resolved. Yet later in the evening, on several occasions, N makes allusion to his clumsiness ("Don't give it to me, you know how klutzy I am"; "Oh God, this stain is looking at me"; "I feel so bad, such a beautiful carpet").

27   A meeting of the members of our block association, held at the house of one of my neighbors. The sofa and chairs are fitted with slip covers, the furniture with cloths to protect the wood, and the table with an oilcloth. Coffee and cake are served in paper cups and on paper plates. Everyone is relaxed, there is no chance of an irreparable accident, everything has been foreseen.

28   Another meeting, at the far more elegant home of one of my colleagues. C, who is about to place his glass of white wine on the coffee table in front of us, stops his gesture halfway and asks our host if the wooden table (modern, elegant) has been treated, "protected." Despite our host's affirmative response, another colleague comes to the rescue and passes C a wooden coaster from a small stack which had been discreetly placed on a table nearby. The glass of cold white wine will leave no trace of its dampness.

29   The recital of cases could go on indefinitely. Those which I have mentioned suffice to illustrate the implicit rules governing American interpersonal exchanges in case of a "minor accident." I will summarize them as follows:

30   1. If I borrow an object from someone, I have an obligation to return it in the very same state as when it was lent to me. If it is a machine that breaks down in my hands, I must repair it, so as to erase all traces of the mishap. (I don't do this in order to hide the accident, which I must mention in any case, but in order to return the object to its previous condition.)

31   2. If the damage is irreparable, I must replace the object by an identical one, no matter how much time and searching are required. I can, however, ask the owner of the object where it was purchased. I must not replace it by an "equivalent," which would mean brushing off as unimportant all the reasons for the owner's choice, or the meaning which a certain object has come to have for its owner. Nor can I replace the object by another similar—but more or less expensive—one (a glass for a glass, for example), because in both cases I would be suggesting that all that counts in my eyes is the price of the object.

32   3. If I have an accident at someone's home, the situation is even more delicate. If I have even slightly damaged a valuable object (an art object or one with sentimental value), I must be grieved by my clumsiness without finding any excuse for myself; I must immediately offer to take the object and to have it repaired (while showing that I know where to go and that I am not going to worsen the damage by leaving the object with nonprofessionals); I must insist on being allowed to do this, if only to relieve my feelings of guilt ("I feel so bad. I wouldn't be able to sleep"). If my host does not wish to signal the end of our relationship, he or she will, out of kindness, allow me to take the object with me, in order to "let me off the hook."

33   If the accident is of a common sort and not very serious, I must do everything in my power to repair the damage then and there, but I must be careful not to insult my host by offering to replace a common item or to pay the cost of cleaning a tablecloth, for instance, because in doing so I would be suggesting that I do not think he or she has the means to take care of it. In this case, I show that I take the accident seriously by mentioning it several times, by berating myself for clumsiness, by making fun of myself—in short, by taking total responsibility for the accident.

34   All this might seem strange, if not "heavy-handed," to a French person. Why make such a fuss? Why put on such an act? Is this yet another example of American "hypocrisy" and "puritanism"?

35   It is nothing of the kind, of course. On the contrary, although their conduct may be completely different from that of the French people mentioned above (in fact it is exactly opposite), the Americans I have focused on sent a message very similar to that expressed by the French people. Indeed, when I (an American) borrow an object from X, I create or confirm a tie with X (I do not borrow things from just anyone). The care I take with this object will

therefore be proportionate to the importance I place on my relationship to the person who lent it to me. Similarly, when I accidentally disturb a home to which I have been invited, my reaction will be interpreted as a conscious commentary on the relationship between my host and myself. If I do everything possible to clean a carpet, it is not for the sake of the endangered carpet (or because my host and I are "materialistic" because we are American) but out of respect for my host. In other words, our relationship does not presuppose that we will "weather difficulties" together (as it does in the French context); it presupposes a tacit pact between the borrower and the lender, the host and the guest, to preserve an equilibrium, without which all relationships of this kind would become impossible. For if I show little concern for something belonging to X which he has put within my reach or at my disposal (thereby trusting me), X has the right to feel wounded, scorned, and to refuse further dealings with me. Meanwhile, the expectation that one will honor this pact is so strong that any avoidance or refusal on my part risks leaving X bewildered, "not knowing what to do," just like the Dear Abby correspondents mentioned earlier. This is, in a sense, because for Americans it is not in the cards that others will behave in ways other than expected (without being criminals, louts, or other types with whom X would not maintain relations).

36   If my "accident" is really major and X refuses to allow me to free myself, as far as is possible, from my debt, X transforms this bond into a shackle, and I have no reason to maintain a relationship with someone so unconcerned with my feelings.

37   In many circumstances, intercultural misunderstandings spring from the fact that surface resemblances and behavioral similarities conceal profound differences in meaning. It is interesting to see here that the inverse is also true.

■ ■ ▨

MEANING

1. In Carroll's view, what cultural differences come into play to explain why Americans tend to respond to "minor accidents" with apologies and self-deprecating remarks, whereas the French barely stop short of "blaming the victim"?

2. From an American point of view, why is it doubly intolerable that someone who damages another's property would not only disclaim responsibility but also attempt to shift the blame by implying that there is something wrong with the positioning of the object or choice of the item?

3. How do Carroll's examples of situations in France in which repairs were made and paid for imply that both parties were unhappier than they would have been if nothing had been done?

4. Before you were aware of Carroll's hypothesis to explain the differences between the ways in which the French and Americans view "minor accidents," what did you think might explain these differences?

TECHNIQUE

1. Which of the examples cited by Carroll (the broken painting, the spilled red wine, the window shade incident, the burned saucepan, etc.) seems to most effectively support her thesis that the French have a different attitude toward "minor accidents" in terms of who is responsible for repairing the damage?

2. Why does Carroll present many more cases illustrating French attitudes than cases illustrating those of Americans to begin her analysis?

3. How does Carroll use examples to show that Americans are guided by different expectations and assumptions than are the French?

4. **Other Patterns.** How does Carroll use **comparison and contrast** to organize her analysis of American versus French attitudes toward "minor accidents"?

LANGUAGE

1. What quoted remarks effectively communicate the different ways in which Americans and the French respond to the same situation?

2. What words and images effectively support the idea that for the French, friendship is above petty concerns about material objects?

3. If you don't know the meaning of the following words, look them up: *proprietorship* (4), *perpetrator* (20), *carafe* (24), *irreparable* (27), *puritanism* (34).

SUGGESTIONS FOR WRITING

1. **Critical Writing.** Do American attitudes reveal what might be called an "investment psychology" in which taking good care of objects is a way of showing others that one is trustworthy?

2. Have you ever borrowed an item from a friend that you accidentally broke, damaged, or lost? What offer of restitution did you make? How did this episode affect your relationship with your friend?

3. Write a short **narrative** specifying what other situations made it obvious to you that people from different cultures rely on different assumptions in interpreting the limits of responsibility?

4. **Thematic Links.** How does Mark Shand's discovery in "An Original Elephant" (Chapter 7, "Process Analysis") about the way in which beggars in India are permitted to use elephants for weddings in the off-season add another perspective to Carroll's analysis?

DANIELA DEANE

The Little Emperors

Daniela Deane is on the staff of the *Washington Post* and has traveled widely in Hong Kong and China and reported on her findings. In the early 1990s, the effects of China's one-child policy became apparent, and Deane wrote the following article for the *Los Angeles Times Magazine* (1992), graphically illustrating these wide-ranging effects in every stratum of Chinese society. This article can serve as a warning against social engineering that can have unpredicted consequences.

BEFORE YOU READ

What are the advantages and disadvantages of being an only child who receives all the attention from parents and grandparents?

■ ■ ▨

1   Xu Ming sits on the worn sofa with his short, chubby arms and legs splayed, forced open by fat and the layers of padded clothing worn in northern China to ward off the relentless chill. To reach the floor, the tubby 8-year-old rocks back and forth on his big bottom, inching forward slowly, eventually ending upright. Xu Ming finds it hard to move.

2   "He got fat when he was about 3," says his father, Xu Jianguo, holding the boy's bloated, dimpled hand. "We were living with my parents and they were very good to him. He's the only grandson. It's a tradition in China that boys are very loved. They love him very much, and so they feed him a lot. They give him everything he wants."

3   Xu Ming weighs 135 pounds, about twice what he should at his age. He's one of hundreds of children who have sought help in the past few years at the Beijing Children's Hospital, which recently began the first American-style fat farm for obese children in what was once the land of skin and bones.

4   "We used to get a lot of cases of malnutrition," says Dr. Ni Guichen, director of endocrinology at the hospital and founder of the weight reduction classes. "But in the last 10 years, the problem has become obese children. The number of fat children in China is growing very fast. The main reason is the one-child policy," she says, speaking in a drab waiting room. "Because parents can only have one child, the families take extra good care of that one child, which means feeding him too much."

5   Bulging waistlines are one result of China's tough campaign to curb its population. The one-child campaign, a strict national directive that seeks to limit each Chinese couple to a single son or daughter, has other dramatic consequences: millions of abortions, fewer girls and a generation of spoiled children.

For a visual to accompany this selection, see color insert photo A-8.

6   The 10-day weight-reduction sessions—a combination of exercise, nutritional guidance and psychological counseling—are very popular. Hundreds of children—some so fat they can hardly walk—are turned away for each class.

7   According to Ni, about 5% of children in China's cities are obese, with two obese boys for every overweight girl, the traditional preference toward boys being reflected in the amount of attention lavished on the child. "Part of the course is also centered on the parents. We try to teach them how to bring their children up properly, not just by spoiling them," Ni says.

8   Ming's father is proud that his son, after two sessions at the fat farm, has managed to halve his intake of *jiaozi*, the stodgy meat-filled dumplings that are Ming's particular weakness, from 30 to 15 at a sitting. "Even if he's not full, that's all he gets," he says. "In the beginning, it was very difficult. He would put his arms around our necks and beg us for more food. We couldn't bear it, so we'd give him a little more."

9   Ming lost a few pounds but hasn't been able to keep the weight off. He's a bit slimmer now, but only because he's taller. "I want to lose weight," says Ming, who spends his afternoons snacking at his grandparents' house and his evenings plopped in front of the television set at home. "The kids make fun of me, they call me a fat pig. I hate the nicknames. In sports class, I can't do what the teacher says. I can run a little bit, but after a while I have to sit down. The teacher puts me at the front of the class where all the other kids can see me. They all laugh and make fun of me."

10   The many fat children visible on China's city streets are just the most obvious example of 13 years of the country's one-child policy. In the vast countryside, the policy has meant shadowy lives as second-class citizens for thousands of girls, or, worse, death. It has made abortion a way of life and a couple's sexual intimacy the government's concern. Even women's menstrual cycles are monitored. Under the directive, couples literally have to line up for permission to procreate. Second children are sometimes possible, but only on payment of a heavy fine.

11   The policy is an unparalleled instrusion into the private lives of a nation's citizens, an experiment on a scale never attempted elsewhere in the world. But no expert will argue that China—by far the world's most populous country with 1.16 billion people—could continue without strict curbs on its population.

12   China's communist government adopted the one-child policy in 1979 in response to the staggering doubling of the country's population during Mao Tse-tung's rule. Mao, who died in 1976, was convinced that the country's masses were a strategic asset and vigorously encouraged the Chinese to produce even-larger families.

13   But large families are now out for the Chinese—20% of the world's population living on just 7% of the arable land. "China has to have a population policy," says Huang Baoshan, deputy director of the State Family Planning Commission. With the numbers ever growing, "how can we feed them, house them?"

14   Dinner time for one 5-year-old girl consists of granddad chasing her through the house, bowl and spoon in hand, barking like a dog or mewing like a cat. If

he performs authentically enough, she rewards him by accepting a mouthful of food. No problem, insists granddad, "it's good exercise for her."

15   An 11-year-old boy never gets up to go to the toilet during the night. That's because his mother, summoned by a shout, gets up instead and positions a bottle under the covers for him. "We wouldn't want him to have to get up in the night," his mother says.

16   Another mother wanted her 16-year-old to eat some fruit, but the teenager was engrossed in a video game. Not wanting him to get his fingers sticky or daring to interrupt, she peeled several grapes and popped one after another into his mouth. "Not so fast," he snapped. "Can't you see I have to spit out the seeds?"

17   Stories like these are routinely published in China's newspapers, evidence that the government-imposed birth-control policy has produced an emerging generation of spoiled, lazy, selfish, self-centered and overweight children. There are about 40 million only children in China. Dubbed the country's "Little Emperors," their behavior toward their elders is likened to that of the young emperor Pu Yi, who heaped indignities on his eunuch servants while making them cater to his whims, as chronicled in Bernardo Bertolucci's film *The Last Emperor.*

18   Many studies on China's only children have been done. One such study confirmed that only children generally are not well liked. The study, conducted by a team of Chinese psychologists, asked a group of 360 Chinese children, half who have siblings and half who don't, to rate each other's behavior. The only children were, without fail, the least popular, regardless of age or social background. Peers rated them more uncooperative and selfish than children with brothers and sisters. They bragged more, were less helpful in group activities and more apt to follow their own selfish interests. And they wouldn't share their toys.

19   The Chinese lay a lot of blame on what they call the "4-2-1" syndrome—four doting grandparents, two overindulgent parents, all pinning their hopes and ambitions on one child.

20   Besides stuffing them with food, Chinese parents have very high expectations of their one *bao bei*, or treasured object. Some have their still-in-strollers babies tested for IQ levels. Others try to teach toddlers Tang Dynasty poetry. Many shell out months of their hard-earned salaries for music lessons and instruments for children who have no talent or interest in playing. They fill their kids' lives with lessons in piano, English, gymnastics and typing.

21   The one-child parents, most of them from traditionally large Chinese families, grew up during the chaotic, 10-year Cultural Revolution, when many of the country's cultural treasures were destroyed and schools were closed for long periods of time. Because many of that generation spent years toiling in the fields rather than studying, they demand—and put all their hopes into—academic achievement for their children.

22   "We've already invested a lot of money in his intellectual development," Wang Zhouzhi told me in her Spartan home in a tiny village of Changping country outside Beijing, discussing her son, Chenqian, an only child. "I don't care how much money we spend on him. We've bought him an organ and we push

him hard. Unfortunately, he's only a mediocre student," she says, looking toward the 10-year-old boy. Chenqian, dressed in a child-sized Chinese army uniform, ate 10 pieces of candy during the half-hour interview and repeatedly fired off his toy pistol, all without a word of reproach from his mother.

23 Would Chenqian have liked a sibling to play with? "No," he answers loudly, firing a rapid, jarring succession of shots. His mother breaks in: "If he had a little brother or sister, he wouldn't get everything he wants. Of course he doesn't want one. With only one child, I give my full care and concern to him."

24 But how will these children, now entering their teen-age years and moving quickly toward adulthood, become the collectivist-minded citizens China's hard-line communist leadership demands? Some think they never will. Ironically, it may be just these overindulged children who will change Chinese society. After growing up doing as they wished, ruling their immediate families, they're not likely to obey a central government that tells them to fall in line. This new generation of egotists, who haven't been taught to take even their parents into consideration, simply may not be able to think of the society as a whole—the basic principle of communism.

25 The need for family planning is obvious in the cities, where living space is limited and the one-child policy is strictly enforced and largely successful. City dwellers are slowly beginning to accept the notion that smaller families are better for the country, although most would certainly want two children if they could have them. However, in the countryside, where three of every four Chinese live—nearly 900 million people—the goal of limiting each couple to only one child has proved largely elusive.

26 In the hinterlands, the policy has become a confusing patchwork of special cases and exceptions. Provincial authorities can decide which couples can have a second child. In the southern province of Guangdong, China's richest, two children are allowed and many couples can afford to pay the fine to have even a third of fourth child. The amounts of the fines vary across the country, the highest in populous Sichuan province, where the fine for a second child can be as much as 25% of a family's income over four years. Special treatment has been given to China's cultural minorities such as the Mongolians and the Tibetans because of their low numbers. Many of them are permitted three or four children without penalty, although some Chinese social scientists have begun to question the privilege.

27 "It's really become a two-child policy in the countryside," says a Western diplomat. "Because of the traditional views on labor supply, the traditional bias toward the male child, it's been impossible for them to enforce a one-child policy outside the cities. In the countryside, they're really trying to stop that third child."

28 Thirteen years of strict family planning have created one of the great mysteries of the vast and remote Chinese countryside: Where have all the little girls gone? A Swedish study of sex ratios in China, published in 1990, and based on China's own census data, concluded that several million little girls are "missing"—up to half a million a year in the years 1985 to 1987—since the policy was introduced in late 1979.

29   In the study, and in demographic research worldwide, sex ratio at birth in humans is shown to be very stable, between 105 and 106 boys for every 100 girls. The imbalance is thought to be nature's way of compensating for the higher rates of miscarriage, stillbirth and infant mortality among boys.

30   In China, the ratio climbed consistently during the 1980s, and it now rests at more than 110 boys to 100 girls. "The imbalance is evident in some areas of the country," says Stirling Scruggs, director of the United Nations Population Fund in China. "I don't think the reason is widespread infanticide. They're adopting out girls to try for a boy, they're hiding their girls, they're not registering them. Throughout Chinese history, in times of famine, and now as well, people have been forced to make choices between boys and girls, and for many reasons, boys always win out."

31   With the dismantling of collectives, families must, once again, farm their own small plots and sons are considered necessary to do the work. Additionally, girls traditionally "marry out" of their families, transferring their filial responsibilities to their in-laws. Boys carry on the family name and are entrusted with the care of their parents as they age. In the absence of a social security system, having a son is the difference between starving and eating when one is old. To combat the problem, some innovative villages have begun issuing so-called girl insurance, an old-age insurance policy for couples who have given birth to a daughter and are prepared to stop at that.

32   "People are scared to death to be childless and penniless in their old age," says William Hinton, an American author of seven books chronicling modern China. "So if they don't have a son, they immediately try for another. When the woman is pregnant, they'll have a sex test to see if it's a boy or a girl. They'll abort a girl, or go in hiding with the girl, or pay the fine, or bribe the official or leave home. Anything. It's a game of wits."

33   Shen Shufen, a sturdy, round-faced peasant woman of 33, has two children—an 8-year-old girl and a 3-year-old boy—and lives in Sihe, a dusty, one-road, mud-brick village in the countryside outside Beijing. Her husband is a truck driver. "When we had our girl, we knew we had to have another child somehow. We saved for years to pay the fine. It was hard giving them that money, 3,000 yuan ($550 in U.S. dollars), in one night. That's what my husband makes in three years. I was so happy when our second child was a boy."

34   The government seems aware of the pressure its policies put on expectant parents, and the painful results, but has not shown any flexibility. For instance, Beijing in 1990 passed a law forbidding doctors to tell a couple the results of ultrasound tests that disclose the sex of their unborn child. The reason: Too many female embryos were being aborted.

35   And meanwhile, several hundred thousand women—called "guerrilla moms"—go into hiding every year to have their babies. They become part of China's 40-million-strong floating population that wanders the country, mostly in search of work, sleeping under bridges and in front of railway stations. Tens of thousands of female children are simply abandoned in rural hospitals.

36   And although most experts say female infanticide is not widespread, it does exist. "I found a dead baby girl," says Hinton. "We stopped for lunch at this mountain ravine in Shaanxi province. We saw her lying there, at the bottom of the creek bed. She was all bundled up, with one arm sticking out. She had been there a while, you could tell, because she had a little line of mold growing across her mouth and nostrils."

37   Death comes in another form, too: neglect. "It's female neglect, more than female infanticide, neglect to the point of death for little girls," says Scruggs of the U.N. Population Fund. "If you have a sick child, and it's a girl," he says, "you might buy only half the dose of medicine she needs to get better."

38   Hundreds of thousands of unregistered little girls—called "black children"—live on the edge of the law, unable to get food rations, immunizations or places in school. Many reports are grim. The government-run China News Service reported last year that the drowning of baby girls had revived to such an extent in Guangxi province that at least 1 million boys will be unable to find wives in 20 years. And partly because of the gender imbalance, the feudalistic practice of selling women has been revived.

39   The alarming growth of the flesh trade prompted authorities to enact a law in January that imposes jail sentences of up to 10 years and heavy fines for people caught trafficking. The government also recently began broadcasting a television dramatization to warn women against the practice. The public-service message shows two women, told that they would be given high-paying jobs, being lured to a suburban home. Instead, they are locked in a small, dark room, and soon realize that they have been sold.

40   Li Wangping is nervous. She keeps looking at the air vents at the bottom of the office door, to see if anyone is walking by or, worse still, standing there listening. She rubs her hands together over and over. She speaks in a whisper. "I'm afraid to get into trouble talking to you," Li confides. She says nothing for a few minutes.

41   "After my son was born, I desperately wanted another baby," the 42-year-old woman finally begins. "I just wanted to have more children, you understand? Anyway, I got pregnant three times, because I wasn't using any birth control. I didn't want to use any. So, I had to have three abortions, one right after the other. I didn't want to at all. It was terrible killing the babies I wanted so much. But I had to."

42   By Chinese standards, Li (not her real name) has a lot to lose if she chooses to follow her maternal yearnings. As an office worker at government-owned CITIC, a successful and dynamic conglomerate, she has one of the best jobs in Beijing. Just being a city dweller already puts her ahead of most of the population.

43   "One of my colleagues had just gotten fired for having a second child. I couldn't afford to be fired," continues Li, speaking in a meeting room at CITIC headquarters. "I had to keep everything secret from the family-planning official at CITIC, from everyone at the office. Of course, I'm supposed to be using birth control. I had to lie. It was hard lying, because I felt so bad about everything."

44   She rubs her hands furiously and moves toward the door, staring continuously at the air slats. "I have to go now. There's more to say, but I'm afraid to tell you. They could find me."

45   China's family-planning officials wield awesome powers, enforcing the policy through a combination of incentives and deterrents. For those who comply, there are job promotions and small cash awards. For those who resist, they suffer stiff fines and loss of job and status within the country's tightly knit and heavily regulated communities. The State Family Planning Commission is the government ministry entrusted with the tough task of curbing the growth of the world's most populous country, where 28 children are born every minute. It employs about 200,000 full-time officials and uses more than a million volunteers to check the fertility of hundreds of millions of Chinese women.

46   "Every village or enterprise has at least one family-planning official," says Zhang Xizhi, a birth-control official in Changping county outside Beijing. "Our main job is propaganda work to raise people's consciousness. We educate people and tell them their options for birth control. We go down to every household to talk to people. We encourage them to have only one child, to marry late, to have their child later."

47   Population police frequently keep records of the menstrual cycles of women of childbearing age, on the type of birth control they use and the pending applications to have children. If they slip up, street committees—half-governmental, half-civilian organizations that have sprung up since the 1949 communist takeover—take up the slack. The street committees, made up mostly of retired volunteers, act as the central government's ear to the ground, snooping, spying and reporting on citizens to the authorities.

48   When a couple wants to have a child—even their first, allotted one—they must apply to the family-planning office in their township or workplace, literally lining up to procreate. "If a woman gets pregnant without permission, she and her husband will get fined, even if it's their first," Zhang says. "It is fair to fine her, because she creates a burden on the whole society by jumping her place in line."

49   If a woman in Nanshao township, where Zhang works, becomes pregnant with a second child, she must terminate her pregnancy unless she or her husband or their first child is disabled or if both parents are only children. Her local family-planning official will repeatedly visit her at home to pressure her to comply. "Sometimes I have to go to people's homes five or six times to explain everything to them over and over to get them to have an abortion," says Zhang Cuiqing, the family-planning official for Sihe village, where there are 2,900 married women of childbearing age, of which 2,700 use some sort of birth control. Of those, 570 are sterilized and 1,100 have IUDs. Zhang recites the figures proudly, adding, "If they refuse, they will be fined between 20,000 and 50,000 yuan (U.S. $3,700 to $9,500)." The average yearly wage in Sihe is 1,500 yuan ($285).

50   The lack of early sexual education and unreliable IUDs are combining to make abortion—which is free, as are condoms and IUDs—a cornerstone of the one-child policy. Local officials are told not to use force, but rather education and persuasion, to meet their targets. However, the desire to fulfill their quotas, coupled with pressure from their bosses in Beijing, can lead to abuses by overzealous officials.

51   "Some local family-planning officials are running amok, because of the targets they have to reach," a Western health specialist says, "and there are a bunch of people willing to turn a blind eye to abuses because the target is so important."

52   The official *Shanghai Legal Daily* last year reported on a family-planning committee in central Sichuan province that ordered the flogging of the husbands of 10 pregnant women who refused to have abortions. According to the newspaper, the family-planning workers marched the husbands one by one into an empty room, ordered them to strip and lie on the floor and then beat them with a stick, once for every day their wives were pregnant.

53   "In some places, yes, things do happen," concedes Huang of the State Family Planning Commission. "Sometimes, family-planning officials do carry it too far."

54   The young woman lies still on the narrow table with her eyes shut and her legs spread while the doctor quickly performs a suction abortion. A few moments, and the fetus is removed. The woman lets out a short, sharp yell. "OK, next," the doctor says.

55   She gets off the table and, holding a piece of cloth between her legs to catch the blood and clutching her swollen womb, hobbles over to a bed and collapses. The next patient gets up and walks toward the abortion table. No one notices a visitor watching. "It's very quick, it only takes about five minutes per abortion," says Dr. Huang Xiaomiao, chief physician at Beijing's Maternity Hospital. "No anesthetic. We don't use anesthetic for abortions or births here. Only for Cesarean sections, we use acupuncture."

56   Down the hall, 32-year-old Wu Guobin waits to be taken into the operating room to have her Fallopian tubes untied—a reversal of an earlier sterilization. "After my son was killed in an accident last year, the authorities in my province said I could try for another." In the bed next to Wu's, a dour-faced woman looks ready to cry. "She's getting sterilized," the nurse explains. "Her husband doesn't want her to, but her first child has mental problems."

57   Although it's a maternity hospital, the Family Planning Unit—where abortions, sterilizations, IUD insertions and the like are carried out—is the busiest department. "We do more abortions than births," says Dr. Fan Huimin, head of the unit. "Between 10 and 20 a day."

58   Abortions are a way of life in China, where about 10.5 million pregnancies are terminated each year. (In the United States, 1.6 million abortions are performed a year, but China's population is four to five times greater than the United States'.) One fetus is aborted for about every two children born and Chinese women often have several abortions. Usually, abortions are performed during the first trimester. But because some women resist, only to cave in under mental bullying further into their terms, abortions are also done in the later months of pregnancy, sometimes up till the eighth month.

59   Because of their population problem, the Chinese have become pioneers in contraceptive research. China will soon launch its own version of the controversial French abortion pill RU-486, which induces a miscarriage. They have perfected a non-scalpel procedure for male sterilization, with no suture required,

allowing the man to "ride his bicycle home within five minutes." This year, the government plans to spend more than the $34 million it spent last year on contraception. The state will also buy some 961 million condoms to be distributed throughout the country, 11% more than in 1991.

60   But even with a family-planning policy that sends a chill down a Westerner's spine and touches every Chinese citizen's life, 64,000 babies are born every day in China and overpopulation continues to be a paramount national problem. Officials have warned that 24 million children will be born in 1992—a number just slightly less than the population of Canada. "The numbers are staggering," says Scruggs, the U.N. Population Fund official, nothing that "170 million people will be added in the 1990s, which is the current population of England, France and Italy combined. There are places in China where the land can't feed that many more people as it is."

61   China estimates that it has prevented 200 million births since the one-child policy was introduced. Women now are having an average of 2.4 children as compared to six in the late '60s. But the individual sacrifice demanded from every Chinese is immense.

62   Large billboards bombard the population with images of happy families with only one child. The government is desperately trying to convince the masses that producing only one child leads to a wealthier, healthier and happier life. But foreigners in China tell a different story, that the people aren't convinced. They tell of being routinely approached—on the markets, on the streets, on the railway and asked about the contraceptive policies of their countries. Expatriate women in Beijing all tell stories of Chinese women enviously asking them how many sons they have and how many children they plan to have. They explain that they only have one child because the government allows them only one.

63   "When I'm out with my three children on the weekend," says a young American father who lives in Beijing, "people are always asking me why am I allowed to have three children. You can feel when they ask you that there is envy there. There's a natural disappointment among the people. They just want to have more children. But there's a resigned understanding, an acceptance that they just can't."

■ ■ ▨

MEANING

1. In what way has China's one-child policy, especially in urban areas, produced an imbalance in the ratio of males to females?

2. What Chinese cultural values and economic factors explain this imbalance?

3. How do the experiences of the parents help to explain the kinds of expectations and hopes they have attached to their "little emperors"?

4. What picture do you get of the extent to which the government monitors everyday life in China? Which examples did you find especially effective in showing this?

TECHNIQUE

1. How do Deane's examples, beginning with the story of the 135-pound eight-year-old child, Xu Ming, graphically illustrate the "little emperor" syndrome?

2. What examples best illustrate the tragic effects and the results of China's one-child policy for female babies?

3. **Other Patterns.** Explain the sequence of **cause and effect** that has produced the specific consequences outlined by Deane.

LANGUAGE

1. How does Deane's style of writing depend on vignettes, snapshots, and short profiles to put a human face on statistics?

2. How does Deane use quotations and testimony of experts to enhance her analysis?

3. If you don't know the meaning of the following words, look them up: *bloated* (2), *demographic* (29), *famine* (30), *infanticide* (30), *suture* (59).

SUGGESTIONS FOR WRITING

1. **Critical Writing.** In an essay, explore the consequences of China's social engineering program in terms of raising individualistic boys. Will these boys be able to find wives and jobs?

2. If you are an only child, to what extent have you been treated similarly to the way in which only children are treated in China? Have you wished you had siblings? If you have siblings, do you ever wish you were an only child?

3. **Compare and contrast** the Chinese preference for male children with the emerging trend in Japan for girls as the preferred gender in their overall decreasing population.

4. **Thematic Links.** Discuss the role of the state in limiting freedoms for the young in Deane's analysis and in Guanlong Cao's "Chopsticks" (in Chapter 3, "Narration").

ROBERT LEVINE AND ELLEN WOLFF

Social Time: The Heartbeat of Culture

In the 1980s, Robert Levine, a social psychologist, researched the variable perceptions that distinguish one culture's attitude toward being on time from other cultures' around the world. The results were published in *Psychology Today* (March 1985) and were correlated with the help of Ellen Wolff. Levine found that in Brazil, Japan, Taiwan, Italy, England, Indonesia, and other countries, he was able to gauge the importance of being on time through quite ordinary means, such as comparing how long it took to buy a stamp at the post office or discovering how accurate clocks in downtown banks were. Levine currently teaches at California State University at Fresno and has written *Power of Persuasion: How We're Bought and Sold* (2003).

BEFORE YOU READ

Are you more likely to be early, on time, or late for appointments and social get-togethers?

■ ■ ▨

1   *"If a man does not keep pace with his companions, perhaps it is because he hears a different drummer."* This thought by Thoreau strikes a chord in so many people that it has become part of our language. We use the phrase "the beat of a different drummer" to explain any pace of life unlike our own. Such colorful vagueness reveals how informal our rules of time really are. The world over, children simply "pick up" their society's time concepts as they mature. No dictionary clearly defines the meaning of "early" or "late" for them or for strangers who stumble over the maddening incongruities between the time sense they bring with them and the one they face in new land.

2   I learned this firsthand, a few years ago, and the resulting culture shock led me halfway around the world to find answers. It seemed clear that time "talks." But what is it telling us?

3   My journey started shortly after I accepted an appointment as visiting professor of psychology at the federal university in Niterói, Brazil, a midsized city across the bay from Rio de Janeiro. As I left home for my first day of class, I asked someone the time. It was 9:05 a.m., which allowed me time to relax and look around the campus before my 10 o'clock lecture. After what I judged to be half an hour, I glanced at a clock I was passing. It said 10:20! In panic, I broke for the classroom, followed by gentle calls of "Hola, professor" and "Tudo bem, professor?" from unhurried students, many of whom, I later realized, were my own. I arrived breathless to find an empty room.

4   Frantically, I asked a passerby the time. "Nine forty-five" was the answer. No, that couldn't be. I asked someone else. "Nine fifty-five." Another said: "Exactly

9:43." The clock in a nearby office read 3:15. I had learned my first lesson about Brazilians: Their timepieces are consistently inaccurate. And nobody minds.

5   My class was scheduled from 10 until noon. Many students came late, some very late. Several arrived after 10:30. A few showed up closer to 11. Two came after that. All of the latecomers wore the relaxed smiles that I came, later, to enjoy. Each one said hello, and although a few apologized briefly, none seemed terribly concerned about lateness. They assumed that I understood.

6   The idea of Brazilians arriving late was not a great shock. I had heard about "mãnha," the Portuguese equivalent of "mañana" in Spanish. This term, meaning "tomorrow" or "the morning," stereotypes the Brazilian who puts off the business of today until tomorrow. The real surprise came at noon that first day, when the end of class arrived.

7   Back home in California, I never need to look at a clock to know when the class hour is ending. The shuffling of books is accompanied by strained expressions that say plaintively, "I'm starving. . . . I've got to go to the bathroom. . . . I'm going to suffocate if you keep us one more second." (The pain usually becomes unbearable at two minutes to the hour in undergraduate classes and five minutes before the close of graduate classes.)

8   When noon arrived in my first Brazilian class, only a few students left immediately. Others slowly drifted out during the next 15 minutes, and some continued asking me questions long after that. When several remaining students kicked off their shoes at 12:30, I went into my own "starving/bathroom/suffocation" routine.

9   I could not, in all honesty, attribute their lingering to my superb teaching style. I had just spent two hours lecturing on statistics in halting Portuguese. Apparently, for many of my students, staying late was simply of no more importance than arriving late in the first place. As I observed this casual approach in infinite variations during the year, I learned that the "mãnha" stereotype oversimplified the real Anglo/Brazilian differences in conceptions of time. Research revealed a more complex picture.

10   With the assistance of colleagues Laurie West and Harry Reis, I compared the time sense of 91 male and female students in Niterói with that of 107 similar students at California State University in Fresno. The universities are similar in academic quality and size, and the cities are both secondary metropolitan centers with populations of about 350,000.

11   We asked students about their perceptions of time in several situations, such as what they would consider late or early for a hypothetical lunch appointment with a friend. The average Brazilian student defined lateness for lunch as 33½ minutes after the scheduled time, compared to only 19 minutes for the Fresno students. But Brazilians also allowed an average of about 54 minutes before they'd consider someone early, while the Fresno students drew the line at 24.

12   Are Brazilians simply more flexible in their concepts of time and punctuality? And how does this relate to the stereotype of the apathetic, fatalistic and irresponsible Latin temperament? When we asked students to give typical reasons for lateness, the Brazilians were less likely to attribute it to a lack of caring than the North Americans were. Instead, they pointed to unforeseen circumstances

that the person couldn't control. Because they seemed less inclined to feel personally responsible for being late, they also expressed less regret for their own lateness and blamed others less when they were late.

13   We found similar differences in how students from the two countries characterized people who were late for appointments. Unlike their North American counterparts, the Brazilian students believed that a person who is consistently late is probably more successful than one who is consistently on time. They seemed to accept the idea that someone of status is expected to arrive late. Lack of punctuality is a badge of success.

14   Even within our own country, of course, ideas of time and punctuality vary considerably from place to place. Different regions and even cities have their own distinct rhythms and rules. Seemingly simple words like "now," snapped out by an impatient New Yorker, and "later," said by a relaxed Californian, suggest a world of difference. Despite our familiarity with these homegrown differences in tempo, problems with time present a major stumbling block to Americans abroad. Peace Corps volunteers told researchers James Spradley of Macalester College and Mark Phillips of the University of Washington that their greatest difficulties with other people, after language problems, were the general pace of life and the punctuality of others. Formal "clock time" may be a standard on which the world agrees, but "social time," the heartbeat of society, is something else again.

15   How a country paces its social life is a mystery to most outsiders, one that we're just beginning to unravel. Twenty-six years ago, anthropologist Edward Hall noted in *The Silent Language* that informal patterns of time "are seldom, if ever, made explicit. They exist in the air around us. They are either familiar and comfortable, or unfamiliar and wrong." When we realize we are out of step, we often blame the people around us to make ourselves feel better.

16   Appreciating cultural differences in time sense becomes increasingly important as modern communications put more and more people in daily contact. If we are to avoid misreading issues that involve time perceptions, we need to understand better our own cultural biases and those of others.

17   When people of different cultures interact, the potential for misunderstanding exists on many levels. For example, members of Arab and Latin cultures usually stand much closer when they are speaking to people than we usually do in the United States, a fact we frequently misinterpret as aggression or disrespect. Similarly, we assign personality traits to groups with a pace of life that is markedly faster or slower than our own. We build ideas of national character, for example, around the traditional Swiss and German ability to "make the trains run on time." Westerners like ourselves define punctuality using precise measures of time: 5 minutes, 15 minutes, an hour. But according to Hall, in many Mediterranean Arab cultures there are only three sets of time: no time at all, now (which is of varying duration) and forever (too long). Because of this, Americans often find difficulty in getting Arabs to distinguish between waiting a long time and a very long time.

18   According to historian Will Durant, "No man in a hurry is quite civilized." What do our time judgments say about our attitude toward life? How can a North

What story does this photograph of a reunion on the Pakistani-Indian border of Kashmir tell, and how does it elicit emotion in ways that are true of all effective narratives?

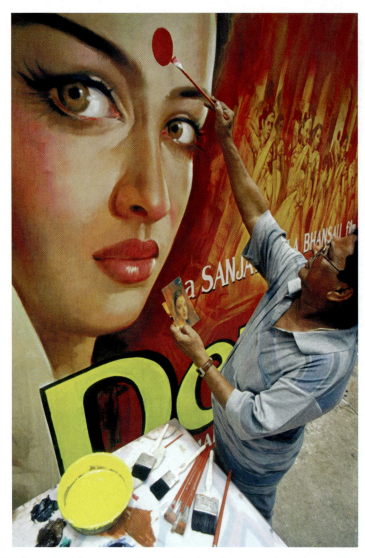

What does this film poster tell you about the qualities that allow a novel to be successfully adapted into a Bollywood film, as related by R. K. Narayan in "Misguided 'Guide'"?

How does this photo of the Basilica di San Marco illustrate the architectural incongruities of St. Mark's Square that Mary McCarthy describes in "The Paradox of St. Mark's"?

Is this how you would have pictured Tepilit Ole Saitoti as a Maasai warrior from his description in "The Initiation of a Maasai Warrior"?

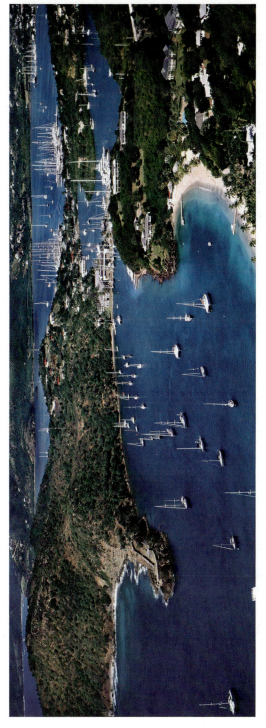

What impression do you get of Antigua from this picture of Galleon Beach, Nelson's Dockyard, and English Harbour? How does it compare with Jamaica Kincaid's depiction of the island in "A Small Place"?

The United States features important public figures such as Washington, Lincoln, Hamilton and Jackson on the national currency; how is it significant that Japan puts the image of the writer Natsume Soseki on their 1000-yen note? See his story "I Am A Cat."

How do the different panels in this cartoon illustrate the generalization that the boy reaches?

How does this picture of a Chinese woman and child outside their home support Daniela Deane's discussion of the status of little boys in China in "The Little Emperors"?

American, coming from a land of digital precision, relate to a North African who may consider a clock "the devil's mill"?

19   Each language has a vocabulary of time that does not always survive translation. When we translated our questionnaires into Portuguese for my Brazilian students, we found that English distinctions of time were not readily articulated in their language. Several of our questions concerned how long the respondent would wait for someone to arrive, as compared with when they hoped for arrival or actually expected the person would come. In Portuguese, the verbs "to wait for," "to hope for" and "to expect" are all translated as "esperar." We had to add further words of explanation to make the distinction clear to the Brazilian students.

20   To avoid these language problems, my Fresno colleague Kathy Bartlett and I decided to clock the pace of life in other countries by using as little language as possible. We looked directly at three basic indicators of time: the accuracy of a country's bank clocks, the speed at which pedestrians walked and the average time it took a postal clerk to sell us a single stamp. In six countries on three continents, we made observations in both the nation's largest urban area and a medium-sized city: Japan (Tokyo and Sendai), Taiwan (Taipei and Tainan), Indonesia (Jakarta and Solo), Italy (Rome and Florence), England (London and Bristol) and the United States (New York City and Rochester).

21   What we wanted to know was: Can we speak of a unitary concept called "pace of life"? What we've learned suggests that we can. There appears to be a very strong relationship between the accuracy of clock time, walking speed and postal efficiency across the countries we studied.

22   We checked 15 clocks in each city, selecting them at random in downtown banks and comparing the time they showed with that reported by the local telephone company. In Japan, which leads the way in accuracy, the clocks averaged just over half a minute early or late. Indonesian clocks, the least accurate, were more than three minutes off the mark.

23   I will be interested to see how the digital-information age will affect our perceptions of time. In the United States today, we are reminded of the exact hour of the day more than ever, through little symphonies of beeps emanating from people's digital watches. As they become the norm, I fear our sense of precision may take an absurd twist. The other day, when I asked for the time, a student looked at his watch and replied, "Three twelve and eighteen seconds."

" 'Will you walk a little faster?' said a whiting to a snail. 'There's a porpoise close behind us, and he's treading on my tail.' "

24   So goes the rhyme from *Alice in Wonderland*, which also gave us that famous symbol of haste, the White Rabbit. He came to mind often as we measured the walking speeds in our experimental cities. We clocked how long it took pedestrians to walk 100 feet along a main downtown street during business hours on clear days. To eliminate the effects of socializing, we observed only people walking alone, timing at least 100 in each city. We found, once again, that the Japanese led the way, averaging just 20.7 seconds to cover the distance. The English nosed out the Americans for second place—21.6 to 22.5 seconds—and the

Indonesians again trailed the pack, sauntering along at 27.2 seconds. As you might guess, speed was greater in the larger city of each nation than its smaller one.

25   Our final measurement, the average time it took postal clerks to sell one stamp, turned out to be less straightforward than we expected. In each city, including those in the United States, we presented clerks with a note in the native language requesting a common-priced stamp—a 20-center in the United States, for example. They were also handed paper money, the equivalent of a $5 bill. In Indonesia, this procedure led to more than we bargained for.

26   At the large central post office in Jakarta, I asked for the line to buy stamps and was directed to a group of private vendors sitting outside. Each of them hustled for my business: "Hey, good stamps, mister!" "Best stamps here!" In the smaller city of Solo, I found a volleyball game in progress when I arrived at the main post office on Friday afternoon. Business hours, I was told, were over. When I finally did get there during business hours, the clerk was more interested in discussing relatives in America. Would I like to meet his uncle in Cincinnati? Which did I like better: California or the United States? Five people behind me in line waited patiently. Instead of complaining, they began paying attention to our conversation.

How does this photo convey the obsession that businesspeople in some countries have with time as analyzed by Robert Levine and Ellen Wolff?

27   When it came to efficiency of service, however, the Indonesians were not the slowest, although they did place far behind the Japanese postal clerks, who averaged 25 seconds. That distinction went to the Italians, whose infamous postal service took 47 seconds on the average.

> "A man who wastes one hour of time has not discovered the meaning of life. . . ."

28   That was Charles Darwin's belief, and many share it, perhaps at the cost of their health. My colleagues and I have recently begun studying the relationship between pace of life and well-being. Other researchers have demonstrated that a chronic sense of urgency is a basic component of the Type A, coronary-prone personality. We expect that future research will demonstrate that pace of life is related to rate of heart disease, hypertension, ulcers, suicide, alcoholism, divorce and other indicators of general psychological and physical well-being.

29   As you envision tomorrow's international society, do you wonder who will set the pace? Americans eye Japan carefully, because the Japanese are obviously "ahead of us" in measurable ways. In both countries, speed is frequently confused with progress. Perhaps looking carefully at the different paces of life around the world will help us distinguish more accurately between the two qualities. Clues are everywhere but sometimes hard to distinguish. You have to listen carefully to hear the beat of even your own drummer.

■ ■ ▨

MEANING

1. What alerted Levine that his concept of time was not shared by his Brazilian students?

2. How did Levine's sense of time differ from that of his students? How does "social time" differ from "clock time"?

3. What three measures did the researchers use to gauge the meaning of a country's sense of time? Are there additional measures that you would have used if you had done this experiment?

4. What assumptions underlie Brazilian attitudes about lateness?

TECHNIQUE

1. What examples best **illustrate** that "social time" was more important than "clock time" to the Brazilian students?

2. Although this article was written for a popular audience, it relies on research techniques used by scientists. How does Levine make these technical features interesting to the reader?

3. **Other Patterns.** How do Levine and Wolff use **comparison and contrast** to underscore the different attitudes toward time in Brazil and in the United States?

LANGUAGE

1. Why did the researchers find it necessary to add meanings to the Portuguese verb *esperar* to elicit the information they needed to obtain?

2. How do Levine and Wolff use quotes by historians, biologists, and famous figures as a way to organize their discussion?

3. If you don't know the meaning of the following words, look them up: *incongruities* (1), *punctuality* (12), *apathetic* (12), *fatalistic* (12).

SUGGESTIONS FOR WRITING

1. **Critical Writing.** What general correlations between pace of life and nationality did the researchers find? What inferences about the cultures involved do you draw from these results?

2. Write a report on Robert Levine's classic *A Geography of Time* (1997) as it relates to this essay.

3. To what extent would your answer about what you would consider being "late" or "early" match the responses of the Brazilian students? What cultural expectations are implicit in your answer?

4. If you performed Levine's experiment with the clocks around your town or campus, what conclusions would you draw? Write a short **narrative** with your findings.

5. **Thematic Links.** How does Sembene Ousmane's story "Her Three Days" (Chapter 8, "Classification and Division") illustrate the social meanings of being late in ways that add to Levine and Wolff's analysis?

GEETA KOTHARI

If You Are What You Eat, Then What Am I?

Geeta Kothari (b. 1928) teaches English at the University of Pittsburgh and directs the writing center there. Her work has appeared in various journals and anthologies, and she is the editor of *Did My Mamma Like to Dance? and Other Stories about Mothers and Daughters* (1994). The following essay, which appeared in *Best American Essays* (2000), provides a wealth of examples that illustrate the profound connection between cultural identity and the foods we eat.

BEFORE YOU READ

How might the foods you normally eat be considered strange by someone from another culture?

■ ■ ▨

> To belong is to understand the tacit codes of the people you live with.
> —Michael Ignatieff, *Blood and Belonging*

I

1 The first time my mother and I open a can of tuna, I am nine years old. We stand in the doorway of the kitchen, in semidarkness, the can tilted toward daylight. I want to eat what the kids at school eat: bologna, hot dogs, salami—foods my parents find repugnant because they contain pork and meat byproducts, crushed bone and hair glued together by chemicals and fat. Although she has never been able to tolerate the smell of fish, my mother buys the tuna, hoping to satisfy my longing for American food.

2 Indians, of course, do not eat such things.

3 The tuna smells fishy, which surprises me because I can't remember anyone's tuna sandwich actually smelling like fish. And the tuna in those sandwiches doesn't look like this, pink and shiny, like an internal organ. In fact, this looks similar to the bad foods my mother doesn't want me to eat. She is silent, holding her face away from the can while peering into it like a half-blind bird.

4 "What's wrong with it?" I ask.

5 She has no idea. My mother does not know that the tuna everyone else's mothers made for them was tuna *salad*.

6 "Do you think it's botulism?"

7 I have never seen botulism, but I have read about it, just as I have read about but never eaten steak and kidney pie.

8 There is so much my parents don't know. They are not like other parents, and they disappoint me and my sister. They are supposed to help us negotiate the world outside, teach us the signs, the clues to proper behavior: what to eat and how to eat it.

9   We have expectations, and my parents fail to meet them, especially my mother, who works full-time. I don't understand what it means, to have a mother who works outside and inside the home; I notice only the ways in which she disappoints me. She doesn't show up for school plays. She doesn't make chocolate-frosted cupcakes for my class. At night, if I want her attention, I have to sit in the kitchen and talk to her while she cooks the evening meal, attentive to every third or fourth word I say.

10   We throw the tuna away. This time my mother is disappointed. I go to school with tuna eaters. I see their sandwiches, yet cannot explain the discrepancy between them and the stinking, oily fish in my mother's hand. We do not understand so many things, my mother and I.

II

11   On weekends, we eat fried chicken from Woolworth's on the back steps of my father's first-floor office in Murray Hill. The back steps face a small patch of garden—hedges, a couple of skinny trees, and gravel instead of grass. We can see the back window of the apartment my parents and I lived in until my sister was born. There, the doorman watched my mother, several months pregnant and wearing a sari, slip on the ice in front of the building.

12   My sister and I pretend we are in the country, where our American friends all have houses. We eat glazed doughnuts, also from Woolworth's, and french fries with ketchup.

III

13   My mother takes a catering class and learns that Miracle Whip and mustard are healthier than mayonnaise. She learns to make egg salad with chopped celery, deviled eggs dusted with paprika, a cream cheese spread with bits of fresh ginger and watercress, chicken liver pâté, and little brown-and-white checkerboard sandwiches that we have only once. She makes chicken à la king in puff pastry shells and eggplant Parmesan. She acquires smooth wooden paddles, whose purpose is never clear, two different eggs slicers, several wooden spoons, icing tubes, cookie cutters, and an electric mixer.

IV

14   I learn to make tuna salad by watching a friend. My sister never acquires a taste for it. Instead, she craves

bologna
hot dogs
bacon
sausages

and a range of unidentifiable meat products forbidden by my parents. Their restrictions are not about sacred cows, as everyone around us assumes; in a pinch, we are allowed hamburgers, though lamb burgers are preferable. A "pinch" means choosing not to draw attention to ourselves as outsiders, impolite visitors who won't eat what their host serves. But bologna is still taboo.

V

15 Things my sister refuses to eat: butter, veal, anything with jeera. The baby-sitter tries to feed her butter sandwiches, threatens her with them, makes her cry in fear and disgust. My mother does not disappoint her; she does not believe in forcing us to eat, in using food as a weapon. In addition to pbj, my sister likes pasta and marinara sauce, bologna and Wonder Bread (when she can get it), and fried egg sandwiches with turkey, cheese, and horseradish. Her tastes, once established, are predictable.

VI

16 When we visit our relatives in India, food prepared outside the house is carefully monitored. In the hot, sticky monsoon months in New Delhi and Bombay, we cannot eat ice cream, salad, cold food, or any fruit that can't be peeled. Definitely no meat. People die from amoebic dysentery, unexplained fevers, strange boils on their bodies. We drink boiled water only, no ice. No sweets except for jalebi, thin fried twists of dough in dripping hot sugar syrup. If we're caught outside with nothing to drink, Fanta, Limca, Thums Up (after Coca-Cola is thrown out by Mrs. Gandhi) will do. Hot tea sweetened with sugar, served with thick creamy buffalo milk, is preferable. It should be boiled, to kill the germs on the cup.

17 My mother talks about "back home" as a safe place, a silk cocoon frozen in time where we are sheltered by family and friends. Back home, my sister and I do not argue about food with my parents. Home is where they know all the rules. We trust them to guide us safely through the maze of city streets for which they have no map, and we trust them to feed and take care of us, the way parents should.

18 Finally, though, one of us will get sick, hungry for the food we see our cousins and friends eating, too thirsty to ask for a straw, too polite to insist on properly boiled water.

19 At my uncle's diner in New Delhi, someone hands me a plate of aloo tikki, fried potato patties filled with mashed channa dal and served with a sweet and a sour chutney. The channa, mixed with hot chilies and spices, burns my tongue and throat. I reach for my Fanta, discard the paper straw, and gulp the sweet orange soda down, huge drafts that sting rather than soothe.

20 When I throw up later that day (or is it the next morning, when a stomachache wakes me from deep sleep?). I cry over the frustration of being singled out, not from the pain my mother assumes I'm feeling as she holds my hair back from my face. The taste of orange lingers in my mouth, and I remember my lips touching the cold glass of the Fanta bottle.

21 At that moment, more than anything, I want to be like my cousins.

VII

22   In New York, at the first Indian restaurant in our neighborhood, my father orders with confidence, and my sister and I play with the silverware until the steaming plates of lamb biryani arrive.

23   What is Indian food? my friends ask, their noses crinkling up.

24   Later, this restaurant is run out of business by the new Indo-Pak-Bangladeshi combinations up and down the street, which serve similar food. They use plastic cutlery and Styrofoam cups. They do not distinguish between North and South Indian cooking, or between Indian, Pakistani, and Bangladeshi cooking, and their customers do not care. The food is fast, cheap, and tasty. Dosa, a rice flour crepe stuffed with masala potato, appears on the same trays as chicken makhani.

25   Now my friends want to know, Do you eat curry at home?

26   One time my mother makes lamb vindaloo for guests. Like dosa, this is a South Indian dish, one that my Punjabi mother has to learn from a cookbook. For us, she cooks everyday food—yellow dal, rice, chapati, bhaji. Lentils, rice, bread, and vegetables. She has never referred to anything on our tables as "curry" or "curried," but I know she has made chicken curry for guests. Vindaloo, she explains, is a curry too. I understand then that curry is a dish created for guests, outsiders, a food for people who eat in restaurants.

VIII

27   I have inherited brown eyes, black hair, a long nose with a crooked bridge, and soft teeth with thin enamel. I am in my twenties, moving to a city far from my parents, before it occurs to me that jeera, the spice my sister avoids, must have an English name. I have to learn that haldi = turmeric, methi = fenugreek. What to make with fenugreek, I do not know. My grandmother used to make methi roti for our breakfast, cornbread with fresh fenugreek leaves served with a lump of homemade butter. No one makes it now that she's gone, though once in a while my mother will get a craving for it and produce a facsimile ("The cornmeal here is wrong") that only highlights what she's really missing: the smells and tastes of her mother's house.

28   I will never make my grandmother's methi roti or even my mother's unsatisfactory imitation of it. I attempt chapati; it takes six hours, three phone calls home, and leaves me with an aching back. I have to write translations down: jeera = cumin. My memory is unreliable. But I have always known garam = hot.

IX

29   My mother learns how to make brownies and apple pie. My father makes only Indian food, except for loaves of heavy, sweet brown bread that I eat with thin slices of American cheese and lettuce. The recipe is a secret, passed on to him by a woman at work. Years later, when he finally gives it to me, when I finally ask for it, I end up with three bricks of gluten that even the birds and my husband won't eat.

X

30 My parents send me to boarding school, outside of London. They imagine that I will overcome my shyness and find a place for myself in this all-girls' school. They have never lived in England, but as former subjects of the British Empire, they find London familiar, comfortable in a way New York—my mother's home for over twenty years by now—is not. American still don't know what to call us; their Indians live on reservations, not in Manhattan. Because they understand the English, my parents believe the English understand us.

31   I poke at my first school lunch—thin, overworked pastry in a puddle of lumpy gravy. The lumps are chewy mushrooms, maybe, or overcooked shrimp.

32   "What is this?" I don't want to ask, but I can't go on eating without knowing.

33   "Steak and kidney pie."

34   The girl next to me, red-haired, freckled, watches me take a bite from my plate. She has been put in charge of me, the new girl, and I follow her around all day, a foreigner at the mercy of a reluctant and angry tour guide. She is not used to explaining what is perfectly and utterly natural.

35   "What, you've never had steak and kidney pie? Bloody hell."

36   My classmates scoff, then marvel, them laugh at my ignorance. After a year, I understand what is on my plate: sausage rolls, blood pudding, Spam, roast beef in a thin, greasy gravy, all the bacon and sausage I could possibly want. My parents do not expect me to starve.

37   The girls at school expect conformity; it has been bred into them, through years of uniforms and strict rules about proper behavior. I am thirteen and contrary, even as I yearn for acceptance. I declare myself a vegetarian and doom myself to a diet of cauliflower, cheese and baked beans on toast. The administration does not question my decision; they assume it's for vague, undefined religious reasons, although my father, the doctor, tells them it's for my health. My reasons, from this distance of many years, remain murky to me.

38   Perhaps I am my parents' daughter after all.

XI

39 When she is three, sitting on my cousin's lap in Bombay, my sister reaches for his plate and puts a chili in her mouth. She wants to be like the grownups, who dip green chilies in coarse salt and eat them like any other vegetable. She howls inconsolable animal pain for what must be hours. She doesn't have the vocabulary for the oily heat that stings her mouth and tongue, burns a trail through her small tender body. Only hot, sticky tears on my father's shoulder.

40   As an adult, she eats red chili paste, mango pickle, kimchee, foods that make my eyes water and my stomach gurgle. My tastes are milder. I order raita at Indian restaurants and ask for food that won't sear the roof of my mouth and scar the insides of my cheeks. The waiters nod, and their eyes shift—a slight once-over that indicates they don't believe me. I am Indian, aren't I? My father seems to agree with them. He tells me I'm asking for the impossible, as if he believes the recipes are immutable, written in stone during the passage from India to America.

XII

41 I look around my boyfriend's freezer one day and find meat: pork chops, ground beef, chicken pieces, Italian sausage. Ham in the refrigerator, next to the home-made bolognese sauce. Tupperware filled with chili made from ground beef and pork.

42 He smells different from me. Foreign. Strange.

43 I marry him anyway.

44 He has inherited blue eyes that turn gray in bad weather, light brown hair, a sharp pointy nose, and excellent teeth. He learns to make chili with ground turkey and tofu, tomato sauce with red wine and portobello mushrooms, roast chicken with rosemary and slivers of garlic under the skin.

45 He eats steak when we are in separate cities, roast beef at his mother's house, hamburgers at work. Sometimes I smell them on his skin. I hope he doesn't notice me turning my face, a cheek instead of my lips, my nose wrinkled at the unfamiliar, musky smell.

XIII

46 And then I realize I don't want to be a person who can find Indian food only in restaurants. One day my parents will be gone and I will long for the foods of my childhood, the way they long for theirs. I prepare for this day the way people on TV prepare for the end of the world. They gather canned goods they will never eat while I stockpile recipes I cannot replicate. I am frantic, disorganized, grabbing what I can, filing scribbled notes haphazardly. I regret the tastes I've forgotten, the meals I have inhaled without a thought. I worry that I've come to this realization too late.

XIV

47 Who told my mother about Brie? One day we were eating Velveeta, the next day Brie, Gouda, Camembert, Port Salut, Havarti with caraway, Danish fontina, string cheese made with sheep's milk. Who opened the door to these foreigners that sit on the refrigerator shelf next to last night's dal?

48 Back home, there is one cheese only, which comes in a tin, looks like Bakelite, and tastes best when melted.

49 And how do we go from Chef Boyardee to fresh pasta and homemade sauce, made with Redpack tomatoes, crushed garlic, and dried oregano? Macaroni and cheese, made with fresh cheddar and whole milk, sprinkled with bread crumbs and paprika. Fresh eggplant and ricotta ravioli, baked with marinara sauce and fresh mozzarella.

50 My mother will never cook beef or pork in her kitchen, and the foods she knew in her childhood are unavailable. Because the only alternative to the super-market, with its TV dinners and canned foods, is the gourmet Italian deli across the street, by default our meals become socially acceptable.

XV

51 If I really want to make myself sick, I worry that my husband will one day leave me for a meat-eater, for someone familiar who doesn't sniff him suspiciously for signs of alimentary infidelity.

XVI

52 Indians eat lentils. I understand this as absolute, a decree from an unidentifiable authority that watches and judges me.

53 So what does it mean that I cannot replicate my mother's dal? She and my father show me repeatedly, in their kitchen, in my kitchen. They coach me over the phone, buy me the best cookbooks, and finally write down their secrets. Things I'm supposed to know but don't. Recipes that should be, by now, engraved on my heart.

54 Living far from the comfort of people who require no explanation for what I do and who I am, I crave the foods we have shared. My mother convinces me that moong is the easiest dal to prepare, and yet it fails me every time: bland, watery, a sickly greenish yellow mush. These imperfect imitations remind me only of what I'm missing.

55 But I have never been fond of moong dal. At my mother's table it is the last thing I reach for. Now I worry that this antipathy toward dal signals something deeper, that somehow I am not my parents' daughter not Indian, and because I cannot bear the touch and smell of raw meat, though I can eat it cooked (charred, dry, and overdone), I am not American either.

56 I worry about a lifetime purgatory in Indian restaurants where I will complain that all the food looks and tastes the same because they've used the same masala.

XVII

57 About the tuna and her attempts to feed us, my mother laughs. She says, "You were never fussy. You ate everything I made and never complained."

58 My mother is at the stove, wearing only her blouse and petticoat, her sari carefully folded and hung in the closet. She does not believe a girl's place is in the kitchen, but she expects me to know that too much hing can ruin a meal, to know without being told, without having to ask or write it down. Hing = asafetida.

59 She remembers the catering class. "Oh, that class. You know, I had to give it up when we got to lobster. I just couldn't stand the way it looked."

60 She says this apologetically, as if she has deprived us, as if she suspects that having a mother who could feed us lobster would have changed the course of our lives.

61 Intellectually, she understands that only certain people regularly eat lobster, people with money or those who live in Maine, or both. In her catering class there were people without jobs for whom preparing lobster was a part of their professional training as caterers. Like us, they wouldn't be eating lobster at home.

For my mother, however, lobster was just another American food, like tuna—different, strange, not natural yet somehow essential to belonging.

62   I learned how to prepare and eat lobster from the same girl who taught me tuna salad. I ate bacon at her house too. And one day this girl, with her houses in the country and Martha's Vineyard, asked me how my uncle was going to pick me up from the airport in Bombay. In 1973, she was surprised to hear that he used a car, not an elephant. At home, my parents and I laughed, and though I never knew for sure if she was making fun of me, I still wanted her friendship.

63   My parents were afraid my sister and I would learn to despise the foods they loved, replace them with bologna and bacon and lose our taste for masala. For my mother, giving up her disgust of lobster, with its hard exterior and foreign smell, would mean renouncing some essential difference. It would mean becoming, decidedly, definitely, American—unafraid of meat in all its forms, able to consume large quantities of protein at any given meal. My willingness to toss a living being into boiling water and then get past its ugly appearance to the rich meat inside must mean to my mother that I am somehow someone she is not.

64   But I haven't eaten lobster in years. In my kitchen cupboards, there is a thirteen-pound bag of basmati rice, jars of lime pickle, mango pickle, and ghee, cans of tuna and anchovies, canned soups, coconut milk, and tomatoes, rice noodles, several kinds of pasta, dried mushrooms, and unlabeled bottles of spices: haldi, jeera, hing. When my husband tries to help me cook, he cannot identify all the spices. He gets confused when I forget their English names and remarks that my expectations of him are unreasonable.

65   I am my parents' daughter. Like them, I expect knowledge to pass from me to my husband without one word of explanation or translation. I want him to know what I know, see what I see, without having to tell him exactly what it is. I want to believe that recipes never change.

■ ■ ▨

MEANING

1. How did Kothari diverge from her mother on the issue of what foods were appropriate to eat?

2. How has Kothari's relationship with her husband also been affected by the food issue?

3. How is being a vegetarian something else that separates Kothari from her husband?

4. Why was it important for Kothari to learn to prepare authentic Indian meals even as she became more culturally assimilated?

TECHNIQUE

1. Why is the example of her mother's attempt to serve her tuna a strong way to start her essay?

2. How does the progression of examples in each of the short sections help to define Kothari's search for an identity?

3. **Other Patterns.** Where does Kothari use **description** to convey the different flavors and fragrances of different foods?

LANGUAGE

1. How does Kothari use striking similes (for example, in paragraph 3 to convey her mother's distaste for typical American food)?
2. How does Kothari's use of so many different names of Indian foods and spices accentuate her wish to have her American-born husband accept who she is?
3. How does the title focus the reader's attention on the central issue?
4. If you don't know the meaning of the following words, look them up: *repugnant* (1), *botulism* (6), *pâté* (13), *taboo* (14), *biryani* (22), *curry* (25), *facsimile* (27), *inconsolable* (39), *immutable* (40).

SUGGESTIONS FOR WRITING

1. Create a series of vignettes using examples from your own experiences that illustrate shifting cultural attitudes in your food preferences.
2. **Critical Writing.** Write a short essay based on examples of your favorite foods, generalizing as to what cultural identity is revealed.
3. Have you ever attempted to cook an unfamiliar ethnic food? If so, what was it? If not, what would you like to try? Write instructions on how to prepare a dish that you made.
4. **Thematic Links.** What insights do Kothari's essay and Ethel Hofman's "An Island Passover" (Chapter 7, "Process Analysis") give you into the importance that ethnic foods have in preserving cultural identity?

LUISA VALENZUELA

The Censors

Argentinian novelist and short story writer Luisa Valenzuela (b. 1938) lived through the period when her country was under military rule in the 1970s. She saw individuals disappear and experienced censorship such as the kind she writes about in the following story (from *The Open Door*, 1988). She later left Argentina for the United States and has taught creative writing at Columbia University. Her works include *The Lizard's Tale* (1983) and *Black Novel: With Argentines* (1992).

BEFORE YOU READ

Do you evaluate the e-mails you send or blogs you create, based on how others might interpret them?

■ ■ ▨

1   Poor Juan! One day they caught him with his guard down before he could even realize that what he had taken as a stroke of luck was really one of fate's dirty tricks. These things happen the minute you're careless, as one often is. Juancito let happiness—a feeling you can't trust—get the better of him when he received from a confidential source Mariana's new address in Paris and knew that she hadn't forgotten him. Without thinking twice, he sat down at his table and wrote her a letter. *The* letter that now keeps his mind off his job during the day and won't let him sleep at night (what had he scrawled, what had he put on that sheet of paper he sent to Mariana?).

2   Juan knows there won't be a problem with the letter's contents, that it's irreproachable, harmless. But what about the rest? He knows that they examine, sniff, feel, and read between the lines of each and every letter, and check its tiniest comma and most accidental stain. He knows that all letters pass from hand to hand and go through all sorts of tests in the huge censorship offices and that, in the end, very few continue on their way. Usually it takes months, even years, if there aren't any snags; all this time the freedom, maybe even the life, of both sender and receiver is in jeopardy. And that's why Juan's so troubled: thinking that something might happen to Mariana because of his letters. Of all people, Mariana, who must finally feel safe there where she always dreamt she'd live. But he knows that the *Censor's Secret Command* operates all over the world and cashes in on the discount in air fares; there's nothing to stop them from going as far as that hidden Paris neighborhood, kidnapping Mariana, and returning to their cozy homes, certain of having fulfilled their noble mission.

3   Well, you've got to beat them to the punch, do what everyone tries to do: sabotage the machinery, throw sand in its gears, get to the bottom of the problem so as to stop it.

4   This was Juan's sound plan when he, like many others, applied for a censor's job—not because he had a calling or needed a job: no, he applied simply to intercept his own letter, a consoling albeit unoriginal idea. He was hired immediately, for each day more and more censors are needed and no one would bother to check on his references.

5   Ulterior motives couldn't be overlooked by the *Censorship Division*, but they needn't be too strict with those who applied. They knew how hard it would be for the poor guys to find the letter they wanted and even if they did, what's a letter or two when the new censor would snap up so many others? That's how Juan managed to join the *Post Office's Censorship Division*, with a certain goal in mind.

6   The building had a festive air on the outside that contrasted with its inner staidness. Little by little, Juan was absorbed by his job, and he felt at peace since he was doing everything he could to get his letter for Mariana. He didn't even worry when, in his first month, he was sent to *Section K* where envelopes are very carefully screened for explosives.

7   It's true that on the third day, a fellow worker had his right hand blown off by a letter, but the division chief claimed it was sheer negligence on the victim's part. Juan and the other employees were allowed to go back to their work, though feeling less secure. After work, one of them tried to organize a strike to demand higher wages for unhealthy work, but Juan didn't join in; after thinking it over, he reported the man to his superiors and thus got promoted.

8   You don't form a habit by doing something once, he told himself as he left his boss's office. And when he was transferred to *Section J*, where letters are carefully checked for poison dust, he felt he had climbed a rung in the ladder.

9   By working hard, he quickly reached *Section E* where the job became more interesting, for he could now read and analyze the letters' contents. Here he could even hope to get hold of his letter, which, judging by the time that had elapsed, had gone through the other sections and was probably floating around in this one.

10   Soon his work became so absorbing that his noble mission blurred in his mind. Day after day he crossed out whole paragraphs in red ink, pitilessly chucking many letters into the censored basket. These were horrible days when he was shocked by the subtle and conniving ways employed by people to pass on subversive messages; his instincts were so sharp that he found behind a simple "the weather's unsettled" or "prices continue to soar" the wavering hand of someone secretly scheming to overthrow the Government.

11   His zeal brought him swift promotion. We don't know if this made him happy. Very few letters reached him in *Section B*—only a handful passed the other hurdles—so he read them over and over again, passed them under a magnifying glass, searched for microprint with an electronic microscope, and tuned his sense of smell so that he was beat by the time he made it home. He'd barely manage to warm up his soup, eat some fruit, and fall into bed, satisfied with having done his duty. Only his darling mother worried, but she couldn't get him back on the right track. She'd say, though it wasn't always true: Lola called, she's

at the bar with the girls, they miss you, they're waiting for you. Or else she'd leave a bottle of red wine on the table. But Juan wouldn't overdo it: any distraction could make him lose his edge and the perfect censor had to be alert, keen, attentive, and sharp to nab cheats. He had a truly patriotic task, both self-denying and uplifting.

12   His basket for censored letters became the best fed as well as the most cunning basket in the whole *Censorship Division.* He was about to congratulate himself for having finally discovered his true mission, when his letter to Mariana reached his hands. Naturally, he censored it without regret. And just as naturally, he couldn't stop them from executing him the following morning, another victim of his devotion to his work.

■ ■ ▨

MEANING

1. What motivates Juan initially in applying for a job as a censor?
2. Was Juan's letter to Mariana dangerous to the government in any way?
3. How does Juan change as he moves up in the hierarchy of the system?
4. What does Juan's ultimate choice reveal about the lure of power?

TECHNIQUE

1. How does Valenzuela use a range of threats that censors must be on guard to detect to express government paranoia?
2. How do the instances in which Juan's mother tries to interest him in leading a normal life reveal how obsessed he has become?
3. **Other Patterns.** How does Valenzuela use a **narrative** to structure her inquiry into how power corrupts?

LANGUAGE

1. How would you characterize Valenzuela's attitude toward Juan as revealed in the story's ending?
2. How effectively does Valenzuela communicate the paranoia of the citizens living under a government that inspects every aspect of one's life?
3. If you do not know the meaning of the following words, look them up: *irreproachable* (2), *albeit* (4).

SUGGESTIONS FOR WRITING

1. **Critical Writing.** Do you believe, as Valenzuela does, that when given the opportunity to wield power, the average citizen will forsake his or her ideals and identify with the authorities? Why or why not?
2. Was the ending foreshadowed, or was it a total surprise to you? Why or why not?

3. Have you or anyone you know bought into a system without admitting that this was the case? **Describe** what happened.

4. **Thematic Links.** How do both Valenzuela's story and Lance Morrow's essay "Advertisements for Oneself" focus on the need to decipher underlying meanings in what you read?

Real-Life Situations: Exemplification

Providing good examples is also important in nonacademic contexts. A letter in which you apply for employment uses examples to substantiate your claim that you would make a good candidate for an advertised position. In the following letter, Samantha Clarke uses examples to emphasize her qualifications that a potential employer could recognize as meeting their needs for a pharmaceutical sales representative. Notice that the letter begins by identifying the position and where it was advertised. She then relates her work experience to the needs of the prospective employer and describes her educational qualifications and current status. She concludes by providing information on how she can be contacted for an interview. If she were granted an interview, she also would write a follow-up thank you note. For the accompanying résumé, see page 417 in Chapter 8, "Classification and Division."

Samantha Clarke
2843 Arcola Ave.
North Hollywood, CA 90402
February 28, 2006

Ms. Marsha Finn, Director
Personnel Dept.
Schering-Plough
680 Wilshire Blvd.
Los Angeles, CA 90656

Dear Ms. Finn:

I am responding to your search for a pharmaceutical sales representative, advertised in your online posting #2750.

I have applicable work experience in the pharmaceutical and medical fields from summer employment at Associates in Primary Care and at Walgreen's. At Associates in Primary Care, I assisted the office manager by scheduling appointments for patients, calling in their prescriptions, maintaining their records and files, and contacting them with lab results. At Walgreen's, I assisted the pharmacist by calling physicians' offices and insurance companies and served the needs of hundreds of customers. These summer jobs gave me experience in sales and in creating and maintaining rapport with customers and patients.

In June 2007 I will graduate from the University of California at Los Angeles with a major in business administration and a minor in botany. In addition to courses in public relations, accounting, statistics, marketing, psychology, and management systems, I have taken courses in botany and plant science. For my senior project, I studied the medical uses of indigenous plants in Costa Rica and reported on my findings.

As the accompanying résumé indicates, my education and experience in closely related fields suggest that I would be an ideal candidate for your advertised position.

If you will add me to your interview roster, I will be available at your convenience. Please contact me at (213) 467-0999 or e-mail me at sclarke@aol.com.

Sincerely,

Samantha Clarke

Samantha Clarke

▨▨▨ STUDENT ESSAY: EXEMPLIFICATION

Helene Santos wrote the following essay as a response to Judith Ortiz Cofer's essay "The Myth of the Latin Woman" and used the pattern of exemplification to organize her analysis. The annotations on Helene's paper (shown without documentation) and the follow-up commentary ("Strategies") are designed to help you understand exemplification.

Santos 1

Refuting the Latina Stereotype

Helene Santos

1   In the musical <u>West Side Story</u>, the beautiful and innocent Maria, newly arrived from Puerto Rico, falls tragically in love with a member of an Anglo gang. The play is filled with memorable songs, but the characters, including Maria and her friend, the Puerto Rican "spitfire" Anita, are familiar stereotypes of Latinas. In "The Myth of the Latin Woman: I Just Met a Girl Named Maria," Judith Ortiz Cofer refutes these sterotypes by contrasting them with the realities of her life as an articulate and accomplished individual.

2   A Puerto Rican writer of some renown, Cofer is offended when strangers make unwarranted assumptions about her. She confesses that since childhood she has been troubled by these cross-cultural misperceptions:

> you can leave the island, master the English language,
> and travel as far as you can, but if you are a Latina,

Introduction gives the background on Cofer's title. The title refers to the thesis statement.

Thesis statement

Quotations for four lines or more are indented one inch.

Santos 2

especially one like me who so obviously belongs to Rita
Moreno's gene pool, the island travels with you (187).

3   Cofer uses personal experiences to show how she has
learned to cope with these misperceptions about her. As a
Puerto Rican growing up in the United States, she was caught
between her parents' Puerto Rican culture and the values of her
Anglo schoolmates. When Cofer was young, "Puerto Rican
mothers . . . encouraged their daughters to dress and act like
women" (188). So on her high school's Career Day, she and her
Puerto Rican friends wore their mothers' flashy jewelry and
clothing, which their teachers and Anglo classmates, who were
attired in "tailored skirts and silk blouses," disapproved (188).

4   Some people might disagree with Cofer's blaming cross-
cultural misunderstandings and feel that she was old enough
and had lived on the mainland long enough to know what
clothes were appropriate. But Cofer was raised in a Puerto
Rican community in New Jersey and had never been out in
the world. Given her background, it was natural for her to
interpret the meaning of "dressing up" in an entirely different
way than her Anglo classmates and teachers. She explains
that "It is custom, . . . not chromosomes, that leads us to
choose scarlet over pale pink" (189).

> Paragraph answers
> an alternative
> viewpoint.

> Ellipsis mark shows
> omission of word
> or words from
> source.

5   Years later, when Cofer was in graduate school at Oxford,
she was unexpectedly treated as a Latina stereotype. On a bus
trip to London, a drunken young passenger knelt before her and
serenaded her with "Maria" from <u>West Side Story</u>. Although her
fellow passengers were "politely amused," Cofer struggled to hide
her anger with her version of "an English smile"—a response that
recalls the "studied indifference" of the young women subjected
to off-color <u>piropos</u> on Saturday nights in the plaza of her
mother's village in Puerto Rico (187).

6   In addition to the assumption that Latinas are sexually
available, there is a second damaging aspect of the stereotype:
that all Latinas are uneducated, socially inferior, and suited
only for menial work. Cofer likens the stereotype of the Hispanic

> Transitional sen-
> tence signals two-
> part structure of
> discussion of
> stereotype.

maid "cooking up a spicy storm in a shiny California kitchen" to the "Mammy" stereotype of black women, which allows them to be treated in ways that would be unthinkable if they were white (190).

7   As an example, Cofer describes an event that happened before her first public poetry reading. Upon arriving at the restaurant, Cofer was called over to a table by an older woman. Cofer walked over, expecting to be asked to autograph a copy of her volume of poems. However, when she reached the table, the woman, who had assumed that Cofer was the waitress, ordered a cup of coffee. Cofer expresses her anger with irony: "Easy enough to mistake my poems for menus, I suppose" (190).

8   The language and the organization of the essay are carefully crafted, demonstrating that Cofer is an accomplished and articulate writer. In the introductory paragraphs, she uses two contrasting metaphors of an island to express what it feels like to be stereotyped. In the first paragraph, the island is Puerto Rico, the vividly colored "tropical paradise" that is the homeland of her parents. But in the second paragraph the island becomes gray and barren, "an Alcatraz, a place nobody wants to visit"—a metaphor for her feeling of isolation in mainland Anglo culture (187).

Transitional sentence signals switch from discussion of content to analysis of style.

9   Cofer's essay has a loosely chronological structure—a series of episodes that trace the development of her reactions to cultural stereotyping from childhood to adulthood. For example, to help the reader understand the differences between Puerto Rican and Anglo customs, Cofer inserts into the chronological series her mother's description of Saturday nights in the town plaza when she was young. There, the flirtations between boys and girls had clear boundaries, and the fundamental rule, says Cofer, was "You may look at my sister, but if you touch her I will

kill you" (189). To illustrate the lack of such boundaries on the mainland, Cofer describes her date's mistaken assumptions and unwanted kiss at her first formal dance.

10   As she gained more experience and more confidence as well as professional success, Cofer's reaction changed to anger at disrespectful behavior that diminished her as a person. When she was accosted in a hotel lobby by a tuxedoed guest singing an off-color version of "La Bamba," she waited in silence until he was finished and then insulted him indirectly but sharply by cautioning his daughter never to ask him what he had done in the army. Later Cofer told her friend that she "had really wanted to push the jerk into the swimming pool" (190).

11   In the last episode of the essay, when she was mistaken for a waitress rather than a poet, Cofer also responded with anger, gazing intently at the offending woman throughout her poetry reading—a tactic that Cofer describes as "punish[ing] her with my full attention" (190).

12   Cofer's adolescent feelings of embarrassment have changed regarding stereotyped assumptions as challenges to "open some avenue for communication" (190). Her goal, she says, is to use her art "to try to replace the old pervasive stereotype . . . with a much more interesting set of realities" (191).

13   Cofer concludes her essay with an example of the art: lines from a poem about Latinas that she calls "a prayer for communication and for respect." Her Latin woman praying "in Spanish to an Anglo god / with a Jewish heritage / . . . fervently hoping / that if not omnipotent, / at least He be bilingual" addresses the realities behind the stereotype of Maria (191).

Conclusion refers back to thesis statement.

Work Cited

Cofer, Judith Ortiz. "The Myth of the Latin Woman: I Just Met a Girl Named Maria." <u>Patterns Across Cultures</u>. Ed. Stuart Hirschberg and Terry Hirschberg. Boston: Houghton, 2009. 187–91.

Strategies for Writing Essays in Exemplification

1. Introduction and Thesis

In her essay "Refuting the Latina Stereotype" Helene responds to an assignment that asks students to identify the thematic focus and literary techniques in an essay that had been previously assigned. Helene begins her introduction by addressing the issue that Judith Ortiz Cofer's essay explores: the way in which she and other Latinas have been dehumanized by being viewed through the lens of popular stereotypes communicated in films and the media. This leads to Helene's thesis that Cofer's article negates these stereotypes by affirming a contrasting value of self-worth and achievement. The final sentence of Helene's introduction serves as both a thesis statement and an organizational plan for her essay.

2. Examples as Evidence

In the body of her essay, Helene supports her thesis with numerous examples that follow a loosely chronological structure. These episodes in Cofer's life, ranging from Puerto Rico to England, illustrate instances of cultural stereotyping. Helene also offers examples of Cofer's achievement as a poet and writer by citing Cofer's skillful use of metaphors and irony and by giving an example of her poetry. The examples that Helene offers are relevant, representative, and specific enough to effectively support her thesis.

3. Point of View and Linking Strategies

The essay that Helene wrote called for her to place the subject in the foreground, and she consistently uses the third-person point of view. She uses linking devices to move the reader smoothly from section to section (for example, "In addition to the assumption that Latinas are sexually available, there is a second damaging aspect of the stereotype").

4. Revision

One aspect of Helene's essay that could be improved is the lack of additional examples drawn from Cofer's essay illustrating her skill as an accomplished writer. Helene needs to provide these to fulfill the expectations she set out in her thesis. Another problem is the uneven shift in focus between summarizing aspects of Cofer's essay and the analysis of key aspects of it to support her thesis. Helene might have spoken up in her own voice, especially in paragraph 4, rather than phrasing her criticism by saying "some people might disagree."

Guidelines for Writing an Essay in Exemplification

- If your assignment requires you to use examples, have you provided a thesis statement that clarifies the idea that your examples illustrate? These examples may be drawn from personal observations and experiences, incidents involving other people, or places and events. They can also be drawn from statistical studies and surveys. Most important, your examples should clarify your thesis.
- Have you provided sufficient examples that are typical and representative with enough detail to enable your readers to grasp your thesis?
- Have you presented the examples in a way that is designed to be both interesting and persuasive to your readers through an easy-to-grasp pattern of organization?
- Have you maintained a consistent third-person point of view (even if some examples are drawn from personal experiences) and provided linking devices to guide the reader smoothly from section to section?

Grammar Tips for Exemplification

Two stylistic issues are especially important in exemplification: (1) varying sentence structure to get away from the pattern of "one example is . . . ," "another example is . . . ," "a third example is . . ." and (2) remembering to separate three or more items—single words, phrases, or clauses—in a series with commas.

1. First drafts frequently contain a jumble of examples one after another, with little variety.

Unedited

One example of the laser's usefulness is in surveying distances. Another example is in microsurgery. A third example is fiber-optic communications. These three applications of the laser make use of its unique capabilities. The directionality of laser beams makes it useful for surveying. Because the laser can be precisely directed and controlled, it can be used to perform surgery. The coherent light beams in tiny fiber-optic cables can carry enormous amounts of data. All three applications show the wide-ranging usefulness of the laser.

In this paragraph, the writer has provided numerous examples but introduces them all in a similar way. The result is choppy and uninteresting.

In the edited passage, the writer consolidates the examples and links them together with a generalization.

continued

Edited

The laser's unique qualities make it especially useful for surveying, microsurgery, and fiber-optic communications. In these applications, the laser's directionality, coherence, precision, and ability to transmit enormous amounts of data have dramatically changed our lives in many areas.

2. In the edited version, notice how commas are used to separate items in a series. In the second sentence, a comma is placed before the coordinating conjunction *and*. A comma comes before the last item in the series of three or more items.

CHECKLIST for Revising an Exemplification Essay

- Does your thesis statement identify the idea that your examples will illustrate, clarify, or explain?
- Have you provided sufficient examples that are typical or representative?
- Are your examples interesting and compelling?
- Are your examples organized in an easy-to-understand pattern?
- Are your examples presented through a consistent third-person viewpoint?
- Do your transitional words and phrases make it easy for the reader to see how your examples support your thesis?

ADDITIONAL WRITING ASSIGNMENTS AND ACTIVITIES

COMMUNICATING WITH DIFFERENT AUDIENCES

1. Write a letter to someone in which you give examples of something you wished you had said earlier but lacked the courage to do so at the time.

2. Write a letter to a film magazine explaining why a movie that has been dubbed should be subtitled or vice versa.

3. You work for an online travel agency, and you are asked to create a short article on the best places to visit in your state or region. Give examples and supporting details for each of these destinations.

4. Write a speech to present to visiting high-school seniors who are considering attending your college, including examples of the benefits and positive features with supporting details.

5. Write a letter to the International Olympic Committee suggesting a sport that should be included in either the summer or winter games with examples that show why the sport is important enough to warrant inclusion.

6. A philanthropic organization holds an open contest in which the organization will fund the winner's choice of a charity or cause. Write an essay giving examples of your cause's unique requirements and needs.

WRITING FOR A NEWSPAPER

Write an editorial giving examples to demonstrate why there should be a traffic light at a certain location.

EXEMPLIFICATION ESSAYS

1. Assemble examples of different kinds of customers for an all-night or late-night diner, laundromat, or video store.

2. Give examples of the different qualities and attributes of fabulous creatures such as angels, minotaurs, or gnomes, and explain why they hold such an appeal.

3. Give examples of times when you felt that you were being contacted by spirits or ghosts and the form the communication took.

4. If you have a lucky charm, talisman, or amulet, what examples can you recall in which it brought you good luck?

5. Give instances that illustrate an abstract idea such as love, hate, depression, ambivalence, or benevolence.

6. If you were stranded on an island, in a desert, or in some other isolated place, what two items would you want to have with you, other than any device with which you could inform the outside world of your predicament?

7. Give examples of survival skills and resourcefulness that you used in a snowstorm, hailstorm, landslide, earthquake, tornado, hurricane, fire, flood, or any other natural disaster.

8. Write about instances that led you to change a belief that you once held that you no longer hold.

9. Describe hypothetical instances in which you might consider telling a lie.

10. Give examples of things that you cannot stand, your pet peeves, and/or phobias.

11. Give examples of pranks that you played or that were played on you and tell what happened.

12. Give examples of cybertalk or slang expressions that are part of your vocabulary and the ideas they allow you to express.

13. Give examples of specialized language or jargon that is used on medical, legal, and/or crime shows on TV and explain what function the special language serves.

RESEARCH SUGGESTIONS

1. Interview someone who has voluntarily given up aspects of their former lifestyle, and compare the person's life then and his or her life now.

2. Research examples of how Elvis Presley or another musician have permeated popular culture in films, books, articles, magazines, artifacts, and song lyrics.

COLLABORATIVE ACTIVITIES

1. Class members can assemble examples of the advantages and disadvantages of belonging to a virtual community in terms of how such communities might serve the same function as the old-fashioned coffeehouse. The examples can address issues of usefulness of information, how these communities meet the needs of their members, and who polices the communities.

2. Class members can assemble examples of various extreme sports such as rock climbing, white-water rafting, paragliding, or snowboarding and discuss the appeal of these activities over conventional sports.

3. Class members can supply examples that illustrate the appeal of their favorite hobby, such as collecting stamps, coins, or comic books; performing magic tricks; playing a musical instrument; or photography.

Comparison and Contrast

6

Exploring Similarities and Differences Across Cultures

Although a poet might extol the virtues of his lady love as being "beyond compare" and an enthusiastic football fan might say the same of his or her team, most things can be compared. Two fishermen trying to decide whether a fish that they have caught is a smallmouth or a largemouth bass or the same fishermen arguing over which kind of fish is tastier are using the intellectual strategy of comparison and contrast.

Writers in all cultures and in many different fields have discovered that distinctive attributes stand out more clearly when the process of comparison and contrast is used: Musicologists study Beethoven's use of the same melody in different compositions, meteorologists compare and contrast barometric pressures in different regions to spot hurricanes, and political scientists use this basic method to explain similarities and differences between the popular vote and the electoral vote.

In "That Lean and Hungry Look," Suzanne Britt uses a point-by-point comparison to create a continual contrast—from paragraph to paragraph and from sentence to sentence—to illuminate the differences between fat people and thin people:

> Thin people believe in logic. Fat people see all sides. The sides fat people see are rounded blobs, usually gray, always nebulous and truly not worth worrying about. But the thin person persists. "If you consume more calories than you burn," says one of my thin friends, "you will gain weight. It's that simple." Fat people always grin when they hear statements like that. They know better.

Britt disputes the negative stereotyped view of fat people by claiming that they have the ability to see all sides of an issue, whereas thin people can see only one view: their own.

Ivan Karp also organizes his essay "Good Marx for the Anthropologist" through a point-by-point comparison. Karp looks at the Marx Brothers' movies in terms of how they show those who are marginalized assuming power, albeit temporarily, from the upper classes for the amusement of audiences. The Marx Brothers' films use a range of techniques to show the values of the upper classes being mocked by immigrants who do not share or even understand the manners, customs, and language of the society into which they have moved:

> **Minister of Finance:** Something must be done! War would mean a prohibitive increase in our taxes.
> **Chico:** Hey, I got an uncle lives in Taxes.
> **Minister of Finance:** No, I'm talking about taxes—money, dollars.
> **Chico:** Dollas! That's-a where my uncle lives. Dollas, Taxes!
> **Minister of Finance:** Aww!

The Marx Brothers use puns, double meanings, and free association to mock sophisticated language and even ordinary logic. They make fools out of those who are in power by confounding them with their misinterpretations and turn the tables so that these people feel frustrated, powerless, and helpless—just the way immigrants who cannot understand the language and are often seen as fools feel.

Another way of arranging a discussion of similarities and differences relies on a subject-by-subject comparison. Using this method, the writer balances a list of relevant points on one side with those on the other. William Bryant Logan uses this subject-by-subject method in "Eiffel and Oak" to present an analysis from the perspective of an arborist of the differences between a stupendous human-made artifact and an imposing natural wonder. He discusses the structure and uses of the Eiffel Tower:

> Vertical members are reinforced by diagonal members and stabilized by cross members. All the parts are joined by rivets, and there is more open space than iron in the volume of the cone. The wind passes freely through the structure, and the jointed frame is even able to adjust slightly to let it through.

Following his discussion of this feature of the Eiffel Tower, Logan retraces the same points as they apply to the oak:

> Far from letting wind pass freely through, the oak tends to catch it and to shake its head furiously in the storms. But the reason it can do this is an internal structure that makes the tower's look rudimentary. The vertical fibers that make up oak flesh are crossed by rays of living cells that stretch inward from the bark to the pith, stabilizing the framework and keeping the vertical fibers from splitting.

The comparative method serves Logan well as a way of getting his audience to perceive the basic differences between the Eiffel Tower and the oak and to understand why one has come to serve as a landmark and the other has come to symbolize nature at its best.

Comparisons, whether arranged point-by-point or subject-by-subject, may be employed to (1) provide insight into the subjects that are being compared or (2) evaluate two subjects in order to decide which is better.

In an evaluative comparison, the writer lists the positive and negative qualities of each side and then decides between the two on the basis of some stipulated criteria. Logan does this when he concludes his essay by asking rhetorically, "If you had to pick one or the other to emulate, which would you choose?"

Dramatic contrast is a favorite device of political commentators and social satirists who expose hypocrisy by reminding us of what people really do, as opposed to what they profess. In "The Prisoner's Dilemma," Stephen Chapman contrasts the punishment of prisoners in Western societies with those practiced in Middle Eastern cultures to deflate the high opinion that Western society has of itself. Chapman contrasts public flogging and amputation in Pakistan and other countries with the overcrowded, unsanitary conditions in Western prisons and asks "would you rather be subjected to a few minutes of intense pain and considerable public humiliation, or to be locked away for two or three years in a prison cell crowded with ill-tempered sociopaths?"

When the comparison is figurative rather than literal and between two subjects in different categories, the writer is using an analogy. Analogies help an audience to understand something that is unfamiliar in terms of what the audience already knows. Analogies are also used to reveal unsuspected resemblances between seemingly different subjects. In "Kill 'Em! Crush 'Em Eat 'Em Raw!" John McMurtry, a former linebacker who became a philosophy professor, creates an intriguing analogy between football and war to ask his audience to consider whether violence in football might be not a result of the game but rather the reason it exists:

> Their principles and practices are alike: mass hysteria, the art of intimidation, absolute command and total obedience, territorial aggression, censorship, inflated insignia and propaganda, blackboard manoeuvres and strategies, drills, uniforms, formations, marching bands and training camps. And the virtues they celebrate are almost identical: hyper-aggressiveness, coolness under fire and suicidal bravery.

McMurty's tactics here are based on getting his readers to agree, point-by-point, that football and war are similar in many respects as expressions of violence and aggression in our society.

Writers also use comparison to build suspense by contrasting inner thoughts with outer events. In his short story "A Canary's Ideas," Machado de Assis compares and contrasts the social view of "a man by the name of Macedo, who had a fancy for ornithology" with Macedo's imagined conversations with his self-centered pet canary.

So too, Immaculée Ilibagiza from Rwanda, in "Left to Tell," builds suspense when she describes how she and five other Tutsi women and children escaped being killed by rampaging Hutus by hiding in the bathroom of her pastor's house:

> My head was burning, but I did hear the killers in the hall, screaming, "kill them! kill them all!"
>
> *No! God is love*, I told the voice. *He loves me and wouldn't fill me with fear. He will not abandon me. He will not let me die cowering on a bathroom floor. He will not let me die in shame!*

Although we might normally think of comparison and contrast as a method for revealing similarities and differences of opinions, objects, or characteristics, Ilibagiza shows us that this pattern can also be used as a powerful technique for presenting dramatic or ironic contrasts between inner mental states and external reality.

You might find that your uses for this technique will not be as dramatic, but in many real-life contexts, you will discover that the ability to reveal similarities and differences will prove invaluable as an organizational tool in your writing.

SUZANNE BRITT

That Lean and Hungry Look

For many years, Suzanne Britt has taught at Meredith College, and her essays and articles have been widely published in such newspapers and magazines as *Newsweek*, the *New York Times*, the *Boston Globe*, and the *Miami Herald*. The results of her research as a teacher of writing appeared in *A Writer's Rhetoric* (1988). In this essay, first published in *Newsweek* in 1978, Britt champions an atypical thesis: Fat people are better adjusted and happier than thin people are. She develops this comparison with humor and vivid observations. She is also the author of *Images: A Centennial Journey* (1993).

BEFORE YOU READ

What preconceptions about body image influence your reaction when you meet someone new?

■ ■ ▨

1   Caesar was right. Thin people need watching. I've been watching them for most of my adult life, and I don't like what I see. When these narrow fellows spring at me, I quiver to my toes. Thin people come in all personalities, most of them menacing. You've got your "together" thin person, your mechanical thin person, your condescending thin person, your tsk-tsk thin person, your efficiency-expert thin person. All of them are dangerous.

2   In the first place, thin people aren't fun. They don't know how to goof off, at least in the best, fat sense of the word. They've always got to be adoing. Give them a coffee break, and they'll jog around the block. Supply them with a quiet evening at home, and they'll fix the screen door and lick S&H green stamps. They say things like "there aren't enough hours in the day." Fat people never say that. Fat people think the day is too damn long already.

3   Thin people make me tired. They've got speedy little metabolisms that cause them to bustle briskly. They're forever rubbing their bony hands together and eyeing new problems to "tackle." I like to surround myself with sluggish, inert, easygoing fat people, the kind who believe that if you clean it up today, it'll just get dirty again tomorrow.

4   Some people say the business about the jolly fat person is a myth, that all of us chubbies are neurotic, sick, sad people. I disagree. Fat people may not be chortling all day long, but they're a hell of a lot *nicer* than the wizened and shriveled. Thin people turn surly, mean and hard at a young age because they never learn the value of a hot-fudge sundae for easing tension. Thin people don't like gooey soft things because they themselves are neither gooey nor soft. They are crunchy and dull, like carrots. They go straight to the heart of the matter while fat people let things stay all blurry and hazy and vague, the way things actually are. Thin people want to face the truth. Fat people know there is no truth. One

of my thin friends is always staring at complex, unsolvable problems and saying, "The key thing is . . ." Fat people never say that. They know there isn't any such thing as the key thing about anything.

5   Thin people believe in logic. Fat people see all sides. The sides fat people see are rounded blobs, usually gray, always nebulous and truly not worth worrying about. But the thin person persists. "If you consume more calories than you burn," says one of my thin friends, "you will gain weight. It's that simple." Fat people always grin when they hear statements like that. They know better.

6   Fat people realize that life is illogical and unfair. They know very well that God is not in his heaven and all is not right with the world. If God was up there, fat people could have two doughnuts and a big orange drink anytime they wanted.

7   Thin people have a long list of logical things they are always spouting off to me. They hold up one finger at a time as they reel off these things, so I won't lose track. They speak slowly as if to a young child. The list is long and full of holes. It contains tidbits like "get a grip on yourself," "cigarettes kill," "cholesterol clogs," "fit as a fiddle," "ducks in a row" "organize" and "sound fiscal management." Phrases like that.

8   They think these 2,000 point plans lead to happiness. Fat people know happiness is elusive at best and even if they could get the kind thin people talk about, they wouldn't want it. Wisely, fat people see that such programs are too dull, too hard, too off the mark. They are never better than a whole cheesecake.

9   Fat people know all about the mystery of life. They are the ones acquainted with the night, with luck, with fate, with playing it by ear. One thin person I know once suggested that we arrange all the parts of a jigsaw puzzle into groups according to size, shape and color. He figured this would cut the time needed to complete the puzzle by at least 50 percent. I said I wouldn't do it. One, I like to muddle through. Two, what good would it do to finish early? Three, the jigsaw puzzle isn't the important thing. The important thing is the fun of four people (one thin person included) sitting around a card table, working a jigsaw puzzle. My thin friend had no use for my list. Instead of joining us, he went outside and mulched the boxwoods. The three remaining fat people finished the puzzle and made chocolate, double-fudged brownies to celebrate.

10   The main problem with thin people is they oppress. Their good intentions, bony torsos, tight ships, neat corners, cerebral machinations and pat solutions loom like dark clouds over the loose, comfortable, spread-out, soft world of the fat. Long after fat people have removed their coats and shoes and put their feet up on the coffee table, thin people are still sitting on the edge of the sofa, looking neat as a pin, discussing rutabagas. Fat people are heavily into fits of laughter, slapping their thighs and whooping it up, while thin people are still politely waiting for the punch line.

11   Thin people are downers. They like math and mortality and reasoned evaluation of the limitations of human beings. They have their skinny little acts together. They expound, prognose, probe and prick.

12   Fat people are convivial. They will like you even if you're irregular and have acne. They will come up with a good reason why you never wrote the great American novel. They will cry in your beer with you. They will put your name in the pot. They will let you off the hook. Fat people will gab, giggle, guffaw, gallumph, gyrate and gossip. They are gluttonous and goodly and great. What you want when you're down is soft and jiggly, not muscled and stable. Fat people know this. Fat people have plenty of room. Fat people will take you in.

MEANING

1. In what respects is the stereotyped view of fat people erroneous, in Britt's view?
2. How does Britt characterize thin people? What do these lists of attributes have in common?
3. Why, in Britt's opinion, are fat people able to see all sides of an issue, better adjusted, and happier than thin people are?
4. How does Britt's analysis make clear that for her, a sense of humor, tolerance, and personal warmth are far more important than superficial appearance?

TECHNIQUE

1. How is Britt's essay constructed as a point-by-point **comparative analysis**?
2. What means does Britt use to counter objections from readers who might believe that thin is in?
3. **Other Patterns.** How do Britt's **descriptions** of typical situations in which fat and thin people react differently from each other add to her comparison?

LANGUAGE

1. How does Britt use a phrase from Shakespeare's play *Julius Caesar* to support her opinion that thin people are pessimistic, power hungry, and untrustworthy?
2. To what extent is Britt's comparison strengthened by her sense of humor, compassion, and conviviality?
3. **Contrast** the terms Britt uses to characterize fat people and thin people.
4. If you don't know the meaning of the following words, look them up: *inert* (3), *neurotic* (4), *nebulous* (5), *cerebral* (10), *gluttonous* (12).

SUGGESTIONS FOR WRITING

1. **Critical Writing.** Choose one of Britt's assertions, and write a few paragraphs agreeing or disagreeing with her. For example, are fat people better adjusted because they see most problems as not worth worrying about?
2. How do cultures have changing **definitions** of what constitutes fat or thin, and how do these ideals alter from era to era?

3. If the person to whom you were engaged suddenly became very thin or very fat, would you still marry him or her? Explain your answer in two paragraphs exploring both possibilities.

4. ***Thematic Links.*** To what extent do Britt and Kim Chernin in "The Flesh and the Devil" (Chapter 9, "Cause and Effect") have similar views but use different methods to reach their conclusions?

IVAN KARP

Good Marx for the Anthropologist

The author of this intriguing analysis, Ivan Karp, is a social anthropologist and a curator at the National Museum of Natural History of the Smithsonian Institution in Washington, D.C. What interests him about the Marx Brothers is the way in which their films act out scenes of rebellion by immigrants against the elite in society who are very uncomfortable in their presence. Karp's scholarship also focuses on disparities of power and class in such works as *Personhood and Agency* (1990) and, most recently, *Museum Frictions: Public Cultures*, with Buntinx, et al. (2006).

BEFORE YOU READ

How is the use of class-based humor in comedy routines effective?

■ ■ ▨

1   The pivot of most of the Marx Brothers' movies is the relationship between Groucho and those he victimizes. They are, by and large, persons in social positions that demand respect and deference, and are naturally offended when they receive less than what they require as their social due. Ambassador Trentino of *Duck Soup*, or Herman Gottlieb, the pompous and self-satisfied manager of the New York Opera from *A Night at the Opera*, are good examples of this type, but the ubiquitous Margaret Dumont, the archetype of the dowager matron, provides us with the purest representative of the kind. There is nothing especially mean or malicious or even particularly self-seeking about Mrs. Teasdale and the other dowagers that Margaret Dumont usually plays. She is merely a pompous woman (often a widow) who either represents or wants to represent the pinnacle of social prestige. She is always wealthy and willing to use her wealth for philanthropic purposes—as she understands them. Groucho, on the other hand, is willing to use her. She is destined to be Groucho's foil. His intention is to flatter her, seduce her, and marry her in order to enjoy her wealth. His exchanges with her start out with Groucho expressing admiration for her beauty, figure, intelligence, culture, or whatever else comes to mind. Groucho's trouble is that he can't keep *his* mind on the job at hand. His distaste for Dumont always gets the better of him, and he winds up expressing his genuine and very funny opinion of her. In *Duck Soup* he impugns her honor, insults her figure, portrays her as overcome by uncontrollable sexual desire, and implies that she drove her husband to his death. Otherwise they get on fine.

2   We might conclude that Groucho is not polite to her. And that is precisely what strikes us as particularly funny about their relationship. Proper behavior in a given situation is very important to the characters that Margaret Dumont plays. She stresses both for herself and the people around her proper dress, proper demeanor, and proper etiquette. The formal garden party and the inaugural

ball are her milieu in *Duck Soup*. Even in her boudoir she presents us with a formally and impeccably well dressed presence. Her major concern appears to be that the social forms are maintained; and she directs a sense of outrage at persons who do not defer to and recognize the importance of such socially eminent persons as ambassadors and cabinet ministers. She is the type of character who remains a stock figure in satires, from Gilbert and Sullivan's *The Mikado* (which has a good deal in common with *Duck Soup*) on to the present.

3   Because of her emphasis on the structural (i.e., public) characteristics of individuals rather than on their personal qualities, she is a stifling and constraining presence. The very existence of Groucho (not to mention what he says and does to her) liberates the audience from Margaret Dumont. In classical structuralist fashion the differences between Rufus T. Firefly as portrayed by Groucho and Mrs. Teasdale as portrayed by Margaret Dumont can be represented through a series of oppositions.

4   Where Teasdale is always impeccably tailored, Firefly is always dressed in an ill-fitting outfit. Both Mrs. Teasdale and Firefly are aware of the rules of etiquette but while she is concerned with upholding the rules of conventional morality, Firefly pokes fun at the people who live by the rules and respond emotionally to their violations. Thus, the net effect of the Groucho-Dumont opposition or the Firefly-Teasdale opposition (they amount to the same thing) is to provide the audience with a spectacular and ongoing relationship of continual status reversal. By victimizing her on the basis of publicly displaying her disconcerting (for her) personal characteristics, her claims to superiority are turned to a position of social inferiority. The relationship is based on Mrs. Teasdale's claims about her superior status vis-à-vis the rest of the world (including Firefly). Firefly exploits those claims by providing information and attitudes that poke fun, often cruel fun, at the pretensions of Teasdale and most of the people he is surrounded by. The audience participates in what becomes the disruption of claims to deference on public occasions. The audience is able, in fact willing, to participate because these claims are based on the assumption that the norms of social behavior express differences of quality between the actors. Firefly expresses what many of the audience will have felt many times but had been forced to repress—that their definition of the situation does not merit the assumption of inequality, which they see themselves as forced to acknowledge and legitimize on public occasions.

5   Firefly and Teasdale represent an important starting point for this analysis. Other dimensions are to be found in the characters played by Chico and Harpo. Chico's character is called, with startling originality, Chicolini while Harpo's character has no name, or at least it is not revealed to the audience.

6   Chicolini is, as with all the characters Chico plays, an immigrant. He wears funny clothes, talks with an accent, and works at what are almost archetypically immigrant occupations. In *Duck Soup* he runs a combination peanut and hot-dog stand and supplements his income with a little espionage on the side. If he were an organ grinder and had a monkey on a string, I don't think we would be surprised. But this is no immigrant made for poking fun at. Although he

represents the image of the greenhorn so dear to vaudeville and later burlesque comedians, he is not the one who is taken in and fleeced. The fleecing, with an appropriately mixed metaphor, is on the other foot. Chico's main contribution to the Marx Brothers' movies in general, and *Duck Soup* in particular, is through a series of outrageous puns. His wit makes no more linear sense than Groucho's or Harpo's. The major difference is that, while Groucho's humor is aimed at deflating pomposity, Chico's humor is aimed at taking advantage of his victim's image of Chico as ignorant and gullible. In *Duck Soup* Chicolini plays with that image by perpetrating on us a series of puns and by taking advantage of the same people that Firefly mocks. Consider the following dialogue:

The Shadow

Trentino: Oh! Now, Chicolini, I want a full detailed report of your investigation.
Chico: All right, I tell you. Monday we watch-a Firefly's house, but he no come out. He wasn't home. Tuesday we go to the ball game, but he fool us. He no show up. Wednesday he go to the ball game, and we fool him. *We* no show up. Thursday was a doubleheader. Nobody show up. Friday it rained all day. There was no ball game, so we stayed home and we listened to it over the radio.
Trentino: Then you didn't shadow Firefly?
Chico: Oh, sure we shadow Firefly. We shadow him all day.
Trentino: But what day was that?
Chico: Shadowday! Hahaha. Atsa some joke, eh, Boss?

(qtd. in Adamson, 1973: 227)

or again when Chicolini is on trial for espionage:

The Trial

Groucho: Chicolini, give me a number from one to ten.
Chico: Eleven.
Groucho: Right.
Chico: Now I ask you one. What is it has a trunk, but no key, weighs 2,000 pounds, and lives in the circus?
Prosecutor: That's irrelevant.
Chico: A relephant! Hey, that's the answer! There's a whole lotter elephants in the circus.
Minister: That sort of testimony we can eliminate.
Chico: Atsa fine. I'll take some.
Minister: You'll take *what?*
Chico: Eliminate. A nice cool glass eliminate.

* * * * * *

Minister of Finance: Something must be done! War would mean a prohibitive increase in our taxes.

Chico: Hey, I got an uncle lives in Taxes.
Minister of Finance: No, I'm talking about taxes—money, dollars.
Chico: Dollas! That's-a where my uncle lives. Dollas, Taxes!
Minister of Finance: Aww!

(qtd. in Adamson, 1973: 242–243)

7   If Groucho inverts the norms and values of the social reality that is accepted by the Teasdales and Trentinos of his world, we may say that Chico has a *tangential* relationship to that same reality. He approaches reality from an oblique angle. Chico, however, does not usually act alone. He is accompanied by Harpo, who presents us with a persona entirely different from Chico and Groucho. *Duck Soup* is Harpo's finest hour. All the innate anarchy and formlessness of his character is expressed in this film. Perhaps his finest scene is during his and Chico's conference with Ambassador Trentino. His voluminous clothes produce an assortment of tools from scissors to a blowtorch used for lighting cigars. He consistently, persistently, and absolutely destroys every premise on which social action can be based until the scene can continue no longer. There is no way that the everyday rationality of the Trentino character can deal with the phenomenon of Harpo.

8   Even Harpo's appearance and manner deny the categories of every day life. He is more than just a stock vaudeville clown figure as he is sometimes interpreted. Immediately, one recognizes that his appearance conveys a remarkable kind of sexual ambiguity. His hair, figure, and face cannot be placed in either of the two sexual categories. Perhaps this is because of his childlike manner. His systematic inarticulateness, his lack of social knowledge, his naiveté and polymorphous sexuality (in *Duck Soup* he winds up in bed with a horse after chasing a voluptuous blonde)[1] are all reminiscent of the condition of infancy, or at least the Freudian version of infancy.

9   For whatever the reason, Harpo is not easily placed into basic and perhaps even universal categories of the social world such a man-woman and child-adult. I suggest that this is because Harpo expresses an attitude to the world that is, to quote Turner, "betwixt and between" the world of structure. Harpo is preeminently a *liminal* figure and as such contradicts the most basic values and distinctions of his and our society. Thus, the figure of Harpo represents for the audience the inversion and obliteration of structure in its most elementary forms.

10   We have in the Marx Brothers' personae three stock figures from drama and comedy, the flimflammer or con man, the immigrant, and the clown. None is admirable by the standards of our society; they are all marginal to the central concerns of anyone trying to get on in life. What these characters have in common, and what the audience responds to, is that they say *NO* to the application of constraints on behavior to which the rest of their world unthinkingly acquiesces. Of course, their very marginality makes them less liable to the imposition of sanctions. They aren't likely to receive the rewards that everyone else is striving so hard to get. Therefore, they are not obliged to accept the discrepancy between the personal perception of a situation and the acknowledgement of a

social norm that is part of the audience's experience of the social world. In the case of Harpo, the audience is given an example of freedom from the constraints imposed on action as a result of being placed by other people into basic social categories such as man-woman or child-adult. With Groucho and Chico, the audience is given an example of freedom from constraints (such as being "nice" or "polite" or "paying attention") that are the necessary baggage that accompanies the achievement of social goals through other people.

11   In fact, I think this is a major aspect of the appeal of the Marx Brothers. Their characters *express* attitudes to the social world that are coterminous with unexpressed attitudes experienced by large portions of the audiences that have appreciated *Duck Soup* and other Marx Brothers films over the years. This is why so many of the Marx Brothers' best scenes are concerned with public occasions such as balls, parties, trials, and operas. On these occasions the presentation of self is limited to the expression of social rather than personal attributes to a far greater degree than on more intimate occasions. In the Marx Brothers films this ritual separation of persons is stood on its head and the brothers and their audience form an unstructured community united through laughter at the structure. Communitas is to be found in the interaction between the audience and the Marx Brothers. In this sense, anyone who attends a performance of *Duck Soup* is engaging in an action akin to taking part in a ritual. How the person responds is, of course, a matter of personal history and temperament. I cannot help but think, however, that the continuing popularity of this movie is based on its ability to strike deep and responsive chords in the experience of the audience.[2]

12   I have tried, through the use of the concept of anti-structure, to discover within *Duck Soup* elements that correspond to the experiences of the audience that enable it to respond to the movie. I have tried to show that the social world of the Marx Brothers has structural features in common with that of the audience. Instead of viewing *Duck Soup* as an entity in itself, I have stressed a relationship between what is expressed in the film and the social experience of the actors. This relationship demonstrates that anti-structure is not chaotic and formless: it derives its form and meaning from structure.[3] In the case, for example, of Groucho and Margaret Dumont the form of anti-structure is derived from an antithetical relationship of deference expressed in the etiquette of hierarchy. In this sense, anti-structure is like Monica Wilson's (1951) definition of witchcraft as "standardized nightmares" that derive their meaning from tensions found in social relationships (Middleton and Winter, 1963). The difference is that in witchcraft beliefs, the uncertainties that are elements in social action are developed into a moral theory of causation. In Marx Brothers' films the irritants that accompany social action are expressed.

13   But what happens as a result of the expression of these irritants? Surely, the audience's interpretation of similar experiences has been altered after seeing *Duck Soup*, just as it would have been altered after seeing any movie—no matter how banal. Since this paper has treated *Duck Soup* as a ritual it should conclude with at least some comments on the consequences for the actors of participation in the affair. Although rituals obviously serve to ease social tensions, in each

society a ritual must be examined anew before such general conclusions can be reaffirmed. In the case of *Duck Soup* it would be easy but incorrect to suggest that after having seen this movie the audience can rest easier in the face of social inequities. If I did suggest that, the analysis would be dialectical in the sense that Turner uses the notion of dialectics. Instead, I wish to suggest that I find it difficult to imagine how anyone can take *Duck Soup* seriously, in the sense of laughing at what it laughs at, and return to the world of structure and accept with reverence and equanimity the received wisdom of public occasions. The consequence of joining with the Marx Brothers in laughing at structure is to formulate and verify for the moviegoer his private and inchoate experience of the structure, and thus to make that experience an objective, social fact.

14   In this sense the title of the paper plays on the historical accident of the identicalness of the surnames of Karl Marx and the Marx Brothers. The young Karl Marx called for "*a ruthless criticism of everything existing . . .* ruthless in two senses: The criticism must not be afraid of its own conclusions, nor of conflict with the powers that be" (Tucker, 1972:9, emphasis in original). The Marx Brothers similarly ask us to take nothing for granted, nor to be afraid of our conclusions. Remember Chico's famous line in *Duck Soup*. Groucho has just left Mrs. Teasdale's boudoir. Chico, dressed as Groucho, crawls out from under the bed. Mrs. Teasdale says, "Why, I can't believe my own eyes." "Lady," replies Chico, "Who you gonna believe? Me or your own eyes?"

NOTES

1. Is this the same horse whose picture he carried next to his heart in *Animal Crackers?*
2. Here again we confront the problem of assertion about the audience. One reader suggested, for example, that an audience composed largely of college students (as seems to be the case for Marx Brothers fans currently) cannot be analyzed in the same fashion as the earlier, predominantly lower-class audiences of *Duck Soup*. I suggest that the continuing popularity of the Marx Brothers can be analyzed in terms of continuities in the experience of the audiences. One such continuity might be the marginal relationship to sources of power in our society of both contemporary college students and the 1930s audiences of the Marx Brothers.
3. It only *seems* chaotic and formless to the participants. Anti-structure derives its form through inverting and contravening the structure.

BIBLIOGRAPHY

Adamson, Joe, 1973, *Groucho, Harpo, Chico and Sometimes Zeppo*. New York: Simon & Schuster.

Evans-Prichard, E. E., 1965, *Theories of Primitive Religion*. London: Oxford University Press.

Gluckman, Max, 1962, *Essays on the Ritual of Social Relations*. Manchester: Manchester University Press.

Goffman, Erving 1959, *Presentation of Self in Everyday Life*. New York: Anchor.

Harris, Grace, 1957, "Possession 'Hysteria' in a Kenya Tribe." *American Anthropologist* 59: 1046–1066.

Leach, E. R., 1954, *Political Systems of Highland Burma.* London: Oxford University Press.

Luckmann, Thomas, 1967, *The Invisible Religion.* New York: Macmillan.

Middleton, J. and E. H. Winter, eds., 1963, *Witchcraft and Sorcery in East Africa.* London: Routledge & Kegan Paul.

Tucker, R. C., 1972, *The Marx-Engels Reader.* New York: Norton.

Turner, V. W., 1967, *The Forest of Symbols.* Ithaca: Cornell University Press.

———— 1968, *The Drums of Affliction.* London: Oxford University Press.

———— 1969, *The Ritual Process.* Chicago: Aldine.

———— 1974, *Dramas, Fields, and Metaphors.* Ithaca: Cornell University Press.

Van Gennep, A., 1960, *The Rites of Passage.* London: Routledge & Kegan Paul.

Wilson, Monica, 1951, "Witch Beliefs and Social Structure." American Journal of Sociology 56: 307–313.

Zimmerman, Paul and Burt Goldblatt, 1968, *The Marx Brothers at the Movies.* New York: New American Library.

How does this photo of the Marx Brothers show another side to their usual on-screen personalities?

MEANING

1. How do the Marx Brothers' movies show immigrants with no social clout turning the tables on those who have power?
2. In what way does comedy act as a release for the audience and a thinly disguised form of aggression?
3. What is Harpo's particular contribution to turning the tables against authority?
4. How does Harpo's method differ from Chico's and Groucho's?

TECHNIQUE

1. How is the contrast between Firefly and Mrs. Teasdale meant to reflect the relationship between immigrants and members of the established society?
2. What examples best illustrate how verbal humor turns the tables on the people in power by making them feel as helpless as immigrants do in not being able to understand what others are saying or doing?
3. **Other Patterns.** Where does Karp use **description** to enable his readers to see the dramatic differences between social classes that he discusses?

LANGUAGE

1. How do the Marx Brothers use puns, double entendres, and free association to mock high society and the authority of English grammar?
2. How does Karp use quotations from anthropologists and historical figures to frame the analysis as a form of cultural inquiry?
3. If you do not know the meanings of the following words, look them up: *pivot* (1), *archetype* (1), *pompous* (1), *pinnacle* (1), *impugns* (1), *milieu* (2), *tangential* (7), *naiveté* (8), *polymorphous* (8), *liminal* (9), *dialectical* (13).

SUGGESTIONS FOR WRITING

1. **Critical Writing.** Apply conclusions reached by Karp to the story line and characters of another of the Marx Brothers' films.
2. Discuss any contemporary movie, such as one by Spike Lee, that expresses social criticism in a satirical form.
3. **Analyze** a performance of any stand-up comic whose humor reflects his or her experiences as an immigrant or as a member of an ethnic minority (for example, Margaret Cho).
4. **Thematic Links.** Compare Karp's analysis with Jamaica Kincaid's in "A Small Place" (Chapter 4, "Description") for the insights they provide through the use of satire to criticize class structure.

JOHN MCMURTRY

Kill 'Em! Crush 'Em! Eat 'Em Raw!

A professor of social and political philosophy, John McMurtry (b. 1939) received his undergraduate degree and played football at the University of Toronto. After a brief career, ended by injuries, in the Canadian Football League, he went on to get a Ph.D. from the University of London. He taught for many years at the University of Guelph in Ontario and has written scholarly works such as *Value Wars: The Global Market Versus the Life Economy* (2002). He has also written for popular magazines such as *Maclean's*, where the following essay first appeared in 1971. McMurtry's startling and insightful analysis of the commonalities between football and war will doubtless be contested by fans of the game.

BEFORE YOU READ

Does violence in football make the game more enjoyable?

■ ■ ▨

1   A few months ago my neck got a hard crick in it. I couldn't turn my head; to look left or right I'd have to turn my whole body. But I'd had cricks in my neck since I started playing grade-school football and hockey; so I just ignored it. Then I began to notice that when I reached for any sort of large book (which I do pretty often as a philosophy teacher at the University of Guelph) I had trouble lifting it with one hand. I was losing the strength in my left arm, and I had such a steady pain in my back I often had to stretch out on the floor of the room I was in to relieve the pressure.

2   A few weeks later I mentioned to my brother, an orthopedic surgeon, that I'd lost the power in my arm since my neck began to hurt. Twenty-four hours later I was in a Toronto hospital not sure whether I might end up with a wasted upper limb. Apparently the steady pounding I had received playing college and professional football in the late Fifties and early Sixties had driven my head into my backbone so that the discs had crumpled together at the neck—"acute herniation"—and had cut the nerves to my left arm like a pinched telephone wire (without nerve stimulation, of course, the muscles atrophy, leaving the arm crippled). So I spent my Christmas holidays in the hospital in heavy traction and much of the next three months with my neck in a brace. Today most of the pain has gone, and I've recovered most of the strength in my arm. But from time to time I still have to don the brace, and surgery remains a possibility.

3   Not much of this will surprise anyone who knows football. It is a sport in which body wreckage is one of the leading conventions. A few days after I went into hospital for that crick in my neck, another brother, an outstanding football

For a visual to accompany this selection, see color insert photo B-1.

player in college, was undergoing spinal surgery in the same hospital two floors above me. In his case it was a lower, more massive herniation, which every now and again buckled him so that he was unable to lift himself off his back for days at a time. By the time he entered the hospital for surgery he had already spent several months in bed. The operation was successful, but, as in all such cases, it will take him a year to recover fully.

4   These aren't isolated experiences. Just about anybody who has ever played football for any length of time, in high school, college or one of the professional leagues, has suffered for it later physically.

5   Indeed, it is arguable that body shattering is the very *point* of football, as killing and maiming are of war. (In the United States, for example, the game results in 15 to 20 deaths a year and about 50,000 major operations on knees alone.) To grasp some of the more conspicuous similarities between football and war, it is instructive to listen to the imperatives most frequently issued to the players by their coaches, teammates and fans. "Hurt 'em!" "Level 'em!" "Kill 'em!" "Take 'em apart!" Or watch for the plays that are most enthusiastically applauded by the fans. Where someone is "smeared," "knocked silly," "creamed," "nailed," "broken in two," or even "crucified." (One of my coaches when I played corner linebacker with the Calgary Stampeders in 1961 elaborated, often very inventively, on this language of destruction: admonishing us to "unjoin" the opponent, "make 'im remember you" and "stomp 'im like a bug.") Just as in hockey, where a fight will bring fans to their feet more often than a skillful play, so in football the mouth waters most of all for the really crippling block or tackle. For the kill. Thus the good teams are "hungry," the best players are "mean," and "casualties" are as much a part of the game as they are of a war.

6   The family resemblance between football and war is, indeed, striking. Their languages are similar: "field general," "long bomb," "blitz," "take a shot," "front line," "pursuit," "good hit," "the draft" and so on. Their principles and practices are alike: mass hysteria, the art of intimidation, absolute command and total obedience, territorial aggression, censorship, inflated insignia and propaganda, blackboard manoeuvres and strategies, drills, uniforms, formations, marching bands and training camps. And the virtues they celebrate are almost identical: hyper-aggressiveness, coolness under fire and suicidal bravery. All this has been implicitly recognized by such jock-loving Americans as media stars General Patton and President Nixon, who have talked about war as a football game. Patton wanted to make his Second World War tank men look like football players. And Nixon, as we know, was fond of comparing attacks on Vietnam to football plays and drawing coachly diagrams on a blackboard for TV war fans.

7   One difference between war and football, though, is that there is little or no protest against football. Perhaps the most extraordinary thing about the game is that the systematic infliction of injuries excites in people not concern, as would be the case if they were sustained at, say, a rock festival, but a collective rejoicing and euphoria. Players and fans alike revel in the spectacle of a combatant felled into semiconsciousness, "blindsided," "clotheslined" or "decapitated." I can remember, in fact, being chided by a coach in pro ball for not "getting my hat"

injuriously into a player who was already lying helpless on the ground. (On another occasion, after the Stampeders had traded the celebrated Joe Kapp to BC, we were playing the Lions in Vancouver and Kapp was forced on one play to run with the ball. He was coming "down the chute," his bad knee wobbling uncertainly, so I simply dropped on him like a blanket. After I returned to the bench I was reproved for not exploiting the opportunity to unhinge his bad knee.)

8   After every game, of course, the papers are full of reports on the day's injuries, a sort of post-battle "body count," and the respective teams go to work with doctors and trainers, tape, whirlpool baths, cortisone and morphine to patch and deaden the wounds before the next game. Then the whole drama is reenacted—injured athletes held together by adhesive, braces and drugs—and the days following it are filled with even more feverish activity to put on the show yet again at the end of the next week. (I remember being so taped up in college that I earned the nickname "mummy.") The team that survives this merry-go-round spectacle of skilled masochism with the fewest incapacitating injuries usually wins. It is a sort of victory by ordeal: "We hurt them more than they hurt us."

9   My own initiation into this brutal circus was typical. I loved the game from the moment I could run with a ball. Played shoeless on a green open field with no one keeping score and in a spirit of reckless abandon and laughter, it's a very different sport. Almost no one gets hurt and it's rugged, open and exciting (it still is for me). But then, like everything else, it starts to be regulated and institutionalized by adult authorities. And the fun is over.

10   So it was as I began the long march through organized football. Now there was a coach and elders to make it clear by their behavior that beating other people was the only thing to celebrate and that trying to shake someone up every play was the only thing to be really proud of. Now there were severe rule enforcers, audiences, formally recorded victors and losers, and heavy equipment to permit crippling bodily moves and collisions (according to one American survey, more than 80% of all football injuries occur to fully equipped players). And now there was the official "given" that the only way to keep playing was to wear suffocating armor, to play to defeat, to follow orders silently and to renounce spontaneity for joyless drill. The game had been, in short, ruined. But because I loved to play and play skillfully, I stayed. And progressively and inexorably, as I moved through high school, college and pro leagues, my body was dismantled. Piece by piece.

11   I started off with torn ligaments in my knee at 13. Then, at the organization and the competition increased, the injuries came faster and harder. Broken nose (three times), broken jaw (fractured in the first half and dismissed as a "bad wisdom tooth," so I played with it for the rest of the game), ripped knee ligaments again. Torn ligaments in one ankle and a fracture in the other (which I remember feeling relived about because it meant I could honorably stop drill-blocking a 270-pound defensive end). Repeated rib fractures and cartilage tears (usually carried, again, through the remainder of the game). More dislocations of the left shoulder than I can remember (the last one I played with because, as the Calgary Stampeder doctor said, it "couldn't be damaged any more"). Occasional

broken or dislocated fingers and toes. Chronically hurt lower back (I still can't lift with it or change a tire without worrying about folding). Separated right shoulder (as with many other injuries, like badly bruised hips and legs, needled with morphine for the games). And so on. The last pro game I played—against Winnipeg Blue Bombers in the Western finals in 1961—I had a recently dislocated left shoulder, a more recently wrenched right shoulder and a chronic pain centre in one leg. I was so tied up with soreness I couldn't drive my car to the airport. But it never occurred to me or anyone else that I miss a play as a corner linebacker.

12   By the end of my football career, I had learned that physical injury—giving it and taking it—is the real currency of the sport. And that in the final analysis the "winner" is the man who can hit to kill even if only half his limbs are working. In brief, a warrior game with a warrior ethos into which (like almost everyone else I played with) my original boyish enthusiasm had been relentlessly taunted and conditioned.

13   In thinking back on how all this happened, though, I can pick out no villains. As with the social system as a whole, the game has a life of its own. Everyone grows up inside it, accepts it and fulfills its dictates as obediently as zealots. Far from ever questioning the principles of the activity, people simply concentrate on executing these principles more aggressively than anybody around them. The result is a group of people who, as the leagues become of a higher and higher class, are progressively insensitive to the possibility that things could be otherwise. Thus, in football, anyone who might question the wisdom or enjoyment of putting on heavy equipment on a hot day and running full speed at someone else with the intention of knocking him senseless would be regarded simply as not really a devoted athlete and probably "chicken." The choice is made straightforward. Either you, too, do your very utmost to efficiently smash and be smashed, or you admit incompetence or cowardice and quit. Since neither of these admissions is very pleasant, people generally keep any doubts they have to themselves and carry on.

14   Of course, it would be a mistake to suppose that there is more blind acceptance of brutal practices in organized football than elsewhere. On the contrary, a recent Harvard study has approvingly argued that football's characteristics of "impersonal acceptance of inflicted injury," an overriding "organization goal," the "ability to turn oneself on and off" and being, above all, "out to win" are of "inestimable value" to big corporations. Clearly, our sort of football is no sicker than the rest of our society. Even its organized destruction of physical well-being is not anomalous. A very large part of our wealth, work and time is, after all, spent in systematically destroying and harming human life. Manufacturing, selling and using weapons that tear opponents to pieces. Making ever bigger and faster predator-named cars with which to kill and injure one another by the million every year. And devoting our very lives to outgunning one another for power in an ever more destructive rat race. Yet all these practices are accepted without question by most people, even zealously defended and honored. Competitive, organized injuring is integral to our way of life, and football is simply one of the

more intelligible mirrors of the whole process: a sort of colorful morality play showing us how exciting and rewarding it is to Smash Thy Neighbor.

15   Now it is fashionable to rationalize our collaboration in all this by arguing that, well, man *likes* to fight and injure his fellows and such games as football should be encouraged to discharge this original-sin urge into less harmful channels than, say, war. Public-show football, this line goes, plays the same sort of cathartic role as Aristotle said stage tragedy does: without real blood (or not much), it releases players and audience from unhealthy feelings stored up inside them.

16   As an ex-player in this seasonal coast-to-coast drama, I see little to recommend such a view. What organized football did to me was make me *suppress* my natural urges and re-express them in an alienating, vicious form. Spontaneous desires for free bodily exuberance and fraternization with competitors were shamed and forced under ("If it ain't hurtin' it ain't helpin'") and in their place were demanded armoured mechanical moves and cool hatred of all opposition. Endless authoritarian drill and dressing-room harangues (ever wonder why competing teams can't prepare for a game in the same dressing room?) were the kinds of mechanisms employed to reconstruct joyful energies into mean and alien shapes. I am quite certain that everyone else around me was being similarly forced into this heavily equipped military precision and angry antagonism, because there was always a mutinous attitude about full-dress practices, and everybody (the pros included) had to concentrate incredibly hard for days to whip themselves into just one hour's hostility a week against another club. The players never speak of these things, of course, because everyone is so anxious to appear tough.

17   The claim that men like seriously to battle one another to some sort of finish is a myth. It only endures because it wears one of the oldest and most propagandized of masks—the romantic combatant. I sometimes wonder whether the violence all around us doesn't depend for its survival on the existence and preservation of this tough guy disguise.

18   As for the effect of organized football on the spectator, the fan is not released from supposed feelings of violent aggression by watching his athletic heroes perform it so much as encouraged in the view that people-smashing is an admirable mode of self-expression. The most savage attackers, after all, are, by general agreement, the most efficient and worthy players of all (the biggest applause I ever received as a football player occurred when I ran over people or slammed them so hard they couldn't get up). Such circumstances can hardly be said to lessen the spectators' martial tendencies. Indeed it seems likely that the whole show just further develops and titillates the North American addiction for violent self-assertion. Perhaps it is for this reason that Trudeau became a national hero when he imposed the "big play," the War Measures Act, to smash the other team, the FLQ and its supporters, at the height of the football season. Perhaps, as well, it helps explain why the greater the zeal of U.S. political leaders as football fans (Johnson, Nixon, Agnew), the more enthusiastic the commitment to hard-line politics. At any rate there seems to be a strong correlation between people who relish tough football and people who relish intimidating and beating the hell out of commies, hippies, protest marchers and other opposition groups.

19   Watching well-advertised strong men knock other people around, make them hurt, is in the end like other tastes. It does not weaken with feeding and variation in form. It grows.

20   I got out of football in 1962. I had asked to be traded after Calgary had offered me a $25-a-week-plus-commissions off-season job as a clothing-store salesman. ("Dear Mr. Finks:" I wrote. [Jim Finks was then the Stampeders' general manager.] "Somehow I do not think the dialectical subtleties of Hegel, Marx and Plato would be suitably oriented amidst the environmental stimuli of jockey shorts and herringbone suits. I hope you make a profitable sale or trade of my contract to the East.") So the Stampeders traded me to Montreal. In a preseason intersquad game with the Alouettes I ripped the cartilages in my ribs on the hardest block I'd ever thrown. I had trouble breathing and I had to shuffle-walk with my torso on a tilt. The doctor in the local hospital said three weeks rest, the coach said scrimmage in two days. Three days later I was back home reading philosophy.

MEANING

1. How do McMurty's observations about commonalities in language, uniforms, control of territory, drills, formations, training camps, tactics, and strategies suggest a kinship between war and football?

2. According to McMurty, how do violence and aggression play an important role in both football and war?

3. How does football develop and increase the spectators' "addiction for violent self-assertion" (paragraph 18)?

4. Why, in McMurtry's view, is aggression self-reinforcing and greeted with more enthusiasm than the skillful execution of plays?

TECHNIQUE

1. What level of knowledge about football does McMurty assume on the part of his readers?

2. Does he organize his comparison on a point-by-point basis or a subject-by-subject basis? Do you find this method effective?

3. **Other Patterns.** How does McMurtry use personal **narrative** to enhance the credibility of his analogy?

LANGUAGE

1. How does the terminology of football enhance McMurtry's comparison?

2. How does the title express McMurtry's thesis?

3. How would you characterize the tone of this essay, and how does this relate to McMurtry's purpose?

4. If you don't know the meaning of any of the following words, look them up: *herniation* (3), *euphoria* (7), *spontaneity* (10), *anomalous* (14), *harangues* (16).

Suggestions for Writing

1. ***Critical Writing.*** What additional points of similarity between football and war can you think of that McMurtry did not include in his essay? For example, are those who rally support for a war akin to cheerleaders for a football team? Are halftime ceremonies comparable to a lull between battles?

2. If you have ever been on any team or are a football fan, create a reply to McMurtry's analysis, examining his assumptions and refuting or supporting his **argument.**

3. To what extent have Superbowl ads become their own art form? What is your favorite one and why?

4. ***Thematic Links.*** Did the United Nations play a role in the Rwandan conflict that is analogous to that of referees in a football game, who make decisions but lack the power to stop the game? (See Immaculée Ilibagiza's "Left to Tell . . .").

WILLIAM BRYANT LOGAN

Eiffel and Oak

A professional arborist and award-winning nature writer, William Bryant Logan writes a column for the *New York Times* and contributes to various gardening magazines. He blends scientific observation with an easy-to-read style in his book *Oak: Frame of Civilization* (2005), where this selection originally appeared. Logan's comparison between the oak tree and the Eiffel Tower is unusual and thought-provoking. He has also written more technical manuals, such as *The Book of Roses* (1984), *Gardener's Book of Sources* (1988), and *Dirt: The Ecstatic Skin of Earth* (1995), which surprisingly, is being made into a feature documentary.

BEFORE YOU READ

Which is more aesthetically pleasing and important—a tree or a metal sculpture?

■ ■ ▧

1   They built the Eiffel Tower for the Paris Exposition of 1889. At precisely three hundred meters tall, it was almost twice as tall as the next largest monolith, the Washington Monument. It took more than 2.5 million rivets to hold together its 18,038 pieces of wrought iron, and the thing weighs more than 7,000 tons. Nevertheless, it took only a little more than two years to build. George Berger, general manager of the fair, declared the meaning of the achievement: "We will give [the people] a view from the steep summit of the slope that has been climbed since the Dark Ages. . . . For the law of progress is inexorable, just as progress itself is infinite."

2   The Eiffel Tower is the founding monument of industrial modernity. It had and has no purpose but to astound. The official Eiffel Tower Web site gives among its statistics the following: "Distinctive Feature: Recognizable throughout the entire world." In short, it is an enormous trademark.

3   At the start, not everyone was mightily pleased with the new view. Before the tower was half completed, a group of Paris artists that included Paul Verlaine, G. K. Huysmans, and Guy de Maupassant wrote a letter of protest that appeared on the front page of *Le Temps*, the chief Paris daily. The artists compared the tower variously to a skeleton, a factory chimney, a gymnast's apparatus, and an immense suppository.

4   Alexandre-Gustav Eiffel responded in *Le Temps* that his structure would be seen as beautiful, because it conformed to the "hidden rules of harmony." He added, "Moreover, there is an attraction in the colossal and a singular delight to which ordinary theories of art are scarcely applicable." It was better *because* it was bigger.

For a visual to accompany this selection, see color insert photo B-2.

5   The French are expert at insults. One of the best hurled against the tower came from a fierce writer named Leon Bloy. Looking on Eiffel's Tower, he was moved to dub it a "truly tragic street lamp."

6   The official Eiffel Tower Web site itself replays this "controversy" in the manner of all good press agents. (Any press, good or bad, is good for business.) And it resolves the dilemma in the accepted way: Two million people visited the tower during the Paris Exposition, and more than 180 million more have visited it since. The people have spoken: The tower is beautiful because it has had so many visitors.

7   But if you will call to mind your own experience in visiting this or any other spectacle of size—the Seattle Space Needle, or the Empire State Building, or the lamented World Trade Center—you may recognize a kind of dutifulness in the visits. You wait forever for the elevator, you crowd into it, and you are disgorged on the summit. After a moment of vertiginous shock, you look around. Dutifully, you continue to look around. You try to recognize monuments dwarfed in the distance. There is a palpitating emptiness to the exercise, as great I don't doubt as the emptiness experienced by nineteenth-century men and women who entered the cathedrals only because it was what everybody had to do.

8   They were supposed to believe in God; we are supposed to believe in progress. But this summit we have reached in these monuments is somehow arid. Perhaps God is not what they had been taught by their priests, and perhaps progress is not what we have been taught by ours. C. S. Lewis wrote that when you are on the wrong road, the shortest way to go forward is to go back to where you made the wrong turn and make the right one.

9   Compare the structure of an oak tree with the Eiffel Tower. There is an obvious analogy. It was noted by D'Arcy Thompson in *On Growth and Form.* Both oak and tower are basically long cones that flare at the base. Eiffel was proud of his tower's basal flare. His mathematical calculations, he said, indicated the dimensions necessary at the base so that the tower could stand up to the wind.

10   The oak too has a pronounced flare at the base, more so than any other tree. If you are walking in a dense forest where all the leaves are high overhead, in fact, you can tell which are oaks by looking for the basal flare. The reason is the same, for though the oak is shorter than the tower and made of lighter materials, it is solid where the tower is skeletal, and its crown catches the wind.

11   But why does the oak have such a pronounced flare when other tall trees do not? A fast-growing tree like poplar or ailanthus has weaker wood than the oak. The fast grower puts its energy into rapid expansion, not into firm structure. Therefore, when a wind- or snowstorm comes, these quick trees respond by shedding branches or even by losing their crowns. The oak seldom does. When an oak fails, it most often fails from the base, usually when the ground gives out. The roots break and the whole tree topples at once. The basal flare is wood added to strengthen the roots at their base and so reduce the chances of failure.

12   The second analogy between the Eiffel Tower and an oak is in their internal structures. Though Eiffel may have noticed the flare at an oak's base, it is unlikely that he ever knew how much the skeletal structure of the tower is a parody of the structure of oak tissue. Two things kept solid stone structures like the

Washington Monument or the Gothic cathedrals from rising even higher: their weight and their resistance to the wind. Eiffel used a skeleton of iron—a material stronger than stone but no heavier—so that he could construct a much taller object without creating unbearable forces of compression. Vertical members are reinforced by diagonal members and stabilized by cross members. All the parts are joined by rivets, and there is more open space than iron in the volume of the cone. The wind passes freely through the structure, and the jointed frame is even able to adjust slightly to let it through. "Eiffel was one of the first," wrote Maurice Besset, "to create a form not as neutral and stable in space, but living and moving." Yes, if you discount the sixty-five-million-year history of the oaks.

13   To all appearances, the tower is just the opposite of the oak, which is quite solid and full of large leafy branches. Far from letting wind pass freely through, the oak tends to catch it and to shake its head furiously in the storms. But the reason it can do this is an internal structure that makes the tower's look rudimentary. The vertical fibers that make up oak flesh are crossed by rays of living cells that stretch inward from the bark to the pith, stabilizing the framework and keeping the vertical fibers from splitting. Furthermore, the living stresses exerted by the tree's own growth—the swelling of the layers of living tissues near the trunk surface—push the fibers together into a tight, hard-to-break bundle. Third, the fibers are woven through each other, but they are also discrete pieces, so that they can flex and slide over one another without shearing or destroying their vital connection. No rivets are needed.

14   Klaus Mattheck, in his continuing study of tree structure, has explained wood structure brilliantly. The tree, he says, has three kinds of structural members: bricks, ropes, and I beams. The bricks are the lignin—strong hydrocarbons that form the framework of every cell in the tree's fibers. They resist the compression that comes from the weight of the tree, and the compression on some fibers when the tree is bent under wind or snow. The ropes are the cellulose, the core of every fiber cell, which are bendable and very hard to break. These, he writes, act to resist tension, for when the tree is bent, some of the cells are necessarily compressed while others are stretched. The I beams are the ray cells—banks of live tissue that stretch from bark to heart. These prevent the fibers from shearing and parting, even when the wind puts twisting loads on the stems. Indeed, it is only thanks to this internal structure that a tree can be solid instead of skeletal. If you put a skin on the Eiffel Tower or gave it branches, the thing would fall down in the first good blow.

15   Iron is harder than wood. This is perhaps the lone advantage of the tower's structure. But this advantage is counteracted by the fact that wood, though softer, is dynamic, while iron is passive. The Eiffel Tower is one large skeletal iron cone. The mature oak is many cones, each sheathed one on top of the other by year after year of annual growth. It is enjoyable to envision the tree—not only the trunk but the roots and branches—as hundreds and hundreds of cones. The outermost cones contain the living cells while the inner cones are filled with plugs and tannins and compounds that further stiffen the structure. Each year, a new set of cones is added, the pressure of growth helping to hold the stems together while the inner wood stiffens to resist both physical and biological stresses.

16   The oak is generative, the tower parasitic. To renew its outer protection, the oak has a cork cambium that annually generates an increment of waxy skin to protect the tree from damage. In fact, it is the cambium's old layers, flaking off as they are squeezed outward by the expanding trunk, that make the rough texture and pattern of the bark that we feel. The Eiffel Tower, instead, needs outside help every seven years to keep it from rusting away. To protect the iron from the weather requires fifty tons of paint and a full year just to apply it.

17   What do the two structures provide in exchange for the energy expended to maintain them? The oak gives oxygen to the air. More than five thousand different species live on, in, or by means of the average oak. Even today, oak is used by man for furniture, packing pallets, railroad ties, flooring, wainscoting, timber frames, basketry, porridge, firewood, and charcoal. On a summer's day, it is up to ten degrees cooler in the shade of a great oak.

18   What does the tower give? A spectacle. To see and to see from. And on a hot summer's day, you practically fry standing on its treeless plaza.

19   If you had to pick one or the other to emulate, which would you choose?

■ ■ ▨

MEANING

1. In what respects has the Eiffel Tower come to serve as a "founding monument of industrial modernity"? Why have visits to the Eiffel Tower become obligatory if you are in Paris?

2. How was the Eiffel Tower originally greeted by Parisian artists and the public?

3. What does Logan mean by his assertion that "The oak is generative, the tower parasitic"?

4. Why does Logan prefer the oak to the Eiffel Tower?

TECHNIQUE

1. What similarities and differences between the oak tree and the Eiffel Tower does Logan discuss?

2. How does Logan foreshadow his preference for the oak above the Eiffel Tower?

3. **Other Patterns.** To what extent do Logan's **descriptions** of the Eiffel Tower and the oak express value judgments?

LANGUAGE

1. How does the language that Logan uses to characterize the Eiffel Tower and the oak further reinforce his perception of the superiority of one over the other?

2. Where does Logan use technical terminology that is familiar to arborists in his analysis while at the same time explaining the terms in everyday language?

3. If you do not know the meaning of the following words, look them up: *infinite* (1), *colossal* (4), *vertiginous* (7), *rudimentary* (13), *emulate* (19).

SUGGESTIONS FOR WRITING

1. **Critical Writing.** In a few paragraphs, answer Logan's final question: "If you had to pick one or the other to emulate, which would you choose?"

2. It you have ever had the occasion to visit the Eiffel Tower, how did your experiences compare with Logan's?

3. **Argue** that artificial plants and flowers are superior or inferior to real ones.

4. **Thematic Links.** How do both Logan and Bernard Rudofsky in "The Unfashionable Human Body" (Chapter 12, "Argument") address the issue of technology versus nature?

IMMACULÉE ILIBAGIZA

Left to Tell

Immaculée Ilibagiza grew up in Rwanda and studied engineering at the National University. In 1994, Rwanda was engulfed by genocide, and most of Ilibagiza's family, who were Tutsis, were killed by the Hutus. She survived by hiding with five other women and children in a small bathroom of a local pastor's home for ninety-one days while machete-wielding mobs hunted for them. In 1998, she emigrated to the United States and began working for the United Nations. In the following chapter from *Left to Tell* (2005), she describes how her faith sustained her during this ordeal.

BEFORE YOU READ

What characteristics distinguish genocide from other events in which large numbers of people are killed?

■ ■ ▨

1 I closed the door behind Vianney and Augustine and joined the other Tutsi women.

2 Pastor Murinzi carried a flashlight and led us down the dark hallway to his bedroom. Our eyes followed the beam of light along the walls until it landed on a door that I assumed opened to the yard.

3 "This is where you'll stay," he said, swinging the door open to reveal our new home: a small bathroom about four feet long and three feet wide. The light shimmered as it bounced off the white enamel tiles on the bottom half of the walls. There was a shower stall at one end and a toilet at the other—the room wasn't big enough for a sink. And there was a small air vent/window near the ceiling that was covered with a piece of red cloth, which somehow made the room feel even smaller.

4 I couldn't imagine how all six of us could possibly fit in this space, but the pastor herded us through the door and packed us in tight. "While you're in here, you must be absolutely quiet, and I mean *silent*," he said. "If you make any noise, you will die. If they hear you, they will find you, and then they will kill you. No one must know that you're here, not even my children. Do you understand?"

5 "Yes, Pastor," we mumbled in unison.

6 "And don't flush the toilet or use the shower." He shone his light along the wall above the toilet. "There's another bathroom on the other side of that wall, which uses the same plumbing. So if you absolutely must flush, wait until you hear someone using the other bathroom, then do so at *exactly* the same time. Do you understand?"

7 "Yes, Pastor."

8 The flashlight clicked off, and his last words were spoken in the dark. "I think that they're going to keep killing for another week, maybe less. If you're careful, you might live through this. I'd hate for the killers to get you . . . I know what they would do."

9   He shut the door and left us standing in blackness, our bodies pressing against one another. The musky heat of our breath, sweat, and skin mingled together and made us feel faint.

10   We tried to sit, but there wasn't enough room for all of us to move at the same time. The four tallest had to push our backs against the wall and slide to the tile floor, then pull the smaller girls down on top of us. It was past 3 A.M. and we were all wide-awake, yet we didn't dare speak. We sat as best we could, listening to the crickets outside and to our own labored breathing.

11   I prayed silently, asking God to protect Vianney and Augustine and keep my parents and Damascene safe. I thanked Him for delivering us to the bathroom— I truly believed that God had guided pastor Murinzi to bring us here, and for the first time in days, I felt safe. If *I* hadn't noticed the bathroom we were currently in after so many visits to the house, no one else would.

12   I asked God to bless Pastor Murinzi for risking his own safety to help us . . . but then I winced at the prayer. A flush of anger burned my cheeks as I remembered how he'd sent my brother and our friend into the night. I prayed that God would eventually help me forgive the pastor.

13   The moon emerged from behind a cloud, and a thin streak of pale light slipped through a crack in the red curtain, providing enough illumination for me to make out the faces of my companions. Sitting beside me was Athanasia, a pretty, dark-skinned 14-year-old with big beautiful eyes that caught the moonlight. Sitting on top of her was 12-year-old Beata, still wearing her school uniform, who looked lost and very frightened. I pulled her onto my lap, cradling her in my arms until she closed her eyes.

14   Across from me was Therese, who, at 55, was the eldest of the group. She wore a colorful, traditional Rwandan wrap-dress popular with married women. She looked more worried than any of us, probably because she only had two of her six children—Claire and Sanda—with her. Claire was very light-skinned, and even though she was my age, she was nervous and withdrawn and wouldn't make eye contact. Her little sister Sanda was only seven, and the youngest of the group. She was cute, sweet, and surprisingly calm. She never once cried or looked frightened, even when the rest of us were trembling—I think she must have been in shock the entire time we were in that bathroom.

15   The pastor's repeated warnings to be quiet had burned into us. We sat in an uncomfortable heap, too afraid to adjust our positions or to even breathe too heavily. We waited for the gray light of dawn to fill the room, then carefully pried ourselves apart to take turns standing and stretching. A two- or three-minute break was all we allowed ourselves before resuming our awkward positions on the floor.

16   When morning broke, the birds in the pastor's shade tree began singing. I was jealous of them, thinking, *How lucky you are to have been born birds and have freedom—after all, look at what we humans are doing to ourselves.*

17   We were so exhausted, hungry, cramped, and hot that our first day in the bathroom passed in a painful haze. It was impossible to sleep—if I dozed off, I was immediately awoken by a leg cramp or someone's elbow knocking against my ribs.

18 In the early evening, we heard Pastor Murinzi talking to someone outside. "No, no, no," he said. "I don't know what you're talking about—I'm a good Hutu, and I'd never hide Tutsis. There are no Tutsis here . . . they left last night."

19 We stared at each other with our eyes wide open. We were terrified.

20 "I don't want any trouble with the government," the pastor continued. "You people know me, and you should protect this house . . . those Tutsi rebels might attack me for being such a good Hutu."

21 Whoever the pastor was talking to left, and we relaxed. Pastor Murinzi had just lied to save us—I felt assured that he wouldn't hand us over to the killers. He had little choice now, because if he turned us in, the killers would know that he'd hidden us. They'd call him a moderate, a traitor to his tribe, and would kill him as surely as they'd kill us.

22 I breathed easier and hugged young Beata, who was lying across my lap. I remembered how my mother sometimes held me in her lap when I was young and frightened. The memory of Mom saddened me—this was the first time in my life that I didn't know the whereabouts of my parents or brothers. I slipped into a half sleep and dreamed of Vianney, Augustine, and Damascene knocking on the pastor's gate, while behind them, our house was burning. I saw my parents sitting on Dad's motorcycle, and my mother asking, "What will happen to my boys?"

23 While I was dreaming, Pastor Murinzi opened the door, and without saying a word, shoved a plate of cold potatoes and beans into the room. It was late, maybe 11 P.M., and none of us had had anything to eat or drink for nearly two days.

24 We attacked the plate, grabbing the food with our dirty fingers and stuffing it into our mouths.

25 When the pastor returned five minutes later with forks, we'd already devoured every bit of food. He stared at the plate, and then looked at us with pity. A moment later he tossed a very thin mattress into the room. "You've traveled down a long road. Now try to get some rest," he said, and closed the door.

26 When we awoke the next day, we took turns stretching our aching muscles. Moving even an inch was a major production because we couldn't talk to one another. We quickly worked out forms of sign language that would become our silent shorthand for the remainder of our stay in the bathroom.

27 I grimaced at the pain in my cramped legs, thinking that I'd have quite a tale of hardship to tell after the war. "Listen to what I had to endure," I'd boast to my friends. "I spent an entire day and night trapped in a tiny bathroom with five strangers. What a hero I am!"

28 No sooner had I begun my little fantasy than I was jolted back to reality by images of my family: my parents fleeing our burning house, Damascene slipping sadly away, and Vianney and Augustine wandering in the open with nowhere to hide. Thank God that Aimable was safely away from Rwanda in another country! But what about the thousands of displaced Tutsis who had sought refuge at our house? What had become of them? Had they found shelter, or were they

lying somewhere bleeding to death? I felt silly and selfish for indulging in my self-pity when thousands were undoubtedly suffering far more.

29   It was my turn to stretch when a commotion erupted outside. There were dozens, maybe hundreds, of voices, some yelling, others chanting. We knew immediately that the killers had arrived.

30   "Let us hunt them in the forests, lakes, and hills; let us find them in the church; let us wipe them from the face of the earth!"

31   I stood on my tiptoes and peeked out the window through a little hole in the curtain. The other ladies grabbed at me, trying to pull me down. Athanasia shook her head wildly, silently mouthing, "Get down! They're looking for us! Get down before they see you!"

32   I ignored them, knocking their hands away and peering through the hole. I immediately regretted my decision because I was petrified by what I saw.

33   Hundreds of people surrounded the house, many of whom were dressed like devils, wearing skirts of tree bark and shirts of dried banana leaves, and some even had goat horns strapped onto their heads. Despite their demonic costumes, their faces were easily recognizable, and there was murder in their eyes.

34   They whooped and hollered. They jumped about, waving spears, machetes, and knives in the air. They chanted a chilling song of genocide while doing a dance of death: "Kill them, kill them, kill them all; kill them big and kill them small! Kill the old and kill the young . . . a baby snake is still a snake, kill it, too, let none escape! Kill them, kill them, kill them all!"

35   It wasn't the soldiers who were chanting, nor was it the trained militiamen who had been tormenting us for days. No, these were my neighbors, people I'd grown up and gone to school with—some had even been to our house for dinner.

36   I spotted Kananga, a young man I'd known since childhood. He was a high school dropout my dad had tried to help straighten out. I saw Philip, a young man who'd been too shy to look anyone in the eye, but who now seemed completely at home in this group of killers. At the front of the pack I could make out two local schoolteachers who were friends of Damascene. I recognized dozens of Mataba's most prominent citizens in the mob, all of whom were in a killing frenzy, ranting and screaming for Tutsi blood. The killers leading the group pushed their way into the pastor's house, and suddenly the chanting was coming from all directions.

37   "Find them, find them, kill them all!"

38   My head was spinning; I fell backward onto the ladies. I couldn't breathe. "Dear God, save us . . ." I whispered, but couldn't remember the words to any of my prayers. A wave of despair washed over me, and I was overwhelmed by fear.

39   That's when the devil first whispered in my ear. *Why are you calling on God? Look at all of them out there . . . hundreds of them looking for you. They are legion, and you are one. You can't possibly survive—you won't survive. They're inside the house, and they're moving through the rooms. They're close, almost here . . . they're going to find you, rape you, cut you, kill you!*

40   My heart was pounding. What was this voice? I squeezed my eyes shut as tightly as I could to resist the negative thoughts. I grasped the red and white

rosary my father had given me, and silently prayed with all my might: *God, in the Bible You said that You can do anything for anybody. Well, I am one of those any-bodies, and I need You to do something for me now. Please, God, blind the killers when they reach the pastor's bedroom—don't let them find the bathroom door, and don't let them see us! You saved Daniel in the lions' den, God, You stopped the lions from ripping him apart . . . stop these killers from ripping us apart, God! Save us, like You saved Daniel!*

41 I prayed more intensely than I'd ever prayed before, but still the negative energy wracked my spirit. The voice of doubt was in my ear again as surely as if Satan himself were sitting on my shoulder. I literally felt the fear pumping through my veins, and my blood was on fire. *You're going to die, Immaculée!* the voice taunted. *You compare yourself to Daniel? How conceited you are . . . Daniel was pure of heart and loved by God—he was a prophet, a saint! What are you? You are nothing . . . you deserve suffering and pain . . . you deserve to die!*

42 I clutched my rosary as though it were a lifeline to God. In my mind and heart I cried out to Him for help: *Yes, I am nothing, but You are forgiving. I am human and I am weak, but please, God, give me Your forgiveness. Forgive my trespasses . . . and please send these killers away before they find us!*

43 My temples pounded. The dark voice was in my head, filling it with fearful, unspeakable images. *Dead bodies are everywhere. Mothers have seen their babies chopped in half, their fetuses ripped from their wombs . . . and you think you should be spared? Mothers prayed for God to spare their babies and He ignored them—why should He save you when innocent babies are being murdered? You are selfish, and you have no shame. Listen, Immaculée . . . do you hear them? The killers are outside your door—they're here for you.*

44 My head was burning, but I did hear the killers in the hall, screaming, "Kill them! Kill them all!"

45 *No! God is love,* I told the voice. *He loves me and wouldn't fill me with fear. He will not abandon me. He will not let me die cowering on a bathroom floor. He will not let me die in shame!*

46 I struggled to form an image of God in my mind, envisioning two pillars of brilliant white light burning brightly in front of me, like two giant legs. I wrapped my arms around the legs, like a frightened child clinging to its mother. I begged God to fill me with His light and strength, to cast out the dark energy from my heart: *I'm holding on to Your legs, God, and I do not doubt that You can save me. I will not let go of You until You have sent the killers away.*

47 The struggle between my prayers and the evil whispers that I was sure belonged to the devil raged in my mind. I never stopped praying . . . and the whispering never relented.

48 In the evening, the pastor opened the door and found us all in a sort of trance. I was bathed in sweat, exhausted, clutching my rosary in both hands, and oblivious to my surroundings. I was still mouthing prayer after prayer while staring vacantly at the others. Therese was using one hand to cover her eyes and the other to hold her Bible firmly on top of her head. And young Beata was crouching on her knees, arms in front of her, hands clasped in prayer.

49   The pastor called our names, but not one of us heard him. Finally, he shook us to awaken us from our stupor. I looked up at him, blinking, confused, and completely taken aback when he began laughing at us.

50   "What are you ladies doing? For heaven's sake, relax. The killers left seven hours ago. I can't believe you're all still praying."

51   To me, those seven hours had passed in what seemed like a few minutes, yet I was utterly drained. In all my years of praying, I'd never focused so completely on God, or been so keenly aware of the presence of darkness. I'd seen evil in the eyes of the killers, and had felt evil all around me while the house was being searched. And I'd listened to the dark voice, letting it convince me that we were about to be slaughtered. Every time I succumbed to my fear and believed the lies of that poisonous whispering, I felt as though the skin were being peeled from my scalp. It was only by focusing on God's positive energy that I was able to pull myself through that first visit by the killers. My father had always said that you could never pray too much . . . now I could see that he was right.

52   I realized that my battle to survive this war would have to be fought inside of me. Everything strong and good in me—my faith, hope, and courage—was vulnerable to the dark energy. If I lost my faith, I knew that I wouldn't be able to survive. I could rely only on God to help me fight.

53   The visit by the killers had left us all spent. Pastor Murinzi brought us a plate of food, but despite our hunger, we were too tired to eat. The food was untouched when he returned around midnight.

54   The pastor returned again in the middle of the night during a heavy storm. The rain beat down so loudly against the iron roof that he was able to talk freely without the fear of being overheard. "We were lucky today. They searched all over the house and looked in every room. They looked in the yard and dug through the dung heap behind the cow pen. They crawled into the ceiling and under the furniture—they even stuck their machetes into my suitcases to make sure that I wasn't hiding Tutsi babies. They were crazed, like rabid animals. Their eyes were glazed and red . . . I think they'd been smoking drugs.

55   "But when they reached my bedroom, they saw that it was neat, so they didn't want to mess it up. They said that they'd leave the bedroom for now but warned that they'd search it next time when they came back."

56   "Next time!" we gasped.

57   I couldn't imagine reliving the same ordeal. Surely God wouldn't put us through that suffering twice!

58   "You never know when they're going to come back," the pastor said. "They could come at any time, and God help us all if they find you."

59   His parting sentence echoed in my mind, keeping me awake all night and throughout the next day.

60   Pastor Murinzi returned the next evening in a panic. "A friend told me that the leader of a death squad thinks the killers did a bad job searching the house yesterday," he hissed. "Some of you were seen in the house a few days ago, and there are rumors that you're hiding here. A different group of killers is being sent to search more thoroughly."

61   I moaned as my body went limp. I simply didn't have the strength to live through another of the killers' hunting expeditions. *God, why don't You just lead them to us now and get it over with?* I entreated. *Why do You let us suffer like this? Why do You torture us?*

62   How could we escape again? The house that once seemed so huge had become my cell, a death trap. I could think of only one escape: I wanted to go to heaven. *Oh, God,* I prayed soundlessly, *I have no heart left to fight. I'm ready to give up . . . please give me strength and protect me from the demons that are all around me. Show me how to make the killers blind again.*

63   I raised my head and opened my eyes. When I saw the pastor standing in the doorway, a crystal clear image flashed through my mind. "I have an idea," I told him in a hushed but insistent voice. "Can you push your wardrobe in front of the bathroom door? It's tall and wide enough to completely cover it, so if the killers can't see the door, they'll never find us. It will be as though they're blind!"

64   Pastor Murinzi thought for a moment and then shook his head. "No, it wouldn't change anything; in fact, it would probably make matters worse. If they look behind the wardrobe and find the door, they will be even more vicious with you."

65   "Oh, no! Pastor, please, you must . . ." I was certain that God had sent me a sign. In my soul, I knew that if the wardrobe were in front of the door, we'd be saved. But the pastor was immovable, so I did something I'd never done in my life: I got on my knees and bowed down to him. "Please, I'm begging you," I said. "I know in my heart that if you don't put the wardrobe in front of the door, they're going to find us the next time they search. Don't worry about making them angry—they can only kill us once. Please do this for us . . . God will reward you if you do."

66   I don't know if it was the sight of me begging on my knees or the fear that I'd be overheard that convinced him, but he relented. "All right, all right. Keep your voice down, Immaculée. I'll move it right now. I hope it helps, but I doubt it will."

67   He disappeared, and a moment later we heard the wardrobe sliding in front of the bathroom door. The other ladies looked at me and whispered, "That was such a good idea—what put it into your head?"

68   I couldn't remember if I'd ever seen the pastor's wardrobe before, but I knew for certain that the idea to move it came to me when I prayed for help.

69   "God," I simply replied.

■   ■   ▨

MEANING

1. How did Ilibagiza discover the power of prayer under the stress of hiding in the pastor's bathroom with five other women and children while a bloodthirsty mob surrounded the house?

2. What does Ilibagiza hear that leads her to believe that the murderers know she and her companions are inside and will continue to search for them?

3. How does her uncertainty as to her family's fate add to her desperation?

4. What inspired idea flashes into Ilibagiza's mind that will allow them to escape a second, more thorough, search of the house?

TECHNIQUE

1. In what way is Ilibagiza's account structured as a violent oscillation between the voices of hope and despair that fill her thoughts?

2. How does Ilibagiza create a positive impression of the pastor who saved her and the other women? Is the portrayal entirely positive?

3. **Other Patterns.** In her **narrative**, how does Ilibagiza employ dialogue to recreate the scene?

LANGUAGE

1. How does the use of italicized words provide an effective contrast to the nonitalicized narrative?

2. How does the language used by the marauding Hutus paint a picture of how brainwashed and brutalized they have become?

3. If you don't know the meaning of the following words, look them up: *grimaced* (27), *cowering* (45), *machetes* (53).

SUGGESTIONS FOR WRITING

1. How does the fact that the murderers are all known to Ilibagiza as neighbors, friends, and prominent citizens test her faith?

2. **Critical Writing.** In an essay, discuss how incidents in the film *Hotel Rwanda* (2004) reflect the conflicts in Ilibagiza's account.

3. As a research project, investigate the events in Rwandan history that led to the 1994 genocide by the Hutus against the Tutsis.

4. Have you ever been in a set of circumstances in which your faith got you through? If so, **describe** the details.

5. **Thematic Links.** How do the accounts by Ilibagiza and C. P. Ellis in "Why I Quit the Klan" (Chapter 9, "Cause and Effect") offer insights into how the stereotype of "the other" comes about?

The Prisoner's Dilemma

Stephen Chapman (b. 1954) has written on a wide range of subjects for the *New Republic* and the *Chicago Tribune* for many years. He grew up in Texas and was educated at Harvard. The following essay (first published in the *New Republic* in 1980) is a profoundly disturbing inside look at practices of punishment in the United States and in Middle Eastern cultures. Chapman graphically describes the brutal, dehumanizing conditions of imprisonment in the West and then challenges his readers to find Eastern methods of punishment, which include public flogging, stoning, and amputation, even more cruel and inhuman.

BEFORE YOU READ

What flaws in the criminal justice system prevent it from achieving worthwhile objectives?

■ ■ ▨

> If the punitive laws of Islam were applied for only one year, all the devastating injustices would be uprooted. Misdeeds must be punished by the law of retaliation; cut off the hands of the thief; kill the murderers; flog the adulterous woman or man. Your concerns, your "humanitarian" scruples are more childish than reasonable. Under the terms of Koranic law, any judge fulfilling the seven requirements (that he have reached puberty, be a believer, know the Koranic laws perfectly, be just, and not be affected by amnesia, or be a bastard, or be of the female sex) is qualified to be a judge in any type of case. He can thus judge and dispose of twenty trials in a single day, whereas the Occidental justice may take years to argue them out.
> —from *Sayings of the Ayatollah Khomeni* (Bantam Books)

1   One of the amusements of life in the modern West is the opportunity to observe the barbaric rituals of countries that are attached to the customs of the dark ages. Take Pakistan, for example, our newest ally and client state in Asia. [In] October [1980] President Zia, in harmony with the Islamic fervor that is sweeping his part of the world, revived the traditional Moslem practice of flogging lawbreakers in public. In Pakistan, this qualified as mass entertainment, and no fewer than 10,000 law-abiding Pakistanis turned out to see justice done to 26 convicts. To Western sensibilities the spectacle seemed barbaric—both in the sense of cruel and in the sense of pre-civilized. In keeping with Islamic custom each of the unfortunates—who had been caught in prostitution raids the previous night and summarily convicted and sentenced—was stripped down to a pair of white shorts, which were painted with a red stripe across the buttocks (the target). Then he was shackled against an easel, with pads thoughtfully placed over the

kidneys to prevent injury. The floggers were muscular, fierce-looking sorts—convicted murderers, as it happens—who paraded around the flogging platform in colorful loincloths. When the time for the ceremony began, one of the floggers took a running start and brought a five-foot stave down across the first victim's buttocks, eliciting screams from the convict and murmurs from the audience. Each of the 26 received from five to 15 lashes. One had to be carried from the stage unconscious.

2   Flogging is one of the punishments stipulated by Koranic law, which has made it a popular penological device in several Moslem countries, including Pakistan, Saudi Arabia, and [. . .], the ayatollah's Iran. Flogging, or *Tá zir*, is the general punishment prescribed for offenses that don't carry an explicit Koranic penalty. Some crimes carry automatic *hadd* punishments—stoning or scourging (a severe whipping) for illicit sex, scourging for drinking alcoholic beverages, amputation of the hands for theft. Other crimes—as varied as murder and abandoning Islam—carry the death penalty (usually carried out in public). Colorful practices like these have given the Islamic world an image in the West, as described by historian G. H. Jansen, "of blood dripping from the stumps of amputated hands and from the striped backs of malefactors, and piles of stones barely concealing the battered bodies of adulterous couples." Jansen, whose book *Militant Islam* is generally effusive in its praise of Islamic practices, grows squeamish when considering devices like flogging, amputation, and stoning. But they are given enthusiastic endorsement by the Koran itself.

3   Such traditions, we all must agree, are no sign of an advanced civilization. In the West, we have replaced these various punishments (including the death penalty in most cases) with a single device. Our custom is to confine criminals in prison for varying lengths of time. In Illinois, a reasonably typical state, grand theft carries a punishment of three to five years; armed robbery can get you from six to 30. The lowest form of felony theft is punishable by one to three years in prison. Most states impose longer sentences on habitual offenders. In Kentucky, for example, habitual offenders can be sentenced to life in prison. Other states are less brazen, preferring the more genteel sounding "indeterminate sentence," which allows parole boards to keep inmates locked up for as long as life. It was under an indeterminate sentence of one to 14 years that George Jackson served 12 years in California prisons for committing a $70 armed robbery. Under a Texas law imposing an automatic life sentence for a third felony conviction, a man was sent to jail for life last year because of three thefts adding up to less than $300 in property value. Texas also is famous for occasionally imposing extravagantly long sentences, often running into hundreds or thousands of years. This gives Texas a leg up on Maryland, which used to sentence some criminals to life plus a day—a distinctive if superfluous flourish.

4   The punishment *intended* by Western societies in sending their criminals to prison is the loss of freedom. But, as everyone knows, the actual punishment in most American prisons is of a wholly different order. The February 2 [1980] riot at New Mexico's state prison in Santa Fe, one of several bloody prison riots in the nine years since the Attica bloodbath, once again dramatized the conditions of life

in an American prison. Four hundred prisoners seized control of the prison before dawn. By sunset the next day 33 inmates had died at the hands of other convicts and another 40 people (including five guards) had been seriously hurt. Macabre stories came out of prisoners being hanged, murdered with blowtorches, decapitated, tortured, and mutilated in a variety of gruesome ways by drug-crazed rioters.

5   The Santa Fe penitentiary was typical of most maximum-security facilities, with prisoners subject to overcrowding, filthy conditions, and routine violence. It also housed first-time, non-violent offenders, like check forgers and drug dealers, with murderers serving life sentences. In a recent lawsuit, the American Civil Liberties Union called the prison "totally unfit for human habitation." But the ACLU says New Mexico's penitentiary is far from the nation's worst.

6   That American prisons are a disgrace is taken for granted by experts of every ideological stripe. Conservative James Q. Wilson has criticized our "crowded, antiquated prisons that require men and women to live in fear of one another and to suffer not only deprivation of liberty but a brutalizing regimen." Leftist Jessica Mitford has called our prisons "the ultimate expression of injustice and inhumanity." In 1973 a national commission concluded that "the American correctional system today appears to offer minimum protection to the public and maximum harm to the offender." Federal courts have ruled that confinement in prisons in 16 different states violates the constitutional ban on "cruel and unusual punishment."

7   What are the advantages of being a convicted criminal in an advanced culture? First there is the overcrowding in prisons. One Tennessee prison, for example, has a capacity of 806, according to accepted space standards, but it houses 2300 inmates. One Louisiana facility has confined four and five prisoners in a single six-foot-by-six-foot cell. Then there is the disease caused by overcrowding, unsanitary conditions, and poor or inadequate medical care. A federal appeals court noted that the Tennessee prison had suffered frequent outbreaks of infectious diseases like hepatitis and tuberculosis. But the most distinctive element of American prison life is its constant violence. In his book *Criminal Violence, Criminal Justice*, Charles Silberman noted that in one Louisiana prison, there were 211 stabbings in only three years, 11 of them fatal. There were 15 slayings in a prison in Massachusetts between 1972 and 1975. According to a federal court, in Alabama's penitentiaries (as in many others), "robbery, rape, extortion, theft and assault are everyday occurrences."

8   At least in regard to cruelty, it's not at all clear that the system of punishment that has evolved in the West is less barbaric than the grotesque practices of Islam. Skeptical? Ask yourself: would you rather be subjected to a few minutes of intense pain and considerable public humiliation, or to be locked away for two or three years in a prison cell crowded with ill-tempered sociopaths? Would you rather lose a hand or spend 10 years or more in a typical state prison? I have taken my own survey on this matter. I have found no one who does not find the Islamic system hideous. And I have found no one who, given the choices mentioned above, would not prefer its penalties to our own.

9   The great divergence between Western and Islamic fashions in punishment is relatively recent. Until roughly the end of the 18th century, criminals in Western countries rarely were sent to prison. Instead they were subjected to an ingenious assortment of penalties. Many perpetrators of a variety of crimes simply were executed, usually by some imaginative and extremely unpleasant method involving prolonged torture, such as breaking on the wheel, burning at the stake, or drawing and quartering. Michel Foucault's book *Discipline and Punishment: The Birth of the Prison* notes one form of capital punishment in which the condemned man's "belly was opened up, his entrails quickly ripped out, so that he had time to see them, with his own eyes, being thrown on the fire; in which he was finally decapitated and his body quartered." Some criminals were forced to serve on slave galleys. But in most cases various corporal measures such as pillorying, flogging, and branding sufficed.

10   In time, however, public sentiment recoiled against these measures. They were replaced by imprisonment, which was thought to have two advantages. First, it was considered to be more humane. Second, and more important, prison was supposed to hold out the possibility of rehabilitation—purging the criminal of his criminality—something that less civilized punishments did not even aspire to. An 1854 report by inspectors of the Pennsylvania prison system illustrates the hopes nurtured by humanitarian reformers:

> Depraved tendencies, characteristic of the convict, have been restrained by the absence of vicious association, and in the mild teaching of Christianity, the unhappy criminal finds a solace for an involuntary exile from the comforts of social life. If hungry, he is fed; if naked, he is clothed; if destitute of the first rudiments of education, he is taught to read and write; and if he has never been blessed with a means of livelihood, he is schooled in a mechanical art, which in after life may be to him the source of profit and respectability. Employment is not his toil nor labor, weariness. He embraces them with alacrity, as contributing to his moral and mental elevation.

11   Imprisonment is now the universal method of punishing criminals in the United States. It is thought to perform five functions, each of which has been given a label by criminologists. First, there is simple *retribution:* punishing the lawbreaker to serve society's sense of justice and to satisfy the victims' desire for revenge. Second, there is *specific deterrence:* discouraging the offender from misbehaving in the future. Third, *general deterrence:* using the offender as an example to discourage others from turning to crime. Fourth, *prevention:* at least during the time he is kept off the streets, the criminals cannot victimize other members of society. Finally, and most important, there is *rehabilitation:* reforming the criminal so that when he returns to society he will be inclined to obey the laws and able to make an honest living.

12   How satisfactorily do American prisons perform by these criteria? Well, of course, they do punish. But on the other scores they don't do so well. Their effect in discouraging future criminality by the prisoner or others is the subject of much debate, but the soaring rates of the last 20 years suggest that prisons

are not a dramatically effective deterrent to criminal behavior. Prisons do isolate convicted criminals, but only to divert crime from ordinary citizens to prison guards and fellow inmates. Almost no one contends anymore that prisons rehabilitate their inmates. If anything, they probably impede rehabilitation by forcing inmates into prolonged and almost exclusive association with other criminals. And prisons cost a lot of money. Housing a typical prisoner in a typical prison costs far more than a stint at a top university. This cost would be justified if prisons did the job they were intended for. But it is clear to all that prisons fail on the very grounds—humanity and hope of rehabilitation—that caused them to replace earlier, cheaper forms of punishment.

13   The universal acknowledgment that prisons do not rehabilitate criminals has produced two responses. The first is to retain the hope of rehabilitation but do away with imprisonment as much as possible and replace it with various forms of "alternative treatment," such as psychotherapy, supervised probation, and vocational training. Psychiatrist Karl Menninger, one of the principal critics of American penology, has suggested even more unconventional approaches, such as "a new job opportunity or a vacation trip, a course of reducing exercises, a cosmetic surgical operation or a herniotomy, some night school courses, a wedding in the family (even one for the patient!), an inspiring sermon." The starry-eyed approach naturally has produced a backlash from critics on the right, who think that it's time to abandon the goal of rehabilitation. They argue that prisons perform an important service just by keeping criminals off the streets, and thus should be used with that purpose in mind.

14   So the debate continues to rage in all the same old ruts. No one, of course, would think of copying the medieval practices of Islamic nations and experimenting with punishments such as flogging and amputation. But let us consider them anyway. How do they compare with our American prison system in achieving the ostensible objectives of punishment? First, do they punish? Obviously they do, and in a uniquely painful and memorable way. Of course any sensible person, given the choice, would prefer suffering these punishments to years of incarceration in a typical American prison. But presumably no Western penologist would criticize Islamic punishments on the grounds that they are not barbaric enough. Do they deter crime? Yes, and probably more effectively than sending convicts off to prison. Now we read about a prison sentence in the newspaper, then think no more about the criminal's payment for his crimes until, perhaps, years later we read a small item reporting his release. By contrast, one can easily imagine the vivid impression it would leave to be wandering through a local shopping center and to stumble onto the scene of some poor wretch being lustily flogged. And the occasional sight of an habitual offender walking around with a bloody stump at the end of his arm no doubt also would serve as a forceful reminder that crime does not pay.

15   Do flogging and amputation discourage recidivism? No one knows whether the scars on his back would dissuade a criminal from risking another crime, but it is hard to imagine that corporal measures could stimulate a higher rate of recidivism than already exists. Islamic forms of punishment do not serve the

favorite new right goal of simply isolating criminals from the rest of society, but they may achieve the same purpose of making further crimes impossible. In the movie *Bonnie and Clyde,* Warren Beatty successfully robs a bank with his arm in a sling, but this must be dismissed as artistic license. It must be extraordinarily difficult, at the very least, to perform much violent crime with only one hand.

16   Do the medieval forms of punishment rehabilitate the criminal? Plainly not. But long prison terms do not rehabilitate either. And it is just as plain that typical Islamic punishments are no crueler to the convict than incarceration in the typical American state prison.

17   Of course there are other reasons besides its bizarre forms of punishment that the Islamic system of justice seems uncivilized to the Western mind. One is the absence of due process. Another is the long list of offenses—such as drinking, adultery, blasphemy, "profiteering," and so on—that can bring on conviction and punishment. A third is all the ritualistic mumbojumbo in pronouncements of Islamic law (like that talk about puberty and amnesia in the ayatollah's quotation at the beginning of this article). Even in these matters, however, a little cultural modesty is called for. The vast majority of American criminals are convicted and sentenced as a result of plea bargaining, in which due process plays almost no role. It has been only half a century since a wave of religious fundamentalism stirred this country to outlaw the consumption of alcoholic beverages. Most states also still have laws imposing austere constraints on sexual conduct. [T]he *Washington Post* reported that the FBI had spent two and a half years and untold amounts of money to break up a nationwide pornography ring. Flogging the clients of prostitutes, as the Pakistanis did, does seem silly. But [. . .] Mayor Koch of New York was proposing that clients caught in his own city have their names broadcast by radio stations. We are not so far advanced on such matters as we often like to think. Finally, my lawyer friends assure me that the rules of jurisdiction for American courts contain plenty of petty requirements and bizarre distinctions that would sound silly enough to foreign ears.

18   Perhaps it sounds barbaric to talk of flogging and amputation, and perhaps it is. But our system of punishment also is barbaric, and probably more so. Only cultural smugness about their system and willful ignorance about our own make it easy to regard the one as cruel and the other as civilized. We inflict our cruelties away from public view, while nations like Pakistan stage them in front of 10,000 onlookers. Their outrages are visible; ours are not. Most Americans can live their lives for years without having their peace of mind disturbed by the knowledge of what goes on in our prisons. To choose imprisonment over flogging and amputation is not to choose human kindness over cruelty, but merely to prefer that our cruelties be kept out of sight, and out of mind.

19   Public flogging and amputation may be more barbaric forms of punishment than imprisonment, even if they are not more cruel. Society may pay a higher price for them, even if the particular criminal does not. Revulsion against officially sanctioned violence and infliction of pain derives from something deeply ingrained in Western conscience, and clearly it is something admirable. Grotesque displays

of the sort that occur in Islamic countries probably breed a greater tolerance for physical cruelty, for example, which prisons do not do precisely because they conceal their cruelties. In fact it is our admirable intolerance for calculated violence that makes it necessary for us to conceal what we have not been able to do away with. In a way this is a good thing, since it holds out the hope that we may eventually find a way to do away with it. But in another way it is a bad thing, since it permits us to congratulate ourselves on our civilized humanitarianism while violating its norms in this one area of our national life.

MEANING

1. What are the five objectives that imprisonment is supposed to achieve in Western culture?
2. How satisfactorily do American prisons perform these functions?
3. How do the practices of punishment in Eastern cultures differ from those in Western societies?
4. What is Chapman's attitude toward Eastern practices in comparison with Western methods?

TECHNIQUE

1. How does Chapman use **comparison and contrast** to clearly illustrate the very different objectives punishment serves in Eastern and Western cultures?
2. Where does Chapman use the testimony of experts as well as statistics to support his analysis?
3. **Other Patterns.** How do Chapman's **descriptions** render alternative choices of punishment in highly graphic and vivid ways?

LANGUAGE

1. Why is it important for readers to understand the specific terms that are stipulated by Koranic law?
2. How does Chapman incorporate the terms used by criminologists (paragraph 11) in his comparative analysis?
3. If you don't know the meaning of the following words, look them up: *penological* (2), *scourging* (2), *flogging* (2), *ostensible* (14), *barbaric* (18).

SUGGESTIONS FOR WRITING

1. **Critical Writing.** Why is it significant that punishment in the West is private and follows secular guidelines, whereas in Eastern cultures, punishment is public and follows Koranic law? Discuss how differences in forms of punishment reveal cultural values.

2. For an interesting research project, compare the Eastern methods of punishment with those used in early New England settlements by the Puritans, who subjected offenders to public derision by imprisoning them in stocks and pillories (frames with holes for the head and hands).

3. In a few paragraphs, create an **argument** that answers Chapman's question as to which form of punishment you would prefer and why.

4. ***Thematic Links.*** How does Michael Levin's essay "The Case for Torture" (Chapter 12, "Argument") take into account both of the choices discussed by Chapman?

MACHADO DE ASSIS

A Canary's Ideas

A biracial self-taught writer, Joaquin Maria Machado de Assis (1839–1908) was born in Rio de Janeiro, had only five years of elementary school, and worked for most of his life as a civil servant. He was an astonishingly prolific writer whose works fill thirty-one volumes, including over one hundred short stories (as well as scores of plays and opera librettos). He is now regarded as one of Brazil's most outstanding authors, and his startlingly original novels include *Epitaph of a Small Winner* (1881) and *Dom Casmurro* (1900). In these works and in the following story, he creates unreliable narrators who see events from an unusual, even warped, perspective. The story is built on a comparison based on a juxtaposition of time frames, characters, and value systems between an obsessed ornithologist and a talking canary.

BEFORE YOU READ

What signs suggest that someone has become obsessed with something?

■   ■   ▨

1   A man by the name of Macedo, who had a fancy for ornithology, related to some friends an incident so extraordinary that no one took him seriously. Some came to believe he had lost his mind. Here is a summary of his narration.

2   At the beginning of last month, as I was walking down the street, a carriage darted past me and nearly knocked me to the ground. I escaped by quickly sidestepping into a secondhand shop. Neither the racket of the horse and carriage nor my entrance stirred the proprietor, dozing in a folding chair at the back of the shop. He was a man of shabby appearance: his beard was the color of dirty straw, and his head was covered by a tattered cap which probably had not found a buyer. One could not guess that there was any story behind him, as there could have been behind some of the objects he sold, nor could one sense in him that austere, disillusioned sadness inherent in the objects which were remnants of past lives.

3   The shop was dark and crowded with the sort of old, bent, broken, tarnished, rusted articles ordinarily found in secondhand shops, and everything was in that state of semidisorder befitting such an establishment. This assortment of articles, though banal, was interesting. Pots without lids, lids without pots, buttons, shoes, locks, a black shirt, straw hats, fur hats, picture frames, binoculars, dress coats, a fencing foil, a stuffed dog, a pair of slippers, gloves, nondescript vases, epaulets, a velvet satchel, two hatracks, a slingshot, a thermometer, chairs, a lithographed portrait by the late Sisson, a backgammon board, two wire masks for some future Carnival—all this and more, which I either did not see or do not remember, filled the shop in the area around the door, propped up, hung, or

displayed in glass cases as old as the objects inside them. Further inside the shop were many objects of similar appearance. Predominant were the large objects—chests of drawers, chairs, and beds—some of which were stacked on top of others which were lost in the darkness.

4   I was about to leave, when I saw a cage hanging in the doorway. It was as old as everything else in the shop, and I expected it to be empty so it would fit in with the general appearance of desolation. However, it wasn't empty. Inside, a canary was hopping about. The bird's color, liveliness, and charm added a note of life and youth to that heap of wreckage. It was the last passenger of some wrecked ship, who had arrived in the shop as complete and happy as it had originally been. As soon as I looked at the bird, it began to hop up and down, from perch to perch, as if it meant to tell me that a ray of sunshine was frolicking in the midst of that cemetery. I'm using this image to describe the canary only because I'm speaking to rhetorical people, but the truth is that the canary thought about neither cemetery nor sun, according to what it told me later. Along with the pleasure the sight of the bird brought me, I felt indignation regarding its destiny and softly murmured these bitter words:

5   "What detestable owner had the nerve to rid himself of this bird for a few cents? Or what indifferent soul, not wishing to keep his late master's pet, gave it away to some child, who sold it so he could make a bet on a soccer game?"

6   The canary, sitting on top of its perch, trilled this reply:

7   "Whoever you may be, you're certainly not in your right mind. I had no detestable owner, nor was I given to any child to sell. Those are the delusions of a sick person. Go and get yourself cured, my friend. . . ."

8   "What?" I interrupted, not having had time to become astonished. "So your master didn't sell you to this shop? It wasn't misery or laziness that brought you, like a ray of sunshine, to this cemetery?"

9   "I don't know what you mean by 'sunshine' or 'cemetery.' If the canaries you've seen use the first of those names, so much the better, because it sounds pretty, but really, I'm sure you're confused."

10   "Excuse me, but you couldn't have come here by chance, all alone. Has your master always been that man sitting over there?"

11   "What master? That man over there is my servant. He gives me food and water every day, so regularly that if I were to pay him for his services, it would be no small sum, but canaries don't pay their servants. In fact, since the world belongs to canaries, it would be extravagant for them to pay for what is already in the world."

12   Astonished by these answers, I didn't know what to marvel at more—the language or the ideas. The language, even though it entered my ears as human speech, was uttered by the bird in the form of charming trills. I looked all around me so I could determine if I were awake and saw that the street was the same, and the shop was the same dark, sad, musty place. The canary, moving from side to side, was waiting for me to speak. I then asked if it were lonely for the infinite blue space. . . .

13   "But, my dear man," trilled the canary, "what does 'infinite blue space' mean?"

14   "But, pardon me, what do you think of this world? What is the world to you?"

15   "The world," retorted the canary, with a certain professorial air, "is a secondhand shop with a small rectangular bamboo cage hanging from a nail. The canary is lord of the cage it lives in and the shop that surrounds it. Beyond that, everything is illusion and deception."

16   With this, the old man woke up and approached me, dragging his feet. He asked me if I wanted to buy the canary. I asked if he had acquired it in the same way he had acquired the rest of the objects he sold and learned that he had bought it from a barber, along with a set of razors.

17   "The razors are in very good condition," he said.

18   "I only want the canary."

19   I paid for it, ordered a huge, circular cage of wood and wire, and had it placed on the veranda of my house so the bird could see the garden, the fountain, and a bit of blue sky.

20   It was my intention to do a lengthy study of this phenomenon, without saying anything to anyone until I could astound the world with my extraordinary discovery. I began by alphabetizing the canary's language in order to study its structure, its relation to music, the bird's appreciation of aesthetics, its ideas and recollections. When this philological and psychological analysis was done, I entered specifically into the study of canaries: their origin, their early history, the geology and flora of the Canary Islands, the bird's knowledge of navigation, and so forth. We conversed for hours while I took notes, and it waited, hopped about, and trilled.

21   As I have no family other than two servants, I ordered them not to interrupt me, even to deliver a letter or an urgent telegram or to inform me of an important visitor. Since they both knew about my scientific pursuits, they found my orders perfectly natural and did not suspect that the canary and I understood each other.

22   Needless to say, I slept little, woke up two or three times each night, wandered about aimlessly, and felt feverish. Finally, I returned to my work in order to reread, add, and emend. I corrected more than one observation, either because I had misunderstood something or because the bird had not expressed it clearly. The definition of the world was one of these. Three weeks after the canary's entrance into my home, I asked it to repeat to me its definition of the world.

23   "The world," it answered, "is a sufficiently broad garden with a fountain in the middle, flowers, shrubbery, some grass, clear air, and a bit of blue up above. The canary, lord of the world, lives in a spacious cage, white and circular, from which it looks out on the rest of the world. Everything else is illusion and deception."

24   The language of my treatise also suffered some modifications, and I saw that certain conclusions which had seemed simple were actually presumptuous. I still could not write the paper I was to send to the National Museum, the Historical

Institute, and the German universities, not due to a lack of material but because I first had to put together all my observations and test their validity. During the last few days, I neither left the house, answered letters, nor wanted to hear from friends or relatives. The canary was everything to me. One of the servants had the job of cleaning the bird's cage and giving it food and water every morning. The bird said nothing to him, as if it knew the man was completely lacking in scientific background. Besides, the service was no more than cursory, as the servant was not a bird lover.

25   One Saturday I awoke ill, my head and back aching. The doctor ordered complete rest. I was suffering from an excess of studying and was not to read or even think, nor was I even to know what was going on in the city or the rest of the outside world. I remained in this condition for five days. On the sixth day I got up, and only then did I find out that the canary, while under the servant's care, had flown out of its cage. My first impulse was to strangle the servant— I was choking with indignation and collapsed into my chair, speechless and bewildered. The guilty man defended himself, swearing he had been careful, but the wily bird had nevertheless managed to escape.

26   "But didn't you search for it?"

27   "Yes, I did, sir. First it flew up to the roof, and I followed it. It flew to a tree, and then who knows where it hid itself? I've been asking around since yesterday. I asked the neighbors and the local farmers, but no one has seen the bird."

28   I suffered immensely. Fortunately, the fatigue left me within a few hours, and I was soon able to go out to the veranda and the garden. There was no sign of the canary. I ran everywhere, making inquiries and posting announcements, all to no avail. I had already gathered my notes together to write my paper, even though it would be disjointed and incomplete, when I happened to visit a friend who had one of the largest and most beautiful estates on the outskirts of town. We were taking a stroll before dinner when this question was trilled to me:

29   "Greetings, Senhor Macedo, where have you been since you disappeared?"

30   It was the canary, perched on the branch of a tree. You can imagine how I reacted and what I said to the bird. My friend presumed I was mad, but the opinions of friends are of no importance to me. I spoke tenderly to the canary and asked it to come home and continue our conversations in that world of ours, composed of a garden, a fountain, a veranda, and a white circular cage.

31   "What garden? What fountain?"

32   "The world, my dear bird."

33   "What world? I see you haven't lost any of your annoying professorial habits. The world," it solemnly concluded, "is an infinite blue space, with the sun up above."

34   Indignant, I replied that if I were to believe what it said, the world could be anything—it had even been a secondhand shop. . . .

35   "A secondhand shop?" it trilled to its heart's content. "But is there really such a thing as a secondhand shop?"

■ ■ ▨

MEANING

1. In your opinion, what kind of person is Macedo, the narrator?
2. Why does he become obsessed with studying every aspect of the canary, especially its ideas?
3. In what different environments does Macedo encounter the canary?
4. How does the canary redefine its view of the world to match each new environment in which it finds itself?

TECHNIQUE

1. How is the story framed as an account reported by the narrator to the author?
2. How does de Assis use the canary's complacency to provide a contrast to the narrator's discontent?
3. **Other Patterns.** Why are de Assis's **descriptions** of different settings indispensable in conveying how the canary's view of the world differs from that of the narrator?

LANGUAGE

1. How do the canary's droll and understated comments communicate its viewpoint?
2. Why is it significant that the canary does not need to use similes and metaphors (paragraphs 4–9) and Macedo does need to do so?
3. If you don't know the meaning of the following words, look them up: *ornithology* (1), *lithographed* (3), *veranda* (19), *aesthetics* (20).

SUGGESTIONS FOR WRITING

1. **Critical Writing.** In what sense could the canary be understood as a symbol of a way of looking at the world that Macedo lacks and desperately needs?
2. Have you ever thought that your pet was talking to you? If so, what did it say?
3. Why is the setting of the story in Rio particularly appropriate, given the story's emphasis on illusion and reality?
4. **Thematic Links.** How do the stories by Machado de Assis and Natsume Soseki (see "I Am A Cat" in Chapter 4, "Description") suggest that writers use animals to present a fresh perspective on human behavior?

▓▓▓ STUDENT ESSAY: COMPARISON AND CONTRAST

The following essay by Naomi Nakamura illustrates the pattern of comparison and contrast. Her analysis is designed to show readers that there are fundamental similarities between seemingly very different philosophies. The annotations on Naomi's paper and the follow-up commentary ("Strategies") are designed to help you understand the pattern of comparison and contrast.

East Meets West: Zen Buddhism and Psychotherapy

Naomi Nakamura

1   Although Zen and psychotherapy are each a characteristic
expression of Eastern and Western thought, respectively, the
similarities between the two outweigh the differences. In general,
psychotherapy and Zen are both concerned with methods of
helping us to fulfill our capacities and to adjust to our
environments. In order to appreciate these deep similarities,
we must become familiar with their basic precepts, tenets, and
concepts.

> Thesis: claim of similarity

2   Zen, a sect of Mahayana Buddhism that originated in China
in the thirteenth century, claims to transmit the spirit or essence
of Buddha (which consists in experiencing the enlightenment,
or satori, that Buddha possessed). All sects of Zen believe in
mind-to-mind instruction from master to disciple, for the purpose
of finding spiritual realization in daily work. In Zen, the teacher is
not a teacher in the Western sense, nor is there rote learning,
memorizing, or the shaping of behavior.

> Description

3   Zen is actually a way of life that involves a resolution of the
struggle between the individual and the environment through an
experience called satori where the self becomes identified with
the world. From this we can infer that satori brings a joy, a
feeling of oneness with all things, and a heightened sense of
reality that cannot be adequately translated into the language of
the everyday world.

> Definition of key term

4   When we turn to psychotherapy, we discover a program
designed to treat all forms of suffering in which emotional factors
play a part. Sigmund Freud was one of the first to observe the
relationship between emotionally charged damaging experiences
in childhood and later mental illness. Often the most significant clue
was provided by the patient's dreams. The theory and practice of
psychoanalysis grew out of these discoveries and greatly influenced
the subsequent development of psychotherapy. Psychotherapy is
essentially a process of reeducation, both emotionally and
intellectually, through which the patient develops better patterns of

> Transition

> Definition

Nakamura 2

adjusting to life. The therapist tries to bring about a reconciliation between the individual's feelings and existing social norms and helps the individual to become self-sufficient without being in conflict with the environment.

5 Thus, we can infer that the basic method used in psychotherapy is to "train" the conscious mind to perceive distortions embedded in the unconscious and to relinquish these fictions. For example, Freud led his patients to see that their dreams in which their siblings died did not reflect their present feelings but rather were surviving wishes from childhood.

Example

6 This realization (or insight) released patients from their feelings of guilt. Effective insight is not thinking but is rather the experience of seeing something as being new and yet as if one had always known it. Authentic therapeutic insight is sudden, like satori. It arrives without being premediated or being forced and cannot be adequately translated into words.

7 As with psychotherapy, the practice of Zen not only leads to seeing into the nature of one's own being, but also liberates energies that are in ordinary circumstances distorted. It is the object of Zen, therefore, to prevent us from becoming mentally ill.

Comparison

8 In summary, Zen and psychoanalysis strive to eliminate unreal perceptions in order to lead the follower to experience a form of enlightenment (or "insight"). Both emphasize the aim of well-being, rather than just freedom from illness. Freud's aim, like that of the Zen masters, was to free man from himself.

Conclusion

9 Psychotherapy, as Freud envisioned it, is a method to help us fulfill our capacities and adjust ourselves to the environment in the most natural and comfortable manner possible. Its goal is to free the individual from the pain and torture suffered as a result of inner conflicts and guilt. Zen, on the other hand, is a technique designed to achieve enlightenment and spiritual freedom. Thus, these two methods of gaining insight into one's own nature are actually quite close despite the many differences in the time periods, and cultural contexts, in which they were conceived.

Restatement of thesis

Strategies for Writing Essays in Comparison and Contrast

1. Purpose and Thesis

This essay was written in response to an assignment in which the student read primary sources in psychology and Zen and was asked to create a comparative essay to clear up misconceptions about either or both.

In "East Meets West: Zen Buddhism and Psychotherapy," Naomi applies the principle of comparison and contrast to demonstrate the striking similarities between the two seemingly different systems of ideas. Naomi uses the title to suggest her point of view and places her thesis at the end of her introduction. This thesis suggests that the essay will focus on similarities between Zen Buddhism and psychotherapy. To support her analysis, she chose to write a point-by-point comparison demonstrating fundamental areas of agreement.

2. Structure

To support her assertion, Naomi provides a context in which to understand the history of both Zen Buddhism and psychotherapy. She then addresses the respective goals of each, that is, satori in Zen and insight in psychotherapy. Naomi then organizes her analysis around the main points of liberating energies in Zen and releasing guilt in psychotherapy.

3. Topic Sentences and Transitions

Naomi uses topic sentences and transitions to organize her comparative analysis and to help her readers to make the connections between paragraphs (for example, "When we turn to psychotherapy, we discover a program designed to treat all forms of suffering in which emotional factors play a part"). Although the entire essay uses a point-by-point method of organization, supporting paragraphs employ the subject-by-subject approach—that is, discussing everything about Zen before shifting to everything about psychotherapy.

In the conclusion, Naomi uses parallel sentence structure to reinforce her thesis.

4. Revision

One area for improvement would require Naomi to consolidate several short paragraphs into longer, more sustained discussions. Also, some readers might be curious about how followers of Zen Buddhism view conventional psychotherapy and how Freudians view Zen Buddhism.

Guidelines for Writing an Essay in Comparison and Contrast

- If your assignment requires you to compare and contrast, have you identified the basis on which the comparison will be developed?
- The purpose that your comparison or contrast is intended to serve should be expressed in a clear thesis statement that tells your readers whether you are focusing on the subjects' similarities or differences or both and what point you are making. Is your essay purely informational or evaluative?
- Decide what points you are going to emphasize for the subjects in your comparison.
- Decide on a clear method of organization. One choice is the one-subject-at-a-time method, in which everything relevant about one subject is discussed before moving to the other. With this method, be sure to cover each point about B in the same order as is used for A. Or choose the point-by-point method of organization in which one aspect of A is covered before you discuss the same aspect of B. (Remember to vary your sentence structure to avoid monotony.)
- Do your transitional words and phrases remind the reader that you are discussing similarities or differences?
- The conclusion should reinforce your original purpose for choosing this pattern.

Grammar Tips for Comparison and Contrast

When writing and revising an essay using comparison and contrast, you need to signal your readers when you are moving from one subject or point to another and when you are discussing parallel features. The two strategies that you can use to accomplish this are (1) using transitional words and phrases to clarify the connections between the points or subjects you are discussing and (2) using parallelism and repetition to link similar or related ideas within a paragraph.

1. Transitions that signal similarities or resemblances include *likewise, similarly, also, again,* and *in the same manner.* Those that signal differences include *by contrast, however, nevertheless, but, even though,* and *whereas.* To further develop a point, you can use *furthermore, in addition, besides, moreover, next,* and *finally.*

2. Use parallel structures to link nouns, verbs, phrases, or clauses that express similar or related ideas. These include:

A. Correlative expressions (*neither/nor, either/or, both/and, not only/but also*) that require parallel structures.

The meal was *not only* delicious *but also* inexpensive.

continued

B. Comparisons and Contrasts (*just as/so too, as/than, on one hand . . . on the other hand*) that have equivalent grammatical form.

Just as scientists have been compelled to recognize global warming as a fact, *so too* have politicians been motivated to include the issue in their policy statements.

Also, notice how comparable points are emphasized by repeated or restated terms ("compelled" and "motivated").

CHECKLIST for Revising Comparison and Contrast Essays

- On what basis will your comparison be developed?
- Does your thesis state clearly what you are comparing and the most important points you intend to make?
- Will your essay be primarily informational or evaluative?
- For a subject-by-subject comparison, do you alert your reader through words and phrases when you are switching from one subject to the other?
- For a point-by-point comparison, do you alert your reader when you alternate from one point to another?
- Do your transitional words and phrases make it easy for your reader to see your comparisons and contrasts?

ADDITIONAL WRITING ASSIGNMENTS AND ACTIVITIES

COMMUNICATING WITH DIFFERENT AUDIENCES

1. Write a letter to yourself adopting a scolding or haranguing tone about a character trait or habit you have, for example, being cheap or a perfectionist or judgmental of others. Write another letter in which you adopt a congratulatory tone and praise yourself for the exact same trait or habit.

2. Create two résumés drawing on the same information with different emphases for two very different positions, either of which you would like to have.

3. Make up a questionnaire that is designed to discover whether a new product would be better received than existing ones already on the market.

4. As a staff member of a city planning committee for your town, write a memo outlining competing choices for a location for a new stop sign and give your recommendation.

5. Write a script for yourself listing pros and cons of an important decision you have made or are currently facing.

WRITING FOR A NEWSPAPER

Write a letter to a newspaper pointing out ways in which their coverage of an event differed from the way in which the event was covered by other media outlets.

COMPARISON AND CONTRAST ESSAYS

1. What analogies would you use to describe colors to someone who was color-blind or music to someone who was deaf?

2. Compare the person you are now to the person you think you will be at the age of sixty.

3. Would you prefer a short, eventful life in which you had unusual powers or a long, uneventful life? Why?

4. What were some experiences you have had that made you aware that time is more subjective than simply counting minutes that pass on the clock?

5. Have you had the experience of moving from one place to another? Compare how you felt living in your former residence with your reactions in the new location.

6. What features in your current environment that you take for granted would you miss the most if you had to live elsewhere?

7. Write about a time when differences in political ideology, beliefs, or values created a conflict between you and someone else.

8. Would you rather be the torturer or the tortured in a situation that you could not avoid? Explain the reasons for your choice.

9. Discuss an event during which you became aware of the way in which rhetoric was used to disguise reality. What happened, and how was reality made to appear?

10. Compare the different sides of a person who seems to be very different while at work or in class from how you ordinarily know the person in his or her personal life.

11. Have you ever traveled to the same place using different kinds of transportation? Compare your experiences.

12. Would you rather have one really close friend or be popular with a group but not have a really close friend? Why?

RESEARCH SUGGESTIONS

1. Compare two works by one author, two films by one director, or the remake of a popular film from the past (for example, *The Omen*). Draw on reviews of both from newspapers or the IMDB (Internet Movie Database).

2. Compare popular toys, children's books, or TV shows of today with those of past years in terms of what they say about our culture.

COLLABORATIVE ACTIVITIES

1. Write your own epitaph, and then compare and contrast yours with your classmates' in terms of effectiveness and being memorable.

2. Write a response to the following: Imagine that you have made a pact with the devil. What do you want in return for your soul? Compare your response with your classmates', and see what contrasts emerge.

3. Interview male and female relatives or acquaintances who overcame obstacles in immigrating to the United States and compare the two accounts with those of other members of the class.

4. If you or any of your classmates have experience with both Eastern (e.g., yoga, tai chi) and Western (e.g., weight lifting, aerobics) forms of exercise, compare and contrast these activities to discover the similarities and differences.

PROCESS ANALYSIS

Cultural Rituals

One of the most effective ways to clarify the nature of something is to explain how it works. Process analysis divides a complex procedure into separate and easy-to-understand steps in order to explain how something works, how something happened, or how an action should be performed.

Process analysis is ideally suited to explaining how a product is manufactured, and it should include data on the equipment used, operations performed, standards used to measure success, and other pertinent technical information. In technical writing, graphs, charts, diagrams, and flowcharts are also useful in helping the reader to visualize the individual phases or steps in a complex procedure.

Process analysis requires the writer to include all necessary steps in the procedure and to demonstrate how each step is related to preceding and subsequent steps in the overall sequence. Writers in fields as diverse as psychology, business, manufacturing, history, cultural anthropology, and journalism all use process analysis to develop, organize, and present information.

Gloria Anzaldúa, in "How to Tame a Wild Tongue," investigates the qualities that characterize Chicano Spanish and the circumstances that have taught her when and where she would feel comfortable speaking it. Anzaldúa analyzes the style of Spanish used in different regions of the country and in different social classes and uses process analysis to organize this information:

> Chicano Spanish sprang out of the Chicanos' need to identify ourselves as a distinct people. We needed a language with which we could communicate with ourselves, a secret language. For some of us, language is a homeland closer than the Southwest— for many Chicanos today live in the Midwest and the East.

297

Anzaldúa's analysis of the sources and varieties of Chicano Spanish begins with this basic principle and then emphasizes the importance of linguistic and ethnic identity in finding her own voice.

Jamaica Kincaid also uses a step-by-step structure in her story "Girl" to present a mother's litany of rules to her daughter about the kinds of things that are necessary to become a respected woman in Antiguan culture:

> This is how to sew on a button; this is how to make a button-hole for the button you have just sewed on; this is how to hem a dress when you see the hem coming down and so to prevent yourself from looking like the slut I know you are so bent on becoming.

The rules that Kincaid lists are passed on from mother to daughter and represent the important social expectations for young women in Antigua.

Jessica Mitford has studied cultural customs from an anthropological perspective. What interests her especially is why our culture attaches such importance to the manner of preparation, arrangement, positioning, and display of the bodies of those who have died. To answer this question, she has done extensive research into the procedures used by undertakers, and in "Mortuary Solaces," she describes the sequence of techniques they use to create, insofar as is possible, the illusion of life:

> Jones is now ready for casketing (this is the present participle of the verb "to casket"). In this operation his right shoulder should be depressed slightly "to turn the body a bit to the right and soften the appearance of lying flat on the back." Positioning the hands is a matter of importance, and special rubber positioning blocks may be used. The hands should be cupped slightly for a more lifelike, relaxed appearance. Proper placement of the body requires a delicate sense of balance. It should lie as high as possible in the casket, yet not so high that the lid, when lowered, will hit the nose. On the other hand, we are cautioned, placing the body too low "creates the impression that the body is in a box."

Mitford's ironic analysis of this process is drawn from undertakers' manuals that give explicit instructions as to the steps that should be taken in preparing and displaying the body. The fastidious concern for how the body will look to the viewing public reveals, for Mitford, a deep cultural need to deny death, which the funeral profession answers with its own macabre form of "make-believe."

Whereas writers such as Anzaldúa and Kincaid create their own instructions to show the inner workings of a linguistic or cultural process, many social and political commentators use process analysis to provide a firsthand account of changes as they occur. Ethel G. Hofman, in "An Island Passover," analyzes the process by which her mother prepared a Passover Seder for her family and hundreds of soldiers stationed on the Shetland Islands during World War II. The emergence of this celebration, which combined both Scottish and Jewish elements, resulted from her mother's determination to keep their tradition and heritage alive in this far-flung outpost:

> Two days before the Holidays, Ma had extra help. There were no freezers, so cooking could not be done very far ahead. Thankfully, in early spring, Shetland weather is cold, so food was stored outside in a meat safe, a wire-mesh box hung high off the ground, or in our unheated, enclosed back porch.

> Putting together the Passover Seder was a family affair and the beginning of weeks of joyful anticipation. "Go fetch a writing pad and pencil," Ma instructed me. Jostling each other to be next to her, we dragged kitchen chairs across the linoleum floor.

Hofman goes beyond reporting the facts and makes her account interesting, lifelike, and dramatic. She creates characters, adds dialogue, and sets the scene while taking us through the steps of preparing the Seder in these unusual circumstances.

To be effective, process analysis should emphasize the significance of each step in the overall sequence and help the reader to understand how each stage emerges from the preceding one and flows into the next.

Process analysis is especially useful in taking an abstract concept or idea and describing how it works by breaking it into a number of distinct and easily understandable phases. Colin Turnbull uses this technique in "The Mbuti Pygmies" to explain how games act as a safety valve to maintain the balance between men and women competitors. Turnbull's research disclosed that the Mbuti play games such as a tug-of-war in which opponents switch sides when either side seems to be winning. This is done to maintain the tribal value of opposition without hostility.

Often, the phenomena that writers study are objectively observable yet appear mysterious. In "An Original Elephant," Mark Shand seeks to correct misconceptions about the uses of elephants in Indian culture. Elephants express the core of religious and social values for broad segments of the Indian population. Shand subdivides the process of acquiring and owning an elephant into a number of distinct and identifiable stages and demonstrates how each stage follows a protocol that is based on religious and social values:

> "An elephant costs about 300 rupees a week to feed, which in India is a great deal of money. From November to March, our marriage season in India, he rents the elephant out. On such occasions it is auspicious to have 'Ganesh' present."

Shand moves the reader through each of the stages of acquiring an elephant and communicates the many meanings, spiritual and commercial, this animal has in Indian society.

Rigoberta Menchú, a Quiché Indian in Guatemala, uses this form of analysis in "Birth Ceremonies" to take her readers behind the scenes during the eight days following the birth of a child to observe firsthand the many steps and various rituals that the Quiché use to initiate the newborn child into the community:

> Candles will be lit for him and his candle becomes part of the candle of the whole community, which now has one more person, one more member. The whole community is at the ceremony, or at least, if not all of it, then some of it. Candles are lit to represent all the things which belong to the universe—earth, water, sun, and man—and the child's candle is put with them, together with incense (what we call *pom*) and lime—our sacred lime.

Menchú separates the overall process of the birth ceremonies into a number of distinct and easy-to-understand stages and describes, step by step, what happens at each stage, starting with the first day of the mother's pregnancy to forty days after the birth of the child. These rituals emphasize the importance the Quiché place on binding the child to the community and preserving tradition.

As these examples illustrate, process analysis can encompass historical, social and cultural phenomena and either explain these processes or provide instructions. When you transfer this type of writing into a real-life context, imagine the responsibility that you incur when you give someone directions (such as how to make a recipe or how to use an unfamiliar tool).

GLORIA ANZALDÚA

How to Tame a Wild Tongue

Chicana poet, essayist, and fiction writer Gloria Anzaldúa (1942–2004) was raised on the Mexican-Texas border and frequently used this location as a metaphor in her writing. Her works address questions of identity, her Mexican Indian heritage, and the role that language plays in helping us to define ourselves. She taught at several universities in Texas and California and wrote a variety of highly praised works including *Borderlands–La Frontera, The New Mestiza* (1987), in which the following essay first appeared. Anzaldúa was a talented editor whose anthology *This Bridge Called My Back: Writings by Radical Women of Color* (1986) won the Before Columbus Foundation American Book Award.

BEFORE YOU READ

How might different forms of a language express the speaker's social class?

■ ■ ▨

1   "We're going to have to control your tongue," the dentist says, pulling out all the metal from my mouth. Silver bits plop and tinkle into the basin. My mouth is a motherlode.

2   The dentist is cleaning out my roots. I get a whiff of the stench when I gasp. "I can't cap that tooth yet, you're still draining," he says.

3   "We're going to have to do something about your tongue," I hear the anger rising in his voice. My tongue keeps pushing out the wads of cotton, pushing back the drills, the long thin needles. "I've never seen anything as strong or as stubborn," he says. And I think, how do you tame a wild tongue, train it to be quiet, how do you bridle and saddle it? How do you make it lie down?

Who is to say that robbing a people of its language is less violent than war?
—RAY GWYN SMITH

4   I remember being caught speaking Spanish at recess—that was good for three licks on the knuckles with a sharp ruler. I remember being sent to the corner of the classroom for "talking back" to the Anglo teacher when all I was trying to do was tell her how to pronounce my name. "If you want to be American, speak 'American.' If you don't like it, go back to Mexico where you belong."

5   "I want you to speak English. *Pa' hallar buen trabajo tienes que saber hablar el inglés bien. Qué vale toda tu educación si todavía hablas inglés con un* 'accent,'" my mother would say, mortified that I spoke English like a Mexican. At Pan American University, I and all Chicano students were required to take two speech classes. Their purpose: to get rid of our accents.

6   Attacks on one's form of expression with the intent to censor are a violation of the First Amendment. *El Anglo con cara de inocente nos arrancó la lengua.* Wild tongues can't be tamed, they can only be cut out.

OVERCOMING THE TRADITION OF SILENCE

Abogadas, escupimos el oscuro.
Peleando con nuestra propia sombra
el silencio nos sepulta.

7   *En boca cerrada no entran moscas.* "Flies don't enter a closed mouth" is a saying I kept hearing when I was a child. *Ser habladora* was to be a gossip and a liar, to talk too much. *Muchachitas bien criadas,* well-bred girls don't answer back. *Es una falta de respeto* to talk back to one's mother or father. I remember one of the sins I'd recite to the priest in the confession box the few times I went to confession: talking back to my mother, *hablar pa' 'tras, repelar. Hocicona, repelona, chismosa,* having a big mouth, questioning, carrying tales are all signs of being *mal criada.* In my culture they are all words that are derogatory if applied to women— I've never heard them applied to men.

8   The first time I heard two women, a Puerto Rican and a Cuban, say the word "*nosotras,*" I was shocked. I had not known the word existed. Chicanas use *nosotros* whether we're male or female. We are robbed of our female being by the masculine plural. Language is a male discourse.

And our tongues have become
dry   the wilderness has
dried out our tongues   and
we have forgotten speech.
                —IRENA KLEPFISZ

9   Even our own people, other Spanish speakers *nos quieren poner candados en la boca.* They would hold us back with their bag of *reglas de academia.*

Oyé como ladra: el lenguaje de la frontera
Quien tiene boca se equivoca.
                —MEXICAN SAYING

10   "*Pocho,* cultural traitor, you're speaking the oppressor's language by speaking English, you're ruining the Spanish language," I have been accused by various Latinos and Latinas. Chicano Spanish is considered by the purist and by most Latinos deficient, a mutilation of Spanish.

11   But Chicano Spanish is a border tongue which developed naturally. Change, *evolución, enriquecimiento de palabras nuevas por invención o adopción* have created variants of Chicano Spanish, *un nuevo lenguaje. Un lenguaje que corresponde a un modo de vivir.* Chicano Spanish is not incorrect, it is a living language.

12   For a people who are neither Spanish nor live in a country in which Spanish is the first language; for a people who live in a country in which English is the reigning tongue but who are not Anglo; for a people who cannot entirely identify with either standard (formal, Castilian) Spanish nor standard English, what recourse is left to them but to create their own language? A language which they can connect their identity to, one capable of communicating the realities

and values true to themselves—a language with terms that are neither *español ni inglés*, but both. We speak a patois, a forked tongue, a variation of two languages.

13   Chicano Spanish sprang out of the Chicanos' need to identify ourselves as a distinct people. We needed a language with which we could communicate with ourselves, a secret language. For some of us, language is a homeland closer than the Southwest—for many Chicanos today live in the Midwest and the East. And because we are a complex, heterogeneous people, we speak many languages. Some of the languages we speak are:

1. Standard English
2. Working class and slang English
3. Standard Spanish
4. Standard Mexican Spanish
5. North Mexican Spanish dialect
6. Chicano Spanish (Texas, New Mexico, Arizona and California have regional variations)
7. Tex-Mex
8. *Pachuco* (called *caló*)

14   My "home" tongues are the languages I speak with my sister and brothers, with my friends. They are the last five listed, with 6 and 7 being closest to my heart. From school, the media and job situations, I've picked up standard and working class English. From Mamagrande Locha and from reading Spanish and Mexican literature, I've picked up Standard Spanish and Standard Mexican Spanish. From *los recién llegados*, Mexican immigrants, and *braceros*, I learned the North Mexican dialect. With Mexicans I'll try to speak either Standard Mexican Spanish or the North Mexican dialect. From my parents and Chicanos living in the Valley, I picked up Chicano Texas Spanish, and I speak it with my mom, younger brother (who married a Mexican and who rarely mixes Spanish with English), aunts and older relatives.

15   With Chicanas from *Nuevo México* or *Arizona* I will speak Chicano Spanish a little, but often they don't understand what I'm saying. With most California Chicanas I speak entirely in English (unless I forget). When I first moved to San Francisco, I'd rattle off something in Spanish, unintentionally embarrassing them. Often it is only with another Chicana *tejana* that I can talk freely.

16   Words distorted by English are known as anglicisms or *pochismos*. The *pocho* is an anglicized Mexican or American of Mexican origin who speaks Spanish with an accent characteristic of North Americans and who distorts and reconstructs the language according to the influence of English. Tex-Mex, or Spanglish, comes most naturally to me. I may switch back and forth from English to Spanish in the same sentence or in the same word. With my sister and my brother Nune and with Chicano *tejano* contemporaries I speak in Tex-Mex.

17   From kids and people my own age I picked up *Pachuco*. *Pachuco* (the language of the zoot suiters) is a language of rebellion, both against Standard Spanish and Standard English. It is a secret language. Adults of the culture and outsiders cannot understand it. It is made up of slang words from both English and Spanish.

Ruca means girl or woman, *vato* means guy or dude, *chale* means no, *simón* means yes, *churro* is sure, talk is *periquiar, pigionear* means petting, *que gacho* means how nerdy, *ponte águila* means watch out, death is called *la pelona*. Through lack of practice and not having others who can speak it, I've lost most of the *Pachuco* tongue.

CHICANO SPANISH

18   Chicanos, after 250 years of Spanish/Anglo colonization have developed significant differences in the Spanish we speak. We collapse two adjacent vowels into a single syllable and sometimes shift the stress in certain words such as *maíz/maiz, cobete/cuete.* We leave out certain consonants when they appear between vowels: *lado/lao, mojado/mojao.* Chicanos from South Texas pronounce *f* as *j* as in *jue* (*fue*). Chicanos use "archaisms," words that are no longer in the Spanish language, words that have been evolved out. We say *semos, truje, haiga, ansina,* and *naiden.* We retain the "archaic" *j,* as in *jalar,* that derives from an earlier *h* (the French *halar* or the Germanic *halon* which was lost to standard Spanish in the 16th century), but which is still found in several regional dialects such as the one spoken in South Texas. (Due to geography, Chicanos from the Valley of South Texas were cut off linguistically from other Spanish speakers. We tend to use words that the Spaniards brought over from Medieval Spain. The majority of the Spanish colonizers in Mexico and the Southwest came from Extremadura—Hernán Cortés was one of them—and Andalucía. Andalucians pronounce *ll* like a *y,* and their *d*'s tend to be absorbed by adjacent vowels; *tirado* becomes *tirao.* They brought *el lenguaje popular, dialectos y regionalismos.*)

19   Chicanos and other Spanish speakers also shift *ll* to *y* and *z* to *s.* We leave out initial syllables, saying *tar* for *estar, toy* for *estoy, hora* for *ahora* (*cubanos* and *puertorriqueños* also leave out initial letters of some words). We also leave out the final syllable such as *pa* for *para.* The intervocalic *y,* the *ll* as in *tortilla, ella, botella,* gets replaced by *tortia* or *tortiya, ea, botea.* We add an additional syllable at the beginning of certain words: *atocar* for *tocar, agastar* for *gastar.* Sometimes we'll say *lavaste las vacijas,* other times *lavates* (substituting the *ates* verb endings for the *aste*).

20   We use anglicisms, words borrowed from English: *bola* from ball, *carpeta* from carpet, *máchina de lavar* (instead of *lavadora*) from washing machine. Tex-Mex argot, created by adding a Spanish sound at the beginning or end of an English word such as *cookiar* for cook, *watchar* for watch, *parkiar* for park, and *rapiar* for rape, is the result of the pressures on Spanish speakers to adapt to English.

21   We don't use the word *vosotros/as* or its accompanying verb form. We don't say *claro* (to mean yes), *imagínate,* or *me emociona,* unless we picked up Spanish from Latinas, out of a book, or in a classroom. Other Spanish-speaking groups are going through the same, or similar, development in their Spanish.

LINGUISTIC TERRORISM

Deslenguadas. Somos los del español deficiente. We are your linguistic nightmare, your linguistic aberration, your linguistic *mestisaje,* the subject of your *burla.*

Because we speak with tongues of fire we are culturally crucified. Racially, culturally and linguistically *somos huérfanos*—we speak an orphan tongue.

22   Chicanas who grew up speaking Chicano Spanish have internalized the belief that we speak poor Spanish. It is illegitimate, a bastard language. And because we internalize how our language has been used against us by the dominant culture, we use our language differences against each other.

23   Chicana feminists often skirt around each other with suspicion and hesitation. For the longest time I couldn't figure it out. Then it dawned on me. To be close to another Chicana is like looking into the mirror. We are afraid of what we'll see there. *Pena*. Shame. Low estimation of self. In childhood we are told that our language is wrong. Repeated attacks on our native tongue diminish our sense of self. The attacks continue throughout our lives.

24   Chicanas feel uncomfortable talking in Spanish to Latinas, afraid of their censure. Their language was not outlawed in their countries. They had a whole lifetime of being immersed in their native tongue; generations, centuries in which Spanish was a first language, taught in school, heard on radio and TV, and read in the newspaper.

25   If a person, Chicana or Latina, has a low estimation of my native tongue, she also has a low estimation of me. Often with *mexicanas y latinas* we'll speak English as a neutral language. Even among Chicanas we tend to speak English at parties or conferences. Yet, at the same time, we're afraid the other will think we're *agringadas* because we don't speak Chicano Spanish. We oppress each other trying to out-Chicano each other, vying to be the "real" Chicanas, to speak like Chicanos. There is no one Chicano language just as there is no one Chicano experience. A monolingual Chicana whose first language is English or Spanish is just as much a Chicana as one who speaks several variants of Spanish. A Chicana from Michigan or Chicago or Detroit is just as much a Chicana as one from the Southwest. Chicano Spanish is as diverse linguistically as it is regionally.

26   By the end of this century, Spanish speakers will comprise the biggest minority group in the U.S., a country where students in high schools and colleges are encouraged to take French classes because French is considered more "cultured." But for a language to remain alive it must be used. By the end of this century English, and not Spanish, will be the mother tongue of most Chicanos and Latinos.

27   So, if you want to really hurt me, talk badly about my language. Ethnic identity is twin skin to linguistic identity—I am my language. Until I can take pride in my language, I cannot take pride in myself. Until I can accept as legitimate Chicano Texas Spanish, Tex-Mex and all the other languages I speak, I cannot accept the legitimacy of myself. Until I am free to write bilingually and to switch codes without having always to translate, while I still have to speak English or Spanish when I would rather speak Spanglish, and as long as I have to accommodate the English speakers rather than having them accommodate me, my tongue will be illegitimate.

28   I will no longer be made to feel ashamed of existing. I will have my voice: Indian, Spanish, white. I will have my serpent's tongue—my woman's voice, my sexual voice, my poet's voice. I will overcome the tradition of silence.

> My fingers
> move sly against your palm
> Like women everywhere, we speak in code . . .
> —MELANIE KAYE/KANTROWITZ

■ ■ ▨

MEANING

1. How have Anzaldúa's experiences over the years in speaking Chicano Spanish taught her the limits as to when and where she can speak?

2. In what sense are language and identity intertwined for Anzaldúa?

3. What different languages does Anzaldúa speak, and what does she value about each?

4. What emphasis does Anzaldúa put on the concept of an "untamed tongue," and how does her essay expand on the meanings of this phrase?

TECHNIQUE

1. In what way are each of the sections of Anzaldúa's essay stages or milestones in her self-education?

2. What aspects of her essay emphasize her aspiration to become comfortable with all the varieties of English and Chicano Spanish?

3. How does Anzaldúa's discussion of countries in which Spanish is the first language parallel her quest to validate Chicano Spanish?

4. *Other Patterns.* How does Anzaldúa use **narrative** vignettes to allow her readers to understand how different kinds of Spanish are spoken in different contexts?

LANGUAGE

1. In what sense is the title of Anzaldúa's essay ironic?

2. How does the use of Spanish words and phrases suggest the richness of the language and its availability to those who are bilingual?

3. If you don't know the meaning of the following words, look them up: *heterogeneous* (13), *archaisms* (18).

SUGGESTIONS FOR WRITING

1. If you are the only one in your family who speaks English, do you find that you function as a translator and intermediary between them and society? Describe your experiences.

2. *Critical Writing.* How is Anzaldúa's essay designed to counter the perception that Chicano Spanish is somehow less legitimate than "pure" Spanish?

3. If you speak another language at home and in your community, **compare** your experiences with those of Anzaldúa.

4. ***Thematic Links.*** How do the essays by Anzaldúa and Luis Alberto Urrea ("Nobody's Son" in Chapter 8, "Classification and Division") provide complementary perspectives on language and identity?

JESSICA MITFORD

Mortuary Solaces

A brilliant investigative reporter and scholar, Jessica Mitford (1917–1996) was born in England, emigrated to the United States in 1939, and worked for civil rights organizations in California and as a professor in sociology at San Jose State College. Mitford's studies of the funeral industry, the government's use of conspiracy laws to punish political opponents, and the abuse of prisoners for experimental medical research are the main areas to which she devoted her efforts. She even conducted seminars in "muckraking" and described her approach in *Poison Penmanship: The Gentle Art of Muckraking* (1979). The following selection, drawn from her classic work *The American Way of Death* (1963), explores the surreal and expensive practices of the funeral industry.

BEFORE YOU READ

What function do funerals serve in our society?

■ ■ ▧

1 Embalming is indeed a most extraordinary procedure, and one must wonder at the docility of Americans who each year pay hundreds of millions of dollars for its perpetuation, blissfully ignorant of what it is all about, what is done, how it is done. Not one in ten thousand has any idea of what actually takes place. Books on the subject are extremely hard to come by. They are not to be found in most libraries or bookshops.

2 In an era when huge television audiences watch surgical operations in the comfort of their living rooms, when, thanks to the animated cartoon, the geography of the digestive system has become familiar territory even to the nursery school set, in a land where the satisfaction of curiosity about almost all matters is a national pastime, the secrecy surrounding embalming can, surely, hardly be attributed to the inherent gruesomeness of the subject. Custom in this regard has within this century suffered a complete reversal. In the early days of American embalming, when it was performed in the home of the deceased, it was almost mandatory for some relative to stay by the embalmer's side and witness the procedure. Today, family members who might wish to be in attendance would certainly be dissuaded by the funeral director. All others, except apprentices, are excluded by law from the preparation room.

3 A close look at what does actually take place may explain in large measure the undertaker's intractable reticence concerning a procedure that has become his major *raison d'être*. Is it possible he fears that public information about embalming might lead patrons to wonder if they really want this service? If the funeral men are loath to discuss the subject outside the trade, the reader may, understandably, be equally loath to go on reading at this point. For those who have the stomach for it, let us part the formaldehyde curtain. . . .

4   The body is first laid out in the undertaker's morgue—or rather, Mr. Jones is reposing in the preparation room—to be readied to bid the world farewell.

5   The preparation room in any of the better funeral establishments has the tiled and sterile look of a surgery, and indeed the embalmer-restorative artist who does his chores there is beginning to adopt the term "dermasurgeon" (appropriately corrupted by some mortician-writers as "demisurgeon") to describe his calling. His equipment, consisting of scalpels, scissors, augers, forceps, clamps, needles, pumps, tubes, bowls and basins, is crudely imitative of the surgeon's as is his technique, acquired in a nine- or twelve-month post-high-school course in an embalming school. He is supplied by an advanced chemical industry with a bewildering array of fluids, sprays, pastes, oils, powders, creams, to fix or soften tissue, shrink or distend it as needed, dry it here, restore the moisture there. There are cosmetics, waxes and paints to fill and cover features, even plaster of Paris to replace entire limbs. There are ingenious aids to prop and stabilize the cadaver: a Vari-Pose Head Rest, the Edwards Arm and Hand Positioner, the Repose Block (to support the shoulders during the embalming), and the Throop Foot Positioner, which resembles an old-fashioned stocks.

6   Mr. John H. Eckels, president of the Eckels College of Mortuary Science, thus describes the first part of the embalming procedure: "In the hands of a skilled practitioner, this work may be done in a comparatively short time and without mutilating the body other than by slight incision—so slight that it scarcely would cause serious inconvenience if made upon a living person. It is necessary to remove the blood, and doing this not only helps in the disinfecting, but removes the principal cause of disfigurements due to discoloration."

7   Another textbook discusses the all-important time element: "The earlier this is done, the better, for every hour that elapses between death and embalming will add to the problems and complications encountered. . . ." Just how soon should one get going on the embalming? The author tells us, "On the basis of such scanty information made available to this profession through its rudimentary and haphazard system of technical research, we must conclude that the best results are to be obtained if the subject is embalmed before life is completely extinct—that is, before cellular death has occurred. In the average case, this would mean within an hour after somatic death." For those who feel that there is something a little rudimentary, not to say haphazard, about this advice, a comforting thought is offered by another writer. Speaking of fears entertained in early days of premature burial, he points out, "One of the effects of embalming by chemical injection, however, has been to dispel fears of live burial." How true, once the blood is removed, chances of live burial are indeed remote.

8   To return to Mr. Jones, the blood is drained out through the veins and replaced by embalming fluid pumped in through the arteries. As noted in *The Principles and Practices of Embalming*, "every operator has a favorite injection and drainage point—a fact which becomes a handicap only if he fails or refuses to forsake his favorites when conditions demand it." Typical favorites are the carotid artery, femoral artery, jugular vein, subclavian vein. There are various choices of embalming fluid. If Flextone is used, it will produce a "mild, flexible rigidity.

The skin retains a velvety softness, the tissues are rubbery and pliable. Ideal for women and children." It may be blended with B. and G. Products Company's Lyf-Lyk tint, which is guaranteed to reproduce "nature's own skin texture . . . the velvety appearance of living tissue." Suntone comes in three separate tints: Suntan; Special Cosmetic Tint, a pink shade "especially indicated for young female subjects"; and Regular Cosmetic Tint, moderately pink.

9   About three to six gallons of a dyed and perfumed solution of formaldehyde, glycerin, borax, phenol, alcohol and water is soon circulating through Mr. Jones, whose mouth has been sewn together with a "needle directed upward between the upper lip and gum and brought out through the left nostril," with the corners raised slightly "for a more pleasant expression." If he should be bucktoothed, his teeth are cleaned with Bon Ami and coated with colorless nail polish. His eyes, meanwhile, are closed with flesh-tinted eye caps and eye cement.

10   The next step is to have at Mr. Jones with a thing called a trocar. This is a long, hollow needle attached to a tube. It is jabbed into the abdomen, poked around the entrails and chest cavity, the contents of which are pumped out and replaced with "cavity fluid." This done, and the hole in the abdomen sewn up, Mr. Jones's face is heavily creamed (to protect the skin from burns which may be caused by leakage of the chemicals), and he is covered with a sheet and left unmolested for a while. But not for long—there is more, much more, in store for him. He has been embalmed, but not yet restored, and the best time to start the restorative work is eight to ten hours after embalming, when the tissues have become firm and dry.

11   The object of all this attention to the corpse, it must be remembered, is to make it presentable for viewing in an attitude of healthy repose. "Our customs require the presentation of our dead in the semblance of normality . . . unmarred by the ravages of illness, disease or mutilation," says Mr. J. Sheridan Mayer in his *Restorative Art.* This is rather a large order since few people die in the full bloom of health, unravaged by illness and unmarked by some disfigurement. The funeral industry is equal to the challenge: "In some cases the gruesome appearance of a mutilated or disease-ridden subject may be quite discouraging. The task of restoration may seem impossible and shake the confidence of the embalmer. This is the time for intestinal fortitude and determination. Once the formative work is begun and affected tissues are cleaned or removed, all doubts of success vanish. It is surprising and gratifying to discover the results which may be obtained."

12   The embalmer, having allowed an appropriate interval to elapse, returns to the attack, but now he brings into play the skill and equipment of sculptor and cosmetician. Is a hand missing? Casting one in plaster of Paris is a simple matter. "For replacement purposes, only a cast of the back of the hand is necessary; this is within the ability of the average operator and is quite adequate." If a lip or two, a nose or an ear should be missing, the embalmer has at hand a variety of restorative waxes with which to model replacements. Pores and skin texture are simulated by stippling with a little brush, and over this cosmetics are laid on. Head off? Decapitation cases are rather routinely handled. Ragged edges are

trimmed, and head joined to torso with a series of splints, wires and sutures. It is a good idea to have a little something at the neck—a scarf or high collar—when time for viewing comes. Swollen mouth? Cut out tissue as needed from inside the lips. If too much is removed, the surface contour can easily be restored by padding with cotton. Swollen necks and cheeks are reduced by removing tissue through vertical incisions made down each side of the neck. "When the deceased is casketed, the pillow will hide the suture incisions . . . as an extra precaution against leakage, the suture may be painted with liquid sealer."

13   The opposite condition is more likely to present itself—that of emaciation. His hypodermic syringe now loaded with massage cream, the embalmer seeks out and fills the hollowed and sunken areas by injection. In this procedure the backs of the hands and fingers and the under-chin area should not be neglected.

14   Positioning the lips is a problem that recurrently challenges the ingenuity of the embalmer. Closed too tightly, they tend to give a stern, even disapproving expression. Ideally, embalmers feel, the lips should give the impression of being ever so slightly parted, the upper lip protruding slightly for a more youthful appearance. This takes some engineering, however, as the lips tend to drift apart. Lip drift can sometimes be remedied by pushing one or two straight pins through the inner margin of the lower lip and then inserting them between the two front upper teeth. If Mr. Jones happens to have no teeth, the pins can just as easily be anchored in his Armstrong Face Former and Denture Replacer. Another method to maintain lip closure is to dislocate the lower jaw, which is then held in its new position by a wire run through holes which have been drilled through the upper and lower jaws at the midline. As the French are fond of saying, *il faut souffrir pour être belle.*[1]

15   If Mr. Jones has died of jaundice, the embalming fluid will very likely turn him green. Does this deter the embalmer? Not if he has intestinal fortitude. Masking pastes and cosmetics are heavily laid on, burial garments and casket interiors are color-correlated with particular care, and Jones is displayed beneath rose-colored lights. Friends will say, "How *well* he looks," Death by carbon monoxide, on the other hand, can be rather a good thing from the embalmer's viewpoint: "One advantage is the fact that this type of discoloration is an exaggerated form of a natural pink coloration." This is nice because the healthy glow is already present and needs but little attention.

16   The patching and filling completed, Mr. Jones is now shaved, washed and dressed. Cream-based cosmetic, available in pink, flesh, suntan, brunette and blond, is applied to his hands and face, his hair is shampooed and combed (and, in the case of Mrs. Jones, set), his hands manicured. For the horny-handed son of toil special care must be taken; cream should be applied to remove ingrained grime, and the nails cleaned. "If he were not in the habit of having them manicured in life, trimming and shaping is advised for better appearance— never questioned by kin."

---

[1] "One must suffer to beautiful."

17   Jones is now ready for casketing (this is the present participle of the verb "to casket"). In this operation his right shoulder should be depressed slightly "to turn the body a bit to the right and soften the appearance of lying flat on the back." Positioning the hands is a matter of importance, and special rubber positioning blocks may be used. The hands should be cupped slightly for a more lifelike, relaxed appearance. Proper placement of the body requires a delicate sense of balance. It should lie as high as possible in the casket, yet not so high that the lid, when lowered, will hit the nose. On the other hand, we are cautioned, placing the body too low "creates the impression that the body is in a box."

18   Jones is next wheeled into the appointed slumber room where a few last touches may be added—his favorite pipe placed in his hand or, if he was a great reader, a book propped into position. (In the case of little Master Jones a Teddy bear may be clutched.) Here he will hold open house for a few days, visiting hours 10 A.M. to 9 P.M.

■ ■ ▨

MEANING

1. Why, in Mitford's view, does our culture envelop mortuary practices in a cloak of secrecy?
2. How do undertakers use a variety of cosmetic techniques to create an illusion of life?
3. Why was this article considered to be an exposé of the funeral industry?
4. From a mortician's point of view, why are deaths from certain causes preferable?

TECHNIQUE

1. Into what stages does Mitford divide the process of "casketing"?
2. How does Mitford use undertakers' instruction manuals in her analysis?
3. **Other Patterns.** What features of objective **description** does Mitford incorporate into her account to emphasize the macabre nature of these practices?

LANGUAGE

1. In her exposé of the funeral industry, how does Mitford use irony and avoid euphemisms?
2. What phrases best capture the irreality and cultural need for denial that are implicit in the procedures adopted by the funeral industry?
3. If you don't know the meaning of the following words, look them up: *embalming* (1), *inherent* (2), *raison d'être* (3), *formaldehyde* (3), *augers* (5), *jaundice* (15).

SUGGESTIONS FOR WRITING

1. **Critical Writing.** To what extent does Mitford overlook the positive aspect of creating an illusion that the dead person is simply sleeping? Might not these funeral practices serve a valuable psychological purpose? Explore this possibility.

2. How might the funeral industry respond to Mitford's exposé?

3. After reading Evelyn Waugh's spoof of Hollywood mortuary customs in his novel *The Loved One* (1948), write an essay relating it to Mitford's analysis.

4. **Compare** the modern techniques that Mitford describes with those used in ancient Egypt, and write an essay about the different cultural and religious purposes they serve.

5. ***Thematic Links.*** Compare the underlying cultural agendas in Mitford's account with those described by Kim Chernin in "The Flesh and the Devil" (Chapter 9, "Cause and Effect").

ETHEL G. HOFMAN

An Island Passover

Ethel G. Hofman grew up in the Shetland Islands in northern Scotland to parents who had emigrated from Russia but resolved to keep their Jewish tradition and heritage in this isolated region. She is a syndicated food journalist, cookbook author, and past president of the International Association of Culinary Professionals. The following chapter, taken from her memoir *Mackerel at Midnight: Growing Up Jewish on a Remote Scottish Island* (2005), takes us through the steps of preparing for a Passover Seder for over 300 Jewish men and women who were stationed in the Shetlands during World War II.

BEFORE YOU READ

What do you know about the Passover celebration?

1   The countdown began exactly two months before Passover. Ma checked the dates on the *Jewish Echo* calendar, which hung on a rusty nail under the mantelpiece, where matchboxes, letters, and china ornaments were crammed together in no particular order.

2   The *Jewish Echo*, now defunct, was the weekly Jewish newspaper, published in Glasgow. The calendar was Ma's guide for Holiday dates as well as Sabbath candle-lighting times. By the time of the High Holidays in September, the pages were well thumbed and grease-stained. Since dusk in the north comes later in summer and earlier in winter, Ma adjusted candle-lighting times accordingly, rationalizing thus: "As long as I light candles, God doesn't mind what time it is."

3   The *Echo* was her only connection to the Glasgow Jewish community. As she scrutinized the births, marriages, and deaths published each week, she could be heard to exclaim, "Oh my, Annie Smith has passed away. We used to go together to the Locarno dances every Saturday night." Or, "Ettie Goldstone has had a baby. . . . That must be Ronnie Goldstone's daughter-in-law."

4   Planning ahead was essential. Deliveries were unreliable. The steamship *St. Magnus*, carrying supplies from the Scottish mainland, arrived in Shetland only twice a week, on Tuesdays and Fridays. And if the weather was stormy, deliveries could be delayed. Shetland sea captains were highly skilled, but none would risk the North Sea crossing from Aberdeen while fighting one-hundred-mile-an-hour gales. "That would be madness," to quote a feisty captain of the 1930s. Besides dealing with this uncertainty over getting food on time, Ma divided her days between working in the shop and cooking for the family.

For a visual to accompany this selection, see color insert photo B-3.

5   Two days before the Holidays, Ma had extra help. There were no freezers, so cooking could not be done very far ahead. Thankfully, in early spring, Shetland weather is cold, so food was stored outside in a meat safe, a wire-mesh box hung high off the ground, or in our unheated, enclosed back porch.

6   Putting together the Passover order was a family affair and the beginning of weeks of joyful anticipation. "Go fetch a writing pad and pencil," Ma instructed me. Jostling each other to be next to her, we dragged kitchen chairs across the linoleum floor. "I want to sit here."

7   "No, I was here first"—this from Roy as he was pushed off the chair.

8   This went on until Ma intervened. "Ethel, you sit on one side and Roy you can sit on the other side."

9   Pencil in hand, she began to compile the list. At first, it was not very detailed. In the 1940s the only Passover items available for the eight-day holiday were *matzo* meal, *matzos*, and wine. And from 1940 to 1945, food was rationed so that coupons in the ration books were saved for special occasions. Lerwick shops stocked sugar, butter, flour, jams, and other basic necessities. But Michael Morrison's delicatessen in Glasgow, still in existence, carried foods we tasted only on holidays: sharp and tangy, sweet and sour, exotic and exciting.

10   Ian Morrison remembers, as a teenager, packing the jars to go to Shetland. "Everything had to be wrapped in two or three sheets of newspaper; then each jar was placed in the box, separated by cardboard. That way, if one jar broke, the contents wouldn't mess up the remaining jars."

11   The list became longer as each of us added our favorite "Jewish foods." Ma yearned for pickles and sauerkraut, which she used to buy in Glasgow whenever she needed to, so half a dozen cans of each was the standard order. Dad insisted on two five-pound wursts (salami). As soon as they were unpacked, the long, fat, garlicky sausages were attached with wooden clothespins to a line strung across the back porch, which served as a natural refrigerator, the temperature in April rarely exceeding fifty degrees. For a Passover snack, Dad sprinted up the steep wooden stairs leading from the back shop, through the kitchen, to the porch. Pulling a silver penknife from his trouser pocket, he cut off a hunk of wurst and ran back to the shop again, savoring small bites on the way. Customers never complained if, at times, he reeked of garlic. And if our supply of olive oil was low, six one-gallon cans were also ordered, Ma never tiring of informing us once more, "I was cooking with olive oil long before it became fashionable."

12   Finally, there was the *matzo* order—fifteen boxes. "How much can one family eat?" came a call from Michael Morrison before mailing the first of many packages to "the Greenwalds in Shetland." Ma began to explain, "I need a box for Granny Hunter, one for the Laurenson family in Hamnavoe, one for the Mullays who live at the top of the lane . . . ," before the exasperated deli owner finally hung up on Lerwick 269, one of his best customers. Most of the *matzos* were delivered to our Christian neighbors, who anxiously waited for the unleavened bread, symbolic of the exodus of the Jews from Egypt—and, in their eyes, we were indeed the Chosen People.

13   When I was eight years old, my birthday fell during Passover. Determined that I should not feel deprived, Ma placed a surprise order. Along with the enormous brown-paper-wrapped boxes containing the Passover order, there was a small package. "Open it," said my mother. I tore off the paper, Ma helping with scissors, and I gasped. Inside, framed in a froth of white tissue-paper, nestled a magnificent, layered, chocolate nut cake. It had been packed so carefully that the swirly rosettes of chocolate frosting, each crowned with a toasted hazelnut, had retained their shapes perfectly—miraculously surviving the fourteen-hour ocean journey in the ship's hold. Memory being enhanced by nostalgia, this remains the most glorious birthday cake I have ever had.

14   We ate fish every day, but meat only occasionally. Like every island household, we stored a barrel of salt herring to carry us over the winter, when the weather was too rough for the fishing boats to go out. We stored our herring in the garage, covering the barrel with a slatted, easily removable wooden lid. It was my job to brave the wind and rain, sprinting from the back door of our house to push open the rickety garage door to "get a *fry*." Of course, that didn't mean the herring would be fried. It is the Shetland expression meaning "enough to feed the family," in our case, a family of five. Ma rinsed and soaked a few herring, as needed, to make pickled herring, chopped herring, and, occasionally, when fresh herring was out of season, to make potted herring (rolled and baked in a vinegar–bay leaf mixture).

15   One month before Passover, she put up a ten-pound jar of pickled herring. First, the fish was soaked in cold water to leach out the salt. Then, in a single slash with a razor-edged knife, the head and backbone, with all the tiny bones attached, were removed, later to be tossed outside to delighted seagulls. The fillets were cut into bite-sized pieces, then packed into an empty ten-pound glass *sweetie* jar, layered with thick onion slices (after the *sweeties* were sold, there was no further use for the jars, except in our house). Finally, vinegary brine was poured over the fish to cover it completely. Bay leaves, peppercorns, and fronds of dill floating throughout helped give a piquant flavor, which mellowed over the weeks. The lid was tightly screwed on, and the jar set on a shelf high above the jams and jellies in the back porch. The pickled herring was perfectly marinated by Passover. To make chopped herring, Ma drained a couple of handfuls of pickled herring and hacked it on a big wooden board with a broad-bladed *messer*. She mixed in chopped onion and hard cooked eggs before spooning the sharp, savory mixture into a bowl. Good plain food—no apples, sugar, mayonnaise, or preservatives added to mask the taste of homespun ingredients.

16   Two days before Passover, our kitchen was the scene of frenzied activity: Ma, Granny Hunter, and "the girl," darting around like hens vying for their daily grain feed. Ma directed culinary operations while she mixed and whisked—never measuring. "Keep that stove stoked . . . bring in more buckets of peat . . . top up the kettle; we need more boiling water." Her cohort cooks followed directions explicitly. The Raeburn stove devoured huge quantities of coal and peat to keep up the oven heat. To boil water, needed to scrub all the pots and cooking utensils, they carried water from the cold-water sink to a stout aluminum kettle on the hob.

17   Before the chicken soup could be started, chickens were plucked of feathers, then singed over a gas flame, to be sure not a scrap of feathers remained. Nothing was wasted, Ma insisting, "Chicken feet have all the flavor." Accordingly, the scaly feet were thoroughly scraped and scalded in boiling water before they were added to the pot, along with an assortment of root vegetables.

18   Fresh beets—boiled, cooled, and peeled—were grated on the coarse side of a grater to make sweet and sour borscht. Ladled over a chunky potato from a Dunrossness *croft* (where the soil was said to help produce the mealy texture) the ruby-red soup, flecked with soured heavy cream, was my father's favorite meal. He would sit back in his chair, licking his lips, pronouncing it the best— a *meichle.*

19   Ma's favorite combination for gefilte fish was halibut and hake, delivered to the door by a neighbor fisherman. He had usually gutted them, but Ma had to skin and bone them. "Pull away the oilcloth," she ordered whoever was around, usually me. "Now hold the grinder steady while I clamp it onto the kitchen table." The grinder was ancient, made of heavy cast iron, but Ma handled it with enviable ease as she pressed the fish through the funnel and into the blade.

20   We always served two varieties of gefilte fish. One big pot contained oval-shaped balls of the chopped-fish mixture, simmered with onion skins; the rest of the mixture was formed into patties and fried in hot olive oil in an enormous black iron skillet. Not just for Passover, fried gefilte fish topped with a dollop of salad cream (Scottish mayonnaise) and eaten at room temperature was a weekly Sabbath dinner.

21   Instead of the rich buttery cakes usually baked each Friday morning, Passover cakes were feathery sponge cakes, each made with a dozen new-laid eggs, beaten to a foam with a hand whisk. Baked and cooled, the cakes were sprinkled with sugar, then snugly wrapped in greaseproof wax paper; wine biscuits, coconut pyramids, and cinnamon balls were stored in tight-lidded, round, five-pound tins, recycled from Quality Sweet chocolates, another item making up the conglomeration of goods sold in Greenwald's shop. The last of the bottled plums and gooseberries were transformed into sweet compotes and *matzo* fruit puddings.

22   Everything was stored on shelves in the back porch. Food poisoning was unheard of. In April, the temperature in the unheated porch was rarely more than fifty degrees. The "girl from the country," the maid, did the menial jobs like scrubbing the floor, then laying down newspapers, "to prevent the floor from getting dirty," as Ma ordered. As for eight days of *matzos,* it was no hardship. We slathered each sheet with fresh, salty Shetland butter, then covered it with a thick layer of Ma's homemade, heather-scented, blackcurrant jam.

23   Although we usually ate all our meals in the kitchen in front of the peat fire, at Passover we dined in the "front room," the parlor, where lace-curtained bay windows overlooked the fields across the one-lane road. The room was large enough to seat family and guests comfortably. The drop-leaf oak table was set with a white lace tablecloth and the best china and glassware (we didn't possess crystal). Our close friends dressed up in their Sunday-best church clothes. Rebe, a few years older than I, arrived in a new black and yellow tartan kilt, her white

satin blouse with a frilly collar peeping out under a black velvet jacket. I was insanely jealous and pestered my parents until, the following year, I was given a similar outfit—not quite the same, but I was happy. Children and adults were silent as my father, in his heavy Russian-accented Shetland dialect, recited parts of the *Haggadah*, first in Hebrew, then in English. I repeated the four questions, and my mother explained the symbolism of the foods on the *Seder* plate. Each year, discussions became more animated, as our devout Christian guests added their comments and views, always in a respectful manner.

24   Our Passover *Seders* continued, even though the peaceful existence of the Shetland community was shattered by the onset of World War II. My parents had an added fear. Norway, only two hundred miles east of the Shetland Islands, was under German occupation. It was obvious from the bold signage above the shop, announcing the name Greenwald, that Jews owned the store. A German invasion would have meant certain death for our family. Fortunately, the islands being well protected, that never happened. With Lerwick's natural harbor a strategic base for naval operations from 1939 until 1945, thousands of troops, including more than three hundred Jewish men and women, were based throughout the islands. They far outnumbered the local community.

25   In 1941, Ma decided to organize a Passover *Seder* for the Jewish soldiers, knowing our flat could not hold all those who would have come to celebrate with us. "These poor souls must have a *Seder*. If there are too many for our house, then we'll hold it at the camp." This became her annual mission. It took an enormous amount of dedicated planning. She called the Commanding Officer (CO) in Lerwick to explain.

26   "Could we have a hut for the evening?"

27   The head of the forces stationed in Shetland knew Ma from coming into the shop, where he was given preferential treatment and often bought items not available in the PX (the soldiers' commissary). He listened to her plans.

28   "What else can we do to help?"

29   "Well, for a start, can we use part of your kitchens?" and, she wheedled, "maybe a couple of helpers. You know, we'll be cooking for about three hundred people."

30   "You just go in and tell the cooks to give you whatever you need. I'll make sure that they work with you."

31   Ma gave a sigh of relief. "That's one hurdle taken care of. I wasn't sure if he would agree." The military's Nissen hut was at the north end of Commercial Road, on the edge of town, but Ma had an army truck with a driver at her disposal. "Just call when you need it," assured the CO. "He'll be there in five minutes."

32   Ma spent days on the telephone, calling Glasgow and London for donations.

33   "Just send it to Jean Greenwald, in care of the Commanding Officer, Shetland Naval Air Station. It'll find me," she said—adding scornfully, after she had hung up, "Ignoramuses. They have no idea where Shetland is."

34   Boxes of *matzos, matzo* meal, pickles, and olive oil arrived. A kosher wine merchant in London agreed to send wine. When the cases were finally unloaded in the camp kitchen, Ma poured a fingerful to taste. She knew good wine. Describing it as "putrid," she ran to the sink, spitting it out. Furious, she immediately

called the liquor store. She screamed into the telephone, with Dad shushing her in the background.

35   "Don't think that because we're in Shetland you can send us inferior wine. This wine is sour . . . it's undrinkable. I will not serve this to the men and women who are fighting for you and your family . . . you should be ashamed!"

36   A fresh shipment arrived on the next boat, along with a letter of profuse apology.

37   "I had *chutzpah*," she later told us. "But I wasn't asking for myself. These soldiers were away from their homes and giving up their lives to protect us. The least these shopkeepers could do was to donate the Passover wine."

38   A team of army cooks and women friends worked together to prepare a complete *Seder* meal, with Ma supervising. They cooked up enormous amounts of chicken soup and *Knaidlach*, chopped herring and gefilte fish (even in wartime, fish was plentiful), roast chicken and potato *kugels*, sponge cake and dried fruit compotes. These dishes were reminiscent of the *Seder* meal they would have had if they had been able to celebrate with their families.

39   But most thrilling for the soldiers and for our family was the arrival of Great Britain's Chief Rabbi, Israel Brodie, the day before the first *Seder*. Ma had arranged for him to come to Shetland to conduct Passover services. The rabbi presented her with two leather-bound Holiday prayer books, signed by him, in appreciation of her tireless work on behalf of the Jewish troops stationed in Shetland in World War II. Now newly bound, the books are a family heirloom. For many of the Holidays, rabbis from England and Scotland made the journey to conduct services in the most northerly point of the British Isles. This continued under my mother's direction until 1945, when the war officially ended and troops were demobbed (demobilized). But the friendships lasted for years, many of the men and women returning with their families to see the Greenwalds, who had given them a Jewish home away from home, and to say thank you.

40   Three thousand miles across the Atlantic in Philadelphia, my Passover table is set with fine china and crystal. An Israeli *Seder* plate, of hand-wrought silver, contains the symbolic foods, and my husband Walter conducts our *Seder* with warmth, compassion, and humor. But the *Seders* that instilled a lasting pride in my heritage and laid the firm foundation for my Jewish identity were held in Lerwick, on the remote Shetland Islands, where the Greenwald family, in the midst of Christian culture, held fast to their faith.

■ ■ ▨

MEANING

1. What obstacles did Hofman's mother have to overcome to create a Passover celebration?

2. How did this Seder celebration in such an isolated setting come to represent a continuing connection to important Jewish values and traditions?

3. What picture do you get of Hofman and her family's living conditions and the time period?

4. What were some of the different steps that had to be performed to stage this event?

TECHNIQUE

1. How does Hofman enhance her account by providing the recipes for the preparation of foods that are crucial to the Passover Seder?
2. **Other Patterns.** How does Hofman's use of **descriptive** details put the reader in the scene of this unfamiliar environment?

LANGUAGE

1. How do the italicized terms blend Jewish and Scottish elements to convey the flavor of the two cultures?
2. How does the conversational style of Hofman's account recreate the event and what it meant to her family?
3. If you don't know the meaning of the following words, look them up: *matzo* (9), *nostalgia* (13), *gefilte fish* (19), *Sabbath* (20), *Seder* (23), *ignoramuses* (33), *chutzpah* (37).

SUGGESTIONS FOR WRITING

1. **Critical Writing.** How did this account change your perception of what it would be like to live as a member of a minority in Scotland?
2. Write a process analysis of the steps you or your family went through in staging a holiday event.
3. Provide **examples** of ethnic foods that are particularly important in your culture's celebrations and how the preparation of these foods creates a sense of community.
4. **Thematic Links.** Compare the ways in which the accounts by Hofman and Rigoberta Menchú in "Birth Ceremonies" describe rituals that are designed to instill a sense of identity and connection to a particular culture.

RIGOBERTA MENCHÚ

Birth Ceremonies

Nobel Prize–winning peace activist Rigoberta Menchú is a Quiché Indian who was born in Guatemala. When a particularly savage regime took over that country in 1978, her family was decimated, and she committed her life to preserving the Quiché traditions. In the following selection from *I, Rigoberta Menchú: An Indian Woman in Guatemala* (1983), she describes the ritual that the Quiché community uses to welcome and bond with a newborn child. This is an especially important ceremony, since the Quiché are in a marginalized and tenuous position in Guatemala and must create a cohesive community if they are to survive.

BEFORE YOU READ

What kinds of gifts are customarily given to newborn babies in your family, and what meanings do the gifts express?

■ ■ ▨

'Whoever may ask where we are, tell them what you know of us and nothing more.'
—Popol Vuh

'Learn to protect yourselves, by keeping our secret.'
—Popol Vuh

1   In our community there is an elected representative, someone who is highly respected. He's not a king but someone whom the community looks up to like a father. In our village, my father and mother were the representatives. Well, then the whole community becomes the children of the woman who's elected. So, a mother, on her first day of pregnancy goes with her husband to tell these elected leaders that she's going to have a child, because the child will not only belong to them but to the whole community, and must follow as far as he can our ancestors' traditions. The leaders then pledge the support of the community and say: 'We will help you, we will be the child's second parents'. They are known as *abuelos*, 'grandparents' or 'forefathers'. The parents then ask the 'grandparents' to help them find the child some godparents, so that if he's orphaned, he shouldn't be tempted by any of the bad habits our people sometimes fall into. So the 'grandparents' and the parents choose the godparents together. It's also the custom for the pregnant mother's neighbours to visit her every day and take her little things, no matter how simple. They stay and talk to her, and she'll tell them all her problems.

For a visual to accompany this selection, see color insert photo B-4.

2   Later, when she's in her seventh month, the mother introduces her baby to the natural world, as our customs tell her to. She goes out in the fields or walks over the hills. She also has to show her baby the kind of life she leads, so that if she gets up at three in the morning, does her chores and tends the animals, she does it all the more so when she's pregnant, conscious that the child is taking all this in. She talks to the child continuously from the first moment he's in her stomach, telling him how hard his life will be. It's as if the mother were a guide explaining things to a tourist. She'll say, for instance; 'You must never abuse nature and you must live your life as honestly as I do.' As she works in the fields, she tells her child all the little things about her work. It's a duty to her child that a mother must fulfill. And then, she also has to think of a way of hiding the baby's birth from her other children.

3   When her baby is born, the mother mustn't have her other children round her. The people present should be the husband, the village leaders, and the couple's parents. Three couples. The parents are often away in other places, so if they can't be there, the husband's father and the wife's mother can perhaps make up one pair. If one of the village leaders can't come, one of them should be there to make up a couple with one of the parents. If none of the parents can come, some aunts and uncles should come to represent the family on both sides, because the child is to be part of the community. The birth of a new member is very significant for the community, as it belongs to the community not just to the parents, and that's why three couples (but not just anybody) must be there to receive it. They explain that this child is the fruit of communal love. If the village leader is not a midwife as well, another midwife is called (it might be a grandmother) to receive the child. Our customs don't allow single women to see a birth. But it does happen in times of need. For instance, I was with my sister when she went into labour. Nobody else was at home. This was when we were being heavily persecuted. Well, I didn't exactly see, but I was there when the baby was born.

4   My mother was a midwife from when she was sixteen right up to her death at forty-three. She used to say that a woman hadn't the strength to push the baby out when she's lying down. So what she did with my sister was to hang a rope from the roof and pull her up, because my brother wasn't there to lift her up. My mother helped the baby out with my sister in that position. It's a scandal if an Indian woman goes to hospital and gives birth there. None of our women would agree to that. Our ancestors would be shocked at many of the things which go on today. Family planning, for example. It's an insult to our culture and a way of swindling the people, to get money out of them.

5   This is part of the reserve that we've maintained to defend our customs and our culture. Indians have been very careful not to disclose any details of their communities, and the community does not allow them to talk about Indian things. I too must abide by this. This is because many religious people have come among us and drawn a false impression of the Indian world. We also find a *ladino* using Indian clothes very offensive. All this has meant that we keep a lot of things to ourselves and the community doesn't like us telling its secrets. This applies

to all our customs. When the Catholic Action[1] arrived, for instance, everyone started going to mass, and praying, but it's not their only religion, not the only way they have of expressing themselves. Anyway, when a baby is born, he's always baptized within the community before he's taken to church. Our people have taken Catholicism as just another channel of expression, not our one and only belief. Our people do the same with other religions. The priests, monks and nuns haven't gained the people's confidence because so many of their things contradict our own customs. For instance, they say; 'You have too much trust in your elected leaders.' But the village elects them *because* they trust them, don't they? The priests say; 'The trouble is you follow those sorcerers,' and speak badly of them. But for our people this is like speaking ill of their own fathers, and they lose faith in the priests. They say; 'Well, they're not from here, they can't understand our world.' So there's not much hope of winning our people's hearts.

6   To come back to the children, they aren't to know how the baby is born. He's born somewhere hidden away and only the parents know about it. They are told that a baby has arrived and that they can't see their mother for eight days. Later on, the baby's companion, the placenta that is, has to be burned at a special time. If the baby is born at night, the placenta is burned at eight in the morning, and if he's born in the afternoon, it'll be burned at five o'clock. This is out of respect for both the baby and his companion. The placenta is not buried, because the earth is the mother and the father of the child and mustn't be abused by having the placenta buried in it. All these reasons are very important for us. Either the placenta is burned on a log and the ashes left there, or else it is put in the *temascal*. This is a stove which our people use to make vapour baths. It's a small hut made of adobe and inside this hut is another one made of stone, and when we want to have a bath, we light a fire to heat the stones, close the door, and throw water on the stones to produce steam. Well, when the woman is about four months pregnant, she starts taking these baths infused with evergreens, pure natural aromas. There are many plants the community uses for pregnant women, colds, headaches, and things like that. So the pregnant mother takes baths with plants prescribed for her by the midwife or the village leader. The fields are full of plants whose names I don't know in Spanish. Pregnant women use orange and peach leaves a lot for bathing and there's another one we call Saint Mary's leaf which they use. The mother needs these leaves and herbs to relax because she won't be able to rest while she's pregnant since our women go on working just as hard in the fields. So, after work, she takes this calming bath so that she can sleep well, and the baby won't be harmed by her working hard. She's given medicines to take as well. And leaves to feed the child. I believe that in practice (even if this isn't a scientific recommendation) these leaves work very well, because many of them contain vitamins. How else would women who endure hunger and hard work, give birth to healthy babies? I think that these plants have helped our people survive.

---

[1] Association created in 1945 by Monsignor Rafael Gonzalez, to try and control the Indian fraternities of the *Altiplano*.

7   The purity with which the child comes into the world is protected for eight days. Our customs say that the new-born baby should be alone with his mother in a special place for eight days, without any of her other children. Her only visitors are the people who bring her food. This is the baby's period of integration into the family; he very slowly becomes a member of it. When the child is born, they kill a sheep and there's a little fiesta just for the family. Then the neighbours start coming to visit, and bring presents. They either bring food for the mother, or something for the baby. The mother has to taste all the food her neighbours bring to show her appreciation for their kindness. After the eight days are over, the family counts up how many visitors the mother had, and how many presents were received; things like eggs or food apart from what was brought for the mother, or clothing, small animals, and wood for the fire, or services like carrying water and chopping wood. If, during the eight days, most of the community has called, this is very important, because it means that this child will have a lot of responsibility towards his community when he grows up. The community takes over all the household expenses for these eight days and the family spends nothing.

8   After eight days everything has been received, and another animal is killed as recognition that the child's right to be alone with his mother is over. All the mother's clothes, bedclothes, and everything she used during the birth, are taken away by our elected leader and washed. She can't wash them in the well, so no matter how far away the river is, they must be carried and washed there. The baby's purity is washed away and he's ready to learn the ways of humanity. The mother's bed is moved to a part of the house which has first been washed with water and lime. Lime is sacred. It strengthens the child's bones. I believe this really is true. It gives a child strength to face the world. The mother has a bath in the *temascal* and puts on clean clothes. Then, the whole house is cleaned. The child is also washed and dressed and put into the new bed. Four candles are placed on the corners of the bed to represent the four corners of the house and show him that this will be his home. They symbolize the respect the child must have for his community, and the responsibility he must feel towards it as a member of a household. The candles are lit and give off an incense which incorporates the child into the world he must live in. When the baby is born, his hands and feet are bound to show him that they are sacred and must only be used to work or do whatever nature meant them to do. They must never steal or abuse the natural world, or show disrespect for any living thing.

9   After the eight days, his hands and feet are untied and he's now with his mother in the new bed. This means he opens the doors to the other members of the community, because neither the family or the community know him yet. Or rather, they weren't shown the baby when he was born. Now they can all come and kiss him. The neighbours bring another animal, and there's big lunch in the new baby's house for all the community. This is to celebrate his integration 'in the universe', as our parents used to say. Candles will be lit for him and his candle becomes part of the candle of the whole community, which now has one more person, one more member. The whole community is at the ceremony,

or at least, if not all of it, then some of it. Candles are lit to represent all the things which belong to the universe—earth, water, sun, and man—and the child's candle is put with them, together with incense (what we call *pom*) and lime— our sacred lime. Then, the parents tell the baby of the suffering of the family he will be joining. With great feeling, they express their sorrow at bringing a child into the world to suffer. To us, suffering is our fate, and the child must be introduced to the sorrows and hardship, but he must learn that despite his suffering, he will be respectful and live through his pain. The child is then entrusted with the responsibility for his community and told to abide by its rules. After the ceremony comes the lunch, and then the neighbours go home. Now, there is only the baptism to come.

10   When the baby is born, he's given a little bag with a garlic, a bit of lime, salt, and tobacco in it, to hang round his neck. Tobacco is important because it is a sacred plant for Indians. This all means that the child can ward off all the evil things in life. For us, bad things are like spirits, which exist only in our imagination. Something bad, for instance, would be if the child were to turn out to be a gossip—not sincere, truthful, and respectful, as a child should be. It also helps him collect together and preserve all our ancestors' things. That's more or less the idea of the bag—to keep him pure. The bag is put inside the four candles as well, and this represents the promise of the child when he grows up.

11   When the child is forty days old, there are more speeches, more promises on his behalf, and he becomes a full member of the community. This is his baptism. All the important people of the village are invited and they speak. The parents make a commitment. They promise to teach the child to keep the secrets of our people, so that our culture and customs will be preserved. The village leaders come and offer their experience, their example, and their knowledge of our ancestors. They explain how to preserve our traditions. Then, they promise to be responsible for the child, teach him as he grows up, and see that he follows in their ways. It's also something of a criticism of humanity, and of the many people who have forsaken their traditions. They say almost a prayer, asking that our traditions again enter the spirits of those who have forsaken them. Then, they evoke the names of our ancestors, like Tecun Umán and others who form part of the ceremony, as a kind of chant. They must be remembered as heroes of the Indian peoples. And then they say (I analyse all this later); 'Let no landowner extinguish all this, nor any rich man wipe out our customs. Let our children, be they workers or servants, respect and keep their secrets'. The child is present for all of this, although he's all wrapped up and can scarcely be seen. He is told that he will eat maize and that, naturally, he is already made of maize because his mother ate it while he was forming in her stomach. He must respect the maize; even the grain of maize which has been thrown away, he must pick up. The child will multiply our race, he will replace all those who have died. From this moment, he takes on this responsibility, and is told to live as his 'grandparents' have lived. The parents then reply that their child promises to accomplish all this. So, the village leaders and the parents both make promises on behalf of the child. It's his initiation into the community.

12   The ceremony is very important. It is also when the child is considered a child of God, our one father. We don't actually have the word God but that is what it is, because the one father is the only one we have. To reach this one father, the child must love beans, maize, the earth. The one father is the heart of the sky, that is, the sun. The sun is the father and our mother is the moon. She is a gentle mother. And she lights our way. Our people have many notions about the moon, and about the sun. They are the pillars of the universe.

13   When children reach ten years old, that's the moment when their parents and the village leaders talk to them again. They tell them that they will be young men and women and that one day they will be fathers and mothers. This is actually when they tell the child that he must never abuse his dignity, in the same way his ancestors never abused their dignity. It's also when they remind them that our ancestors were dishonoured by the White Man, by colonization. But they don't tell them the way that it's written down in books, because the majority of Indians can't read or write, and don't even know that they have their own texts. No, they learn it through oral recommendations, the way it has been handed down through the generations. They are told that the Spaniards dishonoured our ancestors' finest sons, and the most humble of them. And it is to honour these humble people that we must keep our secrets. And no-one except we Indians must know. They talk a lot about our ancestors. And the ten-years ceremony is also when our children are reminded that they must respect their elders, even though this is something their parents have been telling them ever since they were little. For example, if an old person is walking along the street, children should cross over to allow him to pass by. If any of us sees an elderly person, we are obliged to bow and greet them. Everyone does this, even the very youngest. We also show respect to pregnant women. Whenever we make food, we always keep some for any of our neighbours who are pregnant.

14   When little girls are born, the midwives pierce their ears at the same time as they tie their umbilical cords. The little bags around their necks and the thread used to tie their umbilical cord are both red. Red is very significant for us. It means heat, strength, all living things. It's linked to the sun, which for us is the channel to the one god, the heart of everything, of the universe. So red gives off heat and fire and red things are supposed to give life to the child. At the same time, it asks him to respect living things too. There are no special clothes for the baby. We don't buy anything special beforehand but just use pieces of *corte* to wrap him in.

15   When a male child is born, there are special celebrations, not because he's male but because of all the hard work and responsibility he'll have as a man. It's not that *machismo* doesn't exist among our people, but it doesn't present a problem for the community because it's so much part of our way of life. The male child is given an extra day alone with his mother. The usual custom is to celebrate a male child by killing a sheep or some chickens. Boys are given more, they get more food because their work is harder and they have more responsibility. At the same time, he is head of the household, not in the bad sense of the word, but because he is responsible for so many things. This doesn't mean

girls aren't valued. Their work is hard too and there are other things that are due to them as mothers. Girls are valued because they are part of the earth, which gives us maize, beans, plants and everything we live on. The earth is like a mother which multiplies life. So the girl child will multiply the life of our generation and of our ancestors whom we must respect. The girl and the boy are both integrated into the community in equally important ways, the two are inter-related and compatible. Nevertheless, the community is always happier when a male child is born and the men feel much prouder. The customs, like the tying of the hands and feet, apply to both boys and girls.

16   Babies are breast-fed. It's much better than any other sort of food. But the important thing is the sense of community. It's something we all share. From the very first day, the baby belongs to the community, not only to the parents and the baby must learn from all of us . . . in fact, we behave just like bourgeois families in that, as soon as the baby is born, we're thinking of his education, of his well-being. But our people feel that the baby's school must be the community itself, that he must learn to live like all the rest of us. The tying of the hands at birth also symbolizes this; that no-one should accumulate things the rest of the community does not have and he must know how to share, to have open hands. The mother must teach the baby to be generous. This way of thinking comes from poverty and suffering. Each child is taught to live like the fellow members of his community.

17   We never eat in front of pregnant women. You can only eat in front of a pregnant woman if you can offer something as well. The fear is that, otherwise, she might abort the baby or that the baby could suffer if she didn't have enough to eat. It doesn't matter whether you know her or not. The important thing is sharing. You have to treat a pregnant woman differently from other women because she is two people. You must treat her with respect so that she recog-nizes it and conveys this to the baby inside her. You instinctively think she's the image of the baby about to be born. So you love her. Another reason why you must stop and talk to a pregnant woman is because she doesn't have much chance to rest or enjoy herself. She's always worried and depressed. So when she stops and chats a bit, she can relax and feel some relief.

18   When the baby joins the community, with him in the circle of candles—together with his little red bag—he will have his hoe, his machete, his axe and all the tools he will need in life. These will be his playthings. A little girl will have her washing board and all the things she will need when she grows up. She must learn the things of the house, to clean, to wash, and sew her brothers' trousers, for example. The little boy must begin to live like a man, to be respon-sible and learn to love the work in the fields. The learning is done as a kind of game. When the parents do anything they always explain what it means. This includes learning prayers. This is very important to our people. The mother may say a prayer at any time. Before getting up in the morning, for instance, she thanks the day which is dawning because it might be a very important one for the family. Before lighting the fire, she blesses the wood because that fire is going to cook food for the whole family. Since it's the little girl who is closest to her mother, she learns all of this. Before washing the *nixtamal*, the woman blows on

her hands and puts them in the *nixtamal.* She takes everything out and washes it well. She blows on her hands so that her work will bear fruit. She does it before she does the wash as well. She explains all these little details to her daughter, who learns by copying her. With the men it's the same. Before they start work every day, whatever hour of the morning it is, they greet the sun. They remove their hats and talk to the sun before starting to work. Their sons learn to do it too, taking of their little hats to talk to the sun. Naturally, each ethnic group has its own forms of expression. Other groups have different customs from ours. The meaning of their weaving patterns, for example. We realize the others are different in some things, but the one thing we have in common is our culture. Our people are mainly peasants, but there are some people who buy and sell as well. They go into this after they've worked on the land. Sometimes when they come back from working in the *finca,* instead of tending a little plot of land, they'll start a shop and look for a different sort of life. But if they're used to greeting the sun every morning, they still go on doing it. And they keep all their old customs. Every part of our culture comes from the earth. Our religion comes from the maize and bean harvests which are so vital to our community. So even if a man goes to try and make some money, he never forgets his culture springs from the earth.

19   As we grow up we have a series of obligations. Our parents teach us to be responsible; just as they have been responsible. The eldest son is responsible for the house. Whatever the father cannot correct is up to the eldest son to correct. He is like a second father to us all and is responsible for our upbringing. The mother is the one who is responsible for keeping an account of what the family eats, and what she has to buy. When a child is ill, she has to get medicine. But the father has to solve a lot of problems too. And each one of us, as we grow up, has our own small area of responsibility. This comes from the promises made for the child when he is born, and from the continuity of our customs. The child can make the promise for himself when his parents have taught him to do it. The mother, who is closest to the children, does this, or sometimes the father. They talk to their children explaining what they have to do and what our ancestors used to do. They don't impose it as a law, but just give the example of what our ancestors have always done. This is how we all learn our own small responsibilities. For example, the little girl begins by carrying water, and the little boy begins by tying up the dogs when the animals are brought into the yard at night, or by fetching a horse which has wandered off. Both girls and boys have their tasks and are told the reasons for doing them. They learn responsibility because if they don't do their little jobs, well, their father has the right to scold them, or even beat them. So, they are very careful about learning to do their jobs well, but the parents are also very careful to explain exactly why the jobs have to be done. The little girl understands the reasons for everything her mother does. For example, when she puts a new earthenware pot on the fire for the first time, she hits it five times with a branch, so that it knows its job is to cook and so that it lasts. When the little girl asks, 'Why did you do that?', her mother says, 'So that it knows what its job is and does it well.' When it's her turn to cook, the little girl

does as her mother does. Again this is all bound up with our commitment to maintain our customs and pass on the secrets of our ancestors. The elected fathers of the community explain to us that all these things come down to us from our grandfathers and we must conserve them. Nearly everything we do today is based on what our ancestors did. This is the main purpose of our elected leader—to embody all the values handed down from our ancestors. He is the leader of the community, a father to all our children, and he must lead an exemplary life. Above all, he has a commitment to the whole community. Everything that is done today, is done in memory of those who have passed on.

■ ■ ▨

MEANING

1. How does the birth of a child represent continuity and the propagation of tradition for the Quiché?

2. Discuss how the idea of the child's responsibility or obligation toward the community is related to the role the community plays during the first eight days after the child's birth.

3. What aspects of Menchú's account depend on the assumption that the *ladino* way of life would represent a denial of nature and tradition?

4. How does burning the placenta rather than burying it reveal a distinctively Guatemalan Indian cultural attitude toward the earth?

TECHNIQUE

1. Into what stages are the birth ceremonies for a Quiché infant organized?

2. Are all the stages equal in importance, judging by the depth of detail Menchú devotes to them? Which seem to be especially important?

3. **Other Patterns.** How does Menchú use a multitude of **descriptive** details to put the reader in the scene?

LANGUAGE

1. What aspects of Menchú's account reveal the importance she places on preserving tradition and keeping faith with the tribal heritage of the Quiché?

2. In what way does Menchú's narrative style convey a desire to communicate to outsiders what Quiché rituals mean and how they are performed?

3. If you don't know the meaning of the following words, look them up: *ladino* (5), *integration* (7), *machismo* (15), *compatible* (15), *bourgeois* (16), *nixtamal* (18), *finca* (18).

SUGGESTIONS FOR WRITING

1. **Critical Writing.** Which aspects of Menchú's piece surprised you by presenting a culture that is quite different from the culture in which you were raised?

2. In what way is the newborn infant the property of the entire village?

3. **Compare** the conflict that Menchú presents between native Indian beliefs and the belief system of Catholic missionaries. What specific aspects of Indian rituals might missionaries fail to understand?

4. Describe the stages and rituals of birth ceremonies of your ethnic community. Into what steps can the rituals be divided, and which of these do you find the most meaningful?

5. *Thematic Links.* Compare a child brought up among the Quiché with Flavio in Rio de Janeiro as described by Gordon Parks in "Flavio's Home" (Chapter 4, "Description").

COLIN TURNBULL

The Mbuti Pygmies

Colin Turnbull (1924–1994) received undergraduate and graduate degrees from Oxford University and is best known for his ground-breaking anthropological research on two groups: the Ik of northern Uganda and the pygmies of the Ituri forest in the Republic of the Congo. Turnbull's fascination with and admiration for the pygmies was a result of his four years of living and working with them, as described in numerous works, including *In a Pygmy Camp* (1969) and *The Mbuti Pygmies: Change and Adaptation* (1983), where the following selection first appeared. Turnbull describes the enlightened and humane rituals that the pygmies have developed for solving conflicts and teaching children lessons of sharing and cooperation.

BEFORE YOU READ

How do the games that children learn to play express important cultural values, such as competition or cooperation?

■ ■ ▨

THE EDUCATIONAL PROCESS

1   . . . In the first three years of life every Mbuti alive experiences almost total security. The infant is breast-fed for those three years, and is allowed almost every freedom. Regardless of gender, the infant learns to have absolute trust in both male and female parent. If anything, the father is just another kind of mother, for in the second year the father formally introduces the child to its first solid food. There used to be a beautiful ritual in which the mother presented the child to the father in the middle of the camp, where all important statements are made (anyone speaking from the middle of the camp must be listened to). The father took the child and held it to his breast, and the child would try to suckle, crying "*ema, ema*," or "mother." The father would shake his head, and say "no, father . . . *eba*," but like a mother (the Mbuti said), then give the child its first solid food.

2   At three the child ventures out into the world on its own and enters the *bopi*, what we might call a playground, a tiny camp perhaps a hundred yards from the main camp, often on the edge of a stream. The *bopi* were indeed playgrounds, and often very noisy ones, full of fun and high spirits. But they were also rigorous training grounds for eventual economic responsibility. On entry to the *bopi*, for one thing, the child discovers the importance of age as a structural principle, and the relative unimportance of gender and biological kinship. The *bopi* is the private world of the children. Younger youths may occasionally venture in, but if adults or elders try, as they sometimes do when angry at having their afternoon snooze interrupted, they invariably get driven out, taunted, and ridiculed.

Children, among the Mbuti, have rights, but they also learn that they have responsibilities. Before the hunt sets out each day it is the children, sometimes the younger youths, who light the hunting fire.

3   Ritual among the Mbuti is often so informal and apparently casual that it may pass unnoticed at first. Yet insofar as ritual involves symbolic acts that represent unspoken, perhaps even unthought, concepts or ideals, or invoke other states of being, alternative frames of mind and reference, then Mbuti life is full of ritual. The hunting fire is one of the more obvious of such rituals. Early in the morning children would take firebrands from the *bopi*, where they always lit their own fire with embers from their family hearths, and set off on the trail by which the hunt was to leave that day (the direction of each day's hunt was always settled by discussion the night before). Just a short distance from the camp they lit a fire at the base of a large tree, and covered it with special leaves that made it give off a column of dense smoke. Hunters leaving the camp, both men and women, and such youths and children as were going with them, had to pass by this fire. Some did so casually, without stopping or looking, but passing through the smoke. Others reached into the smoke with their hands as they passed, rubbing the smoke into their bodies. A few always stopped, for a moment, and let the smoke envelop them, only then almost dreamily moving off.

4   And indeed it *was* a form of intoxication, for the smoke invoked the spirit of the forest, and by passing through it the hunters sought to fill themselves with that spirit, not so much to make the hunt successful as to minimize the sacrilege of killing. Yet they, the hunters, could not light the fire themselves. After all, they were already contaminated by death. Even youths, who daily joined the hunt at the edges, catching any game that escaped the nets, by hand, if they could, were not pure enough to invoke the spirits of forestness. But young children were uncontaminated, as yet untainted by contact with the original sin of the Mbuti. It was their responsibility to light the fire, and if it was not lit then the hunt would not take place, or, as the Mbuti put it, the hunt *could* not take place.

5   In this way even the children in Mbuti society, at the first of the four age levels that dominate Mbuti social structure, are given very real social responsibility and see themselves as a part of that structure, by virtue of their purity. After all, they have just been born from the source of all purity, the forest itself. By the same reasoning, the elders, who are about to return to that ultimate source of all being, through death, are at least closer to purity than the adults, who are daily contaminated by killing. Elders no longer go on the hunt. So, like the children, the elders have important sacred ritual responsibilities in the Mbuti division of labor by age.

6   In the *bopi* the children play, but they have no "games" in the strict sense of the word. Levi-Strauss has perceptively compared games with rituals, suggesting that whereas in a game the players start theoretically equal but end up unequal, in a ritual just the reverse takes place. All are equalized. Mbuti children could be seen every day playing in the *bopi*, but not once did I see a game, not one activity that smacked of any kind of competition, except perhaps that competition that it

is necessary for us all to feel from time to time, competition with our own private and personal inadequacies. One such pastime (rather than game) was tree climbing. A dozen or so children would climb up a young sapling. Reaching the top, their weight brought the sapling bending down until it almost touched the ground. Then all the children leapt off together, shrieking as the young tree sprang upright again with a rush. Sometimes one child, male or female, might stay on a little too long, either out of fear, or out of bravado, or from sheer carelessness or bad timing. Whatever the reason, it was a lesson most children only needed to be taught once, for the result was that you got flung upward with the tree, and were lucky to escape with no more than a few bruises and a very bad fright.

7   Other pastimes taught the children the rules of hunting and gathering. Frequently elders, who stayed in camp when the hunt went off, called the children into the main camp and enacted a mock hunt with them there. Stretching a discarded piece of net across the camp, they pretended to be animals, showing the children how to drive them into the nets. And, of course, the children played house, learning the patterns of cooperation that would be necessary for them later in life. They also learned the prime lesson of egality, other than for purposes of division of labor making no distinction between male and female, this nuclear family or that. All in the *bopi* were *apua'i* to each other, and so they would remain throughout their lives. At every age level—childhood, youth, adulthood, or old age—everyone of that level is *apua'i* to all the others. Only adults sometimes (but so rarely that I think it was only done as a kind of joke, or possibly insult) made the distinction that the Bira do, using *apua'i* for male and *amua'i* for female. Male or female, for the Mbuti, if you are the same age you are *apua'i*, and that means that you share everything equally, regardless of kinship or gender.

YOUTH AND POLITICS

8   Sometimes before the age of puberty boys or girls, whenever they feel ready, move back into the main camp from the *bopi* and join the youths. This is when they must assume new responsibilities, which for the youths are primarily political. Already, in the *bopi*, the children become involved in disputes, and are sometimes instrumental in settling them by ridicule, for nothing hurts an adult more than being ridiculed by children. The art of reason, however, is something they learn from the youths, and it is the youths who apply the art of reason to the settlement of disputes.

9   When puberty comes it separates them, for the first time in their experience, from each other as *apua'i*. Very plainly girls are different from boys. When a girl has her first menstrual period the whole camp celebrates with the wild *elima* festival, in which the girl, and some of her chosen girl friends, are the center of all attention, living together in a special *elima* house. Male youths sit outside the *elima* house and wait for the girls to come out, usually in the afternoon, for the *elima* singing. They sing in antiphony, the girls leading, the boys responding. Boys come from neighboring territories all around, for this is a time of courtship.

But there are always eligible youths within the camp as well, and the *elima* girl may well choose girls from other territories to come and join her, so there is more than enough excuse for every youth to carry on several flirtations, legitimate or illegitimate. I have known even first cousins to flirt with each other, but learned to be prudent enough not to pull out my kinship charts and point this out—well, not in public anyway.

10   The *elima* is more than a premarital festival, more than a joint initiation of youth into adulthood, and more than a rite of passage through puberty, though it is all those things. It is a public recognition of the opposition of male and female, and every *elima* is used to highlight the *potential* for conflict that lies in that opposition. As at other times of crisis, at puberty, a time of change and uncertainty, the Mbuti bring all the major forms of conflict out into the open. And the one that evidently most concerns them is the male/female opposition.

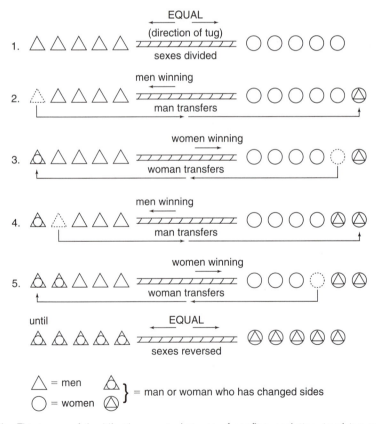

Tug of War. This is one of the Mbuti's many techniques of conflict resolution, involving role reversal and the principle of opposition without hostility.

What insight do you get into the relationship between parents and children among the Mbuti from this picture of a mother painting her daughter's face?

11   The adults begin to play a special form of "tug of war" that is clearly a ritual rather than a game. All the men are on one side, the women on the other.
At first it looks like a game, but quickly it becomes clear that the objective is for
neither side to win. As soon as the women begin to win, one of them will leave
the end of the line and run around to join the men, assuming a deep male voice
and in other ways ridiculing manhood. Then, as the men begin to win, a male
will similarly join the women, making fun of womanhood as he does so. Each
adult on changing sides attempts to outdo all the others in ridiculing the opposite sex. Finally, when nearly all have switched sides, and sexes, the ritual battle
between the genders simply collapses into hysterical laughter, the contestants
letting go of the rope, falling onto the ground, and rolling over with mirth.
Neither side wins, both are equalized very nicely, and each learns the essential
lesson, that there should be *no* contest. . . .

MEANING

1. What are the first rituals in which the child engages?
2. What values do these rituals communicate?
3. Why are only young children allowed to light the fire preceding each day's hunt?
4. What sorts of lessons do children learn in the playground, or *bopi*?

TECHNIQUE

1. How is the way in which Turnbull organizes his description of the tug-of-war game designed to communicate lessons involving conflict resolution and cooperation?

2. How does Turnbull's description of the *bopi* and the rituals that are reserved for certain members of the community reveal that the concept of the peer group determines one's identity within the tribe?

3. **Other Patterns.** The tug-of-war is but one of several **examples** that Turnbull cites of the Mbuti reliance on ritual. What are some others?

LANGUAGE

1. What means does Turnbull use to translate the unfamiliar words and concepts necessary to understand Mbuti culture?

2. Does Turnbull's tone suggest that he has ceased to be an objective observer? Why or why not?

3. If you don't know the meaning of the following words, look them up: *sacrilege* (4), *bravado* (6), *egality* (7).

SUGGESTIONS FOR WRITING

1. **Critical Writing.** In your opinion, why are the games that are played in American culture mostly competitive? What purpose do they serve?

2. What games did you play as a child? Were any noncompetitive? Which attitude toward games do you prefer? Explain your answer.

3. What rituals do children in your culture perform that are based solely on age? **Describe** one of these, its purpose, and the role that the child plays (for example, flower girl or ring bearer at a wedding).

4. **Thematic Links.** Contrast the support system of the Mbuti for children with Flavio's predicament in Gordon Parks's "Flavio's Home" (Chapter 4, "Description").

MARK SHAND

An Original Elephant

Mark Shand's unusual background includes jobs on a sheep farm in Australia and at Sotheby's auction house. He has competed in a transcontinental automobile race, was shipwrecked in the South Pacific, and is the brother of the former Camilla Parker Bowles (the wife of Prince Charles). He often finds himself on unusual quests in strange places and has written of his adventures in widely popular books, including *Travels on My Elephant* (1991), from which this piece is taken, and *River Dog: A Journey Down the Brahma Putra* (2003). This selection describes Shand's efforts to acquire an elephant for a journey that would cover six hundred miles. In the process of finding Tara, he learned a great deal about Indian culture and customs, and he shares his discoveries with us. Tara currently lives in the outskirts of a forest reserve. Shand's continuing interest in the survival of Asian elephants will be seen in a series of documentaries that he is preparing.

BEFORE YOU READ

If you could own any large animal, what would it be?

■ ■ ▨

1   The long arm of coincidence, in which travellers are often held, found the director of the zoo—the very man for whom I had been given a letter of introduction—travelling on the same flight. There were no elephants that he knew of for sale in Orissa, he told us sympathetically. In fact he himself was looking for elephants both for his own establishment and for a temple. He then suggested we try Madras. 'In the meantime visit my zoo. See the white tigers and the kangaroos that have just arrived from Australia.'

2   'Well that's that,' I said glumly after we returned to our seats. 'We might as well catch the next flight back to Delhi.' I turned to Aditya, trying to stay calm. 'What on earth are we going to do?' He was fast asleep.

3   Bhubaneshwar—the city of a thousand temples—was draped in thick black cloud, glistening from the wet kiss of the monsoons. A steamy heat hung in the air. Even the sparrows, those lively occupants of Indian airports, were silent, wilting on top of the announcement speakers.

4   At the hotel the receptionist asked politely, 'Sands, that is your good name?'

5   'No, it's Shand.'

6   'Welcome to the Prachi Hotel, Mr Sands. How long will you be staying?'

7   'Until I find an elephant.'

8   'First class,' he said encouragingly, with a slight inclination of his head.

9   We had barely reached the stairs when a room-boy approached us. 'You are looking for elephants, sir? I have one friend who has many. All sizes. Shall I call him?'

10   A few moments later there came a knock at my door, which I flung open to the surprise of an elderly man wearing a smart two-piece polyester safari suit. Behind him the room-boy struggled with a large suitcase.

11   'My name is Fakir Charan Tripathy,' the man said recovering his composure, 'I have elephants.'

12   'When can we see them?'

13   'Now, of course, sirs,' the man replied, opening the suitcase. Inside were rows of elephants made from ivory, ebony and sandalwood.

14   'Please be making a selection. Finest quality. Most reasonable.'

15   Aditya camouflaged his mouth by pulling on his moustache and explained that these would not meet our requirements. The man seemed confused. Then an expression of wonder crept across his face. 'Aah! You are wanting an o-r-i-g-i-n-a-l elephant.'

16   The room-boy said suddenly, 'I've seen many elephants.'

17   'Where?'

18   'Outside my house, sir. Often they are passing. My children love to see them.' He looked down at his hands in shame. 'I try to keep my family inside. We are very poor and I cannot afford to give away money or food. Only last week three . . .'

19   'Saddhus!' Aditya exclaimed. 'They must be saddhus, and they can't have gone far. They will be stopping at every village and it shouldn't be difficult to follow their route.' He turned to me. 'You see, Mark, the elephant is revered in most parts of India. It represents the elephant-headed deity, Ganesh, our Hindu God of Protection. These elephants are usually ridden by con men masquerading as saddhus, or holy men—a powerful and very lucrative combination. They crisscross the country, begging, living off the consciences of people much worse off than themselves. Now, you are to stay here. If they see that face of yours the price of an elephant will double. Mr Tripathy, will you come with me?'

20   'With pleasure. For a small fee. But there is just one other thing. Why is the gentleman wanting an elephant?'

21   Aditya whispered something into his ear. With a broad smile Mr Tripathy shook my hand before leaving the room.

22   'What did you tell him?' I demanded crossly.

23   'That you are an Englishman.'

24   'Well, so what?'

25   'Everybody knows that the English are mad.'

26   At three o'clock in the morning Aditya returned, tired but elated. They had located the elephants about sixty miles west of Bhubaneshwar in a small town called Daspalla. They were indeed begging elephants owned by saddhus.

27   'Did they want to sell?' I asked anxiously.

28   'We can take our pick. There are two females and one tusker. The tusker comes from Nepal and is a good elephant, or so they tell me. But what the hell do we know about elephants? We must get some expert advice . . .'

29   'What were they like?'

30   'Oh, devious buggers, they . . .'

31   'No, no, not the saddhus, the elephants.'

32   'Big. Like any elephant. I didn't really see them properly. Now let's get some sleep. You'll have plenty of time to look at them tomorrow.'

33   I found I couldn't sleep. All night everything I looked at became an elephant— the shadow of a swaying branch, the moon-filled clouds or even the television set. My obsession had indeed turned to madness.

34   It took most of the day to locate the zoo director who kindly agreed to lend the services of his chief mahout, Bhim. Our party had grown. There were now four of us. Myself, Aditya, Mr Tripathy, with his suitcase of elephants, and a young taxi driver called Indrajit, who had impressed Aditya with his driving skills the previous night. He was a handsome, courteous young man, who radiated energy and had dark fierce eyes—the kind of eyes that remain fierce even in jest. But I wasn't thinking about a chauffeur, I was eagerly waiting to set eyes on my first mahout.

35   In Delhi I had been lent a book on elephants entitled *The Elephant-Lore of the Hindus*, which had detailed the essential qualities required in an elephant driver:

> The supervisor of elephants should be intelligent, king-like, righteous, devoted to his Lord, pure, true to his undertakings, free from vice, controlling his senses, well behaved, vigorous, tried by practice, delighting in kind words, his science learnt from a good teacher, clever, firm, affording protection, renowned for curing disease, fearless, all-knowing.

36   The mahout was waiting at the gates of the zoo. Bhim was a man of indeterminate age, the colour of a walnut, bandy-legged and carried himself like a wounded soldier. As we got out of the car he executed a shaky salute, his arm and leg not quite in co-ordination. From the state of his bloodshot eyes, he was clearly suffering from a hangover. He climbed into the car and yawned, exposing the remains of three yellow teeth which wobbled when he spoke. 'Sleep now, sah. Very good. Haathi later.' He then passed out.

37   Aditya was not wrong about Indrajit. He drove with a cunning recklessness, the tropical landscape passing in a blur outside the window. We had only one accident when he swerved to avoid a bullock cart, clipping the back side-window against one of the animal's enormous horns. The glass exploded like a hand grenade with some of the fragments embedding themselves in Aditya's face. 'Lucky it wasn't my eyes,' he shrugged stoically, picking the glass out of his cheek.

38   It was late at night by the time we reached Daspalla. The town was deserted. There was no sign of the elephants. I felt as if I had been kicked in the stomach. 'Jesus!' I shouted, 'I just can't believe this. We've lost them. They could be anywhere . . .'

39   'No sir,' Mr Tripathy announced calmly, pointing to large mounds like loaves of bread that decorated the road. 'Now we follow shit.'

40   We pushed on deeper into the night, our eyes glued to the black surface of the road, illuminated in the taxi's headlights, searching for the tell-tale signs. At intervals the trail would run dry and Mr Tripathy and Indrajit would make enquiries. Villagers, rudely awoken by the urgent shouting, would appear in their

doorways, cocooned in blankets, looking bewildered and frightened. Reports regarding sightings of the elephants became equally bewildering—anywhere between two hours and six days. We reached a toll gate, where we received more accurate information. The elephants, we were told by the sleepy toll keeper, had definitely passed through. Did he perhaps know how long ago, we asked. No. Unfortunately his watch was not in working order. But he assured us it was not yesterday.

41   We were closer. The droppings were fresher and, as if on cue, Bhim woke up. 'Haathi close,' he said quietly, rubbing his bloodshot eyes, as he poked his nose out of the window. 'Can smell.'

42   We rounded the next bend. Three massive shapes loomed out of the night, their shadows dancing over the glow of a small roadside fire, around which lay bundles of vermilion and saffron rags.

43   'We'll pretend you're a tourist who has never seen an elephant,' Aditya whispered to me. 'Just stare in astonishment.'

44   As I got out of the car the rags suddenly billowed upwards and I found myself transfixed by three pairs of hot eyes that flashed like cash registers, curtained by matted tresses of long black oily hair. I forgot the necessity of our charade. As if drawn by a magnet, I was already moving towards the elephants.

45   Then I saw her. My mouth went dry. I felt giddy, breathless. In that moment the ancient wall crumbled and I walked through. With one hind leg crossed over the other, she was leaning nonchalantly against a tree, the charms of her perfectly rounded posterior in full view, like a prostitute on a street corner. I knew then that I had to have her. Suddenly, nothing else mattered and I realized with some surprise that I had fallen in love with a female Asian elephant.

46   As luck would have it, I had become enamoured with a perfect elephant, an elephant, even Bhim said, that made his heart flutter. She was young, between twenty-five and thirty years old and although in poor condition, due to mishandling and starvation, would in fourteen days in his care, turn into a lovely riding elephant. She had all the attributes—a healthy pink tongue unblemished by black spots, brown kindly eyes with no traces of white, the right amount of toenails, eighteen, five each on the front feet, four on the back, strong and sturdy joints and a perfect arc to her back. The other two elephants, he warned, were dangerous, and would quite likely kill somebody soon if they hadn't done so already. Take her, he advised me, it would be impossible to find better.

47   Anywhere between 10,000 rupees and 2 lakhs, I was told in Delhi when researching the price of elephants. A tusker is usually more expensive due to its ivory and prestige, yet a female is sometimes more desirable due to its temperament.

48   The odds were already stacked heavily in favour of the saddhus. To make matters worse a crowd had mysteriously assembled and was excitedly denouncing the saddhus as robbers and urging the 'rich firinghee' to buy all three elephants. My diary entry for the negotiations reads as follows: 'Their first price was 2 lakhs. Our first price: 60,000 rupees. Their second price: 1 lakh 50,000 rupees. Our second price: 80,000 rupees. Their third price: 1 lakh. Our third price: 85,000 rupees. Their final price: 1 lakh. Problem. Stalemate. Holy men will not budge.

Crowd now very excited. Go away and have urgent discussions over cup of tea. Tea delicious. Tripathy, Indrajit and Bhim advise stick to our price otherwise loss of face. Aditya says loss of elephant more likely. Return and offer 1 lakh. Holy men now refuse. Why? Holy men never go back on word and have hurt feelings. Aditya tells them will bring cash tomorrow. Holy men go back on word and forget about feelings but now want more. How much? 1,000 rupees. Why? In India, even numbers inauspicious, odd numbers auspicious. Bloody crooks. Agree. Crowd very disappointed.' (£1 sterling is approximately 26 rupees, give or take a little depending on fluctuations in the rate of exchange. 1 lakh equals 100,000 rupees, or £4,000.)

49   The mendicants, or beggars, told us that they would bring the elephant back to Daspalla. There they were more likely to find a suitable place to load her on to the truck that we would be bringing the next day. Before leaving I went to see her. I watched her flapping her huge ears, the ends of which were splotched with the palest of pink dots, as if somebody had flicked a paintbrush. I felt ashamed that I had bargained for her at all. I wanted to reach out and touch her, but found I couldn't, terrified that she might reject me. In the car on the way back I realized I didn't even know her name.

50   Mr Tripathy had forgotten about his suitcase full of elephants and now seemed as obsessed with acquiring an original elephant as we were. The next morning he and Indrajit went to organize a truck, while Aditya and I set off to find the zoo director to ask him whether we could keep the elephant there until we departed on our journey, and also if he would allow Bhim to act as mahout. We had reached the decision last night after three bottles of rum. Tripathy and Indrajit had vehemently opposed the idea, saying that he was too old, too weak and too drunk. Whether it was the alcohol or emotion I will never know, but the way that Bhim had accepted his position removed my doubts. 'Sah,' he said proudly, drawing himself up to his full five feet and executing another shaky salute, 'Raja-sahib, Daddy, Mummy, my family now. Bhim look after.'

51   The director was somewhat surprised and sceptical at the speed of our success. He readily agreed to let the elephant reside at the zoo, but wanted it outside the main park due to the quarantine regulations. The place he was suggesting was next to Bhim's house, which suited us perfectly. But, he warned us, although he had no doubts about Bhim's capabilities with elephants, he did have a drink problem. However, if we were prepared to take the risk, he would not stand in our way.

52   We found our transport was waiting for us at the hotel. The truck was a machine of magnificent chaos. It was difficult to ascertain on first inspection which was the front and which the back. It was the hippies' ultimate chariot, a relic of the Sixties and flower power, bedecked with garlands of flowers, effigies of gods, good luck charms and strings of fairy-lights that twinkled on and off prettily on application of the brakes. On the back was written, 'USE HORN PLEASE OK' and underneath, 'TATA' which I thought was a message of farewell, but was in fact the make of the vehicle.

53 We set off to Daspalla stopping for a 'sharpener' in a bottle shop on the way. The proprietor, an ex-serviceman, excited by our visit, took out two bottles of beer and three glasses from a cupboard. The name of the beer was printed over a picture of Mohammed Ali standing over a fallen victim with his arms outstretched—KNOCK OUT, HIGH PUNCH, STRONG BEER, BREWED IN BANGALORE. 'On the houses, gentlemen,' he said, raising his glass. 'To England, India, elephants. God bless and the best of British luck.'

54 'That makes me proud to be an Indian,' Aditya said as we walked back to the truck. 'You have just witnessed something quite unique. In all my travels across this country, that is the first time I have been offered a free drink. It bodes well for our journey, my friend.'

55 'Luckily he didn't know you are a Maratha,' I remarked, 'otherwise his hospitality might have been of a different nature in view of the depredations committed by your ancestors in Orissa two hundred years ago.'

56 'Ah, the sword of the Marathas. Those were the days,' he said dreamily. 'You know, Mark, it was probably right here, on this very spot that my ancestors won yet another brilliant victory.'

57 'Actually it was at a place called Barmul Gorge which is somewhere near here. It was your last stand in Orissa. The English army, led by Marquis Wellesley, wiped you out.'

58 The mendicants were already sleeping by the time we found them in a deserted schoolhouse on the outskirts of Daspalla. I couldn't see the elephants but I could hear them feeding; sharp cracks of breaking branches punctured the still night air like pistol shots. Aditya squatted down beside one of the sleeping forms and I overheard a short, muffled conversation. The mendicant pulled his blanket further over his head, rolled over and went back to sleep. Odd behaviour I thought for a man who is about to receive nearly £4,000. Aditya stood up, his face registering a mixture of anger and disbelief.

59 'They won't sell. They've changed their minds.'

60 'You're joking.'

61 'I am not bloody well joking,' he hissed. 'You know what this bastard told me when I pointed out that he had gone back on his word and put us to a great deal of expense. He said it is our right to give people trouble. We do it all the time.'

62 Indrajit and Tripathy had now joined us. When Aditya explained the situation we had to restrain them forcibly from attacking the mendicants, who were now fully awake clutching an assortment of crude axes and spears, which I realized with horror they had probably used on the elephants.

63 'We are wasting our time,' Aditya said. 'There's only one solution. We will go to the police.'

64 The police station was empty apart from a bat circling a ceiling fan. From the back of the building we heard the sound of snoring. Indrajit disappeared. A few minutes later he returned followed by a disgruntled man with tousled hair, hastily tucking a khaki shirt into a crumpled lunghi. He waved us to a couple of chairs and slid behind a desk. He looked at me, as if he had just awakened from one nightmare and was now about to enter another.

65 Aditya explained the situation. The policeman blinked owlishly and painstakingly scratched out a report.

66 'In my opinion,' he announced finally, pushing back his chair and yawning, 'there is not seeming to be a crime committed.'

67 'There bloody well has been,' I shouted, losing the last vestige of self-control. 'They've got my elephant!' I threw down a visiting-card I had been given by a senior bureaucrat in the Orissa government.

68 To my astonishment, the policeman's eyes widened noticeably. In a matter of moments the entire garrison of the Daspalla Police Force were lined up in front of the desk and ordered to fetch the beggars. The posse returned with the man to whom Aditya had spoken. It would have given us some satisfaction if he had been driven at the point of a bayonet, or at least in handcuffs, but he seemed to be on excellent terms with his captors. He entered the station, helped himself to a cigarette from a packet lying on the desk, lit it from a match proffered by one of the policemen, and squatted down unconcernedly in a corner. A crowd had assembled outside the station. The majority were on our side, but a faction became demonstrative when a local quack told them I was buying the elephant in order to kill it. I would then, with the aid of a huge syringe, extract some magic potion which I would sell as an aphrodisiac. The police chief, sensing a riot, dispersed the crowd.

69 Up until now the mendicant had only revealed his name as Rajpath but when one of the police advanced upon him with a bamboo cane, he broke down in a well-rehearsed fit of histrionics, and whimpered that the elephant did not belong to him but to his boss who lived in a village near Benares in the state of Uttar Pradesh.

70 'Why in hell didn't he tell us that in the first place?' I asked Aditya incredulously.

71 For the next two hours a strange negotiation took place, during which the police acted as go-betweens. At one moment they would be deep in conversation with Aditya, Tripathy and Indrajit, the next with Rajpath through the bars of the station cell, behind which he now reclined. Meanwhile I waited outside and spent a pleasant night discussing the merits of the English and Indian cricket teams with one of the junior policemen.

72 In the early hours of the morning a solution was found. Mysteriously, Rajpath could now sell the elephant. Empowered by the owner, its destiny lay entirely in Rajpath's hands. He would be prepared to sign an affidavit to the effect as well as the sale deeds which we had brought from Bhubaneshwar. Both these documents would be witnessed officially by the police, and Rajpath would then set out immediately for Benares to deliver the money to the owner.

73 The deal was seemingly foolproof, except, I pointed out, for one salient point. In view of his previous attitude how could we trust Rajpath to deliver the money?

74 It was decided that Aditya would accompany him to Benares and conclude the negotiations with the owner personally. I had to fly to Delhi to sort out some visa extension problems. In the meantime, Mr Tripathy and Indrajit would keep watch over the elephant and we would meet back in Bhubaneshwar in a few days.

75   Arriving in Delhi, I found an article had already appeared in a national newspaper about my intended journey. The last paragraph read: 'more than anything else Mr Shand is looking forward to travelling at an elephant's pace in today's era of jet travel because it would enable him to absorb the surrounding elephant.' I assumed the last word to be a misprint; it should perhaps have read 'elements.'

76   My work finished I called on my friend and in his drawingroom ruminated over a name for my elephant. On a table there was a collection of miniature ivory elephants. He picked one up and handed it to me. It was exquisite. The body intricately carved in a pattern of tiny stars.

77   'In Hindi,' he explained, 'the word for star is "tara," more importantly Tara is one of our goddesses. What do you think of that for a name?'

78   'Tara, Tara, Tara,' I rolled it over my tongue. I liked it. It was a beautiful name for a beautiful elephant. A goddess and a star. She deserved nothing less.

79   A jubilant trio was waiting for me in the hotel room in Bhubaneshwar; Aditya handed me an impressive looking document studded with blue seals, a jumble of illegible signatures and a cluster of thumb prints. 'You are now the absolute owner of one female elephant named Toofan Champa.'

80   'Her name is Tara,' I interrupted.

81   'Then you are the absolute owner of one female elephant named Tara, aged about thirty years, height about seven and a half feet, with black forehead and black body, pigmentation spots on both ears, with eighteen toenails, six-inch tusks and healed wound marks on the centre of her back. By the way,' he added, 'Rajpath returned with me. An elephant, he tells me, takes time to get used to a new mahout. He'll work with Bhim.'

82   Over celebratory drinks he told me of his journey. At first he was worried that Rajpath might escape from the train, but the mendicant seemed so sad, and so subdued, that he spent the journey gazing mournfully out of the window until even Aditya began to feel sorry for him. When they arrived in Benares, Aditya employed the services of a lawyer, and they left by taxi to Lakeshar village, about two hours by road northwest of Benares.

83   The owner of the elephant, an elderly man, was obviously a figure of some standing. He lived in the largest house in the village and was not at all surprised to see them. Sitting by his side was one of the other mendicants who, it seemed, had gone on ahead to warn him. The rest of his family were also present. There were fifteen of them. At this moment, Aditya felt concerned. But everything went smoothly. The gentleman wanted to sell the elephant: there was no bargaining and the lawyer drew up the papers which were duly witnessed and signed. The money was then handed over, and each member of the family wanted to count it. This took time. Finally everyone was satisfied and the deal celebrated with cups of hot milk sweetened with sugar. As they were leaving the old man told Aditya that he would now buy another elephant. When he and his brother were young men and first married, their wives were unable to produce a male heir; a saddhu was consulted who advised them to keep 'Ganesh' near the house.

They immediately bought an elephant, and some time later his brother produced a son.

84   'If he has to keep an elephant near his house at all times,' I remarked, 'what's it doing traipsing across Orissa?'

85   'He can't afford to keep it all year round,' Aditya explained. 'An elephant costs about 300 rupees a week to feed, which in India is a great deal of money. From November to March, our marriage season in India, he rents the elephant out. On such occasions, it is auspicious to have "Ganesh" present. During the rest of the year it will just sit eating money, so he makes a deal with mendicants like Rajpath. During the off season, he lends it to them and they make a lucrative living by begging. He also gets a cut of their takings.'

86   I was astounded. 'What a sensible arrangement.'

87   'It's actually quite a large business, particularly in the Benares area. Some of these landlords own up to thirty or forty elephants, or more. In many ways this is a good thing. Sadly, the use of elephants is dying out. Can you imagine India without elephants?'

88   Everyone in the hotel appeared to be involved in Tara's destiny. When I arrived, the receptionist told me my elephant had refused to get on the truck. Aditya laughed. 'It was quite an event. These two'—he nodded towards Tripathy and Indrajit—'were most upset. They wanted her to be waiting for you at the zoo. Indrajit even tried to ride her himself, as if she were some huge taxi. And poor Mr Tripathy nearly got flattened when she shot into reverse. The trouble was caused by the crowd. You can imagine the scenario—the shouting and jeering. She was a nervous wreck.'

89   'Where are they now?'

90   'On the road. Let's go and meet your new girlfriend.'

91   After driving about twenty miles we found them, taking shelter from the sun under the spread of a large banyan tree. It was, I realized, the first time I had seen her in the light of day. As often happens in life and love, she now presented a somewhat different picture. Even to my inexperienced eye, she appeared to be half starved. She lacked that roundness of girth that I had always associated with elephants. Her rib cage was clearly visible and her skin hung in folds like an ill-fitting suit. She looked at that moment exactly what she was—a beggar. It was only then, as I surveyed this immense bag of bones, that the enormity of the situation struck me. She was mine. I was the owner of an elephant, and the idea seemed so ludicrous that I began to laugh. Quickly I controlled myself for I thought—and this was even more absurd—that she might think I was laughing at her, and I had no desire to hurt her feelings.

92   I was also at a loss as to how to effect an introduction. She wasn't exactly an average pet, like a cat or a dog, or even a hamster, which one can pick up and cuddle or stroke and expect a contented purr or a wet lick or, in the case of the hamster, a sharp nip. However, she soon solved that problem. As I approached her nervously she stretched out her trunk and with the utmost delicacy began to explore the front of my shirt. She's making friends with me, I thought happily,

enchanted by this apparent display of affection. It then stopped abruptly in the area of one of my trouser pockets into which she quickly inserted the tip of her trunk and deftly removed my lunch—an apple—and, with a squeak of delight, popped it into her mouth. It seemed the key to Tara's heart was going to be through her stomach. I dispatched Indrajit to buy her some food.

93   After two kilos of rice, which she consumed by poking her trunk into the sacks and sucking the contents out like a vacuum cleaner, four bundles of bananas and twenty-three coconuts, she seemed a little more replete and broke wind loudly as if to say thank you. As I watched her crunch up the last of the coconuts, her eyes, fringed by lashes long enough to suggest that they were false, closed contentedly.

◼ ◼ ▨

MEANING

1. How does the process of acquiring an elephant require Shand to learn a good deal about Indian customs?
2. Ideally, what qualities should an elephant driver, or *mahout*, possess, and how do these compare with the qualities of Bhim?
3. What does the reader discover about how elephants are used to make money in India?
4. What can you infer about the role played by charity in supporting holy men?

TECHNIQUE

1. How is Shand's account structured to emphasize the suspense as to whether he would achieve his objective? What were some of the important steps he had to take?
2. How does the episode about how elephants are employed during the off-season reveal much about Hindu culture?
3. **Other Patterns.** Why is Shand's **description** of his chosen elephant, Tara, invaluable in communicating his happiness in finding her?

LANGUAGE

1. What words and images reveal Shand's attitude toward his newly acquired elephant, and what does the name Tara mean?
2. How does Shand use dialogue to bring out the latent humor in this account?
3. If you don't know the meanings of the following words, look them up: *monsoons* (3), *vehemently* (50), *quarantine* (51), *depredations* (55), *mendicant* (58), *histrionics* (69), *ludicrous* (91), *replete* (93).

SUGGESTIONS FOR WRITING

1. **Critical Writing.** What does buying this elephant mean to Shand? How do the experiences he has gone through allow him to form a close relationship with Tara?

2. What process would you go through in deciding on a name for a pet? Why would you choose this name?

3. Have you ever formed a close bond with an animal? **Describe** your experiences.

4. ***Thematic Links.*** Compare Shand's experiences with those of David R. Counts in "Too Many Bananas" (Chapter 11, "Problem Solving") in terms of what each man learned about the culture.

JAMAICA KINCAID

Girl

Biographical information on Jamaica Kincaid can be found preceding her essay "A Small Place" (Chapter 4, "Description"). This story first appeared in *At the Bottom of the River* (1983) and is a mostly one-sided exchange between a mother and daughter containing the mother's catalog of what to do and what not to do in order to act like a lady. The mother's obsession that her daughter will grow up to be a "slut" tinges her comments. Throughout, Kincaid artfully conveys the rhythms of West Indian speech.

BEFORE YOU READ

Were your parents' expectations for you realistic or unrealistic?

■ ■ ▨

1 Wash the white clothes on Monday and put them on the stone heap; wash the color clothes on Tuesday and put them on the clothesline to dry; don't walk barehead in the hot sun; cook pumpkin fritters in very hot sweet oil; soak your little cloths right after you take them off; when buying cotton to make yourself a nice blouse, be sure that it doesn't have gum on it, because that way it won't hold up well after a wash; soak salt fish overnight before you cook it; is it true that you sing benna[1] in Sunday school?; always eat your food in such a way that it won't turn someone else's stomach; on Sundays try to walk like a lady and not like the slut you are so bent on becoming; don't sing benna in Sunday school; you mustn't speak to wharfrat boys, not even to give directions; don't eat fruits on the street— flies will follow you; *but I don't sing benna on Sundays at all and never in Sunday school*; this is how to sew on a button; this is how to make a button-hole for the button you have just sewed on; this is how to hem a dress when you see the hem coming down and so to prevent yourself from looking like the slut I know you are so bent on becoming; this is how you iron your father's khaki shirt so that it doesn't have a crease; this is how you iron your father's khaki pants so that they don't have a crease; this is how you grow okra—far from the house, because okra tree harbors red ants; when you are growing dasheen, make sure it gets plenty of water or else it makes your throat itch when you are eating it; this is how you sweep a corner; this is how you sweep a whole house; this is how you sweep a yard; this is how you smile to someone you don't like too much; this is how you smile to someone you don't like at all; this is how you smile to someone you like completely; this is how you set a table for tea; this is how you set a table for dinner; this is how you set a table for dinner with an important guest; this is how you set a table for lunch; this is how you set a table for breakfast; this is how to

---

[1] Calypso music.

behave in the presence of men who don't know you very well, and this way they won't recognize immediately the slut I have warned you against becoming; be sure to wash every day, even if it is with your own spit; don't squat down to play marbles—you are not a boy, you know; don't pick people's flowers—you might catch something; don't throw stones at blackbirds, because it might not be a blackbird at all; this is how to make a bread pudding; this is how to make doukona;[2] this is how to make pepper pot; this is how to make a good medicine for a cold; this is how to make a good medicine to throw away a child before it even becomes a child; this is how to catch a fish; this is how to throw back a fish you don't like, and that way something bad won't fall on you; this is how to bully a man; this is how a man bullies you; this is how to love a man, and if this doesn't work there are other ways, and if they don't work don't feel too bad about giving up; this is how to spit up in the air if you feel like it, and this is how to move quick so that it doesn't fall on you; this is how to make ends meet; always squeeze bread to make sure it's fresh; *but what if the baker won't let me feel the bread?*; you mean to say that after all you are really going to be the kind of woman who the baker won't let near the bread?

■ ■ ▨

Can you imagine the mother in this picture of a Caribbean mother and daughter giving the same kind of advice that Jamaica Kincaid dramatizes in her story "Girl"? What clues tell you that the mother is the type of person who will not let anything slip by her?

---

[2] A spicy plantain pudding.

MEANING

1. What picture do you get of the many chores that are involved in keeping house, and how are these related to gender?

2. How would you describe the relationship between the mother and daughter in this story?

3. How do the very different kinds of things a girl is expected to know in this culture tell you the diverse skills she must master if she is to grow from a girl into a woman?

4. Is there any evidence that the mother has any reason to worry about her daughter's morals? If so, what is the evidence? If not, what does this say about the mother?

TECHNIQUE

1. How does Kincaid convey expectations, personal and social, through the mother's litany of instructions?

2. When the girl finally responds, how does Kincaid reveal via the mother's reply tell you what the mother's real intentions are toward her daughter?

3. **Other Patterns.** How is Kincaid's story shaped as a **narrative** that is designed to lead up to her final ironic question?

LANGUAGE

1. What specialized terms give the reader a sense of Antiguan culture?

2. How does the supersaturation of rules and instructions in such a short passage suggest that this advice was delivered over years rather than at one moment?

3. If you don't know the meanings of the following words, look them up: benna (1), wharfrat (1), dasheen (1).

SUGGESTIONS FOR WRITING

1. **Critical Writing.** Are the mother's expectations of the womanly ways passed on from generation to generation still relevant?

2. Provide step-by-step instructions for performing a household task that you are particularly good at.

3. **Narrate** your own version of this story, incorporating the advice, lessons, complaints, and apprehensions that you received from parents or relatives, along with your reactions.

4. **Thematic Links.** Compare the expectations of the mother in this story to those of Fatima Mernissi's mother as described in "Moonlit Nights of Laughter" (Chapter 3, "Narration").

▓▓▓ STUDENT ESSAY: PROCESS ANALYSIS

The following essay by Edison Baquero uses the pattern of process analysis and shows readers step by step what life is like for a gamer. The annotations on Edison's essay and the follow-up assessment ("Strategies") are designed to help you understand the pattern of process analysis.

Baquero 1

True Life: Life as a Gamer

Edison Baquero

1   Ever wonder what a typical day in a land of Arthurian legend would have in store? For Pezzle, a level fifty, Realm Rank eleven, Master Level eleven Briton Friar, living in Albion and completing mythological quests is business as usual. After checking to see if his merchant has sold any of his valuables, it's time to go on hour-long adventures to kill the "Kraken" in its underwater lair, or the Chimera, a mythological creature with the heads of a dragon, a lion and an ornery goat. In the <u>Dark Ages of Camelot</u>, Pezzle is in constant warfare with the minions of the realms of Hibernia and Midgard, the Celtic and Norse realms. For Bryan High, Albion is a second home, quite literally; he has a three-story home there where he keeps Pezzle's belongings and trophies. Bryan is a player in a MMORPG, or Massive Multiplayer Online Role Playing Game. Like most MMO players, Bryan spends a great deal of time playing a role in an imaginary world. Some may look at this gaming as a waste of time, or even a negative influence on habits and behavior, but Bryan and other gamers feel otherwise. Despite having some personality quirks which have developed during his years of gaming, Bryan has shown himself to be a successful person and is liked by nearly everyone he meets. Although Bryan has changed some of his gaming habits, this paper is still an accurate depiction of the life of a hard-core gamer. This is a look into a vastly growing subculture, a culture that is often misunderstood.

2   In high school, Bryan's day in "RL," or real life, was very different from a typical person's. Instead of interacting with others and developing his own personality, he chose to live vicariously

Introduction invites the reader to enter the world of the typical gamer.

Thesis statement essay dispels misconceptions about gamers.

Baquero 2

through his fictional character, Pezzle, the Briton Friar. During a typical day in the school year, Bryan would play from 3 pm until two or four in the morning.

Overview of the process in a gamer's life with the first step: living vicariously through a fictional character.

3   Spending upwards of twelve hours of gaming a day seems like a great deal, but for a gamer like Bryan, it wasn't close to enough time. During the summer, when he logged the most online time for the year, Bryan easily and regularly would play at least eighteen hours a day. On rare occasions, he'd spend entire days, a full twenty-four hours, at the computer.

4   What is it that is so appealing about playing an MMO? It does not seem too appealing to sit in front of a computer screen for hours upon end, but what is going on inside that picture on the screen is actually quite marvelous for some. Being able to traverse beautiful landscapes completing adventures in a seemingly endless world can inspire and satisfy the most adventurous of spirits. In an MMO, you can meet new people, go on fun adventures with friends, and do things you could never do in real life, like kill a dragon. An MMO game also gives its players a powerful sense of accomplishment from completing quests, quests that can take hours to carry out; moreover, these quests can give a sense of recognition to those who may not receive praise in the real world. With statistic boards for each game server showing the highest-ranked players of each class, it's easy for gamers to identify the elite gamers of the moment. Having your accomplishments so widely known can be very satisfying.

Topic sentence serves as transition to the next section.

5   Expert players like Bryan are not the only ones who take gaming seriously. Millions of other people from kids to adults log on to their virtual worlds and take gaming to heart. Bryan, renowned in his gaming world for his skill, decided to take advantage of his ability to see if he could profit from it. The result was over a thousand dollars in RL revenues from playing a video game, payment for what amounted to very little gaming work. A master of his craft, Bryan can accomplish quests that can take from fifteen to fifty "newbs," or unskilled players, with just his one character. By single-handedly killing the Chimera, a quest that normally takes twenty or

Subsequent steps about the rewards gained.

more people, Bryan can sell all the items the Chimera drops after it dies for RL (real life) money. By selling these items, items that are very valuable to players who cannot kill it on their own, this one creature alone can make Bryan anywhere from sixty to eighty dollars. The drops of such high-profile targets are often extremely valuable, and because he doesn't have to split them with group members, he can sell them for all the profit.

6   In spite of a rigorous and obsessive gaming habit, Bryan was still able to excel at school. However, excessive video gaming, reaching a point of addiction, can sometimes be dangerous for the most avid of players. In the most extreme cases, there are instances of players skipping class and work, and in rare cases, players becoming violent. Some excessive gamers find it harder and harder to log off, and their educations, social lives, and careers suffer as a result. Although Bryan's habit did not harm his academic success, a consequence of living life vicariously through Pezzle the Briton Friar was a lack of relationships with the opposite sex during high school, a lack of socializing with his peers, and a deep sense of shyness. Intense gaming was a habit that affected his ability to interact with others.

Writer discusses the problems faced by some avid gamers.

7   Like any enjoyable habit, gaming must be taken in moderation and mixed with other activities. Realizing this, Bryan began to reduce his time spent gaming, opening up more time for him to go out and socialize with others. After going out to various social gatherings, Bryan finally began to shake off his fear of social events and learned to be comfortable with himself around others. Eager to go out and meet new people, but still wanting to play games, Bryan learned to incorporate both gaming and going out into his lifestyle.

8   Contrary to what some may understand, Bryan's time on the computer was not really spent alone. Bryan has made many lasting friendships with people that he met in games. Bryan has recently moved from the <u>Dark Ages of Camelot</u> to the <u>World of Warcraft</u>, but in addition to his game changes, Bryan has also made drastic changes in his social behavior. Without losing any of his love for gaming, Bryan now has toned down his time spent gaming, keeping a balance between games and a social life.

Conclusion echoes the thesis statement in the introduction.

Strategies for Writing an Essay in Process Analysis

1. Purpose and Thesis

Edison's essay is intended as an informational process analysis whose purpose is to describe the process of becoming a gamer. Edison's thesis statement makes clear that although he has some misgivings about the obsessive and compulsive nature of being a gamer, it has redeeming features that explain its growing popularity. Throughout his essay, Edison maintains this even-handed approach as he follows his subject, Bryan, into the virtual world where Bryan has achieved success.

2. Organization and Tone

In explaining the process, Edison wisely provides some background information that his readers will need to know before going into the intricacies of the game world with its levels of play, unique objectives in the form of quests, and financial rewards for those like Bryan who have become masters in this domain. Edison then broadens his analysis by documenting the social rewards—being part of a community—along with the possible dangers of becoming nothing but a gamer with no life outside the game. Edison has chosen an appropriate voice that is nonjudgmental and objective from a third-person point of view.

3. Details

Edison's essay includes helpful descriptive details that allow readers to form an accurate picture of an unfamiliar process. For example, he includes the number of hours Bryan might play continuously, the strange creatures Bryan encounters through his alter ego, and the money Bryan makes selling quest trophies to other, less-accomplished gamers.

4. Transitions and Topic Sentences

To help his readers follow his analysis, Edison introduces paragraphs with clear topic sentences (sometimes phrased as questions) and uses transitions appropriately to identify different stages of this process.

5. Revision

Readers of Edison's essay might feel that some minor revisions would make it more effective. For example, some of the sections seem repetitive, and some of the sentences are overly long.

Guidelines for Writing an Essay in Process Analysis

- If your assignment requires you to use process analysis, decide whether your essay will provide a set of instructions or explain how something works.
- Does your thesis identify the process and suggest why it is important to know about?
- Have you provided necessary background about the process (and defined any technical terms) for readers who might not be familiar with it?
- Have you thought through the steps of the process in advance and identified those that would be especially difficult to understand?
- If the analysis is instructional, address the reader in the second person ("you should first do this, then that"). If the process analysis has an informational purpose, use either the first-person point of view or, more typically, the third-person singular or plural. Avoid shifting the point of view in the middle of the essay. Stay consistent.
- Explain the process one step at a time, using chronological order, along with all the details necessary to explain the process and warnings about possible trouble spots.
- Have you used transitions to clearly signal the separate steps in the process so that readers will know when one is finished and the next has started?
- Does your introduction engage the audience and motivate them to consider the significance of the process? Does your conclusion review key steps and remind readers why the process is important?

Grammar Tips for Process Analysis

In writing a process analysis either as a set of instructions or as an explanation of how something works, two kinds of common problems deserve special attention: (1) shifts in person and (2) shifts in verb tense.

1. In giving instructions, stick to the second person ("you") throughout:

Incorrect:

To prevent getting a shock when installing a dimmer switch, *one* should first turn off the electricity at the main switch. Then *you* should locate the positive, negative, and ground wires in the switch *you* plan to install.

Correct:

To prevent getting a shock when installing a dimmer switch, *you* should first turn off the electricity at the main switch. Then *you* should locate the positive, negative, and ground wires in the switch *you* plan to install.

continued

2. In explaining a process, maintain the same subject throughout:

Incorrect:

The camp *counselor* first assigns each camper a bunk. Then *they* accompany the campers to the central meeting area.

Correct:

Camp *counselors* first assign each camper a bunk. Then *they* accompany the campers to the central meeting area.

In giving instructions or explaining a process, it is best to avoid using passive verb tenses even if this seems to eliminate the problem of an inconsistent subject.

Incorrect:

To prevent getting a shock when installing a dimmer switch, you should first turn off the electricity at the main switch. Then the positive, negative, and ground wires *should be located* in the switch you plan to install.

Incorrect:

First each camper *is assigned* a bunk by the camp counselor. Then the camper *is accompanied* to the central meeting area.

In giving instructions, eliminate passive verbs by using the active form in which the second person ("you") is understood to be the subject.

Correct:

To prevent getting a shock when installing a dimmer switch, first turn off the electricity at the main switch. Then locate the positive, negative, and ground wires in the switch you plan to install.

In explaining a process, it is better to use active verbs performed by a known subject, although you might need to use passive verbs if you do not know who is performing the action.

Correct:

Camp counselors first *assign* each camper a bunk. Then they *accompany* the campers to the central meeting area.

CHECKLIST for Revising Process Analysis Essays

- Will your essay explain how something works or how to do something?
- Have you included a thesis statement that identifies what the process is and why readers should know about it?
- Have you included and defined required technical terms?
- Have you described the process one step at a time from a consistent point of view?
- Have you alerted the reader to potential trouble spots or steps that might be difficult to understand?
- Do your transitional words and phrases make it easy for your reader to clearly understand the differences between separate steps?

ADDITIONAL WRITING ASSIGNMENTS AND ACTIVITIES

COMMUNICATING WITH DIFFERENT AUDIENCES

1. You are an advisor helping students to write résumés to send to prospective employers. What would you tell the students to say or not say? For example, you might want to advise them to include career objectives, a synopsis of work experience, education, personal facts, hobbies, travels, interests, memberships, school and community activities, clubs, awards, providing references on request, how to do well on interviews, and how to write an effective thank-you note.

2. Write a guide for co-workers helping them to understand the steps to take in preparing and sending out a product for distribution.

3. Write a letter to a friend telling him or her how to pick an apartment and what to look for.

4. You are an advice columnist or radio psychologist. What advice would you give to someone whose problem is that his or her parents call every day?

5. You are a volunteer for an emergency squad in your town and have been asked to deliver a talk to trainees. Describe the steps to take in performing an emergency medical procedure (for example, CPR).

6. Make up a brochure for people who are going to take prospective students on a tour of the campus to emphasize its best features, and describe its benefits such as nearby beaches, sushi bars, theaters, malls, and outlets, as well as other inducements that will make them wish to attend your school.

7. Describe the steps to take in preparing a dog, cat, horse, or other animal for a competitive showing.

8. Instruct a new roommate on how to fix up the room or apartment to use the available space most efficiently.

9. Draw on your personal experience to describe the best way to select, set up, and decorate a Christmas tree, to wallpaper or paint a room, or to grill food for a barbeque.

10. As an experienced babysitter, you have been asked to instruct someone else in how to be a good babysitter who will be hired again. Conversely, as a parent, leave detailed instructions for a babysitter.

11. You are a nutritionist who has to design a pamphlet with step-by-step instructions on how to lose weight over a period of time, including details about portion size, when to eat, and meeting nutritional requirements.

12. Without consulting Mapquest or any other electronic aid, give directions on how to get from where you or a friend lives to some specified location, step by step.

13. If you have some expertise in a particular sport, explain one maneuver (for example, flip turns in swimming) in detail so that someone who is not familiar with the maneuver could perform it.

WRITING FOR A NEWSPAPER

For your college newspaper, write an article on the steps to take in choosing a certain electronic product (such as speakers), how to shop for it, and how to buy it for the best price.

PROCESS ANALYSIS ESSAYS

1. Explain the steps that are involved in performing a dance routine.

2. Take readers through a manufacturing process step by step (such as how a certain kind of candy is produced).

3. Take the readers behind the scenes of a movie, and explain the steps that transform a screenplay into a finished film.

4. What are the steps that are involved in any specific religious pilgrimage (for example, to Santiago de Compostela in Spain, Mecca in Saudi Arabia, or Bodh Gaya or Varanasi in India)?

5. What are the ritual preparations for a holiday such as Ramadan, Passover, Easter, Kwanza, or Christmas?

6. For people who were new to a sport or leisure pursuit, what would you tell them, step by step, that they would need to know to participate?

7. Make up an innovative program for getting an incoming group of freshmen to bond with each other in smaller groups or teams by doing some assigned activity, such as a treasure hunt.

8. Explain, step by step, how to plant an herb or decorative garden.

9. From your experience, what are the steps in preparing for and taking an exam, running a marathon, participating in a debate, or performing some other rigorous task?

10. Give instructions on appropriate behavior (including details on what to wear, what to say, and what not to say) at a rock concert, a party, or a meeting with administrators or higher-ups in an office setting.

11. To get your deposit back, you have to restore your apartment to its original condition. Explain step by step the tasks you would perform, the tools you would need, and the length of time you should allocate.

RESEARCH SUGGESTIONS

1. What sequence of behavior modification techniques have proven effective in treating alcoholism, smoking, or other addictive behaviors?

2. What techniques for interrogating suspected terrorists have been devised and/or prohibited in recent years? What sequence of behavior-conditioning techniqes are used at boot camps to transform new recruits into Marines?

3. Research how famous magic tricks actually work. Describe one, and create instructions on how to perform it.

COLLABORATIVE ACTIVITIES

1. What steps do you take to protect your privacy when using electronic means of communication (for example, e-mail, cell phones, or wireless laptops)?

2. Prepare instructions on how to make the different courses (appetizers, entrées, salads, desserts) for a formal sit-down dinner for a new restaurant, including detailed recipes.

3. Describe the objectives, equipment, and rules for a futuristic sport or game that combines aspects of existing ones (for example, rollerball combines motorcycling, football, jai alai, roller derby, and hand-to-hand combat). Alternatively, describe a nontraditional sport such as snowboarding for someone who has never played it.

CLASSIFICATION AND DIVISION

8

Categorizing and Analyzing Cultural Features

Writers use classification to sort, group, and collect things into categories or classes based on one or more criteria. Criteria are features that members of the group all have in common. The purposes of the classifier determine which specific features are selected as the basis of the classification. Effective classifications shed light on the nature of what is being classified by identifying significant features, using these features as criteria in a systematic way, dividing phenomena into at least two different classes on the basis of these criteria, and presenting the results in a logical and consistent manner.

The specific categories into which items are grouped depends on what criteria are being applied. Applying different principles of classification based on designated features will yield different groupings. Most people might classify drugs simply according to the different forms (capsules, pills, liquids, gas, ointments, or powders) in which they appear. Pharmacologists, by contrast, classify drugs according to the different kinds of effects the drugs have on the body. Thus, one category comprises drugs that combat bacteria, such as antibiotics and sulfa drugs. A second category is made up of drugs that prevent disease, such as vaccines and antiserums. A third group consists of drugs that affect the cardiovascular system, such as antiarrhythmics and vasodilators. A fourth group is made up of drugs that affect the body's nervous system, such as analgesics, opiates, anesthetics, stimulants, and depressants. Classification is an invaluable method of imposing a pattern on material that otherwise would remain unorganized.

Equally important, once a classification has been established, it becomes a framework into which new information can be placed. For example, in film studies, critics classify popular films according to genres. Films within genres share certain characteristics of subject matter, character development, and plot. For example, a movie might be identified as a western (*High Noon, Silverado*), a horror film (*Frankenstein,*

361

Poltergeist), a comedy (*It Happened One Night, National Lampoon's Animal House*), a science-fiction film (*The Day the Earth Stood Still, Star Trek IV*), a musical (*The Sound of Music, A Chorus Line*), or an adventure film (*Captain Blood, Raiders of the Lost Ark*).

Amy Tan in "Mother Tongue" uses classification to shed light on the different kinds of "Englishes" that are used in different social settings by her mother, who was born in China:

> But to me, my mother's English is perfectly clear, perfectly natural. It's my mother tongue. Her language, as I hear it, is vivid, direct, full of observation and imagery. That was the language that helped shape the way I saw things, express things, made sense of the world.

Tan uses classification to help her develop her analysis of how she became a better writer when she redrafted her stories so that her mother could understand them.

Luis Alberto Urrea uses classification to identify the different sources of words that have come into the English language:

> English! It's made up of all these untidy *words*, man. Have you noticed?
>
> Native American (*skunk*), German (*waltz*), Danish (*twerp*), Latin (*adolescent*), Scottish (*feckless*), Dutch (*waft*), Caribbean (*zombie*), Nahuatl (*ocelot*), Norse (*walrus*), Eskimo (*kayak*), Tatar (*horde*) words! It's a glorious *wreck* (a good old Viking word, that).

Urrea discusses those specific contributions of various languages, points out scores of Spanish words that have become part of everyday speech, and reflects on the futility of trying to purify English.

Classification is equally well suited to clarifying complex, subjective psychological phenomena. In "Polite Lies," Kyoko Mori classifies the different levels of greetings that are permissible in conversing in Japan. Mori says that on the one hand, politeness may be quite formal depending on the rank and gender of the speakers, while, on the other, it may be informal and casual:

> In Japanese conversations, the two speakers are almost never on an equal footing: one is senior to the other in age, experience, or rank. Various levels of politeness and formality are required according to these differences: it is rude to be too familiar, but people are equally offended if you are too formal, sounding snobbish and untrusting. Gender is as important as rank. Men and women practically speak different languages; women's language is much more indirect and formal than men's.

Mori's purpose in classifying politeness into various kinds is to make it easier for her readers to recognize each type, to evaluate them against each other, and ultimately to sympathize with her.

Margaret Visser in "Fingers" analyzes the role that table manners and etiquette play in cultures that use utensils and in those in which people eat with their hands. Visser shows how the reliance on utensils serves to reinforce distinctions between social classes and how the connotations of left-handedness versus right-handedness have entered the language as value judgments. Visser discusses each of these variables and uses them to organize her ideas and analysis:

> People who eat their food with their hands usually eat it warm rather than steaming, and they grow up preferring it that way. (It is often said that one of the cultural barriers

that divide "developed" from "developing" peoples is this matter of preference in the temperature at which food is eaten.)

In "We Eat What We Are," Mimi Sheraton uses classification as a means of organizing and clarifying the different styles of fellow diners who accompanied her when she was reviewing restaurants. Sheraton identifies a range of types whose agendas reflect categories that we see in society:

> Many Reluctants began every meal by reciting what I have come to call "the Most Amazing Grace," in which they apologized for what they were about to order. "I didn't have a big dinner last night and ate no breakfast today, so I can have the pasta and cheesecake for lunch."

Sheraton discovers that people's attitude toward food when someone else is paying, as she was in her position as a reviewer, can reveal basic character types.

In "Homage to Catalonia," George Orwell discovered, as an on-site observer and combatant, that life in the Army during the Spanish Civil War was organized according to a pragmatic classification:

> In trench warfare five things are important: firewood, food, tobacco, candles, and the enemy. In winter on the Zaragoza front they were important in that order, with the enemy a bad last.

Orwell uses this hierarchy of value to organize his discussion of all aspects of life in the trenches ("We classified according to their burning qualities every plant that grew on the mountain-side"). Orwell uses classification as an analytical tool to reveal how the things that we think would be important in warfare are not and how ordinary things become crucial.

In his short story "Her Three Days," Sembene Ousmane portrays a society in Mali that is maintained through a strict hierarchy based on what number wife a woman is under polygamy. The pivotal character, Noumbe, becomes a tragic figure when her husband Mustapha undercuts her reputation and standing in the community by failing to appear for her designated three days of companionship:

> She deliberately changed the conversation in order to avoid a long discussion about the other three wives. But all the time she was longing to go and find Mustapha. She was being robbed of her three days. And the other wives knew it. Her hours alone with Mustapha were being snatched from her.

The story is shaped to reveal the typical reactions of those who must come to terms with the rules of polygamy and how these rules mirror the cultural bias that permeates the culture of Mali.

Beyond the ways in which writers in this chapter use classification and division to sort information into categories or split a subject into parts, this pattern can be used in a real-life situation. For one example, see the sample résumé at the end of this chapter (pps. 416–417).

AMY TAN

Mother Tongue

Amy Tan, best known for her depiction of relationships between daughters born in America and their Chinese mothers, credits her mother to no small degree for her own success as a writer. The reasons why become apparent when we read the following essay, which was originally published as "Under Western Eyes" in *The Three Penny Review* (1990). Tan was born in 1952 in Oakland, California, to parents who had left China in 1949. She held diverse jobs and studied linguistics before visiting China in 1984, an experience that sparked her desire to become a writer in order to more fully explore her heritage. Her acclaimed work *The Joy Luck Club* (1989) was followed by the equally compelling novel *The Kitchen God's Wife* (1991) and, more recently, by *The Bonesetter's Daughter* (2002) and *Saving Fish from Drowning* (2005).

BEFORE YOU READ

If your parents could not speak English fluently, how would this put you in the role of interpreter?

■ ■ ▨

1   I am not a scholar of English or literature. I cannot give you much more than personal opinions on the English language and its variations in this country or others.

2   I am a writer. And by that definition, I am someone who has always loved language. I am fascinated by language in daily life. I spend a great deal of my time thinking about the power of language—the way it can evoke an emotion, a visual image, a complex idea, or a simple truth. Language is the tool of my trade. And I use them all—all the Englishes I grew up with.

3   Recently, I was made keenly aware of the different Englishes I do use. I was giving a talk to a large group of people, the same talk I had already given to half a dozen other groups. The nature of the talk was about my writing, my life, and my book, *The Joy Luck Club.* The talk was going along well enough, until I remembered one major difference that made the whole talk sound wrong. My mother was in the room. And it was perhaps the first time she had heard me give a lengthy speech, using the kind of English I have never used with her. I was saying things like, "The intersection of memory upon imagination" and "There is an aspect of my fiction that relates to thus-and-thus"—a speech filled with carefully wrought grammatical phrases, burdened, it suddenly seemed to me, with nominalized forms, past perfect tenses, conditional phrases, all the forms of standard English that I had learned in school and through books, the forms of English I did not use at home with my mother.

4   Just last week, I was walking down the street with my mother, and I again found myself conscious of the English I was using, and the English I do use with

her. We were talking about the price of new and used furniture and I heard myself saying this: "Not waste money that way." My husband was with us as well, and he didn't notice any switch in my English. And then I realized why. It's because over the twenty years we've been together I've often used that same kind of English with him, and sometimes he even uses it with me. It has become our language of intimacy, a different sort of English that relates to family talk, the language I grew up with.

5   So you'll have some idea of what this family talk I heard sounds like, I'll quote what my mother said during a recent conversation which I videotaped and then transcribed. During this conversation, my mother was talking about a political gangster in Shanghai who had the same last name as her family's, Du, and how the gangster in his early years wanted to be adopted by her family, which was rich by comparison. Later, the gangster became more powerful, far richer than my mother's family, and one day showed up at my mother's wedding to pay his respects. Here's what she said in part:

6   "Du Yusong having business like fruit stand. Like off the street kind. He is Du like Du Zong—but not Tsung-ming Island people. The local people call putong, the river east side, he belong to that side local people. That man want to ask Du Zong father take him in like become own family. Du Zong father wasn't look down on him, but didn't take seriously, until that man big like become a mafia. Now important person, very hard to inviting him. Chinese way, came only to show respect, don't stay for dinner. Respect for making big celebration, he shows up. Mean gives lots of respect. Chinese custom. Chinese social life that way. If too important won't have to stay too long. He come to my wedding. I didn't see, I heard it. I gone to boy's side, they have YMCA dinner. Chinese age I was nineteen."

7   You should know that my mother's expressive command of English belies how much she actually understands. She reads the *Forbes* report, listens to *Wall Street Week*, converses daily with her stockbroker, reads all of Shirley MacLaine's books with ease—all kinds of things I can't begin to understand. Yet some of my friends tell me they understand 50 percent of what my mother says. Some say they understand 80 to 90 percent. Some say they understand none of it, as if she were speaking pure Chinese. But to me, my mother's English is perfectly clear, perfectly natural. It's my mother tongue. Her language, as I hear it, is vivid, direct, full of observation and imagery. That was the language that helped shape the way I saw things, expressed things, made sense of the world.

8   Lately, I've been giving more thought to the kind of English my mother speaks. Like others, I have described it to people as "broken" or "fractured" English. But I wince when I say that. It has always bothered me that I can think of no way to describe it other than "broken," as if it were damaged and needed to be fixed, as if it lacked a certain wholeness and soundness. I've heard other terms used, "limited English," for example. But they seem just as bad, as if everything is limited, including people's perceptions of the limited English speaker.

9   I know this for a fact, because when I was growing up, my mother's "limited" English limited *my* perception of her. I was ashamed of her English.

I believed that her English reflected the quality of what she had to say. That is, because she expressed them imperfectly her thoughts were imperfect. And I had plenty of empirical evidence to support me: the fact that people in department stores, at banks, and at restaurants did not take her seriously, did not give her good service, pretended not to understand her, or even acted as if they did not hear her.

10   My mother has long realized the limitations of her English as well. When I was fifteen, she used to have me call people on the phone to pretend I was she. In this guise, I was forced to ask for information or even to complain and yell at people who had been rude to her. One time it was a call to her stockbroker in New York. She had cashed out her small portfolio and it just so happened we were going to go to New York the next week, our very first trip outside California. I had to get on the phone and say in an adolescent voice that was not very convincing, "This is Mrs. Tan."

11   And my mother was standing in the back whispering loudly, "Why he don't send me check, already two weeks late. So mad he lie to me, losing me money."

12   And then I said in perfect English, "Yes, I'm getting rather concerned. You had agreed to send the check two weeks ago, but it hasn't arrived."

13   Then she began to talk more loudly. "What he want, I come to New York tell him front of his boss, you cheating me?" And I was trying to calm her down, make her be quiet, while telling the stockbroker, "I can't tolerate any more excuses. If I don't receive the check immediately, I am going to have to speak to your manager when I'm in New York next week." And sure enough, the following week there we were in front of this astonished stockbroker, and I was sitting there red-faced and quiet, and my mother, the real Mrs. Tan, was shouting at his boss in her impeccable broken English.

14   We used a similar routine just five days ago, for a situation that was far less humorous. My mother had gone to the hospital for an appointment, to find out about a benign brain tumor a CAT scan had revealed a month ago. She said she had spoken very good English, her best English, no mistakes. Still, she said, the hospital did not apologize when they said they had lost the CAT scan and she had come for nothing. She said they did not seem to have any sympathy when she told them she was anxious to know the exact diagnosis, since her husband and son had both died of brain tumors. She said they would not give her any more information until the next time and she would have to make another appointment for that. So she said she would not leave until the doctor called her daughter. She wouldn't budge. And when the doctor finally called her daughter, me, who spoke in perfect English—lo and behold—we had assurances the CAT scan would be found, promises that a conference call on Monday would be held, and apologies for any suffering my mother had gone through for a most regrettable mistake.

15   I think my mother's English almost had an effect on limiting my possibilities in life as well. Sociologists and linguists probably will tell you that a person's developing language skills are more influenced by peers. But I do think that the language spoken in the family, especially in immigrant families which are more

insular, plays a large role in shaping the language of the child. And I believe that it affected my results on achievement tests, IQ tests, and the SAT. While my English skills were never judged as poor, compared to math, English could not be considered my strong suit. In grade school I did moderately well, getting perhaps B's, sometimes B-pluses, in English and scoring perhaps in the sixtieth or seventieth percentile on achievement tests. But those scores were not good enough to override the opinion that my true abilities lay in math and science, because in those areas I achieved A's and scored in the ninetieth percentile or higher.

16　　This was understandable. Math is precise, there is only one correct answer. Whereas, for me at least, the answers on English tests were always a judgment call, a matter of opinion and personal experience. Those tests were constructed around items like fill-in-the-blank sentence completion, such as, "Even though Tom was _____, Mary thought he was _____." And the correct answer always seemed to be the most bland combinations of thoughts, for example, "Even though Tom was shy, Mary thought he was charming," with the grammatical structure "even though" limiting the correct answer to some sort of semantic opposites, so you wouldn't get answers like, "Even though Tom was foolish, Mary thought he was ridiculous." Well, according to my mother, there were very few limitations as to what Tom could have been and what Mary might have thought of him. So I never did well on tests like that.

17　　The same was true with word analogies, pairs of words in which you were supposed to find some sort of logical, semantic relationship—for example, "*Sunset* is to *nightfall* as _____ is to _____." And here you would be presented with a list of four possible pairs, one of which showed the same kind of relationship: *red is to stoplight, bus is to arrival, chills is to fever, yawn is to boring.* Well, I could never think that way. I knew what the tests were asking, but I could not block out of my mind the images already created by the first pair, "*sunset* is to *nightfall*"—and I would see a burst of colors against a darkening sky, the moon rising, the lowering of a curtain of stars. And all the other pairs of words—red, bus, stoplight, boring—just threw up a mass of confusing images, making it impossible for me to sort out something as logical as saying: "A sunset precedes nightfall" is the same as "a chill precedes a fever." The only way I would have gotten that answer right would have been to imagine an associative situation, for example, my being disobedient and staying out past sunset, catching a chill at night, which turns into feverish pneumonia as punishment, which indeed did happen to me.

18 I have been thinking about all this lately, about my mother's English, about achievement tests. Because lately I've been asked, as a writer, why there are not more Asian Americans represented in American literature. Why are there few Asian Americans enrolled in creative writing programs? Why do so many Chinese students go into engineering? Well, these are broad sociological questions I can't begin to answer. But I have noticed in surveys—in fact, just last week—that Asian students, as a whole, always do significantly better on math achievement tests than in English. And this makes me think that there are other Asian American students whose English spoken in the home might also be described as "broken" or

"limited." And perhaps they also have teachers who are steering them away from writing and into math and science, which is what happened to me.

19   Fortunately, I happen to be rebellious in nature and enjoy the challenge of disproving assumptions made about me. I became an English major my first year in college, after being enrolled as pre-med. I started writing nonfiction as a free-lancer the week after I was told by my former boss that writing was my worst skill and I should hone my talents toward account management.

20   But it wasn't until 1985 that I finally began to write fiction. And at first I wrote using what I thought to be wittily crafted sentences, sentences that would finally prove I had mastery over the English language. Here's an example from the first draft of a story that later made its way into *The Joy Luck Club*, but without this line: "That was my mental quandary in its nascent state." A terrible line, which I can barely pronounce.

21   Fortunately, for reasons I won't get into today, I later decided I should envision a reader for the stories I would write. And the reader I decided upon was my mother, because these were stories about mothers. So with this reader in mind—and in fact she did read my early drafts—I began to write stories using all the Englishes I grew up with: the English I spoke to my mother, which for lack of a better term might be described as "simple"; the English she used with me, which for lack of a better term might be described as "broken"; my translation of her Chinese, which could certainly be described as "watered down"; and what I imagined to be her translation of her Chinese if she could speak in perfect English, her internal language, and for that I sought to preserve the essence, but neither an English nor a Chinese structure. I wanted to capture what language ability tests can never reveal: her intent, her passion, her imagery, the rhythms of her speech and the nature of her thoughts.

22   Apart from what any critic had to say about my writing, I knew I had succeeded where it counted when my mother finished reading my book and gave me her verdict: "So easy to read."

MEANING

1. What different kinds of Englishes does Tan identify, and what traits characterize each?

2. How has Tan been influenced by her mother's experiences, both positive and negative, with English?

3. How do we know that Tan's mother has greater confidence in reading English than in speaking it?

4. What picture do you get of the complex relationship between Tan and her mother?

TECHNIQUE

1. What principle of classification and division does Tan use to sequence the varieties of Englishes she discusses? How does this classification help her to develop her thesis?

2. How does Tan use the episodes involving her relationship with her mother to reflect the tensions (and different cultural perspectives) between an immigrant parent and a child born in the United States?

3. **Other Patterns.** Where does Tan use **narrative** to provide specific contexts in which her readers can appreciate the distinctions she draws?

LANGUAGE

1. What different meanings does the title of this essay suggest?

2. How does the line Tan quotes from an early draft of *The Joy Luck Club* (paragraph 20) demonstrate how she became a better writer?

3. If you don't know the meaning of the following words, look them up: *wrought* (3), *vivid* (7), *portfolio* (10), *impeccable* (13), *benign* (14), *quandary* (20), *nascent* (20).

SUGGESTIONS FOR WRITING

1. **Critical Writing.** What different Englishes do you use with friends, family, and teachers and in different social settings? How do you choose which English to use?

2. If you speak two languages, in which language do you think, dream, or express feelings? What do you think is the reason for this?

3. Tan imagined that she was writing for her mother. If you were a novelist, for whom would you write? Why?

4. Give some **examples** of different kinds of difficulties that someone whose English was as limited as Tan's mother's was would encounter. Are there instances in which limited English might be an advantage?

5. **Thematic Links.** How do the accounts by Tan and Kyoko Mori in "Polite Lies" address the issue of circumstances in which different variations of a language are appropriate?

LUIS ALBERTO URREA

Nobody's Son

Luis Alberto Urrea's background as a child born in Tijuana to a Mexican father and an American mother informs much of his writing. After graduating from the University of California at San Diego, he served as a volunteer with a charitable organization bringing supplies to the poor living on the Mexican border. He described these experiences in *Across the Wire: Life and Hard Times on the Mexican Border* (1993). Urrea's interest in language, how it affects identity, and the role played by Spanish in shaping conversational English is evident in the following selection from *Nobody's Son: Notes from an American Life* (1998). Urrea is currently a writer in residence at the University of Illinois at Chicago and has also published *The Devil's Highway* (2004) and *The Hummingbird's Daughter* (2005).

BEFORE YOU READ

What common words have come into English from other languages? What are the origins of these words?

■ ■ ▨

1   My mom said, "I'm so sick of your God-damned Mexican bullshit!" I was in bed with my wife at the time. It was 7:30 in the morning. My wife was white. So was my mother.

2   Apparently, the issue of my identity was troubling Mom. She was a good Republican. She tended to work up a good cuss when she was beyond her limit of endurance. I must have come to represent a one-man wave of illegal aliens to her as she sipped her coffee and looked out at a tender New England dawn.

3   I had finally gotten away from the border. I was teaching writing, at Harvard no less. She saw this development as being due to the force of her own will. That's the GOP for you, I'd say in our frequent and spirited political squabbles— taking credit for someone else's achievements while demonizing their ethnicity. (Did you know that *squabble* is a Scandinavian word? So what, you ask? Just keep it in mind, that's all.)

4   I was still being called Mexican, Chicano, Hispanic, Latino, Mexican American, Other. These Ivy-League types were taking my name seriously. It drove my mother to distraction.

5   She barged through the door shouting anti-Mexican rhetoric. Whither goest Mom goest the nation.

6   We had a miniature Proposition 187 anti-immigration rally right there in my bedroom.

For a visual to accompany this selection, see color insert photo B-5.

7   "You are *not* a Mexican!" she cried. "Why can't you be called *Louis* instead of *Luis?*"

8   Go, Mom.

9   "Louis *Woodward* or Louis *Dashiell.* One of *my* names. I'm warning you— someday, they're going to come for you, and you'll be sorry."

10   They.

11   I've been on the lookout for those scoundrels all my life. So has much of my family. (When I mention my family, I mean Mexicans. The Americans were held at bay by my mother for reasons I only later understood. It turns out she was ashamed of the Mexicans. "They spit on the floor," she insisted, though I never saw my *abuelita* hawk up a big one and splash it in the corner. If your mama's saying it, it must be true.) Many of my relatives were afraid of the border patrol. Others were afraid of the Mexican government. Still others were afraid of Republican white people and Democratic black people. Cops. And perhaps my white relatives back East were afraid of all these things, too. But mostly, I got to thinking, they must have been scared of me. I was one of them, but I was also one of *them.*

12   They.

13   "They," Wendell Berry writes, "will want you to kneel and weep / and say you should have been like them."

14   It's a poem called "Do Not Be Ashamed." I read it whenever I'm called upon to give a commencement speech at college graduations. It's not a political poem. It's not a liberal or conservative poem. It's a human poem.

15   Most students seem to understand what Berry's talking about.

16   He goes on to say:

> And once you say you are ashamed,
> reading the page they hold out to you,
> then such light as you have made
> in your history will leave you.
> They will no longer need to pursue you.
> You will pursue them, begging forgiveness.

17   *They.*

18   You can almost see thought bubbles above the students' heads as they listen. *Honkies,* some are thinking. *Liberals,* and *minorities,* and *commies.* And certainly *666* and *the Antichrist* bubble about up in the air: *Hispanics, Yankees, blacks, queers. Democrats. Women. Men.*

19   My mother thought: *Mexicans.*

20   My father, a Mexican, thought: *gringos.*

21   I, for one, think *They* are the ones with the words. You know, the Words. The ones they called my dad and me—like *wetback. Spic. Beaner. Greaser. Pepper-belly. Yellow-belly. Taco-bender. Enchilada-breath.*

22   That was my wife's phrase. She thought it was cute. She's gone now.

23   So is my mom.

24   "Dad?" I said. "What's a greaser?"

25   He used to tell me I was no *God-damned gringo*. I was, however, white. *Speak Spanish, pendejo!* was a common cry when I spoke some unacceptable English phrase. Utterly forbidden English in our house included many taboos, among them: *my old man* (he was sure this was disrespectful and implied he wasn't a virile young thing); *big daddy* (he was certain this meant big penis); *you're kidding* (another disrespect, suggesting he didn't tell the truth at all times—he didn't); *easy rider* (he thought this meant a man married to a whore); *chicano* (from chicanery).

26   His only word for *them* was *gringo*. He didn't see it as all that bad. He said it came from the Mexican-American War. The pop hit the American soldiers sang in those days was "Green Grow the Lilacs." Green grows/*gringos*. It seemed altogether benign compared to yellow bellies.

27   I had been called "greaser" by the son of a retired Navy petty officer in my new, all-white neighborhood. We had fled from the ethnic cleansing taking place in Shelltown, California, to which we had hurried from Tijuana. I couldn't quite fathom the name. Surely I wasn't greasy? But I *felt* greasy. And the vivid image of grease, of some noxious *Mexican* grease, collided in my mind with the word "wetback." And suddenly I was certain that my back was wet with grease. A grease I couldn't see. I had an image in my mind of the back of my shirt soaked through with cooking oil and sticking to me, glistening sickeningly in the sun. Everybody could see the grease drooling down my spine. Except me.

28   My father was whiter than my mother. If he had become an American citizen, he would have voted for Nixon. Twice. Most Mexican immigrants—both "legal" and "illegal"—would vote Republican if given a chance, except the Republicans scare them, so they're forced to support the Clintons and Carters of this nation. It has been estimated that by 2050, Latinos will be the majority population of the world. Not only will America be "brown," but it will also be the home of the new Democrats. The Institutional Revolutionary Catholic Democratic Party ticket of John Kennedy Jr. and Edward James Olmos will sweep the elections. The paradigm will shift, as they say: the bogeyman will become the *chupacabras*. Bullfights at the county fair. Baja California will be the fifty-first state. The Buchanan Brigade Aryan Militia will mount an offensive in the Malibu Hills, holding nineteen gardeners and twelve nannies hostage. NASA will land the first lowrider on the moon. Just watch.

29   "Greaser," my father replied.

30   I believe he had prepared himself for this. On our first day in the neighborhood, he'd been chased out of our driveway by an irate white man. You don't spend two decades living as a Mexican guest of Southern California without becoming fully aware of the genocidal urge that percolates in the human heart.

31   Dad transformed before my eyes into a college lecturer.

32   "During the Americans' westward expansion," he intoned, "the settlers traveled in covered wagons. When they reached the West—Arizona, Texas, California—they often needed repair work done on their wagons after such a long hard trip. A large part of this work consisted of *greasing* the axles, which had dried out.

The only ones who had the skill to fix the wagons were Mexicans. Mexicans greased the axles. You see? *Greasers.* So when they call you that, hold your head up. It's a badge of honor. We helped build America."

33   He's gone now, too.

34   The last time I was interviewed by the Mexican press, I was in Mexico City, the self-appointed home of all true Mexicans. I was startled to find out that I was not a true Mexican. I was any number of things: I was an American, I was "just" a Chicano, I was a *norteño* (which, in Mexico City, is like saying you're one of the Mongol horde). I was lauded for speaking Spanish "just like" a Mexican, or chided for having what amounted to a cowboy accent. That I was born in Tijuana didn't matter a bit: Tijuana, I was informed, is no-man's-land. Mexicans don't come from Tijuana. Tijuanans come from Tijuana.

35   That I was an American citizen was apparently a *faux pas*. That I wrote in English was an insult. That I was blue-eyed, however, allowed me to pass for Mexican high society.

36   I will say this for Mexico City, though: people in La Capital have perfect manners. For all its travails and crises, Mexico City is the most civil city I've ever visited. Imagine a city where a cabbie returns your tip to you because you've paid him too much for his services. Imagine this same city reporting a stunning 700 assaults every day.

37   In the great museum, you can see a famous Aztec mask. One half of it is a smiling face. The other half is a skull.

38   I was told by the editor of the newspaper to be out of town by the time the interview appeared. Someone somewhere decided that what I had to say was somehow dangerous. I thought this was a joke. Then an editor took me to the foyer where several of the paper's reporters had been executed. *All I'm saying*, I protested, *is that poor people should be treated with respect.* She lit a cigarette and said, *Be out of town.*

39   Things that seemed perfectly clear to me turned confusing and opaque.

40   In the interview, I offered the often-quoted comment from *By the Lake of Sleeping Children* that I, as a son of the border, had a barbed-wire fence neatly bisecting my heart. The border, in other words, ran through me. The journalist said, "Aha!" and scribbled with real vigor.

41   When the article came out, however, the comment had been transformed. I'm still not sure what it means. It said: "If you were to cut Urrea's heart open, you would find a border patrol truck idling between his ribs."

42   I was going to write, "Meanwhile, back home . . ." But where is home? Home isn't just a place, I have learned. It is also a language. My words not only shape and define my home. Words—not only for writers—*are* home. Still, where exactly is that?

43   Jimmy Santiago Baca reminds us that "Hispanics" are immigrants in our own land. By the time Salem was founded on Massachusetts Bay, any number of Urreas

had been prowling up and down the Pacific coast of our continent for several decades. Of course, the Indian mothers of these families had been here from the start. But manifest destiny took care of us all—while we greased the wheels.

44   Them wagons is still rollin'.

45   I saw a hand-lettered sign on television. It was held up by a woman in stretch pants and curlers, and it said: America For Americans. A nearby man held up a sign exhorting the universe to speak English or go home.

46   *The official language of the United States.*

47   Well, sure. We speak English and, apparently, Ebonics. I want to call Chicano slang Aztonics while we're at it. *Orale,* Homes—we down, *¿qué no? Simón, vato—* let's trip out the *rucas* of the school board, *ese! Ese torcido rifa, locos!*

48   It's all English. Except for the alligator, which is a Spanish word. Lariat, too, is a Spanish word.

49   In fact, here's a brief list, in no particular order: It might help you score points in a trivia parlor game someday. All words borrowed from Spanish:

Chaps
Savvy
Palaver
Hoosegow
Palomino
Coyote
Pinto
Marijuana
Vamoose
Stampede
Buckaroo
Adobe
Saguaro
Rodeo
Ranch
Rancher
Patio
Key (as in Florida Keys)
Florida
Sarsaparilla
Navajo
Nevada
Machete
Texas
Alfalfa
Bonanza
Bronco
Calaboose

Canyon
Colorado
Fandango
Foofaraw
Guacamole
Hackamore
Beef jerky
Lasso
Abalone
Vanilla
Chocolate
Cigar

50 For example. Perfectly acceptable English. Nary an Aztonic word in sight.

51 You don't believe me about beef jerky, do you? I find it a little hard to believe, my own self. What's more American than a hunk of jerky? Cowboys, rednecks, crackers, wrestlers, mountain men gnaw away on planks of jerked beef!

52 Winfred Blevins, in the marvelous *Dictionary of the American West*, notes: "The word is an Americanized version of the Spanish term for jerked meat, *charqui.*"

53 I don't know what we're going to do. Forget about purifying the American landscape, sending all those ethnic types packing back to their homelands. Those illegal humans. (A straw-hat fool in a pickup truck once told my Sioux brother Duane to go back where he came from. "Where to?" Duane called. "South Dakota?")

54 The humanoids are pretty bad, but how will we get rid of all those pesky foreign *words* debilitating the United States?

55 Those Turkish words (like *coffee*). Those French words (like *maroon*). Those Greek words (like *cedar*). Those Italian words (like *marinate*). Those African words (like *marimba*).

56 English! It's made up of all these untidy *words*, man. Have you noticed?

57 Native American (*skunk*), German (*waltz*), Danish (*twerp*), Latin (*adolescent*), Scottish (*feckless*), Dutch (*waft*), Caribbean (*zombie*), Nahuatl (*ocelot*), Norse (*walrus*), Eskimo (*kayak*), Tatar (*horde*) words! It's a glorious *wreck* (a good old Viking word, that).

58 Glorious, I say, in all of its shambling mutable beauty. People daily speak a quilt work of words, and continents and nations and tribes and even enemies dance all over your mouth when you speak. The tongue seems to know no race, no affiliation, no breed, no caste, no order, no genus, no lineage. The most dedicated Klansman spews the language of his adversaries while reviling them.

59 It's all part of the American palaver and squawk.

60 *Seersucker:* Persian.

61 *Sandalwood:* Sanskrit.

62 Grab a dictionary. It's easy. You at home—play along.

63   The $64,000 question for tonight: What the hell are we speaking? What language (culture, color, race, ethnicity) is this anyway? Who are we?

64   *Abbott:* Aramaic.

65   *Yo-yo:* Philippino.

66   *Muslin:* Iraqi.

67   *Yogurt:* Turkish.

68   I love words so much. Thank God so many people lent us theirs or we'd be forced to point and grunt. When I start to feel the pressure of the border on me, when I meet someone who won't shake my hand because she has suddenly discovered I'm half Mexican (as happened with a landlady in Boulder), I comfort myself with these words. I know how much color and beauty we Others really add to the American mix.

How does this picture of the Beatles holding "All You Need Is Love" signs in different languages suggest that emotions are more universal than the languages that are used to express them?

69   My advice to anyone who wants to close the border and get them Messkins out is this: *don't dare start counting how many of your words are Latin, Baby.*

70   America—there's a Mexican in the woodpile.

■ ■ ▨

MEANING

1. What personal dilemma does Urrea face in trying to appease his parents?

2. How does Urrea's situation place him in an ideal position to appreciate the contribution of Spanish to the English language?

3. What was ironic about Urrea's visit to Mexico in terms of how he thought of himself and how he was perceived?

4. What insights does Urrea offer into the historical derivation of terms, including those that are pejorative?

TECHNIQUE

1. How does Urrea use the different kinds of terms that have entered English from Spanish and other cultures as a way to point out the futility of trying to purify English?

2. What insight does Urrea offer into the way in which ethnic identity is constructed through language?

3. **Other Patterns.** How does Urrea **describe** the concealed connotations of some of the terms that are used to demean Mexicans?

LANGUAGE

1. What does Urrea's conversational tone and free-associative style add to his analysis?

2. How does the history of beef jerky reveal the Spanish-English connection?

3. If you don't know the meaning of the following words, look them up: *squabble* (3), *scoundrels* (10), *abuelita* (10), *gringos* (20), *pendejo* (25), *genocidal* (30), *faux pas* (35), *palaver* (59).

SUGGESTIONS FOR WRITING

1. **Critical Writing.** In what way has the United States become a contact zone where people of diverse racial and ethnic backgrounds must choose how to identify themselves? Provide some examples.

2. Analyze the way in which objectionable ethnic epithets are used to hurt others. Does knowing how they originated diminish their impact? Why or why not?

3. Give some other **examples** of common words that came into English from other languages. Discuss their origins in an essay.

4. **Thematic Links.** In what sense might Urrea be considered an exile as described by Edward Said in "Reflections on Exile" (Chapter 10, "Definition")?

MARGARET VISSER

Fingers

Margaret Visser is a classicist and historian of comparative culture. She has taught at York University in Toronto, is a featured speaker on radio and television programs, and has created and presented a six-part series on European cities for BBC Radio 4 program. In this essay from her award-winning book *The Rituals of Dinner* (1991), Visser surveys the rules that have evolved determining what are acceptable table manners and etiquette in diverse cultures. She is also the author of *Much Depends on Dinner* (1990) and, more recently, *Beyond Fate* (2002).

BEFORE YOU READ

If it were socially acceptable, would you prefer eating with your fingers rather than with utensils?

■ ■ ▨

1   One of the more spectacular triumphs of human "culture" over "nature" is our own determination when eating to avoid touching food with anything but metal implements. Our self-satisfaction with this marvellous instance of artificiality, how-ever, should not lead us to assume that people who habitually eat with their hands are any less determined than we are to behave "properly"; for they too overlay "animal" instincts with manners, and indulge in both the constraints and the ornamentations which characterize polite behaviour. Forks, like handkerchiefs, look like dangerously grubby objects to many people encountering them for the first time. To people who eat with their fingers, hands seem cleaner, warmer, more agile than cutlery. Hands are silent, sensitive to texture and temperature, and graceful—provided, of course, that they have been properly trained.

2   Washing, as we have already remarked, tends to be ostentatious and frequent among polite eaters with their hands. Ancient Romans, like the modern Japan-ese, preferred to bathe all over before dinner. The etiquette of hand-washing in the Middle Ages was very strict. During the washing ritual, precedence was observed as it was in the seating of diners at the table; the bows, genuflections, and ceremonial flourishes of the ewerers or hand-washers were carefully pre-scribed. It was often thought disgusting, as it is in India today, to dip one's hands into the basin of water: a servant had to pour scented water *over* the hands so that it was used only once. (The modern North American preference for showers over baths is similar.) In modern Egypt, the basin is sometimes provided with a perfo-rated cover so that the dirty water disappears at once from view. Hand-washing rules always insist that one must not splash or swish the water; be careful to leave some dry towel for a person washing next; and above all touch as little as possi-ble between washing and beginning to eat. If an Abbasid (ninth-century Arab) guest scratched his head or stroked his beard after washing, everyone present

would wait before beginning to eat, so that he could wash again. An Abbasid, like a modern Egyptian host, would wash first, so that guests need not look as though they were anxious to start the meal; alternatively, washing was done outside, and the meal began directly after the seating, usually when the guest of honour stretched his hand to take the first morsel.

3   Desert Arabs go outside the tent, both before and after the meal, to perform ablutions by rubbing their hands with sand; they often prefer to perform this ritual before washing, even when there is plenty of water available. It is thought very rude to perform one's final washing before everyone else has finished eating; it would be the equivalent of our leaving the table while the meal is in progress. The corollary of this is that people who eat with their hands usually try to finish the meal together, since it is uncomfortable, for one thing, to sit for long when one has finished eating, holding out one greasy hand. Where family eating is done from a shared pot, there are rules about leaving some food over for the children, who eat more slowly than adults do. A great deal of attention, forethought, and control is required in order to finish a meal together, or at a moment agreed on in advance; it is a manoeuvre few of us have been trained to perform.

4   A monstrously greedy Greco-Roman banqueter is said to have accustomed his hands to grasping hot things by plunging them into hot water at the baths; he also habitually gargled with hot water, to accustom his mouth to high temperatures. He would then bribe the cook to serve the meal straight from the stove, so that he could grab as much food as possible and eat it while it was still hot—before anyone else could touch it. The story reminds us that eating food while it is hot is a habit both culture-specific and modern; a taste for it has developed in us, a taste which is dependent both on technology and on the little brothers of technology, the knife, fork, and spoon. People who eat their food with their hands usually eat it warm rather than steaming, and they grow up preferring it that way. (It is often said that one of the cultural barriers that divide "developed" from "developing" peoples is this matter of preference in the temperature at which food is eaten.) Where hot drinks are served, on the other hand (an example is the Arab coffee-drinking habit at mealtimes), people tend to like them very hot, as a contrast, and because the cups or glasses, together with the saucers under them, protect their hands.

5   Delicacy and adroitness of gesture are drummed into people who eat with their hands, from childhood. It might be considered polite, for example, to scoop food up, or it could be imperative to grasp each morsel from above. Politeness works by abjuring whole ranges of behaviour which the body could easily encompass—indeed, very often the easier movement is precisely what is out of bounds. It was once the mark of the utmost refinement in our own culture to deny oneself the use of the fourth and fifth fingers when eating: the thumb and first two fingers alone were allowed. Bones—provided they were small ones—could be taken up, but held between thumb and forefinger only. We hear of especially sophisticated people who used certain fingers only for one dish, so that they had other fingers, still unsticky and ungreasy, held in reserve for taking

food or sauce from a different platter. This form of constraint was possible only if the food was carefully prepared so that no tugging was necessary: the meat must be extremely tender, cut up, or hashed and pressed into small cakes. None but the rich and those with plenty of servants were likely to manage such delicacy; it followed that only they could be truly "refined."

6   Distancing the fourth and fifth fingers from the operation of taking food can be performed by lifting them up, elegantly curled; the constraint has forced them to serve merely as ornament. A hand used in this manner becomes a dramatic expression of the economy of politeness. When a modern tea-drinker is laughed at for holding her cup-handle in three fingers, lifting the two unused digits in the air, we think it is because we find her ridiculously pretentious. What we really mean is that she is conservative to the point that her model of social success is completely out of date, and the constraints and ornaments with which she clothes her behaviour are now inappropriate—which is another way of saying that, although she is trying very hard to be correct, she succeeds merely in being improper. Modern constraints and ornaments are, quite simply, different. We should remember that snobbery has usually delighted in scorning what is passé.

7   Left hands are very commonly disqualified from touching food at dinner. The *Li Chi* tells us that ancient Chinese children were trained from infancy never to use their left hands when eating. Ancient Greeks and Romans leaned on their left elbows when reclining at meals, effectively withdrawing their left hands from use. You *had* to lean on the left elbow even if you were left-handed: if you did not, you ruined the configuration of the party by facing the wrong way. The same problem confronted, even more vitally, an ancient Greek hoplite soldier. He formed part of a phalanx of shields, all which had to be held on left arms so that they could overlap; fighting was done with swords grasped in the right. A shield on the right arm would have created a gap in the closed phalanx. It must have been very difficult to be left-handed in the ancient world.

8   Abbasid Arabs used to hold bread in their left hands because this was the part of the meal not shared from a common dish, and even strict modern Middle Eastern manners permit the use of the left for operations such as peeling fruits; the main thing is not to take from a communal dish with the left, and to avoid bringing the left hand to the mouth. The left hand is traditionally discouraged at table because it is the non-sacred hand, reserved for profane and polluting actions from which the right hand abstains. One example of these tasks is washing after excretion. Now it is invariably important for human beings both culturally and for health reasons to understand that food is one thing and excrement another: the fact that they are "the same thing," that is, different phases of the same process, merely makes it imperative that we should keep the distinction clear, and continually demonstrate to others that we are mindful of it.

9   Eating together is a potent expression of community. Food is sacred, and must also be pure, clean, and undefiled. It crosses the threshold of the mouth, enters, and either feeds or infects the individual who consumes it: anything presented to us as edible which is perceived as impure in any sense immediately revolts us. Homage is paid to the purity of what we eat, and precaution taken to

preserve it, in many different ways: we have already considered washing, white cloths and napkins, dish covers, poison-tastings, prayers, and paper wrappings, and we shall see many more of these. In our culture, lavatories (literally, "wash places"—only euphemisms are permissible for this particular piece of furniture) are kept discreetly closeted, either alone or in a bathroom; a "washroom" or a "toilet" (literally, a "place where there is a towel") is nearly unthinkable without a door for shutting other people out. The lavatory bowl is covered (sometimes the cover is covered as well), usually white, wastefully water-flushed (people even like to tint this water an emphatically artificial blue), and hedged about with special paper rolls and hand-washings.

10   Our fascination when we learn that people exist who will not touch food with their left hands is rather interesting. It begins with our conviction that "civilized" people (ourselves, of course) should eat with knives and forks in the first place—that is, try not to handle food at all. We do not like the reason left hands are most often said to be banned among certain "foreigners," fastening as we do upon one reason when it is only one from a whole category of "profane" actions, because our taboo about washrooms is so strong that we cannot bear to be reminded of excretion—which we are, by the prohibition. In other words, our taboo is even stronger than theirs. Moreover, left hands have in fact an "unclean" connotation in our own culture.

11   "Right," after all, means "correct" or "okay" in English. "Sinister" originally meant "left." In French, a just man is *droit*, meaning both "right" and "straight," while *gauche* ("left") describes one who lacks social assurance, as well as dexterity and adroitness (both of which literally mean "right-handedness"). We raise right hands to take oaths and extend them to shake hands: left-handed people just have to fall in with this. In fact, left-handed people, like left-handed ancient Greeks, have always been regarded as an awkward, wayward minority, to the point where left-handed children have been forced, against their best interests, to use their right hands rather than their left. When sets of opposites (curved and straight, down and up, dark and light, cold and hot, and so forth) are set out, our own cultural system invariably makes "left" go with down, dark, round, cold— and female. Males are straight, up, light, hot—and right. Our metal eating implements free us from denying the left hand—but most of us are right-handed anyway, and knives (quintessentially "male" weapons, by the way) are held in right hands. And as we shall see, North Americans still prefer not only to cut with the right, but to bring food to their mouths with the right hand as well.

12   Eating with the help of both hands at once is very often frowned upon. The Bedouin diner is not permitted to gnaw meat from the bone: he must tear it away and into morsels using only the right hand, and not raise the hand from the dish in order to do so. Sometimes right-handed eaters confronted with a large piece of meat, a chicken, for instance, will share the task of pulling it apart, each of two guests using his right hand and exercising deft coordination; no attention should be drawn to this operation by any movement resembling a wrench or a jerk. Even on formal occasions our own manners permit us, occasionally, to use our fingers—when eating asparagus for example (this is an early

twentieth-century dispensation), or radishes, or apricots. But all of these are taken to the mouth with one hand only. We are still advised that corn kernels should be cut off the cobs in the kitchen, or that corn should, better still, be avoided altogether unless the meal is a very intimate affair. One reason why this vegetable has never become quite respectable is that corn cobs demand to be held in two hands. (More important reasons are of course that teeth come too obviously into play when eating them, and cheeks and chins are apt to get greasy.) When we chew, we should also be careful to fill only one cheek—not too full, to be sure. Two hands and two cheeks both signify indecent enthusiasm; cramming either hands or mouth is invariably rude.

13   People whose custom it is to eat with their hands make a further rule: Never take up and prepare a new morsel while you are still chewing. When left hands are allowed as well as right, it is quite dreadful to be feeding one's mouth with

How does this old photo of students being instructed in proper table manners convey the qualities that become important once utensils take the place of fingers, as described by Visser?

one hand while the other is groping in the dish for more. (We are far more lax than they on this point: we are permitted to use the knives and forks in our hands, and chew at the same time.)

■ ■ ▨

MEANING

1. What kinds of rules and constraints characterize proper behavior in cultures in which people traditionally eat with their hands?

2. In what way is the triumph of "culture over nature" reflected in the reliance on utensils rather than one's hands?

3. How have rituals surrounding eating always had a strong cultural component, and what specific practices are tied to social class and religious-based prohibitions?

4. How is eating with one's hands a far more sensuous experience than eating with utensils?

TECHNIQUE

1. How does Visser highlight the rituals that are used in eating with one's hands to **contrast** them with those that involve the use of utensils?

2. How does Visser's discussion emphasize the way in which the reliance on utensils has served to reinforce distinctions between social classes?

3. **Other Patterns.** How does Visser use **process analysis** to enable her readers to understand the rituals that are embedded in table manners?

LANGUAGE

1. What words and images emphasize the role that good table manners and etiquette play in cultures that use utensils and those in which people eat with their hands?

2. How have the connotations of "right-handed" versus "left-handed" entered the English language as value judgments?

3. If you don't know the meaning of the following words, look them up: *cutlery* (1), *ostentatious* (2), *etiquette* (2), *corollary* (3), *adroitness* (5), *passé* (6), *potent* (9).

SUGGESTIONS FOR WRITING

1. **Critical Thinking.** What are some **examples** of good table manners? What cultural function do good table manners serve?

2. What table manners were you taught while growing up? Have these served you well?

3. How are the differences in the utensils that are used in first class and coach on airplanes and the way in which food is served there connected with differences in social class?

4. **Thematic Links.** Compare the different perspectives on eating with utensils in Visser's essay and in Guanlong Cao's "Chopsticks" (Chapter 3, "Narration").

MIMI SHERATON

We Eat What We Are

Mimi Sheraton is best known for her illuminating and engaging restaurant reviews and her many books and articles about food and wine. She grew up in Brooklyn and attended the New York University School of Commerce and the New York School of Interior Design. She began writing about food when she worked at *Seventeen* magazine. Her passions for food and writing come together in her columns, which have been published in the *Village Voice, Esquire,* and *Mademoiselle.* Between 1975 and 1983, she was the food editor for the *New York Times.* After that, she served as food critic for *Time* magazine and traveled around the world for *Condé Nast Traveler* magazine. Her work has garnered numerous awards. In the following selection from her memoir *Eating My Words: An Appetite for Life* (2004), she offers an amusing appraisal of the dining companions she invited to join her as she investigated various restaurants.

BEFORE YOU READ

What qualities would be important in a dining companion if you were a reviewer who wished to remain anonymous when investigating a new restaurant?

■　■　▨

1   "By their eating habits, ye shall know them" may not be a biblical admonition, but it has become part of my own religious canon. Observing fellow diners throughout the years when we were almost always four at table (unless we were six or eight for a Chinese or Indian meal), I noted their telltale idiosyncrasies of likes and dislikes and prejudices.

2   That is a phenomenon well understood by perceptive filmmakers who use food as props to delineate character. The most outstanding example in my recollection appears in Martin Scorsese's film *Taxi Driver*, when the self-hating hack, Travis Bickle as played by Robert De Niro, eats only junk food such as fast-food burgers, candy and white bread soaked in milk and peach brandy. When he finally manages a lunch date in a restaurant with his much-admired golden girl (Cybill Shepherd), he looks perplexed as she orders a salad. Hesitating in embarrassed desperation over what dish would seem suitably classy, he chooses apple pie. In another scene, he takes a young prostitute (Jodie Foster) to breakfast, and we watch her spread a thick layer of grape jelly on to white bread and then shower it with sugar before folding it over. Wondering how anyone could have invented such bizarre and degrading food, I asked the film's writer, Paul Schrader. He said that he had actually known drug addicts who ate the bread-milk-peach brandy concoction and that he and Scorsese once took a young whore to breakfast and she prepared that exact bread-jelly-sugar sandwich. The message, clearly, was "junk food, junk people."

3   Less menacing, the types I came to recognize at my table were the Reluctants, usually health- or diet-conscious women who came along for the glamour

of being part of a review, or because their husbands really wanted to, or just because we were friends and I needed bodies to try enough dishes. As I indicated their options for ordering, explaining that they had to have the dish the chef's way and could not request their swordfish without butter or oil or other similar culinary obscenities, invariably they expressed displeasure either with an outright form of "yech" or with what they assumed was an inaudible sucking in of breath and tightening of lips. After distributing overly generous samples of their portions to me and anyone else who was interested, the eternal dieters would push the food around on the plate, scattering it to seemingly reduce its mass. It is a trick I recognized from childhood, when I did the same with much hated peas and lima beans, only to watch my mother regroup them and point out how little I had eaten. When pasta was ubiquitous and had to be sampled for reviews, the calorie-watchers would have a taste or two, and then carefully pick off and eat only the sauce. In a most unforgettable incident one such woman, who was a health-oriented food writer and sometime restaurant critic, grimaced openly when presented with an exquisite cold half lobster I had asked her to order.

4   Many Reluctants began every meal by reciting what I have come to call "the Most Amazing Grace," in which they apologized for what they were about to order. "I didn't have a big dinner last night and ate no breakfast today, so I can have the pasta and cheesecake for lunch." Or "I had the swordfish, so I can have the chocolate cake for dessert and I won't eat tomorrow." It is an American litany, still mumbled at almost any meal when I am with anyone other than Dick, a sort of advance confession of gustatory sin to absolve their bodies of calories. It is also phenomenally boring.

5   Similarly, I knew three cooking school teachers and three practicing food writers who if not anorexic, surely were bulimic. Never did I or others I have asked see one of these scraggly, bone-thin creatures swallow a mouthful of food, not even the cooking teachers during classes that I observed. In addition, most were workout fanatics: joggers, weight lifters, crunchers and treadmill addicts. As I understand anorexia, it is not unusual for sufferers to obsessively prepare food for others, and teaching or writing on the subject could be another form of feeding. All of this is not to say that only the overweight make convincing food critics, tasting and leaving being not only acceptable but wise, even if I never could quite manage that myself. As for exercise, acceptable forms to me include turning the pages of a book, beating egg whites with a wire whisk, spinning a salad dryer, walking and window shopping in New York and climbing the three flights of stairs in my house as necessary.

6   Returning to the reviewing table, there were the Grabbers, who always ordered the most expensive items of those I indicated, and their choices narrowed as the visits to a particular restaurant progressed. Only caviar was out of bounds unless it was a specialty of the house as at Petrossian, in which case Dick and I went alone, as expensive duplication was unnecessary, or if caviar was part of a preparation, such as blinis. The most egregious Grabber was the husband of a colleague at the *Times*, who finished one main course of roasted chicken with mashed potatoes and some vegetables, and then asked if he could order a steak. Always happy to see an extra dish, I said yes, although I was relieved that no one else at the table followed suit.

Grabbers also were usually Guzzlers, quaffing Dick's generally terrific wine choices as though they were water, thereby making a second bottle an unnecessary expense.

7   Then there were the Indecisives, those who took forever to order, and occasionally, the Joker—invariably male—who asked what would happen if he did not order what I wanted to see, or wouldn't share for a tasting. My answer was that he would pay for his own meal, a threat that always brought the most recalcitrant around. Sometimes the Joker was a helpful soul who tried to bait waiters on my behalf to provoke an incident that I could recount in salty prose, thereby "showing them." Other so-called friends turned out to be Inside Dopes who dined out on their experiences with me, gossiping widely long before my review was published, and who were nevermore invited, if indeed I ever spoke to them again.

8   There also was the group Dick and I referred to as the Alrightniks. If I did not want to be recognized, neither did I want to invite guests who were in any way intimidating or prepossessing because of face, dress or personal style that might prompt special attention. The Alrightniks, however superb as friends, dressed decently but most unstylishly, suggesting perhaps that they belonged to the bridge-and-tunnel crowd. Unbeknownst to them, I invited or, more candidly, used them at restaurants I suspected of being snooty, to ascertain how they were treated and seated. These unwitting shills were compensated with dinners at some of our very best French, Italian and cutting-edge fusion restaurants.

9   Being human, I have my own personal peeves, now as then, and much magnified when I spent so much time watching others eat. I mark as unknowing those who order big, ice-cold drinks like Bloody Marys before a dinner that will include wine, and, along the same lines, those who end a meal with cappuccino, basically coffee-flavored hot milk best drunk at breakfast or as a midafternoon restorative. I try to turn my eyes away from table companions who chew with their mouths open or who cut long pasta strands with a knife to make them manageable, or who butter an entire slice of bread, then fold and eat it all at once. Then there may be the uncouth eater who, when facing fried eggs at breakfast or brunches, first consumes the white, then puts the entire yolk in his or her mouth and pops it inside, a thought that sends a shudder through me even as I write. Because I like hot foods and beverages to be very, very hot, I get nervous watching slow eaters whose soup or coffee grows cold before my eyes. "Eat quickly," I refrain from saying. "It's getting cold!"

10   That is, in fact, one of the only gustatory points of contention between Dick and me. "Your mouth must be asbestos lined," he admonishes, as I invariably finish my coffee long before he starts his.

11   "If you wanted iced coffee, why didn't you ask for it?" I counter. "Don't you know that your coffee just died? It stopped breathing . . ."

■ ■ ◢

MEANING

1. How have filmmakers used food as props as a means to convey character?
2. How did having their meals paid for by Sheraton prompt her invited guests to reveal what type they were?

3. What basic types did she discover, and what characteristics distinguish them from one another?

4. Which of the types would Sheraton be less likely to invite again and why?

TECHNIQUE

1. How does Sheraton round out her classification by discussing junk food in movies and her pet peeves in addition to the named types?

2. How does Sheraton's analysis emphasize how each of the named types might pose a problem for her when she is concentrating on her forthcoming review?

3. **Other Patterns.** How does Sheraton use **exemplification** to enable her readers to understand the distinguishing features of each type?

LANGUAGE

1. How does Sheraton's choice of words and writing style suggest that she is as discriminating as a food critic as she is as an amateur psychologist?

2. How would you characterize Sheraton's tone and attitude toward the different kinds of invited diners who accompany her to restaurants?

3. If you don't know the meaning of the following words, look them up: *admonition* (1), *canon* (1), *idiosyncracies* (1), *delineate* (2), *concoction* (2), *culinary* (3), *ubiquitous* (3), *litany* (4), *gustatory* (4), *blinis* (6), *egregious* (6), *quaffing* (6), *recalcitrant* (7), *shills* (8), *restorative* (9).

SUGGESTIONS FOR WRITING

1. Of the named categories Sheraton uses (Reluctants, Grabbers, Guzzlers, Indecisives, Jokers, Inside Dopes, and Alrightniks), which most accurately describes you if you had the opportunity to dine with a food critic? If none of these fit your style, what category would you create for yourself?

2. Write a review of your favorite restaurant, and classify your fellow diners into various types.

3. **Critical Thinking.** Rent a movie in which attitudes toward food reveal distinct cultural values, such as *Babette's Feast* (1987), *Eat Drink Man Woman* (1994), *Big Night* (1996), *A Chef in Love* (1996), *Soul Food* (1997), *Like Water for Chocolate* (1998), *Chocolat* (2000), *What's Cooking?* (2000), *Mostly Martha* (2001), *Tortilla Soup* (2001), *My Big Fat Greek Wedding* (2002), *Harold and Kumar Go to White Castle* (2004), and *Supersize Me* (2004). After viewing one or several of these, write an analysis of the way food **exemplifies** the unique values of the culture in the context of the story.

4. **Thematic Links.** Compare the insights you discover about how food can reveal character in Sheraton's essay and in Geeta Kothari's "If You Are What You Eat, Then What Am I?" (Chapter 5, "Exemplification").

Homage to Catalonia

One of the most distinguished observers of political processes and the use of language, George Orwell (born Eric Hugh Blair, 1903–1950) started life in India, was educated at Eton on a scholarship, served with the colonial British government in Burma, and returned to a life of grinding poverty in Paris and London. In 1936, he traveled to Spain to report on the Civil War. Once there, he fought against Franco's fascists until he was gravely wounded. He describes his experiences in *Homage to Catalonia* (1938), in which the following selection first appeared. Here, he introduces us to the haphazard military unit in which he served and classifies the much-needed supplies in order of their importance. Orwell is best known for satire of the Russian Revolution in *Animal Farm* (1945) and his prophecies of a society governed by "Big Brother" in *1984* (1949).

BEFORE YOU READ

Would you prefer to serve in an army in which everyone was equal or in a conventional one with a chain of command?

■ ■ ▨

1 In trench warfare five things are important: firewood, food, tobacco, candles and the enemy. In winter on the Zaragoza front they were important in that order, with the enemy a bad last. Except at night, when a surprise-attack was always conceivable, nobody bothered about the enemy. They were simply remote black insects whom one occasionally saw hopping to and fro. The real preoccupation of both armies was trying to keep warm.

2 I ought to say in passing that all the time I was in Spain I saw very little fighting. I was on the Aragon front from January to May, and between January and late March little or nothing happened on that front, except at Teruel. In March there was heavy fighting round Huesca, but I personally played only a minor part in it. Later, in June, there was the disastrous attack on Huesca in which several thousand men were killed in a single day, but I had been wounded and disabled before that happened. The things that one normally thinks of as the horrors of war seldom happened to me. No aeroplane ever dropped a bomb anywhere near me, I do not think a shell ever exploded within fifty yards of me, and I was only in hand-to-hand fighting once (once is once too often, I may say). Of course I was often under heavy machine-gun fire, but usually at longish ranges. Even at Huesca you were generally safe enough if you took reasonable precautions.

3 Up here, in the hills round Zaragoza, it was simply the mingled boredom and discomfort of stationary warfare. A life as uneventful as a city clerk's, and almost as regular. Sentry-go, patrols, digging; digging, patrols, sentry-go. On every hill-top, Fascist or Loyalist, a knot of ragged, dirty men shivering round their flag and trying to keep warm. And all day and night the meaningless bullets

wandering across the empty valleys and only by some rare improbable chance getting home on a human body.

4   Often I used to gaze round the wintry landscape and marvel at the futility of it all. The inconclusiveness of such a kind of war! Earlier, about October, there had been savage fighting for all these hills; then, because the lack of men and arms, especially artillery, made any large-scale operation impossible, each army had dug itself in and settled down on the hill-tops it had won. Over to our right there was a small outpost, also P.O.U.M., and on the spur to our left, at seven o'clock of us, a P.S.U.C. position faced a taller spur with several small Fascist posts dotted on its peaks. The so-called line zigzagged to and fro in a pattern that would have been quite unintelligible if every position had not flown a flag. The P.O.U.M. and P.S.U.C. flags were red, those of the Anarchists red and black; the Facists generally flew the monarchist flag (red-yellow-red), but occasionally they flew the flag of the Republic (red-yellow-purple).[1] The scenery was stupendous, if you could forget that every mountain-top was occupied by troops and was therefore littered with tin cans and crusted with dung. To the right of us the sierra bent south-eastwards and made way for the wide, veined valley that stretched across to Huesca. In the middle of the plain a few tiny cubes sprawled like a throw of dice; this was the town of Robres, which was in Loyalist possession. Often in the mornings the valley was hidden under seas of cloud, out of which the hills rose flat and blue, giving the landscape a strange resemblance to a photographic negative. Beyond Huesca there were more hills of the same formation as our own, streaked with a pattern of snow which altered day by day. In the far distance the monstrous peaks of the Pyrenees, where the snow never melts, seemed to float upon nothing. Even down in the plain everything looked dead and bare. The hills opposite us were grey and wrinkled like the skins of elephants. Almost always the sky was empty of birds. I do not think I have ever seen a country where there were so few birds. The only birds one saw at any time were a kind of magpie, and the coveys of partridges that startled one at night with their sudden whirring, and, very rarely, the flights of eagles that drifted slowly over, generally followed by rifle-shots which they did not deign to notice.

5   At night and in misty weather patrols were sent out in the valley between ourselves and the Fascists. The job was not popular, it was too cold and too easy to get lost, and I soon found that I could get leave to go out on patrol as often as I wished. In the huge jagged ravines there were no paths or tracks of any kind; you could only find your way about by making successive journeys and noting fresh landmarks each time. As the bullet flies the nearest Fascist post was seven hundred metres from our own, but it was a mile and a half by the only practicable route. It was rather fun wandering about the dark valleys with the stray bullets flying high overhead like redshanks whistling. Better than nighttime were

---

[1] An errata note found in Orwell's papers after his death: "Am not now completely certain that I ever saw Fascists flying the republican flag, though I *think* they sometimes flew it with a small imposed swastika."

the heavy mists, which often lasted all day and which had a habit of clinging round the hill-tops and leaving the valleys clear. When you were anywhere near the Fascist lines you had to creep at a snail's pace; it was very difficult to move quietly on those hill-sides, among the crackling shrubs and tinkling limestones. It was only at the third or fourth attempt that I managed to find my way to the Fascist lines. The mist was very thick, and I crept up to the barbed wire to listen. I could hear the Fascists talking and singing inside. Then to my alarm I heard several of them coming down the hill towards me. I cowered behind a bush that suddenly seemed very small, and tried to cock my rifle without noise. However, they branched off and did not come within sight of me. Behind the bush where I was hiding I came upon various relics of the earlier fighting—a pile of empty cartridge-cases, a leather cap with a bullet-hole in it, and a red flag, obviously one of our own. I took it back to the position, where it was unsentimentally torn up for cleaning-rags.

6   I had been made a corporal, or *cabo*, as it was called, as soon as we reached the front, and was in command of a guard of twelve men. It was no sinecure, especially at first. The *centuria* was an untrained mob composed mostly of boys in their teens. Here and there in the militia you came across children as young as eleven or twelve, usually refugees from Fascist territory who had been enlisted as militiamen as the easiest way of providing for them. As a rule they were employed on light work in the rear, but sometimes they managed to worm their way to the front line, where they were a public menace. I remember one little brute throwing a hand-grenade into the dug-out fire 'for a joke.' At Monte Pocero I do not think there was anyone younger than fifteen, but the average age must have been well under twenty. Boys of this age ought never to be used in the front line, because they cannot stand the lack of sleep which is inseparable from trench warfare. At the beginning it was almost impossible to keep our position properly guarded at night. The wretched children of my section could only be roused by dragging them out of their dug-outs feet foremost, and as soon as your back was turned they left their posts and slipped into shelter; or they would even, in spite of the frightful cold, lean up against the wall of the trench and fall fast asleep. Luckily the enemy were very unenterprising. There were nights when it seemed to me that our position could be stormed by twenty Boy Scouts armed with air-guns, or twenty Girl Guides armed with battledores, for that matter.

7   At this time and until much later the Catalan militias were still on the same basis as they had been at the beginning of the war. In the early days of Franco's revolt the militias had been hurriedly raised by the various trade unions and political parties; each was essentially a political organization, owing allegiance to its party as much as to the central Government. When the Popular Army, which was a 'non-political' army organized on more or less ordinary lines, was raised at the beginning of 1937, the party militias were theoretically incorporated in it. But for a long time the only changes that occurred were on paper; the new Popular Army troops did not reach the Aragon front in any numbers till June, and until that time the militia-system remained unchanged. The essential

point of the system was social equality between officers and men. Everyone from general to private drew the same pay, ate the same food, wore the same clothes, and mingled on terms of complete equality. If you wanted to slap the general commanding the division on the back and ask him for a cigarette, you could do so, and no one thought it curious. In theory at any rate each militia was a democracy and not a hierarchy. It was understood that orders had to be obeyed, but it was also understood that when you gave an order you gave it as comrade to comrade and not as superior to inferior. There were officers and N.C.O.s, but there was no military rank in the ordinary sense; no titles, no badges, no heel-clicking and saluting. They had attempted to produce within the militias a sort of temporary working model of the classless society. Of course there was not perfect equality, but there was a nearer approach to it than I had ever seen or than I would have thought conceivable in time of war.

8   But I admit that at first sight the state of affairs at the front horrified me. How on earth could the war be won by an army of this type? It was what everyone was saying at the time, and though it was true it was also unreasonable. For in the circumstances the militias could not have been much better than they were. A modern mechanized army does not spring up out of the ground, and if the Government had waited until it had trained troops at its disposal, Franco would never have been resisted. Later it became the fashion to decry the militias, and therefore to pretend that the faults which were due to lack of training and weapons were the result of the equalitarian system. Actually, a newly raised draft of militia was an undisciplined mob not because the officers called the privates 'Comrade' but because raw troops are *always* an undisciplined mob. In practice the democratic 'revolutionary' type of discipline is more reliable than might be expected. In a workers' army discipline is theoretically voluntary. It is based on class-loyalty, whereas the discipline of a bourgeois conscript army is based ultimately on fear. (The Popular Army that replaced the militias was midway between the two types.) In the militias the bullying and abuse that go on in an ordinary army would never have been tolerated for a moment. The normal military punishments existed, but they were only invoked for very serious offences. When a man refused to obey an order you did not immediately get him punished; you first appealed to him in the name of comradeship. Cynical people with no experience of handling men will say instantly that this would never 'work,' but as a matter of fact it does 'work' in the long run. The discipline of even the worst drafts of militia visibly improved as time went on. In January the job of keeping a dozen raw recruits up to the mark almost turned my hair grey. In May for a short while I was acting-lieutenant in command of about thirty men, English and Spanish. We had all been under fire for months, and I never had the slightest difficulty in getting an order obeyed or in getting men to volunteer for a dangerous job. 'Revolutionary' discipline depends on political consciousness—on an understanding of *why* orders must be obeyed; it takes time to diffuse this, but it also takes time to drill a man into an automaton on the barrack-square. The journalists who sneered at the militia-system seldom remembered that the militias

had to hold the line while the Popular Army was training in the rear. And it is a tribute to the strength of 'revolutionary' discipline that the militias stayed in the field at all. For until about June 1937 there was nothing to keep them there, except class loyalty. Individual deserters could be shot—were shot, occasionally—but if a thousand men had decided to walk out of the line together there was no force to stop them. A conscript army in the same circumstances—with its battle-police removed—would have melted away. Yet the militias held the line, though God knows they won very few victories, and even individual desertions were not common. In four or five months in the P.O.U.M. militia I only heard of four men deserting, and two of those were fairly certainly spies who had enlisted to obtain information. At the beginning the apparent chaos, the general lack of training, the fact that you often had to argue for five minutes before you could get an order obeyed, appalled and infuriated me. I had British Army ideas, and certainly the Spanish militias were very unlike the British Army. But considering the circumstances they were better troops than one had any right to expect.

9 Meanwhile, firewood—always firewood. Throughout that period there is probably no entry in my diary that does not mention firewood, or rather the lack of it. We were between two and three thousand feet above sea-level, it was mid-winter and the cold was unspeakable. The temperature was not exceptionally low, on many nights it did not even freeze, and the wintry sun often shone for an hour in the middle of the day; but even if it was not really cold, I assure you that it seemed so. Sometimes there were shrieking winds that tore your cap off and twisted your hair in all directions, sometimes there were mists that poured into the trench like a liquid and seemed to penetrate your bones; frequently it rained, and even a quarter of an hour's rain was enough to make conditions intolerable. The thin skin of earth over the limestone turned promptly into a slippery grease, and as you were always walking on a slope it was impossible to keep your footing. On dark nights I have often fallen half a dozen times in twenty yards; and this was dangerous, because it meant that the lock of one's rifle became jammed with mud. For days together clothes, boots, blankets, and rifles were more or less coated with mud. I had brought as many thick clothes as I could carry, but many of the men were terribly underclad. For the whole garrison, about a hundred men, there were only twelve great-coats, which had to be handed from sentry to sentry, and most of the men had only one blanket. One icy night I made a list in my diary of the clothes I was wearing. It is of some interest as showing the amount of clothes the human body can carry. I was wearing a thick vest and pants, a flannel shirt, two pull-overs, a woollen jacket, a pigskin jacket, corduroy breeches, puttees, thick socks, boots, a stout trench-coat, a muffler, lined leather gloves, and a woollen cap. Nevertheless I was shivering like a jelly. But I admit I am unusually sensitive to cold.

10 Firewood was the one thing that really mattered. The point about the firewood was that there was practically no firewood to be had. Our miserable mountain had not even at its best much vegetation, and for months it had been ranged over by freezing militiamen, with the result that everything thicker

than one's finger had long since been burnt. When we were not eating, sleeping, on guard or on fatigue-duty we were in the valley behind the position, scrounging for fuel. All my memories of that time are memories of scrambling up and down the almost perpendicular slopes, over the jagged limestone that knocked one's boots to pieces, pouncing eagerly on tiny twigs of wood. Three people searching for a couple of hours could collect enough fuel to keep the dug-out fire alight for about an hour. The eagerness of our search for firewood turned us all into botanists. We classified according to their burning qualities every plant that grew on the mountain-side; the various heaths and grasses that were good to start a fire with but burnt out in a few minutes, the wild rosemary and the tiny whin bushes that would burn when the fire was well alight, the stunted oak tree, smaller than a gooseberry bush, that was practically unburnable. There was a kind of dried-up reed that was very good for starting fires with, but these grew only on the hill-top to the left of the position, and you had to go under fire to get them. If the Fascist machine-gunners saw you they gave you a drum of ammunition all to yourself. Generally their aim was high and the bullets sang overhead like birds, but sometimes they crackled and chipped the limestone uncomfortably close, whereupon you flung yourself on your face. You went on gathering reeds, however; nothing mattered in comparison with firewood.

11   Beside the cold the other discomforts seemed petty. Of course all of us were permanently dirty. Our water, like our food, came on mule-back from Alcubierre, and each man's share worked out at about a quart a day. It was beastly water, hardly more transparent than milk. Theoretically it was for drinking only, but I always stole a pannikinful for washing in the mornings. I used to wash one day and shave the next; there was never enough water for both. The position stank abominably, and outside the little enclosure of the barricade there was excrement everywhere. Some of the militiamen habitually defecated in the trench, a disgusting thing when one had to walk round it in the darkness. But the dirt never worried me. Dirt is a thing people make too much fuss about. It is astonishing how quickly you get used to doing without a handkerchief and to eating out of the tin pannikin in which you also wash. Nor was sleeping in one's clothes any hardship after a day or two. It was of course impossible to take one's clothes and especially one's boots off at night; one had to be ready to turn out instantly in case of an attack. In eighty nights I only took my clothes off three times, though I did occasionally manage to get them off in the daytime. It was too cold for lice as yet, but rats and mice abounded. It is often said that you don't find rats and mice in the same place, but you do when there is enough food for them.

12   In other ways we were not badly off. The food was good enough and there was plenty of wine. Cigarettes were still being issued at the rate of a packet a day, matches were issued every other day, and there was even an issue of candles. They were very thin candles, like those on a Christmas cake, and were popularly supposed to have been looted from churches. Every dug-out was issued daily with three inches of candle, which would burn for about twenty minutes.

At that time it was still possible to buy candles, and I had brought several pounds of them with me. Later on the famine of matches and candles made life a misery. You do not realize the importance of these things until you lack them. In a night-alarm, for instance, when everyone in the dug-out is scrambling for his rifle and treading on everybody else's face, being able to strike a light may make the difference between life and death. Every militiaman possessed a tinder-lighter and several yards of yellow wick. Next to his rifle it was his most important possession. The tinder-lighters had the great advantage that they could be struck in a wind, but they would only smoulder, so that they were no use for lighting a fire. When the match famine was at its worst our only way of producing a flame was to pull the bullet out of a cartridge and touch the cordite off with a tinder-lighter.

13   It was an extraordinary life that we were living—an extraordinary way to be at war, if you could call it war. The whole militia chafed against the inaction and clamoured constantly to know why we were not allowed to attack. But it was perfectly obvious that there would be no battle for a long while yet, unless the enemy started it. Georges Kopp, on his periodical tours of inspection, was quite frank with us. "This is not a war," he used to say, "it is a comic opera with an occasional death." As a matter of fact the stagnation on the Aragon front had political causes of which I knew nothing at that time; but the purely military difficulties—quite apart from the lack of reserves of men—were obvious to anybody.

14   To begin with, there was the nature of the country. The front line, ours and the Fascists', lay in positions of immense natural strength, which as a rule could only be approached from one side. Provided a few trenches have been dug, such places cannot be taken by infantry, except in overwhelming numbers. In our own position or most of those round us a dozen men with two machine-guns could have held off a battalion. Perched on the hill-tops as we were, we should have made lovely marks for artillery; but there was no artillery. Sometimes I used to gaze round the landscape and long—oh, how passionately!—for a couple of batteries of guns. One could have destroyed the enemy positions one after another as easily as smashing nuts with a hammer. But on our side the guns simply did not exist. The Fascists did occasionally manage to bring a gun or two from Zaragoza and fire a very few shells, so few that they never even found the range and the shells plunged harmlessly into the empty ravines. Against machine-guns and without artillery there are only three things you can do: dig yourself in at a safe distance—four hundred yards, say—advance across the open and be massacred, or make small-scale night-attacks that will not alter the general situation. Practically the alternatives are stagnation or suicide.

15   And beyond this there was the complete lack of war materials of every description. It needs an effort to realize how badly the militias were armed at this time. Any public school O.T.C. in England is far more like a modern army than we were. The badness of our weapons was so astonishing that it is worth recording in detail.

16   For this sector of the front the entire artillery consisted of four trench-mortars with *fifteen rounds* for each gun. Of course they were far too precious to

be fired and the mortars were kept in Alcubierre. There were machine-guns at the rate of approximately one to fifty men; they were oldish guns, but fairly accurate up to three or four hundred yards. Beyond this we had only rifles, and the majority of the rifles were scrap-iron. There were three types of rifle in use. The first was the long Mauser. These were seldom less than twenty years old, their sights were about as much use as a broken speedometer, and in most of them the rifling was hopelessly corroded; about one rifle in ten was not bad, however. Then there was the short Mauser, or *mousqueton*, really a cavalry weapon. These were more popular than the others because they were lighter to carry and less nuisance in a trench, also because they were comparatively new and looked efficient. Actually they were almost useless. They were made out of reassembled parts, no bolt belonged to its rifle, and three-quarters of them could be counted on to jam after five shots. There were also a few Winchester rifles. These were nice to shoot with, but they were wildly inaccurate, and as their cartridges had no clips they could only be fired one shot at a time. Ammunition was so scarce that each man entering the line was only issued with fifty rounds, and most of it was exceedingly bad. The Spanish-made cartridges were all refills and would jam even the best rifles. The Mexican cartridges were better and were therefore reserved for the machine-guns. Best of all was the German-made ammunition, but as this came only from prisoners and deserters there was not much of it. I always kept a clip of German or Mexican ammunition in my pocket for use in an emergency. But in practice when the emergency came I seldom fired my rifle; I was too frightened of the beastly thing jamming and too anxious to reserve at any rate one round that would go off.

17   We had no tin hats, no bayonets, hardly any revolvers or pistols, and not more than one bomb between five or ten men. The bomb in use at this time was a frightful object known as the 'F.A.I. bomb,' it having been produced by the Anarchists in the early days of the war. It was on the principle of a Mills bomb, but the lever was held down not by a pin but a piece of tape. You broke the tape and then got rid of the bomb with the utmost possible speed. It was said of these bombs that they were 'impartial'; they killed the man they were thrown at and the man who threw them. There were several other types, even more primitive but probably a little less dangerous—to the thrower, I mean. It was not till late March that I saw a bomb worth throwing.

18   And apart from weapons there was a shortage of all the minor necessities of war. We had no maps or charts, for instance. Spain has never been fully surveyed, and the only detailed maps of this area were the old military ones, which were almost all in the possession of the Fascists. We had no range-finders, no telescopes, no periscopes, no field-glasses except a few privately-owned pairs, no flares or Very lights, no wire-cutters, no armourers' tools, hardly even any cleaning materials. The Spaniards seemed never to have heard of a pull-through and looked on in surprise when I constructed one. When you wanted your rifle cleaned you took it to the sergeant, who possessed a long brass ramrod which was invariably bent and therefore scratched the rifling. There was not even any gun oil. You greased your rifle with olive oil, when you could get hold of it; at

different times I have greased mine with vaseline, with cold cream, and even with bacon-fat. Moreover, there were no lanterns or electric torches—at this time there was not, I believe, such a thing as an electric torch throughout the whole of our sector of the front, and you could not buy one nearer than Barcelona, and only with difficulty even there.

19   As time went on, and the desultory rifle-fire rattled among the hills, I began to wonder with increasing scepticism whether anything would ever happen to bring a bit of life, or rather a bit of death, into this cock-eyed war. It was pneumonia that we were fighting against, not against men. When the trenches are more than five hundred yards apart no one gets hit except by accident. Of course there were casualties, but the majority of them were self-inflicted. If I remember rightly, the first five men I saw wounded in Spain were all wounded by our own weapons—I don't mean intentionally, but owing to accident or carelessness. Our worn-out rifles were a danger in themselves. Some of them had a nasty trick of going off if the butt was tapped on the ground; I saw a man shoot himself through the hand owing to this. And in the darkness the raw recruits were always firing at one another. One evening when it was barely even dusk a sentry let fly at me from a distance of twenty yards; but he missed me by a yard—goodness knows how many times the Spanish standard of marksmanship has saved my life. Another time I had gone out on patrol in the mist and had carefully warned the guard commander beforehand. But in coming back I stumbled against a bush, the startled sentry called out that the Fascists were coming, and I had the pleasure of hearing the guard commander order everyone to open rapid fire in my direction. Of course I lay down and the bullets went harmlessly over me. Nothing will convince a Spaniard, at least a young Spaniard, that fire-arms are dangerous. Once, rather later than this, I was photographing some machine-gunners with their gun, which was pointed directly towards me.

20   "Don't fire," I said half-jokingly as I focused the camera.

21   "Oh, no, we won't fire."

22   The next moment there was a frightful roar and a stream of bullets tore past my face so close that my cheek was stung by grains of cordite. It was unintentional, but the machine-gunners considered it a great joke. Yet only a few days earlier they had seen a mule-driver accidentally shot by a political delegate who was playing the fool with an automatic pistol and had put five bullets in the mule-driver's lungs.

23   The difficult passwords which the army was using at this time were a minor source of danger. They were those tiresome double passwords in which one word has to be answered by another. Usually they were of an elevating and revolutionary nature, such as *Cultura—progreso*, or *Seremos—invencibles*, and it was often impossible to get illiterate sentries to remember these highfalutin words. One night, I remember, the password was *Cataluña—heroica*, and a moon-faced peasant lad named Jaime Domenech approached me, greatly puzzled, and asked me to explain.

24   "Heroica—what does heroica mean?"

How does this photograph of a crowd of soldiers from the Iberian Anarchist Federation in Barcelona during the Spanish Civil War convey the mood of popular revolt against the fascists that George Orwell describes?

25   I told him that it meant the same as valiente. A little while later he was stumbling up the trench in the darkness, and the sentry challenged him:

26   "Alto! Cataluña!"

27   "Valiente!" yelled Jaime, certain that he was saying the right thing.

28   Bang!

29   However, the sentry missed him. In this war everyone always did miss everyone else, when it was humanly possible.

MEANING

1. What part did Orwell play in the fighting on the Aragon front during the Spanish Civil War?

2. What was the difference between the way in which Orwell's military unit arrived at and carried out military decisions and the way in which decisions are usually made in traditional armies?

3. What ordinary things took on extraordinary importance in combat?

4. What picture do you get of Orwell's fellow soldiers, including their age, training, and discipline?

TECHNIQUE

1. In what way does Orwell's essay develop his first sentence as an implicit classification?

2. How does Orwell extend his classification to include the weaponry the soldiers possessed? What point is he making?

3. **Other Patterns.** How is Orwell's account framed as a **narrative** that incorporates details that illustrate the distinctions he draws?

LANGUAGE

1. How does Orwell's choice of similes and metaphors put the reader into the scene?

2. What is Orwell's attitude toward what he **describes**, and how is this reflected in specific words, phrases, and dialogue?

3. If you do not know the meaning of the following words, look them up: *stupendous* (4), *ravines* (5), *wretched* (6), *hierarchy* (7), *garrison* (9), *pannikinful* (11), *stagnation* (14), *scepticism* (19), *highfalutin* (23).

SUGGESTIONS FOR WRITING

1. **Critical Writing.** If you were a soldier, would you want to belong to an army in which decisions were arrived at by collective agreement or to a traditional army based on following the orders of higher-ranking officers? Why?

2. Research the history of the Spanish Civil War, and write an essay explaining the causes that Orwell identified with.

3. How did the passwords and their accompanying sentiments **contrast** with the reality of Orwell's experience?

4. **Thematic Links.** How do the accounts by Orwell and Yossi Ghinsberg in "Jungle" (Chapter 11, "Problem Solving") illustrate the importance of ingenuity in survival?

Polite Lies

Kyoko Mori (b. 1957) grew up in Japan and left for the United States when she was twenty. Her discomfort at having to modify her behavior and ways of speaking when she periodically returns to Japan underlies her book *Polite Lies: On Being a Woman Caught Between Cultures* (1997), in which the following selection first appeared. Mori's memoir *The Dream of Water* (1995) describes her difficult childhood experiences and helps to explain her sensitivity to young adults, both as a teacher of creative writing at St. Norbert's College in Wisconsin and in her fiction, including *Stone Field, True Arrow* (2000).

BEFORE YOU READ

How, and in what circumstances, does politeness serve as a way of concealing the truth?

■ ■ ▨

1   I don't like to go to Japan because I find it exhausting to speak Japanese all day, every day. What I am afraid of is the language, not the place. Even in Green Bay, when someone insists on speaking to me in Japanese, I clam up after a few words of general greetings, unable to go on.

2   I can only fall silent because thirty seconds into the conversation, I have already failed at an important task: while I was bowing and saying hello, I was supposed to have been calculating the other person's age, rank, and position in order to determine how polite I should be for the rest of the conversation. In Japanese conversations, the two speakers are almost never on an equal footing: one is senior to the other in age, experience, or rank. Various levels of politeness and formality are required according to these differences: it is rude to be too familiar, but people are equally offended if you are too formal, sounding snobbish and untrusting. Gender is as important as rank. Men and women practically speak different languages; women's language is much more indirect and formal than men's. There are words and phrases that women are never supposed to say, even though they are not crude or obscene. Only a man can say *damare* (shut up). No matter how angry she is, a woman must say, *shizukani* (quiet).

3   Until you can find the correct level of politeness, you can't go on with the conversation: you won't even be able to address the other person properly. There are so many Japanese words for the pronoun *you*. *Anata* is a polite but intimate *you* a woman would use to address her husband, lover, or a very close woman friend, while a man would say *kimi*, which is informal, or *omae*, which is so informal that a man would say this word only to a family member; *otaku* is informal but impersonal, so it should be used with friends rather than family.

Though there are these various forms of *you*, most people address each other in the third person—it is offensive to call someone *you* directly. To a woman named Hanako Maeda, you don't say, "Would you like to go out for lunch?" You say, "Would Maeda-san (Miss Maeda) like to go out for lunch?" But if you had known Hanako for a while, maybe you should call her Hanako-san instead of Maeda-san, especially if you are also a woman and not too much younger than she. Otherwise, she might think that you are too formal and unfriendly. The word for *lunch* also varies: *hirumeshi* is another casual word only a man is allowed to say, *hirugohan* is informal but polite enough for friends, *ohirugohan* is a little more polite, *chushoku* is formal and businesslike, and *gochushoku* is the most formal and businesslike.

4   All these rules mean that before you can get on with any conversation beyond the initial greetings, you have to agree on your relationship—which one of you is superior, how close you expect to be, who makes the decisions and who defers. So why even talk, I always wonder. The conversation that follows the mutual sizing-up can only be an empty ritual, a careful enactment of our differences rather than a chance to get to know each other or to exchange ideas.

5   Talking seems especially futile when I have to address a man in Japanese. Every word I say forces me to be elaborately polite, indirect, submissive, and unassertive. There is no way I can sound intelligent, clearheaded, or decisive. But if I did not speak a "proper" feminine language, I would sound stupid in another way—like someone who is uneducated, insensitive, and rude, and therefore cannot be taken seriously. I never speak Japanese with the Japanese man who teaches physics at the college where I teach English. We are colleagues, meant to be equals. The language I use should not automatically define me as second best.

6   Meeting Japanese-speaking people in the States makes me nervous for another reason. I have nothing in common with these people except that we speak Japanese. Our meeting seems random and artificial, and I can't get over the oddness of addressing a total stranger in Japanese. In the twenty years I lived in Japan, I rarely had a conversation with someone I didn't already know. The only exception was the first day of school in seventh grade, when none of us knew one another, or when I was introduced to my friends' parents. Talking to clerks at stores scarcely counts. I never chatted with people I was doing business with. This is not to say that I led a particularly sheltered life. My experience was typical of anyone—male or female—growing up in Japan.

7   In Japan, whether you are a child or an adult, ninety-five percent of the people you talk to are your family, relatives, old friends, neighbors, and people you work or go to school with every day. The only new people you meet are connected to these people you already know—friends of friends, new spouses of your relatives—and you are introduced to them formally. You don't all of a sudden meet someone new. My friends and I were taught that no "nice" girl would talk to strangers on trains or at public places. It was bad manners to gab with shopkeepers or with repair people, being too familiar and keeping them from

work. While American children are cautioned not to speak with strangers for reasons of safety, we were taught not to do so because it wasn't "nice." Even the most rebellious of us obeyed. We had no language in which we could address a stranger even if we had wanted to.

8   Traveling in Japan or simply taking the commuter train in Kobe now, I notice the silence around me. It seems oppressive that you cannot talk to someone who is looking at your favorite painting at a museum or sitting next to you on the train, reading a book that you finished only last week. In Japan, you can't even stop strangers and ask for simple directions when you are lost. If you get lost, you look for a policeman, who will help you because that is part of his job.

9   A Japanese friend and I got lost in Yokohama one night after we came out of a restaurant. We were looking for the train station and had no idea where it was, but my friend said, "Well, we must be heading in the right direction, since most people seem to be walking that way. It's late now. They must be going back to the station, too." After about ten minutes—with no train station in sight yet—my friend said that if she had been lost in New York or Paris, she would have asked one of the people we were following. But in her own country, in her own language, it was unthinkable to approach a stranger.

10   For her, asking was not an option. That's different from when people in the Midwest choose not to stop at a gas station for directions or flag down a store clerk to locate some item on the shelves. Midwestern people don't like to ask because they don't want to call attention to themselves by appearing stupid and helpless. Refusing to ask is a matter of pride and self-reliance—a matter of choice. Even the people who pride themselves on never asking know that help is readily available. In Japan, approaching a stranger means breaking an unspoken rule of public conduct.

11   The Japanese code of silence in public places does offer a certain kind of protection. In Japan, everyone is shielded from unwanted intrusion or attention, and that isn't entirely bad. In public places in the States, we all wish, from time to time, that people would go about their business in silence and leave us alone. Just the other day in the weight room of the YMCA, a young man I had never met before told me that he had been working out for the last two months and gained fifteen pounds. "I've always been too thin," he explained. "I want to gain twenty more pounds, and I'm going to put it all up here." We were sitting side by side on different machines. He indicated his shoulders and chest by patting them with his hand. "That's nice," I said, noncommittal but polite. "Of course," he continued, "I couldn't help putting some of the new weight around my waist, too." To my embarrassment, he lifted his shirt and pointed at his stomach. "Listen," I told him. "You don't have to show it to me or anything." I got up from my machine even though I wasn't finished. Still, I felt obligated to say, "Have a nice workout," as I walked away.

12   I don't appreciate discussing a complete stranger's weight gain and being shown his stomach, and it's true that bizarre conversations like that would never happen in a Japanese gym. Maybe there is comfort in knowing that you will never

have to talk to strangers—that you can live your whole life surrounded by friends and family who will understand what you mean without your saying it. Silence can be a sign of harmony among close friends or family, but silent harmony doesn't help people who disagree or don't fit in. On crowded trains in Kobe or Tokyo, where people won't even make eye contact with strangers, much less talk to them, I feel as though each one of us were sealed inside an invisible capsule, unable to breathe or speak out. It is just like my old dream of being stuck inside a spaceship orbiting the earth. I am alarmed by how lonely I feel—and by how quietly content everyone else seems to be.

■ ■ ▨

MEANING

1. Why is having to speak Japanese on her return to Japan a stressful experience for Mori? What sorts of things does a Japanese speaker evaluate at the start of a conversation?

2. In what way do constraints governing the way in which men and women speak illustrate cultural distinctions between them?

3. How do conversations in Japan differ from those in the United States? What aspects of American conversations does Mori find embarrassing?

4. Why are the protocols for conversations in business environments based more on form than on content?

TECHNIQUE

1. How does Mori's analysis emphasize the different levels of politeness that are negotiated during conversations in Japan?

2. Why does Mori show how the Japanese "code of silence" contributes to a sense of private space?

3. *Other Patterns.* How does Mori use **narrative** vignettes to express her discomfort with both Japanese formality and American informality?

LANGUAGE

1. How are the gradations in permissible styles of address made more comprehensible when we see the original Japanese terms (in paragraph 3)?

2. How does Mori use her recurrent dream as a metaphor for her return trips to Japan?

3. If you don't know the meaning of the following words, look them up: *futile* (5), *oppressive* (8), *option* (10), *noncommittal* (11).

SUGGESTIONS FOR WRITING

1. Are people more or less polite when they are part of a group of strangers who are forced to be together, as in an elevator or on a crowded bus or train? Why or why not?

2. **Critical Writing.** Is Mori's real dilemma that she is a Japanese expatriate living in America who is now between two cultures and at home in neither? Why or why not?

3. Do you prefer people who tell you what they really think or those who are polite but leave you wondering how they really feel? Use a **comparison** format for your answer.

4. **Thematic Links.** What factors govern the different levels of formality and informality in language in the accounts by Mori and Amy Tan in "Mother Tongue"?

SEMBENE OUSMANE

Her Three Days

The renowned filmmaker and novelist Sembene Ousmane (1923–2007) grew up in Senegal, moved to Dakar, and served in the French Army during World War II. Following the war, he became a union organizer, wrote novels, and studied at the Moscow Film School. Films that he directed based on his novels, such as *Zala* (1973), won international recognition. Ousmane was also a prolific writer of short fiction. In the following story, taken from his collection *Tribal Scars* (1974), we meet a woman in Mali whose uncertain position as the third wife of an inconsiderate husband displays Ousmane's empathy and narrative skill.

BEFORE YOU READ

What do you know about polygamy?

■ ■ ▨

1 She raised her haggard face, and her far-away look ranged beyond the muddle of roofs, some tiled, others of thatch or galvanized-iron; the wide fronds of the twin coconut-palms were swaying slowly in the breeze, and in her mind she could hear their faint rustling. Noumbe was thinking of "her three days." Three days for her alone, when she would have her husband Mustapha to herself... It was a long time since she had felt such emotion. To have Mustapha! The thought comforted her. She had heart trouble and still felt some pain, but she had been dosing herself for the past two days, taking more medicine than was prescribed. It was a nice syrup that just slipped down, and she felt the beneficial effects at once. She blinked; her eyes were like two worn buttonholes, with lashes that were like frayed thread, in little clusters of fives and threes; the whites were the colour of old ivory.

2 "What's the matter, Noumbe?" asked Aida, her next-door neighbour, who was sitting at the door of her room.

3 "Nothing," she answered, and went on cutting up the slice of raw meat, helped by her youngest daughter.

4 "Ah, it's your three days," exclaimed Aida, whose words held a meaning that she could not elaborate on while the little girl was present. She went on: "You're looking fine enough to prevent a holy man from saying his prayers properly!"

5 "Aida, be careful what you say," she protested, a little annoyed.

6 But it was true; Noumbe had plaited her hair and put henna on her hands and feet. And that morning she had got the children up early to give her room a thorough clean. She was not old, but one pregnancy after another—and she had five children—and her heart trouble had aged her before her time.

7 "Go and ask Laity to give you five francs' worth of salt and twenty francs' worth of oil," Noumbe said to the girl. "Tell him I sent you. I'll pay for them as soon as your father is here, at midday." She looked disapprovingly at the cut-up meat in the bottom of the bowl.

8   The child went off with the empty bottle and Noumbe got to her feet. She was thin and of average height. She went into her one-room shack, which was sparsely furnished; there was a bed with a white cover, and in one corner stood a table with pieces of china on display. The walls were covered with enlargements and photos of friends and strangers framed in passe-partout.

9   When she came out again she took the Moorish stove and set about lighting it.

10   Her daughter had returned from her errand.

11   "He gave them to you?" asked Noumbe.

12   "Yes, mother."

13   A woman came across the compound to her. "Noumbe, I can see that you're preparing a delicious dish."

14   "Yes," she replied. "It's my three days. I want to revive the feasts of the old days, so that his palate will retain the taste of the dish for many moons, and he'll forget the cooking of his other wives."

15   "Ah-ha! So that his palate is eager for dishes to come," said the woman, who was having a good look at the ingredients.

16   "I'm feeling in good form," said Noumbe, with some pride in her voice. She grasped the woman's hand and passed it over her loins.

17   "*Thieh, souya dome!* I hope you can say the same tomorrow morning . . ."

18   The woman clapped her hands; as if it were a signal or an invitation, other women came across, one with a metal jar, another with a saucepan, which they beat while the woman sang:

> *Sope dousa rafetail,*
> *Sopa nala dousa rafetail*
> *Sa yahi n'diguela.*
> (Worship of you is not for your beauty,
> I worship you not for your beauty
> But for your backbone.)

19   In a few moments, they improvised a wild dance to this chorus. At the end, panting and perspiring, they burst out laughing. Then one of them stepped into Noumbe's room and called the others.

20   "Let's take away the bed! Because tonight they'll wreck it!"

21   "She's right. Tomorrow this room will be . . ."

22   Each woman contributed an earthy comment which set them all laughing hilariously. Then they remembered they had work to do, and brought their amusement to an end; each went back to her family occupations.

23   Noumbe had joined in the laughter; she knew this boisterous "ragging" was the custom in the compound. No one escaped it. Besides, she was an exceptional case, as they all knew. She had a heart condition and her husband had quite openly neglected her. Mustapha had not been to see her for a fortnight. All this time she had been hoping that he would come, if only for a moment. When she went to the clinic for mothers and children she compelled her youngest daughter to stay at home, so that—thus did her mind work—if her husband turned up the child could detain him until she returned. She ought to

have gone to the clinic again this day, but she had spent what little money she possessed on preparing for Mustapha. She did not want her husband to esteem her less than his other wives, or to think her meaner. She did not neglect her duty as a mother, but her wifely duty came first—at certain times.

24   She imagined what the next three days would be like; already her "three days" filled her whole horizon. She forgot her illness and her baby's ailments. She had thought about these three days in a thousand different ways. Mustapha would not leave before the Monday morning. In her mind she could see Mustapha and his henchmen crowding into her room, and could hear their suggestive jokes. "If she had been a perfect wife . . ." She laughed to herself. "Why shouldn't it always be like that for every woman—to have a husband of one's own?" She wondered why not.

25   The morning passed at its usual pace, the shadows of the coconut-palms and the people growing steadily shorter. As midday approached, the housewives busied themselves with the meal. In the compound each one stood near her door, ready to welcome her man. The kids were playing around, and their mothers' calls to them crossed in the air. Noumbe gave her children a quick meal and sent them out again. She sat waiting for Mustapha to arrive at any moment . . . he wouldn't be much longer now.

26   An hour passed, and the men began going back to work. Soon the compound was empty of the male element; the women, after a long siesta, joined one another under the coconut-palms and the sounds of their gossiping gradually increased.

27   Noumbe, weary of waiting, had finally given up keeping a lookout. Dressed in her mauve velvet, she had been on the watch since before midday. She had eaten no solid food, consoling herself with the thought that Mustapha would appear at any moment. Now she fought back the pangs of hunger by telling herself that in the past Mustapha had a habit of arriving late. In those days, this lateness was pleasant. Without admitting it to herself, those moments (which had hung terribly heavy) had been very sweet; they prolonged the sensual pleasure of anticipation. Although those minutes had been sometimes shot through with doubts and fears (often, very often, the thought of her coming disgrace had assailed her; for Mustapha, who had taken two wives before her, had just married another), they had not been too hard to bear. She realized that those demanding minutes were the price she had to pay for Mustapha's presence. Then she began to reckon up the score, in small ways, against the *veudieux*, the other wives. One washed his *boubous*[1] when it was another wife's turn, or kept him long into the night; another sometimes held him in her embrace a whole day, knowing quite well that she was preventing Mustapha from carrying out his marital duty elsewhere.

28   She sulked as she waited; Mustapha had not been near her for a fortnight. All these bitter thoughts brought her up against reality: four months ago Mustapha had married a younger woman. This sudden realization of the facts sent a pain to her heart, a pain of anguish. The additional pain did not prevent

---

[1] *boubous*: a body-length embroidered gown.

her heart from functioning normally, rather was it like a sick person whose sleep banishes pain but who once awake again finds his suffering is as bad as ever, and pays for the relief by a redoubling of pain.

29   She took three spoonfuls of her medicine instead of the two prescribed, and felt a little better in herself.

30   She called her youngest daughter. "Tell Mactar I want him."

31   The girl ran off and soon returned with her eldest brother.

32   "Go and fetch your father," Noumbe told him.

33   "Where, mother?"

34   "Where? Oh, on the main square or at one of your other mothers'."

35   "But I've been to the main square already, and he wasn't there."

36   "Well, go and have another look. Perhaps he's there now."

37   The boy looked up at his mother, then dropped his head again and reluctantly turned to go.

38   "When your father has finished eating, I'll give you what's left. It's meat. Now be quick, Mactar."

39   It was scorching hot and the clouds were riding high. Mactar was back after an hour. He had not found his father. Noumbe went and joined the group of women. They were chattering about this and that; one of them asked (just for the sake of asking), "Noumbe, has your uncle (darling) arrived?" "Not yet," she replied, then hastened to add, "Oh, he won't be long now. He knows it's my three days." She deliberately changed the conversation in order to avoid a long discussion about the other three wives. But all the time she was longing to go and find Mustapha. She was being robbed of her three days. And the other wives knew it. Her hours alone with Mustapha were being snatched from her. The thought of his being with one of the other wives, who was feeding him and opening his waistcloth when she ought to be doing all that, who was enjoying those hours which were hers by right, so numbed Noumbe that it was impossible for her to react. The idea that Mustapha might have been admitted to hospital or taken to a police station never entered her head.

40   She knew how to make tasty little dishes for Mustapha which cost him nothing. She never asked him for money. Indeed, hadn't she got herself into debt so that he would be more comfortable and have better meals at her place? And in the past, when Mustapha sometimes arrived unexpectedly—this was soon after he had married her—hadn't she hastened to make succulent dishes for him? All her friends knew this.

41   A comforting thought coursed through her and sent these aggressive and vindictive reflections to sleep. She told herself that Mustapha was bound to come to her this evening. The certainty of his presence stripped her mind of the too cruel thought that the time of her disfavour was approaching; this thought had been as much a burden to her as a heavy weight dragging a drowning man to the bottom. When all the bad, unfavourable thoughts besetting her had been dispersed, like piles of rubbish on waste land swept by a flood, the future seemed brighter, and she joined in the conversation of the women with childish enthusiasm, unable to hide her pleasure and her hopes. It was like something in a parcel; questioning

eyes wondered what was inside, but she alone knew and enjoyed the secret, drawing an agreeable strength from it. She took an active part in the talking and brought her wit into play. All this vivacity sprang from the joyful conviction that Mustapha would arrive this evening very hungry and be hers alone.

42   In the far distance, high above the tree-tops, a long trail of dark-grey clouds tinged with red was hiding the sun. The time for the *tacousane*, the afternoon prayer, was drawing near. One by one, the women withdrew to their rooms, and the shadows of the trees grew longer, wider and darker.

43   Night fell; a dark, starry night.

44   Noumbe cooked some rice for the children. They clamoured in vain for some of the meat. Noumbe was stern and unyielding: "The meat is for your father. He didn't eat at midday." When she had fed the children, she washed herself again to get rid of the smell of cooking and touched up her toilette, rubbing oil on her hands, feet and legs to make the henna more brilliant. She intended to remain by her door, and sat down on the bench; the incense smelt strongly, filling the whole room. She was facing the entrance to the compound and could see the other women's husbands coming in.

45   But for her there was no one.

46   She began to feel tired again. Her heart was troubling her, and she had a fit of coughing. Her inside seemed to be on fire. Knowing that she would not be going to the dispensary during her "three days," in order to economize, she went and got some wood-ash which she mixed with water and drank. It did not taste very nice, but it would make the medicine last longer, and the drink checked and soothed the burning within her for a while. She was tormenting herself with the thoughts passing through her mind. Where can he be? With the first wife? No, she's quite old. The second then? Everyone knew that she was out of favour with Mustapha. The third wife was herself. So he must be with the fourth. There were puckers of uncertainty and doubt in the answers she gave herself. She kept putting back the time to go to bed, like a lover who does not give up waiting when the time of the rendezvous is long past, but with an absurd and stupid hope waits still longer, self-torture and the heavy minutes chaining him to the spot. At each step Noumbe took, she stopped and mentally explored the town, prying into each house inhabited by one of the other wives. Eventually she went indoors.

47   So that she would not be caught unawares by Mustapha nor lose the advantages which her make-up and good clothes gave her, she lay down on the bed fully dressed and alert. She had turned down the lamp as far as possible, so the room was dimly lit. But she fell asleep despite exerting great strength of mind to remain awake and saying repeatedly to herself, "I shall wait for him." To make sure that she would be standing there expectantly when he crossed the threshold, she had bolted the door. Thus she would be the devoted wife, always ready to serve her husband, having got up at once and appearing as elegant as if it were broad daylight. She had even thought of making a gesture as she stood there, of passing her hands casually over her hips so that Mustapha would hear the clinking of the beads she had strung round her waist and be incited to look at her from head to foot.

48   Morning came, but there was no Mustapha.

49   When the children awoke they asked if their father had come. The oldest of them, Mactar, a promising lad, was quick to spot that his mother had not made the bed, that the bowl containing the stew was still in the same place, by a dish of rice, and the loaf of bread on the table was untouched. The children got a taste of their mother's anger. The youngest, Amadou, took a long time over dressing. Noumbe hurried them up and sent the youngest girl to Laity's to buy five francs' worth of ground coffee. The children's breakfast was warmed-up rice with a meagre sprinkling of gravy from the previous day's stew. Then she gave them their wings, as the saying goes, letting them all out except the youngest daughter. Noumbe inspected the bottle of medicine and saw that she had taken a lot of it; there were only three spoonfuls left. She gave herself half a spoonful and made up for the rest with her mixture of ashes and water. After that she felt calmer.

50   "Why, Noumbe, you must have got up bright and early this morning, to be so dressed up. Are you going off on a long journey?"

51   It was Aida, her next-door neighbour, who was surprised to see her dressed in such a manner, especially for a woman who was having "her three days." Then Aida realized what had happened and tried to rectify her mistake.

52   "Oh, I see he hasn't come yet. They're all the same, these men!"

53   "He'll be here this morning, Aida." Noumbe bridled, ready to defend her man. But it was rather her own worth she was defending, wanting to conceal what an awful time she had spent. It had been a broken night's sleep, listening to harmless sounds which she had taken for Mustapha's footsteps, and this had left its mark on her already haggard face.

54   "I'm sure he will! I'm sure he will!" exclaimed Aida, well aware of this comedy that all the women played in turn.

55   "Mustapha is such a kind man, and so noble in his attitude," added another woman, rubbing it in.

56   "If he weren't, he wouldn't be my master," said Noumbe, feeling flattered by this description of Mustapha.

57   The news soon spread round the compound that Mustapha had slept elsewhere during Noumbe's three days. The other women pitied her. It was against all the rules for Mustapha to spend a night elsewhere. Polygamy had its laws, which should be respected. A sense of decency and common dignity restrained a wife from keeping the husband day and night when his whole person and everything connected with him belonged to another wife during "her three days." The game, however, was not without its underhand tricks that one wife played on another; for instance, to wear out the man and hand him over when he was incapable of performing his conjugal duties. When women criticized the practice of polygamy they always found that the wives were to blame, especially those who openly dared to play a dirty trick. The man was whitewashed. He was a weakling who always ended by falling into the enticing traps set for him by woman. Satisfied with this conclusion, Noumbe's neighbours made common cause with her and turned to abusing Mustapha's fourth wife.

58   Noumbe made some coffee—she never had any herself, because of her heart. She consoled herself with the thought that Mustapha would find more things at her place. The bread had gone stale; she would buy some more when he arrived.

59   The hours dragged by again, long hours of waiting which became harder to bear as the day progressed. She wished she knew where he was . . . The thought obsessed her, and her eyes became glazed and searching. Every time she heard a man's voice she straightened up quickly. Her heart was paining her more and more, but the physical pain was separate from the mental one; they never came together, alternating in a way that reminded her of the acrobatic feat of a man riding two speeding horses.

60   At about four o'clock Noumbe was surprised to see Mustapha's second wife appear at the door. She had come to see if Mustapha was there, knowing that it was Noumbe's three days. She did not tell Noumbe the reason for her wishing to see Mustapha, despite being pressed. So Noumbe concluded that it was largely due to jealousy, and was pleased that the other wife could see how clean and tidy her room was, and what a display of fine things she had, all of which could hardly fail to make the other think that Mustapha had been (and still was) very generous to her, Noumbe. During the rambling conversation her heart thumped ominously, but she bore up and held off taking any medicine.

61   Noumbe remembered only too well that when she was newly married she had usurped the second wife's three days. At that time she had been the youngest wife. Mustapha had not let a day pass without coming to see her. Although not completely certain, she believed she had conceived her third child during this wife's three days. The latter's presence now and remarks that she let drop made Noumbe realize that she was no longer the favourite. This revelation, and the polite, amiable tone and her visitor's eagerness to inquire after her children's health and her own, to praise her superior choice of household utensils, her taste in clothes, the cleanliness of the room and the lingering fragrance of the incense, all this was like a stab in cold blood, a cruel reminder of the perfidy of words and the hypocrisy of rivals; and all part of the world of women. This observation did not get her anywhere, except to arouse a desire to escape from the circle of polygamy and to cause her to ask herself—it was a moment of mental aberration really—"Why do we allow ourselves to be men's playthings?"

62   The other wife complimented her and insisted that Noumbe's children should go and spend a few days with her own children (in this she was sincere). By accepting in principle, Noumbe was weaving her own waist-cloth of hypocrisy. It was all to make the most of herself, to set tongues wagging so that she would lose none of her respectability and rank. The other wife casually added—before she forgot, as she said—that she wanted to see Mustapha, and if mischief-makers told Noumbe that "their" husband had been to see her during Noumbe's three days, Noumbe shouldn't think ill of her, and she would rather have seen him here to tell him what she had to say. To save face, Noumbe dared not ask her when she had last seen Mustapha. The other would have replied with a smile, "The last morning of my three days, of course. I've only come here because it's urgent." And Noumbe would have looked embarrassed and put on an air of innocence. "No, that isn't what I meant. I just wondered if you had happened to meet him by chance."

63   Neither of them would have lost face. It was all that remained to them. They were not lying, to their way of thinking. Each had been desired and

spoilt for a time, then the man, like a gorged vulture, had left them on one side and the venom of chagrin at having been mere playthings had entered their hearts. They quite understood, it was all quite clear to them, that they could sink no lower; so they clung to what was left to them, that is to say, to saving what dignity remained to them by false words and gaining advantages at the expense of the other. They did not indulge in this game for the sake of it. This falseness contained all that remained of the flame of dignity. No one was taken in, certainly not themselves. Each knew that the other was lying, but neither could bring herself to further humiliation, for it would be the final crushing blow.

64   The other wife left. Noumbe almost propelled her to the door, then stood there thoughtful for a few moments. Noumbe understood the reason for the other's visit. She had come to get her own back. Noumbe felt absolutely sure that Mustapha was with his latest wife. The visit meant in fact: "You stole those days from me because I am older than you. Now a younger woman than you is avenging me. Try as you might to make everything nice and pleasant for him, you have to toe the line with the rest of us now, you old carcass. He's slept with someone else—and he will again."

65   The second day passed like the first, but was more dreadful. She ate no proper food, just enough to stave off the pangs of hunger.

66   It was Sunday morning and all the men were at home; they nosed about in one room and another, some of them cradling their youngest in their arms, others playing with the older children. The draught-players had gathered in one place, the card-players in another. There was a friendly atmosphere in the compound, with bursts of happy laughter and sounds of guttural voices, while the women busied themselves with the housework.

67   Aida went to see Noumbe to console her, and said without much conviction, "He'll probably come today. Men always seem to have something to do at the last minute. It's Sunday today, so he'll be here."

68   "Aida, Mustapha doesn't work," Noumbe pointed out, hard-eyed. She gave a cough. "I've been waiting for him now for two days and nights! When it's my three days I think the least he could do is to be here—at night, anyway. I might die . . ."

69   "Do you want me to go and look for him?"

70   "No."

71   She had thought "yes." It was the way in which Aida had made the offer that embarrassed her. Of course she would like her to! Last night, when everyone had gone to bed, she had started out and covered quite some distance before turning back. The flame of her dignity had been fanned on the way. She did not want to abase herself still further by going to claim a man who seemed to have no desire to see her. She had lain awake until dawn, thinking it all over and telling herself that her marriage to Mustapha was at an end, that she would divorce him. But this morning there was a tiny flicker of hope in her heart: "Mustapha will come, all the same. This is my last night."

72   She borrowed a thousand francs from Aida, who readily lent her the money. And she followed the advice to send the children off again, to Mustapha's fourth wife.

73   "Tell him that I must see him at once, I'm not well!"

74   She hurried off to the little market near by and bought a chicken and several other things. Her eyes were feverishly, joyfully bright as she carefully added seasoning to the dish she prepared. The appetizing smell of her cooking was wafted out to the compound and its Sunday atmosphere. She swept the room again, shut the door and windows, but the heady scent of the incense escaped through the cracks between the planks.

75   The children returned from their errand.

76   "Is he ill?" she asked them.

77   "No, mother. He's going to come. We found him with some of his friends at Voulimata's (the fourth wife). He asked about you."

78   "And that's all he said?"

79   "Yes, mother."

80   "Don't come indoors. Here's ten francs. Go and play somewhere else."

81   A delicious warm feeling spread over her. "He was going to come." Ever since Friday she had been harbouring spiteful words to throw in his face. He would beat her, of course . . . But never mind. Now she found it would be useless to utter those words. Instead she would do everything possible to make up for the lost days. She was happy, much too happy to bear a grudge against him, now that she knew he was coming—he might even be on the way with his henchmen. The only means of getting her own back was to cook a big meal . . . then he would stay in bed.

82   She finished preparing the meal, had a bath and went on to the rest of her toilette. She did her hair again, put antimony on her lower lip, eyebrows and lashes, then dressed in a white starched blouse and a hand-woven waist-cloth, and inspected her hands and feet. She was quite satisfied with her appearance.

83   But the waiting became prolonged.

84   No one in the compound spoke to her for fear of hurting her feelings. She had sat down outside the door, facing the entrance to the compound, and the other inhabitants avoided meeting her sorrowful gaze. Her tears overflowed the brim of her eyes like a swollen river its banks; she tried to hold them back, but in vain. She was eating her heart out.

85   The sound of a distant tom-tom was being carried on the wind. Time passed over her, like the seasons over monuments. Twilight came and darkness fell.

86   On the table were three plates in a row, one for each day.

87   "I've come to keep you company," declared Aida as she entered the room. Noumbe was sitting on the foot of the bed—she had fled from the silence of the others. "You mustn't get worked up about it," went on Aida. "Every woman goes through it. Of course it's not nice! But I don't think he'll be long now."

88   Noumbe raised a moist face and bit her lips nervously. Aida saw that she had made up her mind not to say anything. Everything was shrouded in darkness;

no light came from her room. After supper, the children had refrained from playing their noisy games.

89   Just when adults were beginning to feel sleepy and going to bed, into the compound walked Mustapha, escorted by two of his lieutenants. He was clad entirely in white. He greeted the people still about in an oily manner, then invited his companions into Noumbe's hut.

90   She had not stirred.

91   "Wife, where's the lamp?"

92   "Where you left it this morning when you went out."

93   "How are you?" inquired Mustapha when he had lit the lamp. He went and sat down on the bed, and motioned to the two men to take the bench.

94   "God be praised," Noumbe replied to his polite inquiry. Her thin face seemed relaxed and the angry lines had disappeared.

95   "And the children?"

96   "They're well, praise be to God."

97   "Our wife isn't very talkative this evening," put in one of the men.

98   "I'm quite well, though."

99   "Your heart isn't playing you up now?" asked Mustapha, not unkindly.

100   "No, it's quite steady," she answered.

101   "God be praised! Mustapha, we'll be off," said the man, uncomfortable at Noumbe's cold manner.

102   "Wait," said Mustapha, and turned to Noumbe. "Wife, are we eating tonight or tomorrow?"

103   "Did you leave me something when you went out this morning?"

104   "What? That's not the way to answer."

105   "No, uncle (darling). I'm just asking . . . Isn't it right?"

106   Mustapha realized that Noumbe was mocking him and trying to humiliate him in front of his men.

107   "You do like your little joke. Don't you know it's your three days?"

108   "Oh, uncle, I'm sorry, I'd quite forgotten. What an unworthy wife I am!" she exclaimed, looking straight at Mustapha.

109   "You're making fun of me!"

110   "Oh, uncle, I shouldn't dare! What, I? And who would help me into Paradise, if not my worthy husband? Oh, I would never poke fun at you, neither in this world nor the next."

111   "Anyone would think so."

112   "Who?" she asked.

113   "You might have stood up when I came in, to begin with . . ."

114   "Oh, uncle, forgive me. I'm out of my mind with joy at seeing you again. But whose fault is that, uncle?"

115   "And just what are these three plates for?" said Mustapha with annoyance.

116   "These three plates?" She looked at him, a malicious smile on her lips. "Nothing. Or rather, my three days. Nothing that would interest you. Is there anything here that interests you . . . uncle?"

117   As if moved by a common impulse, the three men stood up.

118   Noumbe deliberately knocked over one of the plates. "Oh, uncle, forgive me . . ." Then she broke the other two plates. Her eyes had gone red; suddenly a pain stabbed at her heart, she bent double, and as she fell to the floor gave a loud groan which roused the whole compound.

119   Some women came hurrying in. "What's the matter with her?"

120   "Nothing . . . only her heart. Look what she's done, the silly woman. One of these days her jealousy will suffocate her. I haven't been to see her—only two days, and she cries her eyes out. Give her some ash and she'll be all right," gabbled Mustapha, and went off.

How does this picture of a Malian man with his wives add to your understanding of Ousmane's story?

121   "Now these hussies have got their associations, they think they're going to run the country," said one of his men.

122   "Have you heard that at Bamako they passed a resolution condemning polygamy?" added the other. "Heaven preserve us from having only one wife."

123   "They can go out to work then," pronounced Mustapha as he left the compound.

124   Aida and some of the women lifted Noumbe on to the bed. She was groaning. They got her to take some of her mixture of ash and water . . .

■ ■ ▨

MEANING

1. What is Noumbe's situation relative to those of Mustapha's other wives? How is her status threatened when Mustapha delays his obligatory visit?

2. How is Noumbe's psychological anxiety reflected in the condition for which she takes medicine?

3. How do the preparations that Noumbe makes provide insights into her past and current relationships with her husband and with her friends and neighbors?

4. What changes can you observe in Noumbe's character from the beginning of the story through its conclusion? What does she do or say at the end that demonstrates these changes?

TECHNIQUE

1. How does Ousmane dramatize the range of different privileges and expectations that go along with a wife's status in the hierarchy of a polygamous society in Mali?

2. How does Ousmane's **description** of Noumbe's treatment as each of the three days goes by demonstrate her diminished status now that Mustapha has taken a new wife?

3. **Other Patterns.** What different **narrative** techniques does Ousmane use to enable the reader to share Noumbe's increasing frustration and anger?

LANGUAGE

1. How do the descriptions of Noumbe's preparations (of herself and her living quarters and the supper she makes) put the reader in the scene?

2. How do Noumbe's witty and sarcastic remarks at the conclusion give you insight into her character and situation and her changed attitude?

3. If you do not know the meaning of the following words, look them up: *haggard* (1), *elaborate* (4), *plaited* (6), *palate* (15), *mauve* (27), *chagrin* (63), *polygamy* (122).

SUGGESTIONS FOR WRITING

1. **Critical Writing.** What is Ousmane's attitude toward polygamy and its effect on the relationship between husbands and wives in Mali?

2. What **examples** can you discover in the story that demonstrate that not all communities in Mali are polygamous?

3. Why is it ironic that Mustapha blames the heart attack that Noumbe apparently suffers on jealousy?

4. ***Thematic Links.*** Compare and contrast the role of the wife in this society with her counterpart as discussed by Marilyn Yalom in "The Wife Today" (Chapter 10, "Definition").

Real-Life Situations: Classification

In a resume, you can use the skill that you developed in writing an effective classification to showcase your qualifications, special skills, experience, and education for a prospective employer. Each heading presents information on one topic. The following résumé was written by Samantha Clarke to accompany her letter of application (see Chapter 5, "Exemplification") and provides a useful model. Notice how she begins her resume with the simple heading "OBJECTIVE." This tells potential employers exactly what sort of position she is seeking. She puts the next category, "EXPERIENCE," before "EDUCATION" because her training is relevant and makes her a strong candidate. She begins with her most recent work experience and uses direct action words to emphasize her initiative. She includes a special category, "SKILLS/ABILITIES," that would make her especially useful to a potential employer. Even in "EDUCATION," Samantha included a unique senior project that a pharmaceutical company would consider an asset. Under "REFERENCES," no names or addresses are included. Perhaps most important, her resume is concise and has a clear and clean format.

Samantha Clarke
2843 Arcola Ave.
North Hollywood, CA 90402
(213) 467-0999
sclarke@aol.com

OBJECTIVE

Entry-level position as a pharmaceutical sales representative

EXPERIENCE

<u>Walgreens</u>, North Hollywood, CA, May–August 2005
As an assistant to the pharmacist, worked with customers taking orders for prescriptions
- Called doctor's offices for new prescriptions and refills
- Advised customers that their prescriptions were ready
- Contacted insurance companies to verify customers' drug plans

<u>Associates in Primary Care</u>, North Hollywood, CA, May–August 2004
As an assistant to the office manager, worked with new and regular patients
- Maintained patients' records and files
- Scheduled patients' appointments
- Called in prescriptions from doctors
- Organized records of X-rays and laboratory results

SKILLS/ABILITIES

Fluent in Spanish

EDUCATION

<u>University of California at Los Angeles</u>, 2002–present
Current standing: senior
Major: business administration with a concentration in public relations and a minor in
    botany
Senior project: studied medical uses of indigenous plants in Costa Rica, December
    2005–January 2006.

REFERENCES

Available upon request.

STUDENT ESSAY: CLASSIFICATION AND DIVISION

The following essay by Eunie Park uses the pattern of classification to examine the different attitudes toward wearing high heels. Eunie brings her own experiences with wearing these shoes to her analysis. We have annotated her paper and added a follow-up analysis ("Strategies") to help you understand the principles of classification and division.

Park 1

High on Heels: Society's Obsession with Pain

Eunie Park

1   Shoes are a constant obsession of our society, making appearances on the covers of magazines and on the silver screen and being worn without fail by celebrities on special occasions. They are fetishized and worshipped; shoe-ism could be its own religion. What's with the craze with shoes anyway?

Introduction: writer provides personal context

2   I remember wearing my first pair of high heels. It was in second grade; I was the flower girl for my aunt's wedding. Wearing a gorgeous ivory dress full of frills and embroidery, my satin white pumps gave me the one-and-a-half inches to make me feel like a "big girl." I remember feeling powerful and pretty in front of the mirror in the dressing room before the photo shoot. Not even three hours later, I was hysterical from the foot pain and wanted to chuck my shoes so Mother Goose's Old Woman Who Lived in a Shoe could have a prettier house. My feet were covered in blisters, and for the rest of the night, I was happily running barefoot and dancing with my father at the reception and consequently ruining my perfectly beautiful dress. Aghast, my mom reprimanded me and gave me an excruciating lecture about what the shoes were for.

3   My response? A suitable reaction for a seven-year-old: "My feet hurt, so I took them off, Mom!"

4   The appropriate question here is "What is the purpose of a shoe?" Its original purpose must have been to protect and comfort the foot while treading on rough footpaths of gravel and dirt. This function can be seen perpetuated by the sneaker or the slipper, but as the heel of the shoe rises, the function

Park 2

decreases. In today's society, the heel of the shoe carries much of the definition of the shoe, symbolizing class, stature, power, sexual independence—and for others, pain and female subordination.

Thesis statement: different social values are placed on high heels

5   The history of the heel dates as far back as 1000 B.C., in which "the earliest precursors of stilettos were discovered in the tombs of ancient Egypt" (Schrum 2005). However, the origin of high heels is attributed to Catherine de Medici, daughter of the wealthy de Medici family of the 16th century, who in 1533 married the Duke of Orleans, who later became King Henry II of France. It is said that she traveled to France with several pairs of high heels and wore one for her marriage for grace and "to compensate for her lack of height" (Love 110). The style immediately caught on with the men and women of the French court and spread to neighboring countries as heels were worn as a sign of nobility throughout the seventeenth and eighteenth centuries. For the nobles, height equaled power and status. Women were seen wearing heels as high as five inches. However, in 1793, Marie Antoinette was seen ascending the guillotine scaffold wearing a pair of two-inch heels, and henceforth, the height of the heel varied each year according to that year's vogue (Enders 2006).

Explanation of origins of positive cultural associations with high heels

6   Although vertically challenged men have also donned these shoes, high heels are an exclusively feminine accessory in today's society. High heels are used by some females to demonstrate their femininity and beauty, and the stiletto is known to be the sexiest and most captivating shoe in the industry. Since their advent in the 1950s, stilettos have represented independence and authority. With a heel the width of a pencil, the stiletto shifts the woman's body weight in such a way that "it is impossible for a woman to cower in high heels. She is forced to take a stand, to strike a pose, because anatomically her center of gravity has been displaced forward" (O'Keeffe 71). Stilettos have effectively revolutionized the world of shoes, giving an intoxicating sensation to those who wear them and to those who see them being worn. The word "stiletto" comes from the Latin word

Organization: symbolism of high heels then and now

Discussion of positive modern-day associations with one type of high heel, the stiletto

Park 3

meaning "small dagger," which makes reference to the "thin, sleek silhouette of the pencil-width heel that the shoe rests on" (Emami 2006). As it gives height, it also demands authority, and so high heels are seen by some as the ultimate female power accessory.

7   In addition, for a woman who desires a sexy image, high heels, specifically the stiletto, provide that ultimate sex appeal. Elizabeth Semmelhack, curator of the Bata Shoe Museum in Toronto explains that "stilettos function like lingerie: They reveal a bit about the wearer's private sex life" (Emami 2006). In our society, sex can equal power, and so by extension, heels also equal power for some who choose to wear them.

> Another reason for high heels' popularity

8   In recent times, however, feminists have argued that high heels do nothing but feed the male fantasy of dominance. As much as the heel may seem to demand respect, ironically, heels make a woman extremely vulnerable. The heel enslaves the woman; a woman cannot slouch, run, or walk while teetering on her toes. Women hobble and limp and scowl at the torturous pain the shoes give their precious feet. These limitations subconsciously attract men, giving them the notion that they must save these helpless, beautiful women. High heels are misogynistic devices, like the corset and the chastity belt, created to limit female movement and functionality and perpetuate the idea of feminine weakness and fragility.

> Introduction of category of people who oppose the wearing of high heels

9   Yet no matter how painful the shoes are, some women continue to buy into this obsession. Sarah Jessica Parker, as her shoe-loving character Carrie Bradshaw of Sex and the City explains: "You have to learn how to wear his [Manolo Blahnik] shoes; it doesn't happen overnight. . . . I've destroyed my feet completely, but I don't care. What do you really need your feet for, anyway?" Unlike Carrie, I care deeply about my feet and was mortified to discover the complications high-heeled shoes have for our well being. According to statistics compiled by the Society of Chiropractors and Podiatrists, four times as many women complain of having foot problems as men. They aren't small problems, either. The vast majority of foot surgery patients are female, and the

> Author puts herself into a different category than Carrie Bradshaw based on own attitude toward her feet

Park 4

culprit is often ultra-uncomfortable, tight shoes. Shoes that are too tight and too pointy result in painful bunions and other deformities. Going up on the human anatomy, high heels take a toll on the calf muscles and the Achilles' tendon and cause them to shorten. These injuries result in tendonitis and tears on the Achilles' tendon. Since the body weight is positioned forward, heel strike is also affected. Most of the natural shock absorbers in the body are overwhelmed by this new stance, so the knees must bear the Atlas's burden of the body.

10   Hey, but no pain, no gain? This would be the motto for stiletto lovers. I believe I fall under a different category. While other women can be so-called "slaves to fashion," I will run barefoot, be lectured by my mother again for not being womanly, and tend to my feet with care. Beauty is only skin-deep anyway. I know I can be sexy without the stilettos.

Conclusion: author decides to put herself in anti-high heel category

Works Cited

Emami, Sara. "The Sex Files at Discovery Channel." <u>Discovery Channel.</u> Jan.–Feb. 2006. Discovery Channel. 1 May 2006 <http://www.discovery.com>

Enders, Dave. "The Beauty of Geometry." <u>MIT Alumni Association.</u> 2006. Massachusetts Institute of Technology. 2 May 2006. <https://alum.mit.edu/ne/noteworthy/profiles/insolia.html>

Love, Brenda. <u>Encyclopedia of Unusual Sexual Practices.</u> New York: Barricade, 1992

O'Keeffe, Linda. *Shoes:* <u>A Celebration of Pumps, Sandals, Slippers and More</u>. New York: Workman, 1996

Schrum, Christine. "Health & Beauty: So Sexy It Hurts. High Heels—Arch Enemy or Friend?" <u>The Iowa Source</u> 2005. 20 Apr. 2006. <http://www.iowasource.com/health/health_heels_0504.html>

Strategies for Writing an Essay in Classification and Division

1. Purpose and Thesis

Eunie's purpose as reflected in the title is to inquire into the seemingly bizarre fashion custom of wearing high heels. She uses classification not as an end in itself but as a means of discussing the different associations that high heels have for different people.

2. Organization and Categories

After her opening paragraph, Eunie provides a brief anecdote about the discomfort she experienced in wearing her first pair of high heels when she was seven to lead to her thesis that high heels carry strong cultural associations and values. She implicitly categorizes people based on their attitudes toward high heels, and finally puts herself in the category of people opposed to wearing them.

3. Topic Sentences as Transitions

Eunie effectively uses topic sentences to move her readers from one cultural association of high heels (and related positive or negative attitudes toward it) to the next and provides an easy-to-follow structure within each section.

4. Conclusion and Unusual Insights

In her conclusion, Eunie reinforces her original thesis and has achieved her purpose of convincing her readers that she is in the category of people to whom comfort is most important, rather than being among the so-called "slaves to fashion."

5. Revision

Although this is a classification essay, some readers might feel that Eunie needs to develop the categories of naturalness versus fashionableness more fully. Also, some of her sentences could benefit from rewriting to express her ideas more directly.

Guidelines for Writing an Essay in Classification and Division

- If your assignment requires you to use classification and division, have you identified the principle on which the analysis will be based? Will it be interesting to your readers and disclose a new way of looking at something?

- Have you thought through the categories into which you intend to divide your subject and made sure that they encompass your subject in a consistent way? You might wish to create an outline in order to determine whether your categories make sense and do not overlap.

- Have you created a thesis that names the subject you are going to discuss, identifies the principle underlying the categories, and tells the reader why it is significant?

- Are your categories discussed in comparable detail (touching on equivalent points)? If not, have you explained why one category or class is more important than another? Have you used transitions to clarify the connections between sections and the relationships among the categories?

- What discoveries have you made as a result of your classification and division, and have you stated them as conclusions?

Grammar Tips for Classification and Division

In writing a classification and division essay, there are two techniques that you can use to make it easier for your readers to understand the different categories you will identify and evaluate: (1) using a colon to introduce a list of types, categories, or kinds that your essay will analyze and (2) supplying illustrative examples that make the abstract categories immediately clear to your readers.

1. When you use a colon to set up or introduce the types, categories, or kinds that you are going to analyze, be sure that the words preceding the colon form a complete sentence; the list that follows it, whether it takes the form of a dependent clause, phrase, or single word, should be separated by commas and stated in parallel terms.

Incorrect:

Four different kinds of love are: passionate love, sympathetic love, sensual love, and vanity love.

Correct:

There are four different kinds of love: passionate love, sympathetic love, sensual love, and vanity love.

2. To see the difference between a classification that has been fully developed and an unsupported generalization, compare the first version with the second.

Abbreviated version:

Vanity love is an egotistical expression of self-flattery in which qualities that are attributed to another person enhance the lover's own self-esteem.

Fully developed version:

Vanity love is an egotistical expression of self-flattery in which qualities that are attributed to another person enhance the lover's own self-esteem. For example, in the phenomenon of the "trophy wife," an older man marries a much younger, attractive woman, showing that he is still capable of attracting such a partner and thus boosting his ego.

The second version provides a specific example that illustrates this kind of love.

CHECKLIST for Revising Classification and Division Essays

- On what basis will you classify or divide your material?
- Does your thesis statement explain why readers would find such a classification or division interesting?
- Have you outlined your essay to make sure that your categories are consistent and logically presented?
- Have you developed each category in comparable detail or explained why one is more important?
- Does your conclusion pull together the results of your analysis?
- Do your transitional words or phrases make it easy for your reader to grasp the relationship between your main idea and the categories you analyze?

ADDITIONAL WRITING ASSIGNMENTS AND ACTIVITIES

COMMUNICATING WITH DIFFERENT AUDIENCES

1. You are a professional stand-up comedian giving advice to a new performer who has been booked to appear on a cruise ship. Prepare a talk on different types of personalities that this person can expect to encounter in the audience.

2. As an advisor, create a pamphlet for new students so that they can become familiar with the course requirements for different majors at your school.

3. Classify the kinds of places where one can have lunch near your campus and their typical cuisine, costs, speed of service, and cleanliness.

4. What personas do you create for yourself on the Internet in different contexts, such as video games, chat rooms, or dating services? Or describe the personality types you meet in each context.

5. Choose a category of apparel, and classify the items in it according to principles such as most worn, least worn, expensive, inexpensive, colors, or any other set of principles.

6. Classify the last half-dozen TV shows or films you have seen according to types, and evaluate the degree to which they are original or stereotyped.

WRITING FOR A NEWSPAPER

Write a letter to your local newspaper about kinds of problems that someone of your age, gender, or ethnic group faces in your town, illustrated with specific examples.

CLASSIFICATION AND DIVISION ESSAYS

1. What are the kinds of practical jokes that make you laugh?

2. What kinds of hairstyles for men and women are popular currently (and/or in the past), and what do they say about society?

3. What principles could you use in arranging photo albums or digital files?

4. Create a family tree that is organized according to unusual principles (such as personality types, blood type, fashionableness).

5. What kinds of situations or types of people could provoke you into committing an act of violence?

6. What kinds of friends do you have, and what principles govern each type of friendship (for example, those based on shared interests, people you haven't seen in a long time but still consider to be friends)?

7. What kinds of careers appeal or do not appeal to you and why?

8. What different kinds of information and materials would you require for a particular hobby or craft?

9. What kinds of situations would compel you to intervene to help someone else?

10. What kinds of music do you listen to while studying, exercising, and relaxing?

11. What aspects of yourself (psychological and/or physical) are you satisfied with, and which ones would you change?

12. Describe three different kinds of hypocrisy with examples that illuminate the differences among them.

13. What kinds of pictures or images evoke a feeling of peacefulness, and why?

14. Describe three genres of film and the characteristics of each, giving specific examples.

15. Choose a movie, book, or CD that could be considered to fit into more than one genre, and explain why this is and where *you* think it fits best.

16. Classify the contents of your medicine cabinet first by different types and then by their range of effects.

17. What are at least four different kinds of love, and how do they differ from each other?

18. In what types of situations or locations should the use of cell phones be restricted?

19. Classify the contents of your most cluttered closet, drawer, garage, basement, or attic (what you should throw away, donate, or keep).

20. Classify the kinds of gifts you give to different people on various occasions.

21. Classify different kinds of body modifications, and explain what statements each kind makes about both the person and society.

22. What different kinds of associations do people have about blondes, redheads, brunettes, people with gray hair, or those who are bald?

23. Investigate the different breeds of dogs or another animal, and describe the characteristics of one breed in detail.

RESEARCH SUGGESTIONS

1. What kinds of resources are available to you to do a research paper, and when would each be useful?

2. What types of information could you discover through genetic screening? What would you want to know, and what would you not want to know?

3. What principles govern quotas, visas, and restrictions for people entering the United States from other countries? What cultural agendas do they reflect, and how do they compare with past instances?

4. Research why Pluto was "demoted" from being a planet to it being a "dwarf planet."

5. Research the history of any dance or musical genre, and explore the different forms it can take and/or the elements that it comprises.

6. What principles underlie dietary laws for different religions and cultures (for example, Judaism, Islam, Hinduism, Jainism)?

COLLABORATIVE ACTIVITIES

1. With your classmates, compare kinds of situations in which you feel out of place.
2. Divide into groups. Each group should specify the kinds of things that would be needed for different types of trips (overnight, overseas, by car, on a plane, on a train, on a bus).
3. Describe three different kinds of vacations you would enjoy.
4. What kinds of phobias do different people have, and how do the phobias influence their lives?

CAUSE AND EFFECT

9

Exploring Causal Connections in Society and Culture

Whereas process analysis explains *how* something works, causal analysis seeks to discover *why* something happened, or why it will happen, by dividing an ongoing stream of events into causes and effects. Writers may proceed from a given effect and seek to discover what cause or chain of causes could have produced the observed effect, or they may show how further effects will flow from a known cause.

Causal analysis is an invaluable analytical technique that is used across cultures and in many fields of study. Because of the complexity of causal relationships, writers try to identify, as precisely as possible, the contributing factors in any causal sequence. The direct or immediate causes of the event are those that are most likely to have triggered the actual event. Yet behind direct causes may lie indirect or remote causes that set the stage or create the framework in which the event could occur. By the same token, long-term future effects are much more difficult to identify than are immediate, short-term effects. Causes and effects can also occur in connecting chains of causation, in which each effect itself becomes the cause of a further effect.

Determining with any degree of certainty that *x* caused *y* is more complicated in situations in which one cause may have produced multiple effects or the same effect could have been produced by multiple causes. Causal analysis can get off track when writers confuse sequence with causation. Simply because A preceded B does not necessarily mean that A caused B. Perhaps A and B were both caused by some as yet unknown event C. This confusion of antecedent or correlation with causation is called the *post hoc* fallacy, from the Latin *post hoc, ergo propter hoc* (literally, "after this, therefore because of this").

A common error occurs when a necessary condition is mistaken for the cause. Most college students will agree that taking a course is a necessary condition to receiving an A. It is equally obvious that taking the course, while necessary, does not of itself cause the student to receive the A.

These theoretical considerations become very important in any real-world causal analysis. For example, a specialist in forensic medicine (as reflected in the *CSI* TV series) who is brought in to help investigate a murder will use causal analysis to determine the time and method of death. The approximate time of death can be estimated from the temperature of the body, the amount of clothing worn, the temperature of the surroundings, and the rate at which a dead body normally loses heat. Forensic techniques can also determine the cause of death. Analysis of a stab wound can disclose the size and shape of the weapon that was used, while analysis of a gunshot wound can reveal the distance and angle from which the bullet was fired, the caliber of the bullet, and even the type of gun used. By the same token, forensic chemists can identify from bits of paint the year, make, and model of a car that struck a hit-and-run victim.

In this chapter, we offer a variety of illustrations of different types of causal analyses across a range of cultures. In "The Real Vampire," Paul Barber, a cultural historian, demonstrates how collective paranoia in Eastern European communities expressed itself through scapegoating and a belief in vampires:

> Perhaps foremost among the reasons for urgency with which vampires were sought—and found—was sheer terror. To understand its intensity we need only recall the realities that faced our informants. Around them people were dying in clusters, by agencies that they did not understand.

Barber finds that the predominant cause of the vampire legend can be attributed to a fear of the dead passing on contagion to the living, who sought to prevent this by identifying and staking so-called vampires (who were often ostracized townspeople). He also discovers that the true vampire was quite unlike its fictional or Hollywood counterpart. Barber illustrates how writers use causal analysis to discover the means by which social pressures control the behavior of people in groups.

Kim Chernin, in "The Flesh and the Devil," analyzes a correlation between the artificial and unrealistic image of the female body as portrayed in the media and the observable effect—the willingness of women to starve and exercise to the point of exhaustion:

> What had begun as a vision of harmony between mind and body, a sense of well-being, physical fitness, and glowing health, had become now demonic, driving her always to further exploits, running farther, denying herself more food, losing more weight, always goaded on by the idea that the body's perfection lay just beyond her present achievement.

Although casual analysis seeks to identify specific reasons why a particular event has happened or will happen, it is crucial for writers to be able to distinguish remote causes from immediate ones. Whereas a remote cause may create the possibility for an event to occur, an immediate cause triggers the actual event. For example, Hanan al-Shaykh's story "The Persian Carpet" distinguishes between predisposing and triggering causes to answer the question of why a girl who loves her mother and had looked forward to a visit with her becomes bitterly disillusioned when she sees a Persian carpet in her mother's new home:

> The lines and colours of the Persian carpet were imprinted on my memory. I used to lie on it as I did my lessons; I'd be so close to it that I'd gaze at its pattern and find it looking like slices of red water-melon repeated over and over again.

The first part of the story sketches the remote causes of the narrator's sudden anger (the background events of their mother's divorce and remarriage and the secret visit of the narrator and her sister to their mother's new home). The triggering event is the sight of the carpet that was thought to have been stolen.

Sometimes causal analysis attempts to show how each cause produces an effect, which then acts as a cause of a further effect. This chain of causation is illustrated by Joseph K. Skinner's analysis in "Big Mac and the Tropical Forests" of how the economic incentives of the fast-food industry have led to the destruction of tropical forests to raise cattle:

> Beef production in the tropics may be profitable for the few, but it is taking place at enormous cost for the majority and for the planet as a whole.

Skinner discloses the links between (1) leveling of forests to produce (2) grassland for cattle, (3) the loss of valuable species that could revolutionize treatment of diseases, and (4) irreversible effect on the earth's weather patterns because of rising levels of carbon dioxide that would have been recycled by the trees.

Writers use causal analysis to put events into perspective. C. P. Ellis uses causal analysis for this purpose in "Why I Quit the Klan." He first sets the stage by describing the circumstances that led him to join the Klan and how the Klan's appeal was based on making other groups seem responsible for hardships and inequities that the members had experienced. At a certain point, Ellis began to see that local politicans used the Klan in a divide-and-conquer strategy to maintain power. His dramatic shift in attitude led him to become a union organizer and to leave the Klan:

> When I began to organize, I began to see far deeper. I began to see people again bein used. Blacks against whites. . . . There are two things management wants to keep: all the money and all the say-so.

It is most important that causal analysis demonstrates the means by which an effect could have been produced. Writers are obligated to show how the specific causes that they identify could have produced the effects in question. For example, in "To Kiss: Why We Kiss Under the Mistletoe at Christmas," Vaughn M. Bryant, Jr., and Sylvia Grider investigate how and when this custom began. They found that an ancient Celtic belief in mistletoe became linked with the Roman custom of kissing to seal a betrothal, which Christians adapted for the Christmas season:

> From this original linking of kissing with the mistletoe, and the strong commitments it assumed, came a slow relaxing of the implied commitments and a view of mistletoe kisses as simply part of the joyous celebration of the Christmas season.

In a similar manner, Anwar F. Accawi in "The Telephone" deals with effects that are both real and observable. Most people would not be convinced that the installation of one telephone in a remote rural village in Lebanon would actually destroy the identity of the community. Yet Accawi's experiences led him to conclude that this is exactly what happened:

> And the telephone, as it turned out, was bad news. With its coming, the face of the village began to change. One of the first effects was the shifting of the village's center.

Accawi offers examples, great and small, that illustrate the irreversible effects that the telephone brought to village life.

As you can see, writers are interested in asking and answering questions about what causes events, actions, and shifts in public perception, whether for individuals or societies or in the natural world. In applying this pattern to real-life situations, you might be required to write a report, issue a memo, or draft a proposal specifying the consequences or effects, both intended or unintended, that might occur as a result of some action you took or will take.

The Real Vampire

Paul Barber is the foremost authority on the little-understood history of vampire mythology. His enlightening essay, which was originally published in *Natural History* (October 1990), analyzes the true set of events that caused the vampire myth to be promulgated in a number of guises, the least accurate of which is the Hollywood version. Barber is currently with the Fowler Museum of Cultural History at the University of California at Los Angeles and has written *Vampires, Burial and Death: Folklore and Reality* (1988) and *When They Severed Earth from Sky: How the Human Mind Shapes Myth* (with Elizabeth Wayland Barber, 2005). In the following article, we learn that misinterpretation of forensic clues by terrorized communities in Eastern Europe afflicted by epidemics played a key role in instigating the vampire myth.

BEFORE YOU READ

Why do you think the myth of the vampire has lasted so long?

■ ■ ▨

> I saw the Count lying within the box upon the earth, some of which the rude[1] falling from the cart had scattered over him. He was deathly pale, just like a waxen image, and the red eyes glared with the horrible vindictive look which I knew too well . . .
>
> The eyes saw the sinking sun, and the look of hate in them turned to triumph.
>
> But, on the instant, came the sweep and flash of Jonathan's great knife. I shrieked as I saw it shear through the throat; whilst at the same moment Mr. Morris's bowie knife plunged into the heart.
>
> It was like a miracle; but before our very eyes, and almost in the drawing of a breath, the whole body crumbled into dust and passed from our sight.
>
> —Bram Stoker, *Dracula*

1 If a typical vampire of folklore were to come to your house this Halloween, you might open the door to encounter a plump Slavic fellow with long fingernails and a stubbly beard, his mouth and left eye open, his face ruddy and swollen. He would wear informal attire—a linen shroud—and he would look for all the world like a disheveled peasant.

2 If you did not recognize him, it would be because you expected to see—as would most people today—a tall, elegant gentleman in a black cloak. But that would be the vampire of fiction—the count, the villain of Bram Stoker's novel and countless modern movies, based more or less on Vlad Tepes, a figure in Romanian history who was a prince, not a count; ruled in Walachia, not

---

[1] *rude:* ignorant peasant—*Ed.*

Transylvania; and was never viewed by the local populace as a vampire. Nor would he be recognized as one, bearing so little resemblance to the original Slavic revenant (one who returns from the dead)—the one actually called *upir* or *vampir*. But in folklore, the undead are seemingly everywhere in the world, in a variety of disparate cultures. They are people who, having died before their time, are believed to return to life to bring death to their friends and neighbors.

3   We know the European version of the vampire best and have a number of eyewitness accounts telling of the "killing" of bodies believed to be vampires. When we read these reports carefully and compare their findings with what is now known about forensic pathology, we can see why people believed that corpses came to life and returned to wreak havoc on the local population.

4   Europeans of the early 1700s showed a great deal of interest in the subject of the vampire. According to the *Oxford English Dictionary*, the word itself entered the English language in 1734, at a time when many books were being written on the subject, especially in Germany.

5   One reason for all the excitement was the Treaty of Passarowitz (1718), by which parts of Serbia and Walachia were turned over to Austria. The occupying forces, which remained there until 1739, began to notice, and file reports on, a peculiar local practice: exhuming bodies and "killing" them. Literate outsiders began to attend such exhumations. The vampire craze was an early "media event," in which educated Europeans became aware of practices that were by no means of recent origin.

6   In the early 1730s, a group of Austrian medical officers were sent to the Serbian village of Medvegia to investigate some very strange accounts. A number of people in the village had died recently, and the villagers blamed the deaths on vampires. The first of these vampires, they said, had been a man named Arnold Paole, who had died some years before (by falling off a hay wagon) and had come back to haunt the living.

7   To the villagers, Paole's vampirism was clear: When they dug up his corpse, "they found that he was quite complete and undecayed, and that fresh blood had flowed from his eyes, nose, mouth, and ears; that the shirt, the covering, and the coffin were completely bloody; that the old nails on his hands and feet, along with the skin, had fallen off, and that new ones had grown; and since they saw from this that he was a true vampire, they drove a stake through his heart, according to their custom, whereby he gave an audible groan and bled copiously."

8   This new offensive by the vampires—the one that drew the medical officers to Medvegia—included an attack on a woman named Stanacka, who "lay down to sleep fifteen days ago, fresh and healthy, but at midnight she started up out of her sleep with a terrible cry, fearful and trembling, and complained that she had been throttled by the son of a Haiduk by the name of Milloe, who had died nine weeks earlier, whereupon she had experienced a great pain in the chest and became worse hour by hour, until finally she died on the third day."

9   In their report, *Visum et Repertum* (Seen and Discovered), the officers told not only what they had heard from the villagers but also, in admirable clinical detail, what they themselves had seen when they exhumed and dissected the bodies of the supposed victims of the vampire. Of one corpse, the authors

observed, "After the opening of the body there was found in the *cavitate pectoris* a quantity of fresh extravascular blood. The *vasa* [vessels] of the *arteriae* and *venae*, like the *ventriculis cordis*, were not, as is usual, filled with coagulated blood, and the whole *viscera*, that is, the *pulmo* [lung], *bepar* [liver], *stomachus, lien* [spleen], *et intestina* were quite fresh as they would be in a healthy person." But while baffled by the events, the medical officers did not venture opinions as to their meaning.

10   Modern scholars generally disregard such accounts—and we have many of them—because they invariably contain "facts" that are not believable, such as the claim that the dead Arnold Paole, exhumed forty days after his burial, groaned when a stake was driven into him. If that is untrue—and it surely seems self-evident that it must be untrue—then the rest of the account seems suspect.

11   Yet these stories invariably contain details that could only be known by someone who had exhumed a decomposing body. The flaking away of the skin described in the account of Arnold Paole is a phenomenon that forensic pathologists refer to as "skin slippage." Also, pathologists say that it is no surprise that Paole's "nails had fallen away," for that too is a normal event. (The Egyptians knew this and dealt with it either by tying the nails onto the mummified corpse or by attaching them with little golden thimbles.) The reference to "new nails" is presumably the interpretation of the glossy nail bed underneath the old nails.

12   Such observations are inconvenient if the vampire lore is considered as something made up out of whole cloth. But since the exhumations actually took place, then the question must be, how did our sources come to the conclusion they came to? That issue is obscured by two centuries of fictional vampires, who are much better known than the folkloric variety. A few distinctions are in order.

13   The folklore of the vampire comes from peasant cultures across most of Europe. As it happens, the best evidence of actual exhumations is from Eastern Europe, where the Eastern Orthodox church showed a greater tolerance for pagan traditions than the Catholic church in Western Europe.

14   The fictional vampire, owing to the massive influence of Bram Stoker's *Dracula*, moved away from its humble origin. (Imagine Count Dracula—in formal evening wear—undergoing his first death by falling off a hay wagon.)

15   Most fiction shows only one means of achieving the state of vampirism: people become vampires by being bitten by one. Typically, the vampire looms over the victim dramatically, then bites into the neck to suck blood. When vampires and revenants in European folklore suck blood—and many do not—they bite their victims somewhere on the thorax. Among the Kashubes, a Slavic people of northern Europe, vampires chose the area of the left breast; among the Russians, they left a small wound in the area of the heart; and in Danzig (now Gdansk), they bit the victim's nipples.

16   People commonly believe that those who were different, unpopular, or great sinners returned from the dead. Accounts from Russia tell of people who were unearthed merely because while alive they were alcoholics. A more universal category is the suicide. Partly because of their potential for returning from the dead or for drawing their nearest and dearest into the grave after them, suicides were refused burial in churchyards.

17 One author lists the categories of revenants by disposition as "the godless [people of different faiths are included], evildoers, suicides, sorcerers, witches, and werewolves; among the Bulgarians the group is expanded by robbers, highwaymen, arsonists, prostitutes, deceitful and treacherous barmaids and other dishonorable people."

18 A very common belief, reported not only from Eastern Europe but also from China, holds that a person may become a revenant when an animal jumps over him. In Romania there is a belief that a bat can transform a corpse into a vampire by flying over it. This circumstance deserves remark if only because of its rarity, for as important as bats are in the fiction of vampires, they are generally unimportant in the folklore. Bats came into vampire fiction by a circuitous route: the vampire bat of Central and South America was named after the vampire of folklore, because it sucks (or rather laps up) blood after biting its victim. The bat was then assimilated into the fiction: the modern (fictional) vampire is apt to transform himself into a bat and fly off to seek his victims.

19 Potential revenants could often be identified at birth, usually by some defect, as when (among the Poles of Upper Silesia and the Kashubes) a child was born with teeth or a split lower lip or features viewed as somehow bestial— for example, hair or a taillike extension of the spine. A child born with a red caul, or amniotic membrane, covering its head was regarded as a potential vampire.

20 The color red is related to the undead. Decomposing corpses often acquire a ruddy color, and this was generally taken for evidence of vampirism. Thus, the folkloric vampire is never pale, as one would expect of a corpse; his face is commonly described as florid or of a healthy color or dark, and this may be attributed to his habit of drinking blood. (The Serbians, referring to a red-faced, hard-drinking man, assert that he is "blood red as a vampire.")

21 In various parts of Europe, vampires, or revenants, were held responsible for any number of untoward events. They tipped over Gypsy caravans in Serbia, made loud noises on the frozen sod roofs of houses in Iceland (supposedly by beating their heels against them), caused epidemics, cast spells on crops, brought on rain and hail, and made cows go dry. All these activities attributed to vampires do occur: storms and scourges come and go, crops don't always thrive, cows do go dry. Indeed, the vampire's crimes are persistently "real-life" events. The issue often is not whether an event occurred but why it was attributed to the machinations of the vampire, an often invisible villain.

22 Bodies continue to be active long after death, but we moderns distinguish between two types of activity: that which we bring about by our will (in life) and that which is caused by other entities, such as microorganisms (in death). Because we regard only the former as "our" activity, the body's posthumous movements, changes in dimension, or the like are not real for us, since we do not will them. For the most part, however, our ancestors made no such distinction. To them, if after death the body changed in color, moved, bled, and so on (as it does), then it continued to experience a kind of life. Our view of death has made it difficult for us to understand earlier views, which are often quite pragmatic.

23   Much of what a corpse "does" results from misunderstood processes of decomposition. Only in detective novels does this process proceed at a predictable rate. So when a body that had seemingly failed to decompose came to the attention of the populace, theories explaining the apparent anomaly were likely to spring into being. (Note that when a saint's body failed to decompose it was a miracle, but when the body of an unpopular person failed to decompose it was because he was a vampire.) But while those who exhumed the bodies of suspected vampires invariably noted what they believed was the lack of decomposition, they almost always presented evidence that the body really was decomposing. In the literature, I have so far found only two instances of exhumations that failed to yield a "vampire." (With so many options, the body almost certainly will do something unexpected, hence scary, such as showing blood at the lips.) Our natural bias, then as now, is for the dramatic and the exotic, so that an exhumation that did not yield a vampire could be expected to be an early dropout from the folklore and hence the literature.

24   But however mythical the vampire was, the corpses that were taken for vampires were very real. And many of the mysteries of vampire lore clear up when we examine the legal and medical evidence surrounding these exhumations. "Not without astonishment," says an observer at the exhumation of a Serbian vampire in 1725, "I saw some fresh blood in his mouth, which, according to the common observation, he had sucked from the people killed by him." Similarly, in *Visum et Repertum*, we are told that the people exhuming one body were surprised by a "plumpness" they asserted had come to the corpse in the grave. Our sources deduced a cause-and-effect relationship from these two observations. The vampire was larger than he was because he was full to bursting with the fresh blood of his victims.

25   The observations are clinically accurate: as a corpse decomposes, it normally bloats (from the gases given off by decomposition), while the pressure from the bloating causes blood from the lungs to emerge at the mouth. The blood is real, it just didn't come from "victims" of the deceased.

26   But how was it that Arnold Paole, exhumed forty days after his death, groaned when his exhumers drove a stake into him? The peasants of Medvegia assumed that if the corpse groaned, it must still be alive. But a corpse does emit sounds, even when it is only moved, let alone if a stake were driven into it. This is because the compression of the chest cavity forces air past the glottis, causing a sound similar in quality and origin to the groan or cry of a living person. Pathologists shown such accounts point out that a corpse that did not emit such sounds when a stake was driven into it would be unusual.

27   To vampire killers who are digging up a corpse, anything unexpected is taken for evidence of vampirism. Calmet, an eighteenth-century French ecclesiastic, described people digging up corpses "to see if they can find any of the usual marks which leads them to conjecture that they are the parties who molest the living, as the mobility and suppleness of the limbs, the fluidity of the blood, and the flesh remaining uncorrupted." A vampire, in other words, is a corpse that lacks rigor mortis, has fluid blood, and has not decomposed. As it happens, these

distinctions do not narrow the field very much: Rigor mortis is a temporary condition, liquid blood is not at all unusual in a corpse (hence the "copious bleeding" mentioned in the account of Arnold Paole), and burial slows down decomposition drastically (by a factor of eight, according to a standard textbook on forensic pathology). This being the case, exhumations often yielded a corpse that nicely fit the local model of what a vampire was.

28   None of this explains yet another phenomenon of the vampire lore—the attack itself. To get to his victim, the vampire is often said to emerge at night from a tiny hole in the grave, in a form that is invisible to most people (sorcerers have made a good living tracking down and killing such vampires). The modern reader may reject out of hand the hypothesis that a dead man, visible or not, crawled out of his grave and attacked the young woman Stanacka as related in *Visum et Repertum.* Yet in other respects, these accounts have been quite accurate.

29   Note the sequence of events: Stanacka is asleep, the attack takes place, and she wakes up. Since Stanacka was asleep during the attack, we can only conclude that we are looking at a culturally conditioned interpretation of a nightmare— a real event with a fanciful interpretation.

30   The vampire does have two forms: one of them the body in the grave; the other—and this is the mobile one—the image, or "double," which here appears as a dream. While we interpret this as an event that takes place within the mind of the dreamer, in nonliterate cultures the dream is more commonly viewed as either an invasion by the spirits of whatever is dreamed about (and these can include the dead) or evidence that the dreamer's soul is taking a nocturnal journey.

31   In many cultures, the soul is only rather casually attached to its body, as is demonstrated by its habit of leaving the body entirely during sleep or unconsciousness or death. The changes that occur during such conditions—the lack of responsiveness, the cessation or slowing of breathing and pulse—are attributed to the soul's departure. When the soul is identified with the image of the body, it may make periodic forays into the minds of others when they dream. The image is the essence of the person, and its presence in the mind of another is evidence that body and soul are separated. Thus, one reason that the dead are believed to live on is that their image can appear in people's dreams and memories even after death. For this reason some cultures consider it unwise to awaken someone suddenly: he may be dreaming, and his soul may not have a chance to return before he awakens, in which case he will die. In European folklore, the dream was viewed as a visit from the person dreamed about. (The vampire is not the only personification of the dream: the Slavic *mora* is a living being whose soul goes out of the body at night, leaving it as if dead. The *mora* first puts men to sleep, and then frightens them with dreams, chokes them, and sucks their blood. Etymologically, *mora* is cognate with the *mara* or nightmare, with German *Mahr*, and with the second syllable of the French *cauchemar*.

32   When Stanacka claimed she was attacked by Milloe, she was neither lying nor even making an especially startling accusation. Her subsequent death (probably from some form of epidemic disease; others in the village were dying too)

was sufficient proof to her friends and relatives that she had in fact been attacked by a dead man, just as she had said.

33   This is why our sources tell us seemingly contradictory facts about the vampire. His body does not have to leave the grave to attack the living, yet the evidence of the attack—the blood he has sucked from his victims—is to be seen on the body. At one and the same time he can be both in the grave in his physical form and out of it in his spirit form. Like the fictional vampire, the vampire of folklore must remain in his grave part of the time—during the day—but with few exceptions, folkloric vampires do not travel far from their home towns.

34   And while the fictional vampire disintegrates once staked, the folkloric vampire can prove much more troublesome. One account tells that "in order to free themselves from this plague, the people dug the body up, drove a consecrated nail into its head and stake through its heart. Nonetheless, that did not help: the murdered man came back each night." In many of these cases, vampires were cremated as well as staked.

35   In Eastern Europe the fear of being killed by a vampire was quite real, and the people devised ways to protect themselves from attacks. One of the sources of protection was the blood of the supposed vampire, which was baked in bread, painted on the potential victim, or even mixed with brandy and drunk. (According to *Visum et Repertum*, Arnold Paole had once smeared himself with the blood of a vampire—that is, a corpse—for protection.) The rationale behind this is a common one in folklore, expressed in the saying "similia similiis curantur" (similar things are cured by similar things). Even so, it is a bit of a shock to find that our best evidence suggests that it was the human beings who drank the blood of the "vampires," and not the other way around.

36   Perhaps foremost among the reasons for urgency with which vampires were sought—and found—was sheer terror. To understand its intensity we need only recall the realities that faced our informants. Around them people were dying in clusters, by agencies that they did not understand. As they were well aware, death could be extremely contagious: if a neighbor died, they might be next. They were afraid of nothing less than death itself. For among many cultures it was death that was thought to be passed around, not viruses and bacteria. Contagion was meaningful and deliberate, and its patterns were based on values and vendettas, not on genetic predisposition or the domestic accommodations of the plague-spreading rat fleas. Death came from the dead who, through jealousy, anger, or longing, sought to bring the living into their realm. And to prevent this, the living attempted to neutralize or propitiate the dead until the dead became powerless—not only when they stopped entering dreams but also when their bodies stopped changing and were reduced to inert bones. This whole phenomenon is hard for us to understand because although death is as inescapable today as it was then, we no longer personify its causes.

37   In recent history, the closest parallel to this situation may be seen in the AIDS epidemic, which has caused a great deal of fear, even panic, among people who, for the time being at least, know little about the nature of the

disease. In California, for instance, there was an attempt to pass a law requiring the quarantine of AIDS victims. Doubtless the fear will die down if we gain control over the disease—but what would it be like to live in a civilization in which all diseases were just as mysterious? Presumably one would learn—as was done in Europe in past centuries—to shun the dead as potential bearers of death.

MEANING

1. What forensic clues were misinterpreted or misunderstood by a terror-filled population that was ready to believe that corpses were capable of returning to life to wreak havoc on the local population?

2. What role did persistent epidemics for which no specific cause could be identified play in instigating the formation of teams of vampire hunters?

How does this Hollywood portrayal of Dracula, played by Bela Lugosi in the 1931 film, differ from "The Real Vampire" as analyzed by Barber?

3. How do the "real" vampires described by Barber differ from their fictional and film counterparts?

4. What light does Barber shed on the relationship between those who were staked as vampires after their death and their role as social outcasts in life?

TECHNIQUE

1. Why does Barber disclose poorly understood characteristics of the way corpses decompose?

2. How does Barber **contrast** the disheveled peasant vampire into its glamorous aristocratic version popularized by Bram Stoker?

3. **Other Patterns.** In what different contexts does Barber use **narratives** as evidence of the kinds of stories that have been associated with vampires over the centuries?

LANGUAGE

1. How does Barber use quotations from a wide range of sources to create a historical context within which to understand the emergence of a belief in vampires?

2. How does the etymology of terms having to do with nightmares in paragraph 32 help to explain this aspect of the vampire myth?

3. If you don't know the meaning of the following words, look them up: *forensic* (3), *exhumations* (5), *copiously* (7), *arsonists* (17), *revenants* (19), *amniotic* (19), *decomposition* (23), *glottis* (26), *suppleness* (27), *propitiate* (36).

SUGGESTIONS FOR WRITING

1. **Critical Writing.** Is Barber accurate in equating the causes of the vampire myth and the treatment of AIDS victims as the ostracized "other"? Why or why not?

2. What do film or television portrayals of vampires suggest about contemporary cultural attitudes toward death?

3. Would the idea of a permanent existence as a nocturnal creature who cannot die or ever see the sun be appealing to you? Why or why not? **Argue** for your preference.

4. **Thematic Links.** Discuss the psychology of ostracism as discussed by Barber and as experienced by Lucy Grealy in "Autobiography of a Face" (Chapter 13, "Using Combined Patterns").

JOSEPH K. SKINNER

Big Mac and the Tropical Forests

Although this essay was first published in the Monthly Review *in 1985, Joseph K. Skinner's investigation still applies in large part today. He reveals the far-reaching effects of cutting down tropical forests in Central America to create grazing lands for cattle who supply the beef to fast-food chains in the United States. The loss of the forests with their rare plants that might yield useful medicines and other ecological effects are presented in an organized and compelling way.*

BEFORE YOU READ

What problems might result from cutting down tropical forests to provide grazing land for cattle?

■ ■ ▨

1   Hello, fast-food chains.

2   Goodbye, tropical forests.

3   Sound like an odd connection? The "free-market" economy has led to results even stranger than this, but perhaps none have been as environmentally devastating.

4   These are the harsh facts: the tropical forests are being leveled for commercial purposes at the rate of 150,000 square kilometers a year, an area the size of England and Wales combined.[1]

5   At this rate, the world's tropical forests could be entirely destroyed within seventy-three years. Already as much as a fifth or a quarter of the huge Amazon forest, which constitutes a third of the world's total rain forest, has been cut, and the rate of destruction is accelerating. And nearly two thirds of the Central American forests have been cleared or severely degraded since 1950.

6   Tropical forests, which cover only 7 percent of the Earth's land surface (it used to be 12 percent), support half the species of the world's living things. Due to their destruction, "We are surely losing one or more species a day right now out of the five million (minimum figure) on Earth," says Norman Myers, author of numerous books and articles on the subject and consultant to the World Bank and the World Wildlife Fund. "By the time ecological equilibrium is restored, at least one-quarter of all species will have disappeared, probably a third, and conceivably even more.... If this pattern continues, it could mean the demise of two million species by the middle of next century." Myers calls the destruction

---

[1] Jean-Paul Landley, "Tropical Forest Resources," *FAO Forestry Paper* 30 (Rome: FAO, 1982). This UN statistic is the most accurate to date. For further extrapolations from it, see Nicholas Guppy, "Tropical Deforestation: A Global View," *Foreign Affairs* 62, no. 4 (Spring 1984).

of the tropical forests "one of the greatest biological debacles to occur on the face of the Earth." Looking at the effects it will have on the course of biological evolution, Myers says:

> The impending upheaval in evolution's course could rank as one of the greatest biological revolutions of paleontological time. It will equal in scale and significance the development of aerobic respiration, the emergence of flowering plants, and the arrival of limbed animals. But of course the prospective degradation of many evolutionary capacities will be an impoverishing, not a creative, phenomenon.[2]

7   In other words, such rapid destruction will vacate so many niches so suddenly that a "pest and weed" ecology, consisting of a relatively few opportunistic species (rats, roaches, and the like) will be created.

8   Beyond this—as if it weren't enough—such destruction could well have cataclysmic effects on the Earth's weather patterns, causing, for example, an irreversible desertification of the North American grain belt. Although the scope of the so-called greenhouse effect—in which rising levels of carbon dioxide in the atmosphere heat the planet by preventing infrared radiation from escaping into space—is still being debated within the scientific community, it is not at all extreme to suppose that the fires set to clear tropical forests will contribute greatly to this increase in atmospheric CO_2 and thereby to untold and possibly devastating changes in the world's weather systems.

BIG MAC ATTACK

9   So what does beef, that staple of the fast-food chains and of the North American diet in general, have to do with it?

10   It used to be, back in 1960, that the United States imported practically no beef. That was a time when North Americans were consuming a "mere" 85 pounds of beef per person per year. By 1980 this was up to 134 pounds per person per year. Concomitant with this increase in consumption, the United States began to import beef, so that by 1981 some 800,000 tons were coming in from abroad, 17 percent of it from tropical Latin America and three fourths of that from Central America. Since fast-food chains have been steadily expanding and now are a $5-billion-a-year business, accounting for 25 percent of all the beef consumed in the United States, the connections between the fast-food empire and tropical beef are clear.

---

[2] There are amazingly few scientists in the world with broad enough expertise to accurately assess the widest implications of tropical deforestation; Norman Myers is one of them. His books include *The Sinking Ark* (Oxford: Pergamon Press, 1979). See also *Conversion of Moist Tropical Forests* (Washington, D.C.: National Academy of Sciences, 1980), "The End of the Line," *Natural History* 94, no. 2 (February 1985), and "The Hamburger Connection," *Ambio* 10, no. 1 (1981). I have used Myers extensively in the preparation of this article. The quotes in this paragraph are from "The Hamburger Connection," pp. 3, 4, 5.

11   Cattle ranching is "by far the major factor in forest destruction in tropical Latin America," says Myers. "Large fast-food outlets in the U.S. and Europe foster the clearance of forests to produce cheap beef."[3]

12   And cheap it is, compared to North American beef: by 1978 the average price of beef imported from Central America was $1.47/kg, while similar North American beef cost $3.30/kg.

13   Cheap, that is, for North Americans, but not for Central Americans. Central Americans cannot afford their own beef. Whereas beef production in Costa Rica increased twofold between 1959 and 1972, per capita consumption of beef in that country went down from 30 lbs. a year to 19. In Honduras, beef production increased by 300 percent between 1965 and 1975, but consumption decreased from 12 lbs. per capita per year to 10. So, although two thirds of Central America's arable land is in cattle, local consumption of beef is decreasing; the average domestic cat in the United States now consumes more beef than the average Central American.[4]

14   Brazilian government figures show that 38 percent of all deforestation in the Brazilian Amazon between 1966 and 1975 was attributable to large-scale cattle ranching. Although the presence of hoof-and-mouth disease among Brazilian cattle has forced U.S. lawmakers to prohibit the importation of chilled or frozen Brazilian beef, the United States imports $46 million per year of cooked Brazilian beef, which goes into canned products; over 80 percent of Brazilian beef is still exported, most of it to Western Europe, where no such prohibition exists.

15   At present rates, all remaining Central American forests will have been eliminated by 1990. The cattle ranching largely responsible for this is in itself highly inefficient: as erosion and nutrient leaching eat away the soil production drops from an average one head per hectare—measly in any case—to a pitiful one head per five to seven hectares within five to ten years. A typical tropical cattle ranch employs only one person per 2,000 head, and meat production barely reaches 50 lbs./acre/year. In Northern Europe, in farms that do not use imported feed, it is over 500 lbs./acre/year.

16   This real-term inefficiency does not translate into bad business, however, for although there are some absentee landowners who engage in ranching for the prestige of it and are not particularly interested in turning large profits, others find bank loans for growing beef for export readily forthcoming, and get much help and encouragement from such organizations as the Pan American Health Organization, the Organization of American States, the U.S. Department of Agriculture, and U.S. AID, without whose technical assistance "cattle production in the American tropics would be unprofitable, if not impossible."[5] The ultimate big winner appears to be the United States, where increased imports of Central

---

[3] Myers, "End of the Line," p. 2.

[4] See James Nations and Daniel I. Komer "Rainforests and the Hamburger Society," *Environment* 25, no. 3 (April 1983).

[5] Nations and Komer, "Rainforests and the Hamburger Society," p. 17.

American beef are said to have done more to stem inflation than any other single government initiative.

17   "On the good land, which could support a large population, you have the rich cattle owners, and on the steep slopes, which should be left in forest, you have the poor farmers," says Gerardo Budowski, director of the Tropical Agricultural Research and Training Center in Turrialba, Costa Rica. "It is still good business to clear virgin forest in order to fatten cattle for, say, five to eight years and then abandon it."[6]

18   (Ironically, on a trip I made in 1981 to Morazán, a Salvadoran province largely under control of FMLN guerrillas, I inquired into the guerilla diet and discovered that beef, expropriated from the cattle ranches, was a popular staple.)

SWIFT-ARMOUR'S SWIFT ARMOR

19 The rain forest ecosystem, the oldest on Earth, is extremely complex and delicate. In spite of all the greenery one sees there, it is a myth that rain forest soil is rich. It is actually quite poor, leached of all nutrients save the most insoluble (such as iron oxides, which give lateritic soil—the most common soil type found there—its red color). Rather, the ecosystem of the rain forest is a "closed" one, in which the nutrients are to be found in the biomass, that is, in the living canopy of plants and in the thin layer of humus on the ground that is formed from the matter shed by the canopy. Hence the shallow-rootedness of most tropical forest plant species. Since the soil itself cannot replenish nutrients, nutrient recycling is what keeps the system going.

20   Now, what happens when the big cattle ranchers, under the auspices of the Swift-Armour Meat Packing Co., or United Brands, or the King Ranch sling a huge chain between two enormous tractors, level a few tens of thousands of acres of tropical forest, burn the debris, fly a plane over to seed the ash with guinea grass, and then run their cattle on the newly created grasslands?[7]

21   For the first three years or so the grass grows like crazy, up to an inch a day, thriving on all that former biomass. After that, things go quickly downhill: the ash becomes eroded and leached, the soil becomes exposed and hardens to the consistency of brick, and the area becomes useless to agriculture. Nor does it ever regain anything near its former state. The Amazon is rising perceptibly as a result of the increased runoff due to deforestation.

22   Tractor-and-chain is only one way of clearing the land. Another common technique involves the use of herbicides such as Tordon, 2, 4-D, and 2,4,5-T (Agent Orange). The dioxin found in Agent Orange can be extremely toxic to animal life and is very persistent in the environment.

---

[6] Catherine Caufield, "The Rain Forests," *New Yorker* (January 14, 1985), p. 42. This excellent article was later incorporated in a book, *In the Rainforest* (New York: Knopf, 1985).

[7] Other multinationals with interests in meat packing and cattle ranching in tropical Latin America include Armour-Dial International, Goodyear Tire and Rubber Co., and Gulf and Western Industries, Inc. See Roger Burbach and Patricia Flynn, *Agribusiness in the Americas* (New York: Monthly Review Press, 1980).

23 Tordon, since it leaves a residue deadly to all broad-leaved plants, renders the deforested area poisonous to all plants except grasses; consequently, even if they wanted to, ranchers could not plant soil-enriching legumes in the treated areas, a step which many agronomists recommend for keeping the land productive for at least a little longer.

24 The scale of such operations is a far cry from the traditional slash-and-burn practiced by native jungle groups, which is done on a scale small enough so that the forest can successfully reclaim the farmed areas. Such groups, incidentally, are also being decimated by cattle interests in Brazil and Paraguay—as missionaries, human rights groups, and cattlemen themselves will attest.

25 Capital's "manifest destiny" has traditionally shown little concern for the lives of trees or birds or Indians, or anything else which interferes with immediate profitability, but the current carving of holes in the gene pool by big agribusiness seems particularly short-sighted. Since the tropical forests contain two thirds of the world's genetic resources, their destruction will leave an enormous void in pool of genes necessary for the creation of new agricultural hybrids. This is not to mention the many plants as yet undiscovered—there could be up to 15,000 unknown species in South America alone—which may in themselves contain remarkable properties. (In writing about alkaloids found in the Madagascar periwinkle, which have recently revolutionized the treatment of leukemia and Hodgkin's disease, British biochemist John Humphreys said: "If this plant had not been analyzed, not even a chemist's wildest ravings would have hinted that such structures would be pharmacologically active."[8] Ninety percent of Madagascar's forests have been cut.)

26 But there is no small truth in Indonesian Minister for Environment and Development Emil Salim's complaint that the "South is asked to conserve genes while the other fellow, in the North, is consuming things that force us to destroy the genes in the South."[9]

WHERE'S THE BEEF?

27 The marketing of beef imported into the United States is extremely complex, and the beef itself ends up in everything from hot dogs to canned soup. Fresh meat is exported in refrigerated container ships to points of entry, where it is inspected by the U.S. Department of Agriculture. Once inspected, it is no longer required to be labeled "imported."[10] From there it goes into the hands of customhouse brokers and meat packers, often changing hands many times; and from there it goes to the fast-food chains or the food processors. The financial

[8] Quoted in Caufield, "Rain Forests," p. 60.
[9] Caufield, "Rain Forests," p. 100.
[10] This is one way McDonald's, for example, can claim not to use foreign beef. For a full treatment of McDonald's, see M. Boas and S. Chain, *Big Mac: The Unauthorized Story of McDonald's* (New York: New American Library, 1976).

structures behind this empire are even more complex, involving governments and quasipublic agencies, such as the Export-Import Bank and the Overseas Private Investment Corporation, as well as the World Bank and the Inter-American Development Bank, all of which encourage cattle raising in the forest lands. (Brazilian government incentives to cattle ranching in Amazonia include a 50 percent income-tax rebate on ranchers' investments elsewhere in Brazil, tax holidays of up to ten years, loans with negative interest rates in real terms, and exemptions from sales taxes and import duties. Although these incentives were deemed excessive and since 1979 no longer apply to new ranches, they still continue for existing ones. This cost the Brazilian government $63,000 for each ranching job created.)

28   Beef production in the tropics may be profitable for the few, but it is taking place at enormous cost for the majority and for the planet as a whole. Apart from the environmental destruction, it is a poor converter of energy to protein and provides few benefits for the vast majority of tropical peoples in terms of employment or food. What they require are labor-intensive, multiple-cropping systems.

29   The world is obviously hostage to an ethic which puts short-term profitability above all else, and such catastrophes as the wholesale destruction of the tropical forests and the continued impoverishment of their peoples are bound to occur as long as this ethic rules.

MEANING

1. How does Skinner characterize the extent of ecological damage resulting from the destruction of the tropical forests?

2. What causal link does Skinner point out between hamburgers served in fast-food chains in the United States and the destruction of tropical rain forests in Central America?

3. What is the greenhouse effect, and how is it related to the destruction of tropical forests?

4. Why does Skinner mention the innumerable drugs that are used in modern medicine that were derived from plants in the tropical forests?

TECHNIQUE

1. How does Skinner's strategy in organizing his essay depend on alternating between environments that are not normally thought as bearing any relationship to each other?

2. How does Skinner's discussion of the methods used by cattle ranchers to clear the land underscore his concern about a business ethic that "puts short-term profitability above all else"?

3. How does Skinner use evidence in the form of facts, statistics, and the testimony of experts to support his thesis?

4. *Other Patterns.* How does Skinner use **description** to give his readers a clear picture of both the causes and effects that he analyses?

LANGUAGE

1. How does Skinner use catchy headings in his four-section essay and a thought-provoking title to spark the reader's interest?

2. What transitional words or phrases does Skinner use to link sections of his analysis together and tell an effective story?

3. If you don't know the meaning of the following words, look them up: *kilometer* (4), *debacles* (6), *cataclysmic* (8), *concomitant* (10), *expropriated* (19), *legumes* (24), *hybrids* (26).

SUGGESTIONS FOR WRITING

1. **Critical Writing.** Considering that many modern drugs are derived from plants found in the tropical forests, what other implications of Skinner's thesis can you think of?

2. Skinner recommends switching to a "labor-intensive multiple-cropping system." What steps would be necessary to persuade corporations and governments to do this?

3. Do you think Skinner's analysis would change consumers' attitudes toward eating hamburgers in fast-food restaurants? Why or why not? **Argue** for or against this proposition.

4. **Thematic Links.** What connections can you discover between Skinner's analysis and Elizabeth Kolbert's report in "Shishmaref, Alaska" (Chapter 13, "Using Combined Patterns")?

KIM CHERNIN

The Flesh and the Devil

Kim Chernin (b. 1940) detected the national cultural obsession with being thin as early as 1981 when she wrote about it in *The Obsession: Reflections on the Tyranny of Slenderness*. In the following selection from that book, Chernin explores the damaging effects of these cultural messages on children and depicts the tormented women these girls grow up to be. She draws on personal experience and the results of research studies to analyze the underlying value system that produces such a distorted idea of body image. Her recent works include *In My Mother's House: A Memoir* (2003).

BEFORE YOU READ

Why have Spain and other countries recently prohibited super-skinny models from participating in fashion shows?

■ ■ ▨

We know that every woman wants to be thin. Our images of womanhood are almost synonymous with thinness.
—Susie Orbach

. . . I must now be able to look at my ideal, this ideal of being thin, of being without a body, and to realize: "it is a fiction."
—Ellen West

When the body is hiding the complex, it then becomes our most immediate access to the problem.
—Marian Woodman

1   The locker room of the tennis club. Several exercise benches, two old-fashioned hair dryers, a mechanical bicycle, a treadmill, a reducing machine, a mirror, and a scale.

2   A tall woman enters, removes her towel; she throws it across a bench, faces herself squarely in the mirror, climbs on the scale, looks down.

3   A silence.

4   "I knew it," she mutters, turning to me. "I knew it."

5   And I think, before I answer, just how much I admire her, for this courage beyond my own, this daring to weigh herself daily in this way. And I sympathize. I know what she must be feeling. Not quite candidly, I say: "Up or down?" I am hoping to suggest that there might be people and cultures where gaining weight might not be considered a disaster. Places where women, stepping on scales, might be horrified to notice that they had reduced themselves. A mythical, almost unimaginable land.

For a visual to accompany this selection, see color insert photo B-7.

6   "Two pounds," she says, ignoring my hint. "Two pounds." And then she turns, grabs the towel and swings out at her image in the mirror, smashing it violently, the towel spattering water over the glass. "Fat pig," she shouts at her image in the glass. "You fat, fat pig. . . ."

7   Later, I go to talk with this woman. Her name is Rachel and she becomes, as my work progresses, one of the choral voices that shape its vision.

8   Two girls come into the exercise room. They are perhaps ten or eleven years old, at that elongated stage when the skeletal structure seems to be winning its war against flesh. And these two are particularly skinny. They sit beneath the hair dryers for a moment, kicking their legs on the faded green upholstery, they run a few steps on the eternal treadmill, they wrap the rubber belt of the reducing machine around themselves and jiggle for a moment before it falls off. And then they go to the scale.

9   The taller one steps up, glances at herself in the mirror, looks down at the scale. She sighs, shaking her head. I see at once that this girl is imitating someone. The sigh, the headshake are theatrical, beyond her years. And so, too, is the little drama enacting itself in front of me. The other girl leans forward, eager to see for herself the troubling message imprinted upon the scale. But the older girl throws her hand over the secret. It is not to be revealed. And now the younger one, accepting this, steps up to confront the ultimate judgment. "Oh God," she says, this growing girl. "Oh God," with only a shade of imitation in her voice: "Would you believe it? I've gained five pounds."

10   These girls, too, become a part of my work. They enter, they perform their little scene again and again; it extends beyond them and in it I am finally able to behold something that would have remained hidden—for it does not express itself directly, although we feel its pressure—almost every day of our lives. Something, unnamed as yet, struggling against our emergence into femininity. This is my first glimpse of it, out there. And the vision ripens.

11   I return to the sauna. Two women I have seen regularly at the club are sitting on the bench above me. One of them is very beautiful, the sort of woman Renoir would have admired. The other, who is probably in her late sixties, looks, in the twilight of this sweltering room, very much an adolescent. I have noticed her before, with her tan face, her white hair, her fashionable clothes, her slender hips and jaunty walk. But the effect has not been soothing. A woman of advancing age who looks like a boy.

12   "I've heard about that illness, anorexia nervosa," the plump one is saying, "and I keep looking around for someone who has it. I want to go sit next to her. I think to myself, maybe I'll catch it. . . ."

13   "Well," the other woman says to her, "I've felt the same way myself. One of my cousins used to throw food under the table when no one was looking. Finally, she got so thin they had to take her to the hospital. . . . I always admired her."

14   What am I to understand from these stories? The woman in the locker room who swings out at her image in the mirror, the little girls who are afraid of the coming of adolescence to their bodies, the woman who admires the slenderness of the anorexic girl. Is it possible to miss the dislike these women feel for their bodies?

15   And yet, an instant's reflection tells us that this dislike for the body is not a biological fact of our condition as women—we do not come upon it by nature, we are not born to it, it does not arise for us because of anything predetermined in our sex. We know that once we loved the body, delighting in it the way children will, reaching out to touch our toes and count over our fingers, repeating the game endlessly as we come to knowledge of this body in which we will live out our lives. No part of the body exempt from our curiosity, nothing yet forbidden, we know an equal fascination with the feces we eliminate from ourselves, as with the ear we discover one day and the knees that have become bruised and scraped with falling and that warm, moist place between the legs from which feelings of indescribable bliss arise.

16   From that state to the condition of the woman in the locker room is a journey from innocence to despair, from the infant's naive pleasure in the body, to the woman's anguished confrontation with herself. In this journey we can read our struggle with natural existence—the loss of the body as a source of pleasure. But the most striking thing about this alienation from the body is the fact that we take it for granted. Few of us ask to be redeemed from this struggle against the flesh by overcoming our antagonism toward the body. We do not rush about looking for someone who can tell us how to enjoy the fact that our appetite is large, or how we might delight in the curves and fullness of our own natural shape. We hope instead to be able to reduce the body, to limit the urges and desires it feels, to remove the body from nature. Indeed, the suffering we experience through our obsession with the body arises precisely from the hopeless and impossible nature of this goal.

17   Cheryl Prewitt, the 1980 winner of the Miss America contest, is a twenty-two-year-old woman, "slender, bright-eyed, and attractive."[1] If there were a single woman alive in America today who might feel comfortable about the size and shape of her body, surely we would expect her to be Ms. Prewitt? And yet, in order to make her body suitable for the swimsuit event of the beauty contest she has just won, Cheryl Prewitt "put herself through a grueling regimen, jogging long distances down back-country roads, pedaling for hours on her stationary bicycle." The bicycle is still kept in the living room of her parents' house so that she can take part in conversation while she works out. This body she has created, after an arduous struggle against nature, in conformity with her culture's ideal standard for a woman, cannot now be left to its own desires. It must be perpetually shaped, monitored, and watched. If you were to visit her at home in Ackerman, Mississippi, you might well find her riding her stationary bicycle in her parents' living room, "working off the calories from a large slice of homemade coconut cake she has just had for a snack."

18   And so we imagine a woman who will never be Miss America, a next-door neighbor, a woman down the street, waking in the morning and setting out for her regular routine of exercise. The eagerness with which she jumps up at six o'clock and races for her jogging shoes and embarks upon the cold and arduous toiling up the hill road that runs past her house. And yes, she feels certain that her zeal to take off another pound, tighten another inch of softening flesh, places

her in the school of those ancient wise men who formulated that vision of harmony between mind and body. "A healthy mind in a healthy body," she repeats to herself and imagines that it is love of the body which inspires her this early morning. But now she lets her mind wander and encounter her obsession. First it had been those hips, and she could feel them jogging along there with their own rhythm as she jogged. It was they that had needed reducing. Then, when the hips came down it was the thighs, hidden when she was clothed but revealing themselves every time she went to the sauna, and threatening great suffering now that summer drew near. Later, it was the flesh under the arms—this proved singularly resistant to tautness even after the rest of the body had become gaunt. And finally it was the ankles. But then, was there no end to it? What had begun as a vision of harmony between mind and body, a sense of well-being, physical fitness, and glowing health, had become now demonic, driving her always to further exploits, running farther, denying herself more food, losing more weight, always goaded on by the idea that the body's perfection lay just beyond her present achievement. And then, when she began to observe this driven quality in herself, she also began to notice what she had been thinking about her body. For she would write down in her notebook, without being aware of the violence in what she wrote: "I don't care how long it takes. One day I'm going to get my body to obey me. I'm going to make it lean and tight and hard. I'll succeed in this, even if it kills me."

19   But what a vicious attitude this is, she realizes one day, toward a body she professes to love. Was it love or hatred of the flesh that inspired her now to awaken even before it was light, and to go out on the coldest morning, running with bare arms and bare legs, busily fantasizing what she would make of her body? Love or hatred?

20   "You know perfectly well we hate our bodies," says Rachel, who calls herself the pig. She grabs the flesh of her stomach between her hands. "Who could love this?"

21   There is an appealing honesty in this despair, an articulation of what is virtually a universal attitude among women in our culture today. Few women who diet realize that they are confessing to a dislike for the body when they weigh and measure their flesh, subject it to rigorous fasts or strenuous regimens of exercise. And yet, over and over again, as I spoke to women about their bodies, this antagonism became apparent. One woman disliked her thighs, another her stomach, a third the loose flesh under her arms. Many would grab their skin and squeeze it as we talked, with that grimace of distaste language cannot translate into itself. One woman said to me: "Little by little I began to be aware that the pounds I was trying to 'melt away' were my own flesh. Would you believe it? It never occurred to me before. These 'ugly pounds' which filled me with so much hatred were my body."

22   The sound of this dawning consciousness can be heard now and again among the voices I have recorded in my notebook, heralding what may be a growing awareness of how bitterly the women of this culture are alienated from their bodies. Thus, another woman said to me: "It's true, I never used to like my body." We had been looking at pictures of women from the nineteenth century; they were large women, with full hips and thighs. "What do you think of them?" I said. "They're like me," she answered, and then began to laugh. "Soft, sensual, and inviting."

23   The description is accurate; the women in the pictures, and the woman looking at them, share a quality of voluptuousness that is no longer admired by our
culture:

> When I look at myself in the mirror I see that there's nothing wrong with me—
> now! Sometimes I even think I'm beautiful. I don't know why this began to
> change. It might have been when I started going to the YWCA. It was the first
> time I saw so many women naked. I realized it was the fuller bodies that were
> more beautiful. The thin women, who looked so good in clothes, seemed old
> and worn out. Their bodies were gaunt. But the bodies of the larger women
> had a certain natural mystery, very different from the false illusion of clothes.
> And I thought, I'm like them; I'm a big woman like they are and perhaps my
> body is beautiful. I had always been trying to make my body have the right
> shape so that I could fit into clothes. But then I started to look at myself in the
> mirror. Before that I had always looked at parts of myself. The hips were too
> flabby, the thighs were too fat. Now I began to see myself as a whole. I stopped
> hearing my mother's voice, asking me if I was going to go on a diet. I just looked
> at what was really there instead of what should have been there. What was wrong
> with it? I asked myself. And little by little I stopped disliking my body.[2]

24 This is the starting point. It is from this new way of looking at an old problem
that liberation will come. The very simple idea that an obsession with weight
reflects a dislike and uneasiness for the body can have a profound effect upon
a woman's life.

> I always thought I was too fat. I never liked my body. I kept trying to lose
> weight. I just tortured myself. But if I see pictures of myself from a year or
> two ago I discover now that I looked just fine.
>   I remember recently going out to buy Häagen Dazs ice cream. I had
> decided I was going to give myself something I really wanted to eat. I had to
> walk all the way down to the World Trade Center. But on my way there I began
> to feel terribly fat. I felt that I was being punished by being fat. I had lost the
> beautiful self I had made by becoming thinner. I could hear these voices say-
> ing to me: "You're fat, you're ugly, who do you think you are, don't you know
> you'll never be happy?" I had always heard these voices in my mind but now
> when they would come into consciousness I would tell them to shut up. I saw
> two men on the street. I was eating the Häagen Dazs ice cream. I thought I
> heard one of them say "heavy." I thought they were saying: "She's so fat." But
> I knew that I had to live through these feelings if I was ever to eat what I liked.
> I just couldn't go on tormenting myself any more about the size of my body.
>   One day, shortly after this, I walked into my house. I noticed the scales,
> standing under the sink in the bathroom. Suddenly, I hated them. I was
> filled with grief for having tortured myself for so many years. They looked
> like shackles. I didn't want to have anything more to do with them. I called my
> boyfriend and offered him the scales. Then, I went into the kitchen. I looked
> at my shelves. I saw diet books there. I was filled with rage and hatred of

them. I hurled them all into a box and got rid of them. Then I looked into the ice box. There was a bottle of Weight Watchers dressing. I hurled it into the garbage and watched it shatter and drip down the plastic bag. Little by little, I started to feel better about myself. At first I didn't eat less, I just worried less about my eating. I allowed myself to eat whatever I wanted. I began to give away the clothes I couldn't fit into. It turned out that they weren't right for me anyway. I had bought them with the idea of what my body should look like. Now I buy clothes because I like the way they look on me. If something doesn't fit it doesn't fit. I'm not trying to make myself into something I'm not. I weigh more than I once considered my ideal. But I don't seem fat to myself. Now, I can honestly say that I like my body.[3]

25   Some weeks ago, at a dinner party, a woman who had recently gained weight began to talk about her body.

26   "I was once very thin," she said, "but I didn't feel comfortable in my body. I fit into all the right clothes. But somehow I just couldn't find myself any longer."

27   I looked over at her expectantly; she was a voluptuous woman, who had recently given birth to her first child.

28   "But now," she said as she got to her feet, "now, if I walk or jog or dance, I feel my flesh jiggling along with me." She began to shake her shoulders and move her hips, her eyes wide as she hopped about in front of the coffee table. "You see what I mean?" she shouted over to me. "I love it."

29   This image of a woman dancing came with me when I sat down to write. I remembered her expression. There was in it something secretive, I thought, something knowing and pleased—the look of a woman who has made peace with her body. Then I recalled the faces of women who had recently lost weight. The haggard look, the lines of strain around the mouth, the neck too lean, the tendons visible, the head too large for the emaciated body. I began to reason:

30   There must be, I said, for every woman a correct weight, which cannot be discovered with reference to a weight chart or to any statistical norm. For the size of the body is a matter of highly subjective individual preferences and natural endowments. If we should evolve an aesthetic for women that was appropriate to women it would reflect this diversity, would conceive, indeed celebrate and even love, slenderness in a woman intended by nature to be slim, and love the rounded cheeks of another, the plump arms, broad shoulders, narrow hips, full thighs, rounded ass, straight back, narrow shoulders or slender arms, of a woman made that way according to her nature, walking with head high in pride of her body, however it happened to be shaped. And then Miss America, and the woman jogging in the morning, and the woman swinging out at her image in the mirror might say, with Susan Griffin in *Woman and Nature*:

> And we are various, and amazing in our variety, and our differences multiply, so that edge after edge of the endlessness of possibility is exposed . . . none of us beautiful when separate but all exquisite as we stand, each moment heeded in this cycle, no detail unlovely. . . .[4]

How does this film still of Marines playing football in the desert from the movie *Jarhead* (2004) lend credence to John McMurtry's comparative analogy in "Kill 'Em! Crush 'Em! Eat 'Em Raw!"?

How does this photograph of sunlight filtering through the leaves of oak trees on the Oaklawn Plantation in Natchitoches, Louisiana, show why William Bryan Logan chose the oak tree over the Eiffel Tower in "Eiffel and Oak"?

How does this 1960s photo of a family holding a Passover Seder, commemorating the Jews' escape from slavery in Egypt, convey the importance of the Seder organized by Ethel G. Hofman's mother in "An Island Passover"?

How does this picture of a Mayan woman carrying flowers through a market in Chichicastenago, Guatemala, illustrate life among the Quiché, as also described by Rigoberta Menchú in "Birth Ceremonies"?

What does this image of a Spanish lesson on a chalkboard suggest about the way that concepts translate between languages?

How does this picture of large frozen tuna being sorted for the morning auction at the Tsukiji Fish Market in Tokyo, Japan—the largest in the country—demonstrate the skills necessary to sort and classify?

How does the mood in this photo express the obsession with being thin that Kim Chernin analyzes in "The Flesh and the Devil"?

How does the presence of a sprig of mistletoe permit the action in this photo to take place, as discussed by Vaughn M. Bryant, Jr. and Sylvia Grider in "To Kiss: Why We Kiss Under the Mistletoe"?

NOTES

1. Sally Hegelson, *TWA Ambassador,* July 1980.
2. Private communication.
3. Private communication.
4. Susan Griffin, *Woman and Nature: The Roaring Inside Her,* New York: Harper, 1978.

■ ■ ▨

MEANING

1. What kind of influence do cultural values have in determining how women see themselves?
2. What alternative approach or value system does Chernin suggest to replace the prevailing norms?
3. Why does Chernin believe that dislike of one's body is not natural?
4. To what extent has self-punishment come to be the result of prevailing cultural attitudes?

TECHNIQUE

1. How does the **example** with which Chernin opens her essay illustrate the damaging psychological effects on children of cultural messages about being thin?
2. How do the counterexamples and **narratives** with which Chernin concludes her essay support her conclusions?
3. **Other Patterns.** How does Chernin use **process analysis** in describing the punishing regimen of a former Miss America to illustrate her thesis?

LANGUAGE

1. How does Chernin's title suggest the unwholesome effect of society's values on women?
2. How do the comments by the winner of the Miss America contest underscore the tyranny of the stereotype that dominates women's lives?
3. How do the affirmative connotations of Chernin's concluding paragraph ask women to reclaim their right to be themselves?
4. If you don't know the meaning of the following words, look them up: *candidly* (5), *choral* (7), *elongated* (8), *anorexia* (12), *antagonism* (16), *tautness* (18), *gaunt* (18).

SUGGESTIONS FOR WRITING

1. **Critical Writing.** To what extent are Chernin's assessments still true? Has your self-image been influenced by the cultural stereotypes she describes? How?

2. What cultural messages do you constantly encounter in the media?

3. What **examples** can you present of women who are comfortable in their own bodies and do not buy into the prevailing cultural programming?

4. ***Thematic Links.***   Compare Chernin's essay with Bernard Rudofsky's analysis in "The Unfashionable Human Body" (Chapter 12, "Argument").

C. P. ELLIS

Why I Quit the Klan

Studs Terkel (b. 1912) welcomed the opportunity to interview a former Ku Klux Klan leader, C. P. Ellis (1927–2005), who left the Klan to become a civil rights activist. We can gain a greater understanding of the reasons for racial prejudice in the South from this open and honest interview, which first appeared in Terkel's *American Dreams: Lost and Found* (1980). Ellis later wrote a book, *Best of Enemies* (1996), about his friendship with Ann Atwater, an African American civil rights organizer. Terkel became a familiar figure on the American scene as a moderator for radio programs. Among his many "interview" books are *Working* (1974), *Coming of Age* (1995), *Hope Dies Last* (2003), and *And They All Sang* (2005).

BEFORE YOU READ

How has the KKK attracted new members by exploiting racial antagonisms?

■ ■ ▨

1   All my life, I had work, never a day without work, worked all the overtime I could get and still could not survive financially. I began to see there's something wrong with this country. I worked my butt off and just never seemed to break even. I had some real great ideas about this nation. They say to abide by the law, go to church, do right and live for the Lord, and everything'll work out. But it didn't work out. It just kept gettin worse and worse. . . .

2   Tryin to come out of that hole, I just couldn't do it. I really began to get bitter. I didn't know who to blame. I tried to find somebody. Hatin America is hard to do because you can't see it to hate it. You gotta have somethin to look at to hate. The natural person for me to hate would be black people, because my father before me was a member of the Klan. . . .

3   So I began to admire the Klan. . . . To be part of somethin. . . . The first night I went with the fellas . . . I was led into a large meeting room, and this was the time of my life! It was thrilling. Here's a guy who's worked all his life and struggled all his life to be something, and here's the moment to be something. I will never forget it. Four robed Klansmen led me into the hall. The lights were dim and the only thing you could see was an illuminated cross. . . . After I had taken my oath, there was loud applause goin throughout the buildin, musta been at least four hundred people. For this one little ol person. It was a thrilling moment for C. P. Ellis. . . .

4   The majority of [the Klansmen] are low-income whites, people who really don't have a part in something. They have been shut out as well as blacks. Some are not very well educated either. Just like myself. We had a lot of support from doctors and lawyers and police officers.

5   Maybe they've had bitter experiences in this life and they had to hate some-body. So the natural person to hate would be the black person. He's beginnin to come up, he's beginnin to . . . start votin and run for political office. Here are white people who are supposed to be superior to them, and we're shut out. . . . Shut out. Deep down inside, we want to be part of this great society. Nobody listens, so we join these groups. . . .

6   We would go to the city council meetings, and the blacks would be there and we'd be there. It was a confrontation every time. . . . We began to make some inroads with the city councilmen and county commissioners. They began to call us friend. Call us at night on the telephone; "C. P., glad you came to that meeting last night." They didn't want integration either, but they did it secretively, in order to get elected. They couldn't stand up openly and say it, but they were glad somebody was sayin it. We visited some of the city leaders in their homes and talked to em privately. It wasn't long before councilmen would call me up: "The blacks are comin up tonight and makin outrageous demands. How about some of you people showin up and have a little balance?" . . .

7   We'd load up our cars and we'd fill up half the council chambers, and the blacks the other half. During these times, I carried weapons to the meetings, outside my belt. We'd go there armed. We would wind up just hollerin and fussin at each other. What happened? As a result of our fightin one another, the city council still had their way. They didn't want to give up control to the blacks nor the Klan. They were usin us.

8   I began to realize this later down the road. One day I was walkin downtown and a certain city council member saw me comin. I expected him to shake my hand because he was talkin to me at night on the telephone. I had been in his home and visited with him. He crossed the street [to avoid me]. . . . I began to think, somethin's wrong here. Most of em are merchants or maybe an attorney, an insurance agent, people like that. As long as they kept low-income whites and low-income blacks fightin, they're gonna maintain control. I began to get that feelin after I was ignored in public. I thought: . . . you're not gonna use me any more. That's when I began to do some real serious thinkin.

9   The same thing is happening in this country today. People are being used by those in control, those who have all the wealth. I'm not espousing communism. We got the greatest system of government in the world. But those who have it simply don't want those who don't have it to have any part of it. Black and white. When it comes to money, the green, the other colors make no difference.

10   I spent a lot of sleepless nights. I still didn't like blacks. I didn't want to associate with them. Blacks, Jews or Catholics. My father said: "Don't have anything to do with em." I didn't until I met a black person and talked with him, eyeball to eyeball, and met a Jewish person and talked to him, eyeball to eyeball. I found they're people just like me. They cried, they cussed, they prayed, they had desires. Just like myself. Thank God, I got to the point where I can look past labels. But at that time, my mind was closed.

11 I remember one Monday night Klan meeting. I said something was wrong. Our city fathers were using us. And I didn't like to be used. The reactions of the others were not too pleasant: "Let's just keep fightin them niggers."

12 I'd go home at night and I'd have to wrestle with myself. I'd look at a black person walkin down the street, and the guy'd have ragged shoes or his clothes would be worn. That began to do something to me inside. I went through this for about six months. I felt I just had to get out of the Klan. But I wouldn't get out. . . .

13 [Ellis was invited, as a Klansman, to join a committee of people from all walks of life to make recommendations on how to solve racial problems in the school system. He very reluctantly accepted. After a few stormy meetings, he was elected co-chair of the committee, along with Ann Atwater, a black woman who for years had been leading local efforts for civil rights.]

14 A Klansman and a militant black woman, co-chairmen of the school committee. It was impossible. How could I work with her? But it was in our hands. We had to make it a success. This give me another sense of belongin, a sense of pride. This helped the inferiority feeling I had. A man who has stood up publicly and said he despised black people, all of a sudden he was willin to work with em. Here's a chance for a low-income white man to be somethin. In spite of all my hatred for blacks and Jews and liberals, I accepted the job. Her and I began to reluctantly work together. She had as many problems workin with me as I had workin with her.

15 One night, I called her: "Ann, you and I should have a lot of differences and we got em now. But there's something laid out here before us, and if it's gonna be a success, you and I are gonna have to make it one. Can we lay aside some of these feelins?" She said: "I'm willing if you are." I said: "Let's do it.'"

16 My old friends would call me at night: "C. P., what the hell is wrong with you? You're sellin out the white race." This begin to make me have guilt feelins. Am I doin right? Am I doin wrong? Here I am all of a sudden makin an about-face and tryin to deal with my feelins, my heart. My mind was beginnin to open up. I was beginnin to see what was right and what was wrong. I don't want the kids to fight forever. . . .

17 One day, Ann and I went back to the school and we sat down. We began to talk and just reflect. . . . I begin to see, here we are, two people from the far ends of the fence, havin identical problems, except hers bein black and me bein white. . . . The amazing thing about it, her and I, up to that point, has cussed each other, bawled each other, we hated each other. Up to that point, we didn't know each other. We didn't know we had things in common. . . .

18 The whole world was openin up, and I was learning new truths that I had never learned before. I was beginning to look at a black person, shake hands with him, and see him as a human bein. I hadn't got rid of all this stuff. I've still got a little bit of it. But somethin was happenin to me. . . .

19 I come to work one mornin and some guys says: "We need a union." At this time I wasn't pro-union. My daddy was anti-labor too. We're not gettin paid

much, we're havin to work seven days in a row. We're all starvin to death. . . . I didn't know nothin about organizin unions, but I knew how to organize people, stir people up. That's how I got to be business agent for the union.

20   When I began to organize, I began to see far deeper. I begin to see people again bein used. Blacks against whites. . . . There are two things management wants to keep: all the money and all the say-so. They don't want none of these poor workin folks to have none of that. I begin to see management fightin me with everythin they had. Hire anti-union law firms, badmouth unions. The people were makin $1.95 an hour, barely able to get through weekends. . . .

21   It makes you feel good to go into a plant and . . . see black people and white people join hands to defeat the racist issues [union-busters] use against people. . . .

22   I tell people there's a tremendous possibility in this country to stop wars, the battles, the struggles, the fights between people. People say: "That's an impossible dream. You sound like Martin Luther King." An ex-Klansman who sounds like Martin Luther King. I don't think it's an impossible dream. It's happened in my life. It's happened in other people's lives in America. . . .

23   . . . They say the older you get, the harder it is for you to change. That's not necessarily true. Since I changed, I've set down and listened to tapes of Martin Luther King. I listen to it and tears come to my eyes cause I know what he's sayin now. I know what's happenin."

What does this relatively recent picture (1992) suggest about the appeal of the Klan that Ellis rejected?

MEANING

1. What set of circumstances initially motivated Ellis to become a member of the Klan?

2. How much of the Klan's appeal was due to the way in which it made other groups the scapegoat for inequities and hardships that its members experienced?

3. How was Ellis's decision to become a union organizer related to his discovery that local politicians used the Klan to perpetuate divisions of class and race in order to maintain their own power?

4. How did the problems faced by Ann Atwater in accepting Ellis mirror his own struggle to overcome his stereotyped impressions?

TECHNIQUE

1. What does Ellis's reaction to listening to recordings of Martin Luther King, Jr.'s speeches reveal about how he had changed from being the president of the local chapter of the Klan?

2. What cues in the text remind you that this was an interview and that the original has been edited and formatted?

3. **Other Patterns.** How does Studs Terkel structure his interview with Ellis in the form of a **narrative** so that we can better appreciate Ellis's change of heart?

LANGUAGE

1. How do the colloquialisms add to the authenticity of Ellis's account?

2. What words and phrases capture the essence of Ellis's shift in attitude—what he refers to as having to "wrestle with myself" (paragraph 12)?

3. If you don't know the meaning of the following words, look them up: *Klan* (2), *integration* (6), *despised* (14).

SUGGESTIONS FOR WRITING

1. Have you ever had to change your mind about someone or something because new experiences raised doubts about your original beliefs?

2. Try Studs Terkel's method, and interview someone who has changed his or her beliefs to discover why the person now sees things from a completely different perspective. You might wish to edit and format the results.

3. **Critical Writing.** Do you agree or disagree with Ellis's conclusion that people with wealth and power foment and exploit racism as a means to maintain their position? **Argue** for your point of view.

4. **Thematic Links.** Compare the role of empathy in bringing about a change in the perspectives in Ellis's account and in Margaret Sanger's "The Turbid Ebb and Flow of Misery" (Chapter 13, "Using Combined Patterns").

ANWAR F. ACCAWI

The Telephone

Anwar F. Accawi, a short story writer and essayist, was born in a small town in Lebanon and was later educated in the United States. He began writing fiction as a way of getting his children to understand more about his background. In this essay, written in 1997, he gives a vivid account of the total transformation of village life when the first—and, for a long time, only—telephone was installed. The effects on the community, both large and small, were profound, and not all of them were positive, as might be expected. This essay was selected for the 1998 edition of *Best American Essays*. Accawi currently teaches at the University of Tennessee and has also written *The Boy from the Tower of the Moon* (1999).

BEFORE YOU READ

What would your life have been like before the invention of the telephone?

■ ■ ▨

1   When I WAS growing up in Magdaluna, a small Lebanese village in the terraced, rocky mountains east of Sidon, time didn't mean much to anybody, except maybe to those who were dying, or those waiting to appear in court because they had tampered with the boundary markers on their land. In those days, there was no real need for a calendar or a watch to keep track of the hours, days, months, and years. We knew what to do and when to do it, just as the Iraqi geese knew when to fly north, driven by the hot wind that blew in from the desert, and the ewes knew when to give birth to wet lambs that stood on long, shaky legs in the chilly March wind and baaed hesitantly, because they were small and cold and did not know where they were or what to do now that they were here. The only timepiece we had need of then was the sun. It rose and set, and the seasons rolled by, and we sowed seed and harvested and ate and played and married our cousins and had babies who got whooping cough and chickenpox—and those children who survived grew up and married *their* cousins and had babies who got whooping cough and chickenpox. We lived and loved and toiled and died without ever needing to know what year it was, or even the time of day.

2   It wasn't that we had no system for keeping track of time and of the important events in our lives. But ours was a natural—or rather, a divine—calendar, because it was framed by acts of God. Allah himself set down the milestones with earthquakes and droughts and floods and locusts and pestilences. Simple as our calendar was, it worked just fine for us.

3   Take, for example, the birth date of Teta Im Khalil, the oldest woman in Magdaluna and all the surrounding villages. When I first met her, we had just returned home from Syria at the end of the Big War and were living with Grandma Mariam. Im Khalil came by to welcome my father home and to take

a long, myopic look at his foreign-born wife, my mother. Im Khalil was so old that the skin of her cheeks looked like my father's grimy tobacco pouch, and when I kissed her (because Grandma insisted that I show her old friend affection), it was like kissing a soft suede glove that had been soaked with sweat and then left in a dark closet for a season. Im Khalil's face got me to wondering how old one had to be to look and taste the way she did. So, as soon as she had hobbled off on her cane, I asked Grandma, "How old is Teta Im Khalil?"

4   Grandma had to think for a moment; then she said, "I've been told that Teta was born shortly after the big snow that caused the roof on the mayor's house to cave in."

5   "And when was that?" I asked.

6   "Oh, about the time we had the big earthquake that cracked the wall in the east room."

7   Well, that was enough for me. You couldn't be more accurate than that, now, could you? Satisfied with her answer, I went back to playing with a ball made from an old sock stuffed with other, much older socks.

8   And that's the way it was in our little village for as far back as anybody could remember: people were born so many years before or after an earthquake or a flood; they got married or died so many years before or after a long drought or a big snow or some other disaster. One of the most unusual of these dates was when Antoinette the seamstress and Saeed the barber (and tooth puller) got married. That was the year of the whirlwind during which fish and oranges fell from the sky. Incredible as it may sound, the story of the fish and oranges was true, because men—respectable men, like Abu George the blacksmith and Abu Asaad the mule skinner, men who would not lie even to save their own souls—told and retold that story until it was incorporated into Magdaluna's calendar, just like the year of the black moon and the year of the locusts before it. My father, too, confirmed the story for me. He told me that he had been a small boy himself when it had rained fish and oranges from heaven. He'd gotten up one morning after a stormy night and walked out into the yard to find fish as long as his forearm still flopping here and there among the wet navel oranges.

9   The year of the fish-bearing twister, however, was not the last remarkable year. Many others followed in which strange and wonderful things happened: milestones added by the hand of Allah to Magdaluna's calendar. There was, for instance, the year of the drought, when the heavens were shut for months and the spring from which the entire village got its drinking water slowed to a trickle. The spring was about a mile from the village, in a ravine that opened at one end into a small, flat clearing covered with fine gray dust and hard, marble-sized goat droppings, because every afternoon the goatherds brought their flocks there to water them. In the year of the drought, that little clearing was always packed full of noisy kids with big brown eyes and sticky hands, and their mothers—sinewy, overworked young women with protruding collarbones and cracked, callused brown heels. The children ran around playing tag or hide-and-seek while the women talked, shooed flies, and awaited their turns to fill up their jars with drinking water to bring home to their napping men and wet

babies. There were days when we had to wait from sunup until late afternoon just to fill a small clay jar with precious, cool water.

10   Sometimes, amid the long wait and the heat and the flies and the smell of goat dung, tempers flared, and the younger women, anxious about their babies, argued over whose turn it was to fill up her jar. And sometimes the arguments escalated into full-blown, knockdown-dragout fights; the women would grab each other by the hair and curse and scream and spit and call each other names that made my ears tingle. We little brown boys who went with our mothers to fetch water loved these fights, because we got to see the women's legs and their colored panties as they grappled and rolled around in the dust. Once in a while, we got lucky and saw much more, because some of the women wore nothing at all under their long dresses. God, how I used to look forward to those fights. I remember the rush, the excitement, the sun dancing on the dust clouds as a dress ripped and a young white breast was revealed, then quickly hidden. In my calendar, that year of drought will always be one of the best years of my childhood, because it was then, in a dusty clearing by a trickling mountain spring, I got my first glimpses of the wonders, the mysteries, and the promises hidden beneath the folds of a woman's dress. Fish and oranges from heaven . . . you can get over that.

11   But, in another way, the year of the drought was also one of the worst of my life, because that was the year that Abu Raja, the retired cook who used to entertain us kids by cracking walnuts on his forehead, decided it was time Magdaluna got its own telephone. Every civilized village needed a telephone, he said, and Magdaluna was not going to get anywhere until it had one. A telephone would link us with the outside world. At the time, I was too young to understand the debate, but a few men—like Shukri, the retired Turkish-army drill sergeant, and Abu Hanna the vineyard keeper—did all they could to talk Abu Raja out of having a telephone brought to the village. But they were outshouted and ignored and finally shunned by the other villagers for resisting progress and trying to keep a good thing from coming to Magdaluna.

12   One warm day in early fall, many of the villagers were out in their fields repairing walls or gathering wood for the winter when the shout went out that the telephone-company truck had arrived at Abu Raja's *dikkan*, or country store. There were no roads in those days, only footpaths and dry streambeds, so it took the telephone-company truck almost a day to work its way up the rocky terrain from Sidon—about the same time it took to walk. When the truck came into view, Abu George, who had a huge voice and, before the telephone, was Magdaluna's only long-distance communication system, bellowed the news from his front porch. Everybody dropped what they were doing and ran to Abu Raja's house to see what was happening. Some of the more dignified villagers, however, like Abu Habeeb and Abu Nazim, who had been to big cities like Beirut and Damascus and had seen things like telephones and telegraphs, did not run the way the rest did; they walked with their canes hanging from the crooks of their arms, as if on a Sunday afternoon stroll.

13   It did not take long for the whole village to assemble at Abu Raja's *dikkan*. Some of the rich villagers, like the widow Farha and the gendarme Abu Nadeem,

walked right into the store and stood at the elbows of the two important-looking men from the telephone company, who proceeded with utmost gravity, like priests at Communion, to wire up the telephone. The poorer villagers stood outside and listened carefully to the details relayed to them by the not-so-poor people who stood in the doorway and could see inside.

14   "The bald man is cutting the blue wire," someone said.

15   "He is sticking the wire into the hole in the bottom of the black box," someone else added.

16   "The telephone man with the mustache is connecting two pieces of wire. Now he is twisting the ends together," a third voice chimed in.

17   Because I was small and unaware that I should have stood outside with the other poor folk to give the rich people inside more room (they seemed to need more of it than poor people did), I wriggled my way through the dense forest of legs to get a firsthand look at the action. I felt like the barefoot Moses, sandals in hand, staring at the burning bush on Mount Sinai. Breathless, I watched as the men in blue, their shirt pockets adorned with fancy lettering in a foreign language, put together a black machine that supposedly would make it possible to talk with uncles, aunts, and cousins who lived more than two days' ride away.

18   It was shortly after sunset when the man with the mustache announced that the telephone was ready to use. He explained that all Abu Raja had to do was lift the receiver, turn the crank on the black box a few times, and wait for an operator to take his call. Abu Raja, who had once lived and worked in Sidon, was impatient with the telephone man for assuming that he was ignorant. He grabbed the receiver and turned the crank forcefully, as if trying to start a Model T Ford. Everybody was impressed that he knew what to do. He even called the operator by her first name: "Centralist." Within moments, Abu Raja was talking with his brother, a concierge in Beirut. He didn't even have to raise his voice or shout to be heard.

19   If I hadn't seen it with my own two eyes and heard it with my own two ears, I would not have believed it—and my friend Kameel didn't. He was away that day watching his father's goats, and when he came back to the village that evening, his cousin Habeeb and I told him about the telephone and how Abu Raja had used it to speak with his brother in Beirut. After he heard our report, Kameel made the sign of the cross, kissed his thumbnail, and warned us that lying was a bad sin and would surely land us in purgatory. Kameel believed in Jesus and Mary, and wanted to be a priest when he grew up. He always crossed himself when Habeeb, who was irreverent, and I, who was Presbyterian, were around, even when we were not bearing bad news.

20   And the telephone, as it turned out, was bad news. With its coming, the face of the village began to change. One of the first effects was the shifting of the village's center. Before the telephone's arrival, the men of the village used to gather regularly at the house of Im Kaleem, a short, middle-aged widow with jet-black hair and a raspy voice that could be heard all over the village, even when she was only whispering. She was a devout Catholic and also the village *shlikki*—whore. The men met at her house to argue about politics and drink coffee and

play cards or backgammon. Im Kaleem was not a true prostitute, however, because she did not charge for her services—not even for the coffee and tea (and, occasionally, the strong liquor called arrack) that she served the men. She did not need the money; her son, who was overseas in Africa, sent her money regularly. (I knew this because my father used to read her son's letters to her and take down her replies, as Im Kaleem could not read and write.) Im Kaleem was no slut either—unlike some women in the village—because she loved all the men she entertained, and they loved her, every one of them. In a way, she was married to all the men in the village. Everybody knew it—the wives knew it; the itinerant Catholic priest knew it; the Presbyterian minister knew it—but nobody objected. Actually, I suspect the women (my mother included) did not mind their husbands' visits to Im Kaleem. Oh, they wrung their hands and complained to one another about their men's unfaithfulness, but secretly they were relieved, because Im Kaleem took some of the pressure off them and kept the men out of their hair while they attended to their endless chores. Im Kaleem was also a kind of confessor and troubleshooter, talking sense to those men who were having family problems, especially the younger ones.

21   Before the telephone came to Magdaluna, Im Kaleem's house was bustling at just about any time of day, especially at night, when its windows were brightly lit with three large oil lamps, and the loud voices of the men talking, laughing, and arguing could be heard in the street below—a reassuring, homey sound. Her house was an island of comfort, an oasis for the weary village men, exhausted from having so little to do.

22   But it wasn't long before many of those men—the younger ones especially— started spending more of their days and evenings at Abu Raja's *dikkan.* There, they would eat and drink and talk and play checkers and backgammon, and then lean their chairs back against the wall—the signal that they were ready to toss back and forth, like a ball, the latest rumors going around the village. And they were always looking up from their games and drinks and talk to glance at the phone in the corner, as if expecting it to ring any minute and bring news that would change their lives and deliver them from their aimless existence. In the meantime, they smoked cheap, hand-rolled cigarettes, dug dirt out from under their fingernails with big pocketknives, and drank lukewarm sodas that they called Kacula, Seffen-Ub, and Bebsi. Sometimes, especially when it was hot, the days dragged on so slowly that the men turned on Abu Saeed, a confirmed bachelor who practically lived in Abu Raja's *dikkan,* and teased him for going around barefoot and unshaven since the Virgin had appeared to him behind the olive press.

23   The telephone was also bad news for me personally. It took away my lucrative business—a source of much-needed income. Before the telephone came to Magdaluna, I used to hang around Im Kaleem's courtyard and play marbles with the other kids, waiting for some man to call down from a window and ask me to run to the store for cigarettes or arrack, or to deliver a message to his wife, such as what he wanted for supper. There was always something in it for me: a ten- or even a twenty-five-piaster piece. On a good day, I ran nine or ten of those errands, which assured a steady supply of marbles that I usually lost

to Sami or his cousin Hani, the basket weaver's boy. But as the days went by, fewer and fewer men came to Im Kaleem's, and more and more congregated at Abu Raja's to wait by the telephone. In the evenings, no light fell from her window onto the street below, and the laughter and noise of the men trailed off and finally stopped. Only Shukri, the retired Turkish-army drill sergeant, remained faithful to Im Kaleem after all the other men had deserted her; he was still seen going into or leaving her house from time to time. Early that winter, Im Kaleem's hair suddenly turned gray, and she got sick and old. Her legs started giving her trouble, making it hard for her to walk. By spring she hardly left her house anymore.

24   At Abu Raja's *dikkan*, the calls did eventually come, as expected, and men and women started leaving the village the way a hailstorm begins: first one, then two, then bunches. The army took them. Jobs in the cities lured them. And ships and airplanes carried them to such faraway places as Australia and Brazil and New Zealand. My friend Kameel, his cousin Habeeb, and their cousins and my cousins all went away to become ditch diggers and mechanics and butcher-shop boys and deli owners who wore dirty aprons sixteen hours a day, all looking for a better life than the one they had left behind. Within a year, only the sick, the old, and the maimed were left in the village. Magdaluna became a skeleton of its former self, desolate and forsaken, like the tombs, a place to get away from.

25   Finally, the telephone took my family away, too. My father got a call from an old army buddy who told him that an oil company in southern Lebanon was hiring interpreters and instructors. My father applied for a job and got it, and we moved to Sidon, where I went to a Presbyterian missionary school and graduated in 1962. Three years later, having won a scholarship, I left Lebanon for the United States. Like the others who left Magdaluna before me, I am still looking for that better life.

■ ■ ▨

MEANING

1. How was the pace of life in Accawi's village governed by the seasons?
2. Before the first telephone was installed, how did the people in Accawi's village keep track of important events?
3. After the installation of the telephone, how did the social life in the village begin to change?
4. How did the author's life change as a result of the arrival of technology?

TECHNIQUE

1. How does Accawi portray the effects, both small and large, that were produced by the installation of the telephone?
2. How does delaying the moment when the telephone was installed give the reader a chance to know what the life of the community was like before this event?

3. **Other Patterns.** How do many of the **descriptive** details add texture and a sense of reality to Accawi's account?

LANGUAGE

1. What aspects of Accawi's essay remind the reader that he is reflecting on events that happened when he was a child?

2. How is the conflict of the essay polarized between the two Lebanese terms *shlikki* and *dikkan*?

3. If you don't know the meaning of the following words, look them up: *milestones* (2), *pestilences* (2), *lucrative* (23), *maimed* (24).

SUGGESTIONS FOR WRITING

1. Accawi's essay illustrates the life-changing effects of new technological tools. Pick another technology and describe its impact.

2. If you have ever been away from any means of communicating for some period of time, what effects—negative and positive—did you notice?

3. **Critical Writing.** Do you agree or disagree with Accawi's verdict that life was better before the arrival of the telephone? **Argue** for your point of view.

4. **Thematic Links.** Relate how the installation of the telephone changed the "social time" in Accawi's village to the analysis by Robert Levine and Ellen Wolff in "Social Time: The Heartbeat of Culture" (Chapter 5, "Exemplification").

VAUGHN M. BRYANT, JR., AND SYLVIA GRIDER

To Kiss: Why We Kiss Under the Mistletoe at Christmas

Vaughn M. Bryant, Jr. (b. 1940), and Sylvia Grider (b. 1940), the authors of this selection, which was first published in *The World & I* (1991), are anthropologists at Texas A&M University. They were intrigued by the mysterious origins of this commonplace custom and wondered why mistletoe was associated with Christmas and used as an excuse to "steal a kiss." The results of their research take us back to other ages, other times, and other cultures and open a window into distinctly different values and customs, all centered on this flowering plant. Bryant's research on pollen analysis and its role in prehistoric diets was awarded the 2007 Fryxell Award for interdisciplinary research in archaeology. Grider serves as the president of the American Folklore Society.

BEFORE YOU READ

What do you know about the custom of kissing under the mistletoe at Christmas?

■ ■ ▨

1   While growing up in Texas we were intrigued by a boast, often made by the citizens of Goldthwaite, a small town in west central Texas. On the outskirts of this town is a large sign proclaiming it the Mistletoe Capital of the World. Most Texans like to boast, but this claim, we thought, had to be a joke. Yet, it may be true. Each Christmas season a company in Goldthwaite collects and ships more than one million packages of mistletoe to cities all over North America.

2   Mentioning this boast often brought laughter from the students in our introductory folklore classes at Texas A&M in College Station. But when the laughter stopped, students wondered why this small, parasitic plant had become the basis of a million-dollar commercial industry in our society. Students were even more curious about why we kiss under the mistletoe at Christmas.

3   We had no ready answer. Thus we began our odyssey searching not only for the origins of man's fascination with mistletoe, but also asking why this plant is associated with Christmas and why we traditionally use it as an excuse to steal a kiss.

SEARCH BEGINS WITH CELTS

4   Part of this tradition dates back to the Celts, who dominated Europe from the fifth to the first centuries B.C. Among these aggressive and warlike people an influential priestly caste, called Druids, acted as judges and conducted religious activities. Romans such as Julius Caesar, Pomponius Mela, Tacitus, and Pliny the

---

For a visual to accompany this selection, see color insert photo B-8.

Elder wrote extensively about both the Celts and the Druid rites, and it was among these writings that we found our first clues about the importance of mistletoe.

5   The early writings of Pliny the Elder were most useful. He notes that the Druids revered the oak as the most sacred of trees and that no Druid was ever seen without an oak twig hanging from his apparel. It is because of the Druids' reverence for the oak, and the powerful spirits they believed resided inside its wood, that we still "knock on wood" for good luck. Druids often tapped on oak trees to awaken the sleeping spirits and ask for good luck.

6   Roman historians noted that each year, around November, the Druids presided over the winter celebration of Samhain, which has evolved into our Halloween. By then, the sacred oaks were barren except for the green boughs of mistletoe growing from their branches, a sign, the Druids believed, of eternal fertility. With time, the mistletoe became even more revered than the sacred oak.

7   The Celts believed mistletoe could heal diseases, make poisons harmless, bring fertility to childless women, protect against evil spells, and bring the blessings of the gods. Thus, they customarily carried a sprig of it or placed a bough above the door of their houses. So sacred was the mistletoe that enemies were banned from fighting beneath it, and when Celts met under the mistletoe they were required to greet each other in friendship. Even after they had been conquered by the Roman legions and, later, after their conversion to Christianity, the Celts retained their winter custom of suspending mistletoe above a doorway, as a token of love and peace. Today, the belief in mistletoe's magical powers has spread to many regions, but it is still strongest among the modern descendants of the Celtic peoples. But, as we discovered from the Roman records, the Celts never kissed beneath the mistletoe. The Celts, like most other early European cultures, likely knew nothing about kissing, and there is no recorded evidence that it was ever part of their culture.

8   Today, most of us accept the Christmastime custom of kissing under the mistletoe, and kissing in general, as one of the niceties of our culture. We practice it, we enjoy it, we write about it, we associate it with love and happiness, and most believe that kissing is as universal in human culture as lovemaking. Yet, our research revealed that kissing is a fairly recent phenomenon, and that kissing under the mistletoe did not become common until long after the original Celts had disappeared.

9   If the Celts didn't invent kissing, who did? Maybe the ancient Neanderthals kissed, or at least our more recent predecessors of the last ice age. If so, we may never know. These cultures left no written records, no cave paintings of kissing, and no archaeological records of lovers embracing in a kiss. Even later, when the first towns were settled and the first farmers planted crops of barley and wheat, there was no hint of kissing.

10   The first critics and the earliest writing date to around 3500 B.C. Archaeologists have pieced together the story of our urban beginnings and have deciphered the meanings of the earliest written records. What they found were recipes for making wine and beer, records of crop yields and taxation, and

versions of early laws. Yet, among these earliest texts there are no references to kissing, perhaps suggesting that it was still unknown and unpracticed.

KISSING RITUALIZED IN INDIA

11 This situation changed around 1500 B.C., when the Vedic Sanskrit texts of India were written. In the four major texts of Vedic literature we found references to rituals, spells, and sacred charms, all of which were important to these early Indo-European cultures. Also buried in the verses of the Vedic literature and the accompanying sutra texts are references to the custom of rubbing and pressing noses together. This practice, it is recorded, was a sign of affection, especially between lovers. This is not kissing as we know it today, but we believe it may have been its earliest beginning.

12 The epic *Mahabharata*, written about five hundred to one thousand years later, relates the Vedic priests' attempt to institutionalize the beliefs and practices of their culture. It contains references suggesting that affection was being expressed by lip kissing. By the early fifth century A.D., Vatsyayana had recorded many of the oral verses of the ancient Vedic period in the *Kama Sutra*, a classic text on erotica and other forms of human pleasure. In it, he faithfully records many examples of erotic kissing and even techniques on how to kiss. Among the many examples are detailed instructions on how one should kiss, what parts of the human body should be kissed, and special kissing techniques one should use when dating and after marriage.

13 This information leads us to believe that erotic kissing became part of Indo-European culture between the writing of the early Vedic texts, around 1500 B.C., and the consolidation of Indian culture during the next one thousand years. From India, the custom of kissing seems to have spread slowly westward with other Indo-European cultural traits such as the use of horses.

14 The Greeks were the first Europeans to help the spread of kissing. In 326 B.C. the armies of Alexander the Great conquered parts of India as far eastward as Delhi. During Alexander's campaign, Strabo, Arrian, and other historians chronicled the influences and impressions that Indian culture had on the Greek armies. Although we have not found a specific mention of kissing in the writings about the Greek conquest of India, we believe this is where the Greeks encountered literary references to kissing. Later, when the link between the Greeks and India was strengthened by the formation of the Seleucid Empire in Iran, there was a stronger merging of cultural traits, probably including kissing.

15 After Alexander's death, his empire collapsed. During the subsequent Hellenistic period the remnants of his armies established new empires throughout the eastern Mediterranean region. Although mentioned in the chronicles of these cultures, kissing does not seem to have become an important practice in the eastern Mediterranean region until the Roman era. We are not certain, but we believe that there must have been resistance to the acceptance of kissing by the conquered peoples of the eastern Mediterranean, even though it remained popular among the Greek rulers of those new empires.

16   Despite the Greek contribution, the Romans should be credited with popularizing kissing throughout the Mediterranean and Europe. But even after the conquering legions first introduced the practice to the Celts, kissing was not immediately linked to mistletoe.

17   The Romans had different kinds of kisses. Their *osculum* was a kiss of friendship, most often delivered as a peck on the cheek. It was not a kiss of passion; rather, it was an affectionate way of greeting a friend. So popular did this form of kissing become, that in ancient Rome it was said that one could hardly go anywhere without giving and receiving friendship kisses. In later years, the members of the Roman senate would exchange this type of affectionate kiss at the opening of each session, and nonsenators often kissed a senator's toga as a sign of respect for the person and his office.

18   Today most Western cultures still use the osculum. In the United States, affectionate kisses are bestowed on the cheeks of close relatives or friends, and our custom dictates that males don't kiss males. In some Western cultures, however, such as the Greek, French, and Russian, it is still proper and expected, as it was in Roman times, for males to kiss each other on the cheeks, or even the lips, as a sign of friendship.

ROMAN AND EROTIC KISSING

19   During the first century B.C. another Roman word for kissing began to take on new meaning. In the writings of the poet Catullus we find frequent reference to a more passionate type of kiss called the *basium*. For example, Catullus writes of his loving mistress Lesbia, and asks affectionately about the number of kisses he needs: "as many as the grains of sand in the Libyan deserts, or as the stars that look down, in the silent watches of the night, on the stolen loves of men."

20   It is from this Latin word for passionate kissing that most of the later Romance languages took their word for kissing. In Spanish it is *besar*, and in Italian, *baciare*. In French, however, the verb *baiser*, once used only for kissing, has taken on the specialized meaning of intercourse. The colloquial English word *buss* came into the language originally as *bass*, and both connote noisy, wet, smacking kissing. The present English word *kiss* is from a Germanic word root.

21   Not content with two words for kissing, the Romans added another, *savium*, and its diminutive, preferred by poets like Catullus, *saviolum*, a kiss "sweeter than sweet ambrosia." This was their kiss of wild passion, the ultimate kiss, the one Americans now call the "soul kiss," or "French kiss." In *Amores*, Ovid refers to such "kisses of the tongue" as "shameful," "voluptuous," and "lewdly taught."

22   Kissing became so much a part of Roman culture that laws were passed proclaiming a young woman's right to a man's hand in marriage if he kissed her passionately in public. This was, however, in response to the prevailing custom that placed a greater emphasis on the couple's engagement than on their marriage. When a young couple was ready for marriage, a ceremonial party was held in their honor. At the appropriate time, they would seal their formal engagement with a passionate kiss in view of all those attending. Later, in a simple and quiet civil ceremony, the couple paid a fee for a license and were then considered married.

HOLY KISS OF PEACE

23 Centuries later, Christians shifted the recognition of marriage away from the engagement party to the marriage ceremony. This guaranteed the influence of the church in the important rites of passage in the lives of the faithful. After that, no marriage in the Christian world was considered accepted, in the eyes of God, without the ritual and consent of the church. The public and passionate kiss at the end of the wedding ceremony sealed the eternal bond of love between the bride and groom.

24 In the early Christian period, kissing was not restricted to weddings. However, early codes of behavior regulating many activities, including sexual freedom and kissing, soon became part of established church doctrine.

25 Christianity, the principal religion of Western culture, arose in Judea, one of the eastern provinces governed by Rome, and the people of the region had accepted many Roman customs, including kissing. This is evident in Paul's epistle to the Romans, where he writes, "Salute one another with a holy kiss." The gospel according to Luke tells how a prostitute paid homage to Christ by washing his feet with tears, ". . . and did wipe them with the hairs of her head, and kissed his feet." Both references reveal how Roman customs of kissing were adapted for Christian purposes.

26 In the first reference, the "affectionate kiss" of the Romans becomes the "holy kiss" signifying Christ's affection and blessing to all of humankind, as administered by his representatives, the priests. The "holy kiss," or "kiss of peace," as it was also known, thus becomes an important Christian ritual because it is a visual reinforcement of God's love administered during rites ranging from baptism and confession to marriage and the ordination of priests. Lastly, the celebration of Christ's birth also followed Roman customs of that time. Roman law prescribed that the birth dates of Roman rulers should be celebrated by holidays and festive activities. However, it wasn't until the rule of Constantine I (A.D. 312–37) that the celebration of Christmas, on December 25, was introduced as a special feast day in the Roman Empire. The other kiss, as mentioned by Luke, is also borrowed from a Roman custom: kissing as a visual sign of submission and respect. Throughout the Roman Empire, subjects kissed the robes or signet rings of Roman generals and governors as a sign of respect. Subjects also kissed the statues of Roman gods and other symbols of Roman power and authority to signify their submission and respect. From the beginning of Christianity, the kiss has been an important ritual carried out by faithful Christians and their clergy. Even today it is commonplace to see some Christians kiss the altar, cross, vestments, Bibles, statues and relics of religious importance.

27 Although accepted by Christians as an important ritual of faith, by the late Middle Ages certain kinds of kissing were becoming too erotic for many stoic watchers of the faith. During the fourteenth century, in an attempt to regulate kissing, the church took stern action. At the Council of Vienna in 1311–12, the church passed laws stating that Christians who kissed one another while thinking of fornication were guilty of committing a mortal sin, regardless of their subsequent conduct. The new law also stated that Christians who kissed solely for carnal delight were guilty of committing a venial sin, a less serious offense.

28   Another attempt to stop erotic kissing was the introduction of the *osculatorium,* a metal disk on a handle with ornate engravings depicting images of Christ or various saints. During church services the osculatorium was passed among the congregation, and the faithful would kiss the disk, rather than kissing each other as had become the custom. However, by the Middle Ages, kissing had become so much a part of Western culture that even these efforts to limit kissing met with little success.

29   We suspect that by the Middle Ages it was difficult to prevent the holiday practice of kissing under the mistletoe. Yet, exactly when Christians began kissing under the mistletoe remains a mystery. Even so, based on our research we have developed some intriguing hypotheses. All indications suggest that the earliest practice of kissing under the mistletoe began during the early medieval period in areas of Europe where the influence of ancient Celtic customs remained strong, even after the Roman conquest. This hypothesis is strengthened by the earliest recorded observances of this practice, which reveal a blend of three cultural beliefs: the Celtic belief in the magic powers of the mistletoe, the Roman custom of kissing to seal a betrothal, and the Christian custom of marriage being more important than the betrothal. It was believed that a kiss under the mistletoe was a serious commitment and not to be taken lightly. Such kisses were seen as the physical expression of an eternal love to one another, and more importantly, a promise of marriage. Thus, the couple who sealed their engagement with a kiss under the mistletoe, and then followed through with a church marriage, would be assured of good fortune, fertility, and a long and happy married life together.

30   From this original linking of kissing with the mistletoe, and the strong commitments it assumed, came a slow relaxing of the implied commitments and a view of mistletoe kisses as simply part of the joyous celebration of the Christmas season. This relaxing of custom probably occurred after the Middle Ages, when a renaissance of frivolity became associated with all forms of kissing after the long period of clerical repression.

31   This Christmas season, when you are kissed under a sprig of mistletoe, you may want to tell your "kisser" of the serious commitment and binding pledge that have been evoked. If, on the other hand, kissing frivolity is your goal, at least you will know that the mistletoe, the celebration of Christ's birth, and kissing each originated from different cultural sources yet became forever bonded into one of our favorite Christmas traditions.

■ ■ ▨

MEANING

1. What misconceptions about the supposedly universal meaning of kissing do Bryant and Grider correct? What evidence do they cite?

2. What different cultural and religious influences have shaped the practice and significance of kissing through the ages?

3. What events, traditions, and customs have become associated with kissing under the mistletoe at Christmas?

4. How did the Church try to find a means of using this custom to its benefit?

TECHNIQUE

1. How do Bryant and Grider organize their quest for an answer to the origins of the custom?

2. Where in the authors' investigation can you most clearly see the evolution of this practice through centuries in different cultures?

3. **Other Patterns.** How do the authors use a **narrative** framework to provide a context for their investigation?

LANGUAGE

1. How does the wide range of terms and phrases that are used to refer to kissing in different cultures reflect the meanings kissing has taken on?

2. How would you characterize the authors' tone and their attitude toward their subject?

3. If you don't know the meaning of the following words, look them up: *intrigued* (1), *descendants* (7), *predecessors* (9), *betrothal* (29), *renaissance* (30).

SUGGESTIONS FOR WRITING

1. **Critical Writing.** Do Bryant and Grider's conclusions seem plausible? Why or why not? What examples best illustrate the range of interpretations and meanings that kissing has had over the centuries?

2. Choose another holiday tradition, and research its origins.

3. Choose one aspect of Bryant and Grider's analysis, and try to find representative **examples** in traditional art forms—murals, tapestries, frescoes, paintings—that would provide visual illustrations of their inquiry. How do they complement the written account?

4. **Thematic Links.** Compare the evolution of kissing as discussed in Bryant and Grider's article with the evolution of eating with utensils as described by Margaret Visser in "Fingers" (Chapter 8, "Classification").

The Persian Carpet

One of the best-known writers from the Middle East, Hanan al-Shaykh (b. 1945) was raised in a traditional Shiite family in Lebanon, studied at the American College for Girls in Cairo, and later worked as a journalist in Beirut. Her short stories and novels focus on the cultural pressures to which women are subject, portrayed with great realism. This touching story, first published in *Modern Arabic Short Stories* (1983), translated by Denya Johnson-Davies follows a young girl who is reunited with her mother after her parents' divorce and her mother's remarriage. The title alludes to a dramatic role played by this item and all that it symbolizes. Al-Shaykh's recent works include *Only in London* (2001) and *I Sweep the Sun Off Rooftops* (2002).

BEFORE YOU READ

How might divorce force children to see their parents in a new way?

■ ■ ▨

1   When Maryam had finished plaiting my hair into two pigtails, she put her finger to her mouth and licked it, then passed it over my eyebrows, moaning: "Ah, what eyebrows you have—they're all over the place!" She turned quickly to my sister and said: "Go and see if your father's still praying." Before I knew it my sister had returned and was whispering "He's still at it," and she stretched out her hands and raised them skywards in imitation of him. I didn't laugh as usual, nor did Maryam; instead, she took up the scarf from the chair, put it over her hair and tied it hurriedly at the neck. Then, opening the wardrobe carefully, she took out her handbag, placed it under her arm and stretched out her hands to us. I grasped one and my sister the other. We understood that we should, like her, proceed on tiptoe, holding our breath as we made our way out through the open front door. As we went down the steps, we turned back towards the door, then towards the window. Reaching the last step, we began to run, only stopping when the lane had disappeared out of sight and we had crossed the road and Maryam had stopped a taxi.

2   Our behaviour was induced by fear, for today we would be seeing my mother for the first time since her separation by divorce from my father. He had sworn he would not let her see us, for, only hours after the divorce, the news had spread that she was going to marry a man she had been in love with before her family had forced her into marrying my father.

3   My heart was pounding. This was not from fear or from running but was due to anxiety and a feeling of embarrassment about the meeting that lay ahead. Though in control of myself and my shyness, I knew that I would be incapable—however much I tried—of showing my emotions, even to my mother; I would be unable to throw myself into her arms and smother her with kisses and clasp

her head as my sister would do with such spontaneity. I had thought long and hard about this ever since Maryam had whispered in my ear—and in my sister's—that my mother had come from the south and that we were to visit her secretly the following day. I began to imagine that I would make myself act exactly as my sister did, that I would stand behind her and imitate her blindly. Yet I know myself: I have committed myself to myself by heart. However much I tried to force myself, however much I thought in advance about what I should and shouldn't do, once I was actually faced by the situation and was standing looking down at the floor, my forehead puckered into an even deeper frown, I would find I had forgotten what I had to resolved to do. Even then, though I would not give up hope but would implore my mouth to break into a smile; it would none the less be to no avail.

4   When the taxi came to a stop at the entrance to a house, where two lions stood on columns of red sandstone, I was filled with delight and immediately forgot my apprehension. I was overcome with happiness at the thought that my mother was living in a house where two lions stood at the entrance. I heard my sister imitate the roar of a lion and I turned to her in envy. I saw her stretching up her hands in an attempt to clutch the lions. I thought to myself: She's always uncomplicated and jolly, her gaiety never leaves her, even at the most critical moments—and here she was, not a bit worried about this meeting.

5   But when my mother opened the door and I saw her, I found myself unable to wait and rushed forward in front of my sister and threw myself into her arms. I had closed my eyes and all the joints of my body had grown numb after having been unable to be at rest for so long. I took in the unchanged smell of her hair, and I discovered for the first time how much I had missed her and wished that she would come back and live with us, despite the tender care shown to us by my father and Maryam. I couldn't rid my mind of that smile of hers when my father agreed to divorce her, after the religious sheikh had intervened following her threats to pour kerosene over her body and set fire to herself if my father wouldn't divorce her. All my senses were numbed by that smell of her, so well perserved in my memory. I realized how much I had missed her, despite the fact that after she'd hurried off behind her brother to get into the car, having kissed us and started to cry, we had continued with the games we were playing in the lane outside our house. As night came, and for the first time in a long while we did not hear her squabbling with my father, peace and quiet descended upon the house—except that is for the weeping of Maryam, who was related to my father and had been living with us in the house ever since I was born.

6   Smiling, my mother moved me away from her so that she could hug and kiss my sister, and hug Maryam again, who had begun to cry. I heard my mother, who was in tears, say to her "Thank you," and she wiped her tears with her sleeve and looked me and my sister up and down, saying: "God keep them safe, how they've sprung up!" She put both arms round me, while my sister buried her head in my mother's waist, and we all began to laugh when we found that it was difficult for us to walk like that. Reaching the inner room, I was convinced her new husband was inside because my mother said, sniffing: "Mahmoud loves you very much and he would like it if your father would give you to me so that you can live with us

and become his children too." My sister laughed and answered: "Like that we'd have two fathers." I was still in a benumbed state, my hand placed over my mother's arm, proud at the way I was behaving, at having been able without any effort to be liberated from myself, from my shackled hands, from the prison of my shyness, as I recalled to mind the picture of my meeting with my mother, how I had spontaneously thrown myself at her, something I had thought wholly impossible, and my kissing her so hard I had closed my eyes.

7   Her husband was not there. As I stared down at the floor I froze. In confusion I looked at the Persian carpet spread out on the floor, then gave my mother a long look. Not understanding the significance of my look, she turned and opened a cupboard from which she threw me an embroidered blouse, and moving across to a drawer in the dressing-table, she took out an ivory comb with red hearts painted on it and gave it to my sister. I stared down at the Persian carpet, trembling with burning rage. Again I looked at my mother and she interpreted my gaze as being one of tender longing, so she put her arms round me, saying: "You must come every other day, you must spend the whole of Friday at my place." I remained motionless, wishing that I could remove her arms from around me and sink my teeth into that white forearm. I wished that the moment of meeting could be undone and re-enacted, that she could again open the door and I could stand there—as I should have done—with my eyes staring down at the floor and my forehead in a frown.

8   The lines and colours of the Persian carpet were imprinted on my memory. I used to lie on it as I did my lessons; I'd be so close to it that I'd gaze at its pattern and find it looking like slices of red water-melon repeated over and over again. But when I sat down on the couch, I would see that each slice of melon had changed into a comb with thin teeth. The cluster of flowers surrounding its four sides were purple-coloured. At the beginning of summer my mother would put mothballs on it and on the other ordinary carpets and would roll them up and place them on top of the cupboard. The room would look stark and depressing until autumn came, when she would take them up to the roof and spread them out. She would gather up the mothballs, most of which had dissolved from the summer's heat and humidity, then, having brushed them with a small broom, she'd leave them there. In the evening she'd bring them down and lay them out where they belonged. I would be filled with happiness as their bright colours once again brought the room back to life. This particular carpet, though, had disappeared several months before my mother was divorced. It had been spread out on the roof in the sun and in the afternoon my mother had gone up to get it and hadn't found it. She had called my father and for the first time I had seen his face flushed with anger. When they came down from the roof, my mother was in a state of fury and bewilderment. She got in touch with the neighbors, all of whom swore they hadn't seen it. Suddenly my mother exclaimed: "Ilya!" Everyone stood speechless: not a word from my father or from my sister or from our neighbours Umm Fouad and Abu Salman. I found myself crying out: "Ilya? Don't say such a thing, it's not possible."

9   Ilya was an almost blind man who used to go round the houses of the quarter repairing cane chairs. When it came to our turn, I would see him, on my arrival back from school, seated on the stone bench outside the house with piles of straw

in front of him and his red hair glinting in the sunlight. He would deftly take up the strands of straw and, like fishes, they'd slip through the mesh. I would watch him as he coiled them round with great dexterity, then bring them out again until he had formed a circle of straw for the seat of the chair, just like the one that had been there before. Everything was so even and precise: it was as though his hands were a machine and I would be amazed at the speed and nimbleness of his fingers. Sitting as he did with his head lowered, it looked as though he were using his eyes. I once doubted that he could see more than vague shapes in front of him, so I squatted down and looked into his rosy-red face and was able to see his half-closed eyes behind his glasses. They had in them a white line that pricked at my heart and sent me hurrying off to the kitchen, where I found a bag of dates on the table, and I heaped some on a plate and gave them to Ilya.

10   I continued to stare at the carpet as the picture of Ilya, red of face and hair, appeared to me. I was made aware of his hand as he walked up the stairs on his own; of him sitting on his chair, of his bargaining over the price for his work, of how he ate and knew that he had finished everything on the plate, of his drinking from the pitcher, with the water flowing easily down his throat. Once at midday, having been taught by my father that before entering a Muslim house he should say "Allah" before knocking at the door and entering, as a warning to my mother in case she were unveiled, my mother rushed at him and asked him about the carpet. He made no reply, merely making a sort of sobbing noise. As he walked off, he almost bumped into the table and, for the first time, tripped. I went up to him and took him by the hand. He knew me by the touch of my hand, because he said to me in a half-whisper: "Never mind, child." Then he turned round to leave. As he bent over to put on his shoes, I thought I saw tears on his cheeks. My father didn't let him leave before saying to him: "Ilya, God will forgive you if you tell him the truth." But Ilya walked off, steadying himself against the railings. He took an unusually long time as he felt his way down the stairs. Then he disappeared from sight and we never saw him again.

■ ■ ▨

MEANING

1. What circumstances led to the mother's divorcing the father?
2. What made it necessary for the narrator and her sister to visit their mother secretly?
3. Why does seeing the Persian carpet dramatically change the narrator's attitude toward her mother?
4. What role does Ilya, the blind man, play in explaining the girl's shift in feelings toward her mother?

TECHNIQUE

1. Why does al-Shaykh reconstruct events leading up to the disappearance of the carpet?
2. How does al-Shaykh make the reader understand what the blind man meant to the narrator in order to understand why she became so angry?

3. **Other Patterns.** In what way do the many **descriptive** details, both subjective and objective, make this story more dramatic?

LANGUAGE

1. What words communicate that the normally self-possessed narrator first wants to love her mother and then is bitterly disillusioned?

2. How does al-Shaykh knit the story together using the images, colors, and shapes within the Persian carpet? In what instances can you find the color red mentioned, and what does it symbolize?

3. If you don't know the meaning of the following words, look them up: *sheikh* (5), *benumbed* (6), *spontaneously* (6).

SUGGESTIONS FOR WRITING

1. Have you ever been disillusioned with someone to such an extent that the experience was a turning point in your relationship? If so, discuss your experience.

2. **Critical Writing.** In what way can material possessions become surrogates for a failed relationship?

3. What object holds associations for you connected with your parents, grandparents, or other relatives? Write a **narrative** exploring the history of this object and the context in which it acquired its meaning.

4. **Thematic Links.** In a few paragraphs, contrast the mother-daughter relationship in this story with that in Jamaica Kincaid's story "Girl" (Chapter 7, "Process Analysis").

▨▨▨ STUDENT ESSAY: CAUSE AND EFFECT

The following essay by Cassandra Bjork analyzes the causes and effects of the rise in the rates of obesity among American adults and children. Cassandra is clearly alarmed by this trend and structures her essay to examine the factors that are most likely to be responsible for this increasingly widespread threat to the health of our nation. We have annotated her paper and added a follow-up analysis ("Strategies") to help you understand the principles of cause and effect.

Bjork 1

Americans: Bigger by the Day

Cassandra Bjork

1   Why are Americans getting bigger by the day? And what's so bad about that anyway? Studies have shown that there are many negative effects associated with obesity. Obesity has been accused of contributing to many long-term conditions, such as

Introduction

Bjork 2

heart disease, stroke, high blood pressure, osteoarthritis, diabetes, and cancer (Pennybacker 15). Along with the fact that obesity is the most common form of malnutrition in the Western world, it also affects sixty-four percent of Americans (Pennybacker 15; Brownell 1). Obesity is one of today's most visible yet most neglected conditions, affecting more Americans each day.

Thesis statement

2   Obesity is defined as "a condition characterized by excessive bodily fat" (Merriam-Webster). Moreover, the Centers for Disease Control and Prevention have labeled the obesity problem an "epidemic" (Brownell 1). Basically, obesity is the long-term result of a diet that delivers more calories than are consumed through daily activity. Nevertheless, obesity is a serious medical condition that affects a high percentage of Americans and should be treated with concern.

Definition of condition of obesity

Description of need to investigate causes

3   There are many possible factors for the rise in the number of overweight and obese Americans. Brownell outlines these factors very well in <u>Food Fight</u> and writes, "The reasons for this growing problem are simple and complex at the same time. People eat too much and exercise too little" (Brownell 2). Furthermore, by taking a look at the modern lifestyle of our world today, one could say it does not discourage obesity in the least way. One obstacle Americans need to overcome is to find the time in their busy schedules to exercise. It is much too easy to travel in cars, as opposed to walking or biking. Many people sit all day in an office, and do not get much physical activity at all. The conveniences and technology of today contribute to a very sedentary lifestyle for much of the population. According to <u>Food Fight</u>, one study found that twenty-three percent of all deaths from major chronic disease could be attributed to sedentary lifestyles (Brownell 70). The lack of exercise is one of the main causes of obesity in the United States.

Analysis of a contributing cause

4   Another possible contribution to obesity, which is still in the process of being further researched, is genetics. According to the Centers for Disease Control and Prevention, studies indicate that inherited genetic variation is an important risk factor for obesity. It was also pointed out that genetic factors are starting to be questioned as to the degree of effectiveness of diet and physical

Identifies another likely cause

Bjork 3

activity interventions for weight reduction ("Obesity and Genetics"). Learning how genetic variations affect obesity will make it much easier to prevent and treat the condition of obesity.

5   In addition to the many other causes of obesity, fast food receives much of the blame. With the continual growth of the fast-food industry in the United States, obesity is becoming a bigger problem every day. The connection between fast food and obesity is one of the primary criticisms in the book Fast Food Nation by Eric Schlosser. Due to the high-calorie, high-fat food choices offered at many restaurants, both consumers and experts are quick to point their fingers at fast-food restaurants. In the book, Schlosser states, "If you look at the rise of the obesity rate in the United States, it's grown pretty much in step with the rise of fast-food consumption . . . and now it's the second leading cause of death in the United States, after smoking" (1). When McDonald's was asked to respond to Schlosser's charges, they stated that forty-five million customers make the choice to dine at McDonald's every single day ("Fast Food"). The point McDonald's was trying to get across is that the fast-food restaurant customers are responsible for the persistent growth of the fast-food industry. Customers are the ones choosing to put this type of food into their digestive systems. Fast-food restaurants would not be so profitable if it were not for the high demand for their food products by consumers. Another source provided a statement from Dr. Cathy Kapica, former Global Director of Nutrition for McDonald's, regarding the responsibility of the customer: "It is not where you eat, but the food choices you make, and especially how much you eat." She then addressed the fact that McDonald's offers a wide variety of different foods and portion styles that can be a significant part of a healthy diet ("Meet McDonald's").

6   An opposing opinion on the correlation between fast food and obesity came from HeartInfo.org. According to Amanda Gardner, a study was conducted on individuals' dietary habits. There were 3,301 adults surveyed between ages eighteen and thirty. The results showed that individuals who ate fast food more than twice a week gained an extra ten pounds in just six months

> Identifies a third likely cause

> Statistics that illustrate effects

and had a twofold greater increase in insulin resistance than people who ate fast food less than once a week (Gardner). The outcome of the study indicates that eating a high-fat diet can lead to weight gain and, eventually, obesity.

7   Although fast food is often blamed because of its high caloric content, it is simply a contributing factor. Obesity is caused by overeating, poor food choices, genetics, and lack of exercise as well. Whether it is from fast food or not, extra weight is put on by not burning as many calories as the number taken in. Dining in restaurants can encourage this unhealthy habit by providing enough food for two or more people on a single plate. Frequent visits to restaurants can then compound the effect of too much food too often. According to Kelly Brownell, more than forty percent of adults eat at a restaurant on a typical day. The frequency of eating out is associated with higher calorie and fat intake and increased body weight, while eating meals at home is associated with better calorie intake (Brownell 36). When it comes to healthy eating, it can be easier for one to make better healthful choices in his or her own kitchen.

8   In our world today, obesity affects people of all ages. A common misconception is that obesity is only an adult problem. In the United States, more children suffer from obesity than ever before. The Centers for Disease Control estimate that twenty-three percent of American children are overweight, in comparison to only four percent in the 1960s. Obesity causes the young to be at risk for problems that used to be common only in adults, such as cardiovascular disease, high cholesterol and blood pressure, and type 2 diabetes (Pennybacker 15).

Transition: Cassandra moves from the effects on adults to the effects on children of previously identified causes

Statistics that illustrate effects

9   There are many different suggestions for the prevention of and fight against obesity. The first and most obvious recommendation is to lose weight. Because obesity is a condition requiring continuous attention, any behavioral changes required to maintain weight loss must be lifelong. In order to lose weight, it is necessary to decrease caloric intake, increase caloric expenditure, or do both ("Fast Food"). According to Greg Critser in Fatlands, the response is simple but not always easy: We need to burn at

Possible solutions to modify effects

Bjork 5

least as many calories as we take in (Schlosser 2). It has been proven that physical activity is a vital component of a healthy lifestyle, whether a person is overweight or not. It is recommended to participate in moderate levels of physical activity for thirty to forty minutes, three to five times each week (Mathur). It can be difficult to meet this recommendation, but it eventually causes a positive long-term result.

10   Obesity is one of today's most visible yet most neglected conditions, affecting more Americans each day. The possible causes of obesity include fast food, genetics, and lack of physical activity. Although it is a growing problem, today we have the resources and knowledge available to overcome obesity. It is up to Americans to assist in the prevention of this condition that affects such a high percentage of our people.

> Conclusion: summarizes causes and echoes thesis statement in the introduction

Works Cited

Brownell, Kelly D. Food Fight. Boston: McGraw, 2004.

"Fast Food, Fat Children." CBSNews.com. 21 Apr. 2001. CBS News. 15 Sept. 2007 <http://www.cbsnews.com>

Gardner, Amanda. "Fast Food Linked to Obesity." HeartInfo.org. 30 Dec. 2005. 15 Sept. 2007 <http://www.heartinfo.org/ms/ news/523168/main.html>

Mathur, Ruchi. "Obesity (Weight Loss)." Ed. Dennis Lee. MedicineNet.com. 22 July 2003. 15 Sept. 2007 <http:// www.medicinenet.com/obesity_weight_loss/article.htm>

"Meet McDonald's Nutrition Expert, Dr. Cathy Kapica." McDonald's.com. 2005. McDonald's Corporation 15 Sept. 2007 <http://www.rhmc.com/usa!_eat/nutritionist.html>

"Obesity." Merriam-Webster's Collegiate Dictionary. 11th ed.

Pennybaker, Mindy. "Reducing 'Globesity' Begins at Home." World Watch Sept./Oct. 2005: 15.

Schlosser, Eric. Fast Food Nation: The Dark Side of the All-American Meal. Boston: Houghton, 2001.

United States. Centers for Disease Control and Prevention. "Obesity and Genetics." June 2006. 15 Sept. 2007 <http://www.cdc.gov/ genomics/training/perspectives/files/obesedit.htm>

Strategies for Writing Essays in Cause and Effect

1. Introduction and Thesis

Cassandra's essay analyzes the causes and effects of a nationwide trend as American adults and children grow increasingly obese. Cassandra then connects this phenomenon to Americans' sedentary lifestyle, genetic predispositions, and reliance on fast food rather than home-cooked meals. She uses the first paragraph to characterize this trend and then moves to her thesis: "Obesity is one of today's most visible yet most neglected conditions, affecting more Americans each day."

2. Purpose and Structure

Cassandra's purpose is not simply to provide information, but to reinforce the conclusions she reaches on the basis of her causal analysis. To do this, she must demonstrate the existence of complex cause-and-effect relationships linking lifestyle, genetic factors, and the growth of the fast-food industry with obesity. Her structure supports this approach by documenting with statistics the links between a sedentary lifestyle and mortality, current research on genetic factors, and marketing surveys linking fast-food indulgence to weight gain. The remaining sections of her essay show how children as well as adults are affected by this problem and present possible solutions to lessen this threat.

3. Topic Sentences and Transitions

Cassandra uses succinct topic sentences either as questions (paragraph 1) or statements (paragraph 3) to focus the reader's attention on the causes and effects of this trend. These topic sentences also serve as transitions to introduce new aspects of her analysis (as in paragraph 5: "In addition to the many different causes of obesity, fast food receives much of the blame").

4. Revision

One way for Cassandra to improve her essay would be to change the title to more accurately reflect the focus of her paper. Some sentences could be rewritten to be less tentative and express her ideas more directly. For example, the third sentence in the third paragraph includes a vague hypothetical phrase ("one could say it does not discourage obesity in the least way"). Also, she briefly touches on the role of genetics in causing obesity but does not provide a supporting analysis as she does with the sedentary lifestyle and the role of fast food. Finally, she uses the same wording to state her thesis at the end of the first paragraph and at the beginning of the last. She should vary the wording of her thesis in the conclusion.

Guidelines for Writing an Essay in Cause and Effect

- If your assignment requires you to analyze causes, effects, or both, have you created a thesis statement that focuses on the purpose and significance of your causal analysis? Essays that discuss causes and effects can go beyond providing information and can adopt a persuasive tone.
- Have you carefully identified possible causes and effects and, if necessary, distinguished between the chief cause and contributing causes? Have you also identified the immediate causes and effects and those that are remote?
- For causes, you need to know what happened, the reasons why, and who or what was involved. For effects, you need to know what happened, who or what was involved, and what consequences (both positive and negative) resulted from what happened.
- Does the organization of your essay reflect your analysis? If a chain of causes and effects is involved, a chronological order might work best. Otherwise, go from the least-well-understood (or mistaken) aspects of the situation to a discovery of the real causes and effects—a sequence that your readers will find convincing.
- After completing your causal analysis, double-check to make sure that you have avoided the *post hoc* fallacy, which assumes that because one event followed another, the first one caused the second.
- Have you used transitional words and phrases to signal the reader when you are discussing causes and/or effects and when you are analyzing the relationship between them?
- If appropriate, does your tone reflect a sense of likelihood rather than certainty?

Grammar Tips for Cause and Effect

Whether you are analyzing causes and effects to inform, to speculate, or to argue, you will be faced with two kinds of problems: (1) organizing your analysis in a clear and concise way and (2) using *affect* and *effect* correctly.

1. Causal essays in particular require close and careful editing to isolate the sequence of causes and effects that might be buried in paragraphs that are filled with redundancies, false starts, wordiness, and material that is out of order. Revise these by identifying the correct sequence, discovering the true focus of your analysis, and revising sentences for clarity and directness. To do this, you have to eliminate unnecessary words, combine sentences that repeat material, and use verbs in the active voice.

Unedited:

For example, consider how the following passage of an early draft has a provocative thesis but needs a clearer sequence:

College costs are rising faster than the rate of inflation. The proportion of students borrowing money is also going up. Income to pay back student loans would be easier for a beginning engineer than for a beginning teacher or social worker. The amount they owe could influence the choice of majors. Therefore, students major in fields that pay higher to finance their education even if they would have preferred to major in something else.

Edited:

We can observe the writer following an intriguing line of thought as a chain of causation without crystallizing it into a clear thesis and concise sequence. In a later draft, the central idea becomes clear:

Do students choose careers that do not correspond to their prime interests because they have to repay sizable debts originally incurred to attend college? The average student indebtedness has dramatically increased as college costs have escalated. The percentage of income available to repay federal loans would be more for some fields—such as engineering, computer science, or business—than for teaching, social work, or music. Therefore, we should not be surprised if students who borrow money for college are more influenced by economics than by personal talents and interests.

2. *Affect* and *effect* are commonly confused. It is especially important in essays analyzing causes and effects that you use these terms correctly. If you wish to express the idea "to have an influence on," use the verb *affect*. For example:

It should be obvious that student indebtedness *affects* the majors they choose.

If you wish to express the idea of a "result," use the noun *effect*. For example:

Thus, the *effect* of economics on career choices is substantial and unfortunate.

Or, you might wish to express the idea "to cause to happen" by using *effect* as a verb. For example:

For this reason, politicians need to *effect* changes in public financing for higher education.

> **CHECKLIST for Revising Cause and Effect Essays**
>
> - Will your essay analyze causes, effects, or both?
> - Does your thesis statement tell your readers why an analysis of causes and/or effects is worth knowing?
> - Have you drawn up a list of possible causes and/or potential effects and then identified the most significant cause and/or effect?
> - Does your essay require you to distinguish between causes in the distant past and those that are more recent?
> - Have you clearly identified the means by which the cause could have produced the effect?
> - Does your analysis require you to demonstrate a causal chain rather than a single cause?
> - Has your analysis avoided the *post hoc* fallacy of confusing coincidence with causation?
> - Do you use transitional words and phrases that show the relationship between causes and effects?

ADDITIONAL WRITING ASSIGNMENTS AND ACTIVITIES

COMMUNICATING WITH DIFFERENT AUDIENCES

1. You work for a tutorial service or at the campus writing center. Prepare a sheet of guidelines to advise students on how to address problems that could cause them to fail to complete work for a course or have to drop it.

2. Outline a series of talking points that you can use to advise a local community action group on the causes and effects of gangs in order to help them better understand the challenges they face.

WRITING FOR A NEWSPAPER

1. Write a letter to your local newspaper stating the effects of your college winning a major award or championship.

2. Write a letter to your college newspaper in which you analyze the effects of a campus speech code.

3. Write an op-ed piece to a newspaper analyzing the causes (strikes, collective bargaining, TV fees, player's salaries) and effects of trends in professional sports (high price of tickets) on the average fan.

CAUSE AND EFFECT ESSAYS

1. How do photojournalists shape our view of history?

2. What are the effects of film scores on your experience of viewing a movie?

3. What effect has a rock group, for example, the Rolling Stones, had on society?

4. Analyze the role of any causal mechanism in the natural world, for example, migration patterns in different species such as butterflies, whales, or birds.

5. Discuss some historical events that have been explained through the use of causal analysis.

6. What causal mechanisms have been discovered by researchers in social psychology experiments such as Stanley Milgram and Philip G. Zimbardo?

7. Argue for or against the idea that violent video games cause violent behavior in people who play them.

8. What are the effects of allowing cars in national parks?

9. Identify causes that were responsible for your decision to attend your present college or university.

10. What were the effects of an invention that changed the world, for example, the laser?

11. How much do negative reviews influence the public's decision whether or not to see a movie, buy a CD, go to a restaurant, or watch a TV show?

12. What are the effects of long-distance relationships, other than high telephone bills?

13. What are the current or foreseeable effects of a culture of fear of terrorism on the United States?

14. What factors influence the kind of medical care that is available to you?

15. How have devices such as the iPod changed the way in which people relate to each other?

16. What are the causes and effects of twenty-somethings moving back in with their parents?

17. What are the causes and effects of the rise of Islamic fundamentalism, the popularity of country music, or any other feature or trend of modern society?

18. Describe the effects of a strong personal emotional response such as jealousy, envy, infatuation, resentment, or hope.

19. Describe the causes and effects of the breakup of a relationship.

20. Describe the causes and effects of a time when you tried to be someone you were not.

21. What are the effects of dreams you have had that seemed to express premonitions?

RESEARCH SUGGESTIONS

1. How do the episodes of *CSI* rely on causal analysis and forensic medical techniques to connect all the elements of a case in order to solve the crime?

2. Research the question of whether distant prayer can help terminally ill patients to recover. You might wish to check NIH studies.

3. How has the use of e-mail and other short-lived electronic records undermined the nature of permanent historical records?

4. What are the causes and effects of global warming?

5. Research a current medical problem in terms of cause and effect, for example, the presumed role of mercury-based preservatives such as thimerosal in vaccines as a cause of autism, which now affects one out of every 166 children.

6. What are the causes and effects of such mysterious maladies such as Alzheimer's disease, obsessive-compulsive disorder, dyslexia, Tourette's syndrome, or any other physical or neurological disorder?

COLLABORATIVE ACTIVITIES

1. As a class, examine or analyze any proposed local or national law to see whether or not it would have a positive or negative effect on the environment, community, or nation.

2. Analyze the cause of any marketing mistake, for example Ford's Edsel, New Coke, or the Susan B. Anthony dollar.

DEFINITION

10

Identifying Meanings in Different Cultures

efinition is a useful method for specifying the basic nature of any phe-nomenon, idea, or thing. Discussing whether Jack has a "sense of humor" or Jill has "charisma" depends on establishing a clearly defined, commonly agreed-upon meaning for the terms involved. Frequently, we arrive at the mean-ing of a concept, such as a "sense of humor," by giving synonyms such as "playful," "witty," or "droll" to clarify the meaning of the terms or phrase in question.

By contrast, dictionaries use a more formal method for establishing exact mean-ings. Dictionaries place the subject to be defined in the context of the general class of things to which it belongs and then give distinguishing features that differenti-ate the item from all other subjects in its class with which it might be confused. For example, *tepee* is defined as "an American Indian skin-tent." The modifiers "American Indian" and "skin" are necessary to distinguish this particular type of tent from all other kinds of tent (for example, a canvas army tent) in the same general class. The terms that are used to define a word should be more specific, clear, and familiar than the actual term in question. Of course, in many cases, a dictionary definition is not adequate because the dictionary does not delve into specific criteria, characteristics, and qualities a writer might need to explore in developing an essay.

Traditional methods of definition are useful as long as the meaning of the term that is being defined has already been established, is generally agreed upon, or does not change in a different context. Many disciplines need to define new terms or concepts or redefine old ones as the results of new research become known. Thus, the term *node* is defined one way in anatomy (a concentrated swelling, as in "lymph node"), another in physics (as the point in a string where the least vibra-tion occurs), still differently in botany (as the stem joint out of which a leaf grows), and has yet another meaning in astronomy (a point where a planet's orbit appears to cross the sun's apparent path across the heavens).

491

The range of methods available to writers for defining technical terms, concepts, and processes goes well beyond the concise, formulaic type of definition that is found in dictionaries. Writers can draw on any or all of the writing strategies previously discussed—narration, description, exemplification, comparison and contrast, process analysis, classification and division, and cause and effect—to clarify and define the basic nature of any idea, term, condition, or phenomenon.

In "The Married Woman," for example, Simone de Beauvoir employs narration and description in a series of anecdotes that allow her readers to perceive how much of the married woman's life is defined by a fruitless struggle against dirt, dust, and disorder:

> The maniac housekeeper wages her furious war against dirt, blaming life itself for the rubbish all living growth entails. When any living being enters her house, her eye gleams with a wicked light: "Wipe your feet, don't tear the place apart, leave that alone!" She wishes those of her household would hardly breathe; everything means more thankless work for her. Severe, preoccupied, always on the watch, she loses *joie de vivre*, she becomes overprudent and avaricious. She shuts out the sunlight, for along with that come insects, germs, and dust, and besides, the sun ruins silk hangings and fades upholstery; she scatters naphthalene, which scents the air. She becomes bitter and disagreeable and hostile to all that lives: the end is sometimes murder.

Simone de Beauvoir's descriptive anecdote allows her readers to immediately see the features and specific qualities (repetitive, never-ending household tasks) that she considers essential in defining her subject.

Marilyn Yalom offers a range of examples in "The Wife Today" to illustrate the ways in which patterns of child-rearing, social relationships, joint financial responsibilities, and moral commitment have become defining values for today's wives and mothers:

> Wives, spouses, partners, companions, and lovers all wish to be confirmed by their chosen mates and to share a profound, mutual connection. Such a union demands commitment and recommitment. Ironically, we may come to think of marriage as a vocation requiring the kind of devotion that was once expected only of celibate monks and nuns. To be a wife today when there are few prescriptions or proscriptions is a truly creative endeavor.

Another useful method for defining concepts is by comparing and contrasting. Yalom also does this as a way of organizing the examples of the alternatives she cites:

> The number of Americans living alone (a quarter of all households) has never been higher. The number of men and women living together without marrying has also reached a record high, with heterosexual couples often taking years to decide whether they will or will not become husband and wife.

Yalom identifies the essential characteristics of "The Wife Today" in American culture by citing evidence that clearly distinguishes this role from the traditional wife of past generations.

Sometimes the best way of clarifying an unfamiliar technical process is to define it in terms of its function. In "Tortillas," Jose Antonio Burciaga uses this type of operational definition to give his readers insight into the distinctive nature of this essential Mexican food:

> For Mexicans over the centuries, the *tortilla* has served as the spoon and the fork, the plate and the napkin. . . . When you had no money for the filling, a poor man's *taco* could be made by placing a warm *tortilla* on the left palm, applying a sprinkle of salt, then rolling the *tortilla* up quickly with the fingertips of the right hand.

The broad range of applications that Burciaga describes gives the reader insight into the unique properties that make the tortilla such an indispensable food.

We can also see process analysis at work alongside definition in "Transformation" by Lydia Minatoya. As a daughter of Japanese American immigrants, Minatoya describes her parents's elaborate search for a suitable name for her:

> And so I received my uncommon conventional name. It really did not provide the camouflage my parents had anticipated. I remained unalterably alien. For Dr. Spock had been addressing *American* families, and in those days, everyone knew real American families were white.

The care her parents took in choosing her name revealed the importance of the acceptance they sought for their daughter.

Liliana Heker also uses process analysis in her story "The Stolen Party" as the chief means of showing that her main character, Rosaura, comes to believe that she is the social equal of her mother's employer's daughter, for whom the party is given.

> "I'll die if I don't go," she whispered, almost without moving her lips.
>
> And she wasn't sure whether she had been heard, but on the morning of the party she discovered that her mother had starched her Christmas dress. And in the afternoon, after washing her hair, her mother rinsed it in apple vinegar so that it would be all nice and shiny. Before going out, Rosaura admired herself in the mirror, with her white dress and glossy hair, and thought she looked terribly pretty.

This and other step-by-step passages offer insight into how Rosaura sees herself and illuminate the meaning of the title.

The need to have a clear grasp of the nature of the thing being defined can be readily seen in "A Look Behind the Veil," which represents Elizabeth W. Fernea and Robert A. Fernea's research to develop a useful definition of the practice of veiling. In the past, discussion of veiling has been hampered by the lack of a commonly agreed-upon definition. In creating their definition, the Ferneas use classification to systematically group veiling practices together in order to isolate the controlling characteristic that defines it:

> The veil and the all-enveloping garments that inevitably accompany it . . . are only the outward manifestations of a cultural pattern and idea that is rooted deep in Mediterranean society.

The Ferneas believe that a clearer conception of the principles that explain veiling will, in turn, make possible an understanding of its cultural meaning.

Another useful strategy for defining a phenomenon, idea, or process is to identify the circumstances that brought it about or the principles and laws that control its operation. This type of definition seeks to establish causes or consequences. In "Reflections on Exile," Edward Said examines a condition that has come to define much of the world's population. To help his readers understand the complexities of the term, he begins by looking at its historical causes:

> Although it is true that anyone prevented from returning home is an exile, some distinctions can be made between exiles, refugees, expatriates and émigrés. Exile originated in the age-old practice of banishment. Once banished, the exile lives an anomalous and miserable life, with the stigma of being an outsider.

Said clearly distinguishes the condition of exile from other states with which it might be confused and illuminates a pattern of causes and effects so that it becomes a way of looking at the world. Said's essay also illustrates how writers define a term by looking at its etymology or history as an important clue to illuminating its meaning.

Thus, as we have seen, writers across cultures are concerned with formulating new definitions of ideas, conditions, and phenomena or redefining old terms or concepts in light of the results of current study. They reveal that words change meaning and take on different cultural weight over time as part of wider historical processes.

In nonacademic contexts—on the job, for example—you might employ definition in preparing a report, brochure, or newsletter in which you need to explain the meaning of a key term. A brief definition might not be sufficient; you might have to use a combination of rhetorical strategies. Most important, you need to communicate the defining features of the term or idea in ways that will be clear to your audience.

EDWARD SAID

Reflections on Exile

A distinguished scholar and professor of English and comparative literature at Columbia University, whose literary criticism caused a revolution in prevalent attitudes towards Islam, Edward Said (1935–2003) was born in Jerusalem. Said was educated first in Cairo and then at Princeton and Harvard, where he received a Ph.D. He is best known for critical works, including *Orientalism* (1978), *Culture and Imperialism* (1993), and *Out of Place: A Memoir* (1999) that received *The New Yorker*'s award for nonfiction. Said also wrote music criticism for *The Nation* that was collected posthumously in *On Late Style: Music and Literature Against the Grain* (2006). In the following selection, which originally was published in *Granta* in 1984, Said defines the uniquely disorienting nature of exile and shows us how many great literary figures wrote under this condition.

BEFORE YOU READ

What kinds of difficulties do you imagine people who grew up in another country would have fitting into your community?

■ ■ ▨

1   Exile is strangely compelling to think about but terrible to experience. It is the unhealable rift forced between a human being and a native place, between the self and its true home: its essential sadness can never be surmounted. And while it is true that literature and history contain heroic, romantic, glorious, even triumphant episodes in an exile's life, these are no more than efforts meant to overcome the crippling sorrow of estrangement. The achievements of exile are permanently undermined by the loss of something left behind for ever.

2   Exiles look at non-exiles with resentment. *They* belong in their surroundings, you feel, whereas an exile is always out of place. What is it like to be born in a place, to stay and live there, to know that you are of it, more or less for ever?

3   Although it is true that anyone prevented from returning home is an exile, some distinctions can be made between exiles, refugees, expatriates and émigrés. Exile originated in the age-old practice of banishment. Once banished, the exile lives an anomalous and miserable life, with the stigma of being an outsider. Refugees, on the other hand, are a creation of the twentieth-century state. The word 'refugee' has become a political one, suggesting large herds of innocent and bewildered people requiring urgent international assistance, whereas 'exile' carries with it, I think, a touch of solitude and spirituality.

4   Expatriates voluntarily live in an alien country, usually for personal or social reasons. Hemingway and Fitzgerald were not forced to live in France. Expatriates may share in the solitude and estrangement of exile, but they do not suffer under its rigid proscriptions. Émigrés enjoy an ambiguous status. Technically, an émigré is anyone who emigrates to a new country. Choice in the matter is certainly a

possibility. Colonial officials, missionaries, technical experts, mercenaries and military advisers on loan may in a sense live in exile, but they have not been banished. White settlers in Africa, parts of Asia and Australia may once have been exiles, but as pioneers and nation-builders the label 'exile' dropped away from them.

5   Much of the exile's life is taken up with compensating for disorienting loss by creating a new world to rule. It is not surprising that so many exiles seem to be novelists, chess players, political activists, and intellectuals. Each of these occupations requires a minimal investment in objects and places a great premium on mobility and skill. The exile's new world, logically enough, is unnatural and its unreality resembles fiction. Georg Lukács, in *Theory of the Novel*, argued with compelling force that the novel, a literary form created out of the unreality of ambition and fantasy, is *the* form of 'transcendental homelessness.' Classical epics, Lukács wrote, emanate from settled cultures in which values are clear, identities stable, life unchanging. The European novel is grounded in precisely the opposite experience, that of a changing society in which an itinerant and disinherited middle-class hero or heroine seeks to construct a new world that somewhat resembles an old one left behind for ever. In the epic there is no *other* world, only the finality of *this* one. Odysseus returns to Ithaca after years of wandering; Achilles will die because he cannot escape his fate. The novel, however, exists because other worlds *may* exist, alternatives for bourgeois speculators, wanderers, exiles.

6   No matter how well they may do, exiles are always eccentrics who *feel* their difference (even as they frequently exploit it) as a kind of orphanhood. Anyone who is really homeless regards the habit of seeing estrangement in everything modern as an affectation, a display of modish attitudes. Clutching difference like a weapon to be used with stiffened will, the exile jealously insists on his or her right to refuse to belong.

7   This usually translates into an intransigence that is not easily ignored. Wilfulness, exaggeration, overstatement: these are characteristic styles of being an exile, methods for compelling the world to accept your vision—which you make more unacceptable because you are in fact unwilling to have it accepted. It is yours, after all. Composure and serenity are the last things associated with the work of exiles. Artists in exile are decidedly unpleasant, and their stubbornness insinuates itself into even their exalted works. Dante's vision in *The Divine Comedy* is tremendously powerful in its universality and detail, but even the beatific peace achieved in the *Paradiso* bears traces of the vindictiveness and severity of judgement embodied in the *Inferno*. Who but an exile like Dante, banished from Florence, would use eternity as a place for settling old scores?

8   James Joyce *chose* to be in exile: to give force to his artistic vocation. In an uncannily effective way—as Richard Ellmann has shown in his biography—Joyce picked a quarrel with Ireland and kept it alive so as to sustain the strictest opposition to what was familiar. Ellmann says that 'whenever his relations with his native land were in danger of improving. [Joyce] was to find a new incident to solidify his intransigence and to reaffirm the rightness of his voluntary absence.' Joyce's fiction concerns what in a letter he once described as the state of being 'alone and friendless.' And although it is rare to pick banishment as a way of life, Joyce perfectly understood its trials.

9   But Joyce's success as an exile stresses the question lodged at its very heart: is exile so extreme and private that any instrumental use of it is ultimately a trivialization? How is it that the literature of exile has taken its place as a *topos* of human experience alongside the literature of adventure, education or discovery? Is this the *same* exile that quite literally kills Yanko Goorall and has bred the expensive, often dehumanizing relationship between twentieth-century exile and nationalism? Or is it some more benign variety?

10   Much of the contemporary interest in exile can be traced to the somewhat pallid notion that non-exiles can share in the benefits of exile as a redemptive motif. There is, admittedly, a certain plausibility and truth to this idea. Like medieval itinerant scholars or learned Greek slaves in the Roman Empire, exiles—the exceptional ones among them—do leaven their environments. And naturally 'we' concentrate on that enlightening aspect of 'their' presence among us, not on their misery or their demands. But looked at from the bleak political perspective of modern mass dislocations, individual exiles force us to recognize the tragic fate of homelessness in a necessarily heartless world.

11   A generation ago, Simone Weil posed the dilemma of exile as concisely as it has ever been expressed. 'To be rooted,' she said, 'is perhaps the most important and least recognized need of the human soul.' Yet Weil also saw that most remedies for uprootedness in this era of world wars, deportations and mass exterminations are almost as dangerous as what they purportedly remedy. Of these, the state—or, more accurately, statism—is one of the most insidious, since worship of the state tends to supplant all other human bonds.

12   Weil exposes us anew to that whole complex of pressures and constraints that lie at the centre of the exile's predicament, which, as I have suggested, is as close as we come in the modern era to tragedy. There is the sheer fact of isolation and displacement, which produces the kind of narcissistic masochism that resists all efforts at amelioration, acculturation and community. At this extreme the exile can make a fetish of exile, a practice that distances him or her from all connections and commitments. To live as if everything around you were temporary and perhaps trivial is to fall prey to petulant cynicism as well as to querulous lovelessness. More common is the pressure on the exile to join— parties, national movements, the state. The exile is offered a new set of affiliations and develops new loyalties. But there is also a loss—of critical perspective, of intellectual reserve, of moral courage.

13   It must also be recognized that the defensive nationalism of exiles often fosters self-awareness as much as it does the less attractive forms of self-assertion. Such reconstitutive projects as assembling a nation out of exile (and this is true in this century for Jews and Palestinians) involve constructing a national history, reviving an ancient language, founding national institutions like libraries and universities. And these, while they sometimes promote strident ethnocentrism, also give rise to investigations of self that inevitably go far beyond such simple and positive facts as 'ethnicity.' For example, there is the self-consciousness of an individual trying to understand why the histories of the Palestinians and the Jews have certain patterns to them, why in spite of oppression and the threat of extinction a particular ethos remains alive in exile.

14   Necessarily, then, I speak of exile not as a privilege, but as an *alternative* to the mass institutions that dominate modern life. Exile is not, after all, a matter of choice: you are born into it, or it happens to you. But, provided that the exile refuses to sit on the sidelines nursing a wound, there are things to be learned: he or she must cultivate a scrupulous (not indulgent or sulky) subjectivity.

15   Perhaps the most rigorous example of such subjectivity is to be found in the writing of Theodor Adorno, the German-Jewish philosopher and critic. Adorno's masterwork, *Minima Moralia*, is an autobiography written while in exile: it is sub-titled *Reflexionen aus dem beschädigten Leben (Reflections from a Mutilated Life)*. Ruth-lessly opposed to what he called the 'administered' world, Adorno saw all life as pressed into ready-made forms, prefabricated 'homes.' He argued that every-thing that one says or thinks, as well as every object one possesses, is ultimately a mere commodity. Language is jargon, objects are for sale. To refuse this state of affairs is the exile's intellectual mission.

16   Adorno's reflections are informed by the belief that the only home truly available now, though fragile and vulnerable, is in writing. Elsewhere, 'the house is past. The bombings of European cities, as well as the labour and concentra-tion camps, merely precede as executors, with what the immanent development of technology had long decided was to be the fate of houses. These are now good only to be thrown away like old food cans.' In short, Adorno says with a grave irony, 'it is part of morality not to be at home in one's home.'

17   To follow Adorno is to stand away from 'home' in order to look at it with the exile's detachment. For there is considerable merit in the practice of not-ing the discrepancies between various concepts and ideas and what they actu-ally produce. We take home and language for granted; they become nature, and their underlying assumptions recede into dogma and orthodoxy.

18   The exile knows that in a secular and contingent world, homes are always provisional. Borders and barriers, which enclose us within the safety of familiar territory, can also become prisons, and are often defended beyond reason or necessity. Exiles cross borders, break barriers of thought and experience.

19   Hugo of St Victor, a twelfth-century monk from Saxony, wrote these haunt-ingly beautiful lines:

> It is, therefore, a source of great virtue for the practised mind to learn, bit by bit, first to change about invisible and transitory things, so that after-wards it may be able to leave them behind altogether. The man who finds his homeland sweet is still a tender beginner; he to whom every soil is as his native one is already strong; but he is perfect to whom the entire world is as a foreign land. The tender soul has fixed his love on one spot in the world; the strong man has extended his love to all places: the perfect man has extinguished his.

Erich Auerbach, the great twentieth-century literary scholar who spent the war years as an exile in Turkey, has cited this passage as a model for anyone wishing to transcend national or provincial limits. Only by embracing this attitude can a historian begin to grasp human experience and its written records in their diversity and particularity; otherwise he or she will remain committed more to the exclusions and reactions of prejudice than to the freedom that accompanies knowledge. But note that Hugo twice makes it clear that the 'strong' or 'perfect' man achieves independence and detachment by *working through* attachments, not by rejecting them. Exile is predicated on the existence of, love for, and bond with, one's native place; what is true of all exile is not that home and love of home are lost, but that loss is inherent in the very existence of both.

20   Regard experiences as if they were about to disappear. What is it that anchors them in reality? What would you save of them? What would you give up? Only someone who has achieved independence and detachment, someone whose homeland is 'sweet' but whose circumstances makes it impossible to recapture that sweetness, can answer those questions. (Such a person would also find it impossible to derive satisfaction from substitutes furnished by illusion or dogma.)

21   This may seem like a prescription for an unrelieved grimness of outlook and, with it, a permanently sullen disapproval of all enthusiasm or buoyancy of spirit. Not necessarily. While it perhaps seems peculiar to speak of the pleasures of exile, there are some positive things to be said for a few of its conditions. Seeing 'the entire world as a foreign land' makes possible originality of vision. Most people are principally aware of one culture, one setting, one home; exiles are aware of at least two, and this plurality of vision gives rise to an awareness of simultaneous dimensions, an awareness that—to borrow a phrase from music— is *contrapuntal*.

22   For an exile, habits of life, expression or activity in the new environment inevitably occur against the memory of these things in another environment. Thus both the new and the old environments are vivid, actual, occurring together contrapuntally. There is a unique pleasure in this sort of apprehension, especially if the exile is conscious of other contrapuntal juxtapositions that diminish orthodox judgement and elevate appreciative sympathy. There is also a particular sense of achievement in acting as if one were at home wherever one happens to be.

23   This remains risky, however: the habit of dissimulation is both wearying and nerve-racking. Exile is never the state of being satisfied, placid, or secure. Exile, in the words of Wallace Stevens, is 'a mind of winter' in which the pathos of summer and autumn as much as the potential of spring are nearby but unobtainable. Perhaps this is another way of saving that a life of exile moves according to a different calendar, and is less seasonal and settled than life at home. Exile is life led outside habitual order. It is nomadic, decentred, contrapuntal; but no sooner does one get accustomed to it than its unsettling force erupts anew.

■ ■ ▨

MEANING

1. What distinction does Said draw between being an exile (that is, someone who is prevented from returning home) and being a refugee or an émigré?

2. Why are so many exiles chess players, novelists, and intellectuals?

3. How much of the exile's life is "taken up with compensating for disorienting loss by creating a new world to rule"?

4. How does the exile's awareness of the culture that was left behind and the one currently being inhabited produce a dual perspective?

TECHNIQUE

1. How does Said use literary works to show how writers project into imaginative form the psychological characteristics of being an exile?

2. What aspects of Said's essay illuminate the difficulties exiles have of not being able to put down roots?

3. **Other Patterns.** How does Said use **comparison and contrast** to distinguish the condition of exile from other seemingly similar states with which it might be confused?

LANGUAGE

1. How does the quotation from Hugo of St. Victor (in paragraph 19) communicate the unanticipated beneficial effects of being exiled?

2. What terms and images does Said use to define *exile* as a psychological state rather than a literal dislocation from one's homeland?

3. If you don't know the meaning of the following words, look them up: *exile* (1), *rift* (1), *estrangement* (1), *expatriates* (3), *anomalous* (3), *proscriptions* (4), *itinerant* (5), *modish* (6), *insinuates* (7), *beatific* (7), *topos* (9), *dogma* (17).

SUGGESTIONS FOR WRITING

1. Have you or members of your family experienced the psychological condition of exile that Said describes? Write a few paragraphs explaining what it is like to be between cultures and at home in neither.

2. Discuss some recent developments that have brought the condition of exile into the public awareness.

3. **Critical Writing.** After reading any of the works by Joyce, Dante, or other writers mentioned by Said, write an essay analyzing how they **illustrate** his thesis.

4. **Thematic Links.** To what extent are the family members in Ethel G. Hofman's "An Island Passover" (Chapter 7, "Process Analysis") exiles?

LYDIA MINATOYA

Transformation

Seldom has the drama of what to name a child been depicted with greater humor and urgency than in the case of Lydia Minatoya (b. 1950). Her Japanese parents wanted her to have an American name, and this event—described in the following selection, a chapter from her book *Talking to High Monks in the Snow* (1992)—was a decisive moment for her. We can trace the importance of this back to the family's isolation in Albany, New York, in the late 1950s when she was growing up. We can also see additional evidence in her need to be the "teacher's pet," as her elder sister had been before her. Minatoya went on to receive a doctorate in psychology from the University of Maryland, traveled widely throughout Asia, and currently resides in Seattle, where she is a community college teacher and counselor. A more recent publication is *The Strangeness of Beauty* (1999).

BEFORE YOU READ

How might the name immigrant parents give to a child express a wish for the child's future?

■ ■ ▨

1   Perhaps it begins with my naming. During her pregnancy, my mother was reading Dr. Spock. "Children need to belong," he cautioned. "An unusual name can make them the subject of ridicule." My father frowned when he heard this. He stole a worried glance at my sister. Burdened by her Japanese name, Misa played unsuspectingly on the kitchen floor.

2   The Japanese know full well the dangers of conspicuousness. "The nail that sticks out gets pounded down," cautions an old maxim. In America, Relocation was all the proof they needed.

3   And so it was, with great earnestness, my parents searched for a conventional name. They wanted me to have the full true promise of America.

4   "I will ask my colleague Froilan," said my father. "He is the smartest man I know."

5   "And he has poetic soul," said my mother, who cared about such things.

6   In due course, Father consulted Froilan. He gave Froilan his conditions for suitability.

7   "First, if possible, the full name should be alliterative," said my father. "Like Misa Minatoya." He closed his eyes and sang my sister's name. "Second, if not an alliteration, at least the name should have assonantal rhyme."

8   "Like Misa Minatoya?" said Froilan with a teasing grin.

9   "Exactly," my father intoned. He gave an emphatic nod. "Finally, most importantly, the name must be readily recognizable as conventional." He peered at Froilan with hope. "Do you have any suggestions or ideas?"

10   Froilan, whose own American child was named Ricardito, thought a while.

11   "We already have selected the name for a boy," offered my Father. "Eugene."

12   "Eugene?" wondered Froilan. "But it meets none of your conditions!"

13   "Eugene is a special case," said my father, "after Eugene, Oregon, and Eugene O'Neill. The beauty of the Pacific Northwest, the power of a great writer."

14   "I see," said Froilan, who did not but who realized that this naming business would be more complex than he had anticipated. "How about Maria?"

15   "Too common," said my father. "We want a *conventional* name, not a common one."

16   "Hmmm," said Froilan, wondering what the distinction was. He thought some more and then brightened. "Lydia!" he declared. He rhymed the name with media. "Lydia for *la bonita infanta!*"

17   And so I received my uncommon conventional name. It really did not provide the camouflage my parents had anticipated. I remained unalterably alien. For Dr. Spock had been addressing *American* families, and in those days, everyone knew all real American families were white.

18   Call it denial, but many Japanese Americans never quite understood that the promise of America was not truly meant for them. They lived in horse stalls at the Santa Anita racetrack and said the Pledge of Allegiance daily. They rode to Relocation Camps under armed guard, labeled with numbered tags, and sang "The Star-Spangled Banner." They lived in deserts or swamps, ludicrously imprisoned—where would they run if they ever escaped—and formed garden clubs, and yearbook staffs, and citizen town meetings. They even elected beauty queens.

19   My mother practiced her okoto and was featured in a recital. She taught classes in fashion design and her students mounted a show. Into exile she had carried an okoto and a sewing machine. They were her past and her future. She believed in Art and Technology.

20   My mother's camp was the third most populous city in the entire state of Wyoming. Across the barren lands, behind barbed wire, bloomed these little oases of democracy. The older generation bore the humiliation with pride. "*Kodomo no tame ni,*" they said. For the sake of the children. They thought that if their dignity was great, then their children would be spared. Call it valor. Call it bathos. Perhaps it was closer to slapstick: a sweet and bitter lunacy.

21   Call it adaptive behavior. Coming from a land swept by savage typhoons, ravaged by earthquakes and volcanoes, the Japanese have evolved a view of the world: a cooperative, stoic, almost magical way of thinking. Get along, work hard, and never quite see the things that can bring you pain. Against the tyranny of nature, of feudal lords, of wartime hysteria, the charm works equally well.

22   And so my parents gave me an American name and hoped that I could pass. They nourished me with the American dream: Opportunity, Will, Transformation.

23   When I was four and my sister was eight, Misa regularly used me as a comic foil. She would bring her playmates home from school and query me as I sat amidst the milk bottles on the front steps.

24   "What do you want to be when you grow up?" she would say. She would nudge her audience into attentiveness.

25   "A mother kitty cat!" I would enthuse. Our cat had just delivered her first litter of kittens and I was enchanted by the rasping tongue and soft mewings of motherhood.

26   "And what makes you think you can become a cat?" Misa would prompt, gesturing to her howling friends—wait for this; it gets better yet.

27   "This is America," I stoutly would declare. "I can grow up to be anything that I want!"

28   My faith was unshakable. I believed. Opportunity. Will. Transformation.

29 When we lived in Albany, I always was the teachers' pet. "So tiny, so precocious, so prettily dressed!" They thought I was a living doll and this was fine with me.

30   My father knew that the effusive praise would die. He had been through this with my sister. After five years of being a perfect darling, Misa had reached the age where students were tracked by ability. Then, the anger started. Misa had tested into the advanced track. It was impossible, the community declared. Misa was forbidden entry into advanced classes as long as there were white children being placed below her. In her defense, before an angry rabble, my father made a presentation to the Board of Education.

31   But I was too young to know of this. I knew only that my teachers praised and petted me. They took me to other classes as an example. "Watch now, as Lydia demonstrates attentive behavior," they would croon as I was led to an empty desk at the head of the class. I had a routine. I would sit carefully, spreading my petticoated skirt neatly beneath me. I would pull my chair close to the desk, crossing my swinging legs at my snowy white anklets. I would fold my hands carefully on the desk before me and stare pensively at the blackboard.

32   This routine won me few friends. The sixth-grade boys threw rocks at me. They danced around me in a tight circle, pulling at the corners of their eyes. "Ching Chong Chinaman," they chanted. But teachers loved me. When I was in first grade, a third-grade teacher went weeping to the principal. She begged to have me skipped. She was leaving to get married and wanted her turn with the dolly.

* * *

33 When we moved, the greatest shock was the knowledge that I had lost my charm. From the first, my teacher failed to notice me. But to me, it did not matter. I was in love. I watched her moods, her needs, her small vanities. I was determined to ingratiate.

34   Miss Hempstead was a shimmering vision with a small upturned nose and eyes that were kewpie doll blue. Slender as a sylph, she tripped around the classroom, all saucy in her high-heeled shoes. Whenever I looked at Miss Hempstead, I pitied the Albany teachers whom, formerly, I had adored. Poor old Miss Rosenberg. With a shiver of distaste, I recalled her loose fleshy arms, her mottled hands, the scent of lavender as she crushed me to her heavy breasts.

35   Miss Hempstead had a pet of her own. Her name was Linda Sherlock. I watched Linda closely and plotted Miss Hempstead's courtship. The key was the

piano. Miss Hempstead played the piano. She fancied herself a musical star. She sang songs from Broadway revues and shaped her students' reactions. "Getting to know you," she would sing. We would smile at her in a staged manner and position ourselves obediently at her feet.

36   Miss Hempstead was famous for her ability to soothe. Each day at rest time, she played the piano and sang soporific songs. Linda Sherlock was the only child who succumbed. Routinely, Linda's head would bend and nod until she crumpled gracefully onto her folded arms. A tousled strand of blonde hair would fall across her forehead. Miss Hempstead would end her song, would gently lower the keyboard cover. She would turn toward the restive eyes of the class. "Isn't she sweetness itself!" Miss Hempstead would declare. It made me want to vomit.

What clues in this picture of a student at her desk (who is not Minatoya) might allow you to imagine Lydia Minatoya when she was in her model student phase?

37   I was growing weary. My studiousness, my attentiveness, my fastidious grooming and pert poise: all were failing me. I changed my tactics. I became a problem. Miss Hempstead sent me home with nasty notes in sealed envelopes: Lydia is a slow child, a noisy child, her presence is disruptive. My mother looked at me with surprise, *"Nani desu ka?* Are you having problems with your teacher?" But I was tenacious. I pushed harder and harder, firmly caught in the obsessive need of the scorned.

38   One day I snapped. As Miss Hempstead began to sing her wretched lullabies, my head dropped to the desk with a powerful CRACK! It lolled there, briefly, then rolled toward the edge with a momentum that sent my entire body catapulting to the floor. Miss Hempstead's spine stretched slightly, like a cat that senses danger. Otherwise, she paid no heed. The linoleum floor was smooth and cool. It emitted a faint pleasant odor: a mixture of chalk dust and wax.

39   I began to snore heavily. The class sat electrified. There would be no drowsing today. The music went on and on. Finally, one boy could not stand it. "Miss Hempstead," he probed plaintively, "Lydia has fallen asleep on the floor!" Miss Hempstead did not turn. Her playing grew slightly strident but she did not falter.

40   I lay on the floor through rest time. I lay on the floor through math drill. I lay on the floor while my classmates scraped around me, pushing their sturdy little wooden desks into the configuration for reading circle. It was not until penmanship practice that I finally stretched and stirred. I rose like Sleeping Beauty and slipped back to my seat. I smiled enigmatically. A spell had been broken. I never again had a crush on a teacher.

■ ■ ▨

MEANING

1. From the parents' perspective, what cultural assumptions determine the name that is given to a child?

2. Why does Minatoya believe that many Japanese Americans were in a state of denial as to their true identity?

3. What events involving her sister preceded Minatoya's entry into the public school system?

4. How does the author's "transformation" involve liberating herself from being cast as the teacher's pet?

TECHNIQUE

1. How does Minatoya's **description** of internment camps for the Japanese during World War II provide insight into why her parents chose "Lydia" for her name?

2. How does Minatoya cause the reader to sympathize with her revolt against the stereotyped role into which she has allowed herself to be cast?

3. *Other Patterns.* How does Minatoya use **narration** at the opening of her account to frame the issues her essay will explore?

LANGUAGE

1. How does Minatoya's attitude toward her given name differ from the expectations of her parents when they gave her this name?
2. How does referring to herself as "the dolly" reveal the animosity she feels toward this role?
3. If you don't know the meaning of the following words, look them up: *conspicuousness* (2), *alliterative* (7), *assonantal* (7), *conventional* (15), *feudal* (21), *pensively* (31), *ingratiate* (33), *mottled* (34), *soporific* (36), *tenacious* (37), *catapulting* (38).

SUGGESTIONS FOR WRITING

1. ***Critical Writing.*** Have you ever rebelled against a role into which you had been cast? If so, what happened? **Compare** your experiences with Minatoya's.
2. What **causes** are responsible for the choice of your name?
3. ***Thematic Links.*** In what ways do Minatoya and Frank McCourt in "Irish Step Dancing" (Chapter 3, "Narration") both rebel against the roles that they were expected to play?

The Married Woman

The renowned novelist, essayist, and pioneering feminist Simone de Beauvoir (1908–1986) was born in Paris, studied philosophy at the Sorbonne, and helped to found the French existentialist movement along with her longtime companion, Jean-Paul Sartre. The following selection, which originally appeared in *The Second Sex* (1949, trans. 1956)— so named because it describes the subservient status of woman—offers a brilliant analysis of the isolated life of married women when compared with the independence and opportunities available to their husbands. De Beauvoir's keen intellectual gifts are also apparent in *The Mandarins* (1954), which won the prestigious Prix Goncourt, and *All Said and Done* (1972), an engrossing memoir.

BEFORE YOU READ

What tasks in your daily life do you dislike most?

■ ■ ▨

1   Few tasks are more like the torture of Sisyphus than housework, with its endless repetition: the clean becomes soiled, the soiled is made clean, over and over, day after day. The housewife wears herself out marking time, she makes nothing, simply perpetuates the present. She never senses conquest of a positive Good, but rather indefinite struggle against negative Evil. A young pupil writes in her essay: "I shall never have house-cleaning day"; she thinks of the future as constant progress toward some unknown summit; but one day, as her mother washes the dishes, it comes over her that both of them will be bound to such rites until death. Eating, sleeping, cleaning—the years no longer rise up toward heaven, they lie spread out ahead, gray and identical. The battle against dust and dirt is never won.

2   Washing, ironing, sweeping, ferreting out rolls of lint from under wardrobes—all this halting of decay is also the denial of life: for time simultaneously creates and destroys, and only its negative aspect concerns the housekeeper. Hers is the position of the Manichaeist, regarded philosophically. The essence of Manichaeism is not solely to recognize two principles, the one good, the other evil; it is also to hold that the good is attained through the abolition of evil and not by positive action. In this sense Christianity is hardly Manichaeist in spite of the existence of the devil, for one fights the demon best by devoting oneself to God and not by endeavoring to conquer the evil one directly. Any doctrine of transcendence and liberty subordinates the defeat of evil to progress toward the good. But woman is not called upon to build a better world: her domain is fixed and she has only to keep up the never ending struggle against the evil principles that creep into it; in her war against dust, stains, mud, and dirt she is fighting sin, wrestling with Satan.

3   But it is a sad fate to be required without respite to repel an enemy instead of working toward positive ends, and very often the housekeeper submits to it in a kind of madness that may verge on perversion, a kind of sado-masochism. The maniac housekeeper wages her furious war against dirt, blaming life itself for the rubbish all living growth entails. When any living being enters her house, her eye gleams with a wicked light: "Wipe your feet, don't tear the place apart, leave that alone!" She wishes those of her household would hardly breathe; everything means more thankless work for her. Severe, preoccupied, always on the watch, she loses *joie de vivre*, she becomes overprudent and avaricious. She shuts out the sunlight, for along with that come insects, germs, and dust, and besides, the sun ruins silk hangings and fades upholstery: she scatters naphthalene, which scents the air. She becomes bitter and disagreeable and hostile to all that lives: the end is sometimes murder.

4   The healthy young woman will hardly be attracted by so gloomy a vice. Such nervousness and spitefulness are more suited to frigid and frustrated women, old maids, deceived wives, and those whom surly and dictatorial husbands condemn to a solitary and empty existence. I knew an old beldame, once gay and coquettish, who got up at five each morning to go over her closets; married to a man who neglected her, and isolated on a lonely estate, with but one child, she took to orderly housekeeping as others take to drink. In this insanity the house becomes so neat and clean that one hardly dares live in it; the woman is so busy she forgets her own existence. A household, in fact, with its meticulous and limitless tasks, permits to woman a sado-masochistic flight from herself as she contends madly with the things around her and with herself in a state of distraction and mental vacancy. And this flight may often have a sexual tinge. It is noteworthy that the rage for cleanliness is highest in Holland, where the women are cold, and in puritanical civilizations, which oppose an ideal of neatness and purity to the joys of the flesh. If the Mediterranean Midi lives in a state of joyous filth, it is not only because water is scarce there: love of the flesh and its animality is conducive to toleration of human odor, dirt, and even vermin.

5   The preparation of food, getting meals, is work more positive in nature and often more agreeable than cleaning. First of all it means marketing, often the bright spot of the day. And gossip on doorsteps, while peeling vegetables, is a gay relief for solitude; to go for water is a great adventure for half-cloistered Mohammedan women; women in markets and stores talk about domestic affairs, with a common interest, feeling themselves members of a group that—for an instant—is opposed to the group of men as the essential to the inessential. Buying is a profound pleasure, a discovery, almost an invention. As Gide says in his *Journal*, the Mohammedans, not knowing gambling, have in its place the discovery of hidden treasure; that is the poetry and the adventure of mercantile civilizations. The housewife knows little of winning in games, but a solid cabbage, a ripe Camembert, are treasures that must be cleverly won from the unwilling storekeeper; the game is to get the best for the least money; economy means not so much helping the budget as winning the game. She is pleased with her passing triumph as she contemplates her well-filled larder.

6   Gas and electricity have killed the magic of fire, but in the country many women still know the joy of kindling live flames from inert wood. With her fire going, woman becomes a sorceress; by a simple movement, as in beating eggs, or through the magic of fire, she effects the transmutation of substances: matter becomes food. There is enchantment in these alchemies, there is poetry in making preserves; the housewife has caught duration in the snare of sugar, she has enclosed life in jars. Cooking is revolution and creation; and a woman can find special satisfaction in a successful cake or a flaky pastry, for not everyone can do it: one must have the gift.

7   Here again the little girl is naturally fond of imitating her elders, making mud pies and the like, and helping roll real dough in the kitchen. But as with other housework, repetition soon spoils these pleasures. The magic of the oven can hardly appeal to Mexican Indian women who spend half their lives preparing tortillas, identical from day to day, from century to century. And it is impossible to go on day after day making a treasure-hunt of the marketing or ecstatically viewing one's highly polished faucets. The male and female writers who lyrically exalt such triumphs are persons who are seldom or never engaged in actual housework. It is tiresome, empty, monotonous, as a career. If, however, the individual who does such work is also a producer, a creative worker, it is as naturally integrated in life as are the organic functions; for this reason housework done by men seems much less dismal; it represents for them merely a negative and inconsequential moment from which they quickly escape. What makes the lot of the wife-servant ungrateful is the division of labor which dooms her completely to the general and the inessential. Dwelling-place and food are useful for life but give it no significance: the immediate goals of the housekeeper are only means, not true ends. She endeavors, naturally, to give some individuality to her work and to make it seem essential. No one else, she thinks, could do her work as well; she has her rites, superstitions, and ways of doing things. But too often her "personal note" is but a vague and meaningless rearrangement of disorder.

8   Woman wastes a great deal of time and effort in such striving for originality and unique perfection; this gives her task its meticulous, disorganized, and endless character and makes it difficult to estimate the true load of domestic work. Recent studies show that for married women housework averages about thirty hours per week, or three fourths of a working week in employment. This is enormous if done in addition to a paid occupation, little if the woman has nothing else to do. The care of several children will naturally add a good deal to woman's work: a poor mother is often working all the time. Middle-class women who employ help, on the other hand, are almost idle; and they pay for their leisure with ennui. If they lack outside interests, they often multiply and complicate their domestic duties to excess, just to have something to do.

9   The worst of it all is that this labor does not even tend toward the creation of anything durable. Woman is tempted—and the more so the greater pains she takes—to regard her work as an end in itself. She sighs as she contemplates the perfect cake just out of the oven: "it's a shame to eat it!" It is really too bad to have

husband and children tramping with their muddy feet all over her waxed hard-wood floors! When things are used they are soiled or destroyed—we have seen how she is tempted to save them from being used; she keeps preserves until they get moldy; she locks up the parlor. But time passes inexorably; provisions attract rats; they become wormy; moths attack blankets and clothing. The world is not a dream carved in stone, it is made of dubious stuff subject to rot; edible material is as equivocal as Dali's fleshy watches: it seems inert, inorganic, but hidden larvae may have changed it into a cadaver. The housewife who loses herself in things becomes dependent, like the things, upon the whole world: linen is scorched, the roast burns, chinaware gets broken; these are absolute disasters, for when things are destroyed, they are gone forever. Permanence and security cannot possibly be obtained through them. The pillage and bombs of war threaten one's wardrobes, one's house.

10   The products of domestic work, then, must necessarily be consumed; a con-tinual renunciation is required of the woman whose operations are completed only in their destruction. For her to acquiesce without regret, these minor holo-causts must at least be reflected in someone's joy or pleasure. But since the housekeeper's labor is expended to maintain the *status quo*, the husband, com-ing into the house, may notice disorder or negligence, but it seems to him that order and neatness come of their own accord. He has a more positive interest in a good meal. The cook's moment of triumph arrives when she puts a suc-cessful dish on the table: husband and children receive it with warm approval, not only in words, but by consuming it gleefully. The culinary alchemy then pur-sues its course, food becomes chyle and blood.

11   Thus, to maintain living bodies is of more concrete, vital interest than to keep a fine floor in proper condition; the cook's effort is evidently transcended toward the future. If, however, it is better to share in another's free transcendence than to lose oneself in things, it is not less dangerous. The validity of the cook's work is to be found only in the mouths of those around her table; she needs their approba-tion, demands that they appreciate her dishes and call for second helpings; she is upset if they are not hungry, to the point that one wonders whether the fried pota-toes are for her husband or her husband for the fried potatoes. This ambiguity is evident in the general attitude of the housekeeping wife: she takes care of the house for her husband; but she also wants him to spend all he earns for furnishings and an electric refrigerator. She desires to make him happy; but she approves of his activities only in so far as they fall within the frame of happiness she has set up.

12   There have been times when these claims have in general found satisfac-tion: times when such felicity was also man's ideal, when he was attached above all to his home, to his family, and when even the children chose to be charac-terized by their parents, their traditions, and their past. At such times she who ruled the home, who presided at the dinner table, was recognized as supreme; and she still plays this resplendent role among certain landed proprietors and wealthy peasants who here and there perpetuate the patriachal civilization.

13   But on the whole marriage is today a surviving relic of dead ways of life, and the situation of the wife is more ungrateful than formerly, because she still has the same duties but they no longer confer the same rights, privileges, and honors.

Man marries today to obtain an anchorage in immanence, but not to be himself confined therein; he wants to have hearth and home while being free to escape therefrom; he settles down but often remains a vagabond at heart; he is not contemptuous of domestic felicity, but he does not make of it an end in itself; repetition bores him; he seeks after novelty, risk, opposition to overcome, companions and friends who take him away from solitude *à deux.* The children, even more than their father, want to escape beyond family limits: life for them lies elsewhere, it is before them; the child always seeks what is different. Woman tries to set up a universe of permanence and continuity; husband and children wish to transcend the situation she creates, which for them is only a given environment. This is why, even if she is loath to admit the precarious nature of the activities to which her whole life is devoted, she is nevertheless led to impose her services by force: she changes from mother and housewife into harsh stepmother and shrew.

14   Thus woman's work within the home gives her no autonomy; it is not directly useful to society, it does not open out on the future, it produces nothing. It takes on meaning and dignity only as it is linked with existent beings who reach out beyond themselves, transcend themselves, toward society in production and action. That is, far from freeing the matron, her occupation makes her dependent upon husband and children; she is justified through them; but in their lives she is only an inessential intermediary. That "obedience" is legally no longer one of her duties in no way changes her situation; for this depends not on the will of the couple but on the very structure of the conjugal group. Woman is not allowed to *do* something positive in her work and in consequence win recognition as a complete person. However respected she may be, she is subordinate, secondary, parasitic. The heavy curse that weighs upon her consists in this: the very meaning of her life is not in her hands. That is why the successes and the failures of her conjugal life are much more gravely important for her than for her husband; he is first a citizen, a producer, secondly a husband; she is before all, and often exclusively, a wife; her work does not take her out of her situation; it is from the latter on the contrary, that her work takes its value, high or low. Loving, generously devoted, she will perform her tasks joyously; but they will seem to her mere dull drudgery if she performs them with resentment. In her destiny they will never play more than an inessential role; they will not be a help in the ups and downs of conjugal life. We must go on to see, then, how woman's condition is concretely experienced in life—this condition which is characterized essentially by the "service" of the bed and the "service" of the housekeeping and in which woman finds her place of dignity only in accepting her vassalage.

■ ■ ▨

Meaning

1. What characteristics are encompassed within de Beauvoir's definition of the married woman?

2. What aspects of housework undermine the married woman's independence and subordinate her individuality?

3. Why is preparing food a more desirable kind of task than other chores of the married woman?

4. What is the purpose of de Beauvoir's analysis, and who might her audience have been?

TECHNIQUE

1. How is de Beauvoir's definition strengthened by comparison with tasks performed by women in many cultures?

2. How does de Beauvoir **contrast** the tasks of the married woman with work that men do outside the home to emphasize the disadvantages of the married woman's life?

3. *Other Patterns.* What **examples** did you find particularly effective in illustrating de Beauvoir's thesis?

LANGUAGE

1. Why does the legend of Sisyphus characterize the tasks housewives must perform?

2. How would you characterize de Beauvoir's tone and her attitude toward her subject?

3. If you don't know the meaning of the following words, look them up: *Sisyphus* (1), *sado-masochism* (3), *joie de vivre* (3), *avaricious* (3), *coquettish* (4), *meticulous* (4), *alchemies* (6), *inconsequential* (7), *Dali* (9), *acquiesce* (10), *status quo* (10), *approbation* (11), *à deux* (13), *autonomy* (14), *vassalage* (14).

SUGGESTIONS FOR WRITING

1. Are there positive features that de Beauvoir omits from her definition of the married woman? If so, what are they?

2. *Critical Writing.* Using de Beauvoir's essay as a model, write an essay defining the single woman in today's world.

3. Read Terry Keefe's *Simone de Beauvoir* (1998), and write an essay exploring how de Beauvoir's own life illustrated her views, as expressed in this essay.

4. To what extent have changes in society since de Beauvoir wrote this essay altered her observations? Write a few paragraphs exploring the **causes** for these changes, and include examples that illustrate how things have changed and how they have remained the same.

5. *Thematic Links.* Compare the picture painted by de Beauvoir ("the magic of the oven can hardly appeal to Mexican Indian women who spend half their lives preparing tortillas") with that given in Jose Antonio Burciaga's essay "Tortillas."

MARILYN YALOM

The Wife Today

Marilyn Yalom (b. 1932) in this essay from *The History of the Wife* (2001) investigates ways in which the role of the wife today entails radically different responsibilities and allows greater freedom than was possible in previous eras. Yalom was born in Chicago, educated at Wellesley, and received advanced degrees from Harvard (M.A., 1956) and Johns Hopkins (Ph.D., 1963). Her work has put her at the forefront of feminist scholarship and has appeared in publications including *A History of the Breast* (1997) and *The Birth of the Chess Queen: How Her Majesty Transformed the Game* (2004). At present, she is a senior scholar at the Institute for Research on Women and Gender at Stanford University.

Before You Read

Are marriages more of a partnership today than they were in previous generations?

■ ■ ▨

1   American wives and mothers, most of whom work inside and outside the home, are constantly improvising and juggling to provide adequate day care and schooling for their children, comfortable housing, wholesome meals, decent clothing, weekly entertainment, and summertime vacations. Little wonder that they complain and that some return, when economically feasible, to full-time homemaking.

2   Yet, as Stephanie Coontz argues in *The Way We Really Are*, wives and mothers will continue to work outside the home for more than financial reasons. Most women enjoy the satisfactions offered by their jobs. "They consistently tell interviewers they like the social respect, self-esteem, and friendship networks they gain from the job, despite the stress they may face finding acceptable childcare and negotiating household chores with their husbands." In support of this position, Coontz points to a 1995 Harris survey reporting that less than a third of working women would stay at home, if money were no object.[1]

3   There are several reasons married women like to work. In the first place, they do not want to be economically dependent on their husbands. They have absorbed the lessons of early feminists—Charlotte Perkins Gilman and Simone de Beauvior, among others—arguing that women will always be the second sex as long as they depend on men for support. Some remember their own mothers asking their husbands for allowances and having little say in how the family income was spent. Many feel that earning an income puts them on an equal footing with their husbands, as expressed by one dual-career wife in the following manner: "I'm in the relationship because I want to be, not because somebody's taking care

---

[1] Stephanie Coontz. *The Way We Really Are* (New York: Basic Books, 1997), p. 58.

of me. . . . I feel like I don't have to say, 'Well, you're bringing in the money that's putting food on the table, that's keeping me alive.' I'm putting in money, too."[2]

4   Most women understand intuitively the theory of "bargaining power" outlined by gender theorists Strober and Chan. Put succinctly, "the more resources, particularly economic resources, a spouse brings to a marriage, the greater is his or her bargaining power."[3] Bargaining power affects the decisions couples make about almost everything, from the advancement of one partner's career over the other's to the division of household tasks. This hard-nosed, economic view of spousal relations is by no means the exclusive purview of academic theory. Even women's magazines have become more forthright about the clout a wife commands when she, too, brings home a paycheck. Clinical psychologist Judith Sills, writing in that bastion of domesticity *Family Circle* (March 7, 2000), states bluntly, "The power balance in a marriage changes when one person either stops or starts earning money. . . . Power automatically accrues to the one who earns the money."

5   Some wives and husbands keep their income in separate accounts. With divorce an eventuality for half of all marriages, both parties feel they must be cautious in money matters, just in case. Even women in secure marriages, who would like to take time off when they have young children, are afraid of losing both salary and seniority, because, if they divorced, they would find themselves in dire financial straits.[4]

6   Social Security also penalizes the person who takes time off from work. One CPA wife and mother, who stayed at home when her children were little, accurately observed: "For every quarter a mother stays home to take care of her kids, she gets zero on her Social Security. And all those zeros will be averaged into her final payment. . . . I froth at the mouth every time I get my statement from Social Security. Every zero year is factored in."[5]

7   A second, and in my opinion, equally important reason why married women choose to work is that they do not want to be confined to the perimeters of the home. They do not want to operate within the cagelike frame of traditional domesticity. Greater education for women has meant that their horizons extend far beyond the kitchen, the parlor, and the garden. Once again, we must remember that higher education for women is a relatively recent phenomenon. The American women's colleges and most coed universities were a late-nineteenth-century creation admitting only a very small percentage of females, mostly from the upper and middle classes. As late as 1950, there were three male students

---

[2] Rosanna Hertz, *More Equal than Others: Women and Men in Dual-Career Marriages* (Berkeley, Los Angeles, London: University of California Press, 1986), p. 101.

[3] Myra H. Strober and Agnes Miling Keneko Chan. *The Road Winds Uphill All the Way: Gender, Work and Family in the United States and Japan* (Cambridge, MA, and London: MIT Press, 1999), p. 87.

[4] David Elkind. *Ties That Stress: The New Family Imbalance* (Cambridge, MA, and London: Cambridge University Press. 1994). p. 51.

[5] *Wellesley*, Winter 2000, p. 25.

granted a BA for every female college graduate.[6] Today, females receive educations comparable to males—55 percent of BAs, over 50 percent of law and medical degrees, and 45 percent of PhDs. Like the men in their college courses, they expect to use their minds for the rest of their lives. Paid employment can present a challenge to one's intelligence, as well as to one's interpersonal skills. It allows a person the opportunity to interact with others in the workplace, and sometimes even to make a difference in their lives.

8   I have no illusions about the nature of work in general. It does not always challenge the intellect, and rarely allows for innovation and imagination. It can produce stress and pain and damage to private life. Yet I cannot imagine the world of the immediate future without it. Wives, like husbands, look to the work world for satisfactions that few can find within themselves or within the four walls of their houses. Most husbands today assume that their wives will have a commitment outside the home, and many husbands are credited with being their wives' "strongest supporters." In addition, many husbands count on their wives to share the economic burdens of supporting a family.

9   Of course, there are some women who refuse this scenario, some wives who prefer to be the domestic anchor for their husbands and children. They find satisfaction in caring for their children, driving them to and from school, attending their soccer and baseball games, cooking, cleaning, washing and ironing, gardening, sewing, shopping, and taking care of a parent or sick relative. Theoretically, housewives, especially those with the means to pay for a maid or a team of housecleaners, should have more time than employed women to read, answer e-mail, surf the Internet, look at television, play tennis, do yoga, go to the gym, take hikes, practice the piano, listen to music, paint, entertain, write letters or creative literature, do volunteer work, meet with friends, and follow their own rhythms. But few full-time homemakers, especially those with children, think of their lives as leisurely. Obligations to home, family, and the community always seem to expand into the hours one tries to sequester for oneself, perhaps because homemaking is, by nature, always open to the unpredictable—a sick child, a broken washing machine, storm damage to the roof. Moreover, without the extra income of a second wage earner, housewives often have to sacrifice material rewards in order to stay at home. For some women, being available to their children when they are small is reward enough. The life of a housewife (or house husband) can be fulfilling if it is freely chosen, if the other spouse's income is adequate, or if the wife has sufficient assets of her own. A relatively small percentage of married women today are economically able to choose this life.

10   With the increased longevity of women, the child-raising period takes up a relatively short part of the life span. If a woman waits until her late twenties to have a child, as many do, and lives until she is eighty, as statistics say she will, she will spend only a third of her life in the active phase of mothering. Before

---

[6] Cynthia Fuchs Epstein, *Woman's Place: Options and Limits in Professional Careers* (Berkeley, Los Angeles, London: University of California Press, 1971), p. 57.

and after her child-rearing years, there are long stretches of time for paid employment or sustained volunteer work. Most wives, even those who take time off when their children are young, work for economic reasons, and many wives, even those who do not have to, work because they want to.

11   Every societal revolution has a conservative reaction that eventually forces it to retreat partially, if not wholly, from acquired ground. The backlash symbolized by the election of President Ronald Reagan in 1980 and invoked in the battle cry "family values" undid some of the victories claimed by the sexual and feminist revolutions. During the eighties, abortion rights began to be curtailed. ERA was all but buried. Androgyny gave way to a renewed femininity featuring sexy underwear, breast implants, and pushup bras. Expensive weddings with brides in elaborate white gowns came back into fashion. Women's paid employment came under attack, with wives accused of undermining their husbands, and mothers indicted for sacrificing their children on the altar of professional success. The popular press remained skeptical over women's ability to have both a successful marriage and a successful career, and castigated the working woman who wanted to "have it all."[7]

12   Documenting the backlash in 1992, author Susan Faludi exploded some of the antifeminist myths that had proliferated during the eighties.[8] Magazines and newspapers eager to discredit women's gains exploited questionable research, such as the 1986 Harvard-Yale marriage study announcing that unwed women over thirty had very little likelihood of ever marrying at all, or sociologist Lenore Weitzman's 1985 finding that divorced women had a 73 percent drop in their standard of living a year after divorce. Subsequent research proved both of these findings to be greatly exaggerated. The gloom-and-doom picture of liberated women promulgated by the media and the glowing pictures of mothers who had chosen to give up demanding careers in favor of domesticity were clearly intended to stop the clock and send women scurrying back to the safety of home.

13   Yet, according to historian Ruth Rosen's assessment, "By the end of the 20th century, feminist ideas had burrowed too deeply into our culture for any resistance or politics to root them out.[9] Even those who lamented the excesses of the sexual and feminist revolutions were not about to ask their daughters or sweethearts to remain virgins until marriage or to retreat full-time to the kitchen once they had become wives. Increasingly, men sizing up prospective spouses expected them to carry their weight in both the bedroom and the boardroom.

14   One sign of the times is that the old jokes about nagging, frigid, dumb, unattractive wives have run their course. Remember comedian Henny Youngman's repertoire of wife jokes? "Take my wife, please!" "My wife has a black belt in shopping." "She got a mudpack and looked great for two days. Then the mud

---

[7] Dana Vannoy-Hiller and William W. Philliber, *Equal Partners: Successful Women in Marriage* (Newbury Park, CA: Sage Publications, 1989), pp. 16–17.

[8] Susan Faludi, *Backlash: The Undeclared War Against American Women* (New York; Crown Publishers, Inc. 1992).

[9] Ruth Rosen. *The World Split Open: How the Modern Women's Movement Changed America* (New York: Viking, 2000), p. xv.

fell off." "I've been in love with the same woman for forty-nine years. If my wife ever finds out, she'll kill me." Wives are no longer the targets of such easy ridicule coming from husbands confident of their superiority. If anything, jokes about husbands have become more numerous, as in the following examples currently circulating on e-mail:

> "I think—therefore I'm single." Attributed to Lizz Winstead.

> "I never married because there was no need. I have three pets at home which answer the same purpose as a husband. I have a dog which growls every morning, a parrot which swears all afternoon and a cat that comes home late at night." Attributed to Marie Corelli.

> "Behind every successful man is a surprised woman." Attributed to Maryon Pearson.

15   In the vein of the last witticism, here is a joke that was frequently repeated in 1999. "Hillary and Bill Clinton drive into a gas station. The man at the pump is particularly warm toward the First Lady, and when they drive away, she tells her husband that he had been one of her first boyfriends. Bill says smugly: 'Aren't you glad you married me instead of a gas station attendant?' To which she replies. 'If I had married him, he'd be the president.'"

INTIMATIONS OF THE NEW WIFE

16   The story of Hillary and Bill Clinton played out on the national stage some of the ambiguities inherent in the role of the new wife. Like 1990s soap operas, theirs was a dramatic saga of dual-career ambitions, marriage, infidelity, forgiveness, and love. In 1992, America was not ready for Hillary Rodham Clinton. After Nancy Reagan and Barbara Bush, women who had incarnated the traditional wife par excellence, a lawyer first lady on a par with her husband was just too threatening for much of the American public. They viewed her political activities with suspicion and felt vindicated when her health care plan went down to defeat. During Clinton's first term in office, Hillary was constantly changing her tactics and her hairdo so as to meet public approval. But whatever she did, there were numerous Americans who made no secret of the revulsion they felt for her.

17   All of this changed, of course, when she became an injured wife. As the gross details of President Clinton's marital infidelity with Monica Lewinsky became daily pap for the media, and Hillary maintained her dignity in spite of everything, her popularity with the American people soared. She became the woman who "stood by her man," a wife with whom other American women could identify. The damage to Clinton's reputation did not spill over similarly to his spouse. She emerged from their sensational story with a determination to pursue her own career, even at the expense of abandoning the role of first lady during her husband's last year in office. As I write these pages, she has just been elected to the United States Senate. Is the American public now ready for wives who are as well educated, assertive, and as ambitious as Hillary Rodham Clinton?

18   Fundamental aspects of the new wife can be observed in those reliable standards, the women's magazines. At the start of the new millennium, they focus on homemaking, recipes, diet, health, work, children, love, and sex. The most venerable of these magazines known as "the seven sisters" (*Ladies' Home Journal, Redbook, McCall's, Good Housekeeping, Family Circle, Woman's Day*, and *Better Homes and Gardens*), originally oriented toward traditional wives with children, have been obliged to move with the times. Today, they are claiming the sexually explicit content that used to be the exclusive purview of magazines intended for single women (e.g., *Glamour, Cosmopolitan*, and *Mademoiselle*).

19   "101 Ways to Sex Up Your Marriage," in the January 2000 *Ladies' Home Journal*, assumes that spouses occasionally need to bring "more sizzle" into the bedroom, and that it's the wife's responsibility to make this happen. The February *Redbook* presents "Your 39 Most Embarrassing Sex Questions" in graphic detail, as well as an insightful piece titled "What Happy Couples Know about Marriages That Last." *More*, the magazine for older women put out by *Ladies' Home Journal*, offers a surprisingly frank and relatively guilt-free article titled "I Am the Other Woman," confessing the trials and tribulations of an anonymous woman in love with a married man.

20   Even financial matters have to be sexy. An article titled "Creating Financial Intimacy: A Couple's Guide to Getting Rich" (January 2000 *Good Housekeeping*) insinuates sex into the process of buying stock. It reads:

> Consider buying a stock for your beloved. It's surprising how sexy (yes, sexy) such a gift can be. . . . Sneak off to a financial seminar together one evening instead of to a movie; sit in the back, dress up, and wear your best perfume. Scan the newstand for a financial magazine that features an article reflecting your family's situation, and share it during a quiet moment alone. All powerful and positive acts, acts that will help you and your money grow, and you and your husband grow closer.

21   While the sexed-up prose is downright silly, the article does point to the central nexus of sex and money in the maintenance of a marriage. It argues convincingly that shared responsibility for money matters makes for a powerful bond between spouses. Whereas men once had total control over families finances, today, in more egalitarian marriages, both sex and money are often considered joint ventures capable of drawing spouses more closely together—that is, if they don't drive them further apart. It's not surprising that the year 2000 began with paeans in the popular press to both sources of empowerment for wives, with sexual performance hyped far beyond any other wifely virtue. Kinsey's midcentury belief that good sex is indispensable to enduring unions has by now become an American cliché, and, like most clichés, one that tends to obscure competing truths. While sexual satisfaction is generally recognized as a sensitive index of marital happiness, especially in the early years, there are undoubtedly some good marriages with bad or minimal sex, and some bad marriages with great sex.[10]

---

[10] See, for example, Mirra Komarovsky (with the collaboration of Jane H. Philips). *Blue-Collar Marriage*, 2nd ed. (New Haven, CT: Yale University Press, 1987), pp. 94–111.

22   And what of love, that romantic feeling that gained primacy in the early nineteenth century and that has been claiming special status ever since? In the past, at least among middle- and upper-class couples, love was supposed to precede sex, indeed, to make sex possible. Today it is usually the other way around. Young people engage in sex with several partners, then "fall in love" with one of them. Subsequently some combination of sexual desire and romantic love impels the couple to vow to stay together forever. But sex and romance do not, in and of themselves, cement a relationship, at least not for a lifetime. Common interests, values, and goals, mutual respect and moral commitment, may, in the long run, prove as valuable as sex, love, and money in the preservation of a union.

23   Young women today, marrying on average around twenty-five, often have at least some college education and work experience behind them when they become wives. They enter into marriage on a relatively equal footing with their husbands, and expect to maintain this parity for the rest of their lives. The old ideal of companionate marriage has been reformulated under such new labels as egalitarian marriage, equal partnership, and marital equality.

24   Unfortunately, married life today is not yet truly equal. According to a 1997 research study, which follows the lead of sociologist Jessie Bernard in *The Future of Marriage* (1972), "his" marriage continues to be better than "hers."[11] The data on marital satisfaction, garnered from surveys, interviews, and personal assessments, indicate that husbands have a more positive view of marriage than their wives, and that wives fall behind husbands on numerous measures of marital satisfaction. One consistent finding is that single men do *worse* than married men on almost all measures of mental health (e.g., suicide, depression, nervous breakdown), whereas single women do *better* than married women on these same measures.[12] All agree that wives experience greater stress than husbands from their career/family obligations, and that women put more time into caring for children, aged parents, and sick relatives.

25   When couples divorce, it is almost always the ex-wife who loses out financially. According to the latest statistics, divorce produces a 27 percent decline in women's standard of living and 10 percent increase in that of men.[13] This represents an almost 40 percent gap between what ex-wives and what ex-husbands experience financially in the aftermath of a divorce. Part of this difference is attributable to the fact that mothers, in the great majority of cases, are granted custody of the children. Even when the mother is awarded child support, it is frequently insufficient and not always forthcoming. Another factor is the lower earning power of women on the whole—75 percent of what men earn. Many women are still segregated in low-paying jobs and hindered in advancement by

[11] Janice M. Steil, *Marital Equality: Its Relationship to the Well-Being of Husbands and Wives* (Thousand Oaks, London, New Delhi: Sage Publications, 1997), p. xix. See also differences in his and her appraisals of marriage in Alford-Cooper, *For Keeps*, p. 107.
[12] Faludi. *Backlash*, pp. 17, 36–37.
[13] Richard R. Peterson, "A Re-Evaluation of the Economic Consequences of Divorce." *American Sociological Review*, Vol. 61, No. 3, June 1996, pp. 528–536.

home and childcare responsibilities, as well as by the sacrifices they have made promoting their husbands' careers rather than their own.

26   In addition to the disadvantageous financial consequences of divorce for many women and their children, the emotional distress is often deep and long-lasting. While no-fault divorce, first instituted in California in 1970 and subsequently adopted in most of the United States, was intended to remove the blame and acrimony from prolonged adversarial litigation, today's divorces are still often as bitter as those of the past. Divorce continues to be a major family disruption with prolonged consequences for the spouses, their offspring, and extended kin.

27   Here is how Susan Straight, an articulate ex-wife and mother of three school-aged children, described the devastation that divorce brought into her life, a devastation she shared with her best friend, who had been widowed.

> My best friend on the street, Jeannine, whose four kids had baby-sat mine and played with them, lost her husband, too. He was killed in a car accident. Jeannine and I were both thirty-five that year. We couldn't believe we had to do this alone. Seven kids. Old houses with flickering electrical wires and flooding basements and overgrown hedges and missing shingles. Jeannine was in her last year of nursing school. I was working. We were stunned.
>
> . . . Some nights we were both mad. She'd met her husband at fourteen, like me. After we talked, I would lie in bed, my body aching, my hands raw from dishes and floors and branches and baby shampoo, thinking that when I got married, I always assumed I'd work hard, have kids and a house and some fun. . . .
>
> And when my husband first left. I thought, So I work a little harder. But now, the realization has set in, piled high and crackling as the mulberry leaves falling from those spear straight branches one more year; I have to do all of this forever. Fix the vacuum cleaner, kill the spiders, correct the spelling and make the math flash cards and pay for pre-school and trim the tree. Trim the tree.
>
> Now, sometimes, I feel like a burro. A small frame, feet hard as hooves, back sagging a little. Now the edges of my life are a bit ragged, and things don't always get done as they should.[14]

28   Susan Straight's story is, unfortunately, writ over and over again in the lives of myriad American mothers whose husbands have left them, or who have themselves chosen to leave an unhappy marriage, or who never had a husband in the first place. In her words, she and the other ex-wives have no "backup," and backup is "what marriage is really about." So if she and her children look "slightly

---

[14] Susan Straight, "One Drip at a Time," in *Mothers Who Think: Tales of Real-Live Parenthood,* ed. Camille Perl and Kate Moses (New York: Villard Books, 1999), pp. 50, 51, 55. For a sensitive appraisal of divorce in America, see Barbara Defoe Whitehead. *The Divorce Culture: Rethinking Our Committments to Marriage and Family* (New York: Vintage Books, 1998).

askew," she asks us not to blame her. "When you see us, don't shake your heads and think, How irresponsible. Responsible is all I'm good at anymore."

29   In serial marriages, the husband often "marries down" in terms of age and is far more likely to start a new family. The ex-wife who remarries has a selection of males usually her own age or older, but fewer candidates to choose from, since there are more older women than older men. For the same reasons, widows remarry less frequently than widowers. Another difference between older men and older women lies in the ability to reproduce. After menopause, a woman is unable to become pregnant (without technological intervention), in contrast to men, who usually can go on reproducing in their fifties, sixties, and beyond. Whether this is advisable, given the father's probable death when his children are still young, the ability to reproduce at any age does confer a fundamental existential advantage to men.

30   At the same time, females have certain advantages over males. They live approximately seven years longer. They have the amazing possibility of carrying babies within their bodies and of establishing a unique connection to their offspring through pregnancy and lactation. They are probably more flexible than men in terms of sexual orientation, moving more easily between heterosexual and same-sex relations (though not everyone will see this as an advantage). They more frequently establish close bonds of friendship with other women that are sources of deep pleasure and ongoing support, whereas men, in general, have fewer intimate friends.

31   One thing many women have learned during the past twenty to thirty years is that wifehood is not one's only option. With women no longer economically dependent on men, they do not have to marry for the mere sake of survival. Business and professional women tend to defer marriage during early adulthood and sometimes do not marry at all. Susan Faludi's assertion that "the more women are paid, the less eager they are to marry" should not surprise us.[15] And even more than marriage per se, motherhood has become problematic for working women, given the "mommy gap" in wages between mothers and non-mothers. While the hourly wages of women without children are roughly 90 percent of men's, the comparable figure for women with children is 70 percent.[16] Thus women concerned about their present and future economic well-being are obliged to consider the effects of both marriage and motherhood on their working lives.

32   In the case of black women, the "marriage-market" theory advanced by sociologist Henry Walker attributes their low incidence of marriage to their new earning power, which is now roughly the same as that of black men. Perhaps even more important, black women have a smaller pool of economically viable black men to choose from, as compared to white women in relation to white

[15] Faludi, *Backlash*, p. 16.

[16] *Boston Globe*, May 13, 2000, A19, citing the work of economist Jane Waldfogel of Columbia University.

men, since black men are more likely to have been killed, more likely to be incarcerated, and more likely to be unemployed than white men.[17]

33   Not surprisingly, careers loom larger than ever for women of all races, with many companies and institutions providing a kind of ersatz "family." Many people now look to their jobs for close interpersonal relations and for a sense of meaning they have not found either in their families or in their communities. Indeed, this growing job orientation is beginning to cause concern to many societal observers, who believe the workplace is replacing the home as the center of American life.

34   Another issue of concern is the "merging" of home life and work life that often occurs when people work out of their homes. Now that computers have made it possible for both men and women to earn substantial incomes without leaving the house, there is the danger that paid work will cannibalize the time needed for quality family life. While this may present a problem for some workaholics, it can also be a boon for parents needing flexible schedules for childcare. In some ways we may be returning to a preindustrial mode, when artisans, professionals, and shopkeepers did indeed work out of their homes, with children always in the wings or underfoot.

35   Alternatives to marriage come in numerous forms. The number of Americans living alone (a quarter of all households) has never been higher. The number of men and women living together without marrying has also reached a record high, with heterosexual couples often taking years to decide whether they will or will not become husband and wife. Same-sex couples cohabitate without the legal and economic benefits that a marriage license confers, although many are taking advantage of the "domestic partnerships" offered by numerous cities, states, and institutions. In the future, Vermont-style "civil unions" will probably serve the needs not only of gay couples, but also of heterosexuals opting for an intermediary step between cohabitation and marriage.

36   Similarly, childlessness is no longer seen as a curse for adult females. The proportion of childless women aged forty to forty-four was 19 percent in 1998 (up from 10 percent in 1980), and many of these women are childless by choice, according to some demographers.[18] At the same time, single parenting is on the ascendency, without the stigma of past eras. Unmarried girls and women who become pregnant accidentally often decide to bear and raise the child, rather than have an abortion or give the baby up for adoption. Some unmarried women, especially those around forty, are now choosing to be mothers without intending to marry the baby's father. All of these girls and women take on a formidable challenge when they raise a child on their own: at present, their children are much more likely to be brought up in poverty than children in two-parent families.

---

[17] Henry A. Walker, "Black-White Differences in Marriage and Family Patterns," in *Feminism*, ed. Dornbusch and Strober, pp. 87–112.

[18] Margaret L. Usdansky, "Numbers Show Families Growing Closer as They Pull Apart," *The New York Times*, March 8, 2000, D10.

37   Some single mothers manage to extend the family network by living with relatives or friends. In black communities, where single mothers greatly outnumber married mothers, children often grow up in female households headed by a mother or grandmother. Private and government programs to bring fathers back into the picture may, in time, reverse this trend somewhat, but it is unlikely that the nuclear family consisting of a married couple and their children, which peaked numerically for blacks in 1950 and for whites in 1960, will return to its former hegemonic position in American society.[19]

38   What, then, can a woman today anticipate, or at at least hope, when she becomes a wife? Surely she hopes that her marriage will be among the 50 percent that adheres to a lifelong script. Despite the well-known statistics on divorce, people usually marry with the belief that *their* marriage is "for keeps"—86 percent, according to a survey conducted by the *New York Times Magazine* (May 7, 2000). And most women still hope to become mothers. In fact, motherhood has remained central to most women's core conception of self and may even have "supplanted marriage as a source of romantic fantasy for many young single women," in the judgment of Peggy Orenstein, the astute author of *School Girls* and *Flux*.[20]

39   The new wife will not be able to count on children to keep the marriage intact, as in the past when people often did stay together "for the children." In fact, children are known to bring conflict into a marriage, especially when they are very young and again in adolescence. Those spouses who make it past the stress-filled child-rearing years are likely to experience a bonus in later life. Older couples often enjoy a special bond based on their shared history—a level of intimacy paid for in past tears and joys. In the words of Mark Twain: "No man or woman really knows what perfect love is until they have been married a quarter of a century."[21]

40   When one vows at the onset of a marriage to live together "for better, for worse," one anticipates little of the "for worse" scenario. Yet heartache, tragedy, sickness, and death are invariably a part of marriage, especially in the later years. Then one is particularly grateful for the support and love of a lifelong partner— someone who remembers you as you once were and who continues to care for you as you are now. To be the intimate witness of another person's life is a privilege one can fully appreciate only with time. To have weathered the storms of early and middle marriage—the turmoil of children, the unfaithfulness of one or both spouses, the death of one's parents, the adult struggles of one's own children—can create an irreplaceable attachment to the person who has shared that history with you.

41   What I have referred to as "unfaithfulness" can, of course, make it impossible for a couple to go on as before. Many marriages do come to an end when one of

---

[19] Walker, "Black-White Differences," in *Feminism*, ed. Dornbusch and Strober, pp. 92–93.

[20] Peggy Orenstein, *Flux: Women on Sex, Work, Kids, Love, and Life in a Half-Changed World* (New York: Doubleday, 2000), p. 39.

[21] This paragraph draws from Susan Turk Charles and Laura L. Carstensen, "Marriage in Old Age," in *Inside the American Couple*, ed. Marilyn Yalom and Laura Carstensen (Berkeley: University of California Press, [2002]).

the spouses has an affair. But many don't. Many continue to think of their marital union as the "essential" relationship, even while they engage in an extramarital affair. Since young people today have the opportunity to make love to more than one potential partner before they marry and since they tend to marry at a supposedly mature age, they *should* be ready to settle down to a monogamous union when they exchange vows. Yet, as we know, the "shoulds" sometimes falter in the face of unexpected passion. Even when one is seriously committed to one's spouse, temptations do arise, and married women as well as married men are more likely today than in the past to give in to these temptations. This does not necessarily lead to divorce, or even permanent bitterness, though it often creates turmoil and suffering. When a husband or wife has an affair, it is usually for a cluster of reasons, of which sex per se is only a part. The affair can act as a catalyst that forces the spouses to look more closely at their own relationship, to renegotiate the terms of their union, and to rededicate themselves to one another.

42   The present statistics on lifelong marriages being what they are, I do not envy today's young women the pain that will come from divorce, the hardships they will endure as single parents, the poverty in which many will live. But I do believe in their expanded possibilities, which are greater now than ever before and which contrast dramatically to the more circumscribed lives most married women accepted in the past and still experience today in many parts of the world. Above all, I wish them the courage to persevere toward that ideal of equality in marriage that has been in the making for several centuries.

43   Wives, spouses, partners, companions, and lovers all wish to be confirmed by their chosen mates and to share a profound, mutual connection. Such a union demands commitment and recommitment. Ironically, we may come to think of marriage as a vocation requiring the kind of devotion that was once expected only of celibate monks and nuns. To be a wife today when there are few prescriptions or proscriptions is a truly creative endeavor. It is no longer sufficient to "think back through our mothers," in the words of Virginia Woolf; we must project ahead into the future and ask ourselves what kind of marital legacy we want to leave for our daughters and sons.

44   While the traditional wife who submerged her identity into that of her husband may no longer represent a viable model for most women. Americans are not giving up on wifehood. Instead, they are straining to create more perfect unions on the basis of their new status as coearners and their husbands' fledgling status as co-homemakers. I suspect that the death of the "little woman" will not be grieved by the multitude, even if society must endure severe birth pangs in producing the new wife.

■ ■ ▨

MEANING

1. In Yalom's view, what are the defining features of the role of the wife today?

2. How does this role differ from the traditional role of the past in terms of economic, legal, and social issues?

3. According to Yalom, what role does bargaining power play in explaining how women have come to define themselves?

4. What alternatives to traditional marriage have emerged, and what different forms do they take?

TECHNIQUE

1. How does Yalom use statistics and a wide range of evidence from scholarly and popular sources to support her analysis?

2. How does Yalom use anecdotal evidence such as the account by Susan Straight (in paragraph 27) to reinforce her profile of those who have been excluded from the traditional role of the wife?

3. How does Yalom strengthen her analysis by documenting the range of different definitions that have been attributed to the role of the wife?

4. **Other Patterns.** How does Yalom use **comparison and contrast** to underscore the differences between the traditional role of the wife and contemporary alternatives?

LANGUAGE

1. What is Yalom's attitude toward the notion of romantic love, based on paragraph 22?

2. What is the tone of Yalom's conclusion?

3. If you don't know the meaning of the following words, look them up: *improvising* (1), *succinctly* (4), *dire* (5), *longevity* (10), *androgyny* (11), *promulgated* (12), *paeans* (21), *acrimony* (26), *ersatz* (33), *formidable* (36), *hegemonic* (37).

SUGGESTIONS FOR WRITING

1. **Critical Writing.** Does Yalom's definition still apply to the role of the wife in today's society? Why or why not? What kind of marriage would you hope to have in relation to the realities she discusses?

2. In your opinion, how are children influenced by the changing nature of the wife's role defined by Yalom?

3. **Compare** a selection of articles in magazines such as *Ladies' Home Journal*, *Redbook*, *Family Circle*, or other traditional magazines to discover how they express current realities and expectations regarding marriage.

4. **Thematic Links.** Contrast the role of the wife today as described by Yalom with Simone de Beauvoir's characterization in "The Married Woman." How has the definition of the wife changed from de Beauvoir's day to today?

JOSÉ ANTONIO BURCIAGA

Tortillas

José Antonio Burciaga (1940–1996) was a poet, artist, muralist, and community leader. He was born in El Chuco, Texas, and after serving in the Air Force, he graduated from the University of Texas at El Paso in 1968. He was a founder of a Chicano publishing company and started a comedy troupe, Culture Clash. His prolific output includes collections of poetry, fiction, essays, and drawings and numerous articles. In "Tortillas," originally titled "I Remember Masa," which first appeared in *Weedee Peepo* (1988), Burciaga expands on the commonplace definition of this essential Mexican food.

BEFORE YOU READ

What memories do you have of tortillas or any other ethnic food?

■ ■ ▨

1   My earliest memory of *tortillas* is my *Mamá* telling me not to play with them. I had bitten eyeholes in one and was wearing it as a mask at the dinner table.

2   As a child, I also used *tortillas* as hand warmers on cold days, and my family claims that I owe my career as an artist to my early experiments with *tortillas*. According to them, my clowning around helped me develop a strong artistic foundation. I'm not so sure, though. Sometimes I wore a *tortilla* on my head, like a *yarmulke*, and yet I never had any great urge to convert from Catholicism to Judaism. But who knows? They may be right.

3   For Mexicans over the centuries, the *tortilla* has served as the spoon and the fork, the plate and the napkin. *Tortillas* originated before the Mayan civilizations, perhaps predating Europe's wheat bread. According to Mayan mythology, the great god Quetzalcoatl, realizing that the red ants knew the secret of using maize as food, transformed himself into a black ant, infiltrated the colony of red ants, and absconded with a grain of corn. (Is it any wonder that to this day, black ants and red ants do not get along?) Quetzalcoatl then put maize on the lips of the first man and woman, Oxomoco and Cipactonal, so that they would become strong. Maize festivals are still celebrated by many Indian cultures of the Americas.

4   When I was growing up in El Paso, *tortillas* were part of my daily life. I used to visit a *tortilla* factory in an ancient adobe building near the open *mercado* in Ciudad Juárez. As I approached, I could hear the rhythmic slapping of the *masa* as the skilled vendors outside the factory formed it into balls and patted them into perfectly round corn cakes between the palms of their hands. The wonderful aroma and the speed with which the women counted so many dozens of *tortillas* out of warm wicker baskets still linger in my mind. Watching them at work convinced me that the most handsome and *deliciosas tortillas* are handmade.

For a visual to accompany this selection, see color insert photo C-1.

Although machines are faster, they can never adequately replace generation-to-generation experience. There's no place in the factory assembly line for the tender slaps that give each *tortilla* character. The best thing that can be said about mass-producing *tortillas* is that it makes it possible for many people to enjoy them.

5   In the *mercado* where my mother shopped, we frequently bought *taquitos de nopalitos*, small tacos filled with diced cactus, onions, tomatoes, and *jalapeños*. Our friend Don Toribio showed us how to make delicious, crunchy *taquitos* with dried, salted pumpkin seeds. When you had no money for the filling, a poor man's *taco* could be made by placing a warm *tortilla* on the left palm, applying a sprinkle of salt, then rolling the *tortilla* up quickly with the fingertips of the right hand. My own kids put peanut butter and jelly on *tortillas*, which I think is truly bicultural. And speaking of fast foods for kids, nothing beats a *quesadilla*, a *tortilla* grilled-cheese sandwich.

6   Depending on what you intend to use them for, *tortillas* may be made in various ways. Even a run-of-the-mill *tortilla* is more than a flat corn cake. A skillfully cooked homemade *tortilla* has a bottom and a top; the top skin forms a pocket in which you put the filling that folds your *tortilla* into a taco. Paper-thin *tortillas* are used specifically for *flautas*, a type of taco that is filled, rolled, and then fried until crisp. The name *flauta* means *flute*, which probably refers to the Mayan bamboo flute; however, the only sound that comes from an edible *flauta* is a delicious crunch that is music to the palate. In México *flautas* are sometimes made as long as two feet and then cut into manageable segments. The opposite of *flautas* is *gorditas*, meaning *little fat ones*. These are very thick small *tortillas*.

7   The versatility of *tortillas* and corn does not end here. Besides being tasty and nourishing, they have spiritual and artistic qualities as well. The Tarahumara Indians of Chihuahua, for example, concocted a corn-based beer called *tesgüino*, which their descendants still make today. And everyone has read about the woman in New Mexico who was cooking her husband a *tortilla* one morning when the image of Jesus Christ miraculously appeared on it. Before they knew what was happening, the man's breakfast had become a local shrine.

8   Then there is *tortilla* art. Various Chicano artists throughout the Southwest have, when short of materials or just in a whimsical mood, used a dry *tortilla* as a small, round canvas. And a few years back, at the height of the Chicano movement, a priest in Arizona got into trouble with the Church after he was discovered celebrating mass using a *tortilla* as the host. All of which only goes to show that while the *tortilla* may be a lowly corn cake, when the necessity arises, it can reach unexpected distinction.

■ ■ ▨

MEANING

1. How would you define a tortilla?
2. In what ways is the tortilla integral to Mexican cuisine and culture?
3. What sense do you get of the importance of the tortilla to Burciaga personally?
4. What innovative uses for the tortilla does Burciaga mention?

TECHNIQUE

1. How does Burciaga use **examples** to demonstrate the versatility and ubiquity of the tortilla in Mexican culture?
2. Why does Burciaga work up to a final judgment about the tortilla rather than stating it at the outset?
3. **Other Patterns.** How does Burciaga use **narration** to create a framework in which to define the characteristics of tortillas?

LANGUAGE

1. Why do you think Burciaga defines only a few of the Spanish terms he uses? Can you infer the meaning of the others from the context?
2. How would you characterize Burciaga's tone and his attitude toward his subject?
3. If you don't know the meaning of the following words, look them up: *tortillas* (1), *yarmulke* (2), *absconded* (3), *maize* (3), *adobe* (4), *concocted* (7).

SUGGESTIONS FOR WRITING

1. **Critical Writing.** What do you think is the cultural significance of food-eating contests, such as Nathan's Famous Hot Dog Eating Contest on Coney Island?
2. Explore the significance and history of a local or regional specialty, for example, saltwater taffy, key lime pie, or jambalaya.
3. Is there some specific ethnic or other food that means as much to you as the tortilla does to Burciaga? If so, **describe** it in detail and explain what it means to you.
4. **Thematic Links.** How do both Burciaga's account and Guanlong Cao's "Chopsticks" (Chapter 3, "Narration") illustrate how commonplace items or foods can acquire symbolic meanings in their respective cultures?

ELIZABETH W. FERNEA AND ROBERT A. FERNEA

A Look Behind the Veil

The veiling of women in Muslim cultures is a topic of current debate in many countries because of political, religious, and social pressures. Definitive studies of this issue have been done by Elizabeth W. Fernea, a professor of Middle Eastern Studies at the University of Texas at Austin, and Robert A. Fernea. Together, they have written *The Arab World: Personal Encounters* (1987) and the follow-up study, *The Arab World: Forty Years of Change* (1997). Elizabeth Fernea has also written *Remembering Childhood in the Middle East: Memoirs from a Century of Changes* (2002). In the following essay, first published in *Human Nature* (1979), the authors use interviews and the results of their extensive travels in Iraq, Morocco, Egypt, and Afghanistan to decipher the meanings and messages that are communicated through veiling.

BEFORE YOU READ

What do you know about the practice of veiling women in Middle Eastern societies?

■ ■ ▨

1   What objects do we notice in societies other than our own? Ishi, the last of a "lost" tribe of North American Indians who stumbled into 20th Century California in 1911, is reported to have said that the truly interesting objects in the white man's culture were pockets and matches. Rifa'ah Tahtawi, one of the first young Egyptians to be sent to Europe to study in 1826, wrote an account of French society in which he noted that Parisians used many unusual articles of dress, among them something called a belt. Women wore belts, he said, apparently to keep their bosoms erect, and to show off the slimness of their waists and the fullness of their hips. Europeans are still fascinated by the Stetson hats worn by American cowboys; an elderly Dutch lady of our acquaintance recently carried six enormous Stetsons back to The Hague as presents for the male members of her family.

2   Many objects signify values in society and become charged with meaning, a meaning that may be different for members of the society and for observers of that society. The veil is one object used in Middle Eastern societies that stirs strong emotions in the West. "The feminine veil has become a symbol: that of the slavery of one portion of humanity," wrote French ethnologist Germaine Tillion in 1966. A hundred years earlier, Sir Richard Burton, British traveler, explorer, and translator of the *Arabian Nights*, recorded a different view. "Europeans inveigh against this article [the face veil] . . . for its hideousness and jealous concealment of charms made to be admired," he wrote in 1855. "It is, on the contrary, the most coquettish article of woman's attire . . . it conceals coarse

---

For a visual to accompany this selection, see color insert photo C-2.

skins, fleshy noses, wide mouths and vanishing chins, whilst it sets off to best advantage what in these lands is most lustrous and liquid—the eye. Who has not remarked this at a masquerade ball?"

3   In the present generation, the veil and purdah, or seclusion, have become a focus of attention for Western writers, both popular and academic, who take a measure of Burton's irony and Tillion's anger to equate modernization of the Middle East with the discarding of the veil. "Iranian women return to veil in a resurgence of spirituality," headlines one newspaper; another writes, "Iran's 16 million women have come a long way since their floor-length cotton veil officially was abolished in 1935." The thousands of words written about the appearance and disappearance of the veil and of purdah do little to help us understand the Middle East or the cultures that grew out of the same Judeo-Christian roots as our own. The veil and the all-enveloping garments that inevitably accompany it (the *milayah* in Egypt, the *abbayah* in Iraq, the *chadoor* in Iran, the *yashmak* in Turkey, the *burqa* in Afghanistan, and the *djellabah* and the *haik* in North Africa) are only the outward manifestations of a cultural pattern and idea that is rooted deep in Mediterranean society.

4   "Purdah" is a Persian word meaning curtain or barrier. The Arabic word for veiling and secluding comes from the root *hajaba*. A *hijab* is an amulet worn to keep away the evil eye; it also means a diaphragm used to prevent conception. The gatekeeper or doorkeeper who guards the entrance to a government minister's office is a *hijab,* and in casual conversation a person might say, "I want to be more informal with my friend so-and-so, but she always puts a *hijab* (barrier) between us."

5   In Islam, the Koranic verse that sanctions the barrier between men and women is called the Sura of the *hijab* (curtain): "Prophet, enjoin your wives, your daughters and the wives of true believers to draw their veils close round them. That is more proper, so that they may be recognized and not molested. Allah is forgiving and merciful."

6   Certainly seclusion and some forms of veiling had been practiced before the time of Muhammad, at least among the upper classes, but it was his followers who apparently felt that his women should be placed in a special category. According to history, the *hijab* was established after a number of occasions on which Muhammad's wives were insulted by people who were coming to the mosque in search of the prophet. When chided for their behavior, they said they had mistaken Muhammad's wives for slaves. The *hijab* was established, and in the words of the historian Nabia Abbott, "Muhammad's women found themselves, on the one hand, deprived of personal liberty, and on the other hand, raised to a position of honor and dignity."

7   The veil bears many messages and tells us many things about men and women in Middle East society; but as an object in and of itself it is far less important to members of the society than the values it represents. Nouha al Hejailan, wife of the Saudi Arabian ambassador to London, told Sally Quinn of *The Washington Post,* "If I wanted to take it all off (her *abbayah* and veil), I would have long ago. It wouldn't mean as much to me as it does to you." Early Middle Eastern

feminists felt differently. Huda Sh'arawi, an early Egyptian activist who formed the first Women's Union, made a dramatic gesture of removing her veil in public to demonstrate her dislike of society's attitudes toward women and her defiance of the system. But Basima Bezirgan, a contemporary Iraqui feminist, says, "Compared to the real issues that are involved between men and women in the Middle East today, the veil is unimportant." A Moroccan linguist who buys her clothes in Paris laughs when asked about the veil. "My mother wears a *djellabah* and a veil. I have never worn them. But so what? I still cannot get divorced as easily as a man, and I am still a member of my family group and responsible to them for everything I do. What is the veil? A piece of cloth."

8   "The seclusion of women has many purposes," states Egyptian anthropologist Nadia Abu Zahra. "It expresses men's status, power, wealth, and manliness. It also helps preserve men's image of virility and masculinity, but men do not admit this; on the contrary they claim that one of the purposes of the veil is to guard women's honor." The veil and purdah are symbols of restriction, to men as well as to women. A respectable woman wearing a veil on a public street is signaling, "Hands off. Don't touch me or you'll be sorry." Cowboy Jim Sayre of Deadwood, South Dakota, says, "If you deform a cowboy's hat, he'll likely deform you." In the same way, a man who approaches a veiled woman is asking for trouble; not only the woman but also her family is shamed, and serious problems may result. "It is clear," says Egyptian anthropologist Ahmed Abou Zeid, "that honor and shame which are usually attributed to a certain individual or a certain kinship group have in fact a bearing on the total social structure, since most acts involving honor or shame are likely to affect the existing social equilibrium."

9   Veiling and seclusion almost always can be related to the maintenance of social status. Historically, only the very rich could afford to seclude their women, and the extreme example of this practice was found among the sultans of pre-revolutionary Turkey. Stories of these secluded women, kept in harems and guarded by eunuchs, formed the basis for much of the Western folklore concerning the nature of male-female relationships in Middle East society. The stereotype is of course contradictory; Western writers have never found it necessary to reconcile the erotic fantasies of the seraglio with the sexual puritanism attributed to the same society.

10   Poor men could not always afford to seclude or veil their women, because the women were needed as productive members of the family economic unit, to work in the fields and in cottage industries. Delta village women in Egypt have never been veiled, nor have the Berber women of North Africa. But this lack of veiling placed poor women in ambiguous situations in relation to strange men.

11   "In the village, no one veils, because everyone is considered a member of the same large family," explained Aisha bint Mohammed, a working-class wife of Marrakech. "But in the city, veiling is *sunnah*, required by our religion." Veiling is generally found in towns and cities, among all classes, where families feel that it is necessary to distinguish themselves from other strangers in the city.

12   Veiling and purdah not only indicate status and wealth, they also have some religious sanction and protect women from the world outside the home. Purdah

delineates private space, distinguishes between the public and private sectors of society, as does the traditional architecture of the area. Older Middle Eastern houses do not have picture windows facing the street, nor walks leading invitingly to front doors. Family life is hidden from strangers; behind blank walls may lie courtyards and gardens, refuges from the heat, the cold, the bustle of the outside world, the world of non-kin that is not to be trusted. Outsiders are pointedly excluded.

13   Even within the household, among her close relatives, a traditional Muslim woman veils before those kinsmen whom she could legally marry. If her maternal or paternal male cousins, her brothers-in-law, or sons-in-law come to call, she covers her head, or perhaps her whole face. To do otherwise would be shameless.

14   The veil does more than protect its wearers from known and unknown intruders; it can also be used to conceal identity. Behind the anonymity of the veil, women can go about a city unrecognized and uncriticized. Nadia Abu Zahra reports anecdotes of men donning women's veils in order to visit their lovers undetected; women may do the same. The veil is such an effective disguise that Nouri Al-Said, the late prime minister of Iraq, attempted to escape death by wearing the *abbayah* and veil of a woman; only his shoes gave him away.

15   Political dissidents in many countries have used the veil for their own ends. The women who marched, veiled, through Cairo during the Nationalist demonstrations against the British after World War I were counting on the strength of Western respect for the veil to protect them against British gunfire. At first they were right. Algerian women also used the protection of the veil to carry bombs through French army checkpoints during the Algerian revolution. But when the French discovered the ruse, Algerian women discarded the veil and dressed like Europeans to move about freely.

16   The multiple meanings and uses of purdah and the veil do not explain how the pattern came to be so deeply embedded in Mediterranean society. Its origins lie somewhere in the basic Muslim attitudes about men's roles and women's roles. Women, according to Fatima Mernissi, a Moroccan sociologist, are seen by men in Islamic societies as in need of protection because they are unable to control their sexuality, are tempting to men, and hence are a danger to the social order. In order words, they need to be restrained and controlled so that society may function in an orderly way.

17   The notion that women present a danger to the social order is scarcely limited to Muslim society. Anthropologist Julian Pitt-Rivers has pointed out that the supervision and seclusion of women is also to be found in Christian Europe, even though veiling was not usually practiced there. "The idea that women not subjected to male authority are a danger is a fundamental one in the writings of the moralists from the Archpriest of Talavera to Padre Haro, and it is echoed in the modern Andalusian *pueblo*. It is bound up with the fear of ungoverned female sexuality which had been an integral element of European folklore ever since prudent Odysseus lashed himself to the mast to escape the sirens."

18   Pitt-Rivers is writing about Mediterranean society, which, like all Middle Eastern societies, is greatly concerned with honor and shame rather than with individual

guilt. The honor of the Middle Eastern extended family, its ancestors and its descendants, is the highest social value. The misdeeds of the grandparents are indeed visited on the children. Men and women always remain members of their natal families. Marriage is a legal contract but a fragile one that is often broken; the ties between brother and sister, mother and child, father and child are lifelong and enduring. The larger family is the group to which the individual belongs and to which the individual owes responsibility in exchange for the social and economic security that the family group provides. It is the group, not the individual, that is socially shamed or socially honored.

19   Male honor and female honor are both involved in the honor of the family, but each is expressed differently. The honor of a man, *sharaf*, is a public matter, involving bravery, hospitality, piety. It may be lost, but it may also be regained. The honor of a woman, *'ard*, is a private matter involving only one thing, her sexual chastity. Once lost, it cannot be regained. If the loss of female honor remains only privately known, a rebuke—and perhaps a reveiling—may be all that takes place. But if the loss of female honor becomes public knowledge, the other members of the family may feel bound to cleanse the family name. In extreme cases, the cleansing may require the death of the offending female member. Although such killings are now criminal offenses in the Middle East, suspended sentences are often given, and the newspapers in Cairo and Baghdad frequently carry sad stories of runaway sisters "gone bad" in the city and revenge taken upon them in the name of family honor by their brothers or cousins.

20   This emphasis on female chastity, many say, originated in the patrilineal society's concern with the paternity of the child and the inheritance that follows the male line. How does a man know that the child in his wife's womb is his own, and not that of another man? Obviously he cannot know unless his wife is a virgin at marriage. From this consideration may have developed the protective institutions called variously purdah, seclusion, or veiling.

21   Middle Eastern women also look upon seclusion as practical protection. In the Iraqi village where we lived from 1956 to 1958, one of us (Elizabeth) wore the *abbayah* and found that it provided a great sense of protection from prying eyes, dust, heat, flies. Parisian ladies visiting Istanbul in the 16th Century were so impressed by the ability of the all-enveloping garment to keep dresses clean of mud and manure and to keep women from being attacked by importuning men that they tried to introduce it into French fashion.

22   Perhaps of greater importance for many women reared in traditional cultures is the degree to which their sense of personal identity is tied to the use of the veil. Many women have told us that they felt self-conscious, vulnerable, and even naked when they first walked on a public street without the veil and *abbayah*—as if they were making a display of themselves.

23   The resurgence of the veil in countries like Morocco, Libya, and Algeria, which have recently established their independence from colonial dominance, is seen by some Middle Eastern and Western scholars as an attempt by men to reassert their Muslim identity and to reestablish their roles as heads of families.

The presence of the veil is a sign that the males of the household are once more able to assume the responsibilities that were disturbed or usurped by foreign colonial powers.

24   But a veiled woman is seldom seen in Egypt or in many parts of Lebanon, Syria, Iran, Tunisia, Turkey, or the Sudan. And as respectable housewives have abandoned the veil, in some of these Middle Eastern countries prostitutes have put it on. They indicate their availability by manipulating the veil in flirtatious ways, but as Burton pointed out more than a century ago, prostitutes are not the first to discover the veil's seductiveness. Like women's garments in the West, the veil can be sturdy, utilitarian, and forbidding—or it can be filmy and decorative, hinting at the charms beneath it.

25   The veil is the outward sign of a complex reality. Observers are often deceived by the absence of that sign, and fail to see that in most Middle Eastern societies (and in many parts of Europe) basic attitudes are unchanged. Women who have taken off the veil continue to play the old roles within the family, and their chastity remains crucial. A woman's behavior is still the key to the honor and the reputation of her family.

26   In Middle Eastern societies, feminine and masculine continue to be strong polarities of identification. This is marked contrast to Western society, where for more than a generation social critics have been striving to blur distinctions in dress, in status, and in type of labor. Almost all Middle Eastern reformers (most of whom are middle and upper class) are still arguing from the assumption of a fundamental difference between men and women. They do not demand an end to the veil (which is passing out of use anyway) but an end to the old principles, which the veil symbolizes, that govern patrilineal society. Middle Eastern reformers are calling for equal access to divorce, child custody, and inheritance; equal opportunities for education and employment; abolition of female circumcision and "crimes of honor"; and a law regulating the age of marriage.

27   An English woman film director, after several months in Morocco, said in an interview, "This business about the veil is nonsense. We all have our veils, between ourselves and other people. That's not what the Middle East is about. The question is what veils are used for, and by whom." The veil triggers Western reactions simply because it is the dramatic, visible sign of vexing questions, questions that are still being debated, problems that have still not been solved, in the Middle East or in Western societies.

28   Given the biological differences between men and women, how are the sexes to be treated equitably? Men and women are supposed to share the labor of society and yet provide for the reproduction and nurture of the next generation. If male fear and awe of women's sexuality provokes them to control and seclude women, can they be assuaged? Rebecca West said long ago that "the difference between men and women is the rock on which civilization will split before it can reach any goal that could justify its expenditure of effort." Until human beings come to terms with this basic issue, purdah and the veil, in some form, will continue to exist in both the East and the West.

REFERENCES

Abou-Zeid, Ahmed, "Honor and Shame among the Bedouins of Egypt," *Honor and Shame: The Values of Mediterranean Society*, ed. by J. G. Peristiany, University of Chicago Press, 1966.

Fernea, Elizabeth Warnock, *Guests of the Sheik: An Ethnology of an Iraqi Village*, Doubleday/Anchor, 1969.

Fernea, Elizabeth Warnock, and Basima Qattan Bezirgan, eds., *Middle Eastern Muslim Women Speak*, University of Texas Press, 1977.

Levy, Reuben, *The Social Structure of Islam*, Cambridge University Press, 1965.

Mernissi, Fatima, *Beyond the Veil: Male-Female Dynamics in a Modern Muslim Society*, Schenkman Publishing Company, 1975.

Pitt-Rivers, Julian, *The Fate of Schechem: or The Politics of Sex*, Cambridge University Press, 1977.

■ ■ ▨

MEANING

1. What meanings and messages are communicated through the practice of veiling?

2. According to the authors, why is the practice of veiling most frequently found in male-dominated extended families in the Middle East?

3. What insight do the authors provide into the historical basis of veiling?

4. What attitudes toward female sexuality help to explain the veiling of women and the practice of *purdah*?

TECHNIQUE

1. How do the authors use interviews and the testimony of experts to explain why veiling and *purdah* are still important in Middle Eastern societies?

2. What aspects of this essay explore the wearing of or removal of the veil as a gesture of adherence to or defiance of the political system?

3. **Other Patterns.** How do the detailed **descriptions** of the articles of clothing analyzed by theFerneas clarify their definition?

LANGUAGE

1. How do the terms *sharaf* and *'ard* express values that are important in Islamic societies?

2. How does the explanation for the root meaning of *hijab* (see paragraph 4) reveal its religious and time-honored place in Middle Eastern culture?

3. If you don't know the meaning of the following words, look them up: *ethnologist* (2), *lustrous* (2), *resurgence* (3), *mosque* (6), *equilibrium* (8), *eunuchs* (9), *seraglio* (9).

SUGGESTIONS FOR WRITING

1. **Critical Writing.** What insight do the authors provide into the pressures on women to wear veils in Middle Eastern cultures?

2. If you were a man who lived in a Middle Eastern country, would you want women to be veiled completely, partially, or not at all? If you were a woman in a Middle Eastern country, would you choose to wear the veil? Explain your answer.

3. In what ways do saris in India, kimonos in Japan, and high heels (or other examples you can think of) communicate precise but different images of the ways in which women should present themselves? Write an essay providing **examples** that illustrate your analysis.

4. ***Thematic Links.*** Discuss the contrast between the desire to hide or control female sexuality as discussed by the Ferneas with the overt need to display it as analyzed by Kim Chernin in "The Flesh and the Devil" (Chapter 9, "Cause and Effect").

LILIANA HEKER

The Stolen Party

Differences in social class can intrude even into something as ordinary as a birthday party for a child. But what happens if the child who is being slighted is slow to realize it? This is the predicament that Liliana Heker (b. 1943), an Argentinian writer, dramatizes in the following story, which first appeared in translation by Alberto Manguel in *Other Fires: Short Fiction by Latin American Women* (1985). Heker's career is unusual in that she edited a literary magazine (*The Platypus*) during the time of the military dictatorship in Argentina and her magazine was the only forum in which many writers could be published. An important theme in her work, such as *Hermanas de Shakespeare* [*Shakespeare's Sisters*] (1999), is the clash of the privileged with the underclass, whether due to gender or to economic forces.

BEFORE YOU READ

Do you try to anticipate the results of important choices you make?

■ ■ ▨

1   As soon as she arrived she went straight to the kitchen to see if the monkey was there. It was: what a relief! She wouldn't have liked to admit that her mother had been right. *Monkeys at a birthday?* her mother had sneered. *Get away with you, believing any nonsense you're told!* She was cross but not because of the monkey, the girl thought; it's just because of the party.

2   "I don't like you going," she told her. "It's a rich people's party."

3   "Rich people go to Heaven too," said the girl, who studied religion at school.

4   "Get away with Heaven," said the mother. "The problem with you, young lady, is that you like to fart higher than your ass."

5   The girl didn't approve of the way her mother spoke. She was barely nine, and one of the best in her class.

6   "I'm going because I've been invited," she said. "And I've been invited because Luciana is my friend. So there."

7   "Ah yes, your friend," her mother grumbled. She paused. "Listen, Rosaura," she said at last. "That one's not your friend. You know what you are to them? The maid's daughter, that's what."

8   Rosaura blinked hard: she wasn't going to cry. Then she yelled: "Shut up! You know nothing about being friends!"

9   Every afternoon she used to go to Luciana's house and they would both finish their homework while Rosaura's mother did the cleaning. They had their tea in the kitchen and they told each other secrets. Rosaura loved everything in the big house, and she also loved the people who lived there.

10   "I'm going because it will be the most lovely party in the whole world, Luciana told me it would. There will be a magician, and he will bring a monkey and everything."

11   The mother swung around to take a good look at her child, and pompously put her hands on her hips.

12   "Monkeys at a birthday?" she said. "Get away with you, believing any nonsense you're told!"

13   Rosaura was deeply offended. She thought it unfair of her mother to accuse other people of being liars simply because they were rich. Rosaura too wanted to be rich, of course. If one day she managed to live in a beautiful palace, would her mother stop loving her? She felt very sad. She wanted to go to that party more than anything else in the world.

14   "I'll die if I don't go," she whispered, almost without moving her lips.

15   And she wasn't sure whether she had been heard, but on the morning of the party she discovered that her mother had starched her Christmas dress. And in the afternoon, after washing her hair, her mother rinsed it in apple vinegar so that it would be all nice and shiny. Before going out, Rosaura admired herself in the mirror, with her white dress and glossy hair, and thought she looked terribly pretty.

16   Señora Ines also seemed to notice. As soon as she saw her, she said:

17   "How lovely you look today, Rosaura."

18   Rosaura gave her starched skirt a slight toss with her hands and walked into the party with a firm step. She said hello to Luciana and asked about the monkey. Luciana put on a secretive look and whispered into Rosaura's ear. "He's in the kitchen. But don't tell anyone, because it's a surprise."

19   Rosaura wanted to make sure. Carefully she entered the kitchen and there she saw it: deep in thought, inside its cage. It looked so funny that the girl stood there for a while, watching it, and later, every so often, she would slip out of the party unseen and go and admire it. Rosaura was the only one allowed into the kitchen. Señora Ines had said: "You yes, but not the others, they're much too boisterous, they might break something." Rosaura had never broken anything. She even managed the jug of orange juice, carrying it from the kitchen into the dining-room. She held it carefully and didn't spill a single drop. And Señora Ines had said: "Are you sure you can manage a jug as big as that?" Of course she could manage. She wasn't a butterfingers, like the others. Like that blonde girl with the bow in her hair. As soon as she saw Rosaura, the girl with the bow had said:

20   "And you? Who are you?"

21   "I'm a friend of Luciana," said Rosaura.

22   "No," said the girl with the bow, "you are not a friend of Luciana because I'm her cousin and I know all her friends. And I don't know you."

23   "So what," said Rosaura. "I come here every afternoon with my mother and we do our homework together."

24   "You and your mother do your homework together?" asked the girl, laughing.

25   "I and Luciana do our homework together," said Rosaura, very seriously.

26   The girl with the bow shrugged her shoulders.

27   "That's not being friends," she said. "Do you go to school together?"

28   "No."

29   "So where do you know her from?" said the girl, getting impatient.

30   Rosaura remembered her mother's words perfectly. She took a deep breath.

31   "I'm the daughter of the employee," she said.

32   Her mother had said very clearly: "If someone asks, you say you're the daughter of the employee; that's all." She also told her to add: "And proud of it." But Rosaura thought that never in her life would she dare say something of the sort.

33   "What employee?" said the girl with the bow. "Employee in a shop?"

34   "No," said Rosaura angrily. "My mother doesn't sell anything in any shop, so there."

35   "So how come she's an employee?" said the girl with the bow.

36   Just then Señora Ines arrived saying *shh shh*, and asked Rosaura if she wouldn't mind helping serve out the hot-dogs, as she knew the house so much better than the others.

37   "See?" said Rosaura to the girl with the bow, and when no one was looking she kicked her in the shin.

38   Apart from the girl with the bow, all the others were delightful. The one she liked best was Luciana, with her golden birthday crown; and then the boys. Rosaura won the sack race, and nobody managed to catch her when they played tag. When they split into two teams to play charades, all the boys wanted her for their side. Rosaura felt she had never been so happy in all her life.

39   But the best was still to come. The best came after Luciana blew out the candles. First the cake. Señora Ines had asked her to help pass the cake around, and Rosaura had enjoyed the task immensely, because everyone called out to her, shouting "Me, me!" Rosaura remembered a story in which there was a queen who had the power of life or death over her subjects. She had always loved that, having the power of life or death. To Luciana and the boys she gave the largest pieces, and to the girl with the bow she gave a slice so thin one could see through it.

40   After the cake came the magician, tall and bony, with a fine red cape. A true magician, he could untie handkerchiefs by blowing on them and make a chain with links that had no openings. He could guess what cards were pulled out from a pack, and the monkey was his assistant. He called the monkey "partner." "Let's see here, partner," he would say, "Turn over a card." And, "Don't run away, partner: time to work now."

41   The final trick was wonderful. One of the children had to hold the monkey in his arms and the magician said he would make him disappear.

42   "What, the boy?" they all shouted.

43   "No, the monkey!" shouted back the magician.

44   Rosaura thought that this was truly the most amusing party in the whole world.

45   The magician asked a small fat boy to come and help, but the small fat boy got frightened almost at once and dropped the monkey on the floor. The magician picked him up carefully, whispered something in his ear, and the monkey nodded almost as if he understood.

46   "You mustn't be so unmanly, my friend," the magician said to the fat boy.

47   "What's unmanly?" said the fat boy.

48   The magician turned around as if to look for spies.

49   "A sissy," said the magician. "Go sit down."

50   Then he stared at all the faces, one by one. Rosaura felt her heart tremble.

51   "You, with the Spanish eyes," said the magician. And everyone saw that he was pointing at her.

52   She wasn't afraid. Neither holding the monkey, nor when the magician made him vanish; not even when, at the end, the magician flung his red cape over Rosaura's head and uttered a few magic words . . . and the monkey reappeared, chattering happily, in her arms. The children clapped furiously. And before Rosaura returned to her seat, the magician said:

53   "Thank you very much, my little countess."

54   She was so pleased with the compliment that a while later, when her mother came to fetch her, that was the first thing she told her.

55   "I helped the magician and he said to me, 'Thank you very much, my little countess.'"

56   It was strange because up to then Rosaura had thought that she was angry with her mother. All along Rosaura had imagined that she would say to her: "See that the monkey wasn't a lie?" But instead she was so thrilled that she told her mother all about the wonderful magician.

57   Her mother tapped her on the head and said: "So now we're a countess!"

58   But one could see that she was beaming.

59   And now they both stood in the entrance, because a moment ago Señora Ines, smiling, had said: "Please wait here a second."

60   Her mother suddenly seemed worried.

61   "What is it?" she asked Rosaura.

62   "What is what?" said Rosaura. "It's nothing; she just wants to get the presents for those who are leaving, see?"

63   She pointed at the fat boy and at a girl with pigtails who were also waiting there, next to their mothers. And she explained about the presents. She knew, because she had been watching those who left before her. When one of the girls was about to leave, Señora Ines would give her a bracelet. When a boy left, Señora Ines gave him a yo-yo. Rosaura preferred the yo-yo because it sparkled, but she didn't mention that to her mother. Her mother might have said: "So why don't you ask for one, you blockhead?" That's what her mother was like. Rosaura didn't feel like explaining that she'd be horribly ashamed to be the odd one out. Instead she said:

64   "I was the best-behaved at the party."

65   And she said no more because Señora Ines came out into the hall with two bags, one pink and one blue.

66   First she went up to the fat boy, gave him a yo-yo out of the blue bag, and the fat boy left with his mother. Then she went up to the girl and gave her a bracelet out of the pink bag, and the girl with the pigtails left as well.

67   Finally she came up to Rosaura and her mother. She had a big smile on her face and Rosaura liked that. Señora Ines looked down at her, then looked up at her mother, and then said something that made Rosaura proud:

68   "What a marvellous daughter you have, Herminia."

69   For an instant, Rosaura thought that she'd give her two presents: the bracelet and the yo-yo. Señora Ines bent down as if about to look for something. Rosaura also leaned forward, stretching out her arm. But she never completed the movement.

70   Señora Ines didn't look in the pink bag. Nor did she look in the blue bag. Instead she rummaged in her purse. In her hand appeared two bills.

71   "You really and truly earned this," she said handing them over. "Thank you for all your help, my pet."

72   Rosaura felt her arms stiffen, stick close to her body, and then she noticed her mother's hand on her shoulder. Instinctively she pressed herself against her mother's body. That was all. Except her eyes. Rosaura's eyes had a cold, clear look that fixed itself on Señora Ines's face.

73   Señora Ines, motionless, stood there with her hand outstretched. As if she didn't dare draw it back. As if the slightest change might shatter an infinitely delicate balance.

■ ■ ▨

MEANING

1. Over the course of the party, what special favors or privileges does Rosaura receive that lead her to believe that she is going to receive a gift?

2. How do the incidents in which she is chosen to distribute the cake and to hold the monkey contribute to Rosaura's feelings of acceptance?

3. How has Rosaura's view of herself as Luciana's friend and social equal changed by the end of the party?

4. In what sense is the party "stolen"?

TECHNIQUE

1. What means does Heker use to alert the reader that Rosaura's perceptions are incorrect and that her mother does not wish her daughter to be disappointed?

2. How does Heker use the monkey to parallel Rosaura's true social status?

3. **Other Patterns.** How does Heker use **narrative** containing dialogue to create the scene for the reader?

LANGUAGE

1. How does Señora Ines's comment that Rosaura is a "marvellous daughter" (paragraph 68) become ironic?

2. How does Heker use language to convey the nuances of social class in Argentinian society?

3. If you don't know the meaning of the following words, look them up: *pompously* (11), *boisterous* (19), *butterfingers* (19), *furiously* (52), *rummaged* (70).

Suggestions for Writing

1. **Critical Writing.** Does Rosaura's mother want to protect her from being disillusioned, or is she really proud of Rosaura in spite of herself?

2. Did you ever discover that your sense of belonging and being accepted was not as secure as you thought it was? If so, describe the details of your experience.

3. **Argue** for or against the idea that it is Rosaura who is trying to steal the party.

4. **Thematic Links.** Discuss the impact of social class in this story and in Margaret Sanger's account "The Turbid Ebb and Flow of Misery" (Chapter 13, "Using Combined Patterns").

▓▓▓ STUDENT ESSAY: DEFINITION

The following essay by Geeta Patel, who grew up in Mumbai, defines the "dabbawalas" who provide a unique and indispensable service for workers in this major city in India. We have annotated her essay and added a follow-up analysis ("Strategies") to help you understand the important principles of definition.

Patel 1

Dabbawalas in Action
Geeta Patel

1   A term with which residents of Mumbai (or Bombay) are very familiar that is largely unknown in the West is "dabbawala." To understand what it means, imagine the following:

Introduction

2   What if you could have a home-cooked meal delivered to you promptly at lunchtime every day where you work? This unique service is provided to over half the office workers in Mumbai by a network of thousands of food transporters known as Dabbawalas. The term "dabbawala" can be translated as "lunchbox carrier." In Hindi, "dabba" refers to a box (although they are actually cylindrical metal containers), while "wala" denotes someone who practices a trade. In order to appreciate the astounding service dabbawalas provide, we need to investigate the history, logistical delivery system, customers, and social implications of their service in what is still a caste-based society.

Formal definition

Thesis and overview

3   Dabbawalas are predominantly drawn from unskilled rural workers who would earn far less as farmers. Currently, they earn between $40 and $80 a month. This trade has existed for over 125 years. Although most dabbawalas are illiterate, they have evolved an amazingly sophisticated system based on simple color codes painted on the lunch boxes (or tiffins).

Description

4   We can appreciate the unique level of efficiency these workers have achieved when we consider that each day between 4500 and 5000 dabbawalas travel by bicycles, railways, and on foot to deliver nearly 200,000 lunches. Their system is so efficient that according to <u>Forbes</u> magazine (1998) dabbawalas only made one mistake out of eight million deliveries, an error rate that would be the envy of any business in our technologically advanced society.

Exemplification

5   The way the system works is that the lunchboxes are collected from the homes in the morning, taken to the nearest railway station, sorted according to destination, and placed in luggage cars. At their destination they are picked up by other dabbawallas, who deliver each meal to an individual's office workplace. At the end of the day the process is reversed. We should keep in mind that each dabba changes hands eight times in its journey (four going and four returning) without being lost or confused with other lunchboxes.

Process analysis

6   Customers include government, factory, and office workers and even students. Each customer is charged a few hundred rupees for daily service for a month—a bargain when you consider how much we pay to have a pizza delivered. The service provided by dabbawalas is so popular in Mumbai because many people adhere to hygienic or dietary restrictions or simply want inexpensive and tasty home-cooked food. Restaurant meals would be many times more expensive, and most office workers live too far from their homes to be able to return there for lunch. Also, Mumbai residents prefer homemade meals over the ubiquitous fast food Americans prefer. There is also a personal factor involved, since customers get to know and trust their dabbawalas (each of whom serves approximately 40 people). This is important since in India there are many castes and religions, each with their own dietary laws. Ironically, the only thing these groups may have in common is the dabbawala who delivers their lunch.

Cause and effect

Comparison/ contrast

7   Dabbawalas wearing their white Gandhi caps and carrying up to forty tiffins in a wire case are a familiar and welcome sight at lunchtime in Mumbai. This service has met the needs of their customers for over a century and has not been interrupted even during the annual monsoons that deluge the city.

Conclusion

Strategies for Writing Essays in Definition

1. Introduction:

Geeta Patel's assignment was to write an extended definition of a term that she believed would be unfamiliar to her readers. Although she grew up in Mumbai and knew a lot about her subject, she also knew that her American readers would need a detailed explanation and some background information to fully understand her analysis. She uses an engaging hypothetical example to open her essay and then follows it with a formal definition of the term "dabbawala." Geeta then concludes her introductory paragraph with a thesis and overview of the topics she will discuss.

2. Organization:

To support her extended definition, Geeta first provides a vivid description of who the dabbawalas are, how much they earn, and what system they use to route the lunches they will deliver. She follows this with examples that illustrate the magnitude and efficiency of the dabbawala delivery system.

The organizational strategy of her entire essay reflects the thesis in her introduction, and she succeeds in providing a context so that her readers can understand what is to them an unfamiliar term.

She uses several techniques to add interest: She (1) contrasts the efficiency achieved by the semiliterate dabbawalas with far more error-prone Western companies and (2) uses a rhetorical question to engage her readers.

3. Patterns of Development:

Geeta uses a number of strategies that are found in extended definitions. She provides a formal definition, **describes** the dabbawalas and gives **examples** to illustrate the scale and efficiency of their operation. She also uses **process analysis** to explain how the meals get delivered, **causal analysis** to explain why Mumbai residents use this service to such a large extent, and **comparison and contrast** to highlight the differences in food preferences between American and Indian cultures.

Her conclusion echoes her thesis in the introduction and creates a final lasting image that communicates the integral nature of the dabbawalas in Mumbai society.

4. Revision:

Although Geeta is effective in defining an unfamiliar term and communicates the reality of the dabbawala system, her essay might benefit from editing to eliminate repetitive words such as "efficiency . . . efficient" in the fourth paragraph. The next-to-last paragraph rambles a bit and needs more focus. Geeta might consider dividing it into two paragraphs at the point at which she changes the subject to the unique role that dabbawalas play in uniting the segments of Mumbai society and then expanding on this point.

Guidelines for Writing an Essay in Definition

- If your assignment requires you to write an essay using definition, have you created a thesis that clearly identifies the term to be defined and the method you plan to use?

- Have you provided a formal definition (in your introduction) that identifies the unique characteristics of the subject and other important supplementary terms that will enable your audience to clearly understand its boundaries?

- Have you identified a means by which you can extend your definition through one or several of the other patterns? You might explain the nature of something by telling when and where it occurs (**narration**), by describing its dominant features (**description**), by giving examples of it in different situations (**exemplification**), by comparing or contrasting it to something else (**comparison and contrast**), by telling how it works (**process analysis**), by identifying its component parts or the different forms it can take (**classification and division**), and/or by identifying its causes or consequences (**cause and effect**).

- What other techniques (such as providing synonyms or analogies or tracing the etymology of the term) can you use to clarify and enlarge your definition?

- Does the organization of your essay fulfill your objective in defining this particular term for a specified audience? If you use several patterns, have you opened each paragraph with a topic sentence that signals the approach you will follow?

- Does your conclusion restate the thesis or summarize key aspects of the term you have defined?

Grammar Tips for Definition

Writing an extended definition essay will usually require you to provide a dictionary definition of an important term and also use a variety of rhetorical methods to explore and clarify it. Each of these poses a particular pitfall: (1) using only the dictionary definition plus "is when" or "is where" and/or (2) being sidetracked by any of the rhetorical patterns you use and not relating the term back to your thesis.

1. Dictionaries use an analytical method that puts the term to be defined into a general class and then provides distinguishing features that differentiate the term from other things in its class with which it might be confused. If you simply refer to an instance using the phrase "is where" or "is when," your definition lacks the context in which the reader can judge its distinguishing features.

Faulty:

Charisma "is when" a special quality gives an individual influence or authority over large numbers of people.

continued

Correct:

Charisma is the special quality that gives an individual influence or authority over large numbers of people.

Faulty:

A *hazard* "is where" there is a danger which one can foresee but cannot avoid.

Correct:

A *hazard* is a danger that one can foresee but cannot avoid.

This mistake can be corrected by simply using "is" before an abstract noun ("special quality" and "danger") and omitting "is when" or "is where."

2. The variety of rhetorical methods that are used to define your term within their own paragraphs or sections need to be explicitly connected to your thesis.

For example, each section of Elizabeth W. Fernea and Robert A. Fernea's essay "A Look Behind the Veil" defines and clarifies the basic phenomenon of veiling by bringing different rhetorical methods into play by looking at its history, current practices, etymology, religious and political symbolism, and as an indicator of social class. The writers could have gotten sidetracked by any one of these interesting issues but always connected their analyses with the central concept they set out to define.

CHECKLIST for Revising a Definition Essay

- Does your thesis clearly identify the idea, term, or phrase that you will define?
- Does your introduction contain a formal definition and suggest the approach you plan to take?
- Have you used a variety of rhetorical patterns to develop your definition?
- What additional methods, such as tracing the history of the term or providing synonyms or analogies, can you use to clarify your definition?
- Do you need to define important supplementary terms in order for your readers to understand your main term?
- When your essay uses multiple patterns to define a term, do you use topic sentences to prepare your reader for each section of your analysis?

ADDITIONAL WRITING ASSIGNMENTS AND ACTIVITIES

COMMUNICATING WITH DIFFERENT AUDIENCES

1. As an office manager, write a definition of sexual harrassment for new employees so that they will understand your company's policy.

2. Make up an ad with a job description—including the qualifications you are looking for and the tasks and responsibilities that the job entails—to be posted on the Internet.

WRITING FOR A NEWSPAPER

Write an editorial to a national newspaper on a term that you use (such as a slang term or a term related to one of your hobbies) that not everyone would know. Use a variety of rhetorical methods (as in Geeta Patel's essay) to explain the term.

DEFINITION ESSAYS

1. Define any of the following terms in an essay, using any of the previous patterns or other methods such as giving the etymology or history of the term:

   dowry, addiction, depression, diversity, melting pot, assimilation, cross-cultural, multicultural, anxiety, stress, truth, bullshit, obsession, culture, stereotype, subculture, prejudice, racism, ageism, speciesism, sexism, freedom, poverty, propaganda, euphemism, the "other," icon, ethics, masala, egotist, conscience, karma, untouchable, hypocrisy, genocide, muckraker, obscene, shame, plagiarism, *déjà vu*, virtual, kitsch, *hijab*, inalienable rights, date rape, autism, chic, insight.

2. What are the defining characteristics of a good parent, child, or sibling?

3. Define an abstract idea such as love, hate, good, evil, jealousy, or benevolence, and support your definition with concrete examples.

4. Have you ever experienced what is known as "culture shock"? If so, describe the circumstances and your perception of this phrase.

5. Define a phrase or saying that is widely used in your family or region but that might be unfamiliar to a larger audience.

RESEARCH SUGGESTIONS

1. Look up the history of a term as given in the *Oxford English Dictionary*, and bring it up to date in your own words. (You might wish to read one of Simon Winchester's books, *The Professor and the Madman* (1999) and/or *A Crack in the Edge of the World* (2005), for a glimpse of how this authoritative source came into being.)

2. How did the term *Ms.* come into being, and what are its implications today?

3. What are the origins, evolution, and social history of the name of a popular food, such as *hot dogs, Buffalo wings,* or *Baby Ruth* bars?

4. On the basis of research, write an extended essay on the qualities and characteristics of a school of art, architecture, music, or literature (for example, Impressionism).

COLLABORATIVE ACTIVITIES

1. Create a riddle describing an object, animal, or natural force, using metaphors and/or similes that define its main characteristics. For example, "I am fruity, transparent, colorful, sweet, and shaky—what am I?"

2. Define a current slang term that expresses a value judgment such as *sweet, awesome, bling, dis, freak,* or any other term that you often use, or the name of a current trend such as *downsizing* or *outsourcing.*

3. How has the meaning of the term *salsa* broadened and evolved into a cultural designation beyond referring to a sauce?

Problem Solving

11

Resolving Cultural Dilemmas

Although problem solving is not a rhetorical strategy as such, the techniques that writers use to identify problems, apply theoretical models, define constraints, pose and investigate solutions, and check solutions against relevant criteria are techniques you will find useful in your own writing.

The process by which problems are solved usually involves recognizing and defining the problem, using various research techniques to discover a solution, verifying the solution, and communicating it to a particular audience, who might need to know the history of the problem, the success or failure of previous attempts to solve it, and possible consequences if the problem is not solved.

 RECOGNIZING THE EXISTENCE
AND NATURE OF THE PROBLEM

The first step in solving a problem is recognizing that a problem exists. Often the magnitude of the problem is obvious from serious effects that the problem is causing. For Thor Heyerdahl, who originated the *Kon-Tiki* and *Ra* expeditions, the dramatic effects of midocean pollution were warning signals, as he describes in "How to Kill an Ocean":

> We treat the ocean as if we believed that it is not part of our planet—as if the blue waters curved into space somewhere beyond the horizon where our pollutants would fall off the edge, as ships were believed to do before the days of Christopher Columbus. . . . What we consider too dangerous to be stored under technical control ashore we dump forever out

of sight at sea, whether toxic chemicals or nuclear waste. Our only excuse is the still-surviving image of the ocean as a bottomless pit.

Heyerdahl redefines the popular conception of the "boundless oceans" to emphasize its vulnerability and uses dramatic illustrations and statistical evidence to support his recommendations for protecting and preserving it.

DEFINING THE PROBLEM

It is often helpful to present the problem with a single, clear-cut example that describes the context in which the problem occurs, the limits and constraints within which the problem must be solved, and the nature of the choices that are involved. In "Daisy," Luis Sepúlveda takes us inside a prison in Chile where he was confined and tortured. One of the guards, whom Sepúlveda nicknames "Daisy," is an aspiring poet who wants Sepúlveda, a well-known writer, to review his work:

> We went into an office. On the desk I saw a tin of cocoa and a carton of cigarettes which were obviously there to reward my comments on his literary work.
> "Did you read my poesy?" he asked, offering me a seat.
> Poesy. Daisy said poesy, not poetry. A man covered with pistols and grenades can't say "poesy" without sounding ridiculous and effete. At that moment he revolted me, and I decided that even if it meant pissing blood, hissing when I spoke and being able to charge batteries just by touching them, I wasn't going to lower myself to flattering a plagiarising faggot in uniform.

Sepúlveda confronts a problem that is moral and practical, and he must decide which is the most important criterion in making his decision.

All problem-solving situations presented in writing must include a description of the initial state, the goal to be reached, the actions that can be performed, and the restrictions that limit what can and cannot be done.

REPRESENTING THE PROBLEM IN RELEVANT FORM

Often problems are so complex that it is useful to represent them in simplified form. Expert problem solvers find it useful to construct a mental picture of the problem or to put it in writing, whether in the form of a mathematical equation, displayed as a diagram, or represented conceptually in language. For example, in "An Incident in Hong Kong," the case history reported by Gina Kolata recounts the efforts of researchers trying to solve the problem of why a three-year-old boy suddenly had died of an unidentified strain of the flu:

> The child's doctors sent washings from his throat to a government virology lab for analysis. The samples, tests revealed, contained just one kind of virus, an influenza virus.

Then the difficulty occurred. Try as they might, the lab scientists could not identify the strain of influenza.

Experts differ from inexperienced problem solvers in having the ability to draw on a greater range of knowledge and recognize a variety of distinct problem types that are important in their particular field of study. The better the problem solver, the greater the repertoire of types, models, or concepts from which he or she can draw. In this case, solving the problem required the doctors to "think outside the box" and check strains of flu viruses that infect birds that "no one had ever expected to see in humans."

 ## USING DIFFERENT TECHNIQUES TO FIND A SOLUTION

Search techniques allow problem solvers to find their way through the maze of the problem and evaluate different paths by which the solution can be reached. Usually, new information that is gained along the way gradually leads to new, more productive approaches. However, in many situations, it would be impractical to try every possible combination in the time available.

Better methods of searching for a solution include "working backwards," which assumes that the goal has been reached and asks what step immediately before the goal would have been taken. Means-ends analysis identifies the actions that can be taken, step by step, to close the gap between the original problem and the goal. For example, David A. Counts's essay "Too Many Bananas" is structured as a three-part narrative that records his progressive insights into a culture (in Papua, New Guinea) that was an enigma to him, as it relied on reciprocity and an unusual barter system:

> We hadn't quite reached the point of being crowded off our veranda by the stalks of fruit, but it was quite close. Another factor was that we were tired of playing the gift game. We had acquiesed in playing it—no one was permitted to sell us anything, and in turn we only gave things away, refusing under any circumstances to sell tobacco (or anything else) for money. But there had to be a limit.

Counts learned in the village where he was residing that money should not be offered for goods given or services rendered; instead, "gifts" should be given as a sign of appreciation for the goods or services that he received. Each of the three "lessons" Counts learned brings him closer to solving the problem, from an anthropological perspective, of understanding a culture based on reciprocity.

 ## BREAKING THE PROBLEM INTO EASIER-TO-SOLVE SUBPROBLEMS

Sometimes the most effective strategy consists of breaking the problem into "subproblems" that are easier to solve. A top-down approach to problem solving replaces a complex problem with several simpler, easier-to-handle individual problems. In his account of being lost, alone, and near starvation in a remote Bolivian rain forest, Yossi Ghinsberg, in "Jungle," is clear-headed in using the few items that he has with him:

> I secured the edges of the mosquito netting with rocks so that no snakes could come slithering in. The flashlight was near my knee. I kept hold of it for fear that I wouldn't be able to find it in the dark if I should need it.

In Robert Frost's poem "The Road Not Taken," the speaker presents himself as having to decide which of two roads to take as they diverge at a crossroads in the forest. He looks down each as far as he can, observes their differences, and strikes out on the one that "was grassy and wanted wear." The solution to this problem is not what the speaker (or the reader) might imagine but resides in the speaker's unique way of looking at the choice that Frost so adroitly presents.

USING ANALOGIES TO REFORMULATE THE PROBLEM THROUGH A CHANGE IN PERSPECTIVE

With some types of problems, a useful and creative technique is to use an analogy to reformulate the problem through a change in perspective. For example, Alexander Graham Bell's invention of the telephone was based on a direct analogy between the mechanical linkage of the membranes and bones of the human ear and the magnetic linkage in a receiver between a metal diaphragm and an electromagnet.

The Dalai Lama in "The Role of Religion in Modern Society" uses analogous thinking to address the age-old problem of intolerance between religions:

> I sometimes think of religion in terms of medicine for the human spirit. Independent of its usage and suitability to a particular individual in a particular condition, we really cannot judge a medicine's efficacy.... Similarly with different religious traditions, we can say that this one is the most effective for this particular individual.

DESIGNING EXPERIMENTS TO IDENTIFY AND DETERMINE THE MOST IMPORTANT VARIABLE

Besides these search techniques, including trial and error, means-end analysis, working backwards, breaking problems into subproblems, and discovering useful analogies, another technique exists for efficiently allocating problem-solving resources: designing an experiment to isolate the single most important variable within a problem.

The use of experiments that are designed to isolate and measure a single important factor is common to researchers in a variety of disciplines. Social scientists and psychologists use control groups as the constant framework against which to measure results. The experimental group differs from the control group in one important feature that is manipulated. By holding all but one variable fixed, experimenters can control and measure what they suspect to be the most important factor. Today, powerful computers make it possible to simulate the effects of different variables in a whole range of situations from automobile design to cell proliferation.

Although this overview of problem solving has described various search techniques, or heuristics, there is no set order that determines whether one strategy should be tried before another. Frequently, results will depend on using an entire range of search techniques, because the more alternatives that are generated, the better the chances of finding a solution to the problem. Also, any search may uncover facts that require the problem to be redefined; this is typical of the process of scientific analysis, whereby observation of facts leads to a hypothesis, which additional facts either support or refute. For example, in "The Bittersweet Science," Austin Bunn tells the story of the efforts through the centuries to find a cure for diabetes. This disease causes the body to be unable to properly manufacture or store glucose. The ancient Greeks identified its symptoms of unquenchable thirst and an inability to put on weight and called it *diabetes*. The idea of starvation as a means of staving off this wasting disease occurred in 1871 during the Siege of Paris, when a French doctor noticed that "though hundreds were starving to death, his diabetic patients strangely improved." This type of treatment was administered to Elizabeth Hughes in the early twentieth century. The discovery of insulin in 1922 isolated the key factor in what caused diabetes and made it possible to keep the disease under control:

> In the summer of 1922, two young clinicians in Toronto named Frederick Banting and Charles Best surgically removed the pancreases from dozens of dogs, causing the dogs to "get" diabetes. They found that by injecting the dogs with a filtered solution of macerated pancreases (either the dogs' own or from calf fetuses), the glucose level in the dogs' blood dropped to normal. The researchers had discovered insulin.

Insulin made it possible for Elizabeth Hughes and others suffering from diabetes to gain weight and lead a normal life. Bunn's account is an excellent example of writing in the problem-solving format: He provides a historical context in which to understand the nature of the problem, and he discusses the importance of chance discoveries and the trial-and-error methods that were used before the Canadian researchers conducted an experiment that verified their hypothesis.

New interpretations of known facts, solutions generated by problem-solving techniques, and new theoretical models through which fields of study evolve must gain acceptance and be seen as valid by the intended audience. This chapter and the next, "Argument," take up the question of how writers rely on strategies of argument to convince specific audiences of the accuracy of their investigations and the validity of their conclusions.

Problem solving in the workplace often takes the form of proposals designed to secure funding for a project or to change an existing policy. In this type of writing, you begin by demonstrating the need for the action or policy and how those needs can best be met. Your readers need to understand what the potential costs will be and the feasibility of what you recommend. For an illustration of how problem solving can be used in a real-life situation, see the sample letter of complaint later in this chapter (pps. 603–04).

AUSTIN BUNN

The Bittersweet Science

Austin Bunn is a journalist whose essays and reviews run the gamut from video games to medical research. He grew up in Princeton, New Jersey, received a B.A. from Yale, and has taught at Fordham College. His articles have appeared in *Wired*, the *Village Voice*, *Salon*, and *The New York Times Magazine*, where the following essay on the discovery of insulin and the torturous road to understanding diabetes first appeared in March 2003. This essay was chosen for inclusion in *Best American Science and Nature Writing* (2004). More recently, Bunn has coauthored *Big Picture, Little Picture* with Christine Vachon (2005).

BEFORE YOU READ

How does having a chronic disease that requires daily treatment change a person's life?

▨ ▪ ▨

1   Eleven-year-old Elizabeth Hughes was, in retrospect, the ideal patient: bright, obedient, uncomplaining, and wholly unprepared to die. Born in 1907 in the New York State governor's mansion, Elizabeth was the daughter of Charles Evans Hughes, who later became a justice on the Supreme Court, ran against Woodrow Wilson in 1916, and served as secretary of state under Harding. Elizabeth had a perfectly normal, aristocratic youth until she seemed to become allergic to childhood. She would come home from friends' birthday parties with an insatiable thirst, drinking almost two quarts of water at a sitting. By winter, she had become thin, constantly hungry, and exhausted. Her body turned into a sieve: No matter how much water she drank, she was always thirsty.

2   In early 1919, Elizabeth's parents took her to a mansion in Morristown, New Jersey, recently christened the Physiatric Institute and run by Dr. Frederick Allen. A severe, debt-ridden clinician with a pockmarked résumé, Allen had written the authoritative account on treating her condition. He prolonged hundreds of lives and was the girl's best chance. Allen examined Elizabeth and diagnosed diabetes—her body was not properly processing her food into fuel—and told her parents what they would never tell their daughter: that her life expectancy was one year, three at the outside. Even that was a magnificent extension of previous fatality rates. "The diagnosis was like knowing a death sentence had been passed," wrote one historian. Then Dr. Allen did what many doctors at the time would have done for Elizabeth, except that this doctor was exceptionally good, if not the finest in the world, at it. He began to starve her.

3   The history of medicine "is like the night sky," says the historian Roy Porter in his book *The Greatest Benefit to Mankind: A Medical History of Humanity*. "We see a few stars and group them into mythic constellations. What is chiefly visible is the darkness."

4   Diabetes doesn't come from simply eating too much sugar; nor is it cured, as was once thought, by a little horseback riding. It is not the result of a failing kidney, overactive liver, or phlegmy disposition, though these were the authoritative answers for centuries. Diabetes happens when the blood becomes saturated with glucose, the body's main energy source, which is normally absorbed by the cells—which is to say that the pathology of diabetes is subtle and invisible, so much so that a third of the people who have it don't even know it. Until the prohibition against autopsies was gradually lifted (by 1482, the pope had informally sanctioned it), what we knew of human anatomy came through the tiny window of war wounds and calamitous gashes—and even then it took centuries for doctors to decide just what the long, lumpy organ called the pancreas actually did or, in the case of diabetes, didn't do. We like to think surgically about the history of medicine, that it moved purposefully from insight to insight, angling closer to cure. But that is only the luxury of contemporary life. Looked at over time, medicine doesn't advance as much as grope forward, with remedies—like bloodletting; quicksilver ointments; and simple, unendurable hunger—that blurred the line between treatment and torture.

5   Diabetes was first diagnosed by the Greek physician Aretaeus of Cappadocia, who deemed it a "wonderful affection . . . being a melting down of the flesh and limbs into urine." For the afflicted, "life is disgusting and painful; thirst unquenchable . . . and one cannot stop them from drinking or making water." Since the classical period forbade dissection, Porter notes, "hidden workings had to be deduced largely from what went in and what came out." An early diagnostic test was to swill urine, and to the name *diabetes*, meaning "siphon," was eventually added *mellitus*, meaning "sweetened with honey." Healers could often diagnose diabetes without the taste test. Black ants were attracted to the urine of those wasting away, drawn by the sugar content. Generations later, doctors would make a similar deduction by spotting dried white sugar spots on the shoes or pants of diabetic men with bad aim.

6   For the Greeks, to separate disease symptoms from individual pain while isolating them from magical causes was itself an enormous intellectual leap. "We should be really impressed with Aretaeus," says Dr. Chris Feudtner, author of the coming *Bittersweet: Diabetes, Insulin, and the Transformation of Illness*. "He was able to spot the pattern of diabetes in a dense thicket of illness and suffering."

7   But for centuries, this increasing precision in disease recognition was not followed by any effective treatment—more details didn't make physicians any less helpless. At the time, they were unknowingly confusing two kinds of diabetes: Type 1, known until recently as "juvenile diabetes," which is more extreme but less common than Type 2, or "adult onset," which seems to be related to obesity and overeating. With Type 1 (what Elizabeth Hughes had), the pancreas stops secreting insulin, a hormone that instructs the body to use the sugar in the blood for energy. With Type 2, the pancreas produces insulin (at least initially), but the tissues of the body stop responding appropriately. By 1776, doctors were still just boiling the urine of diabetics to conclusively determine that they were passing sugar, only to watch their patients fall into hyperglycemic comas and die.

8   If dangerous levels of glucose were pumping out of diabetics, one idea was obvious: Stop it from going in. That demanded a more sophisticated understanding of food itself. In the long tradition of grotesque scientific experimentation, an insight came through a lucky break: a gaping stomach wound. In 1822, William Beaumont, a surgeon in the U.S. Army, went to the Canadian border to treat a nineteen-year-old trapper hit by a shotgun. The boy recovered, but he was left with a hole in his abdomen. According to Porter, Beaumont "took advantage of his patient's unique window" and dropped food in on a string. The seasoned beef took the longest to digest. Stale bread broke down the quickest. The digestion process clearly worked differently depending on what was eaten. Then during the 1871 siege of Paris by the Germans, a French doctor named Apollinaire Bouchardat noticed that, though hundreds were starving to death, his diabetic patients strangely improved. This became the basis for a new standard of treatment. *Mangez le moins possible*, he advised them. Eat as little as possible.

9   In the spring of 1919, when Elizabeth Hughes came under Dr. Allen's care, she weighed seventy-five pounds and was nearly five feet tall. For one week, he fasted her. Then he put her on an extremely low-calorie diet to eradicate sugar from her urine. If the normal caloric intake for a girl her age is between 2,200 and 2,400 calories daily, Elizabeth took in 400 to 600 calories a day for several weeks, including one day of fasting each week. Her weight, not surprisingly, plummeted. As Michael Bliss notes in his book *The Discovery of Insulin*, the Hughes family brought in a nurse to help weigh and supervise every gram of food that she ate. Desserts and bread were verboten. "She lived on lean meat, eggs, lettuce, milk, a few fruits, tasteless bran rusks, and tasteless vegetables (boiled three times to make them almost totally carbohydrate-free)," Bliss writes. Instead of a birthday cake, she had to settle for "a hat box covered in pink and white paper with candles on it. On picnics in the summertime she had her own little frying pan to cook her omelet in while the others had chops, fresh fish, corn on the cob, and watermelon."

10   You could say that Elizabeth Hughes was on a twisted precursor of the Zone diet: Her menu relied on proteins and fats, with the abolishment of carbohydrates like bread and pasta. In fact, Allen's maniacal scrutiny of his patients' nutrition—fasting them, weighing each meal, counting calories—was one of the first "diets" in the modern sense. At the time Elizabeth entered the clinic, being well fed was a sign of good health. But the new science of nutrition fostered the idea of weight reduction as a standard of health and not illness.

11   Allen's "starvation diet" was a particular cruelty. Patients came to him complaining of hunger and rapid weight loss, and Allen demanded further restrictions, further weight loss. "Yes, the method was severe; yes, many patients could not or would not follow it," writes Bliss. "But what was the alternative?" Over the years, doctors recommended opium, even heaps of sugar (which only accelerated death, but since nothing else worked, why not enjoy the moment?). But nobody had a better way than Allen to extend lives. If the fasting wasn't working and symptoms got worse, Allen insisted on more rigorous undernourishment. In his campaigns to master their disease, Allen took his patients right to the edge of death, but he

justified this by pointing out that patients faced a stark choice: die of diabetes or risk "inanition," which Allen explained as "starvation due to inability to acquire tolerance for any living diet." The Physiatric Institute became a famine ward.

12   Some of Allen's patients survived levels of inanition not thought possible, Bliss writes. One twelve-year-old patient, blind from diabetes when he was admitted, still occasionally showed sugar in his urine. The clinic became convinced that the kid—so weak he could barely get out of bed—was somehow stealing food. "It turned out that his supposed helplessness was the very thing that gave him opportunities which other persons lacked," Allen later wrote in his book, *Total Dietary Regulation in the Treatment of Diabetes.* "Among unusual things eaten were toothpaste and birdseed, the latter being obtained from the cage of a canary which he had asked for." The staff, thinking he was pilfering food, cut his diet back and further back. The boy weighed less than forty pounds when he died from starvation.

13   No one explained to Elizabeth Hughes why the friends she made at Allen's clinic stopped writing her letters. Death was kept hidden, though it must have been obvious from the halls of the clinic, where rows of gaunt children stared from their beds. "It would have been unendurable if only there had not been so many others," one Allen nurse wrote. Dutifully, Elizabeth—strong enough just to read and sew—hardly ever showed sugar. Her attendant punished her severely the one time she caught her stealing turkey skin from the kitchen after Thanksgiving. Still, she was wasting away. By April 1921, thirteen years old and two years into her treatment, Elizabeth was down to fifty-two pounds and averaged 405 calories a day. In letters to her parents, she talked about getting married and what she would do on her twenty-first birthday. Reading the letters "must have been heartbreaking," writes Bliss. "Elizabeth was a semi-invalid."

14   In the history of illness, there are countless medicines, over time and across cultures, with varying degrees of suffering and success. There is only one kind of cure—the one that invariably, irrefutably works. Insulin is not a cure. It is a treatment, but it changed everything. In the summer of 1922, two young clinicians in Toronto named Frederick Banting and Charles Best surgically removed the pancreases from dozens of dogs, causing the dogs to "get" diabetes. They found that by injecting the dogs with a filtered solution of macerated pancreas (either the dogs' own or from calf fetuses), the glucose level in the dogs' blood dropped to normal. The researchers had discovered insulin.

15   But in August 1922, Dr. Frederick Allen had patients who could not wait, like Elizabeth. Allen left for Toronto to secure insulin. While he was gone, word leaked through his clinic about the breakthrough. Patients "who had not been out of bed for weeks began to trail weakly about, clinging to walls and furniture," wrote one nurse. "Big stomachs, skin-and-bone necks, skull-like faces . . . they looked like an old Flemish painter's depiction of a resurrection after famine. It was a resurrection, a crawling stirring, as of some vague springtime."

16   On the night Allen returned to the clinic, he found his patients—"silent as the bloated ghosts they looked like"—waiting in the hallway for him, wrote the nurse. "When he appeared through the open doorway, he caught the full beseeching of a hundred pair of eyes. It stopped him dead. Even now I am

sure it was minutes before he spoke to them. . . . 'I think,' he said. 'I think we have something for you?" He did, but not nearly enough. Though the results were striking—with the insulin, sugar vanished from the urine of "some of the most hopelessly severe cases of diabetes I have ever seen," wrote Allen—he did not have enough extract to treat all his patients, including Elizabeth. So her parents got her to Toronto. When Banting saw Elizabeth, she was three days away from her fifteenth birthday. She weighed forty-five pounds. He wrote: "Patient extremely emaciated . . . hair brittle and thin . . . muscles extremely wasted. . . . She was scarcely able to walk."

17   He started her insulin treatment immediately. The first injections cleared the sugar from her urine, and by the end of the first week, she was up to 1,220 calories a day, still without sugar. By the next, she was at 2,200 calories. Banting advised her to eat bread and potatoes, but she was incredulous. It had been three and a half years since she had them. That fall, she was one of several hundred North American diabetics pulled back from the edge. By November, she went home to her parents in Washington, and by January, she weighed 105 pounds. The same year, the thirty-one-year-old Banting won the Nobel Prize. Meanwhile, Dr. Allen, proprietor of an expensive clinic whose patients no longer needed him, went broke. Insulin was a miracle drug, resurrecting diabetics from comas and putting flesh on skeletons and, since it needed to be administered at least twice daily, it was a miracle that would be performed over and over. The era of chronic medical care had begun.

18   That may be the most poignant part of the history of Allen's clinic. The end of the famine of Elizabeth Hughes is really the start of another hunger: for the drugs that will keep us well for the rest of our lives. Elizabeth went to Barnard, reared three children, drank and smoked, but kept her diabetes a secret almost her entire life. She died of a heart attack in 1981, more than 43,000 injections of insulin later. But if the discovery of insulin took away the terror of diabetes, it replaced the miraculous with the routine. Healing lost one major ingredient: awe. "To think that I'll be leading a normal, healthy existence is beyond all comprehension," Elizabeth wrote to her mother, days after her first injection, in 1922. "It is simply too wonderful for words."

■ ■ ▨

MEANING

1. What problems did the inability of physicians to treat diabetes present in centuries past?

2. How does the case of Elizabeth Hughes illustrate how diabetes was treated before the discovery of insulin?

3. How did the discoveries by Frederick Banting and Charles Best make it possible to treat, if not cure, diabetes?

4. What impact did the discovery of insulin in 1922 have on patients in Dr. Allen's clinic?

TECHNIQUE

1. How does Bunn provide a historical context to help the reader understand how diabetes was treated in the past and the importance of chance discoveries (such as that of William Beaumont)?

2. How does Bunn's account emphasize the impact that the difficulty in diagnosing diabetes had on finding successful treatment?

3. **Other Patterns.** How does Bunn use **cause and effect** to explain the relationship between diminished insulin production and diabetes?

LANGUAGE

1. What is the significance of the medical terms used to diagnose *diabetes mellitus*?

2. Explain in your own words why the beginning of "the era of chronic medical care . . . may be the most poignant part of the history of Allen's clinic."

3. If you don't know the meaning of the following words, look them up: *retrospect* (1), *insatiable* (1), *phlegmy* (4), *calamitous* (4), *pancreas* (4), *insulin* (7), *hyperglycemic* (7), *verboten* (9), *precursor* (10), *inanition* (11), *pilfering* (12), *macerated* (14), *poignant* (18).

SUGGESTIONS FOR WRITING

1. **Critical Writing.** Elizabeth Hughes kept her diabetes a secret for most of her life. How has society's attitude toward this disease as well as other chronic diseases dramatically changed?

2. If you know someone who is suffering from a chronic illness or disease, discuss the impact of new medications or treatments on their lives.

3. Research the history of another well-known medical treatment or medicine (such as penicillin) and use **causal analysis** and **process analysis** to explain how and why it was developed.

4. **Thematic Links.** Compare the problem-solving methods used by medical researchers discussed by Bunn with those described by Gina Kolata in "An Incident in Hong Kong."

THOR HEYERDAHL

How to Kill an Ocean

The daring Norwegian explorer and anthropologist Thor Heyerdahl (1914–2002) won international renown through his seafaring odysseys that sought to establish that pre-Inca inhabitants of Peru could have sailed from there and settled in Polynesia. Heyerdahl recreated primitive boats using balsa and, later, papyrus and reeds, and successfully sailed from Peru to the South Pacific (1947), from Morocco to the West Indies (1970), and from Iraq to Djibouti (1977). On his journeys, it grew ever more obvious that the oceans far from land were being polluted to an extent that had previously been thought impossible. The following essay, which first appeared in *Saturday Review* (1975), sounded the alarm and was later incorporated into an important United Nations report. Heyerdahl's travels and observations are available in *The Kon-Tiki Expedition* (1948), among other works, and, most recently in *In the Footsteps of Adam* (2000).

BEFORE YOU READ

Why would evidence of pollution in an environment that you thought was pristine be alarming?

■ ■ ▨

1   Since the ancient Greeks maintained that the earth was round and great navigators like Columbus and Magellan demonstrated that this assertion was true, no geographical discovery has been more important than what we all are beginning to understand today: that our planet has exceedingly restricted dimensions. There is a limit to all resources. Even the height of the atmosphere and the depth of soil and water represent layers so thin that they would disappear entirely if reduced to scale on the surface of a commonsized globe.

2   The correct concept of our very remarkable planet, rotating as a small and fertile oasis, two-thirds covered by life-giving water, and teeming with life in a solar system otherwise unfit for man, becomes clearer for us with the progress of moon travel and modern astronomy. Our concern about the limits to human expansion increases as science produces ever more exact data on the measurable resources that mankind has in stock for all the years to come.

3   Because of the population explosion, land of any nature has long been in such demand that nations have intruded upon each other's territory with armed forces in order to conquer more space for overcrowded communities. During the last few years, the United Nations has convened special meetings in Stockholm, Caracas, and Geneva in a dramatic attempt to create a "Law of the Sea" designed to divide vast sections of the global ocean space into national waters. The fact that no agreement has been reached illustrates that in our ever-shriveling world there is not even ocean space enough to satisfy everybody. And only one

generation ago, the ocean was considered so vast that no one nation would bother to lay claim to more of it than the three-mile limit which represented the length of a gun shot from the shore.

4   It will probably take still another generation before mankind as a whole begins to realize fully that the ocean is but another big lake, landlocked on all sides. Indeed, it is essential to understand this concept for the survival of coming generations. For we of the 20th century still treat the ocean as the endless, bottomless pit it was considered to be in medieval times. Expressions like "the bottomless sea" and "the boundless ocean" are still in common use, and although we all know better, they reflect the mental image we still have of this, the largest body of water on earth. Perhaps one of the reasons why we subconsciously consider the ocean a sort of bottomless abyss is the fact that all the rain and all the rivers of the world keep pouring constantly into it and yet its water level always remains unchanged. Nothing affects the ocean, not even the Amazon, the Nile, or the Ganges. We know, of course, that this imperviousness is no indicator of size, because the sum total of all the rivers is nothing but the return to its own source of the water evaporated from the sea and carried ashore by drifting clouds.

5   What is it really then that distinguishes the ocean from the other more restricted bodies of water? Surely it is not its salt content. The Old and the New World have lakes with a higher salt percentage than the ocean has. The Aral Sea, the Dead Sea, and the Great Salt Lake in Utah are good examples. Nor is it the fact that the ocean lacks any outlet. Other great bodies of water have abundant input and yet no outlet. The Caspian Sea and Lake Chad in Central Africa are valid examples. Big rivers, among them the Volga, enter the Caspian Sea, but evaporation compensates for its lack of outlet, precisely as is the case with the ocean. Nor is it correct to claim that the ocean is open while inland seas and lakes are landlocked. The ocean is just as landlocked as any lake. It is flanked by land on all sides and in every direction. The fact that the earth is round makes the ocean curve around it just as does solid land, but a shoreline encloses the ocean on all sides and in every direction. The ocean is not even the lowest body of water on our planet. The surface of the Caspian Sea, for instance, is 85 feet below sea level, and the surface of the Dead Sea is more than 1,200 feet below sea level.

6   Only when we fully perceive that there is no fundamental difference between the various bodies of water on our planet, beyond the fact that the ocean is the largest of all lakes, can we begin to realize that the ocean has something else in common with all other bodies of water: it is vulnerable. In the long run the ocean can be affected by the continued discharge of all modern man's toxic waste. One generation ago no one would have thought that the giant lakes of America could be polluted. Today they are, like the largest lakes of Europe. A few years ago the public was amazed to learn that industrial and urban refuse had killed the fish in Lake Erie. The enormous lake was dead. It was polluted from shore to shore in spite of the fact that it has a constant outlet through Niagara Falls, which carries pollutants away into the ocean in a never-ending flow. The ocean receiving all this pollution has no outlet but represents a dead end, because only pure water

evaporates to return into the clouds. The ocean is big; yet if 10 Lake Eries were taken and placed end to end, they would span the entire Atlantic from Africa to South America. And the St. Lawrence River is by no means the only conveyor of pollutants into the ocean. Today hardly a creek or a river in the world reaches the ocean without carrying a constant flow of nondegradable chemicals from industrial, urban, or agricultural areas. Directly by sewers or indirectly by way of streams and other waterways, almost every big city in the world, whether coastal or inland, makes use of the ocean as mankind's common sink. We treat the ocean as if we believed that it is not part of our own planet—as if the blue waters curved into space somewhere beyond the horizon where our pollutants would fall off the edge, as ships were believed to do before the days of Christopher Columbus. We build sewers so far into the sea that we pipe the harmful refuse away from public beaches. Beyond that is no man's concern. What we consider too dangerous to be stored under technical control ashore we dump forever out of sight at sea, whether toxic chemicals or nuclear waste. Our only excuse is the still-surviving image of the ocean as a bottomless pit.

7   It is time to ask: is the ocean vulnerable? And if so, can many survive on a planet with a dead ocean? Both questions can be answered, and they are worthy of our attention.

8   First, the degree of vulnerability of any body of water would of course depend on two factors: the volume of the water and the nature of the pollutants. We know the volume of the ocean, its surface measure, and its average depth. We know that it covers 71 percent of the surface of our planet, and we are impressed, with good reason, when all these measurements are given in almost astronomical figures. If we resort to a more visual image, however, the dimensions lose their magic. The average depth of all oceans is only 1,700 meters. The Empire State Building is 448 meters high. If stretched out horizontally instead of vertically, the average ocean depth would only slightly exceed the 1,500 meters than an Olympic runner can cover by foot in 3 minutes and 35 seconds. The average depth of the North Sea, however, is not 1,700 meters, but only 80 meters, and many of the buildings in downtown New York would emerge high above water level if they were built on the bottom of this sea. During the Stone Age most of the North Sea was dry land where roaming archers hunted deer and other game. In this shallow water, until only recently, all the industrial nations of Western Europe have conducted year-round routine dumping of hundreds of thousands of tons of their most toxic industrial refuse. All the world's sewers and most of its waste are dumped into waters as shallow as, or shallower than, the North Sea. An attempt was made at a recent ocean exhibition to illustrate graphically and in correct proportion the depths of the Atlantic, the Pacific, and the Indian oceans in relation to a cross section of the planet earth. The project had to be abandoned, for although the earth was painted with a diameter twice the height of a man, the depths of the world oceans painted in proportion became so insignificant that they could not be seen except as a very thin pencil line.

9   The ocean is in fact remarkably shallow for its size. Russia's Lake Baikal, for instance, less than 31 kilometers wide, is 1,500 meters deep, which compares

well with the average depth of all oceans. It is the vast *extent* of ocean surface that has made man of all generations imagine a correspondingly unfathomable depth.

10   When viewed in full, from great heights, the ocean's surface is seen to have definite, confining limits. But at sea level, the ocean seems to extend outward indefinitely, to the horizon and on into blue space. The astronauts have come back from space literally disturbed upon seeing a full view of our planet. They have seen at first hand how cramped together the nations are in a limited space and how the "endless" oceans are tightly enclosed with in cramped quarters by surrounding land masses. But one need not be an astronaut to lose the sensation of a boundless ocean. It is enough to embark on some floating logs tied together, as we did with the *Kon-Tiki* in the Pacific, or on some bundles of papyrus reeds, as we did with the *Ra* in the Atlantic. With no effort and no motor we were pushed by the winds and currents from one continent to another in a few weeks.

11   After we abandon the outworn image of infinite space in the ocean, we are still left with many wrong or useless notions about biological life and vulnerability. Marine life is concentrated in about 4 percent of the ocean's total body of water, whereas roughly 96 percent is just about as poor in life as is a desert ashore. We all know, and should bear in mind, that sunlight is needed to permit photosynthesis for the marine plankton on which all fishes and whales directly or indirectly base their subsistence. In the sunny tropics the upper layer of light used in photosynthesis extends down to a maximum depth of 80 to 100 meters. In the northern latitudes, even on a bright summer's day, this zone reaches no more than 15 to 20 meters below the surface. Because much of the most toxic pollutants are buoyant and stay on the surface (notably all the pesticides and other poisons based on chlorinated hydrocarbons), this concentration of both life and venom in the same restricted body of water is most unfortunate.

12   What is worse is the fact that life is not evenly distributed throughout this thin surface layer. Ninety percent of all marine species are concentrated above the continental shelves next to land. The water above these littoral shelves represents an area of only 8 percent of the total ocean surface, which itself represents only 4 percent of the total body of water, and means that much less than half a percent of the ocean space represents the home of 90 percent of all marine life. This concentration of marine life in shallow waters next to the coasts happens to coincide with the area of concentrated dumping and the outlet of all sewers and polluted river months, not to mention silt from chemically treated farm-land. The bulk of some 20,000 known species of fish, some 30,000 species of mollusks, and nearly all the main crustaceans lives in the most exposed waters around the littoral areas. As we know, the reason is that this is the most fertile breeding ground for marine plankton. The marine plant life, the phytoplankton, find here their mineral nutriments, which are brought down by rivers and slit and up from the ocean bottom through coastal upwellings that bring back to the surface the remains of decomposed organisms which have sunk to the bottom through the ages. When we speak of farmable land in any country, we do not include deserts or sterile rock in our calculations. Why then shall we deceive

ourselves by the total size at the ocean when we know that not even 1 percent of its water volume is fertile for the fisherman?

13   Much as been written for or against the activities of some nations that have dumped vast quantities of nuclear waste and obsolete war gases in the sea and excused their actions on the grounds that it was all sealed in special containers. In such shallow waters as the Irish Sea, the English Channel, and the North Sea there are already enough examples of similar "foolproof" containers moving about with bottom currents until they are totally displaced and even crack open with the result that millions of fish are killed or mutilated. In the Baltic Sea, which is shallower than many lakes and which—except for the thin surface layer—has already been killed by pollution, 7,000 tons of arsenic were dumped in cement containers some 40 years ago. These containers have now started to leak. Their combined contents are three times more than is needed to kill the entire population of the earth today.

14   Fortunately, in certain regions modern laws have impeded the danger of dumpings; yet a major threat to marine life remains—the less spectacular but more effective ocean pollution through continuous discharge from sewers and seepage. Except in the Arctic, there is today hardly a creek or a river in the world from which it is safe to drink at the outlet. The more technically advanced the country, the more devastating the threat to the ocean. A few examples picked at random will illustrate the pollution input from the civilized world:

15   French rivers carry 18 billion cubic meters of liquid pollution annually into the sea. The city of Paris alone discharges almost 1.2 million cubic meters of untreated effluent into the Seine every day.

16   The volume of liquid waste from the Federal Republic of Germany is estimated at over 9 billion cubic meters per year, or 25.4 million cubic meters per day, not counting cooling water, which daily amounts to 33.6 million cubic meters. Into the Rhine alone 50,000 tons of waste are discharged daily, including 30,000 tons of sodium chloride from industrial plants.

17   A report from the U.N. Economic and Social Council, issued prior to the Stockholm Conference on the Law of the Sea four years ago, states that the world had then dumped an estimated billion pounds of DDT into our environment and was adding an estimated 100 million more pounds per year. The total world production of pesticides was estimated at more than 1.3 billion pounds annually, and the United States alone exports more than 400 million pounds per year. Most of this ultimately finds its way into the ocean with winds, rain, or silt from land. A certain type of DDT sprayed on crops in East Africa a few years ago was found and identified a few months later in the Bay of Bengal, a good 4,000 miles away.

18   The misconception of a boundless ocean makes the man in the street more concerned about city smog than about the risk of killing the ocean. Yet the tallest chimney in the world does not suffice to send the noxious smoke away into space; it gradually sinks down, and nearly all descends, mixed with rain, snow, and silt, into the ocean. Industrial and urban areas are expanding with the population explosion all over the world, and in the United States alone, waste

products in the form of smoke and noxious fumes amount to it total of 390,000 tons of pollutants every day, or 142 million tons every year.

19   With this immense concentration of toxic matter, life on the continental shelves would in all likelihood have been exterminated or at least severely decimated long since if the ocean had been immobile. The cause for the delayed action, which may benefit man for a few decades but will aggravate the situation for coming generations, is the well-known fact that the ocean rotates like boiling water in a kettle. It churns from east to west, from north to south, from the bottom to the surface, and down again, in perpetual motion. At a U.N. meeting one of the developing countries proposed that if ocean dumping were prohibited by global or regional law, they would offer friendly nations the opportunity of dumping in their own national waters—for a fee, of course!

20   It cannot be stressed too often, however, that it is nothing but a complete illusion when we speak of national waters. We can map and lay claim to the ocean bottom, but not to the mobile sea above it. The water itself is in constant transit. What is considered to be the national waters of Morocco one day turns up as the national waters of Mexico soon after. Meanwhile Mexican national water is soon on its way across the North Atlantic to Norway. Ocean pollution abides by no law.

21   My own transoceanic drifts with the *Kon-Tiki* raft and the reed vessels *Ra I* and *II* were eye-openers to me and my companions as to the rapidity with which so-called national waters displace themselves. The distance from Peru to the Tuamotu Islands in Polynesia is 4,000 miles when it is measured on a map. Yet the *Kon-Tiki* raft had only crossed about 1,000 miles of ocean surface when we arrived. The other 3,000 miles had been granted us by the rapid flow of the current during the 101 days our crossing lasted. But the same raft voyages taught us another and less pleasant lesson: it is possible to pollute the oceans, and it is already being done. In 1947, when the balsa raft *Kon-Tiki* crossed the Pacific, we towed a plankton net behind. Yet we did not collect specimens or even see any sign of human activity in the crystal-clear water until we spotted the wreck of an old sailing ship on the reef where we landed. In 1969 it was therefore a blow to us on board the papyrus raft-ship *Ra* to observe, shortly after our departure from Morocco, that we had sailed into an area filled with ugly clumps of hard asphalt-like material, brownish to pitch black in color, which were floating at close intervals on or just below the water's surface. Later on, we sailed into other areas so heavily polluted with similar clumps that we were reluctant to dip up water with our buckets when we needed a good scrub-down at the end of the day. In between these areas the ocean was clean except for occasional floating oil lumps and other widely scattered refuse such as plastic containers, empty bottles, and cans. Because the ropes holding the papyrus reeds of *Ra I* together burst, the battered wreck was abandoned in polluted waters short of the island of Barbados, and a second crossing was effectuated all the way from Safi in Morocco to Barbados in the West Indies in 1970. This time a systematic day-by-day survey of ocean pollution was carried out, and samples of oil lumps collected were sent to the United Nations together with a detailed report on the observations. This was published

by Secretary-General U Thant as an annex to his report to the Stockholm Conference on the Law of the Sea. It is enough here to repeat that sporadic oil clots drifted by within reach of our dip net during 43 out of the 57 days our transatlantic crossing lasted. The laboratory analysis of the various samples of oil clots collected showed a wide range in the level of nickel and vanadium content, revealing that they originated from different geographical localities. This again proves that they represent not the homogeneous spill from a leaking oil drill or from a wrecked super-tanker, but the steadily accumulating waste from the daily routine washing of sludge from the combined world fleet of tankers.

22   The world was upset when the *Torrey Canyon*'s unintentionally spilled 100,000 tons of oil into the English Channel some years ago; yet this is only a small fraction of the intentional discharge of crude oil sludge through less spectacular, routine tank cleaning. Every year more than *Torrey Canyon*'s spill of a 100,000 tons of oil is intentionally pumped into the Mediterranean alone, and a survey of the sea south of Italy yielded 500 liters of solidified oil for every square kilometer of surface. Both the Americans and the Russians were alarmed by our observations of Atlantic pollution in 1970 and sent out specially equipped oceanographic research vessels to the area. American scientists from Harvard University working with the Bermuda Biological Station for Research found more solidified oil than seaweed per surface unit in the Sargasso Sea and had to give up their plankton catch because their nets were completely plugged up by oil sludge. They estimated, however, a floating stock of 86,000 metric tons of tar in the Northwest Atlantic alone. The Russians, in a report read by the representative of the Soviet Academy of Sciences at a recent pollution conference in Prague, found that pollution in the coastal areas of the Atlantic had already surpassed their tentative limit for what had been considered tolerable, and that a new scale of tolerability would have to be postulated.

23   The problem of oil pollution is in itself a complex one. Various types of crude oil are toxic in different degrees. But they all have one property in common: they attract other chemicals and absorb them like blotting paper, notably the various kinds of pesticides. DDT and other chlorinated hydrocarbons do not dissolve in water, nor do they sink: just as they are absorbed by plankton and other surface organisms, so are they drawn into oil slicks and oil clots, where in some cases they have been rediscovered in stronger concentrations than when originally mixed with dissolvents in the spraying bottles. Oil clots, used as floating support for barnacles, marine worms, and pelagic crabs, were often seen by us from the *Ra*, and these riders are attractive bait for filter-feeding fish and whales, which cannot avoid getting gills and baleens cluttered up by the tarlike oil. Even sharks with their rows of teeth plastered with black oil clots are now reported from the Caribbean Sea. Yet the oil spills and dumping of waste from ships represent a very modest contribution compared with the urban and industrial refuse released from land.

24   That the ocean, given time, will cope with it all, is a common expression of wishful thinking. The ocean has always been a self-purifying filter that has taken care of all global pollution for millions of years. Man is not the first polluter. Since

the morning of time nature itself has been a giant workshop, experimenting, inventing, decomposing, and throwing away waste: the incalculable billions of tons of rotting forest products, decomposing flesh, mud, silt, and excrement. If this waste had not been recycled, the ocean would long since have become a compact soup after millions of years of death and decay, volcanic eruptions, and global erosion. Man is not the first large-scale producer, so why should he become the first disastrous polluter?

25   Man has imitated nature by manipulating atoms, taking them apart and grouping them together in different compositions. Nature turned fish into birds and beasts into man. It found a way to make fruits out of soil and sunshine. It invented radar for bats and whales, and shortwave transceivers for beetles and butterflies. Jet propulsion was installed on squids, and unsurpassed computers were made as brains, for mankind. Marine bacteria and plankton transformed the dead generations into new life. The life cycle of spaceship earth is the closest one can ever get to the greatest of all inventions, *perpetuum mobile*—perpetual-motion machine. And the secret is that nothing was composed by nature that could not be recomposed, recycled, and brought back into service again in another form as another useful wheel in the smoothly running global machinery.

26   This is where man has sidetracked nature. We put atoms together into molecules of types nature had carefully avoided. We invent to our delight immediately useful materials like plastics, pesticides, detergents, and other chemical products hitherto unavailable on planet earth. We rejoice because we can get our laundry whiter than the snow we pollute and because we can exterminate every trace of insect life. We spray bugs and bees, worms and butterflies. We wash and flush the detergents down the drain out to the oysters and fish. Most of our new chemical products are not only toxic: they are in fact created to sterilize and kill. And they keep on displaying these same inherent abilities wherever they end up. Through sewers and seepage they all head for the ocean, where they remain to accumulate as undesired nuts and bolts in between the cog wheels of a so far smoothly running machine. If it had not been for the present generation, man could have gone on polluting the ocean forever with the degradable waste he produced. But with ever-increasing speed and intensity we now produce and discharge into the sea hundreds of thousands of chemicals and other products. They do not evaporate nor do they recycle, but they grow in numbers and quantity and threaten all marine life.

27   We have long known that our modern pesticides have begun to enter the flesh of penguins in the Antarctic and the brains of polar bears and the blubber of whales in the Arctic, all subsisting on plankton and plankton-eating crustaceans and fish in areas far from cities and farmland. We all know that marine pollution has reached global extent in a few decades. We also know that very little or nothing is being done to stop it. Yet there are persons who tell us that there is no reason to worry, that the ocean is so big and surely science must have everything under control. City smog is being fought through intelligent legislation. Certain lakes and rivers have been improved by leading the sewers down to the sea. But where, may we ask, is the global problem of ocean pollution under control?

What important features of the vessel from which Heyerdahl made his observations can you observe in this photo?

28   No breathing species could live on this planet until the surface layer of the ocean was filled with phytoplankton, as our planet in the beginning was only surrounded by sterile gases. These minute plant species manufactured so much oxygen that it rose above the surface to help form the atmosphere we have today. All life on earth depended upon this marine plankton for its evolution and continued subsistence. Today, more than ever before, mankind depends on the welfare of this marine plankton for his future survival as a species. With the population explosion we need to harvest even more protein from the sea. Without plankton there will be no fish. With our rapid expansion of urban and industrial areas and the continuous disappearance of jungle and forest, we shall be ever more dependent on the plankton for the very air we breathe. Neither man nor any other terrestrial beast could have bred had plankton not preceded them. Take away this indispensable life in the shallow surface areas of the sea, and life ashore will be unfit for coming generations. A dead ocean means a dead planet.

■ ■ ▨

MEANING

1. Why was it important for Heyerdahl to challenge the concept that the ocean was immune to pollution?

2. In Heyerdahl's view, what accounts for the mistaken impression that there is a funda-mental difference between the ocean and other large bodies of water?

3. To what types of pollution is the ocean most vulnerable? Why does one form of pollu-tion make other kinds worse?

4. What catastrophic scenarios does Heyerdahl mention, and how might they be expected to alter his audience's perceptions?

TECHNIQUE

1. How do Heyerdahl's illustrations of midocean pollution dramatize the extent of the problem?

2. How does Heyerdahl use statistics and comparisons with both buildings and smaller bodies of water to support his conclusions?

3. **Other Patterns.** Where does Heyerdahl use **process analysis** to explain the sequence by which bodies of water become polluted?

LANGUAGE

1. Why does Heyerdahl challenge the popular concepts of "the bottomless sea" and "the boundless ocean"?

2. How does Heyerdahl use references to his own pioneering voyages (on the *Ra* and the *Kon-Tiki*) to add credibility to his analysis?

3. If you don't know the meaning of the following words, look them up: *abyss* (4), *vulnerable* (7), *astronomical* (8), *diameter* (8), *photosynthesis* (11), *buoyant* (11), *crustaceans* (12), *annex* (21), *indispensable* (28).

SUGGESTIONS FOR WRITING

1. **Critical Writing.** What are the foremost environmental issues today? Discuss one. How was the problem diagnosed, and what attempts, if any, have been made to solve it?

2. How has the premium that is put on excessive packaging of products in a throwaway society made the problem worse?

3. There have been dramatic reversals in our treatment of the natural world since Heyerdahl wrote this essay in 1975. Identify one of these, and write a short report incorporating the **process** that has been taken to solve the problem.

4. **Thematic Links.** Compare the impacts of civilization on the environment in the accounts by Heyerdahl and by Joseph K. Skinner in "Big Mac and the Tropical Forests" (Chapter 9, "Cause and Effect").

DALAI LAMA

The Role of Religion in Modern Society

The preeminent religious authority in Buddhism, the Dalai Lama, Tenzin Gyatso (b. 1935), was born into a farming family in northeastern Tibet. His ascension to this role began when he was two years old and was found to be the reborn soul of the thirteenth Dalai Lama. After a period of extensive studies in religion and philosophy, he attained what is equivalent to a doctorate in Buddhist studies. China's invasion of Tibet in 1950 propelled him into a position of leadership, but he was forced to flee to northern India in 1959; there, he established a community of exiled Tibetans. He wrote about this difficult time in *Freedom in Exile: The Autobiography of the Dalai Lama* (1990). This firsthand experience of religious intolerance and many other examples around the world of religion as a divisive rather than a uniting force was the impetus for his writing *The Ethics for a New Millennium* (1999), in which the following essay first appeared. His message goes beyond merely advocating tolerance and seeks to promote compassion as the essential quality necessary for interreligious harmony. The Dalai Lama's lifelong nonviolent campaign to seek freedom for Tibet and his inspiring personal example were recognized with the Nobel Peace Prize in 1989. A recent work, *The Universe in a Single Atom: The Convergence of Science and Spirituality* (2005), continues the Dalai Lama's unique way of bringing disparate realms together.

Before You Read

What do you know about the way problems are approached in Buddhism (or another religion)?

■ ■ ▨

1   It is a sad fact of human history that religion has been a major source of conflict. Even today, individuals are killed, communities destroyed, and societies destabilized as a result of religious bigotry and hatred. It is no wonder that many question the place of religion in human society. Yet when we think carefully, we find that conflict in the name of religion arises from two principal sources. There is that which arises simply as a result of religious diversity—the doctrinal, cultural, and practical differences between one religion and another. Then there is the conflict that arises in the context of political, economic, and other factors, mainly at the institutional level. Interreligious harmony is the key to overcoming conflict of the first sort. In the case of the second, some other solution must be found. Secularization and in particular the separation of the religious hierarchy from the institutions of the state may go some way to reducing such institutional problems. Our concern in this chapter is with interreligious harmony, however.

For a visual to accompany this selection, see color insert photo C-3.

2   This is an important aspect of what I have called universal responsibility. But before examining the matter in detail, it is perhaps worth considering the question of whether religion is really relevant in the modern world. Many people argue that it is not. Now I have observed that religious belief is not a precondition either of ethical conduct or of happiness itself. I have also suggested that whether a person practices religion or not, the spiritual qualities of love and compassion, patience, tolerance, forgiveness, humility, and so on are indispensable. At the same time, I should make it clear that I believe that these are most easily and effectively developed within the context of religious practice. I also believe that when an individual sincerely practices religion, that individual will benefit enormously. People who have developed a firm faith, grounded in understanding and rooted in daily practice, are in general much better at coping with adversity than those who have not. I am convinced, therefore, that religion has enormous potential to benefit humanity. Properly employed, it is an extremely effective instrument for establishing human happiness. In particular it can play a leading role in encouraging people to develop a sense of responsibility toward others and of the need to be ethically disciplined.

3   On these grounds, therefore, I believe that religion is still relevant today. But consider this too: some years ago, the body of a Stone Age man was recovered from the ice of the European Alps. Despite being more than five thousand years old, it was perfectly preserved. Even its clothes were largely intact. I remember thinking at the time that were it possible to bring this individual back to life for a day, we would find that we have much in common with him. No doubt we would find that he too was concerned for his family and loved ones, for his health and so on. Differences of culture and expression notwithstanding, we would still be able to identify with one another on the level of feeling. And there could be no reason to suppose any less concern with finding happiness and avoiding suffering on his part than on ours. If religion, with its emphasis on overcoming suffering through the practice of ethical discipline and cultivation of love and compassion, can be conceived of as relevant in the past, it is hard to see why it should not be equally so today. Granted that in the past the value of religion may have been more obvious, in that human suffering was more explicit due to the lack of modern facilities. But because we humans still suffer, albeit today this is experienced more internally as mental and emotional affliction, and because religion in addition to its salvific truth claims is concerned to help us overcome suffering, surely it must still be relevant.

4   How then might we bring about the harmony that is necessary to overcome interreligious conflict? As in the case of individuals engaged in the discipline of restraining their response to negative thoughts and emotions and cultivating spiritual qualities, the key lies in developing understanding. We must first identify the factors that obstruct it. Then we must find ways to overcome them.

5   Perhaps the most significant obstruction to interreligious harmony is lack of appreciation of the value of others' faith traditions. Until comparatively recently, communication between different cultures, even different communities, was slow or nonexistent. For this reason, sympathy for other faith traditions was not necessarily very important—except of course where members of different religions

lived side by side. But this attitude is no longer viable. In today's increasingly complex and interdependent world, we are compelled to acknowledge the existence of other cultures, different ethnic groups, and, of course, other religious faiths. Whether we like it or not, most of us now experience this diversity on a daily basis.

6   I believe that the best way to overcome ignorance and bring about understanding is through dialogue with members of other faith traditions. This I see occurring in a number of different ways. Discussions among scholars in which the convergence and perhaps more importantly the divergence between different faith traditions are explored and appreciated are very valuable. On another level, it is helpful when there are encounters between ordinary but practicing followers of different religions in which each shares their experiences. This is perhaps the most effective way of appreciating others' teachings. In my own case, for example, my meetings with the late Thomas Merton, a Catholic monk of the Cistercian order, were deeply inspiring. They helped me develop a profound admiration for the teachings of Christianity. I also feel that occasional meetings between religious leaders joining together to pray for a common cause are extremely useful. The gathering at Assisi in Italy in 1986, when representatives of the world's major religions gathered to pray for peace, was, I believe, tremendously beneficial to many religious believers insofar as it symbolized the solidarity and a commitment to peace of all those taking part.

7   Finally, I feel that the practice of members of different faith traditions going on joint pilgrimages together can be very helpful. It was in this spirit that in 1993 I went to Lourdes, and then to Jerusalem, a site holy to three of the world's great religions. I have also paid visits to various Hindu, Islamic, Jain, and Sikh shrines both in India and abroad. More recently, following a seminar devoted to discussing and practicing meditation in the Christian and Buddhist traditions, I joined an historic pilgrimage of practitioners of both traditions in a program of prayers, meditation, and dialogue under the Bodhi tree at Bodh Gaya in India. This is one of Buddhism's most important shrines.

8   When exchanges like these occur, followers of one tradition will find that, just as in the case of their own, the teachings of others' faiths are a source both of spiritual inspiration and of ethical guidance to their followers. It will also become clear that irrespective of doctrinal and other differences, all the major world religions are concerned with helping individuals to become good human beings. All emphasize love and compassion, patience, tolerance, forgiveness, humility, and so on, and all are capable of helping individuals to develop these. Moreover, the example given by the founders of each major religion clearly demonstrates a concern for helping others find happiness through developing these qualities. So far as their own lives were concerned, each conducted themselves with great simplicity. Ethical discipline and love for all others was the hallmark of their lives. They did not live luxuriously like emperors and kings. Instead, they voluntarily accepted suffering—without consideration of the hardships involved—in order to benefit humanity as a whole. In their teachings, all placed special emphasis on developing love and compassion and renouncing selfish

desires. And each of them called on us to transform our hearts and minds. Indeed, whether we have faith or not, all are worthy of our profound admiration.

9   At the same time as engaging in dialogue with followers of other religions, we must, of course, implement in our daily life the teachings of our own religion. Once we have experienced the benefit of love and compassion, and of ethical discipline, we will easily recognize the value of other's teachings. But for this, it is essential to realize that religious practice entails a lot more than merely saying, "I believe" or, as in Buddhism, "I take refuge." There is also more to it than just visiting temples, or shrines, or churches. And taking religious teachings is of little benefit if they do not enter the heart but remain at the level of intellect alone. Simply relying on faith without understanding and without implementation is of limited value. I often tell Tibetans that carrying a *mala* (something like a rosary) does not make a person a genuine religious practitioner. The efforts we make sincerely to transform ourselves spiritually are what make us genuine religious practitioners.

10   We come to see the overriding importance of genuine practice when we recognize that, along with ignorance, individuals' unhealthy relationships with their beliefs is the other major factor in religious disharmony. Far from applying the teachings of their religion in our personal lives, we have a tendency to use them to reinforce our self-centered attitudes. We relate to our religion as something we own or as a label that separates us from others. Surely this is misguided? Instead of using the nectar of religion to purify the poisonous elements of our hearts and minds, there is a danger when we think like this of using these negative elements to poison the nectar of religion.

11   Yet we must acknowledge that this reflects another problem, one which is implicit in all religions. I refer to the claims each has of being the one "true" religion. How are we to resolve this difficulty? It is true that from the point of view of the individual practitioner, it is essential to have a single-pointed commitment to one's own faith. It is also true that this depends on the deep conviction that one's own path is the sole mediator of truth. But at the same time, we have to find some means of reconciling this belief with the reality of a multiplicity of similar claims. In practical terms, this involves individual practitioners finding a way at least to accept the validity of the teachings of other religions while maintaining a wholehearted commitment of their own. As far as the validity of the metaphysical truth claims of a given religion is concerned, that is of course the internal business of that particular tradition.

12   In my own case, I am convinced that Buddhism provides me with the most effective framework within which to situate my efforts to develop spiritually through cultivating love and compassion. At the same time, I must acknowledge that while Buddhism represents the best path for me—that is, it suits my character, my temperament, my inclinations, and my cultural background—the same will be true of Christianity for Christians. For them, Christianity is the best way. On the basis of my conviction, I cannot, therefore, say that Buddhism is best for everyone.

13   I sometimes think of religion in terms of medicine for the human spirit. Independent of its usage and suitability to a particular individual in a particular condition, we really cannot judge a medicine's efficacy. We are not justified

in saying this medicine is very good because of such and such ingredients. If you take the patient and the medicine's effect on that person out of the equation, it hardly makes sense. What is relevant is to say that in the case of this particular patient with its particular illness, this medicine is the most effective. Similarly with different religious traditions, we can say that this one is most effective for this particular individual. But it is unhelpful to try to argue on the basis of philosophy or metaphysics that one religion is better than another. The important thing is surely its effectiveness in individual cases.

14   My way to resolve the seeming contradiction between each religion's claim to "one truth and one religion" and the reality of the multiplicity of faiths is thus to understand that in the case of a single individual, there can indeed be only one truth, one religion. However, from the perspective of human society at large, we must accept the concept of "many truths, many religions." To continue with our medical analogy, in the case of one particular patient, the suitable medicine is in fact the one medicine. But clearly that does not mean that there may not be other medicines suitable to other patients.

15   To my way of thinking, the diversity that exists among the various religious traditions is enormously enriching. There is thus no need to try to find ways of saying that ultimately all religions are the same. They are similar in that they all emphasize the indispensability of love and compassion in the context of ethical discipline. But to say this is not to say that they are all essentially one. The contradictory understanding of creation and beginninglessness articulated by Buddhism, Christianity, and Hinduism, for example, means that in the end we have to part company when it comes to metaphysical claims, in spite of the many practical similarities that undoubtedly exist. These contradictions may not be very important in the beginning stages of religious practice. But as we advance along the path of one tradition or another, we are compelled at some point to acknowledge fundamental differences. For example, the concept of rebirth in Buddhism and various other ancient Indian traditions may turn out to be incompatible with the Christian idea of salvation. This need not be a cause for dismay, however. Even within Buddhism itself, in the realm of metaphysics there are diametrically opposing views. At the very least, such diversity means that we have different frameworks within which to locate ethical discipline and the development of spiritual values. That is why I do not advocate a super or a new world religion. It would mean that we would lose the unique characteristics of the different faith traditions.

16   Some people, it is true, hold that the Buddhist concept of *shunyata*, or emptiness, is ultimately the same as certain approaches to understanding the concept of God. Nevertheless, there remain difficulties with this. The first is that while of course we can interpret these concepts, to what extent can we be faithful to the original teachings if we do so? There are compelling similarities between the Mahayana Buddhist concept of *Dharmakaya*, *Sambogakaya*, and *Nirmanakaya* and the Christian trinity of God as Father, Son, and Holy Spirit. But to say, on the basis of this, that Buddhism and Christianity are ultimately the same is to go a bit far, I think! As an old Tibetan saying goes, we must beware of trying to put a yak's head on a sheep's body—or vice versa.

17   What is required instead is that we develop a genuine sense of religious pluralism in spite of the different claims of different faith traditions. This is especially true if we are serious in our respect for human rights as a universal principle. In this regard, I find the concept of a world parliament of religions very appealing. To begin with, the word "parliament" conveys a sense of democracy, while the plural "religions" underlines the importance of the principle of a multiplicity of faith traditions. They truly pluralist perspective on religion which the idea of such a parliament suggests could, I believe be, of great help. It would avoid the extremes of religious bigotry on the one hand, and the urge toward unnecessary syncretism on the other.

18   Connected with this issue of interreligious harmony, I should perhaps say something about religious conversion. This is a question which must be taken extremely seriously. It is essential to realize that the mere fact of conversion alone will not make an individual a better person, that is to say, a more disciplined, a more compassionate, and a warm-hearted person. Much more helpful, therefore, is for the individual to concentrate on transforming themselves spiritually through the practice of restraint, virtue, and compassion. To the extent that the insights or practices of other religions are useful or relevant to our own faith, it is valuable to learn from others. In some cases, it may even be helpful to adopt certain of them. Yet when this is done wisely, we can remain firmly committed to our own faith. This way is best because it carries with it no danger of confusion, especially with respect to the different ways of life that tend to go with different faith traditions.

19   Given the diversity to be found among individual human beings, it is of course bound to be the case that out of many millions of practitioners of a particular religion, a handful will find that another religion's approach to ethics and spiritual development is more satisfactory. For some, the concept of rebirth and karma will seem highly effective in inspiring the aspiration to develop love and compassion within the context of responsibility. For others, the concept of a transcendent, loving creator will come to seem more so. In such circumstances, it is crucial for those individuals to question themselves again and again. They must ask, "Am I attracted to this other religion for the right reasons? Is it merely the cultural and ritual aspects that are appealing? Or is it the essential teachings? Do I suppose that if I convert to this new religion it will be less demanding than my present one?" I say this because it has often struck me that when people do convert to a religion outside their own heritage, quite often they adopt certain superficial aspects of the culture to which their new faith belongs. But their practice may not go very much deeper than that.

20   In the case of a person who decides after a process of long and mature reflection to adopt a different religion, it is very important that they remember the positive contribution to humanity of each religious tradition. The danger is that the individual may, in seeking to justify their decision to others, criticize their previous faith. It is essential to avoid this. Just because that tradition is no longer effective in the case of one individual does not mean it is no longer of benefit to humanity. On the contrary, we can be certain that it has been an inspiration

to millions of people in the past, that it inspires millions today, and that it will inspire millions in the path of love and compassion in the future.

21 The important point to keep in mind is that ultimately the whole purpose of religion is to facilitate love and compassion, patience, tolerance, humility, forgiveness, and so on. If we neglect these, changing our religion will be of no help. In the same way, even if we are fervent believers in our own faith, it will avail us nothing if we neglect to implement these qualities in our daily lives. Such a believer is no better off than a patient with some fatal illness who merely reads a medical treatise but fails to undertake the treatment prescribed.

22 Moreover, if we who are practitioners of religion are not compassionate and disciplined, how can we expect it of others? If we can establish genuine harmony derived from mutual respect and understanding, religion has enormous potential to speak with authority on such vital moral questions as peace and disarmament, social and political justice, the natural environment, and many other matters affecting all humanity. But until we put our own spiritual teachings into practice, we will never be taken seriously. And this means, among other things, setting a good example through developing good relations with other faith traditions.

■ ■ ■

Meaning

1. Why does the Dalai Lama begin his essay by citing the role of religion as a devisive force in human history?

2. What was the significance of the Dalai Lama's meeting with a Catholic monk, Thomas Merton?

3. How does the Dalai Lama suggest that we overcome one of the main obstacles to religious harmony, that is, the claim of each religion that it is the one "true" religion?

4. Why is compassion the essential quality in developing interreligious harmony?

Technique

1. How does the analogy drawn from medicine illustrate the need to develop tolerance toward the teachings and practices of other people's faiths?

2. What aspects of the Dalai Lama's proposal emphasize the need to preserve the unique differences among religions?

3. **Other Patterns.** At what points does the Dalai Lama insert a personal **narrative** to illustrate the benefits of interreligious harmony?

Language

1. Where does the Dalai Lama explain terms and concepts in Buddhism that might be unfamiliar to his readers?

2. How would you characterize the Dalai Lama's tone? Would this essay have been equally effective if you did not know who the author was?

3. If you don't know the meaning of the following words, look them up: *destabilized* (1), *bigotry* (1), *secularization* (1), *viable* (5), *diversity* (5), *implement* (9), *nectar* (10), *metaphysical* (11), *syncretism* (17), *karma* (19).

SUGGESTIONS FOR WRITING

1. **Critical Writing.** The Dalai Lama asserts that the pursuit of spiritual qualities is "most easily and effectively developed within the context of religious practice." Would this be equally possible in a secular context? Why or why not?
2. For a study of interreligious commonalities, see Denise Lardner Carmody's *In the Path of the Masters: Understanding the Spirituality of Buddha, Confucius, Jesus, and Muhammad* (1994). Read this text, and write an essay exploring the relationship between it and the Dalai Lama's ideas.
3. What current events **illustrate** the Dalai Lama's main concerns?
4. **Thematic Links.** Discuss the problem-solving methods of the Dalai Lama in overcoming religious intolerance in relation to how C. P. Ellis overcame racial intolerance in "Why I Quit the Klan" (Chapter 9, "Cause and Effect").

GINA KOLATA

An Incident in Hong Kong

News alerts are issued periodically for occurrences of bird flu, and scientists are watchful for evidence that it is mutating into a pandemic like the one in 1918 that killed millions of people. But few people know that the first alarm went off in 1997 when a three-year-old boy in Hong Kong died suddenly of a mysterious disease. A science writer for the *New York Times* since 1987, Gina Kolata (b. 1948), in the following excerpt from *Flu: The Story of the Great Influenza Pandemic of 1918 and the Search for the Virus that Caused It* (1999), retraces the complex search for clues by medical researchers who needed to know whether this event was likely to be a harbinger of things to come. The result is a real-life detective story that is as compelling as any fictionalized one. Kolata's background includes a degree in molecular biology from MIT and a M.A. in mathematics from the University of Maryland. She has published numerous books, including *Rethinking Thin: The New Science of Weight Loss and the Myths and Realities of Dieting* (2007).

BEFORE YOU READ

How does the diagram on page 579 complement Kolata's account?

■ ■ ▨

1   Dr. Nancy Cox was on vacation in Wyoming when she got the call from her lab in Atlanta. Virologists there had done what they thought would be a routine test to determine the strain of an influenza virus isolated from a patient that past May. The sample had been stored at the lab for about a month and taken up in its turn for analysis. But when Cox, who directs the influenza lab at the Centers for Disease Control and Prevention heard the result, her heart started to pound and she felt adrenaline rush through her body. The virus was of type H5N1. It was a flu strain that should never have infected a human being. Even worse, Cox was told, the person it infected was a child, a three-year-old boy in Hong Kong. And he had died.

2   It was August 1997. Jeffery Taubenberger had just published his initial analysis of the 1918 flu virus genes that he had extracted from Private Vaughan's lung tissue. But it was too soon to say what had made the 1918 flu virus so lethal. The flu virologists in Cox's group had no way of knowing whether the virus that had killed the Hong Kong boy shared deadly features with the 1918 flu and whether, like the 1918 virus, the Hong Kong virus would sweep the world, spreading a swath of devastation in its wake. The question leaped to Cox's mind: Was this the first sounding of a fatal pandemic? On the other hand, she realized, it might instead be a repeat of the sort of false alarm raised by the soldier who died of a swine flu virus in 1976.

For a visual to accompany this selection, see color insert photo C-4.

How bird flu can turn deadly

Strains of influenza similar to the one that caused a pandemic in 1918 are found in water birds, and one of them could mutate, or change its genes, and threaten humans again.

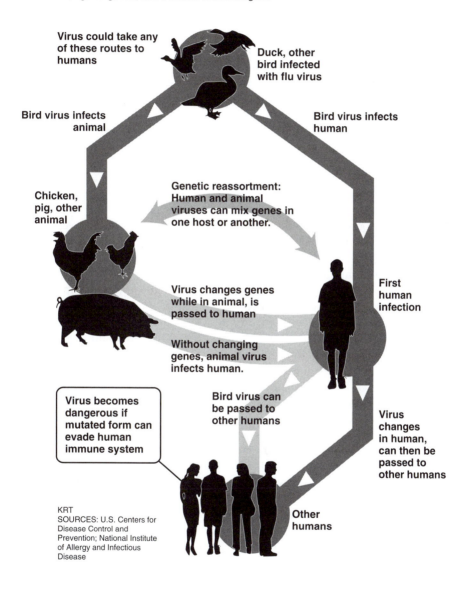

Virus could take any of these routes to humans

Duck, other bird infected with flu virus

Bird virus infects animal

Bird virus infects human

Genetic reassortment: Human and animal viruses can mix genes in one host or another.

Chicken, pig, other animal

Virus changes genes while in animal, is passed to human

First human infection

Without changing genes, animal virus infects human.

Virus becomes dangerous if mutated form can evade human immune system

Bird virus can be passed to other humans

Virus changes in human, can then be passed to other humans

Other humans

KRT
SOURCES: U.S. Centers for Disease Control and Prevention; National Institute of Allergy and Infectious Disease

3   Cox spent long afternoons in conference calls with her staff and other scientists discussing what to do. She tossed in bed through several long, sleepless nights worrying. The flu virologists of the world could not afford to make a mistake.

4   Until that moment, there was little reason to panic over the viral infection. Yes, the boy's illness had been frightening, but his doctors were not even convinced that a virus had killed him.

5   The boy had died on May 9, in a hospital tethered to a respirator. He had been healthy and entirely normal, striding into his preschool class, playing with his friends, with no illnesses other than the usual runny noses and earaches that plague young children. Then, one day in early May, he got a respiratory infection that quickly turned into viral pneumonia. Soon he was hospitalized, unable to breathe on his own. His doctors diagnosed viral pneumonia complicated by Reye's syndrome, a disorder that sometimes follows viral infections like influenza or chicken pox. It is a rare disease that strikes children and teenagers and it can be fatal. The patient's brain fills with fluid, creating so much pressure inside the skull that the brain starts to compress the delicate nerves at its base, the brain stem, that control breathing and heart rate. When the brain stem is damaged, Reye's victims die.

6   So even though the child died within days of becoming ill, it was not clear what had killed him—a viral illness or Reye's syndrome. Nonetheless, the hospital staff was frightened and saddened and sought answers. What kind of virus had precipitated this death? How could a vibrant and robust child have become so sick and died so quickly? The child's doctors sent washings from his throat to a government virology lab for analysis. The samples, tests revealed, contained just one kind of virus, an influenza virus. Then the difficulty occurred. Try as they might, the lab scientists could not identify the strain of influenza.

7   Labs, like the one in Hong Kong that analyzed the throat washings from the three-year-old boy, keep a set of antibodies that recognize the most common types of the viral surface proteins—hemagglutinin and neuraminidase—that define flu strains. Scientists mark the antibodies with chemicals that will glow if the antibodies latch on to a flu virus. Then they swish a solution of these antibodies onto a petri dish where the flu virus is growing. If the antibodies hook up with a flu virus, the petri dish's contents will glisten red.

8   The boy's virus never elicited such an effect. Even though the lab workers tested the boy's flu virus with every antibody they had, they came up empty-handed. Nothing matched.

9   The lab workers in Hong Kong were not alarmed. After all, their set of antibodies would attach to the most likely strains of flu viruses, but they by no means had a complete set of antibodies. They passed the sample on to a specialty lab in Rotterdam for further testing.

10   Since the Hong Kong scientists did not convey a sense of urgency, the Rotterdam scientists simply put the specimen on their list of things to do. In July, they sent some of the sample to Cox's group at the Centers for Disease Control and Prevention.

11   "They didn't send us any paperwork indicating that it was anything unusual," Cox said. "As far as they knew, it was just another influenza virus." And so her

group put the specimen in its queue. "It was processed along with other viruses," Cox notes.

12   That meant that it was a month before Cox's group got around to looking at it. The Atlanta lab, one of four in the world that keep a lookout for emerging flu strains, is awash in flu samples, receiving several thousand specimens each year. It's part of the global flu surveillance network that allows virologists to discern the first signs of the next year's predominant flu strain—in time to start making vaccines—and that lets them keep an ever-vigilant watch for new strains of flu.

13   The surveillance network evolved over the years so that now, in the United States, about 110 local influenza centers collect flu viruses in their own regions and determine their type. About eighty-four countries are linked in an international network. The group from the Centers for Disease Control and Prevention looks at flu viruses submitted from all of them. Some places send in just a subset of their viruses, a representative sample. Others send in everything they come across.

14   "We ask for viruses isolated early and late in the flu season—that sometimes gives us a clue to what is going to happen in the season that is coming or the next season. We ask for isolates from the peak of flu activity and we ask for typical strains and unusual strains," Cox said.

15   The Hong Kong virus came through that surveillance network.

16 As a reference lab for influenza, Cox's lab—and the one in Rotterdam—had sets of antibodies to flu strains that no one ever expected to see in humans. These were strains of flu viruses that infect birds. While very occasionally a bird flu mutates and kills birds, for the most part bird flus are entirely benign. Instead of infecting cells of the lung and causing sickness, the virus lives peacefully in cells of the birds' intestines, causing no symptoms. In theory, a bird flu could not infect a human because the virus should require cellular enzymes found in bird intestinal cells but not in human lung cells. Yet if, against all odds, a bird flu virus was infecting people, it would have hemagglutinin and neuraminidase proteins that had never been seen before by a human being. No human would be immune to such a virus. The whole world was at risk.

17   Worse yet, if a bird flu did jump to humans, and if the event happened in Asia, the scenario fit all too well into a chilling story developed by two leading flu virologists, Dr. Robert Webster of St. Jude Children's Research Hospital in Memphis and Dr. Kennedy Shortridge of the University of Hong Kong.

18   Webster proposed that the worst flu pandemics, the one in 1918 being at the far end of bad, start with a bird flu. But before it can infect a person, it has to be humanized—that is, to change in a way that would allow it to keep the birdlike features that make it so infectious and yet acquire human flu-like properties that would allow it to grow in the lung cells of a human being. That crucial step, Webster said, typically takes place in pigs. Pigs bridge the gap between birds and humans—both bird flu strains and human flu strains can grow in pigs' bodies.

19   An unfortunate pig that happens to be infected with both a bird and human virus at the same time can become a mixing bowl, with the genes from the two

types of flu viruses recombining in its cells to form a new hybrid virus that can infect humans but has some genes from the bird flu, genes that make the newly emerging virus more dangerous than any that had been around before. Thus the stage can be set for a worldwide pandemic.

20   As evidence for his hypothesis, Webster posited that the 1918 virus probably started out in a bird, moved to a pig, and then infected people, which is why those who lived through the epidemic had antibodies to swine flu. Moreover, the only two pandemics in which flu viruses had been isolated, the "Asian" flu of 1957 and the "Hong Kong" flu of 1968, involved virus strains that seem to have come, indirectly, from birds. (Earlier pandemics took place before virologists knew how to test flu strains and there were no subsequent pandemics.)

21   Kennedy Shortridge elaborated from there. Asia, he said, is the influenza epicenter. The virus thrives in ducks, in particular, that are omnipresent in southern China. Those birds have served as a reservoir for dangerous viral strains that have become converted into human flus because of an ingenious system devised by Chinese rice farmers that inadvertently ensures that the flu strains have plenty of opportunity to jump from ducks to pigs to people.

22   As early as the seventeenth century, these farmers discovered a way to keep their rice crops free of weeds and insects and, at the same time, keep a flock of plump ducks around for food. While the rice is growing, they put ducks on the flooded fields. The ducks eat insects and even weeds, but do not touch the rice. When the rice starts to blossom, the farmers remove the ducks from the rice fields and put them on waterways and ponds. After the rice is harvested, the farmers put the ducks back on the dry rice fields, where they eat the grains of rice that have fallen to the ground. Now the ducks are ready for slaughter.

23   The problem, however, is that the farmers also keep pigs that live alongside the ducks. And so, Shortridge said, "when you domesticate the duck, you unwittingly bring the flu virus to humans."

24   Shortridge notes that influenza epidemics always seem to start in Asia—in southern China in particular, exactly the place where the rice-duck-pig system is in place. "Historical records always refer to this part of the world," he said.

25   Now, as Cox looked at the lab records from the little boy who died in Hong Kong, she knew she was seeing an unprecedented and possibly horrifying event. Here was a flu virus. It came from Hong Kong. It was a bird virus, but unlike any other bird flu virus ever known, it seemed to have skipped the pig step altogether since it had hemagglutinin and neuraminidase proteins that are characteristic of bird, but not pig, flus. It infected a three-year-old boy. And it killed him.

■ ■ ▨

MEANING

1. Why was it crucial for scientists to understand the means by which the three-year-old boy who died was infected?

2. Why didn't scientists in Hong Kong attach any sense of urgency to the specimen they had obtained from the three-year-old boy?

3. Why do influenza epidemics seem to begin in the same place, that is, southern China?

4. Why is it important to determine the link between swine flu, bird flu, and influenza to understand why a recurrence of a 1918-style outbreak could occur?

TECHNIQUE

1. How does the case history of the doctor who sought to discover why a three-year-old boy died in Hong Kong define the problem in human terms?

2. How does the problem-solving procedure that was followed in this case require ruling out false causes?

3. **Other Patterns.** What role does **classification** play in the search for an exact cause of the boy's death?

LANGUAGE

1. How does Kolata make technical procedures comprehensible to the general reader?

2. How is the title intended to provoke curiosity as to what started the quest to forestall a possible epidemic?

3. If you don't know the meaning of the following words, look them up: *influenza* (1), *adrenaline* (1), *surveillance* (15), *mutates* (16), *pandemics* (18), *epidemics* (24).

SUGGESTIONS FOR WRITING

1. What insight does Kolata offer into the resources that can be applied to the problem of detecting new incidences of bird flu?

2. Along with the possible recurrence of bird flu, what other previous diseases might be reappearing, and what is being done to prevent this?

3. **Critical Writing.** Describe the measures that are being taken to prevent the recurrence of the 1918-style pandemic.

4. **Thematic Links.** In what ways do medical researchers benefit from having a case history in which they can examine the variables as they attempt to solve a problem, as in Kolata's account and Austin Bunn's "The Bittersweet Science"?

DAVID R. COUNTS

Too Many Bananas

Gift giving and the obligation it creates to return a comparable gift are widely recognized as the basis for many small-scale societies. Anthropologist David R. Counts (b. 1934) studied a striking instance of this when he lived with his wife and children in Papua New Guinea and discovered that the rules of reciprocity were far more intricate than he had assumed. We can share his amazement in the following selection from *The Humbled Anthropologist: Tales from the Pacific* (1990). Currently, Counts teaches at Okanagan University College in British Columbia.

BEFORE YOU READ

How would receiving a gift, even one that you did not want, obligate you to reciprocate?

■ ■ ▨

NO WATERMELON AT ALL

1   The woman came all the way through the village, walking between the two rows of houses facing each other between the beach and the bush, to the very last house standing on a little spit of land at the mouth of the Kaini River. She was carrying a watermelon on her head, and the house she came to was the government "rest house," maintained by the villagers for the occasional use of visiting officials. Though my wife and I were graduate students, not officials, and had asked for permission to stay in the village for the coming year, we were living in the rest house while the debate went on about where a house would be built for us. When the woman offered to sell us the watermelon for two shillings, we happily agreed, and the kids were delighted at the prospect of watermelon after yet another meal of rice and bully beef. The money changed hands and the seller left to return to her village, a couple of miles along the coast to the east.

2   It seemed only seconds later that the woman was back, reluctantly accompanying Kolia, the man who had already made it clear to us that he was the leader of the village. Kolia had no English, and at that time, three or four days into our first stay in Kandoka Village on the island of New Britain in Papua New Guinea, we had very little Tok Pisin. Language difficulties notwithstanding, Kolia managed to make his message clear: The woman had been outrageously wrong to sell us the watermelon for two shillings and we were to return it to her and reclaim our money immediately. When we tried to explain that we thought the price to be fair and were happy with the bargain, Kolia explained again and finally made it clear that we had missed the point. The problem wasn't that we had paid too much; it was that we had paid at all. Here he was,

---

For a visual to accompany this selection, see color insert photo C-5.

a leader, responsible for us while we were living in his village, and we had shamed him. How would it look if he let guests in his village *buy* food? If we wanted watermelons, or bananas, or anything else, all that was necessary was to let him know. He told us that it would be all right for us to give little gifts to people who brought food to us (and they surely would), but *no one* was to sell food to us. If anyone were to try—like this woman from Lauvore—then we should refuse. There would be plenty of watermelons without us buying them.

3   The woman left with her watermelon, disgruntled, and we were left with our two shillings. But we had learned the first lesson of many about living in Kandoka. We didn't pay money for food again that whole year, and we did get lots of food brought to us . . . but we never got another watermelon. That one was the last of the season.

Lesson 1:
In a society where food is shared or gifted as part of social life, you may not buy it with money.

TOO MANY BANANAS

4 In the couple of months that followed the watermelon incident, we managed to become at least marginally competent in Tok Pisin, to negotiate the construction of a house on what we hoped was neutral ground, and to settle into the routine of our fieldwork. As our village leader had predicted, plenty of food was brought to us. Indeed, seldom did a day pass without something coming in— some sweet potatoes, a few taro, a papaya, the occasional pineapple, or some bananas—lots of bananas.

5   We had learned our lesson about the money, though, so we never even offered to buy the things that were brought, but instead made gifts, usually of tobacco to the adults or chewing gum to the children. Nor were we so gauche as to haggle with a giver over how much of a return gift was appropriate, though the two of us sometimes conferred as to whether what had been brought was a "two-stick" or a "three-stick" stalk, bundle, or whatever. A "stick" of tobacco was a single large leaf, soaked in rum and then twisted into a ropelike form. This, wrapped in half a sheet of newsprint (torn for use as cigarette paper), sold in the local trade stores for a shilling. Nearly all of the adults in the village smoked a great deal, and they seldom had much cash, so our stocks of twist tobacco and stacks of the Sydney *Morning Herald* (all, unfortunately, the same day's issue) were seen as a real boon to those who preferred "stick" to the locally grown product.

6   We had established a pattern with respect to the gifts of food. When a donor appeared at our veranda we would offer our thanks and talk with them for a few minutes (usually about our children, who seemed to hold a real fascination for the villagers and for whom most of the gifts were intended) and then we would inquire whether they could use some tobacco. It was almost never refused, though occasionally a small bottle of kerosene, a box of matches, some laundry soap, a cup of rice, or a tin of meat would be requested instead of (or even in

addition to) the tobacco. Everyone, even Kolia, seemed to think this arrangement had worked out well.

7   Now, what must be kept in mind is that while we were following their rules— or seemed to be—we were *really still buying food.* In fact we kept a running account of what came in and what we "paid" for it. Tobacco as currency got a little complicated, but since the exchange rate was one stick to one shilling, it was not too much trouble as long as everyone was happy, and meanwhile we could account for the expenditure of "informant fees" and "household expenses." Another thing to keep in mind is that not only did we continue to think in terms of our buying the food that was brought, we thought of them as *selling it.* While it was true they never quoted us a price, they also never asked us if we needed or wanted whatever they had brought. It seemed clear to us that when an adult needed a stick of tobacco, or a child wanted some chewing gum (we had enormous quantities of small packets of Wrigley's for just such eventualities) they would find something surplus to their own needs and bring it along to our "store" and get what they wanted.

8   By late November 1966, just before the rainy season set in, the bananas were coming into flush, and whereas earlier we had received banana gifts by the "hand" (six or eight bananas in a cluster cut from the stalk), donors now began to bring bananas, "for the children," by the *stalk!* The Kaliai among whom we were living are not exactly specialists in banana cultivation—they only recognize about thirty varieties, while some of their neighbors have more than twice that many—but the kinds they produce differ considerably from each other in size, shape, and taste, so we were not dismayed when we had more than one stalk hanging on our veranda. The stalks ripen a bit at the time, and having some variety was nice. Still, by the time our accumulation had reached *four* complete stalks, the delights of variety had begun to pale a bit. The fruits were ripening progressively and it was clear that even if we and the kids ate nothing but bananas for the next week, some would still fall from the stalk onto the floor in a state of gross overripeness. This was the situation as, late one afternoon, a woman came bringing yet another stalk of bananas up the steps of the house.

9   Several factors determined our reaction to her approach: one was that there was literally no way we could possibly use the bananas. We hadn't quite reached the point of being crowded off our veranda by the stalks of fruit, but it was close. Another factor was that we were tired of playing the gift game. We had acquiesced in playing it—no one was permitted to sell us anything, and in turn we only gave things away, refusing under any circumstances to sell tobacco (or anything else) for money. But there had to be a limit. From our perspective what was at issue was that the woman wanted something and she had come to trade for it. Further, what she had brought to trade was something we neither wanted nor could use, and it should have been obvious to her. So we decided to bite the bullet.

10   The woman, Rogi, climbed the stairs to the veranda, took the stalk from where it was balanced on top of her head, and laid it on the floor with the words, "Here are some bananas for the children." Dorothy and I sat near her on the floor and thanked her for her thought but explained, "You know, we really have

too many bananas—we can't use these; maybe you ought to give them to some-one else. . . ." The woman looked mystified, then brightened and explained that she didn't want anything for them, she wasn't short of tobacco or anything. They were just a gift for the kids. Then she just sat there, and we sat there, and the bananas sat there, and we tried again. "Look," I said, pointing up to them and counting, "we've got four stalks already hanging here on the veranda—there are too many for us to eat now. Some are rotting already. Even if we eat only bananas, we can't keep up with what's here!"

11   Rogi's only response was to insist that these were a gift, and that she didn't want anything for them, so we tried yet another tack: "Don't *your* children like bananas?" When she admitted that they did, and that she had none at her house, we suggested that she should take them there. Finally, still puzzled, but convinced we weren't going to keep the bananas, she replaced them on her head, went down the stairs, and made her way back through the village toward her house.

12   As before, it seemed only moments before Kolia was making his way up the stairs, but this time he hadn't brought the woman in tow. "What was wrong with those bananas? Were they no good?" he demanded. We explained that there was nothing wrong with the bananas at all, but that we simply couldn't use them and it seemed foolish to take them when we had so many and Rogi's own children had none. We obviously didn't make ourselves clear because Kolia then took up the same refrain that Rogi had—he insisted that we shouldn't be worried about taking the bananas, because they were a gift for the children and Rogi hadn't wanted anything for them. There was no reason, he added, to send her away with them—she would be ashamed. I'm afraid we must have seemed as if were hard of hearing or thought he was, for our only response was to repeat our reasons. We went through it again—there they hung, one, two, three, *four* stalks of bananas, rapidly ripening and already far beyond our capacity to eat—we just weren't ready to accept any more and let them rot (and, we added to ourselves, pay for them with tobacco, to boot).

13   Kolia finally realized that we were neither hard of hearing nor intentionally offensive, but merely ignorant. He stared at us for a few minutes, thinking, and then asked: "Don't you frequently have visitors during the day and evening?" We nodded. Then he asked, "Don't you usually offer them cigarettes and coffee or milo?" Again, we nodded. "Did it ever occur to you to suppose," he said "that your visitors might be hungry?" It was at this point in the conversation, as we recall, that we began to see the depth of the pit we had dug for ourselves. We nodded, hesitantly. His last words to us before he went down the stairs and stalked away were just what we were by that time afraid they might be. "When your guests are hungry, *feed them bananas!*"

Lesson 2:
Never refuse a gift, and never fail to return a gift. If you cannot use it, you can always give it away to someone else—there is no such thing as too much—there are never too many bananas.

NOT ENOUGH PINEAPPLES

14   During the fifteen years between that first visit in 1966 and our residence there in 1981 we had returned to live in Kandoka village twice during the 1970s, and though there were a great many changes in the village, and indeed for all of Papua New Guinea during that time, we continued to live according to the lessons of reciprocity learned during those first months in the field. We bought no food for money and refused no gifts, but shared our surplus. As our family grew, we continued to be accompanied by our younger children. Our place in the village came to be something like that of educated Kaliai who worked far away in New Guinea. Our friends expected us to come "home" when we had leave, but knew that our work kept us away for long periods of time. They also credited us with knowing much more about the rules of their way of life than was our due. And we sometimes shared the delusion that we understood life in the village, but even fifteen years was not long enough to relieve the need for lessons in learning to live within the rules of gift exchange.

15   In the last paragraph I used the word *friends* to describe the villagers intentionally, but of course they were not all our friends. Over the years some really had become friends, others were acquaintances, others remained consultants or informants to whom we turned when we needed information. Still others, unfortunately, we did not like at all. We tried never to make an issue of these distinctions, of course, and to be evenhanded and generous to all, as they were to us. Although we almost never actually refused requests that were made of us, over the long term our reciprocity in the village was balanced. More was given to those who helped us the most, while we gave assistance or donations of small items even to those who were not close or helpful.

16   One elderly woman in particular was a trial for us. Sara was the eldest of a group of siblings and her younger brother and sister were both generous, informative, and delightful persons. Her younger sister, Makila, was a particularly close friend and consultant, and in deference to that friendship we felt awkward in dealing with the elder sister.

17   Sara was neither a friend nor an informant, but she had been, since she returned to live in the village at the time of our second trip in 1971, a constant (if minor) drain on our resources. She never asked for much at a time. A bar of soap, a box of matches, a bottle of kerosene, a cup of rice, some onions, a stick or two of tobacco, or some other small item was usually all that was at issue, but whenever she came around it was always to ask for something—or to let us know that when we left, we should give her some of the furnishings from the house. Too, unlike almost everyone else in the village, when she came, she was always empty-handed. We ate no taro from her gardens, and the kids chewed none of her sugarcane. In short, she was, as far as we could tell, a really grasping, selfish old woman—and we were not the only victims of her greed.

18   Having long before learned the lesson of the bananas, one day we had a stalk that was ripening so fast we couldn't keep up with it, so I pulled a few for our own use (we only had one stalk at the time) and walked down through the village to Ben's house, where his five children were playing. I sat down on his steps to talk, telling him that I intended to give the fruit to his kids. They never

got them. Sara saw us from across the open plaza of the village and came rushing over, shouting, "My bananas!" Then she grabbed the stalk and went off gorging herself with them. Ben and I just looked at each other.

19 Finally it got to the point where it seemed to us that we had to do something. Ten years of being used was long enough. So there came the afternoon when Sara showed up to get some tobacco—again. But this time, when we gave her the two sticks she had demanded, we confronted her.

20 First, we noted the many times she had come to get things. We didn't mind sharing things, we explained. After all, we had plenty of tobacco and soap and rice and such, and most of it was there so that we could help our friends as they helped us, with folktales, information, or even gifts of food. The problem was that she kept coming to get things, but never came to talk, or to tell stories, or to bring some little something that the kids might like. Sara didn't argue—she agreed. "Look," we suggested, "It doesn't have to be much, and we don't mind giving you things—but you can help us. The kids like pineapples, and we don't have any—the next time you need something, bring something—like maybe a pineapple." Obviously somewhat embarrassed, she took her tobacco and left, saying that she would bring something soon. We were really pleased with ourselves. It had been a very difficult thing to do, but it was done, and we were convinced that either she would start bringing things or not come. It was as if a burden had lifted from our shoulders.

21 It worked. Only a couple of days passed before Sara was back, bringing her bottle to get it filled with kerosene. But this time, she came carrying the biggest, most beautiful pineapple we had seen the entire time we had been there. We had a friendly talk, filled her kerosene container, and hung the pineapple up on the veranda to ripen just a little further. A few days later we cut and ate it, and whether the satisfaction it gave came from the fruit or from its source would be hard to say, but it was delicious. That, we assumed, was the end of that irritant.

22 We were wrong, of course. The next afternoon, Mary, one of our best friends for years (and no relation to Sara), dropped by for a visit. As we talked, her eyes scanned the veranda. Finally she asked whether we hadn't had a pineapple there yesterday. We said we had, but that we had already eaten it. She commented that it had been a really nice-looking one, and we told her that it had been the best we had eaten in months. Then, after a pause, she asked, "Who brought it to you?" We smiled as we said, "Sara!" because Mary would appreciate our coup— she had commented many times in the past on the fact that Sara only *got* from us and never gave. She was silent for a moment, and then she said, "Well, I'm glad you enjoyed it—my father was waiting until it was fully ripe to harvest it for you, but when it went missing I thought maybe it was the one you had here. I'm glad to see you got it. I thought maybe a thief had eaten it in the bush."

Lesson 3:
Where reciprocity is the rule and gifts are the idiom, you cannot demand a gift, just as you cannot refuse a request.

23   It says a great deal about the kindness and patience of the Kaliai people that they have been willing to be our hosts for all these years despite our blunders and lack of good manners. They have taught us a lot, and these three lessons are certainly not the least important things we learned.

■ ■ ▨

MEANING

1. How does Counts's intitial experience of offering money for watermelon teach him his first important lesson about the culture of New Guinea?
2. What important principle of reciprocity did Counts learn from receiving an unlimited supply of bananas?
3. What incidents reveal to Counts that he is actually "paying" for goods that the villagers considered "gifts"?
4. In what way is Counts's experience with Sara ironic, and what does it teach him?

TECHNIQUE

1. How is the essay structured in order to record Counts's insights into a culture that still remains an enigma?
2. How does Counts attempt to use a problem-solving method to understand and control his situation?
3. **Other Patterns.** How are the **descriptive** details in Counts's narrative essential in communicating the nature of the problem he faced?

LANGUAGE

1. How does Counts's ironic realization about how little he has learned about New Guinea culture influence the tone of his account?
2. How do the villagers use euphemisms (or talk "around" the issue) as part of their cultural communication?
3. If you don't know the meaning of the following words, look them up: *disgruntled* (3), *marginally* (4), *gauche,* (5), *acquiesced* (9), *delusion* (14), *reciprocity* (14).

SUGGESTIONS FOR WRITING

1. **Critical Writing.** Does the barter system as practiced in New Guinea have advantages over a money-based economy? Why or why not?
2. If you have had experiences in trading goods for services or vice versa, what lessons did you learn about reciprocity?
3. How does Counts's essay **illustrate** the typical problems faced by anthropologists who work in other cultures?
4. **Thematic Links.** Discuss the theme of reciprocity in Counts's essay and in Mark Salzman's "Lessons" (Chapter 4, "Description")?

YOSSI GHINSBERG

Jungle

Yossi Ghinsberg was born and raised in Israel and served for three years in the Israeli Navy. He graduated from Tel Aviv University and chose to leave a comfortable life to trek through South America with three friends. His experiences of being near starvation and lost and alone in a remote Bolivian rain forest form the basis of his best-selling book *Jungle* (1986), from which the following excerpt is drawn. The Discovery Channel has made a documentary film based on this book. In 1995, Ghinsberg became vice president of a center devoted to the treatment of addictions and established his own clinic in Australia, where he lives with his wife and three daughters. His latest work is *The Laws of the Jungle* (2007).

BEFORE YOU READ

What is the most terrifying experience in a jungle that you can imagine?

■ ■ ▨

1   It was growing dark, and I could find no shelter. There were no crags or cliffs, no caves or niches. Where could I spend the night? I had to choose a campsite quickly and get a fire going while there was still daylight. I chose a level area, cleared away the damp leaves, and replaced them with fresh, dry ones. I took out one of the mosquito nets and tied it down to four tree stumps with vines, so that it formed a long, narrow, translucent green pup tent. I looked for dry wood but didn't find any. I gathered a few branches and tried to break them and strip them away to the dry inner parts. It was impossible without a machete. My attempts at lighting a fire only wasted the fluid in the lighter and brought me to a state of despair. Reluctantly I crawled under the tent of mosquito netting and wrapped myself in the remaining net and red poncho. I took my arsenal out of the pack: the flashlight, the lighter, the mosquito repellent, and the snakebite serum. To these I added a tin can and a spoon. If any wild animal should approach me, I would make a horrendous clatter and scare it away. So I thought.

2   I tried to close my eyes, to escape into my fantasies, but I was too tense, uneasy. My stomach was growling with hunger, for I hadn't eaten anything all day. The fear, however, was harder to bear. I was in the heart of the jungle, totally vulnerable, with no means of protecting myself, no cave to hide myself in, no fire. I kept hearing animal calls, the cries of birds, and the buzz of insects. I secured the edges of the mosquito netting with rocks so that no snakes could come slithering in. The flashlight was near my knee. I kept hold of it for fear that I wouldn't be able to find it in the dark if I should need it. Off in the distance I could hear bloodcurdling screeches. A jaguar must have caught a monkey or some other prey.

3   A few hours went by; I was in total darkness. Suddenly I heard the snapping of branches, the stealthy thud of footsteps, something coming. Fear gripped me. It's only your imagination, I kept telling myself, only your imagination, but the rustle of the leaves and branches on the ground was so clear. I stuck my head out from under my covers, moved one of the rocks away from the mosquito net, and peered into the darkness. I turned on the flashlight. I couldn't see a thing. I sighed with relief but didn't really feel any better. The fear weighed upon me; I had never been so terrified. I tried to lie back down and cover myself up, but I kept hearing sounds all around me, and my heart was pounding frantically.

4   *God, just don't let a wild animal devour me.*

5   I ran my fingers over my makeshift weapons, afraid that I might become hysterical. Again I heard rustling sounds around me. I sat up with a jolt, gripped the spoon, and started banging on the tin can. It made a dull sound, and I called out, "Shoo! Shoo! Go away! Shoo!" as if I were about to be set upon by a flock of chickens. I lay back down, my heart thumping. The sounds drew closer.

6   *No, it's nothing. There's nothing out there. It's only your imagination. It's all in your mind.*

7   I heard the rustle again, too close and too real to ignore. I clutched the flashlight, stuck my head out of the mosquito net, turned it on … and found myself face-to-face with a jaguar.

8   It was large, covered with black spots. One of its paws was raised off the ground, as if it had been about to take another step. When I turned the light on it, it put its foot down without stepping forward. It stood at a distance of about twelve feet. Just stood there looking at me. It wasn't blinded by the light, but it stopped and looked me over. It didn't appear particularly menacing; it wasn't roaring or licking its chops. Its eyes were neither ferocious nor meek. They were just great cat's eyes, staring at me. The jaguar stood perfectly still; only its tail waved slowly back and forth.

9   "Go away," I whined. "Get out of here. Beat it. Do you hear me? Get away."

10   I was trembling and started to scream loudly at the jaguar. "Get out of here, you son of a bitch! Go away! I'll burn you up! Get away!"

11   The flashlight had a chain to hang it from. I clamped it between my teeth in order to have both hands free. I felt around on the ground by my knees and found the repellent spray and the lighter. I held the lighter in my left hand and the spray in my right hand. Now I was calm. I didn't scream or tremble.

12   *Maybe I shouldn't try it.* I hesitated. *It might just make him mad, and then he might attack me.* But then I pushed down on the spray button and lit the lighter.

13   It worked. The spray caught fire and spewed an enormous blaze. I could smell the scorched hair on my left hand, and I was completely blinded. I held it for a few minutes, until the spray ran out and the flame of the lighter grew weaker. My makeshift flame-thrower was exhausted.

14   My sight returned gradually, in concentric circles of fading darkness, and finally I could see the beam of the flashlight. The jaguar was gone. I shined the light around in fear, right and left, in back of me. The jaguar had vanished.

I thought I could hear receding footsteps. Had it worked? Had I scared it off? I felt neither joy nor relief. I kept the flashlight on for a while but was afraid of running it down and turned it off.

15   I sat inside the mosquito net, wide awake, my heart jumping wildly at every sound until the merciful morning light. The sunlight gave me a tremendous sense of security, as if no danger could befall me. I packed up my gear while I murmured a hasty prayer of thanks and got out of there as fast as I could.

16   Now that the sun was shining, I remembered exactly in which direction the river should be and walked on rapidly. "Straight and to the left, straight and to the left." I sang out the rhythm of my steps as I made for the river along a diagonal course. Singing helped to keep my spirits up.

17   There was far less foliage on the higher ground, and I progressed quite rapidly. From time to time I came across a stream and stopped to drink. I felt I could safely empty the two big cans of water, and my shoulders were greatly relieved.

18   After a few hours' walk, however, I once again felt the dread of uncertainty. The sun was directly overhead, and I hadn't the slightest idea where I was. I feared that I might well be marching away from the river. I might end up on the other side of the mountain, lost forever where no one would find me. It was so easy to lose one's way and one's wits.

■ ■ ▨

MEANING

1. In what predicament does Ghinsberg find himself, and why is it so dangerous?
2. How is his verbal response to the jaguar both absurd and understandable?
3. Given the choices available to him, what means does he use to cope with the situation?
4. What landmarks does he use the next day to begin his journey back?

TECHNIQUE

1. How does Ghinsberg's narrative allow the reader to understand the desperate nature of his situation and his ingenuity in using the few tools he has available?
2. How does Ghinsberg emphasize that by remaining calm, he could begin to solve his problem?
3. **Other Patterns.** How do Ghinsberg's **descriptions** appeal to sight, sound, touch, smell, and taste and enhance our ability to identify with him?

LANGUAGE

1. How do the italicized comments add a subjective dimension to his objective account?
2. How do Ghinsberg's comments to the curious jaguar reveal how much a creature of civilization the author is?
3. If you don't know the meaning of the following words, look them up: *translucent* (1), *reluctantly* (1), *scorched* (14), *makeshift* (14), *foliage* (18).

Suggestions for Writing

1. ***Critical Writing.*** If you had found yourself in the same situation as Ghinsberg, what would you have done?

2. What encounters have you or someone you know had with animals that were dangerous? Describe how you or your acquaintance handled the situation.

3. Write a **narrative** of an experience you have had in which you were concerned for your safety or were "out of your element."

4. ***Thematic Links.*** How do both Ghinsberg and Immaculée Ilibagiza in "Left to Tell" (in Chapter 6, "Comparison and Contrast") display great presence of mind in life-threatening situations?

LUIS SEPÚLVEDA

Daisy

Imagine being imprisoned in a squalid cell and tortured for information that you could not possibly possess and then having to flatter your torturer, who had literary aspirations. If this sounds absurd, you will understand why the Chilean writer Luis Sepúlveda, now an expatriate, had to develop a tough skin and an ironic sensibility to withstand this condition. He describes his experience in this chapter from *Full Circle: A South American Journey* (1996). Sepúlveda is an accomplished writer in different genres, including screenplays such as *Zorba and Lucky* (1998), detective stories, essays, and novels such as *Hot Line* (2002).

BEFORE YOU READ

What kinds of relationships might arise in a prison between guards and prisoners?

■ ■ ▰

1   The military had rather inflated ideas of our destructive capacity. They questioned us about plans to assassinate all the officers in American military history, to blow up bridges and seal off tunnels, and to prepare for the landing of a terrible foreign enemy whom they could not identify.

2   Temuco is a sad, grey, rainy city. No-one would call it a tourist attraction, and yet the barracks of the Tucapel regiment came to house a sort of permanent international convention of sadists. The Chileans, who were the hosts, after all, were assisted in the interrogations by primates from Brazilian military intelligence—they were the worst—North Americans from the State Department, Argentinian paramilitary personnel, Italian neo-fascists and even some agents of Mossad.

3   I remember Rudi Weismann, a Chilean with a passion for the South and sailing, who was tortured and interrogated in the gentle language of the synagogues. This infamy was too much for Rudi, who had thrown in his lot with Israel: he had worked on a kibbutz, but in the end his nostalgia for Tierra del Fuego had brought him back to Chile. He simply could not understand how Israel could support such a gang of criminals, and though till then he had always been a model of good humour, he dried up like a neglected plant. One morning we found him dead in his sleeping bag. No need for an autopsy, his face made it clear: Rudi Weismann had died of sadness.

4   The commander of the Tucapel regiment—a basic respect for paper prevents me from writing his name—was a fanatical admirer of Field Marshal Rommel. When he found a prisoner he liked, he would invite him to recover from the interrogations in his office. After assuring the prisoner that everything that happened in the barracks was in the best interests of our great nation, the commander would offer him a glass of Korn—somebody used to

send him this insipid, wheat-based liquor from Germany—and make him sit through a lecture on the Afrika Korps. The guy's parents or grandparents were German, but he couldn't have looked more Chilean: chubby, short-legged, dark untidy hair. You could have mistaken him for a truck driver or a fruit vendor, but when he talked about Rommel he became the caricature of a Nazi guard.

5   At the end of the lecture he would dramatise Rommel's suicide, clicking his heels, raising his right hand to his forehead to salute an invisible flag, muttering "Adieu geliebtes Vaterland," and pretending to shoot himself in the mouth. We all hoped that one day he would do it for real.

6   There was another curious officer in the regiment: a lieutenant struggling to contain a homosexuality that kept popping out all over the place. The soldiers had nicknamed him Daisy, and he knew it.

7   We could all tell that it was a torment for Daisy not to be able to adorn his body with truly beautiful objects, and the poor guy had to make do with the regulation paraphernalia. He wore a .45 pistol, two cartridge clips, a commando's curved dagger, two hand grenades, a torch, a walkie-talkie, the insignia of his rank and the silver wings of the parachute corps. The prisoners and the soldiers thought he looked like a Christmas tree.

8   This individual sometimes surprised us with generous and apparently disinterested acts—we didn't know that the Stockholm syndrome could be a military perversion. For example, after the interrogations he would suddenly fill our pockets with cigarettes or the highly prized aspirin tablets with vitamin C. One afternoon he invited me to his room.

9   "So you're a man of letters," he said, offering me a can of Coca-Cola.

10   "I've written a couple of stories. That's all," I replied.

11   "You're not here for an interrogation. I'm very sorry about what's happening, but that's what war is like. I want us to talk as one writer to another. Are you surprised? The army has produced some great men of letters. Think of Don Alonso de Ercilla y Zúñiga, for example."

12   "Or Cervantes," I added.

13   Daisy included himself among the greats. That was his problem. If he wanted adulation, he could have it. I drank the Coca-Cola and thought about Gracés, or rather, about his chicken, because, incredible as it seems, the cook had a chicken called Dulcinea, the name of Don Quixote's mistress.

14   One morning it jumped the wall which separated the common-law prisoners from the POWs, and it must have been a chicken with deep political convictions, because it decided to stay with us. Garcés caressed it and sighed, saying: "If I had a pinch of pepper and a pinch of cumin, I'd make you a chicken marinade like you've never tasted."

15   "I want you to read my poems and give me your opinion, your honest opinion," said Daisy, handing me a notebook.

16   I left that room with my pockets full of cigarettes, caramel sweets, tea bags and a tin of US Army marmalade. That afternoon I started to believe in the brotherhood of writers.

17   They transported us from the prison to the barracks and back in a cattle truck. The soldiers made sure there was plenty of cow shit on the floor of the truck before ordering us to lie face down with our hands behind our necks. We were guarded by four of them, with North American machine guns, one in each corner of the truck. They were almost all young guys brought down from northern garrisons, and the harsh climate of the South kept them flu-ridden and in a perpetually filthy mood. They had orders to fire on the bundles—us—at the slightest suspect movement, or on any civilian who tried to approach the truck. But as time wore on, the discipline gradually relaxed and they turned a blind eye to the packet of cigarettes or piece of fruit thrown from a window, or the pretty and daring girl who ran beside the truck blowing us kisses and shouting: "Don't give up, comrades! We'll win!"

18   Back in prison, as always, we were met by the welcoming committee organised by Doctor "Skinny" Pragnan, now an eminent psychiatrist in Belgium. First he examined those who couldn't walk and those who had heart problems, then those who had come back with a dislocation or with ribs out of place. Pragnan was expert at estimating how much electricity had been put into us on the grill, and patiently determined who would be able to absorb liquids in the next few hours. Then finally it was time to take communion: we were given the aspirin with vitamin C and an anticoagulant to prevent internal haematomas.

19   "Dulcinea's days are numbered," I said to Garcés, and looked for a corner in which to read Daisy's notebook.

20   The elegantly inscribed pages were redolent of love, honey, sublime suffering and forgotten flowers. By the third page I knew that Daisy hadn't even gone to the trouble of reusing the ideas of the Mexican poet Amado Nervo—he'd simply copied out his poems word for word.

21   I called out to Peyuco Gálvez, a Spanish teacher, and read him a couple of lines.

22   "What do you think, Peyuco?"

23   "Amado Nervo. The book is called *The Interior Gardens.*"

24   I had got myself into a real jam. If Daisy found out that I knew the work of this sugary poet Nervo, then it wasn't Garcés's chicken whose days were numbered, but mine. It was a serious problem, so that night I presented it to the Council of Elders.

25   "Now, Daisy, would he be the passive or the active type?" enquired Iriarte.

26   "Stop it, will you. My skin's at risk here," I replied.

27   "I'm serious. Maybe our friend wants to have an affair with you, and giving you the notebook was like dropping a silk handkerchief. And like a fool you picked it up. Perhaps he copied out the poems for you to find a message in them. I've known queens who seduced boys by lending them *Demian* by Hermann Hesse. If Daisy is the passive type, this business with Amado Nervo means he wants to test your nerve, so to speak. And if he's the active type, well, it would have to hurt less than a kick in the balls."

28   "Message my arse. He gave you the poems as his own, and you should say you liked them a lot. If he was trying to send a message, he should have given

the notebook to Garcés, he's the only one who has an interior garden. Or maybe Daisy doesn't know about the pot plant," remarked Andrés Müller.

29   "Let's be serious about this. You have to say something to him, and Daisy mustn't even suspect that you know Nervo's poems," declared Pragnan.

30   "Tell him you liked the poems, but that the adjectives strike you as a bit excessive. Quote Huidobro: when an adjective doesn't give life, it kills. That way you'll show him that you read his poems carefully and that you are criticising his work as a colleague," suggested Gálvez.

31   The Council of Elders approved of Gálvez's idea, but I spent two weeks on tenterhooks. I couldn't sleep. I wished they would come and take me to be kicked and electrocuted so I could give the damned notebook back. In those two weeks I came to hate good old Garcés:

32   "Listen, mate, if everything goes well, and you get a little jar of capers as well as the cumin and the pepper, we'll have such a feast with that chicken."

33   After a fortnight, I found myself at last stretched out face down on the mattress of cowpats with my hands behind my neck. I thought I was going mad: I was happy to be heading towards a session of the activity known as torture.

34   Tucapel barracks. Service Corps. In the background, the perpetual green of Cerro Ñielol, sacred to the Mapuche Indians. There was a waiting room outside the interrogation cell, like at the doctor's. There they made us sit on a bench with our hands tied behind our backs and black hoods over our heads. I never understood what the hoods were for, because once we got inside they took them off, and we could see the interrogators—the toy soldiers who, with panic-stricken faces, turned the handle of the generator, and the health officers who attached the electrodes to our anuses, testicles, gums and tongue, and then listened with stethoscopes to see who was faking and who had really passed out on the grill.

35   Lagos, a deacon of the Emmaus International ragmen, was the first to be interrogated that day. For a year they had been working him over to find out how the organisation had come by a couple of dozen old military uniforms which had been found in their warehouses. A trader who sold army surplus gear had donated them. Lagos screamed in pain and repeated over and over what the soldiers wanted to hear: the uniforms belonged to an invading army which was preparing to land on the Chilean coast.

36   I was waiting for my turn when someone took off the hood, It was Lieutenant Daisy.

37   "Follow me," he ordered.

38   We went into an office. On the desk I saw a tin of cocoa and a carton of cigarettes which were obviously there to reward my comments on his literary work.

39   "Did you read my poesy?" he asked, offering me a seat.

40   Poesy. Daisy said poesy, not poetry. A man covered with pistols and grenades can't say "poesy" without sounding ridiculous and effete. At that moment he revolted me, and I decided that even if it meant pissing blood, hissing when I spoke and being able to charge batteries just by touching them, I wasn't going to lower myself to flattering a plagiarising faggot in uniform.

41   "You have pretty handwriting, Lieutenant. But you know these poems aren't yours," I said, giving him back the notebook.

42   I saw him begin to shake. He was carrying enough arms to kill me several times over, and if he didn't want to stain his uniform, he could order someone else to do it. Trembling with anger he stood up, threw what was on the desk onto the floor and shouted:

43   "Three weeks in the cube. But first, you're going to visit the chiropodist, you piece of subversive shit!"

44   The chiropodist was a civilian, a landholder who had lost several thousand hectares in the land reform, and who was getting his revenge by participating in the interrogations as a volunteer. His speciality was peeling back toenails, which led to terrible infections.

45   I knew the cube. I had spent my first six months of prison there in solitary confinement: it was an underground cell, one and a half metres wide by one and a half metres long by one and a half metres high. In the old days there had been a tannery in the Temuco jail, and the cube was used to store fat. The walls still stank of fat, but after a week your excrement fixed that, making the cube very much a place of your own.

46   You could only stretch out across the diagonal, but the low temperatures of southern Chile, the rainwater and the soldiers' urine made you want to curl up hugging your legs and stay like that wishing yourself smaller and smaller, so that eventually you could live on one of the islands of floating shit, which conjured up images of dream holidays. I was there for three weeks, running through Laurel and Hardy films, remembering the books of Salgari, Stevenson and London word by word, playing long games of chess, licking my toes to protect them from infection. In the cube I swore over and over again never to become a literary critic.

■ ■ ▨

MEANING

1. What aspects of Sepúlveda's predicament make clear what life was like for a political prisoner?

2. How does the fact that his torturers needed information and therefore could not actually kill him explain the paradoxical mixture of sadism and after-torture comforts?

3. What unusual combination of character traits and aspirations makes the prison guard, Daisy, unique?

4. What challenge does Sepúlveda confront, and what does he decide to do?

TECHNIQUE

1. How does Sepúlveda's description of prison life provide a context for the reader to understand the choice Sepúlveda must make?

2. What details most clearly dramatize Daisy's strange and unnerving alternation between readiness to torture and chummy familiarity with Sepúlveda?

3. *Other Patterns.* How does Sepúlveda use **process analysis** to communicate the interrogation techniques that are used on prisoners?

LANGUAGE

1. What is the significance of the guard's nickname, "Daisy"?

2. What are some of the instances in which Sepúlveda's ironic sense of humor allows him to detach himself from his horrendous predicament?

3. If you don't know the meaning of the following words, look them up: *autopsy* (3), *caricature* (4), *paraphernalia* (7), *marinade* (14), *garrisons* (17).

SUGGESTIONS FOR WRITING

1. *Critical Writing.* If you had been in the same situation as Sepúlveda, would you have lied or told the truth, as Sepúlveda does despite the torture that awaits him? Explain your answer.

2. Compare Sepúlveda's account with other prison narratives such as Aleksandr Solzhenitsyn's *One Day in the Life of Ivan Denisovich* (1962).

3. In your opinion, what central issue **defines** Sepúlveda's unwillingness to simply go along with Daisy's pretense?

4. *Thematic Links.* Compare Sepúlveda's account with George Orwell's "Homage to Catalonia" (Chapter 8, "Classification") in terms of the authors' use of irony and humor in dire circumstances.

ROBERT FROST

The Road Not Taken

One of America's foremost poets, Robert Frost (1874–1963) was not born in New England, the region of the country that most people associate with him, but in San Francisco. He did, however, grow up in Massachusetts because his father, shortly before dying, requested that he be buried there, and Mrs. Frost could not afford the return trip to California. After a year at Dartmouth, where he had a full scholarship, Frost took odd jobs in a woolen mill and as a newspaper reporter. He then studied for two years at Harvard but left to pursue his career as a poet. In the years that followed, he tried to support his wife and four children by raising poultry and teaching various subjects at Pinkerton Academy. With money from the sale of his farm, he moved his family to England in 1912, and his books of poems *A Boy's Will* (1913) and *North of Boston* (1914) were published there. With the outbreak of World War I, Frost returned to New England and flourished as a writer-in-residence and professor of English, first at Amherst College, then at the University of Michigan, and later at Harvard. The different paths Frost was trying to travel down simultaneously and the need to choose between them might well have been the personal impulse underlying his popular poem that follows, written in 1916. In addition to receiving the Pulitzer Prize for poetry on four separate occasions, Frost is vividly remembered for his recitation of a poem at John F. Kennedy's inauguration in 1961.

BEFORE YOU READ

Why is it important to anticipate the possible results before making life-changing choices?

■ ■ ▨

Two roads diverged in a yellow wood,
And sorry I could not travel both
And be one traveler, long I stood
And looked down one as far as I could
5 To where it bent in the undergrowth;

Then took the other, as just as fair,
And having perhaps the better claim,
Because it was grassy and wanted wear;
Though as for that the passing there
10 Had worn them really about the same,

And both that morning equally lay
In leaves no step had trodden black.
Oh, I kept the first for another day!
Yet knowing how way leads on to way,
15 I doubted if I should ever come back.

I shall be telling this with a sigh
Somewhere ages and ages hence:
Two roads diverged in a wood, and I—
I took the one less traveled by,
20 And that has made all the difference.

■ ■ ▨

MEANING

1. What dilemma confronts the speaker? Why will he have to live with the consequences of his choice?

2. Before making his choice, how does the speaker evaluate what each choice represents?

3. Now, years later, as the speaker looks back on the choice he made is he happy with his choice or simply resigned to it?

TECHNIQUE

1. How does the fact that there are only two end rhymes in each stanza underscore the reality of the two choices?

2. How does the repetition of the first-person pronoun in lines 18 and 19 reflect the speaker's moment of decision?

3. **Other Patterns.** What **descriptive** details enable us to visualize the scene as it originally appeared to the speaker?

LANGUAGE

1. How does the down-home Yankee speech of the poem express a sophisticated sensibility?

2. Is the title ironic in light of the ending? Why or why not?

3. If you don't know the meaning of the following words, look them up: *diverged* (line 1), *trodden* (line 12).

SUGGESTIONS FOR WRITING

1. **Critical Writing.** Is the speaker rationalizing earlier choices that he can no longer make? Explain.

2. What would be the less-traveled road for you, and would you choose it?

3. Revisit a choice that you made to better understand why you made it, and **narrate** the experience and the insights you gained.

4. **Thematic Links.** Apply Frost's method to C. P. Ellis's predicament in "Why I Quit the Klan" (Chapter 9, "Cause and Effect").

Real-Life Situations: Problem Solving

An extremely useful kind of letter to know how to write and one that applies problem-solving skills is the letter of complaint. In it, you identify the problem (such as damaged merchandise, improper billing, unsatisfactory service) and request that it be resolved. A complaint letter is a business letter and you should be courteous and focus on the issue.

As the following example shows, you should try to identify the person in the company who can help you. Otherwise, your letter should be addressed to the department within the company that handles consumer complaints. Begin by describing the problem in as much detail as possible so as to allow the person reading your letter to investigate your claims.

Next, describe the inconvenience or disruption that resulted from the problem. Then, state clearly what you want the company to do. Supply supporting evidence that might be required such as receipts for expenses incurred. End your letter politely but firmly. As with all business letters, keep to one page and edit for typos and grammar.

614 East 74th Street
Kansas City, Missouri 64131
March 17, 2007

Jonathan Steele
Director of Customer Relations
Western Airlines
2601 Newberry Street
Houston, Texas 77058

Dear Mr. Steele:

When my wife and I and our two small children flew on Western Airlines from Kansas City to San Francisco, we were abandoned in Houston overnight and had to fend for ourselves by locating a hotel room and paying for all the associated costs.

We arrived on your flight #2800 to Houston on March 4th at 2:07 p.m. and were scheduled to pick up your connecting flight #2447 to San Francisco at 5:10 p.m. After we landed in Houston, our connecting flight was cancelled because of mechanical problems and we were rescheduled on a 7:00 a.m. flight the next day, March 5th.

Your agents informed us that it was our responsibility to find a hotel room for the night. After checking the availability for hotels near the airport we discovered that there were no vacancies. When we finally located a hotel room it was on the other side of Houston. The taxi fare was steep, as was the return fare back to the airport early the next morning. Since our luggage had been checked from Kansas City through to San Francisco, we only had the clothes we were wearing and what was in our carry-ons.

Other expenses we incurred included room service for our family since we were in no condition to go to the dining room with our exhausted and crying children.

This was a most horrendous experience and we feel that the very least you can do is to reimburse us for the expenses we incurred. Copies of our receipts are enclosed. We look forward to your prompt attention to this matter.

Sincerely,

Brian Bigelow

Brian Bigelow

STUDENT ESSAY: PROBLEM SOLVING

The following essay by Brandon Porter applies the principles of problem solving to an important social issue. As you read his essay, notice how he uses the principles of problem solving and presents his personal experiences as evidence to support his thesis. Brandon documents his sources in MLA style and includes a list of Works Cited at the end of his paper. Annotations on Brandon's essay and the follow-up commentary ("Strategies") will help you to understand the important principles of problem solving.

Porter 1

Medicinal Marijuana

Brandon Porter

1   The word "relief" would best describe the effects of a marijuana-induced state of being. It's this relief, the emancipation from the present psychological mindset into a temporary asylum, that makes marijuana one of the most commonly used drugs of the past century. The "hippy generation" of the 1960s made marijuana the most popular recreational drug for adolescents and adults alike. Many people of this era openly smoked marijuana without concern for the legal ramifications. Those who indulged in a marijuana-induced high felt that it expanded their senses and enhanced their music experience. This same liberation and relief experienced by concertgoers can also be experienced by those lying in a hospital bed, fighting the most malignant disease on Earth—cancer. Legislatures today, however, will not allow it. It is because of this opposition that the legalization of medicinal marijuana is under extreme debate. The use of medicinal marijuana should be legalized all across the nation because its benefits of controlling nausea, relieving pain, and stimulating

Introduction

Problem defined

Thesis statement

Porter 2

appetite in people suffering from life-threatening diseases largely outweigh the potential harmful effects.

2   Over the past several years, the controversy of legalizing marijuana for medicinal purposes has been debated in both medical and political fields. Because of the excessive use of marijuana for recreational purposes, the incredible benefits that can result from its medicinal purposes are being strongly disputed by the Drug Enforcement Administration (DEA) and the United States Congress.

The causes of the problem identified

3   Despite the constant debate over this issue, there is still a large support system within the public and medical community to bring a halt to the prevention of medicinal marijuana. Recent polls have consistently shown that nearly 75% of Americans are in favor of legalizing this drug strictly for medical purposes. Although the DEA continues to favor prohibiting medicinal marijuana, the U.S. Congress has the overall right to change the federal laws to benefit those who are critically ill, thus giving the general population hope for the future ("Medicinal Marijuana Briefing").

4   In 1986, the U.S. Food and Drug Administration tried to experiment with this issue and approved a drug in pill form called Marinol. It contains one of the major active ingredients in marijuana and is administered ·for treatment of nausea and other side effects caused by chemotherapy. Unfortunately, the pill proved to be much less effective than marijuana because only a small amount of the oral dosage was absorbed, which left the majority of the drug filtered through the kidneys and liver with minimal medicinal effects. The key to quality medical care is to ensure that there is prompt and effective relief of the symptoms. The patient is already experiencing turmoil in life and the goal should therefore be, one might phrase it, "to take him/her away from this horrible place and help him/her feel better."

Past attempts to solve the problem

5   Because of these factors, most would agree that this oral drug option for marijuana is not sufficient. Marijuana for medicinal purposes should be legalized, as it will have a major impact and bring a smile to those suffering from fatal diseases like cancer ("Medicinal Marijuana," CNN). So far, marijuana seems to be the most effective drug in providing relief to cancer patients.

Porter 3

If there is anything that can help these patients in getting them through their treatments, it should be implemented, regardless of the legislation for its recreational use. In today's society, with today's technology, people die every day from cancer. This leads to much frustration on the part of patients, knowing that there is a drug out there that can be used to effectively treat symptoms, but the government is not allowing it. Legalizing a drug strictly to improve the quality of life of those in need should be, without question, taken into serious consideration.

Evidence supporting the thesis from medical websites and news service

6   Marijuana is one of the safest active substances that has been experimented with for the purpose of controlling nausea, vomiting, and stimulating appetites for patients suffering from cancer and AIDS. The cause of this nausea and loss of appetite comes directly from the chemotherapy the patient is receiving as part of the treatment necessary to cure the disease they are fighting. Marijuana does not affect every person the same way—some of those with AIDS and cancer never obtain relief from smoking the drug— however, the majority experience temporary relief.

7   Despite the diverse reactions to the drug, it has been scientifically and medically proven that, for the most part, people will respond well to the marijuana and reap the benefits ("Medicinal Marijuana," About). Some people against the notion of legalizing marijuana might argue that if a patient tries it and it does not provide them with any relief, then he or she has just done harm to the body for no reason. Although that may be true, if you lost a loved one and knew that there was a drug available that could have alleviated some of their suffering, wouldn't you want it legalized?

8   I happen to know first hand what suffering from nausea induced by chemotherapy actually feels like, as I am a cancer survivor myself. Just two years ago in my junior year of high school, when I thought all was going well, I was diagnosed with leukemia, a form of cancer centralized in the bloodstream. I suddenly went from being active on the tennis court to lying in a hospital bed receiving intense chemotherapy. I never in my life had experienced such agony and sickness, caused mainly by the strong medicine itself. There were times when I just wanted to

Personal experience as to the serious nature of the problem

Porter 4

be put out of my own misery and not have to deal with the extreme vomiting. The depth of nausea caused by chemotherapy was completely overwhelming and began consuming my life.

9   Most people understand nausea as a simple gastrointestinal illness that has symptoms associated with a viral gastrointestinal illness. That is in fact marginal compared to the nausea I personally went through. Whenever I had to go to the hospital, I dreaded receiving the medicine, as I knew what was to come. Although they gave me certain drugs to try to alleviate the nausea, I still never felt at peace. The two main drugs that they gave me had certain side effects including fatigue or loss of appetite, and after a short while, it started to become a mind game. If I could have gone into the hospital knowing that I could rely on smoking marijuana to help get me through the horrible side effects of chemotherapy, it would have made my treatments that much easier. My experience shows that people need to think strongly about this and come to realize that using marijuana for medicinal purposes really can impact a person's life in a positive manner.

10   Aside from controlling nausea and vomiting and stimulating a person's appetite, smoking marijuana is also said to relieve patients from chronic pain caused by diseases such as multiple sclerosis, glaucoma, and other numerous disorders and injuries. Multiple sclerosis, an inflammatory disease of the brain and spinal cord, is a serious condition that unfortunately affects many people throughout the world. By using legal marijuana, many of the patients will be able to reduce the muscle spasms and pains caused by this disease and live a happier, less excruciating life. It is also suggested, yet not clinically proven, that smoking marijuana will improve migraine symptoms that these patients also experience ("Medicinal Marijuana Briefing"). Glaucoma, another disease, is the leading cause of blindness in the United States, but some of its symptoms can be limited by smoking marijuana. The main symptoms, high intraocular pressure as well as damage to the eyes, can be reduced by marijuana ("Medicinal Marijuana Briefing"). There are many other conditions and medical problems that smoking marijuana can cure, yet it still remains illegal under the federal law.

Additional evidence of other benefits supporting the thesis

Porter 5

11   Although there are many benefits of smoking marijuana for
medicinal purposes, there are also some harmful effects. It is
commonly known that marijuana is damaging to the lungs and
should never be used as a recreational drug, but when it comes to
terminal patients suffering from different diseases, its rewards greatly
outweigh its risks. Many of those against legalization will never
understand the reason for its legalization unless a life-threatening
circumstance, in which the major source of relief is marijuana,
occurs in their own lives. Another claim is that smoking marijuana is
bad for one's immune system. This claim still remains unclear, as
scientists have not fully proven it to be true. Lastly, marijuana
carries a stigma with it that it is a very addictive drug once a person
begins smoking. This is valid only to a certain extent, as research
has shown that it is not nearly as addicting as other drugs, especially alcohol, which is legal at the age of twenty-one ("Medicinal
Marijuana," About). Few marijuana users become dependent on the
drug, and more often than not the dependence appears to be even
less severe when it is used for patients fighting off deadly diseases
because they know that their lives are at stake. For these types of
patients, the medical harm related to smoking marijuana
is of little concern and they feel that the medical benefits most
definitely outweigh the harmful effects.

> States opposing viewpoints

> Concedes one aspect of opposing viewpoint and refutes others

> Conclusion

12   The legalization of marijuana for medicinal purposes is
undoubtedly a beneficial proposal. It offers relief from a variety of
symptoms that result from intensive treatment, and it allows those
whose lives have been burdened to experience temporary liberation.
Unfortunately, marijuana has a reputation as the gateway into many
societal delinquencies. It has become associated with lack of motivation,
increased health risks, and addiction. It is because of this societal
perception that has developed over the past thirty years that its use in
aiding those who may be alive for only a couple more months, weeks,
or even days, is objectionable. It is a good thing everyone in this
world is not affected by something as detrimental as cancer or AIDS
because they would not be able to legally use marijuana. But perhaps
this would convince people to support legalization.

> Restatement of the thesis

> Summary of supporting reasons

Works Cited

"Medicinal Marijuana: A Continuing Controversy." <u>About.com.</u>
    12 Aug. 1997. 17 Sept. 2005 <http://arthritis.about.com/cs/
    medmarijuanadebate.htm>.

"Medicinal Marijuana Briefing Paper." Marijuana Policy Project. Dec.
    2004. 17 Sept. 2005 <http://www.mmp.org/omedicine.html>.

"Medicinal Marijuana: The Struggle for Legalization." <u>CNN.com</u>
    1997. Cable News Network. 17 Sept. 2005 <http://www.cnn
    .com/HEALTH/9702/weed.wars/issues/background/>.

In your paper,
the works cited
would begin on
a separate page

Strategies for Problem Solving

1. The Nature and History of the Problem

Brandon describes the problem as a reaction to the 1960s drug culture and provides evidence from recent polls showing that a majority of Americans are in favor of legalizing marijuana for medicinal purposes. He cites an unsuccessful earlier attempt to administer the ingredient in pill form and dramatizes the need for legalization by describing his own experiences as a cancer patient suffering the side effects of chemotherapy. He also cites research on the proven efficacy of marijuana in controlling pain in other chronic diseases.

2. Evaluating Alternative Solutions

Brandon examines why past attempts to solve the problem have failed by explaining why an FDA-approved drug in pill form (called Marinol) containing the active ingredient in marijuana proved ineffective. By evaluating the rewards against the risks, he also answers objections that marijuana depresses the immune system, damages the lungs, and can become addictive.

3. Considering the Audience

Brandon enhances his analysis by adopting an analytical tone and not exploiting his own suffering as a cancer patient. His approach involves separating the idea of legalizing marijuana for medicinal purposes from the audience's assumed preexisting negative associations.

4. Organizing the Essay

Brandon employs several aspects of problem-solving techniques that were covered earlier in this chapter. The introduction demonstrates his awareness that preconceptions about marijuana use in the 1960s have undermined efforts to legalize it for medical purposes in the present. This defines the problem in a way that his audience can understand and specifies the constraints that limit the problem being solved. This leads to his thesis that frames the problem and solution in terms of risk versus reward.

In the next phase of his essay, Brandon cites current polls favoring legalization and casts the DEA in the role of naysayer while Congress presumably is still flexible. At this point, Brandon recalls the past attempt to use Marinol to combat nausea and other effects of chemotherapy. He uses his own experience as a graphic illustration of how his proposed solution would have worked in a specific example. He also attempts to quell his audience's concerns that legalizing marijuana would cause undesirable consequences for the users and for society.

In Brandon's conclusion, he restates his thesis and summarizes the benefits of legalizing marijuana for medicinal purposes that he identified in the course of his essay.

5. Suggestions for Revision

Overall, this is a strong essay, but some areas for change can be identified. One of these is the conclusion, which might strike some readers as too hypothetical or even bullying in its use of scare tactics. In a few instances, Brandon's zeal in his attempt to transfer the benefits of marijuana use for recreational purposes to those who are really suffering results in inappropriate rhetoric (such as "bring a smile to those suffering from fatal diseases like cancer" in paragraph 5).

Guidelines for Writing a Problem-Solving Essay

- If your assignment requires you to solve a problem, your introduction should clearly establish that a problem exists that is serious enough to need solving. Your introduction should state the history of the problem and the success or failure of previous attempts to solve it. Although not a rhetorical strategy as such, problem-solving techniques are an invaluable part of many effective kinds of writing. The process by which problems are solved involves recognizing and defining the problem, specifying constraints that limit the way the problem can be solved, proposing and investigating a solution, verifying the solution, and communicating it to a particular audience.

- Identify the causes of the problem. Describe the circumstances that create it, explain who suffers because of it, and speculate about what would happen if the problem were not solved. Present a clear-cut example that dramatizes the consequences of failing to solve the problem.

- Assess alternative solutions. Which solution appears to be the most feasible and effective? Which would cause the least undesirable consequences? Help the reader to visualize how a solution would work through specific examples or hypothetical scenarios. Why have past attempts to solve the problem failed? Provide sound reasons for rejecting alternative solutions. Would any of these be too expensive, inefficient, unworkable, impractical, disruptive of the status quo, or unacceptable on moral or ethical grounds?

- Adopt an appropriate tone. Present yourself as a reasonable person who is well informed on the issue and sensitive to the needs and concerns of those to whom you will be presenting your recommended solution.

- Describe how the solution might be enacted. Conclude by restating your recommendation using the term "should," "ought," or "must," or words to that effect, and reinforce the audience's motivation to approve the actions that are recommended.

Grammar Tips for Problem Solving

When you write a problem-solving essay, it is important to pay attention to grammatical cues that signal complex relationships. You can use (1) coordinating conjunctions to connect or equate ideas and/or (2) subordinating conjunctions to express the relationship between ideas that depend on each other.

1. Coordinating conjunctions connect two complete sentences or two independent clauses by using *and, but, or, nor, for, so, yet*. For example:

Early studies have suggested a link between mercury-based preservatives in vaccines and autism, *yet* later studies have not confirmed this relationship.

Shelters for the homeless are by no means secure or crime free, *and* they expose their residents to the risk of being attacked.

Notice that a comma always precedes the coordinating conjunction that joins the two independent clauses.

If your essay contains too many of these compound sentences (that is, two or more simple sentences or independent clauses connected by a coordinating conjunction), you might wish to rewrite one or more as follows:

a. You can change a compound sentence into a simple sentence with a compound predicate.

Shelters for the homeless *are* by no means secure *and expose* their residents to the risk of being attacked.

b. You can change a compound sentence into a complex sentence made up of a simple sentence or independent clause and one or more dependent clauses.

Because shelters for the homeless are by no means secure, they expose their residents to the risk of being attacked.

2. As we have just seen, complex sentences use subordinating conjunctions to connect dependent to independent clauses. Subordinating conjunctions are used to express specific relationships that are especially important in problem-solving essays.

To express time: *before, after, since, until, when, as, once, whenever, while* (in the sense of "during the time that")

To express causation: *because, since*

To express limitation: *even if, if, unless, provided that*

To express contrast: *even though, although, though, rather than, as if, despite*

continued

To express purpose: *so that, in order that, that*
To express place: *where, wherever*

Remember to put a comma after a dependent clause when it precedes the independent clause. Conversely, do not use a comma when the dependent clause follows the independent clause.

Comma required:

Although she was a graduate student in animal behavior, Lisa had never heard of a tree kangaroo.

Comma not required:

Lisa had never heard of a tree kangaroo *although* she was a graduate student in animal behavior.

CHECKLIST for Revising Problem-Solving Essays

- What problem is the basis of your essay?
- Have you established that the problem is serious enough to need solving?
- Does your thesis include a recommendation as to how to solve the problem?
- Have you identified the causes of the problem and the reasons why it has not been solved thus far?
- Have you fairly stated and provided sound reasons for rejecting alternative solutions?
- Does your essay have a clear pattern of development that incorporates patterns (for example, clearly defining the problem, establishing its cause, comparing and contrasting proposed solutions)?
- Do you use transitional words and phrases that show the relationship between the problem you identify and the solution you propose?

 # ADDITIONAL WRITING ASSIGNMENTS AND ACTIVITIES

COMMUNICATING WITH DIFFERENT AUDIENCES

1. Are privately operated prisons a good idea? Why or why not? Write a letter to your congressman or senator stating your opinion.

2. Should the United States adopt a national health care program? Why or why not? Write a letter to your congressman or senator stating your opinion.

3. Write a letter to the president of a company requesting your money back for a defective product or an unsatisfactory service. Explain how the product or service was lacking and why you should be compensated.

WRITING FOR A NEWSPAPER

Write a review for the op-ed column of a controversial or problematic book (for example, Bob Woodward's 2006 book *Iraq: State of Denial*), movie (for example, Michael Moore's *Fahrenheit 911*), television program (for example, *Boston Legal*), play (David Mamet's *Edmund*), or concert (Madonna's crucifixion tableau) stating your criteria and comparing your opinion to judgments made by other reviewers.

PROBLEM-SOLVING ESSAYS

1. If you ever have been romantically involved with someone from a different racial, political, or religious background, what kinds of problems did this create and what steps did you take to solve them?
2. What contemporary work of film or literature has contributed to your understanding of problems of gender, social class, and/or ethnicity and how members of that group dealt with the problems?
3. What should be done about the presence of gangs in major cities?
4. If you had a child who was dying and the only thing that could save him or her was the bone marrow of a sibling, would you consider having another child to facilitate what was almost sure to be a positive bone-marrow transplant?
5. What item would you save in a fire (other than a person or pet), and what does your choice reveal about what is important to you?
6. If Mount Rushmore had to be recarved to display the faces of four athletes or four other celebrities, whom would you choose and why?
7. Describe an invention that does not yet exist but that would make the world a better place.
8. If you are female, would you consider keeping your maiden name after you are married? If you are male, would you consider taking your wife's name? Why or why not?
9. Would you be willing to add five years to your life if it meant taking five years away from the life of someone you did not know? Would your decision change if you knew who the person was?
10. Imagine you have been incapacitated or have a disability. Write an essay that will help your readers to understand the visible and psychological aspects of discrimination that the disabled endure every day. What measures did you take to cope with the problem?
11. What problems have you had with a pet? What did you do to solve the problem?

RESEARCH SUGGESTIONS

1. Visit the website of Pulitzer-Prize winners for photography at http://www.pulitzer.org and analyze one of the photos for the current year in terms of the issue or problem it addresses. What occasion prompted this image, and what purpose is this image designed to serve?

2. Should the FDA suspend the normally required testing periods for new drugs to provide seriously ill people with access to the most promising drugs and treatment?

COLLABORATIVE ACTIVITIES

Divide into small groups of two to four students to explore different problems and problem-solving strategies for any of these topics. After you have presented your analyses and recommendations (if possible using projected visual aids and tables, graphs, and charts), the rest of the class will decide which team made the most persuasive analysis.

1. Why don't eighteen-year-olds (who would seem to have a vested interest in who is elected) vote as often as other age groups do, and what should be done about it?

2. What problems confront students at your college or university? Which of these do you think is most important and should be solved as soon as possible? Analyze it in terms of the people who suffer because of it, the reasons why it exists, and the consequences of its failing to be solved. Offer a proposed solution specifying who has the power to solve it and the benefits and costs that would be involved. Why is your proposed solution better than alternative ones?

3. What is the most pressing issue facing America today, and what should be done about it? Follow the same steps in question 2 above in making a case for your solution.

ARGUMENT

12

Taking a Stand on Issues

An argument states an opinion and then presents one or more reasons and evidence to support that opinion. Arguments differ from expressions of personal preferences because they depend on evidence and on a pattern of logical reasoning that an audience will find credible. In the following editorial, "Fan Manipulation," for example, Nicholas F. Filla argues that the average fan is being exploited by decisions made by those who have the power to decide under what conditions we can view professional sports events:

> Professional sports management often means fan management, fan manipulation, and exploitation of the fans' fantasies. Professional sports management has made viewing the game, in person or on television, less accessible, less affordable, and less enjoyable. . . .
>
> Professional sports management has successfully adjusted to the demands of TV by orchestrating, what, when, and how we view professional sports. The marriage of sports management to television, players to agents, and the games to show business are the result of economic decisions that have sidelined the fan, discarded him like a ticket stub after a home-game loss.
>
> The scenario runs like this: Make the "product" so desirable that ticket prices are unattainable for the average family. Introduce mismanagement scenarios such as strikes, lockouts, and collective bargaining. Demand higher TV rights fees, send players' salaries up, and increase the cost to the fans, regardless of the quality of the game.
>
> And when TV revenue decreases, make sure pay-per-view is forced down fans' throats so the bottom line remains intact.
>
> That is what professional sports management has done. And the American sports fan is tired, disgusted, and wants a change.

Thus, argument is a form of advocacy that is designed to increase the likelihood that an audience will accept the truth of a claim or assertion. It also can be used to refute a claim that you believe to be untrue or answer criticisms of your own position.

THE DIFFERENCE BETWEEN ARGUMENT AND PERSUASION

Arguments present reasons and evidence to gain an audience's agreement with the validity of a proposition. This process of reasoning is designed to appeal to an audience's intellect and sense that the case being presented is well constructed and logical. By contrast, persuasion also includes appeals to the emotional needs and values of the audience and to the impact the speaker's character or personality could have. As Aristotle observed, real-world arguments appeal to the intellect, the emotions, and the audience's confidence in the speaker. Because audiences vary in the degree to which they are receptive, neutral, or hostile to the proposition being advanced, it is up to the arguer to determine the balance he or she will use. But most important, audiences expect arguers to present a well-reasoned and fair case.

WRITING EFFECTIVE ARGUMENTS

Selecting an Issue

An essay that advances an argument will not be interesting to you or your audience unless it is on an issue that is genuinely debatable. Moreover, the topic that you choose must be specific enough that you will be able to explore it in depth within the number of pages you have been assigned and the time you have available to do the assignment. Often, the best topics or issues involve questions about which knowledgeable people disagree or situations that are open to more than one interpretation. You will also need to consider the objective or goal you wish to achieve in your argument. Beyond winning an audience's intellectual agreement, do you want them to take some action or approve a course of action that you recommend?

Stating Your Position

The assertion or claim that will serve as the focus of your essay should be stated in the form of a *thesis statement*. The way you phrase the thesis statement is particularly important, since you will be required to develop your argument by supplying reasons and evidence that would convince someone who held the opposite point of view. For example, suppose you assert the following:

> It is immoral to keep animals in zoos for our entertainment and education.

Your claim or thesis statement meets the central requirement of being debatable, as many people would disagree and say that zoos are important for our education and to preserve endangered species. In your argument you will have to define exactly what you mean by *immoral* and answer the objections of those who disagree with your position.

Considering Your Audience

Next, after selecting a debatable topic and making sure it is narrow enough to be developed, you must consider the specific audience for whom you are writing your argument. Are they predisposed to accept your claim, to be neutral, or known to have a vested interest that would make them resist your assertion? For most arguers, the best approach to take is to construct your case with clear logic and persuasive evidence to get a fair hearing even from those who are opposed to your position. For example, you might anticipate that you would have no problem convincing a general audience that tax money should not be used to subsidize tobacco growers, since the government requires health warnings on every pack of cigarettes and prohibits advertising for cigarettes on radio and television. But the same could not be said if your audience consisted of legislators or lobbyists from states in which tobacco was grown. For this audience, your argument might stress the double standard of requiring health warnings while giving money to the same companies about whose products the public is being warned.

Providing Evidence

A well-reasoned argument not only makes a claim, but also presents reasons and evidence that will convince an audience that the claim is true. Evidence can appear in a variety of forms, including examples drawn from personal experience, statistics, and the opinions of experts on a set of facts.

Examples drawn from personal experience are relevant if your experiences clearly illustrate, document, or substantiate your thesis.

Statistics are among the most compelling kinds of proof a writer can offer to support a thesis.

Expert opinion is not a substitute for the process of reasoning by which you arrive at your conclusion, but a well-known authority in the field can add credibility to your argument. For example, because a great many people use cell phones while driving, an argument that sought to convince your audience that the likelihood of having an accident was greater under these circumstances could benefit from citing an expert opinion. You might cite the result of a study released in 2005 by the Insurance Institute for Highway Safety in Perth, Australia. Researchers studied patterns of cell phone use by several hundred drivers who were treated in an emergency room for injuries after car accidents and discovered that the use of a cell phone within ten minutes of the accident was associated with a fourfold increase in the likelihood of an accident. In this case, the expert opinion might supplement your reasoning based on the commonsense assumption that being distracted while driving increases the risk of a crash. When considering whether to quote an authority, remember that the expert must be an authority in that field and that the opinion must be free from bias, subject to verification, relevant, and timely.

Evaluating Evidence

There are certain considerations to keep in mind when you are evaluating what kind of evidence and how much evidence would be needed to convince your audience to give your case a fair hearing. First, your evidence should be appropriate, that is, it should directly pertain to the assertion you wish your audience to accept. For example, if you were trying to persuade an audience of office workers about the need for or dangers of corporate surveillance of personal e-mail, an example drawn from the government's use of phone records to locate Japanese citizens for internment during World War II would be irrelevant. Next, the evidence, in whatever form it appears, should reflect positions on different sides of the issue so that your readers will feel that you are being fair and are acknowledging opposing positions besides providing compelling evidence to support your own views. For example, in an essay in which you discuss the causal relationship between vaccines with the mercury-based preservative thimerosal and increased rates of autism, you would want to supplement opinions supporting your position with expert opinions drawn from those on the opposing side. Finally, your evidence should be ample and proportionate to the length of your essay. Moreover, you would need more evidence for an audience that was not in agreement with your thesis than you would for an audience that already agreed with you and wanted reinforcement for their views.

Documenting Your Sources

Occasionally, the evidence that you generate will be based on your own experiences. More often, you will need to explore your topic by drawing on books, journals, and other printed materials as well as online sources of information available in your library and on the Internet. As you gather this evidence, you need to document all information that is not common knowledge (the recommended format is that of the Modern Language Association, discussed in detail in Chapter 2). You must give proper credit to avoid plagiarism and to acknowledge that these ideas belong to others. By identifying your sources, you also enable your audience to judge the authenticity of the evidence you present.

Refuting Opposing Viewpoints

In the course of developing your argument, you are likely to encounter opposing viewpoints. Your argument will be more persuasive if you acknowledge these viewpoints and refute them convincingly. Readers of arguments often wonder what someone on the other side would say and will fault you if you are perceived as ignoring these objections. To refute opposing arguments, you might look at the reasons and evidence that are advanced to support them. Is the reasoning flawed or based on unsound assumptions? Are key terms defined adequately? Has the writer successfully demonstrated clear causal connections? Are the recommended courses of action feasible? Is the evidence offered skewed or insufficient? Does your argument present more compelling evidence on the same points? A critical analysis of opposing viewpoints also requires that you acknowledge when the opposition has a good point. You can then go on to show that the writer did not take into account additional points that are the basis for your argument.

Using Rogerian Argument

The audience that you are trying to persuade might already have formed strong opinions and beliefs. You might wish to use the approach recommended by the psychologist Carl Rogers. He pointed out that people on both sides of an argument fail to hear each other and instead identify with their position so strongly that they find it difficult even to consider another point of view. Rogers suggested that for many writers, a reasonable goal is not so much to change the readers' mind as to persuade them to give the writer's opposing point of view a fair hearing. He recommended that

> [t]he next time you get into an argument with your wife, or your friend, or with a small group of friends, just stop the discussion for a moment and for an experiment, institute this rule. "Each person can speak up for himself only *after* he has restated the ideas and feelings of the previous speaker accurately, and to that speaker's satisfaction."

You can incorporate this method in your own arguments by summarizing an opponent's viewpoint on an issue in a fair way and thus increasing the chance that your audience will be receptive to your point of view.

REASONING IN DEDUCTIVE AND INDUCTIVE ARGUMENTS

There are two basic methods of drawing conclusions from the evidence you have gathered. In **deductive reasoning**, you begin with an assumption or generalization that is widely agreed upon and apply this to a specific case to draw a valid conclusion. In deductive reasoning, the conclusion is logically certain or valid because it necessarily follows from premises that are taken to be true. The other method of drawing conclusions is called **inductive reasoning** because it always requires an inference or **inductive leap** to reach a generalization from individual cases, facts, and examples. Both forms of reasoning operate in oral and written arguments, since they complement each other: The generalizations that are the starting point for deductive reasoning are the conclusions that are reached through inductive reasoning. Let's look at each of these methods.

Deductive Arguments

A **syllogism** is the basic form of deductive arguments and consists of a *major premise* (a general statement), a *minor premise* (a specific statement), and a *conclusion* which is drawn from these premises. For example:

Major premise: All human beings are mortal.
Minor premise: Mary is a human being.
Conclusion: Therefore, Mary is mortal.

Notice how deductive reasoning applies a general statement about an entire group or class to a particular case that identifies an individual as a member of that class to draw a logical conclusion that what is true of the group is true of the individual.

Conclusions that are drawn by means of deductive reasoning are both logically certain and valid. If either the major or minor premise is not true, then the conclusion, although logical, will not be true either. But what are we to make of the following syllogism?

Major premise: All giraffes are mammals.
Minor premise: Socrates is a mammal.
Conclusion: Therefore, Socrates is a giraffe.

This syllogism is defective because it illustrates the fallacy of what is called the *undistributed middle term*; that is, the minor premise does not refer to an item in the class covered in the major premise.

In deductive arguments expressed in ordinary language (not syllogisms), one premise is generally implicit and understood rather than actually stated. Also, the conclusion may be implied rather than being explicitly stated. The result is called an *enthymeme*. For example, Charles de Gaulle once rhetorically asked, "How can you be expected to govern a country that has 246 kinds of cheese?" This enthymeme takes for granted the unexpressed major premise that might be stated as "Any country whose citizens have hundreds of preferences in cheese is unlikely to unite behind one political leader." It is often helpful to make the unexpressed major premise explicit in order to evaluate the soundness of different parts of the argument. Deductive reasoning is useful when an audience might reject a conclusion if it were stated at the outset. But a writer who can get an audience to agree with the assumptions on which the argument is based has a better chance of getting the audience to agree with the conclusion that follows logically from the premises.

Inductive Arguments

Unlike deductive reasoning, which reaches conclusions based on premises, inductive reasoning draws inferences from particular cases to create a hypothesis that is highly probable rather than certain. Writers use inductive reasoning to draw inferences from evidence in order to convince an audience to accept a claim. For example, suppose the question you wished to investigate was "Why are twenty-somethings moving back in with their parents at an increased rate?" The evidence that you would consider would include data from surveys, newspaper reports, magazine articles, films such as *Failure to Launch* (2006), and anecdotal reports from friends and/or personal experiences. Your conclusion might be that it is hard to find jobs after graduation that will pay for increased costs of living. This conclusion involves an inductive leap, since it would be impossible to observe every new graduate who is faced with the choice of living at the poverty level or moving back home into one's old room, perhaps with the benefit of laundry facilities, cable TV, and meals. Writers using inductive reasoning must be careful not to draw conclusions from limited or atypical instances. This logical fallacy is called a **hasty** or **sweeping generalization**. Arguments that generalize from a broader variety of sources will be more convincing than arguments that generalize from fewer examples.

Understanding Toulmin's Logic

The British logician and philosopher Stephen Toulmin devised another useful means of identifying important features of arguments as they are engaged in by people in real life. Its advantage is that by charting the different parts of an argument, it can help us to develop a more accurate picture of the unstated and implicit assumptions on which the argument is based. In Toulmin's model, the three basic elements to be considered in any argument include (1) the **claim** or proposition the audience is to consider; (2) the **evidence**, support, or grounds the writer will have to produce to back up the claim; and (3) the **warrant**, or underlying assumption, belief, or inference that spells out the relationship between the claim and the evidence offered to support it.

In its basic form, an argument in Toulmin's model would appear as follows:

Claim: Sara should not be found guilty of murder, since she has been declared mentally incompetent.

Grounds: The defendant has been found to be mentally incompetent by court-appointed psychiatrists.

Warrant: The law does not punish people who lack the capacity for choice.

What Toulmin refers to as the *warrant* is what is known as the *major premise* in a deductive argument: the overall justification for drawing a particular conclusion from the evidence offered to support a claim. For an argument to be persuasive, the warrant should be clear and be one on which the writer and the audience agree.

Identifying Common Fallacies

Fallacies give the appearance of being reasonable and sound but, when looked at closely, are based on faulty reasoning and/or appeals to prejudices and preconceptions. They can undermine the audience's confidence in what might otherwise be a convincing argument. The following are some of the more common fallacies.

Begging the Question (Circular Reasoning) A pseudo-argument that offers as proof the claim that the argument itself exists to prove.

Congress should require manufacturers of unreliable cars such as gas-electric hybrids to warn consumers about costs and how often they break down.

This argument begs the question because it assumes that readers will accept the claim that such cars are unreliable.

Argument from Analogy An unwarranted assumption that because two things are comparable in some respects, they are comparable in other ways as well.

Darrell F. Gates in his book *Chief: My Life in the LAPD* equates the release of convicted criminals who are then convicted of new crimes as being the same as a leaky pipe: "If you had a leaky pipe, you wouldn't keep calling a plumber to patch it up—you would get a new pipe. It would be fixed, and the leak controlled. We need to begin to control our criminals' leak too, putting an end to the faulty patchwork."

Personal Attack (Argumentum ad Hominem) An attack against the person instead of the issue.

Senator X had an affair while married, so how can we listen to his pleas for federal funding for homeless shelters?

Hasty or Sweeping Generalization An erroneous judgment based on too few instances or on atypical or inadequate examples.

Because my Uncle John wears suspenders and has no sense of humor, I am sure that all men who wear suspenders have no sense of humor.

False Dilemma (Either/Or) A simplistic characterization suggesting that there are only two choices in a particular situation.

We must remedy the illegal immigration problem by building a fence along the Mexican border or watch the economies of California and Texas collapse.

Equivocation A key term takes on different meanings at different points in the claim. For example, consider Zsa Zsa Gabor's observation that "a man in love is incomplete until he has married. Then he's finished." Notice how the term "incomplete" takes on two different meanings.

Red Herring The bringing in of a tangential or irrelevant point to divert attention from the real issue.

The conservative commentator Rush Limbaugh responded to news that dolphins may be almost as intelligent as humans by saying, "Could somebody please show me one hospital built by a dolphin?"

You Also (Tu Quoque) Discounting an opponent's claim on the grounds that he or she has not followed the advice given to others.

How could you take the advice of that marriage counselor when everyone knows that she is divorced?

Appeal to Doubtful Authority   Citing of an authority outside the field of his or her relevant expertise.

Derek Jeter of the Yankees baseball team asserts that E. coli contamination poses a greater threat to public health than bird flu.

Misleading Statistics   Distorted statistics that convey an erroneous impression by omitting a context in which to make an interpretation. Someone who reads that "nine out of ten dentists who recommend chewing gum recommend XYZ gum" might not recognize that the sample has been distorted to refer to survey only those dentists who recommend chewing gum, an atypical and minuscule subgroup of all dentists.

Post Hoc Ergo Propter Hoc (after this, therefore because of this)   The incorrect inference that simply because B follows A, A has caused B.

After Tom started listening to his iPod while studying, he got better grades. Therefore, his iPod made him a better student.

Non Sequitur (it does not follow)   The introduction of irrelevant evidence to support a claim.

Lawrence P. Goldman, chief executive of NJPAC (New Jersey Performing Arts Center), was reported as saying, "We're not going to let a developer put up an ugly building— there have to be shops and galleries, and cafes, because that's in our DNA."

Slippery Slope   A failure to provide evidence to support predictions that one event will lead to a chain of events, usually catastrophic.

In 1901, Henry T. Finck forecast dire consequences if women were given the vote: "Doctors tell us … that thousands of children would be harmed or killed before birth by the injurious effect of untimely political excitement on their mothers."

▓▓▓▓ TRANSITIONS

Transitional words and phrases are invaluable in an argument in informing the reader how paragraphs are related to each other. Transitions can serve several purposes. Some transitions signal your reader that you are following a sequential or chronological order (with terms such as *first, second, third,* and *last*). Other linking words express causal relationships, such as *as a result, since, consequently, because, therefore,* and *thus.* Still other guide words express amplification, such as *furthermore, really, in addition, ultimately,* and *moreover.* Words that alert your reader that you are examining opposing arguments include *although, however, yet,* and *granted.* An especially important category of words that signal that you have reached a conclusion include *it follows that, in summary, which shows that,* and *as a result.* These terms help your reader to understand the organization of your essay and the relationship between the sections and the central idea expressed in your thesis.

ORGANIZING AN ARGUMENT ESSAY

The choices that are open to the writer in organizing an argument essay depend on the nature of the thesis, the kind of claim on which the thesis is based, and, perhaps most important, the anticipated attitude of the audience toward this claim. Like other kinds of essays, the traditional argument essay has three parts: the introduction, middle or body, and conclusion.

The function of the introduction is to engage the reader in the central issue and to present your claim regarding the question at hand. If you intend to disagree with widely held views or if the nature of the issue is complex or unfamiliar to your readers, you might use the first few paragraphs to briefly summarize relevant background information before explicitly stating your thesis.

The middle portion, or body, of the essay presents reasons and evidence that support your thesis. Some parts can be structured inductively by offering evidence that leads to and supports the thesis. Other parts can be structured deductively and use the pattern of major premise, minor premise, and conclusion to prove the thesis. The middle portion may also contain a critical analysis of opposing arguments along with reasons why your opinion should be accepted as more persuasive.

Your conclusion should restate the thesis (although you should use different words), summarize important points and evidence that you developed within the essay, and conclude on a note of certainty that makes your readers feel that you fulfilled your obligation to prove your thesis.

Martin Luther King, Jr.'s speech, "I Have a Dream," to the quarter of a million people who had assembled in Washington, D.C., in 1963 exemplifies many aspects of an effective argument. The speech was intended to commemorate the centennial of Lincoln's Emancipation Proclamation freeing slaves in the Confederate states. King uses the occasion to state his thesis that the rights guaranteed in the Declaration of Independence have not been granted to blacks. King connects his aspirations with the dreams of America's founding fathers of a new nation where prejudice does not exist. To prove his point, he cites evidence in the form of a litany of injustices, including segregated facilities, racial prejudice, police brutality, the refusal to allow blacks such basic rights as riding at the front of buses and lodging in all motels, and the dismal condition of life in the slums and ghettos, sanctioned by a system which deprived blacks of their most basic right to vote.

Throughout his speech, King uses vivid metaphors and analogies to take the abstract idea of "inalienable rights" and translate it into a concrete image of a bad check stamped "insufficient funds." Because King was adamantly against violence, he stresses that the battle for equality had to be carried out through acts of peaceful protest. This portion of his speech refutes apprehensions that the civil rights movement would degenerate into violence. In his conclusion, King eloquently frames his appeal for all groups, whites and blacks, to continue the struggle for freedom and incorporates lyrics from "My Country, 'Tis of Thee." This classic speech uses a range of argumentation strategies that are well suited to King's purpose, audience, and occasion.

When you approach a topic that you have chosen, let your thesis, purpose, audience, and, if relevant, occasion, determine the kind of organization you will use. For instance, suppose you were assigned the following paper topic in a sociology class:

> Would the legalization of drugs be beneficial or harmful to American society?
> Choose one aspect of this broad topic, and write a short paper addressed to those who hold an opposing viewpoint. Remember to take into account, fairly summarize, and refute possible objections to your argument.

You are aware of this issue because recent newspaper articles have published the results of medical studies showing the usefulness of a chemical in marijuana in delaying the acceleration of Alzheimer's disease. You have also traveled to countries such as the Netherlands that have legalized drugs without seemingly adverse effects. As a result, you believe that you can make a strong case for legalization and reply to the arguments of those who disagree with you.

In outline form, your proposed argument might appear as follows:

> Overview of the issue: Should drugs be legalized?
>
> Thesis statement: Although those who are opposed to legalization claim that it would result in a dramatic increase in drug abuse and crime, legalization most likely would reduce the level of drug-related violence and would save the government billions of dollars a year without endangering public health.
>
> Support: (via deductive reasoning) Explain that drug users commit crimes to support their addiction and that these crimes would diminish if drugs were made readily available.
>
> Support: (via inductive reasoning) Present recent examples of government studies linking street trafficking and drug-related violence to gangs that control the drug market. Present statistics showing how much prison space is taken by nonviolent drug users that would become available for violent criminals.
>
> Support: (via deductive reasoning) Explain how the drug policies of other nations that have legalized drugs and suffered little or no adverse effects could be applied to the United States.
>
> Refuting objections: Fairly state and respond to those who say that legalization would increase addiction by making drugs readily available. Respond to

opponents' views that drugs themselves cause crimes by showing that crimes are caused by the user's need for money to buy drugs. Concede that it is still an open question whether drug education will work.

Conclusion: Restate your thesis, and emphasize the common ground with you and your audience—that the magnitude of the problem requires a different approach.

WILLIAM SALETAN

Overabundance, Not Hunger, Is the World's New Peril

With the widely reported stories of starvation in the Third World, one might assume that scarcity of food is a pressing problem. But William Saletan, chief national correspondent for Slate.com, claims that the opposite is true: The availability of filling, but not nutritious, food and the resulting obesity around the world, with its concomitant diseases, are the real problem. He presents this atypical view in the following article, which first appeared in the *Washington Post* (2006). Saletan grew up in Texas and currently lives in Maryland. He honed his skills as a reporter covering the 2004 Republican Convention and is the author of *Bearing Right: How Conservatives Won the Abortion War* (2003).

BEFORE YOU READ

What have you observed that might suggest that obesity rather than starvation has become a worldwide problem?

■ ■ ▨

1   Over the past four decades, global population has doubled, but food output, driven by increases in productivity, has outpaced it. Poverty, infant mortality and hunger are receding. For the first time in our planet's history, a species no longer lives at the mercy of scarcity. We have learned to feed ourselves.

2   We've learned so well, in fact, that we're getting fat. Not just the United States or Europe, but the whole world. Egyptian, Mexican and South African women are now as fat as Americans. Far more Filipino adults are now overweight than underweight. In China, one in five adults is too heavy, and the rate of overweight children is 28 times higher than it was two decades ago. In Kuwait, Thailand and Tunisia, obesity, diabetes and heart disease are soaring.

3   Hunger is far from conquered. But since 1990, the global rate of malnutrition has declined an average of 1.7 percent a year. Based on data from the World Health Organization and the U.N. Food and Agriculture Organization, for every two people who are malnourished, three are now overweight or obese. Among women, even in most African countries, overweight has surpassed underweight. The balance of peril is shifting.

4   Fat is no longer a rich man's disease. For middle- and high-income Americans, the obesity rate is 29 percent. For low-income Americans, it's 35 percent. Fourteen percent of middle- and high-income kids age 15 to 17 are overweight. For low-income kids in the same age bracket, it's 23 percent.

5   Globally, weight has tended to rise with income. But a recent study in Vancouver, Canada, found that preschoolers in "food-insecure" households were twice as likely as other kids to be overweight or obese. In Brazilian cities, the poor have become fatter than the rich.

6 Technologically, this is a triumph. In the early days of our species, even the rich starved. Barry Popkin, a nutritional epidemiologist at the University of North Carolina, divides history into several epochs. In the hunter-gatherer era, if we didn't find food, we died. In the agricultural era, if our crops perished, we died. In the industrial era, famine receded, but infectious diseases killed us.

7 Now we've achieved such control over nature that we're dying not of starvation or infection, but of abundance. Nature isn't killing us. We're killing ourselves.

8 You don't have to go hungry anymore; we can fill you with fats and carbs more cheaply than ever. You don't have to chase your food; we can bring it to you. You don't have to cook it; we can deliver it ready to eat. You don't have to eat it before it spoils; we can pump it full of preservatives so it lasts forever. You don't even have to stop when you're full. We've got so much food to sell, we want you to keep eating.

9 What happened in America is happening everywhere, only faster. Fewer farmers markets, more processed food. Fewer whole grains, more refined ones. More sweeteners, salt and transfats. Cheaper meat, more animal fat. Less cooking, more eating out. Bigger portions, more snacks.

10 Kentucky Fried Chicken and Pizza Hut are spreading across the planet. Coca-Cola is in more than 200 countries. Half of McDonald's business is outside the United States. In China, animal fat intake has tripled in 20 years. By 2020, meat consumption in developing countries will grow by 106 million metric tons, outstripping growth in developed countries by a factor of more than five. Forty years ago, to afford a high-fat diet, your country needed a gross national product per capita of nearly $1,500. Now the price is half that. You no longer have to be rich to die a rich man's death.

11 Soon it'll be a poor man's death. The rich have Whole Foods, gyms and personal trainers. The poor have 7-11, Popeye's and streets unsafe for walking. When money's tight, you feed your kids at Wendy's and stock up on macaroni and cheese. At a lunch buffet, you do what your ancestors did: store all the fat you can.

12 That's the punch line: Technology has changed everything but us. We evolved to survive scarcity. We crave fat. We're quick to gain weight and slow to lose it. Double what you serve us; we'll double what we eat. Thanks to technology, the deprivation that made these traits useful is gone. So is the link between flavors and nutrients. The food industry can sell you sweetness without fruit, salt without protein, creaminess without milk. We can fatten and starve you at the same time.

13 And that's just the diet side of the equation. Before technology, adult men expended about 3,000 calories a day. Now they expend about 2,000. The folks fielding customer service calls in Bangalore are sitting at desks. Nearly everyone in China has a television set. Remember when Chinese rode bikes? In the past six years, the number of cars there has grown from 6 million to 20 million. More than one in seven Chinese has a motorized vehicle, and households with such vehicles have an obesity rate 80 percent higher than their peers.

14 The answer to these trends is simple. We have to exercise more and change the food we eat, donate and subsidize. [In 2007], for example, the U.S. Women, Infants, and Children program, which subsidizes groceries for impoverished

youngsters, will begin to pay for fruits and vegetables. For 32 years, the program has fed toddlers eggs and cheese but not one vegetable. And we wonder why poor kids are fat.

15   The hard part is changing our mentality. We have a distorted body image. We're so used to not having enough, as a species, that we can't believe the problem is too much. From China to Africa to Latin America, people are trying to fatten their kids. I just got back from a vacation with my Jewish mother and Jewish mother-in-law. They told me I need to eat more.

16   The other thing blinding us is liberal guilt. We're so caught up in the idea of giving that we can't see the importance of changing behavior rather than filling bellies. We know better than to feed buttered popcorn to zoo animals, yet we send it to a food bank and call ourselves humanitarians. Maybe we should ask what our fellow humans actually need.

■ ■ ▨

MEANING

1. According to Saletan, why is the food problem that the world confronts today ironic in view of past fears?

2. What income factors does Saletan find contributing to the problem?

3. What kinds of adjustments will have to be made in terms of education and cultural expectations, in Saletan's view?

4. How have modern changes in lifestyle made the problem harder to solve?

TECHNIQUE

1. How does Saletan use statistics and comparisons to support his argument?

2. How does Saletan use the link between social class and obesity to support his analysis?

3. *Other Patterns.* How does Saletan's essay depend on his **definition** of overabundance as the problem to be solved?

LANGUAGE

1. How would you characterize the tone of Saletan's essay? Where does he use irony to underscore his thesis (for example, in paragraph 14)?

2. How does Saletan use antithesis (for example, in paragraph 11) to make his point?

3. If you don't know the meaning of the following words, look them up: *epidemiologist* (6), *infectious* (6), *Bangalore* (11), *impoverished* (12), *humanitarians* (14).

SUGGESTIONS FOR WRITING

1. *Critical Writing.* To what extent have you been subject to the same kind of cultural programming regarding overeating that Saletan discusses?

2. How can Saletan's observations be reconciled with the predictions of too many people and not enough food that Thomas Robert Malthus (1766–1834) made in "An Essay on the Principle of Population" (1798)?

3. What steps are being taken to alert the public about the problem in regard to exactly what they are eating?

4. Evaluate the causes that Saletan cites to support his argument. Which ones are objective and measurable, and which ones are simply his opinion?

5. *Thematic Links.* In what respects do Saletan and Alan T. Durning in "Asking How Much Is Enough" offer complementary perspectives on overconsumption?

ALAN T. DURNING

Asking How Much Is Enough

The radical disparity between affluent societies' wasteful use of natural resources compared with the rest of the world requires, according to Alan T. Durning, a radical solution. Durning makes his case in the following selection from the "State of the World Report" of the Worldwatch Institute (1991), where Durning is currently a senior researcher. This article was published in the same year by the *San Francisco Chronicle*. Durning, who was educated at Oberlin College, expresses these environmental concerns in much of what he writes, including *This Place on Earth 2000: Measuring What Matters* (2002).

BEFORE YOU READ

What are the consequences for society when consuming more becomes the goal?

■ ■ ◪

1 Early in the age of affluence that followed World War II, an American retailing analyst named Victor Lebow proclaimed, "Our enormously productive economy . . . demands that we make consumption our way of life, that we convert the buying and use of goods into rituals, that we seek our spiritual satisfaction, our ego satisfaction, in consumption. . . . We need things consumed, burned up, worn out, replaced and discarded at an ever increasing rate."

2 Americans have responded to Lebow's call, and much of the world has followed.

3 Consumption has become a central pillar of life in industrial lands and is even embedded in social values. Opinion surveys in the world's two largest economies—Japan and the United States—show consumerist definitions of success becoming ever more prevalent.

4 In Taiwan, a billboard demands "Why Aren't You a Millionaire Yet?" The Japanese speak of the "new three sacred treasures": color television, air conditioning and the automobile.

5 The affluent life-style born in the United States is emulated by those who can afford it around the world. And many can: the average person today is 4.5 times richer than were his or her great-grandparents at the turn of the century.

6 Needless to say, that new global wealth is not evenly spread among the earth's people. One billion live in unprecedented luxury; 1 billion live in destitution. Even American children have more pocket money—$230 a year—than the half-billion poorest people alive.

7 Overconsumption by the world's fortunate is an environmental problem unmatched in severity by anything but perhaps population growth. Their surging exploitation of resources threatens to exhaust or unalterably disfigure forests, soils, water, air and climate.

8   Ironically, high consumption may be a mixed blessing in human terms, too. The time-honored values of integrity of character, good work, friendship, family and community have often been sacrificed in the rush to riches.

9   Thus many in the industrial lands have a sense that their world of plenty is somehow hollow—that, hoodwinked by a consumerist culture, they have been fruitlessly attempting to satisfy what are essentially social, psychological and spiritual needs with material things.

10   Of course, the opposite of overconsumption—poverty—is no solution to either environmental or human problems. It is infinitely worse for people and bad for the natural world too. Dispossessed peasants slash-and-burn their way into the rain forests of Latin America, and hungry nomads turn their herds out onto fragile African rangeland, reducing it to desert.

11   If environmental destruction results when people have either too little or too much, we are left to wonder how much is enough. What level of consumption can the earth support? When does having more cease to add appreciably to human satisfaction?

12   Answering these questions definitively is impossible, but for each of us in the world's consuming class, asking is essential nonetheless. Unless we see that more is not always better, our efforts to forestall ecological decline will be overwhelmed by our appetites.

13   In simplified terms, an economy's total burden on the ecological systems that undergird it is a function of three factors: the size of the population, average consumption and the broad set of technologies—everything from mundane clothesline to the most sophisticated satellite communications system—the economy uses to provide goods and services.

14   Changing agricultural patterns, transportation systems, urban design, energy uses and the like could radically reduce the total environmental damage caused by the consuming societies, while allowing those at the bottom of the economic ladder to rise without producing such egregious effects.

15   Japan, for example, uses a third as much energy as the Soviet Union to produce a dollar's worth of goods and services, and Norwegians use half as much paper and cardboard apiece as their neighbors in Sweden, though they are equals in literacy and richer in monetary terms.

16   Some guidance on what the earth can sustain emerges from an examination of current consumption patterns around the world.

17   For three of the most ecologically important types of consumption—transportation, diet and use of raw materials—the world's people are distributed unevenly over a vast range. Those at the bottom clearly fall below the "too little" line, while those at the top, in what could be called the cars-meat-and-disposables class, clearly consume too much.

18   About 1 billion people do most of their traveling, aside from the occasional donkey or bus ride, on foot, many of them never going more than 500 miles from their birthplaces. Unable to get to jobs easily, attend school or bring their

complaints before government offices, they are severely hindered by the lack of transportation options.

19   The massive middle class of the world, numbering some 3 billion, travels by bus and bicycle. Mile for mile, bikes are cheaper than any other vehicles, costing less than $100 new in most of the Third World and requiring no fuel.

20   The world's automobile class is relatively small: only 8 percent of humans, about 400 million people, own cars. Their cars are directly responsible for an estimated 13 percent of carbon dioxide emissions from fossil fuels worldwide, along with air pollution, acid rain and a quarter-million traffic fatalities a year.

21   Car owners bear indirect responsibility for the far-reaching impacts of their chosen vehicle. The automobile makes itself indispensable: cities sprawl, public transit atrophies, shopping centers multiply, workplaces scatter. As suburbs spread, families start to need a car for each driver.

22   One-fifth of American households own three or more vehicles, more than half own at least two, and 65 percent of new American houses are built with two-car garages.

23   Today, working Americans spend nine hours a week behind the wheel. To make these homes-away-from-home more comfortable, 90 percent of new cars have air conditioning, doubling their contributions to climate change and adding emissions of ozone-depleting chlorofluorocarbons.

24   Some in the auto class are also members of a more select group: the global jet set. Although an estimated 1 billion people travel by air each year, the overwhelming majority of trips are taken by a small group. The 4 million Americans who account for 41 percent of domestic trips, for example, cover five times as many miles a year as average Americans.

25   Furthermore, because each mile traveled by air uses more energy than one traveled by car, jetsetters consume six-and-half times as much energy for transportation as other car-class members.

26   The global food consumption ladder has three rungs. At the bottom, the world's 630 million poorest people are unable to provide themselves with a healthy diet, according to the latest World Bank estimates.

27   On the next rung, the 3.4 billion grain eaters of the world's middle class get enough calories and plenty of plant-based protein, giving them the healthiest basic diet of the world's people. They typically receive less than 20 percent of their calories from fat, a level low enough to protect them from the consequences of excessive dietary fat.

28   The top of the ladder is populated by the meat eaters, those who obtain close to 40 percent of their calories from fat. These 1.25 billion people eat three times as much fats per person as the remaining 4 billion, mostly because they eat so much red meat. The meat class pays the price of its diet in high death rates from the so-called diseases of affluence—heart disease, stroke and certain types of cancer.

29   The earth also pays for the high-fat diet. Indirectly, the meat-eating quarter of humanity consumes nearly 40 percent of the world's grain—grain that fattens the livestock they eat. Meat production is behind a substantial share of the environmental strains induced by the present global agricultural system, from soil erosion to overpumping of underground water.

30   In the extreme case of American beef, producing 2 pounds of steak requires 10 pounds of grain and the energy equivalent of 2 gallons of gasoline, not to mention the associated soil erosion, water consumption, pesticide and fertilizer runoff, groundwater depletion and emissions of the greenhouse gas methane.

31   Beyond the effects of livestock production, the affluent diet rings up an ecological bill through its heavy dependence on long-distance transport. North Europeans eat lettuce trucked from Greece and decorate their tables with flowers flown in from Kenya. Japanese eat turkey from the United States and ostrich from Australia.

32   One-fourth of the grapes eaten in the United States are grown 5,500 miles away, in Chile, and the typical mouthful of American food travels 1,000 miles from farm field to dinner plate.

33   Processing and packaging add further resource costs to the way the affluent eat. Extensively packaged foods are energy gluttons, but even seemingly simple foods need a surprising amount of energy to prepare ounce for ounce, getting canned corn to the consumer takes 10 times the energy of providing fresh corn in season. Frozen corn, if left in the freezer for much time, takes even more energy.

34   To be sure, canned and frozen vegetables make a healthy diet easy even in the dead of winter; more of a concern are the new generation of microwave-ready instant meals. Loaded with disposable pans and multilayer packaging, their resource inputs are orders of magnitude larger than preparing the same dishes at home from scratch.

35   In raw material consumption, the same pattern emerges.

36   In the throwaway economy, packaging becomes an end in itself, disposables proliferate, and durability suffers. Four percent of consumer expenditures on goods in the United States goes for packaging—$225 a year.

37   Likewise, the Japanese use 30 million "disposable" single-roll cameras each year, and the British dump 12.5 billion diapers. Americans toss away 180 million razors annually, enough paper and plastic plates and cups to feed the world a picnic six times a year, and enough aluminum cans to make 6,000 DC-10 airplanes.

38   Where disposability and planned obsolescence fail to accelerate the trip from cash register to junk heap, fashion sometimes succeeds. Most clothing goes out of style long before it is worn out; lately, the realm of fashion has even colonized sports footwear. Kevin Ventrudo, chief financial officer of California-based L. A. Gear, which saw sales multiply 50 times in four years, told the Washington Post, "If you talk about shoe performance, you only need one or two pairs. If you're talking fashion, you're talking endless pairs of shoes."

39   In transportation, diet and use of raw materials, as consumption rises on the economic scale, so does waste—both of resources and of health. Bicycles and public transit are cheaper, more efficient and healthier transport options than cars. A diet founded on the basics of grains and water is gentle to the earth and the body.

40   And a lifestyle that makes full use of raw materials for durable goods without succumbing to the throwaway mentality is ecologically sound while still affording many of the comforts of modernity.

■ ■ ▨

MEANING

1. What traditional values became less important as overconsumption became the norm?
2. What factors help to explain why the ethic of "throwaway" consumption has become the dominant value in American culture?
3. In Durning's view, what are the penalties for the ethic of increased consumption that has become the dominant way of life in the United States and other industrialized countries?
4. In Durning's view, into what three divisions can worldwide food consumption be categorized? Why is the top level so wasteful?

TECHNIQUE

1. How does Durning's analysis depend on documenting the inequities and consequences of excessive use of fuel, wasteful consumption of food, and inefficient use of resources?
2. What phase of Durning's argument is designed to show the extent to which consumption has become identified with our social values?
3. **Other Patterns.** How does Durning use **classification and division** to emphasize the enormous disparity between tiers of the world's population with access to basic resources?

LANGUAGE

1. How does the title Durning has chosen focus on the central issue of his essay?
2. How does the quote in paragraph 1, with which Durning begins his analysis, illustrate the values that his essay assails?
3. If you do not know the meaning of the following words, look them up: *unprecedented* (6), *exploitation* (7), *egregious* (14), *affluence* (28), *obsolescence* (37).

SUGGESTIONS FOR WRITING

1. **Critical Writing.** Has Durning's argument persuaded you to make any changes in your lifestyle that you otherwise would not have? Why or why not?
2. What environmental impacts of everyday products are an issue on your campus or in your community?
3. In an essay, explore the **casual** relationship between planned obsolescence and fashion.
4. **Thematic Links.** What additional insight does Thor Heyerdahl in "How to Kill an Ocean" (Chapter 11, "Problem Solving") give you into Durning's thesis?

MARTIN LUTHER KING, JR.

I Have a Dream

The central figure in the civil rights movement and a persuasive champion of nonviolent means for producing social change, Martin Luther King, Jr. (1929–1968), was born in Atlanta, Georgia, and was ordained as a Baptist minister when he was nineteen. He earned advanced degrees from Chicago Theological Seminary (D.D., 1957) and Boston University (Ph.D., 1955; D.D., 1959). He led a successful boycott of the segregated bus system in Montgomery, Alabama in 1955 founded the Southern Christian Leadership Conference; and he used nonviolent means to help bring about the Civil Rights Act of 1964 and the Voting Rights Act of 1965. King was awarded the Nobel Prize for Peace in 1964. The previous year, he delivered the following speech from the steps of the Lincoln Memorial to 250,000 people who had come to commemorate the centennial of Lincoln's Emancipation Proclamation. King's life ended when he was assassinated in Memphis, Tennessee, on April 4, 1968. His many inspirational writings include *Where Do We Go From Here: Community or Chaos?* (1967) and *Letter from Birmingham Jail* (published in 1968).

BEFORE YOU READ

In what ways has the civil rights movement achieved its goals?

■ ■ ▞

1   I am happy to join with you today in what will go down in history as the greatest demonstration for freedom in the history of our nation.

2   Five score years ago, a great American, in whose symbolic shadow we stand today, signed the Emancipation Proclamation.[1] This momentous decree came as a great beacon light of hope to millions of Negro slaves who had been seared in the flames of withering injustice. It came as a joyous daybreak to end the long night of their captivity. But one hundred years later, the Negro is still not free. One hundred years later, the life of the Negro is still sadly crippled by the manacles of segregation and the chains of discrimination. One hundred years later, the Negro lives on a lonely island of poverty in the midst of a vast ocean of material prosperity. One hundred years later, the Negro is still languishing in the corners of American society and finds himself in exile in his own land. And so we have come here today to dramatize a shameful condition.

3   In a sense we have come to our nation's capital to cash a check. When the architects of our republic wrote the magnificent words of the Constitution and the Declaration of Independence, they were signing a promissory note to which

---

[1] The Emancipation Proclamation: the executive order abolishing slavery in the confederacy that President Abraham Lincoln signed on January 1, 1863.

every American was to fall heir. This note was the promise that all men—yes, black men as well as white men—would be guaranteed the inalienable rights of life, liberty, and the pursuit of happiness.

4 It is obvious today that America has defaulted on this promissory note insofar as her citizens of color are concerned. Instead of honoring this sacred obligation, America has given the Negro people a bad check, a check which has come back marked "insufficient funds." But we refuse to believe that the bank of justice is bankrupt. We refuse to believe that there are insufficient funds in the great vaults of opportunity of this nation; and so we have come to cash this check, a check that will give us upon demand the riches of freedom and the security of justice.

5 We have also come to this hallowed spot to remind America of the fierce urgency of *now*. This is no time to engage in the luxury of cooling off or to take the tranquilizing drug of gradualism. *Now* is the time to make real the promises of democracy. *Now* is the time to rise from the dark and desolate valley of segregation to the sunlit patch of racial justice. *Now* is the time to lift our nation from the quicksands of racial injustice to the solid rock of brotherhood. *Now* is the time to make justice a reality for all of God's children.

6 It would be fatal for the nation to overlook the urgency of the moment. This sweltering summer of the Negro's legitimate discontent will not pass until there is an invigorating autumn of freedom and equality. Nineteen sixty-three is not an end, but a beginning. And those who hope that the Negro needed to blow off steam and will now be content will have a rude awakening if the nation returns to business as usual. There will be neither rest nor tranquility in America until the Negro is granted his citizenship rights. The whirlwinds of revolt will continue to shake the foundations of our nation until the bright day of justice emerges.

7 But there is something that I must say to my people who stand on the warm threshold which leads into the palace of justice. In the process of gaining our rightful place, we must not be guilty of wrongful deeds. Let us not seek to satisfy our thirst for freedom by drinking from the cup of bitterness and hatred. We must forever conduct our struggle on the high plane of dignity and discipline. We must not allow our creative protest to degenerate into physical violence. Again and again we must rise to the majestic heights of meeting physical force with soul force. And the marvelous new militancy which has engulfed the Negro community must not lead us to a distrust of all white people; for many of our white brothers, as evidenced by their presence here today, have come to realize that their destiny is tied up with our destiny, and they have come to realize that their freedom is inextricably bound to our freedom.

8 We cannot walk alone. And as we walk we must make the pledge that we shall always march ahead. We cannot turn back. There are those who are asking the devotees of civil rights, "When will you be satisfied?" We can never be satisfied as long as the Negro is the victim of the unspeakable horrors of police brutality. We can never be satisfied as long as our bodies, heavy with the fatigue of travel, cannot gain lodging in the motels of the highways and the hotels of

the cities. We cannot be satisfied as long as the Negro's basic mobility is from a smaller ghetto to a larger one. We can never be satisfied as long as our children are stripped of their selfhood and robbed of their dignity by signs stating "For Whites Only." We cannot be satisfied as long as the Negro in Mississippi cannot vote and a Negro in New York believes he has nothing for which to vote. No, no, we are not satisfied, and we will not be satisfied until justice rolls down like waters and righteousness like a mighty stream.

9   I am not unmindful that some of you have come here out of great trials and tribulations. Some of you have come fresh from narrow jail cells. Some of you have come from areas where your quest for freedom left you battered by the storms of persecution and staggered by the winds of police brutality. You have been the veterans of creative suffering. Continue to work with the faith that unearned suffering is redemptive.

10   Go back to Mississippi, and go back to Alabama. Go back to South Carolina. Go back to Georgia. Go back to Louisiana. Go back to the slums and ghettos of our Northern cities, knowing that somehow this situation can and will be changed. Let us not wallow in the valley of despair.

11   I say to you today, my friends, even though we face the difficulties of today and tomorrow, I still have a dream. It is a dream deeply rooted in the American dream. I have a dream that one day this nation will rise up and live out the true meaning of its creed: "We hold these truths to be self-evident, that all men are created equal." I have a dream that one day, on the red hills of Georgia, sons of former slaves and the sons of former slave owners will be able to sit down together at the table of brotherhood. I have a dream that one day even the state of Mississippi, a state sweltering with the heat of injustice, sweltering with the heat of oppression, will be transformed into an oasis of freedom and justice. I have a dream that my four little children will one day live in a nation where they will not be judged by the color of their skin, but by the content of their character.

12   I have a dream today. I have a dream that one day down in Alabama—with its vicious racists, with its governor's lips dripping with the words of interposition and nullification—one day right there in Alabama, little black boys and black girls will be able to join hands with little white boys and white girls as sisters and brothers.

13   I have a dream today. I have a dream that one day every valley shall be exalted and every hill and mountain shall be made low, the rough places will be made plain and the crooked places will be made straight, and the glory of the Lord shall be revealed, and all flesh shall see it together.

14   This is our hope. This is the faith that I go back to the South with. And with this faith we will be able to hew out of the mountain of despair a stone of hope. With this faith we will be able to transform the jangling discords of our nation into a beautiful symphony of brotherhood. With this faith we will be able to work together, to play together, to struggle together, to go to jail together, to stand up for freedom together, knowing that we will be free one day.

15   And this will be the day—this will be the day when all of God's children will be able to sing with new meaning.

My country, 'tis of thee,
Sweet land of liberty,
   Of thee I sing;
Land where my fathers died,
Land of the Pilgrims' pride,
From every mountainside
   Let freedom ring.

And if America is to be a great nation, this must become true.

16   And so let freedom ring from the prodigious hilltops of New Hampshire. Let freedom ring from the mighty mountains of New York. Let freedom ring from the heightening Alleghenies of Pennsylvania. Let freedom ring from the snow-capped Rockies of Colorado. Let freedom ring from the curvaceous slopes of California.

17   But not only that. Let freedom ring from Stone Mountain of Georgia. Let freedom ring from Lookout Mountain of Tennessee. Let freedom ring from every hill and molehill of Mississippi. "From every mountainside let freedom ring."

18   And when this happens—when we allow freedom to ring, when we let it ring from every village and every hamlet, from every state and every city—we will be able to speed up that day when all of God's children, black men and white men, Jews and Gentiles, Protestants and Catholics, will be able to join hands and sing in the words of the old Negro spiritual: "Free at last! Free at last! Thank God Almighty. We are free at last!"

■ ■ ▨

MEANING

1. According to King, in what sense does the civil rights movement put into action ideas that are implicit in great struggles in American history?
2. What injustices have been overcome to reach this historic moment?
3. What importance does King place on the idea of nonviolent protest?
4. What dream does King project as an attainable ideal?

TECHNIQUE

1. How does King use the analogy of a check that has come due that must now be honored?
2. How can we tell that King recognizes that he is speaking to many different groups of people and how does King employ appeals directed at these different groups?
3. **Other Patterns.** How is King's speech enhanced by **descriptive** passages that evoke sensory impressions?

LANGUAGE

1. How does King employ biblical phrases and cadences to create an emotional bond with his listeners?

2. How does King use language from the Emancipation Proclamation to remind his audience that this speech was delivered on the centennial of Lincoln's freeing the slaves? Why is this ironic?

3. If you don't know the meaning of the following words, look them up: *momentous* (2), *manacles* (2), *languishing* (2), *gradualism* (5), *degenerate* (7), *inextricably* (7), *redemptive* (9), *tribulations* (8), *nullification* (16), *curvaceous* (16), *hamlet* (18), *prodigious* (21).

SUGGESTIONS FOR WRITING

1. *Critical Writing.* To what extent has King's dream come true, and in what areas is it still unfulfilled?

2. Research the roots of nonviolence in Henry David Thoreau's *Civil Disobedience* and in the life and works of Mahatma Gandhi, and write a **causal analysis** showing how King adapted the principle of passive resistance to the civil rights movement to effect change.

3. In your opinion, what combination of elements in this speech have made it a classic?

4. *Thematic Links.* Compare King's speech to Frederick Douglass's account in "Learning to Read and Write" (Chapter 3, "Narration") in terms of how they use rhetorical skill to persuasively address racial prejudice.

BERNARD RUDOFSKY

The Unfashionable Human Body

Austrian-born writer, architect, designer, and social critic Bernard Rudofsky (1905–1988) has always been fascinated by the role of fashion and the extraordinary measures people take to adapt their bodies to current styles in various cultures. He expresses these views with verve and intelligence in the following selection, which originally appeared in *The Unfashionable Human Body* (1971). The extent of his scholarship can be assessed by the fact that he held professorships at both Yale and Tokyo's Waseda University and received Ford, Fulbright, and Guggenheim fellowships. Between 1945 and 1965 he created popular and controversial exhibitions for New York's Museum of Modern Art.

BEFORE YOU READ

Why do fashionable clothes and shoes have to be so uncomfortable?

■ ■ ▨

1   Every generation has its own demented ideas on supporting some part of the human anatomy. Older people still remember a time when everybody went through life ankle-supported. Young and old wore laced boots. A shoe that did not reach well above the ankle was considered disastrous to health. What, one asks, has become of ankle support, once so warmly recommended by doctors and shoe salesmen? What keeps our ankles from breaking down in these days of low-cut shoes?

2   Ankle support has given way to arch support; millions of shoe-buying people are determined to "preserve their metatarsal arch" without as much as suspecting that it does not exist. Nevertheless, the fiction of the arch is being perpetuated to help sell "supports" and "preservers" on an impressive scale.

3   The dread of falling arches is, however, a picayune affair compared to that other calamity the feet's asymmetry. I am not talking about the difference within a single pair of feet, that is, the difference between the right and left foot of a person; I mean the asymmetry of the foot itself.

4   Few of us are truly aware that an undeformed foot's outline is *not* symmetrical. It is distinctly lopsided. Let us have a close look at it: The big toe extends from one to two inches beyond the fifth toe. More importantly, the five toes spread out fanlike. They do not converge to a point in front as one would expect from the shape of the shoe. Quite the contrary, they converge to a point in back of the heel. It should be obvious, even to the least observant person, that to conform to the outline of a shoe, the big toe ought to be in the place of the third one, i.e. in the center.

5   Shoe manufacturers have shown admirable patience with nature. Despite or because of the absence of feet that live up to their commercial ideals of

anatomy, they doggedly go on producing symmetrical shoes. And although their customers' feet have not changed in the course of time, they spare no effort and expense to come up every season with a new (symmetrical) shoe for the same old foot. (The pathological hate of the natural form of the foot is nowhere more forcibly expressed than in the commandments of the Shakers which say that "it is contrary to order to have right and left shoes.")

6   By some atavistic quirk of nature, every normal baby is born with undeformed feet. The forepart of the foot—measured across the toes—is about twice as wide as the heel. The toes barely touch each other and are as nimble as fingers. Were the child able to keep up his toe-twiddling, he might easily retain as much control over his feet as over his hands. Not that we see anything admirable in nimble toes; they strike us as freakish perhaps because we associate prehensile feet with primitive civilizations. To our twisted mind, the foot in its undamaged state is anachronistic, if not altogether barbaric. Ever since the shoe became the badge of admission to Western civilization—in rural countries such as Portugal and Brazil the government exhorts peasants to wear shoes in the name of progress—we look down on barefooted or sandaled nations.

7   Since wearing shoes is synonymous with wearing *bad* shoes, the modern shoe inevitably becomes an instrument of deformation. The very concept of the modern shoe does not admit of an intelligent solution; it is not made to fit a human foot but to fit a wooden last whose shape is determined by the whims of the "designer." Whereas a tailor allows for a customer's unequal shoulders and arms; an optometrist prescribes different lenses for the right and left eye, we buy shoes of identical size and dimensions for our right and left foot, conveniently forgetting—or ignoring—that, as a rule, they are not of the same width and length. Even in countries where it is still possible to find an artisan willing to make a pair of shoes to order, chances are that he works on mass-produced lasts and comes up with a product that, shapewise, is not much different from the industrial one.

8   In both the manufacturer's and the customer's opinion the shoe comes before the foot. It is less intended to protect the foot from cold and dirt than to mold it into a fashionable shape. Infants' very first shoes are liable to dislocate the bones, and bend the foot into the shoe shape. The child does not mind the interference; "never expect the child to complain that the shoe is hurting him," says podiatrist Dr. Simon Wikler, "for the crippling process is painless." According to a ten-year study of the Podiatry Society of the State of New York, 99 percent of all feet are perfect at birth, 8 percent have developed troubles at one year, 41 percent at the age of five, and 80 percent at twenty; "we limp into adulthood," the report concludes. "Medical schools," says Dr. DePalma, "fail almost completely in giving the student a sound grounding and a sane therapeutic concept of foot conditions." And in *Military Medicine* one reads that "there has been no objective test that could be readily incorporated in physical examinations, or taught to medical students, pediatricians, or physicians in military and industrial medicine, that would enable them to recognize deformities of the foot . . ." In sum, physicians leave it to the shoe designer to decide the fate of our feet.

9   To top it all, modern man, perhaps unknown to himself, is afflicted with a diffuse shoe-fetishism. Inherited prejudices derived from the Cinderella complex; practices whose origins and reasons escape him, and traditional obtuseness combine to make him tolerate the deformities inflicted by his shoes. In this respect his callousness matches that of the Chinese of old. In fact, if he ever felt a need to justify the shoes' encroachments on his anatomy, he could cite Lily feet (provided he had ever heard of them), the Chinese variety of the "correctly shaped" foot.

10   This exotic custom which lasted nearly one thousand years did not extend over the whole country; the Manchu, including the imperial family, never practiced foot-binding. Small feet are a racial characteristic of Chinese women, and the desire to still further reduce their size in the name of beauty and for reasons indicated earlier, seems to have been strong enough to make women tolerate irrevocable mutilation. As so often happens, people derive infinitely greater satisfaction from an artifact, however crude, than from nature's product. Besides, not only were a woman's stunted feet highly charged with erotic symbolism, they made her eligible for marriage. Without them she was reduced to spinsterhood. Her desirability as a love object was in direct proportion to her inability to walk. It ought to be easy for our women to understand the Chinese men's mentality; "every woman knows that to wear 'walking shoes'—as derogatory a term as 'sensible shoes'—puts a damper on a man's ardor. The effect of absurdly impractical shoes, on the other hand, is as intoxicating as a love potion. The girl child who puts on a pair of high-heeled shoes is magically propelled into womanhood."

11   Modern woman is not averse to maltreating her feet for reasons similar to those of her Chinese sisters, and therefore makes allowance for bunions, calluses, corns, ingrown toenails and hammer toes. But she draws the line at a major interference with her foot skeleton. Unwilling to bother with growing her own, organic high heels, she has to get along with artificial ones.

12   As costume props go, the high heel's history is relatively short. In the middle of the seventeenth century this new device for corrupting the human walk was added to the footwear of the elegant, putting them, as it were, on tiptoe. The ground, indoors and outdoors, came to a tilt, so to speak, and, for fashion's sake, people began to walk on a portable incline. As the ordinary folk continued to wear flat-bottomed shoes, heeled footwear, combined with a strutting walk, became a mark of distinction. Withal, the times were anything but favorable to the new invention. On the street the well-heeled had to avail themselves of a sedan chair to avoid the cobblestones underfoot, while indoors they found it difficult to negotiate the polished parquets and marble floors that were the pride of the epoch. And yet, men took to high heels as enthusiastically as women did. To judge from paintings of the time, fashionable men could not have cared less for "walking shoes."

13   Did men's high-heeled shoes and fine stockings turn a woman's head? Were women smitten with the sight of a man's well-turned ankle and slender leg? For whereas their own legs remained hidden by crinolines, men proudly displayed their calves and gave as much attention to them as to their wigs. Silicon

injections still being centuries away, a skinny fellow made up by padding for any natural deficiency. Eventually, the French Revolution brought men and women down to earth. Dandies and *élégantes* wore paper-thin flat soles without, it seems, depriving themselves of their mutual attraction. Years later, when high heels reappeared on the fashionable scene, they were relegated to woman's domain; men never left the ground again.

14   In lucid moments we look with amazement at the fraud we perpetrate on ourselves—the bruises, mutilations, and dislocated bones—but if we feel at all uncomfortable, it is not for long. An automatic self-defense mechanism blurs our judgment, and makes right and wrong exchange places. Moreover, some violations of the body are sanctioned by religion, while others are simply the price of a man's admittance to his tribe, regardless of whether he lives in the bush or in a modern metropolis. The sense of superiority he derives from, say, circumcision is no less real than that of the owner of a pair of Lily feet. Physicians have always been of two minds about it; "to cut off the top of the uppermost skin of the secret parts," maintained the intrepid Dr. Bulwer, "is directly against the honesty of nature, and an injurious unsufferable trick put upon her." And a contemporary pediatrician, E. Noel Preston, writing in the *Journal of the American Medical Association*, considers circumcision "little better than mutilation." The very real dangers of the operation such as infection and hemorrhage outweigh the fancied advantages of cancer prevention. "If a child can be taught to tie his shoes or brush his teeth or wash behind the ears," said Dr. Preston, "he can also be taught to wash beneath his foreskin."

15   A change of allegiance may lead to double mutilation, as in the paradoxical phenomenon of uncircumcision: After the subjugation of Palestine by Alexander the Great, those Jews who found it desirable to turn into Gentiles, underwent a painful operation that restored to them the missing prepuce. (1 Cor. 7:18 ff; 1 Macc. 1:15)

16   Sometimes such mutilation reaches a high degree of ferocity. Among some Arabian tribes circumcision is performed as an endurance test for youths who have come of age; "it consists," writes the Hebrew scholar Raphael Patai, "in cutting off the skin across the stomach below the navel and thence down the thighs, after which it is peeled off, leaving the stomach, the pelvis, the scrotum, and the inner legs uncovered and flayed. Many young men are said to have succumbed to the ordeal which in recent times has been prohibited by the Saudi Arabian government." However, the custom has not disappeared, doubtless as a result of its sex appeal. The ceremony takes place in female company, that is, in the presence of the young men's brides-to-be, who may refuse to marry their intended if they betray their agony by as much as an air of discomfort.

17   Man's obsession with violating his body is not just of anthropological interest, it helps us to understand the irrationality of dress. The devices for interfering with human anatomy are paralleled by a host of contraptions that simulate deformation or are simply meant to cheat the eye: bustles, pads, heels, wedges, braguettes, brassières, and so forth. Once, thirty years marked the end of a woman's desirability. In time, this age limit was gradually extended and pushed to a point where it got

lost altogether. In order not only to look eternally young but also fashionable, woman had to obey ever-changing body ideals. Thus a woman born at the turn of the century was a buxom maiden in accordance with the dictates of the day. Photographs testify to the generosity of her charms although her tender age ought to raise doubts about their authenticity. In the nineteen-twenties, when maturity and motherhood had come to her, pictures record an angular, lean, flat-chested creature. Since she did not want to renounce her attractiveness, she had to submit to an extremely unfeminine beauty ideal. Twenty years later, she was rotund again and commanded the undiminished attention of the other sex. Today, she is still in the running, ever ready to overhaul her body to prolong her youth beyond biological limits. She has inflamed three generations of men each loyal to a different image of perfection.

In what way does this picture of a recent high-fashion offering confirm Bernard Rudofsky's thesis in "The Unfashionable Human Body"?

18   Alas, an aged body, however arresting and deceptive be the results of its updating and remodeling, imparts to its owner only a limited sense of youth. It serves mainly as a stylish peg for clothes. In other words, it is the clothed body that triumphs, not the naked one. As Herbert Spencer said; "The consciousness of being perfectly dressed may bestow a peace such as religion cannot give."

MEANING

1. What are some of the unnatural alterations to which feet are subjected, and what does this tell us about civilization?
2. How is the modern woman's wearing of high heels similar to the deforming foot-binding practices of pre-Communist China?
3. Why do some cultures fixate on certain features of the human body and try to reconstruct them to reflect cultural values?
4. What reasons does Rudofsky give to support his view that we make our bodies conform to fashion rather than making our clothes fit our bodies?

TECHNIQUE

1. How does Rudofsky use the example of wearing high-laced boots for ankle support to illustrate the generational nature of fashion trends? How does he use the human foot's asymmetry to support his argument?
2. By alluding to the fairy tale *Cinderella*, Rudofsky invokes the myth equating virtue with small foot size. How did this myth operate in China, and what use does Rudofsky make of it in his argument?
3. **Other Patterns.** How does Rudofsky support his thesis by **causal analysis** of the deforming effects of bizarre myths and beliefs about the human form?

LANGUAGE

1. How does Rudofsky's characterization of fashions in footwear and their connection to circumcision and devices for "interfering with human anatomy" support his thesis?
2. How does Rudofsky use quotations from podiatrists, pediatricians, and scholars to **illustrate** how the bizarre becomes the norm?
3. If you don't know the meaning of the following words, look them up: *metatarsal* (2), *picayune* (3), *symmetrical* (4), *prehensile* (6), *anachronistic* (6), *callousness* (9), *irrevocable* (10), *crinolines* (13), *metropolis* (14), *braguettes* (17).

SUGGESTIONS FOR WRITING

1. **Critical Writing.** What current fashion practices require transforming the body in the interest of style in ways that would appear bizarre if they were not accepted as "normal"?

2. Why are shoes that conform to the natural foot invariably seen as less attractive than those that are seen as sexy and appealing but that disable the wearer?

3. Discuss a custom that is shoe related, such as removing one's shoes when entering a religious site or a Japanese home.

4. **Thematic Links.** How does Kim Chernin's analysis in "The Flesh and the Devil" (Chapter 9, "Cause and Effect") support Rudofsky's thesis?

Circumcision of Girls

An Egyptian physican and internationally acclaimed writer whose work focuses on injustices to which Arab women are subject, Nawal El Saadawi (b. 1931) completed her secondary and college education in Egypt and later studied at Columbia University. She has worked as an internist and psychiatrist in both Cairo and the rural areas of Egypt. Her outspoken opposition to restrictions placed on women, as expressed in her first book *Women and Sex* (1972), led to her imprisonment by Anwar Sadat, and many of her books are still banned in Middle Eastern countries. In the following essay, orginally published in *The Hidden Face of Eve: Women in the Arab World* (1980), El Saadawi documents and condemns a practice that causes physical and psychological damage to young girls. Her autobiography was published under the title *Walking Through Fire: A Life of Nawal El Saadawi* (2002), translated by her husband, Dr. Sherif Hetata.

BEFORE YOU READ

Is it acceptable for another culture to practice a custom that our own culture finds morally wrong? Do we have an obligation to end the practice?

■ ■ ▨

1   The practice of circumcising girls is still a common procedure in a number of Arab countries such as Egypt, the Sudan, Yemen and some of the Gulf states.

2   The importance given to virginity and an intact hymen in these societies is the reason why female circumcision still remains a very widespread practice despite a growing tendency, especially in urban Egypt, to do away with it as something outdated and harmful. Behind circumcision lies the belief that, by removing parts of girls' external genital organs, sexual desire is minimized. This permits a female who has reached the 'dangerous age' of puberty and adolescence to protect her virginity, and therefore her honour, with greater ease. Chastity was imposed on male attendants in the female harem by castration which turned them into inoffensive eunuchs. Similarly female circumcision is meant to preserve the chastity of young girls by reducing their desire for sexual intercourse.

3   Circumcision is most often performed on female children at the age of seven or eight (before the girl begins to get menstrual periods). On the scene appears the *daya* or local midwife. Two women members of the family grasp the child's thighs on either side and pull them apart to expose the external genital organs and to prevent her from struggling—like trussing a chicken before it is slain. A sharp razor in the hand of the *daya* cuts off the clitoris.

4   During my period of service as a rural physician, I was called upon many times to treat complications arising from this primitive operation, which very often jeopardized the life of young girls. The ignorant *daya* believed that effective circumcision necessitated a deep cut with the razor to ensure radical

amputation of the clitoris, so that no part of the sexually sensitive organ would remain. Severe hemorrhage was therefore a common occurrence and sometimes led to loss of life. The *dayas* had not the slightest notion of asepsis, and inflammatory conditions as a result of the operation were common. Above all, the lifelong psychological shock of this cruel procedure left its imprint on the personality of the child and accompanied her into adolescence, youth and maturity. Sexual frigidity is one of the after-effects which is accentuated by other social and psychological factors that influence the personality and mental make-up of females in Arab societies. Girls are therefore exposed to a whole series of misfortunes as a result of outdated notions and values related to virginity, which still remains the fundamental criterion of a girl's honour. In recent years, however, educated families have begun to realize the harm that is done by the practice of female circumcision.

5   Nevertheless a majority of families still impose on young female children the barbaric and cruel operation of circumcision. The research that I carried out on a sample of 160 Egyptian girls and women showed the 97.5% of uneducated families still insisted on maintaining the custom, but this percentage dropped to 66.2% among educated families.[1]

6   When I discussed the matter with these girls and women it transpired that most of them had no idea of the harm done by circumcision, and some of them even thought that it was good for one's health and conducive to cleanliness and 'purity.' (The operation in the common language of the people is in fact called the cleansing or purifying operation.) Despite the fact that the percentage of educated women who have undergone circumcision is only 66.2%, as compared with 97.5% among uneducated women, even the former did not realize the effect that this amputation of the clitoris could have on their psychological and sexual health. The dialogue that occurred between these women and myself would run more or less as follows:

7   'Have you undergone circumcision?'

8   'Yes.'

9   'How old were you at the time?'

10   'I was a child, about seven or eight years old.'

11   'Do you remember the details of the operation?'

12   'Of course. How could I possibly forget?'

13   'Were you afraid?'

14   'Very afraid. I hid on top of the cupboard [in other cases she would say under the bed, or in the neighbour's house], but they caught hold of me, and I felt my body tremble in their hands.'

15   'Did you feel any pain?'

16   'Very much so. It was like a burning flame and I screamed. My mother held my head so that I could not move it, my aunt caught hold of my right arm and my grandmother took charge of my left. Two strange women whom I had not seen before tried to keep me from moving my thighs by pushing them as far apart as possible. The *daya* sat between these two women, holding a sharp razor in her hand which she used to cut off the clitoris. I was scared and suffered such

great pain that I lost consciousness at the flame that seemed to sear me through and through.'

17 'What happened after the operation?'

18 'I had severe bodily pains, and remained in bed for several days, unable to move. The pain in my external genital organs led to retention of urine. Every time I wanted to urinate the burning sensation was so unbearable that I could not bring myself to pass water. The wound continued to bleed for some time, and my mother used to change the dressing for me twice a day.'

19 'What did you feel on discovering that a small organ in your body had been removed?'

20 'I did not know anything about the operation at the time, except that it was very simple, and that it was done to all girls for purposes of cleanliness, purity and the preservation of a good reputation. It was said that a girl who did not undergo this operation was liable to be talked about by people, her behaviour would become bad, and she would start running after men, with the result that no one would agree to marry her when the time for marriage came. My grandmother told me that the operation had only consisted in the removal of a very small piece of flesh from between my thighs, and that the continued existence of this small piece of flesh in its place would have made me unclean and impure, and would have caused the man whom I would marry to be repelled by me.'

21 'Did you believe what was said to you?'

22 'Of course I did. I was happy the day I recovered from the effects of the operation, and felt as though I was rid of something which had to be removed, and so had become clean and pure.'

23 Those were more or less the answers that I obtained from all those interviewed, whether educated or uneducated. One of them was a medical student from Ein Shams School of Medicine. She was preparing for her final examinations and I expected her answers to be different but in fact they were almost identical to the others. We had quite a long discussion which I reproduce here as I remember it.

24 'You are going to be a medical doctor after a few weeks, so how can you believe that cutting off the clitoris from the body of a girl is a healthy procedure, or at least not harmful?'

25 'This is what I was told by everybody. All the girls in my family have been circumcised. I have studied anatomy and medicine, yet I have never heard any of the professors who taught us explain that the clitoris had any function to fulfill in the body of a woman, neither have I read anything of the kind in the books which deal with the medical subjects I am studying.'

26 'That is true. To this day medical books do not consider the science of sex as a subject which they should deal with. The organs of a woman worthy of attention are considered to be only those directly related to reproduction, namely the vagina, the uterus and the ovaries. The clitoris, however, is an organ neglected by medicine, just as it is ignored and disdained by society.'

27   'I remember a student asking the professor one day about the clitoris. The professor went red in the face and answered him curtly, saying that no one was going to ask him about this part of the female body during examinations, since it was of no importance.'

28   My studies led me to try and find out the effect of circumcision on the girls and women who had been made to undergo it, and to understand what results it had on the psychological and sexual life. The majority of the normal cases I interviewed answered that the operation had no effect on them. To me it was clear that in the face of such questions they were much more ashamed and intimidated than the neurotic cases were. But I did not allow myself to be satisfied with these answers, and would go on to question them closely about their sexual life both before and after the circumcision was done. Once again I will try to reproduce the dialogue that usually occurred.

29   'Did you experience any change of feeling or of sexual desire after the operation?'

30   'I was a child and therefore did not feel anything.'

31   'Did you not experience any sexual desire when you were a child?'

32   'No, never. Do children experience sexual desire?'

33   'Children feel pleasure when they touch their sexual organs, and some form of sexual play occurs between them, for example, during the game of bride and bridegroom usually practised under the bed. Have you never played this game with your friends when still a child?'

34   At these words the young girl or woman would blush, and her eyes would probably refuse to meet mine, in an attempt to hide her confusion. But after the conversation had gone on for some time, and an atmosphere of mutual confidence and understanding had been established, she would begin to recount her childhood memories. She would often refer to the pleasure she had felt when a man of the family permitted himself certain sexual caresses. Sometimes these caresses would be proffered by the domestic servant, the house porter, the private teacher or the neighbour's son. A college student told me that her brother had been wont to caress her sexual organs and that she used to experience acute enjoyment. However after undergoing circumcision she no longer had the same sensation of pleasure. A married woman admitted that during intercourse with her husband she had never experienced the slightest sexual enjoyment, and that her last memories of any form of pleasurable sensation went back twenty years, to the age of six, before she had undergone circumcision. A young girl told me that she had been accustomed to practise masturbation, but had given it up completely after removal of the clitoris at the age of ten.

35   The further our conversations went, and the more I delved into their lives, the more readily they opened themselves up to me and uncovered the secrets of childhood and adolescence, perhaps almost forgotten by them or only vaguely realized.

36   Being both a woman and a medical doctor I was able to obtain confessions from these women and girls which it would be almost impossible, except in very rare cases, for a man to obtain. For the Egyptian woman, accustomed as she is

to a very rigid and severe upbringing built on a complete denial of any sexual life before marriage, adamantly refuses to admit that she has even known, or experienced, anything related to sex before the first touches of her husband. She is therefore ashamed to speak about such things with any man, even the doctor who is treating her.

37   My discussions with some of the psychiatrists who had treated a number of the young girls and women in my sample, led me to conclude that there were many aspects of the life of these neurotic patients that remained unknown to them. This was due either to the fact that the psychiatrist himself had not made the necessary effort to penetrate deeply into the life of the woman he was treating, or to the tendency of the patient herself not to divulge those things which her upbringing made her consider matters not to be discussed freely, especially with a man.

38   In fact the long and varied interchanges I had over the years with the majority of practising psychiatrists in Egypt, my close association with a large number of my medical colleagues during the long periods I spent working in health centres and general or specialized hospitals and, finally, the four years I spent as a member of the National Board of the Syndicate of Medical Professions, have all led me to the firm conclusion that the medical profession in our society is still incapable of understanding the fundamental problems with which sick people are burdened, whether they be men or women, but especially if they are women. For the medical profession, like any other profession in society, is governed by the political, social and moral values which predominate, and like other professions is one of the institutions which is utilized more often than not to protect these values and perpetuate them.

39   Men represent the vast majority in the medical profession, as in most professions. But apart from this, the mentality of women doctors differs little, if at all, from that of the men, and I have known quite a number of them who were even more rigid and backward in outlook than their male colleagues.

40   A rigid and backward attitude towards most problems, and in particular towards women and sex, predominates in the medical profession, and particularly within the precincts of the medical colleges in the Universities.

41   Before undertaking my research study on 'Women and Neurosis' at Ein Shams University, I had made a previous attempt to start it at the Kasr El Eini Medical College in the University of Cairo, but had been obliged to give up as a result of the numerous problems I was made to confront. The most important obstacle of all was the overpowering traditionalist mentality that characterized the professors responsible for my research work, and to whom the word 'sex' could only be equated to the word 'shame.' 'Respectable research' therefore could not possibly have sex as its subject, and should under no circumstances think of penetrating into areas even remotely related to it. One of my medical colleagues in the Research Committee advised me not to refer at all to the question of sex in the title of my research paper, when I found myself obliged to shift to Ein Shams University. He warned me that any such reference would most probably lead to fundamental objections which would jeopardize my chances of

going ahead with it. I had initially chosen to define my subject as 'Problems that confront the sexual life of modern Egyptian women,' but after prolonged negotiations I was prevailed to delete the word 'sexual' and replace it by 'psychological.' Only thus was it possible to circumvent the sensitivities of the professors at the Ein Shams Medical School and obtain their consent to go ahead with the research.

42   After I observed the very high percentages of women and girls who had been obliged to undergo circumcision, or who had been exposed to different forms of sexual violation or assault in their childhood, I started to look for research undertaken in these two areas, either in the medical colleges or in research institutes, but in vain. Hardly a single medical doctor or researcher had ventured to do any work on these subjects, in view of the sensitive nature of the issues involved. This can also be explained by the fact that most of the research carried out in such institutions is of a formal and superficial nature, since its sole aim is to obtain a degree or promotion. The path of safety is therefore the one to choose, and safety means to avoid carefully all subjects of controversy. No one is therefore prepared to face difficulties with the responsible academic and scientific authorities, or to engage in any form of struggle against them, or their ideas. Nor is anyone prepared to face up to those who lay down the norms of virtue, morals and religious behaviour in society. All the established leaderships in the area related to such matters suffer from a pronounced allergy to the word 'sex,' and any of its implications, especially if it happens to be linked to the word 'woman.'

43   Nevertheless I was fortunate enough to discover a small number of medical doctors who had the courage to be different, and therefore to examine some of the problems related to the sexual life of women. I would like to cite, as one of the rare examples, the only research study carried out on the question of female circumcision in Egypt and its harmful effects. This was the joint effort of Dr. Mahmoud Koraim and Dr. Rushdi Ammar, both from Ein Shams Medical College, and which was published in 1965. It is composed of two parts, the first of which was printed under the title *Female Circumcision and Sexual Desire*,[2] and the second, under the title *Complications of Female Circumcision*.[3] The conclusions arrived at as a result of this research study, which covered 651 women circumcised during childhood, may be summarized as follows:

44   1. Circumcision is an operation with harmful effects on the health of women, and is the cause of sexual shock to young girls. It reduces the capacity of a woman to reach the peak of her sexual pleasure (i.e., orgasm) and has a definite though lesser effect in reducing sexual desire.

45   2. Education helps to limit the extent to which female circumcision is practiced, since educated parents have an increasing tendency to refuse the operation for their daughters. On the other hand, uneducated families still go in for female circumcision in submission to prevailing traditions, or in the belief that removal of the clitoris reduces the sexual desire of the girl, and therefore helps to preserve her virginity and chastity after marriage.

46   3. There is no truth whatsoever in the idea that female circumcision helps in reducing the incidence of cancerous disease of the external genital organs.

47   4. Female circumcision in all its forms and degrees, and in particular the fourth degree known as Pharaonic or Sudanese excision, is accompanied by immediate or delayed complications such as inflammations, haemorrhage, disturbances in the urinary passages, cysts or swellings that can obstruct the urinary flow or the vaginal opening.

48   5. Masturbation in circumcised girls is less frequent than was observed by Kinsey in girls who have not undergone this operation.

49   I was able to exchange views with Dr. Mahmoud Koraim during several meetings in Cairo. I learnt from him that he had faced numerous difficulties while undertaking his research, and was the target of bitter criticism from some of his colleagues and from religious leaders who considered themselves the divinely appointed protectors of morality, and therefore required to shield society from such impious undertakings, which constituted a threat to established values and moral codes.

50   The findings of my research study coincide with some of the conclusions arrived at by my two colleagues on a number of points. There is no longer any doubt that circumcision is the source of sexual and psychological shock in the life of the girl, and leads to a varying degree of sexual frigidity according to the woman and her circumstances. Education helps parents realize that this operation is not beneficial, and should be avoided, but I have found that the traditional education given in our schools and universities, whose aim is simply some certificate, or degree, rather than instilling useful knowledge and culture, is not very effective in combating the long-standing, and established traditions that govern Egyptian society, and in particular those related to sex, virginity in girls, and chastity in women. These areas are strongly linked to moral and religious values that have dominated and operated in our society for hundreds of years.

51   Since circumcision of females aims primarily at ensuring virginity before marriage, and chastity throughout, it is not to be expected that its practice will disappear easily from Egyptian society or within a short period of time. A growing number of educated families are, however, beginning to realize the harm that is done to females by this custom, and are therefore seeking to protect their daughters from being among its victims. Parallel to these changes, the operation itself is no longer performed in the old primitive way, and the more radical degrees approaching, or involving, excision are dying out more rapidly. Nowadays, even in upper Egypt and the Sudan, the operation is limited to the total, or more commonly the partial, amputation of the clitoris. Nevertheless, while undertaking my research, I was surprised to discover, contrary to what I had previously thought, that even in educated urban families over 50% still consider circumcision as essential to ensure female virginity and chastity.

52   Many people think that female circumcision only started with the advent of Islam. But as a matter of fact it was well known and widespread in some areas of the world before the Islamic era, including in the Arab peninsula. Mahomet

the Prophet tried to oppose this custom since he considered it harmful to the sexual health of the woman. In one of his sayings the advice reported as having been given by him to Om Attiah, a woman who did tattooings and circumcision, runs as follows: 'If you circumcise, take only a small part and refrain from cutting most of the clitoris off . . . The woman will have a bright and happy face, and is more welcome to her husband, if her pleasure is complete.'[4]

53   This means that the circumcision of girls was not originally an Islamic custom, and was not related to monotheistic religions, but was practised in societies with widely varying religious backgrounds, in countries of the East and the West, and among peoples who believed in Christianity, or in Islam, or were atheistic . . . Circumcision was known in Europe as late as the 19th century, as well as in countries like Egypt, the Sudan, Somaliland, Ethiopia, Kenya, Tanzania, Ghana, Guinea and Nigeria. It was also practised in many Asian countries such as Sri Lanka and Indonesia, and in parts of Latin America. It is recorded as going back far into the past under the Pharaonic Kingdoms of Ancient Egypt, and Herodotus mentioned the existence of female circumcision seven hundred years before Christ was born. This is why the operation as practised in the Sudan is called 'Pharaonic excision.'

54   For many years I tried in vain to find relevant sociological or anthropological studies that would throw some light on the reasons why such a brutal operation is practised on females. However I did discover other practices related to girls and female children which were even more savage. One of them was burying female children alive almost immediately after they were born, or even at a later stage. Other examples are the chastity belt, or closing the aperture of the external genital organs with steel pins and a special iron lock.[5] This last procedure is extremely primitive and very much akin to Sudanese circumcision where the clitoris, external lips and internal lips are completely excised, and the orifice of the genital organs closed with a flap of sheep's intestines leaving only a very small opening barely sufficient to let the tip of the finger in, so that the menstrual and urinary flows are not held back. This opening is slit at the time of marriage and widened to allow penetration of the male sexual organ. It is widened again when a child is born and then narrowed down once more. Complete closure of the aperture is also done on a woman who is divorced, so that she literally becomes a virgin once more and can have no sexual intercourse except in the eventuality of marriage, in which case the opening is restored.

55   In the face of all these strange and complicated procedures aimed at preventing sexual intercourse in women except if controlled by the husband, it is natural that we should ask ourselves why women, in particular, were subjected to such torture and cruel suppression. There seems to be no doubt that society, as represented by its dominant classes and male structure, realized at a very early stage that sexual desire in the female is very powerful, and that women, unless controlled and subjugated by all sorts of measures, will not submit themselves to the moral, social, legal and religious constraints with which they have been surrounded, and in particular the constraints related to monogamy. The patriarchal system, which came into being when society had reached a certain stage of development and which necessitated the imposition of one husband on the

woman whereas a man was left free to have several wives, would never have been possible, or have been maintained to this day, without the whole range of cruel and ingenious devices that were used to keep her sexuality in check and limit her sexual relations to only one man, who had to be her husband. This is the reason for the implacable enmity shown by society towards female sexuality, and the weapons used to resist and subjugate the turbulent force inherent in it. The slightest leniency in facing this 'potential danger' meant that woman would break out of the prison bars to which marriage had confined her, and step over the steely limits of a monogamous relationship to a forbidden intimacy with another man, which would inevitably lead to confusion in succession and inheritance, since there was no guarantee that a strange man's child would not step into the waiting line of descendants. Confusion between the children of the legitimate husband and the outside lover would mean the unavoidable collapse of the patriarchal family built around the name of the father alone.

56   History shows us clearly that the father was keen on knowing who his real children were, solely for the purpose of handing down his landed property to them. The patriarchal family, therefore, came into existence mainly for economic reasons. It was necessary for society simultaneously to build up a system of moral and religious values, as well as a legal system capable of protecting and maintaining these economic interests. In the final analysis we can safely say that female circumcision, the chastity belt and other savage practices applied to women are basically the result of the economic interests that govern society. The continued existence of such practices in our society today signifies that these economic interests are still operative. The thousands of *dayas*, nurses, paramedical staff and doctors, who make money out of female circumcision, naturally resist any change in these values and practices which are a source of gain to them. In the Sudan there is a veritable army of *dayas* who earn a livelihood out of the series of operations performed on women, either to excise their external genital organs, or to alternately narrow and widen the outer aperture according to whether the woman is marrying, divorcing, remarrying, having a child or recovering from labour.[6]

57   Economic factors and, concomitantly, political factors are the basis upon which such customs as female circumcision have grown up. It is important to understand the facts as they really are, the reasons that lie behind them. Many are the people who are not able to distinguish between political and religious factors, or who conceal economic and political motives behind religious arguments in an attempt to hide the real forces that lie at the basis of what happens in society and in history. It has very often been proclaimed that Islam is at the root of female circumcision, and is also responsible for the under-privileged and backward situation of women in Egypt and the Arab countries. Such a contention is not true. If we study Christianity it is easy to see that this religion is much more rigid and orthodox where women are concerned than Islam. Nevertheless, many countries were able to progress rapidly despite the preponderance of Christianity as a religion. This progress was social, economic, scientific and also affected the life and position of women in society.

58   That is why I firmly believe that the reasons for the lower status of women in our societies, and the lack of opportunities for progress afforded to them, are not due to Islam, but rather to certain economic and political forces, namely those of foreign imperialism operating mainly from the outside, and of the reactionary classes operating from the inside. These two forces cooperate closely and are making a concerted attempt to misinterpret religion and to utilize it as an instrument of fear, oppression and exploitation.

59   Religion, if authentic in the principles it stands for, aims at truth, equality, justice, love and a healthy wholesome life for all people, whether men or women. There can be no true religion that aims at disease, mutilation of the bodies of female children, and amputation of an essential part of their reproductive organs.

60   If religion comes from God, how can it order man to cut off an organ created by Him as long as that organ is not diseased or deformed? God does not create the organs of the body haphazardly without a plan. It is not possible that He should have created the clitoris in woman's body only in order that it be cut off at an early stage in life. This is a contradiction into which neither true religion nor the Creator could possibly fall. If God has created the clitoris as a sexually sensitive organ, whose sole function seems to be the procurement of sexual pleasure for women, it follows that He also considers such pleasure for women as normal and legitimate, and therefore as an integral part of mental health. The psychic and mental health of women cannot be complete if they do not experience sexual pleasure.

61   There are still a large number of fathers and mothers who are afraid of leaving the clitoris intact in the bodies of their daughters. Many a time they have said to me that circumcision is a safeguard against the mistakes and deviations into which a girl may be led. This way of thinking is wrong and even dangerous because what protects a boy or a girl from making mistakes is not the removal of a small piece of flesh from the body, but consciousness and understanding of the problems we face, and a worthwhile aim in life, an aim which gives it meaning and for whose attainment we exert our mind and energies. The higher the level of consciousness to which we attain, the closer our aims draw to human motives and values, and the greater our desire to improve life and its quality, rather than to indulge ourselves in the mere satisfaction of our senses and the experience of pleasure, even though these are an essential part of existence. The most liberated and free of girls, in the true sense of liberation, are the least preoccupied with sexual questions, since these no longer represent a problem. On the contrary, a free mind finds room for numerous interests and the many rich experiences of a cultured life. Girls that suffer sexual suppression, however, are greatly preoccupied with men and sex. And it is a common observation that an intelligent and cultured woman is much less engrossed in matters related to sex and to men than is the case with ordinary women, who have not got much with which to fill their lives. Yet at the same time such a woman takes much more initiative to ensure that she will enjoy sex and experience pleasure, and acts with a greater degree of boldness than others. Once sexual satisfaction is attained, she is able to turn herself fully to other important aspects of life.

62   In the life of liberated and intelligent women, sex does not occupy a disproportionate position, but rather tends to maintain itself within normal limits. In contrast, ignorance, suppression, fear and all sorts of limitations exaggerate the role of sex in the life of girls and women, and cause it to swell out of all proportion and to end up by occupying the whole, or almost the whole, of their lives.

REFERENCES

1. This research study was carried out in the years 1973 and 1974 in the School of Medicine, Ein Shams University, under the title: *Women and Neurosis.*
2. *Female Circumcision and Sexual Desire*, Mahmoud Koraim and Rushdi Ammar (Ein Shams University Press, Cairo, 1965).
3. *Complications of Female Circumcision*, the same authors (Cairo, 1965).
4. See *Dawlat El Nissa'a*, Abdel Rahman El Barkouky, first edition (Renaissance Bookshop, Cairo, 1945).
5. Desmond Morris, *The Naked Ape* (Corgi, 1967), p. 76.
6. Rose Oldfield, 'Female genital mutilation, fertility control, women's roles, and patrilineage in modern Sudan,' *American Ethnologist*, Vol. II, No. 4, November 1975.

■ ■ ▨

MEANING

1. What factors explain the practice of female circumcision in many Middle Eastern countries?
2. In her research, what effects on girls, both physical and psychological, did El Saadawi find?
3. What assumptions underlie the importance ascribed to female virginity in Middle Eastern cultures?
4. What prevailing beliefs did Koraim and Ammar's study about the supposed medical benefits of circumcision disclose to be baseless?

TECHNIQUE

1. Did the number of interviews El Saadawi conducted provide a sample large enough to form the basis for generalizations?
2. What role do personal narratives and case histories play in authenticating El Saadawi's account? In particular, why is the interview with the female medical student significant?
3. How does El Saadawi use the framework of **argumentation** to support her claim that female circumcision was not originally an Islamic custom and should be eliminated?
4. **Other Patterns.** How does El Saadawi use **definition** to explain the practice, **narration** to provide anecdotal evidence based on interviews, and **causal analysis** to discover its effects in women's lives?

LANGUAGE

1. What aspects of the essay show that El Saadawi approaches her subject as a physician who honestly believes that scientists and colleagues will be persuaded by her findings?
2. Where can you detect El Saadawi's surprise and dismay that educated women and even some medical colleagues at the University of Cairo saw no reason to question this practice?
3. How would you characterize El Saadawi's tone in this article? What words and phrases reveal her attitude most clearly? What is the relationship between the tone she uses and the purpose of her essay?
4. If you don't know the meanings of the following words, look them up: *circumcising* (1), *chastity* (2), *castration* (2), *eunuchs* (2), *trussing* (3), *asepsis* (4), *anatomy* (25), *proffered* (34), *jeopardize* (41), *Herodotus* (53), *aperture* (54), *suppression* (55), *monogamy* (55), *patriarchal* (55), *leniency*, (55), *veritable* (56).

SUGGESTIONS FOR WRITING

1. How plausible do you find El Saadawi's reasoning when she argues that God would not have created an organ in the human body only for it to be removed at an early age? Explain your answer.
2. **Critical Writing.** In what way does the issue of female circumcision focus on the connection between cultural customs and women's freedom of choice?
3. Is there any outdated custom or practice in contemporary society that you would wish to make a case against? Formulate your response as an argument, citing evidence and reasons to support your views. You should also anticipate objections that opponents might raise and respond to these objections.
4. Should the United States and other Western societies let the practice of female circumcision go on in Middle Eastern communities in their own countries? Why or why not? Develop your answer by using **comparison and contrast** and giving **examples** in your argument.
5. **Thematic Links.** Compare the different culturally defined values of female circumcision, as described by El Saadawi, with male circumcision among the Maasai, as described by Tepilit Ole Saitoti (Chapter 4, "Description"). For example, how is one intended to restrict and limit while the other is intended to empower?

DEBATE: TRENDS IN ANIMAL RESEARCH

CAROL GRUNEWALD

Monsters of the Brave New World

Few taboos are as ingrained as the one against creating hybrid experimental creatures that are mixtures of different species or, worse, part human and part animal. This is precisely what megacorporations have done in pilot programs and intend to do on a large scale in the future, according to Carol Grunewald. She works for the National Humane Society, is a former editor for the magazine *Animal Rights Agenda*, and is currently a reporter for the *Times Mirror* newspaper in London. In the following essay, which first appeared in the *New Internationalist* (1991), Grunewald raises concerns about genetically hybridized species from a moral and practical viewpoint.

BEFORE YOU READ

What would be the effects if corporations were able to copyright new life forms?

■ ■ ▨

1　It's probably no accident that some of the most fearsome monsters invented by the human mind have been composed of body parts of various animal—including human—species.

2　Ancient and mediaeval mythology teem with "transgenic' creatures who have served through the ages as powerful symbols and movers of the human subconscious. In Greek mythology the Chimera—a hideous fire-breathing she-monster with the head of a lion, the body of a goat and a dragon's tail—was darkness incarnate and a symbol of the underworld.

3　At the beginning of the industrial or technological age, the collective consciousness conjured monsters from a new but related fear—the consequences of human interference with nature. Fears of science and technology gone out of control created the stories of *Dr. Jekyll and Mr. Hyde*[1] and *Dr. Frankenstein*[2].

---

[1] *Dr Jekyll and Mr. Hyde:* a person marked by a dual personality, one aspect of which is good and the other evil, after the protagonist of Robert Louis Stevenson's novel, *The Strange Case of Dr. Jekyll and Mr. Hyde* (1886).

[2] *Dr. Frankenstein:* a person who creates a destructive agency that cannot be controlled or brings about the ruin of the creator. A character from the 1818 novel by Mary Shelley.

4   The contemporary monster is apt to be a real human being, but an amoral, sociopathic one—a Mengele[3] or an Eichmann[4] who imposes his evil will not in the heat of passion, but in cold detachment.

DEEPEST HUMAN FEARS

5   Our nightmares, our mythologies, our movies, our real-life monsters reveal many of our deepest human fears: of the unknown, of the unnatural, of science gone berserk and of the dark side of the human psyche. With such an intense subliminal heritage, no wonder many people are instinctively wary of the new and revolutionary science of generic engineering—a science born just 15 years ago but which is already creating its own monsters. They have good reason to be afraid.

6   The goal of genetic engineering is to break the code of life and to reform and "improve" the biological world according to human specifications. It is the science of manipulating genes either within or between organisms. Genes are the fundamental and functional units of heredity; they are what make each of us similar to our species but individually different.

7   There are two astonishing aspects to this new science. For the first time, humankind has the capacity to effect changes in the genetic code of individual organisms which will be passed down to future generations.

8   Equally startling, humankind now has the ability to join not only various animal species that could never mate in nature but also to cross the fundamental biological barriers between plants and animals that have always existed.

9   Experiments have already produced a few animal monstrosities. "Geeps," part goat, part sheep, have been engineered through the process of cell-fusion—mixing cells of goat and sheep embryos. A pig has been produced whose genetic structure was altered by the insertion of a human gene responsible for producing a growth hormone. The unfortunate animal (nicknamed "super-pig") is so riddled with arthritis she can barely stand, is nearly blind, and prone to developing ulcers and pneumonia. No doubt researchers will create many such debilitated and pain-racked animals until they get it right.

CUSTOM-DESIGNED CREATURES

10   Meanwhile, the world's knowledge of genetic engineering is growing apace. Much of what is now only theoretically possible will almost certainly be realized. With the world's genetic pool at a scientist's disposal, the possibilities are endless. It's just a matter of time.

---

[3]*Josef Mengele (1911–1979):* nicknamed "the angel of death" because of his role in deciding who would live and die at the Auschwitz concentration camp.

[4]*Adolf Eichmann (1906–1962):* German Nazi official responsible for the killing of millions of Jews during the Holocaust. In 1962, he was hanged for crimes against humanity by the government of Israel.

11   But two historic events spurred the growth in what is now referred to as the "biotech industry." In 1980 the U.S. Supreme Court ruled, in a highly controversial 5–4 vote, that "man-made" micro-organisms can be patented. Then in April 1987, without any public debate, the U.S. Patent Officer suddenly announced that all forms of life—including animals but excluding human beings—may be considered "human inventions." These could qualify as "patentable subject matter," provided they had been genetically engineered with characteristics not attainable through classical breeding techniques.

12   The economic incentives were impossible for researchers and corporations to resist. The genetic engineering of animals was a biological gold mine waiting to be exploited. In hope o getting rich off the "inventions," scientists have so far "created" thousands of animals nature could never have made. Now more than 90 parents are pending for transgenic animals, and some 7,000 are pending for genetically engineered plant and animal micro-organisms.

13   Until now animal rights activists have been the foremost opponents of genetic engineering. The reason: animals are already the worse for it. Because they are powerless, animals have always suffered at the hands of humankind. When a new technology comes along, new ways are devised to exploit them. But genetic engineering represents the most extreme and blatant form animal exploitation yet.

14   Genetic engineers do not see animals as they are: inherently valuable, sentient creatures with sensibilities very similar to ours and lives of their own to live. To them, animals are mere biological resources, bits of genetic code that can be manipulated at will and "improved" to serve human purposes. They can then be patented like a new toaster or tennis ball.

15   In a recent article, the U.S. Department of Agriculture crows that "the face of animal production in the twenty-first century could be . . . broilers blooming to market size 40 percent quicker, miniature hens cranking out eggs in double time, a computer 'cookbook' of recipes for custom-designed creatures."

16   The trade journal of the American beef industry boasts that in the year 2014 farmers will be able to order, "from a Sears-type catalog, specific breeds or mixtures of breeds of (genetically engineered) cattle identified by a model number and name. Just like the 2014's new model pick-up truck, new model animals can be ordered for specific purposes."

17   A university scientist says, "I believe it's completely feasible to specifically design an animal for a hamburger."

18   A Canadian researcher speaking at a farmers' convention eagerly tells the group that "at the Animal Research Institute we are trying to breed animals without legs and chickens without feathers."

19   Huge profits are to be made from new cows, pigs, chickens and other farm animals whose genetic scripts will be written and "improved" to grow faster and leaner on less food and on new foods such as sawdust, cardboard and industrial and human waste.

20   Researchers have been straining at the bit to design and patent new animal "models" of human disease—living, breathing "tools" who will be experimented

to death in the laboratory. Scientists have also created "medicine factories" out of mice by implanting in them human genes for producing human enzymes, proteins and drugs that can be harvested. Cows, sheep and other milk-producing animals have been targeted for further experimentation in this area.

21   Animals already suffer abominably in intensive-confinement factory farms and laboratories. Genetic manipulations will result in further subjugation of animals and increase and intensify their stress, pain, and mental suffering.

22   But genetic engineering also imposes risks on wildlife and the environment. Many questions need to be asked. For example, what will happen when genetically-altered animals and plants are released into the environment? Once they're out there we can't get them back. What if they run amok? Carp and salmon are currently engineered to grow twice as large as they do in nature. But will they also consume twice as much food? Will they upset the ecological balance and drive other animal or plant species to extinction?

23   Indeed, the genetic engineering of animals will almost certainly endanger species and reduce biological diversity. Once researchers develop what is considered to be the "perfect carp" or "perfect chicken" these will be the ones that are reproduced in large numbers. All other "less desirable" species would fall by the wayside and decrease in number. The "perfect" animals might even be cloned—reproduced as exact copies—reducing even further the pool of available genes on the planet.

24   Such fundamental human control over all nature would force us to view it differently. Which leads us to the most important examination of all: our values.

HOW HUMAN?

25   "We need to ask ourselves what are the long term consequences for civilization of reducing all of life to engineering values." These are the words of Foundation on Economic Trends President Jeremy Rifkin, the leading opponent of genetic engineering in the U.S. Rifkin warns that the effects of new technologies are pervasive. They reach far beyond the physical, deep into the human psyche and affect the well-being of all life on earth.

26   In the brave new world of genetic engineering will life be precious? If we could create living beings at will—and even replace a being with an exact clone if it died—would life be valued? The patenting of new forms of life has already destroyed the distinction between living things arid inanimate objects. Will nature be just another form of private property?

27   The intermingling of genes from various species, including the human species, will challenge our view of what it means to be human. If we inject human genes into animals, for example, will they become part human? If animal genes are injected into humans will we become more animal? Will the distinctions be lost? And if so, what will the repercussions be for all life?

28   And will humans be able to create, patent, and thus own a being that is, by virtue of its genes, part human? In other words, how human would a creature have to be in order to be included in the system of rights and protections that are accorded to "full humans" today?

29   We may already know the answer to that question. Chimpanzees share 99 percent of our human genetic inheritance, yet nowhere in the world is there a law that prevents these nearly 100-percent human beings from being captured, placed in leg-irons, owned, locked in laboratory and zoo cages and dissected in experiments.

30   The blurring of the lines between humans and animals could have many interesting consequences. All of us (humans and animals) are really made of the same "stuff" and our genes will be used interchangeably. Since we are already "improving" animals to serve our needs, why not try and improve ourselves as well? With one small step, we could move from animal eugenics to human eugenics and, by means of genetic engineering, make the plans of the Nazis seem bumbling and inefficient.

LIFE AS PROPERTY

31 Finally, who will control life? Genetic technology is already shoring up the mega-multinational corporations and consolidating and centralizing agribusiness. Corporate giants like General Electric, Du Pont, Upjohn, Ciba-Geigy, Monsanto, and Dow Chemical have multibillion-dollar investments in genetic engineering technology. It is becoming increasingly clear that we are placing the well-being of the planet and all its inhabitants in the hands of a technological elite. Our scientists, corporations and military are playing with, and may eventually own, our genes.

32   The arrogance and foolishness of humankind! With everything on the planet existing just to be used and exploited—with nothing existing without a "reason" and a "use"—where is the joy of life? What is the reason for living?

33   People and animals are inseparable; our fates are inextricably linked. People are animals. What is good for animals is good for the environment is good for people. What is bad for them is bad for us.

34   The first line of resistance should be to scrap the patenting of animals. And the release of any genetically altered organisms into the environment should be prohibited.

35   Finally, we must remember that the mind that views animals as pieces of coded genetic information to be manipulated and exploited at will is the mind that would view human beings in a similar way. People who care about people should listen carefully to what Animals Rights activists and environmentalists have to say about obtaining justice for, and preserving the integrity of, *all* life.

■ ■ ▨

MEANING

1. How do classic myths and modern horror movies tap into the profound human apprehensions about producing experimental mixtures of different species?

2. How has the potential of genetic engineering raised concerns for a whole new category of abuse of animals in the course of conducting research?

3. What hybridized creatures illustrate the ill-advised nature of this project?

4. How do changes in patent law provide a powerful new incentive for creating transgenic animals?

Technique

1. In what way does Grunewald's argument rest on a philosophical position that is opposed to manipulation or exploitation of animals?

2. What aspects of Grunewald's argument explore the dangers of potential interaction between laboratory-produced animals and existing species?

3. **Other Patterns.** How does Grunewald's essay amplify and expand the **definition** of what a transgenic creature might be?

Language

1. How does Grunewald attempt to influence the reader by evoking parallels to the eugenic programs of the Nazis?

2. Where dues Grunewald use quoted terms to express her skepticism about the plans to create hybrid species?

3. If you don't know the meaning of the following words, look them up: *transgenic* (2), *pervasive* (25), *eugenics* (30), *inextricably* (33).

Suggestions for Writing

1. **Critical Writing.** Do you agree with any of Grunewald's assumptions? If so, which ones? Would you necessarily draw the same conclusions she does? If not, why not?

2. What science-fiction films have featured transgenic characters (such as *Spider Man*, *X-Men*)? Do they show this process as beneficial or harmful?

3. What **examples** of genetically altered animals and foods have appeared since Grunewald wrote this in 1991, and what has been the public response to them?

4. **Thematic Links.** Compare how Grunewald and Caroline Murphy in "Genetically Engineered Animals" use the example of the transgenic pig to support their respective arguments.

CAROLINE MURPHY

Genetically Engineered Animals

In Caroline Murphy's view, the apprehensions about transgenic creations are unduly alarmist and overlook real benefits that genetic engineering of animals could produce in medicine, pharmacology, and agriculture. Her viewpoint is expressed in the following essay, reprinted from *The Biorevolution*, edited by Peter Wheale and Ruth McNally (1990). Murphy's credentials are impressive: She is the education officer for the Royal Society for the Prevention of Cruelty to Animals in England and holds advanced degrees in medicine, biology, and genetics.

BEFORE YOU READ

To what extent have science fiction and monster movies scared us away from creating hybrid species?

■ ■ ▨

1   Making animals that are a mixture of different species is not a new idea, but it is a new reality. One consequence of this is that there is a common ground that we all share when we start thinking about the type of genetic engineering that we call the transgenic manipulation of animals. Here I describe briefly what transgenic manipulation is, and point out some implications which may be both reassuring and disconcerting.

2   For many people, the transgenic manipulation of animals is a very frightening concept. The reason why we should find this application of modern genetics so disturbing lies at least partly in our cultural heritage. The fantasy of animals with a mix of characteristics of various species can be found in the culture of many ancient, and not so ancient, civilisations. When trying to decide what our reactions to transgenic animals should be we must be aware that many of us will have seen, or chosen not to see, feature films about mad scientists who have shut themselves away from the world and set about producing half-human, half-beast monsters. Mary Shelley's *Frankenstein* nightmare has produced many abiding cultural images and exposed deep-seated fears about the consequences of mankind's interference with nature. When we look at transgenic animals we must be aware that our reactions to them are unlikely to be based on the rational analysis of facts ably presented; the nightmare images from past fantasies are too likely to escape from the Pandora's Box of our imagination and distort our vision.

TRANSGENIC MANIPULATION

3   Transgenic manipulation is a type of genetic engineering. It can loosely be described as taking genes from one organism and inserting them into the genetic

For a visual to accompany this selection, see color insert photo C-6.

material of another. A gene is a length, or a series of lengths, of DNA which carries the code for the sequence of amino acids that make up a protein. Every different protein has a unique amino acid sequence: that sequence is coded for in a gene. The genes lie interspersed with regulatory DNA in a fixed order along the chromosomes. There are gene-bearing chromosomes in the nuclei of all actively dividing cells and they are large enough to be seen under a light-microscope in a dividing cell nucleus. A gene is too small to see with the light-microscope, but banding patterns, generated by staining techniques, help us to 'map' the location of genes on chromosomes fairly accurately. For example, using a variety of gene mapping techniques, we have identified that the gene for the blood protein alpha globin is, in humans, on chromosome 16. In transgenic manipulation, a gene from one species relocates permanently—the scientists hope—into one of the chromosomes of another species.

4   When a sperm fertilises an egg, the chromosomes of the mother and father pair up to produce the unique genetic characteristics of the offspring. Today's genetic engineering of transgenic animals involves the insertion of relatively small amounts of DNA. The amount of foreign DNA inserted into the chromosomes is so small that it does not interfere with this chromosome pairing process. Therefore transgenic animals are able to interbreed with each other and with other (nontransgenic) members of their species. It is hoped that the foreign gene, like any other gene, is passed on to about half the offspring. The normal transmission of half of each parent's genes to each offspring can apply to transgenic animals so successfully that, by normal mating of two different transgenics, young are born carrying both transgenes.

5   The first experiments with transgenic manipulation were undertaken with bacteria and viruses. The commercial application of this work offers possibilities to people and animals. Bacteria carrying the gene for making the human insulin protein have already been produced. These bacteria have been cultured to produce commercial quantities of human insulin for use in place of insulin derived from pig or cow pancreases. However, many patients find it harder to control their diabetes using the new genetically engineered human insulin than using the insulins extracted from pigs or cows.

6   Nowadays transgenic plants and animals are being created in the laboratory. If wheat could be genetically engineered to fix nitrogen from the air (as the legumes can, naturally), wildlife could benefit from reduced run-off from nitrogenous fertilisers into streams and rivers.

7   But what about the genetic engineering of animals? The science magazine *Nature* introduced the reality of transgenic animals to the world with a spectacular front cover (*Nature* 1982). The cover depicted two apparently perfectly healthy mice; one of normal size, together with a 'giant' transgenic sibling with the growth hormone gene of a rat in every cell of its body. This 'giant' mouse was one of only seven transgenics produced from 170 specially treated egg cells. The researchers who had genetically engineered these transgenic mice nonetheless recognised that: 'the implicit possibility is to use this technology to stimulate the rapid growth of commercially valuable animals. Benefit would presumably

come from a shorter production time and possibly from increased efficiency of food utilisation.'

8   The pigs carrying human growth hormone genes produced by USDA [United States Department of Agriculture] scientists at Beltsville in Maryland, USA, were among the first and most widely publicised transgenic animals. These pigs expressed high levels of growth hormone and developed severe arthritic deformities, probably as result of the regulatory gene sequence attached to the human growth hormone gene.

APPLICATIONS

9   There are three main types of genetic engineering of vertebrates being carried out at the moment. These are the production of animal disease models for use in medical research, the production of pharmaceutically useful human proteins in animals, and the production of 'improved' agricultural animals. Each of these applications of genetic engineering may have both a positive and a negative side. The sheep which produce Factor IX in their milk are fit and healthy. Factor IX is the human blood-clotting factor missing in a type of haemophilia called 'Christmas disease.' If sheep could similarly be genetically engineered so that they lactate Factor VIII, the absence of which is the most common cause of haemophilia, haemophiliacs the world over could benefit.

10   Much valuable grazing land in Africa cannot be used by farmers because of tsetse flies which carry various trypanosome parasites that cause diseases in cattle and humans, notably 'sleeping-sickness.' If cows could be genetically engineered to be resistant to these parasites, the farmers would be able to graze more land. In the short term, this might be good for the farmers and their stock, but the wild animals which are already resistant to 'sleeping-sickness' would be deprived of undisturbed grazing land, and their numbers would be bound to fall further as they were pushed to more marginal land.

11   The first patented mouse had a human cancer gene inserted into its genome so that it could act as a more 'accurate' model of human cancer than the mice that were already used. These patented mice are already on the market and were first imported into the UK in the spring of 1989. . . .

12   Poultry producers, worried about the spread of infectious disease through the large flocks of intensively reared birds, are very interested in the prospect of transgenic birds resistant to highly infectious viral infections, such as 'Newcastle Disease' (avian influenza). Those concerned about the birds' welfare question the humaneness of battery production systems. 'The Trojan horse' of disease resistance may provide a means whereby genetic engineers can design animals to cope with conditions that no animal, genetically engineered or not, should be expected to endure.

13   Another proposal is the production of cows which do not metabolise and break down their naturally produced growth hormone protein—bovine somatotropin (BST). Such cows could be genetically engineered so that they contain extra copies of the BST gene. The consequence of this would be cows, possibly patentable, producing high milk yields due to abnormal levels of their own BST. . . .

14   I have drawn attention to the important cultural role of mythical beasts—human-animal and animal-animal hybrids—in providing us all with nightmarish preconceptions about the crossing of species barriers. Scientists and welfarists alike must guard the Pandora's Box of our imaginations in assessing future realities. The Pandora's Box of the human imagination tempts scientists to out-do Doctor Frankenstein, and tempts welfarists to shut the lid on what may offer a cornucopia of opportunities. We must neither assume that all genetic engineering is evil, nor be seduced into thinking that the bright light of science can offer only progress. The genetic engineering of animals is here to stay. It offers both possibilities and problems that we must address intelligently. While the mythical 'transgenic' creatures of the past were thought to control our destiny, the power to control the genetic engineering of animals lies in our hands. We must ensure that we regulate and control this new technique to the benefit of both ourselves and other animals.

■ ■ ▨

Meaning

1. How does Murphy seek to calm apprehensions regarding transgenic creations? According to Murphy, why are these fears irrational?
2. What successful instances of transgenic engineering does Murphy cite?
3. In what three areas has the commercial application of transgenic animals been beneficial?
4. Why does Murphy believe that genetic engineering is here to stay and with careful regulation will benefit humans and animals?

Technique

1. How does Murphy's discussion of transgenic manipulation provide the general reader with a context in which to understand this new research?
2. What real or anticipated benefits of the genetic engineering of animals in the areas of medicine, pharmacology, and agriculture does Murphy cite to support her argument?
3. **Other Patterns.** Where does Murphy use **classification** to discuss the kinds of benefits genetic engineering could produce?

Language

1. To what extent does Murphy strike a balance between admitting problems and citing benefits?
2. How would you characterize Murphy's tone and the language she uses and the purpose it serves?
3. If you don't know the meaning of the following words, look them up: *chromosomes* (3), *haemophilia* (9), *Trojan horse* (12), *Pandora's Box* (14).

SUGGESTIONS FOR WRITING

1. **Critical Writing.** In your opinion, do the benefits of transgenic engineering outweigh the risks? Why or why not?

2. To your knowledge, have you or a loved one benefited directly or indirectly from the kind of research Murphy describes? How might you benefit in the future?

3. Choose one of the problems related to or arising as a consequence of genetic engineering. Research it, and in a few paragraphs, summarize your findings and suggest policies that you think would be effective in solving it.

4. **Thematic Links.** Which argument, Murphy's or Carol Grunewald's in "Monsters of the Brave New World," did you find more persuasive in terms of the issues raised, rhetorical strategies used, evidence presented, and conclusions drawn?

DEBATE: TORTURE AND TERRORISM

MICHAEL LEVIN

The Case for Torture

A philosopher and scholar, Michael Levin (b. 1943) is a professor at the City College of the City University of New York. He was educated at Michigan State University and Columbia University (where he taught philosophy from 1968 to 1980). Levin, who is no stranger to controversy, has applied scholarly rigor to a number of provocative issues in works such as *Why Race Matters: Race Differences and What They Mean* (1997) and *Sexual Orientation and Human Rights* (1999). The truly prophetic set of insights that Levin presents in the following essay, which first appeared in *Newsweek* (1982), are only now being appreciated. The scenarios that Levin foresees in which the immediate use of torture would be necessary to prevent the death of millions have now become more real than hypothetical.

BEFORE YOU READ

Are different standards required for extracting information from suspected terrorists because of the terrorist attacks on September 11, 2001?

■ ■ ▨

1   It is generally assumed that torture is impermissible, a throwback to a more brutal age. Enlightened societies reject it outright, and regimes suspected of using it risk the wrath of the United States.

2   I believe this attitude is unwise. There are situations in which torture is not merely permissible but morally mandatory. Moreover, these situations are moving from the realm of imagination to fact.

DEATH

3   Suppose a terrorist has hidden an atomic bomb on Manhattan Island which will detonate at noon on July 4 unless . . . (here follow the usual demands for money and release of his friends from jail). Suppose, further, that he is caught at 10 A.M. of the fateful day, but—preferring death to failure—won't disclose where the bomb is. What do we do? If we follow due process—wait for his lawyer, arraign him—millions of people will die. If the only way to save those lives is to subject the terrorist to the most excruciating possible pain, what grounds can there be for not doing so? I suggest there are none. In any case, I ask you to face the question with an open mind.

4   Torturing the terrorist is unconstitutional? Probably. But millions of lives surely outweigh constitutionality. Torture is barbaric? Mass murder is far more barbaric. Indeed, letting millions of innocents die in deference to one who flaunts his guilt is moral cowardice, an unwillingness to dirty one's hands. If *you*

caught the terrorist, could you sleep nights knowing that millions died because you couldn't bring yourself to apply the electrodes?

5   Once you concede that torture is justified in extreme cases, you have admitted that the decision to use torture is a matter of balancing innocent lives against the means needed to save them. You must now face more realistic cases involving more modest numbers. Someone plants a bomb on a jumbo jet. He alone can disarm it, and his demands cannot be met (or if they can, we refuse to set a precedent by yielding to his threats). Surely we can, we must, do anything to the extortionist to save the passengers. How can we tell 300, or 100, or 10 people who never asked to be put in danger, "I'm sorry, you'll have to die in agony, we just couldn't bring ourselves to . . ."

6   Here are the results of an informal poll about a third, hypothetical, case. Suppose a terrorist group kidnapped a newborn baby from a hospital. I asked four mothers if they would approve of torturing kidnappers if that were necessary to get their own newborns back. All said yes, the most "liberal" adding that she would like to administer it herself.

7   I am not advocating torture as punishment. Punishment is addressed to deeds irrevocably past. Rather, I am advocating torture as an acceptable measure for preventing future evils. So understood, it is far less objectionable than many extant punishments. Opponents of the death penalty, for example, are forever insisting that executing a murderer will not bring back his victim (as if the purpose of capital punishment were supposed to be resurrection, not deterrence or retribution). But torture, in the cases described, is intended not to bring anyone back but to keep innocents from being dispatched. The most powerful argument against using torture as a punishment or to secure confessions is that such practices disregard the rights of the individual. Well, if the individual is all that important—and he is—it is correspondingly important to protect the rights of individuals threatened by terrorists. If life is so valuable that it must never be taken, the lives of the innocents must be saved even at the price of hurting the one who endangers them.

8   Better precedents for torture are assassination and pre-emptive attack. No Allied leader would have flinched at assassinating Hitler, had that been possible. (The Allies did assassinate Heydrich.) Americans would be angered to learn that Roosevelt could have had Hitler killed in 1943—thereby shortening the war and saving millions of lives—but refused on moral grounds. Similarly, if nation A learns that nation B is about to launch an unprovoked attack, A has a right to save itself by destroying B's military capability first. In the same way, if the police can by torture save those who would otherwise die at the hands of kidnappers or terrorists, they must.

IDEALISM

9   There is an important difference between terrorists and their victims that should mute talk of the terrorists' "rights." The terrorist's victims are at risk unintentionally, not having asked to be endangered. But the terrorist knowingly initiated his actions. Unlike his victims, he volunteered for the risks of his deed. By

threatening to kill for profit or idealism, he renounces civilized standards, and he can have no complaint if civilization tries to thwart him by whatever means necessary.

10   Just as torture is justified only to save lives (not extort confessions or recantations) it is justifiably administered only to those *known* to hold innocent lives in their hands. Ah, but how can the authorities ever be sure they have the right malefactor? Isn't there a danger of error and abuse? Won't We turn into Them?

11   Questions like these are disingenuous in a world in which terrorists proclaim themselves and perform for television. The name of their game is public recognition. After all, you can't very well intimidate a government into releasing your freedom fighters unless you announce that it is your group that has seized its embassy. "Clear guilt" is difficult to define, but when 40 million people see a group of masked gunmen seize an airplane on the evening news, there is not much question about who the perpetrators are. There will be hard cases where the situation is murkier. Nonetheless, a line demarcating the legitimate use of torture can be drawn. Torture only the obviously guilty, and only for the sake of saving innocents, and the line between Us and Them will remain clear.

12   There is little danger that the Western democracies will lose their way if they choose to inflict pain as one way of preserving order. Paralysis in the face of evil is the greater danger. Some day soon a terrorist will threaten tens of thousands of lives, and torture will be the only way to save them. We had better start thinking about this.

■ ■ ▨

MEANING

1. How does the hypothetical scenario that Levin creates compel his readers to consider his claim that "the decision to use torture is a matter of balancing innocent lives against the means necessary to save them"?

2. What historical parallel does Levin apply to strengthen his case?

3. Ultimately, what criteria, in Levin's view, should determine whether torture in a particular case is warranted?

TECHNIQUE

1. How does Levin control his argument by setting up the alternatives of "inflict[ing] pain as one way of preserving order" versus becoming paralyzed "in the face of evil"?

2. How does Levin's argumentation strategy depend on working from extreme cases to more realistic ones?

3. How does Levin use the results of an informal poll of four mothers to augment his case that torture can be a viable option under the right circumstances?

4. **Other Patterns.** How does Levin use **comparison and contrast** to forestall his readers' desire to apply normal ethical standards?

LANGUAGE

1. Does the language that Levin uses suggest that he is playing the role of devil's advocate? Why or why not?

2. Why do you think Levin selects the atomic bomb, Manhattan Island, and July 4th as the conditions for the hypothetical scenario?

3. If you don't know the meaning of the following words, look them up: *excruciating* (3), *barbaric* (4), *deterrence* (7), *retribution* (7), *disingenuous* (11), *perpetrators* (11).

SUGGESTIONS FOR WRITING

1. **Critical Writing.** Does Levin make assumptions that, if untrue, would undercut his argument? If so, what are they?

2. How have the scenarios and the issues connected with them that Levin wrote about in 1982 come to pass?

3. In your opinion, has the issue of torture produced ethical, legal, and/or moral ambiguities? Explore one of these (for example, transferring detainees to countries where they can be legally tortured or creating a protocol for torture that could not be controlled).

4. **Thematic Links.** From what different philosophical and historical perspectives do Levin and Henry Porter in "Now the Talk Is About Bringing Back Torture" view this issue?

HENRY PORTER

Now the Talk Is About Bringing Back Torture

In the aftermath of September 11, 2001, torture of terrorists to gain information to forestall future attacks became a central issue. Henry Porter (b. 1953), London editor of *Vanity Fair* magazine, has profound misgivings about this policy and voices his reservations in the following essay, which first appeared in *The Observer* (November 11, 2001). Porter's articles appear regularly in the *Guardian*, *Evening Standard*, and *Sunday Telegraph* newspapers. He also has a career as a novelist specializing in political thrillers, including *Empire State* (2003) and *Brandenburg* (2005).

BEFORE YOU READ

Should the Geneva Conventions, which set the standard for treating prisoners in previous wars, be redefined now?

■ ■ ▨

1   For America's supporters, the blind cohesion of the United States is impressive but also worrying. Two months after the attacks there is still no real debate about the fundamentals of U.S. policy or any real criticism of the way the Bush White House conducted itself prior to the September attacks. More surprising is that the country appears nowhere near ready for the total review and overhaul of the institutions—the FBI, CIA and State Department—which failed the people so drastically.

2   If these things were discussed as vigorously as they are here, the U.S. would be stronger and able to present a more convincing case to the world about its current action. Instead much necessary self-examination is suppressed in the cause of unity and to reassure a president whose lack of rhetorical subtlety and modulation does seem to betray a pretty basic intellect—even to Americans.

3   It is in this fiercely uncritical mood that the issue of torture has been raised. Columnists and TV discussion shows have begun to ask at what stage the authorities might consider torturing suspects who have information vital to the security of the American people. *Newsweek*'s Jonathan Alter wrote that in this 'autumn of anger' even a liberal wondered whether torture would 'jump-start the stalled investigation into the greatest crime in American history'. He refers to the wall of silence which has met investigators questioning the small number of material witnesses among the 1,147 suspects currently held by the U.S. in connection with the attacks. Little has been learnt about al-Qaeda from them and nothing about future attacks on America and its overseas assets.

For a visual to accompany this selection, see color insert photo C-7.

4   Similar frustrations surfaced on the Fox and CNN TV networks and in the *Wall Street Journal*, where the academic Jay Winick explained how a terrorist named Abdul Hakim Murad had been tortured by the Philippine authorities in 1995 and revealed a plot to crash 11 U.S. airliners into the Pacific and one into the CIA headquarters at Langley, Virginia. He went on to wonder what would have happened if Murad had been held by the U.S. authorities, his implication being that hundreds, maybe thousands, of lives might have been lost because of the U.S.'s respect for human rights.

5   Today, when a sealed container of smallpox virus or a nuclear suitcase bomb are seen as real threats in the U.S., the case of Abdul Murad seems especially relevant. What if one of these suspects or some future detainee is thought to know about plans to cause thousands of American deaths? Surely the nation should steel itself to do anything necessary to avert the deaths?

6   A round-up of these speculations in the *New York Times* made plain that torture was still unthinkable to commentators and to most of the American public: the U.S. is still a long way off using torture in its war against terrorism, was the conclusion. But how true is that? After all, America is capable of inflicting great pain and fear in the execution of convicted murderers. There are now about 70 executions a year in the U.S. This is despite the anguish of the people placed on a gurney to wait for, and sometimes hear about, temporary reprieves; despite the reports which show that those who are executed are almost always unable to afford the best legal representation; despite the UN convention that prohibits the execution of people who committed their crimes when they were under 18 years of age. (Only Somalia and the U.S. refused to sign.)

7   This inadvertent torture, delivered as a by-product of the people's vengeance, is nothing like the act which sets out to inflict pain in order to extract information or to terrorise a section of the population. There is a world of difference in the intention, if not in some cases, the effect, and that makes a lot of difference to the American conscience.

8   Even if this was so, America has in the last few decades been remarkably close to regimes which routinely practise torture. The U.S. Ambassador to the United Nations, John Negroponte, is someone who could testify to this, but he won't because as Ambassador to Honduras between 1981 and 1985 he was involved with the fight against communist insurgents in neighbouring countries.

9   This included the torture of more than 100 women who fled El Salvador and were disposed of by being thrown from helicopters. The U.S. also supported General Pinochet's regime in Chile where the socialist opposition was terrorised with unbelievable barbarity. This is to say nothing of the torture used in Saudi Arabia and to a lesser degree in Israel, both countries which enjoy U.S. support.

10   To the perversely legal mind, torture could be regarded as morally less of a crime than state-sponsored killing, because the victim stands a chance of surviving the ordeal. The targets of the CIA, which is armed with new authority from President Bush and is contemplating clandestine operations aimed at killing specific members of al-Qaeda, will not live. If you have authorised assassinations, then why not torture? The first is final; the second is not—necessarily.

11   The legal answer to this, as Amnesty International points out, is that America ratified the UN convention against torture and it would be impossible to derogate from that stand. But this answer assumes that the American authorities would feel compelled to admit that they had used torture when faced with a suspect who possessed information crucial to the safety of large numbers of U.S. citizens. They wouldn't because it has been the wisdom of successive administrations that the American people would often prefer to be kept in the dark about what has been done in their interests.

12   So in a way it is good that the issue of torture has been raised in the U.S. for at least the issue is not being consigned to that area of affairs where Americans prefer not to go. But it is not encouraging that American commentators have so little grasp of the profound and terrible concession which is made to bin Laden if a single person is tortured during the prosecution of the war against him. Torture is an absolute evil and there can be no allowances, especially in a country which stands for liberty and spends a good deal of time distinguishing itself from the Taliban and al-Qaeda on those grounds.

13   Americans have broadly shown indifference to the violated human rights of the majority of the 1,147 people detained, often without charge, since 11 September. It is to be hoped that their very understandable fears do not lead to a further deterioration of human rights.

■ ■ ▨

MEANING

1. In what context does Porter feel the need to voice his opposition to the use of torture?
2. How does Porter use the distinction between torture and capital punishment in his argument?
3. Why does Porter unambiguously oppose torture in any circumstances? What evil effects does he associate with the use of torture?
4. What historical precedence does Porter include as a way of strengthening his case?

TECHNIQUE

1. What objections does Porter raise to those who would want torture to be considered as a real option? Does he fairly summarize their position?
2. Why does Porter conclude his argument by mentioning the 1,147 prisoners who were detained, "often without charge" after September 11th?
3. **Other Patterns.** How does Porter use both real and hypothetical **examples** to illustrate the difficulty of defining torture?

LANGUAGE

1. How does the title suggest what Porter's thesis will be?
2. What words and phrases reveal Porter's attitude toward the subject?

3. If you don't know the meaning of the following words, look them up: *cohesion* (1), *overhaul* (1), *modulation* (2), *gurney* (6), *inadvertent* (7), *insurgents* (8), *clandestine* (10), *concession* (12).

SUGGESTIONS FOR WRITING

1. **Critical Writing.** Porter characterizes the national state of mind as being reluctant to carry out a vigorous self-examination on the issue of torture. Is that statement still true? Why or why not?

2. To what extent did the events at Abu Ghraib and the accompanying photographs change the public's view on the issue of torture?

3. What Supreme Court rulings are there on the issue of the government's claim that detainees can be kept indefinitely without charge or given a trial in accordance with the Geneva Conventions? Write an essay **describing** the issues involved.

4. **Thematic Links.** How does Luis Sepúlveda's "Daisy" (Chapter 11, "Problem Solving".) illustrate Porter's concerns?

DEBATE: STEROIDS IN SPORTS

THOMAS H. MURRAY

The Coercive Power of Drugs in Sports

Ethicist Thomas H. Murray (b. 1946) is frequently interviewed on the issue of doping in sports, whether the subject is the Tour de France or Olympic competitions. He currently directs public policy at the Institute for Medical Humanities at the University of Texas in Galveston. His opposition to the use of performance-enhancing drugs on a number of grounds is expressed in the following article, which first appeared in the *Hastings Center Report* (1983). He also has expertise in the less competitive areas of child care and elder care as presented in *The Worth of a Child* (1996) and *The Cultures of Caregiving*, a volume that he coedited with Carol Levine (2004).

BEFORE YOU READ

Why would athletes who do not resort to doping be at a disadvantage in competing with those who do?

■ ■ ◢

1   Our images of the nonmedical drug user normally include the heroin addict nodding in the doorway, the spaced-out marijuana smoker, and maybe, if we know that alcohol is a drug, the wino sprawled on the curb. We probably do not think of the Olympic gold medalist, the professional baseball player who is a shoo-in for the Hall of Fame, or the National Football League lineman. Yet these athletes and hundreds, perhaps thousands of others regularly use drugs in the course of their training, performance, or both. I am talking not about recreational drug use—athletes use drugs for pleasure and relaxation probably no more or less than their contemporaries with comparable incomes—but about a much less discussed type of drug use: taking drugs to enhance performance.

2   It is a strange idea. Most of us think of drugs in one of two ways. Either they are being properly used by doctors and patients to make sick people well or at least to stem the ravages of illness and pain, or they are being misused— we say "abused"—by individuals in pursuit of unworthy pleasures. Performance-enhancing drug use is so common and so tolerated in some forms that we often fail to think of it as "drug" use. The clearest example is the (caffeinated) coffee pot, which is as much a part of the American workplace as typewriters and time-clocks. We drink coffee (and tea and Coke) for the "lift" it gives us. The source of "that Pepsi feeling" and the "life" added by Coke is no mystery—it is caffeine or some of its close chemical relatives, potent stimulants to the human central nervous system. Anyone who has drunk too much coffee and felt caffeine "jitters," or drunk it too late at night and been unable to sleep can testify to its pharmacological potency. Caffeine and its family, the xanthines, can stave off

mental fatigue and help maintain alertness, very important properties when we are working around a potentially dangerous machine, fighting through a boring report, or driving for a long stretch.

3   Caffeine, then, is a performance-enhancing drug. Using caffeine to keep alert is an instance of the nonmedical use of a drug. So, too, is consuming alcohol at a cocktail party for the pleasure of a mild inebriation, or as a social lubricant to enable you to be charming to people you find intolerably boring when you are sober. In the first case, alcohol is a pleasure-enhancer; in the second, it is a performance-enhancer. What the drug is used for and the intention behind the use—not the substance itself—determines whether we describe it as medical or nonmedical; as pleasure, performance, or health-enhancing.

4   The area of human endeavor that has seen the most explosive growth in performance-enhancing drug use is almost certainly sport. At the highest levels of competitive sports, where athletes strain to improve performances already at the limits of human ability, the temptation to use a drug that might provide an edge can be powerful. Is this kind of drug use unethical? Should we think of it as an expression of liberty? Or do the special circumstances of sport affect our moral analysis? In particular, should liberty give way when other important values are threatened, and when no one's good is advanced? These questions frame the discussion that follows. . . .

5   May athletes use drugs to enhance their athletic performance? The International Olympic committee [IOC] has given an answer of sorts by flatly prohibiting "doping" of any kind. This stance creates at least as many problems as it solves. It requires an expensive and cumbersome detection and enforcement apparatus, turning athletes and officials into mutually suspicious adversaries. It leads Olympic sports medicine authorities to proclaim that drugs like steroids are ineffective, a charge widely discounted by athletes, and thereby decreases the credibility of Olympic officials. Drug use is driven underground, making it difficult to obtain sound medical data on drug side effects.

6   The enforcement body, in an attempt to balance firmness with fairness, bans athletes "for life" only to reinstate them a year later, knowing that what distinguishes these athletes from most others is only that they were caught.

7   Any argument for prohibiting or restricting drug use by Olympic athletes must contend with a very powerful defense based on our concept of individual liberty. We have a strong legal and moral tradition of individual liberty that proclaims the right to pursue our life plans in our own way, to take risks if we so desire and, within very broad limits, do with our own bodies what we wish. This right in law has been extended unambiguously to competent persons who wish to refuse even life-saving medical care. More recently, it has been extended to marginally competent persons who refuse psychiatric treatment. Surely, competent and well-informed athletes have a right to use whatever means they desire to enhance their performance.

8   Those who see performance-enhancing drug use as the exercise of individual liberty are unmoved by the prospect of some harm. They believe it should be up to the individual, who is assumed to be a rational, autonomous, and

uncoerced agent, to weigh probable harms against benefits, and choose according to his or her own value preferences. It would be a much greater wrong, they
would say, to deny people the right to make their own choices. Why should we
worry so much about some probabilistic future harm for athletes while many other
endeavors pose even greater dangers? High-steel construction work and coal-
mining, mountain-climbing, hang-gliding, and auto-racing are almost certainly more
dangerous than using steroids or other common performance-enhancing drugs.

9   Reasons commonly given to limit liberty fall into three classes: those that claim
that the practice interferes with capacities for rational choice; those that emphasize harms to self; and those that emphasize harm to others. The case of performance-enhancing drugs and sport illustrates a fourth reason that may justify
some interference with liberty, a phenomenon we can call "inherent coerciveness."
But first the other three reasons.

10   There is something paradoxical about our autonomy: we might freely choose
to do something that would compromise our future capacity to choose freely.
Selling oneself into slavery would be one way to limit liberty, by making one's
body the property of another person. If surrendering autonomous control over
one's body is an evil and something we refuse to permit, how much worse is it
to destroy one's capacity to *think* clearly and independently? Yet that is one thing
that may happen to people who abuse certain drugs. We may interfere with
someone's desire to do a particular autonomous act if that act is likely to cause
a general loss of the capacity to act autonomously. In this sense, forbidding selling yourself into slavery and forbidding the abuse of drugs likely to damage your
ability to reason are similar *restrictions* on liberty designed to *preserve* liberty.

11   This argument applies only to things that do in fact damage our capacity to
reason and make autonomous decisions. While some of the more powerful
pleasure-enhancing drugs might qualify, no one claims that performance-
enhancing drugs like the steroids have any deleterious impact on reason. This
argument, then, is irrelevant to the case of performance-enhancing drugs. . . .

12   A second class of reasons to limit liberty says that we may interfere with some
actions when they result in wrong to others. The wrong done may be direct—
lying, cheating, or other forms of deception are unavoidable when steroid use
is banned. Of course, we could lift the ban, and then the steroid use need no
longer be deceptive; it could be completely open to the same extent as other
training aids. Even with the ban forcing steroids into the pale of secrecy, it would
be naive to think that other athletes are being deceived when they all know that
steroids are in regular use. The public may be deceived, but not one's competitors. There is no lie when no one is deceived. Using steroids may be more
like bluffing in poker than fixing the deck, at least for your competitors.

13   The wrong we do to others may be indirect. We could make ourselves incapable of fulfilling some duty we have to another person. For example, a male
athlete who marries and promises his wife that they will have children makes
himself sterile with synthetic anabolic steroids (a probable side effect). He has
violated his moral duty to keep a promise. This objection could work, but only
where the duty is clearly identifiable and not overly general, and the harm is

reasonably foreseeable: Duties to others must have a limited, clear scope or become absurdly general or amorphous. We may believe that parents have the duty to care for their children, but we do not require parents to stay by their children's bedside all night, every night, to prevent them from suffocating in their blankets. The duty is narrower than that. In order to avoid being too vague, we would have to be able to specify what the "duty to care for one's children" actually includes. Except for cases like the sterile athlete reneging on his promise, instances where athletes make themselves incapable of fulfilling some specific duty to others would probably be rare. In any case, we cannot get a general moral prohibition on drug use in sports from this principle, only judgments in particular cases.

14   We may also do a moral wrong to others by taking unnecessary risks and becoming a great burden to family, society, or both. The helmetless motorcyclist who suffers severe brain damage in an accident is a prototype case. Increasingly, people are describing professional boxing in very similar terms. While this might be a good reason to require motorcyclists to wear helmets or to prohibit professional boxing matches, it is not a sound reason to prohibit steroid use. No one claims that the athletes using steroids are going to harm themselves so grievously that they will end up seriously brain-damaged or otherwise unable to care for themselves.

15   Olympic and professional sport, as a social institution, is an intensely competitive endeavor, and there is tremendous pressure to seek a competitive advantage. If some athletes are believed to have found something that gives them an edge, other athletes will feel pressed to do the same, or leave the competition. Unquestionably, coerciveness operates in the case of performance-enhancing drugs and sport. Where improved performance can be measured in fractions of inches, pounds, or seconds, and that fraction is the difference between winning and losing, it is very difficult for athletes to forego using something that they believe improves their competitors' performance. Many athletes do refuse; but many others succumb; and still others undoubtedly leave rather than take drugs or accept a competitive handicap. Under such pressure, decisions to take performance-enhancing drugs are anything but purely "individual" choices.

16   Can we say that "freedom" has actually been diminished because others are using performance-enhancing drugs? I still have a choice whether to participate in the sport at all. In what sense is my freedom impaired by what the other athletes may be doing? If we take freedom or liberty in the very narrow sense of noninterference with my actions, then my freedom has not been violated, because no one is prohibiting me from doing what I want, whether that be throwing the discus, taking steroids, or selling real estate. But if we take freedom to be one of a number of values, whose purpose is to support the efforts of persons to pursue reasonable life plans without being forced into unconscionable choices by the actions of others, then the coerciveness inherent when many athletes use performance-enhancing drugs and compel others to use the same drugs, accept a competitive handicap, or leave the competition can be seen as a genuine threat

to one's life plan. When a young person has devoted years to reach the highest levels in an event, only to find that to compete successfully he or she must take potentially grave risks to health, we have as serious a threat to human flourishing as many restrictions on liberty.

17   At this point it might be useful to consider the social value we place on improved performance in sport. It is a truism that you win a sports event by performing better than any of your competitors. The rules of sport are designed to eliminate all influences on the outcome except those considered legitimate. Natural ability, dedication, cleverness are fine; using an underweight shot-put, taking a ten-yard head start, fielding twelve football players are not. The rules of sport are man-made conventions. No natural law deems that shot puts shall weigh sixteen pounds, or that football teams shall consist of eleven players. Within these arbitrary conventions, the rules limit the variations among competitors to a small set of desired factors. A willingness to take health risks by consuming large quantities of steroids is *not* one of the desired, legitimate differences among competitors.

18   Changing the rules of a sport will alter performances, but not necessarily the standing of competitors, If we use a twelve-lb. shot-put, everyone will throw it farther than the sixteen-lb. one, but success will still depend on strength and technique, and the best at sixteen pounds will probably still be best at twelve pounds. Giving all shot-putters 10 mg. of Dianabol [a steroid] a day will have a similar impact, complicated by variations in physiological response to the drug. Noncatastrophic changes in the rules may shift some rankings, but will generally preserve relations among competitors. Changes that do not alter the nature of a sport, but greatly increase the risk to competitors are unconscionable. Changes that affirmatively tempt athletes to take the maximum health risk are the worst. Lifting the ban on performance-enhancing drugs would encourage just that sort of brinksmanship. On the other hand, an effective policy for eliminating performance-enhancing drug use would harm no one, except those who profit from it.

19   My conclusions are complex. First, the athletes who are taking performance-enhancing drugs that have significant health risks are engaging in a morally questionable practice. They have turned a sport into a sophisticated game of "chicken." Most likely, each athlete feels pressed by others to take drugs, and does not feel he or she is making a free choice. The "drug race" is analogous to the arms race.

20   Second, since the problem is systemic, the solution must be too. The IOC has concentrated on individual athletes, and even then it has been inconsistent. This is the wrong place to look. Athletes do not use drugs because they like them, but because they feel compelled to. Rather than merely punishing those caught in the social trap, why not focus on the system? A good enforcement mechanism should be both ethical and efficient. To be ethical, punishment should come in proportion to culpability and should fall on *all* the guilty parties—not merely the athletes. Coaches, national federations, and political bodies that encourage, or fail to strenuously discourage, drug use are all guilty. Current policy punishes only the athlete.

21   To be efficient, sanctions should be applied against those parties who can most effectively control drug use. Ultimately, it is the athlete who takes the pill or injection, so he or she ought to be one target of sanctions. But coaches are in an extraordinarily influential position to persuade athletes to take or not to take drugs. Sanctions on coaches whose athletes are caught using drugs could be very effective. Coaches, not wanting to be eliminated from future competitions, might refuse to take on athletes who use performance-enhancing drugs.

22   Finally, although I am not in a position to elaborate a detailed plan to curtail performance-enhancing drug use in sports, I have tried to establish several points. Despite the claims of individual autonomy, the use of performance-enhancing drugs is ethically undesirable because it is coercive, has significant potential for harm, and advances no social value. Furthermore, any plan for eliminating its use should be just and efficient, in contrast to current policies.

23   Can we apply this analysis of drug use in sports to other areas of life? One key variable seems to be the social value that the drug use promotes, weighed against the risks it imposes. If we had a drug that steadied a surgeon's hand and improved her concentration so that surgical errors were reduced at little or no personal risk, I would not fault its use. If, on the other hand, the drug merely allowed the surgeon to operate more quickly and spend more time on the golf course with no change in surgical risk, its use would be at best a matter of moral indifference. Health, in the first case, is an important social value, one worth spending money and effort to obtain. A marginal addition to leisure time does not carry anywhere near the same moral weight.

24   A careful, case-by-case, practice-by-practice weighing of social value gained against costs and risks appears to be the ethically responsible way to proceed in deciding on the merits of performance-enhancing drugs.

MEANING

1. How has the pervasive acceptance of drugs in all walks of life made it harder to argue against the use of drugs in sports, according to Murray?
2. Why does Murray believe that performance-enhancing drugs should be banned?
3. What harm do performance-enhancing drugs do to the athletes who use them and to the sports in which these athletes compete?
4. What responsibility do coaches bear along with the athletes who use drugs?

TECHNIQUE

1. How does Murray's argument depend on the premise that the athlete's freedom of choice is compromised if drugs are part of the game?
2. How does Murray use the difference between steroids and other drugs such as heroin and cocaine to explore the idea of impaired judgment?

3. **Other Patterns.** How does Murray use **classification** to clarify the issue of autonomy versus coercion that is central to his argument?

LANGUAGE

1. How do Murray's definitions of coercion and freedom play a key role in the way in which he develops his argument?
2. Murray never defines the term *performance-enhancing*. Does this take away from his argument, or would most readers understand what he means by this term?
3. If you don't know the meaning of the following words, look them up: *xanthines* (2), *adversaries* (5), *probabilistic* (8), *steroids* (8), *phenomenon* (9), *amorphous* (13), *prototype* (14), *culpability* (20).

SUGGESTIONS FOR WRITING

1. **Critical Writing.** Are the standards that have been established for drug testing and punishment commensurate in all sports, or do different sports have different standards for their players? Why do you think this is the case?
2. What recent events in world-class sports (such as the Olympic Games, Major League baseball, and the Tour de France) have brought this problem to public attention, and with what results?
3. Have you ever participated in or known about a sports competition in which athletes were pressured by coaches or fellow players to take drugs? If so, write a **narrative** about your experiences.
4. **Thematic Links.** Does Norman C. Fost in "Ethical and Social Issues in Antidoping Strategies in Sport" effectively refute Murray's argument? Why or why not?

NORMAN C. FOST

Ethical and Social Issues in Antidoping Strategies in Sport

Norman C. Fost, a professor of pediatrics, disputes the moral assumptions that opponents to his position advance on the issue of doping in sports. He presents this position in the following essay, which was originally published in *Sport: The Third Millennium* (1991). Fost is the director of the Medical Ethics Program at the University of Wisconsin at Madison. He is particularly careful to point out inconsistencies in logic and the instances of hypocrisy in those who disagree with him.

BEFORE YOU READ

Is the use of steroids inherently wrong when compared with all the other means (better equipment, better coaches, better training regimens, better diets) that athletes use to remain competitive?

■ ■ ▧

1   My purpose . . . is to question the claim that athletes who use performance enhancing drugs, such as anabolic steroids, violate moral principles other than the obvious duty to obey the rules of competition. I will conclude that the prohibition of such drugs is based on no apparent moral principles, and must therefore serve some other purpose. Finally, I will suggest that the extreme outrage and vilification cast on the Canadian sprinter Ben Johnson is so disproportionate to whatever offense he may have committed, as to raise questions as to the true source of the campaign to discredit him. The task of analyzing the moral basis of prohibiting performance enhancing drugs is complicated by the virtual absence of any strict rationale in the rules governing the subject. Neither has there been much discussion of the moral basis of these rules in the voluminous and raucous literature on the subject over the past decade. I must begin therefore by taking the opponent's view and offering whatever moral arguments might be proposed as a basis for prohibiting drugs in sport.

2   As best as I can infer from reading commentaries on the subject, there seem to be four moral or quasi-moral concerns:

1. Such drugs provide users with an *unfair advantage* over opponents.
2. The drugs commonly used, particularly anabolic steroids, are *harmful* and there is a duty to protect athletes from harming themselves.
3. The use of such drugs forces competitors to use them, placing them in a situation of *coercion.*
4. Such drugs are *unnatural*, and constitute a perversion of the essence of sports in which they are used.

3   The problems associated with each of these claims will be examined in turn.

THE "UNFAIR ADVANTAGE" CLAIM

4   It should be obvious that merely seeking or gaining an advantage over an opponent is not *implicitly* unfair. It is the essence of sport that athletes have or seek to gain an advantage over their opponents. The most obvious advantages are those created by different genetic endowments. We do not say it is unfair that one runner is faster than another, or a wrestler stronger than his opponent, if these differences are due to natural *endowments*. Questions of morality arise only when humans choose certain courses of action. But simply trying or succeeding in gaining an advantage beyond what nature confers is not implicitly immoral. Most athletic training and preparation is indeed guided by the very desire to gain an advantage over one's opponents. Sometimes these efforts are as simple as routine practice and training procedures. But since the first Olympiad, both ancient and modern athletes have explored an infinite variety of natural and unnatural advantages, ranging from better shoes or swimsuits, to better coaches or training equipment, or better diets or nutrition advisors. The mere seeking of an advantage is not implicitly unfair, nor is the gaining of an advantage implicitly unfair. To label it unfair, and prohibit such a practice on the basis of that claim, requires more argumentation than simply showing that an athlete seeks or indeed gains an advantage. Conversely, seeking an advantage by a practice which, in fact, confers no advantage, would not be judged clearly immoral, nor would a ban on such practice seem appropriate. To facilitate discussion of the moral issues I will thus assume for this discussion that anabolic steroids *do* confer an advantage in that they allow some athletes to improve their maximum performance over that which they could have achieved without using steroids. I believe it has been clearly demonstrated that some athletes in some events, particularly weightlifting, can improve upon their previous best performance by adding anabolic steroids to an already intensive training regimen. Whether or not this advantage extends to sprinters, and whether or not Ben Johnson himself in fact was able to run faster *because* of the use of steroids, is less clear. But let us assume for the purpose of this discussion that he was, in fact, able to run faster as a result of using steroids so that we can get to the question of whether he would have violated any moral rule by so doing, and whether officials have a moral basis for prohibiting such a practice.

STEROIDS AND GREASY SWIMSUITS

5   One factor which might constitute a moral claim that a given practice confers an *unfair* advantage would be unequal access. In the 1972 Olympic Games, for example, the American pole vaulter Bob Seagren sought to gain an advantage by using a fibreglass pole, a clear improvement on the traditional poles made of other materials. Because his opponents had not had the opportunity to obtain or practice with the new device, it was prohibited. Four years later, when access had been "equalized," the use of that device was permitted. Thus far, I have seen no claim that access to steroids is unequal. On the contrary, it is acknowledged that they are nowadays readily available and widely used. Indeed, it is also widely

acknowledged that Johnson is distinguishable from many of his competitors not because he *used* steroids but because he was *caught*. The sophisticated athlete and/or his managers know that the use of such drugs must be scheduled in such a way that hormonal balance is restored at the time of testing; *i.e.*, it is necessary to use the drugs on a schedule that is coordinated with testing, which heretofore has been rather predictable, since it was done primarily at the time of championship events.

6   In the eyes of many, it is ironic, at least, and hypocritical, at worst, that Johnson was punished and castigated beyond punishment for a practice that had little unfairness (of accessibility), while others publicly boasted of achieving medals by using other types of unnatural assists to victory in ways that appear more clearly unfair. The American swimming coach, for example, gleefully displayed a "greasy" swimsuit which allowed the women swimmers to improve upon their previous best times with the marginal advantage of reducing friction between the swimsuit and the water. He acknowledged that this small differential might well have been the difference between victory and defeat. Similarly, the American volleyball team claimed they had substantially improved their leaping ability with the assistance of expensive computer analyses of their movements and consultation with experts in kinesiology and biomechanics. These advantages, *if* real, could by the same token be judged unfair in that they were *intended* to be kept secret so that opponents would *not* have access to the same technology, even if they could afford it. If there is a rational basis for the ubiquitous steroids to be considered unfair, and the secret greasy swimsuits to be considered objects of praise and admiration, it has not yet been explained.

THE "HARMFUL" CLAIM

7   Most published discussions of the steroid controversy emphasize the health hazards and medical harms. A list of dangerous side effects has become a virtual mantra—liver cancer, heart attacks, sterility, hirsutism, psychopathic behavior and others. But good ethics starts with good facts and the first question is whether, in fact, there is unambiguous evidence that steroids, in the doses and duration commonly used by world class athletes, have been shown to cause such harm and, if so, in what incidence.

8   Much of the data published thus far is anecdotal and of little scientific use. A case report of even a rare event, such as liver cancer in a young adult who had used anabolic steroids, does not prove *causation* or even statistically significant association. Either longterm prospective studies are needed, or at least better retrospective case control studies with careful design and analysis by expert epidemiologists. Many adverse effects which are unquestionably caused by anabolic steroids—such as hirsutism and infertility—are reversible for the vast majority of individuals. But as with the "unfair advantage" argument, we can get to the moral question by stipulating the facts. Let us assume, for the sake of discussion, that steroids do in fact, cause serious, irreversible longterm physical harm, including perhaps death, in some users. What would follow from such a finding? It would not follow that such consequences would justify prohibition

among competent adults. Approximately two-thirds of premature mortality in the United States is attributable to personal behavior: smoking, heavy drinking, high fat diets, lack of exercise, inadequate use of seat belts, and so on. For skeptics who would dispute this, there are simpler examples: skiing, sky diving, or automobile racing, to name a few. Indeed, sport itself carries *per se* a substantial risk of death and permanent disability. The majority of professional football players who play for five years or more develop permanent disability. Far more deaths have been attributed to football than to steroids. Quite obviously, it does not follow from these observations that such sports should be banned, or that officials would be morally justified in prohibiting individuals from pursuing these activities. Such paternalism is generally opposed on philosophical and political grounds in western society, particularly in North America. As stated by John Stuart Mill, the dealings of society with the individual should be governed by "one very simple principle":

> [. . .] that the sole end for which mankind are warranted, individually or collectively, in interfering with the liberty of action of any of their members, is self-protection. . . . His own good, either physical or moral, is not a sufficient warrant. He cannot rightfully be compelled to do or forebear because it will be better for him to do so, because it will make him happier, because in the opinion of others, to do so would be wise, or even right. These are good reasons for remonstrating with him, or reasoning with him, or persuading him, or entreating him, but not for compelling him, or visiting him with any evil in case he do otherwise.

9   Even proving that an activity is harmful is therefore not a sufficient reason for preventing a *competent* person from pursuing that activity. While there are some exceptions to the general prohibition against paternalism, the burden is on those who would practice it to justify their intrusion into the liberty of those athletes who choose to pursue whatever risks are entailed in exchange for the benefits of athletic success.

PROTECTING ATHLETES

10 The claim that the ban on steroids is justified by concern for the well-being of the athletes is not only paternalistic without justification, but disingenuous. In sports such as football and hockey, where disability and mayhem are ubiquitous, it is implausible that a drug with few proven harms is singled out as part of a beneficent program to protect athletes from physical harm. If the consequence of roughing the passer were a three point penalty, the practice would disappear and far more disability would be prevented than has been attributed to steroids by even their most severe critics. Similarly, illegal violence in ice-hockey, with its attendant risks, could be dramatically reduced with harsher penalties. The failure of leaders to curtail these clearly dangerous activities suggests that protecting athletes from harm is obviously not the highest priority; presumably, it is balanced with the entertainment objectives, and therefore the economic value, associated with violence. If the health of the athletes were truly

the concern and responsibility of the leaders of organized sports, then screening athletes for evidence of heavy smoking and drinking would seem a more justifiable or efficient program.

11   In summary, the proposition that steroids *are* harmful claims too little and too much. There is little evidence that whatever harms they cause can match numerous other self-destructive activities of world class athletes, including sport itself. And further, the demonstration that any of these behaviors are harmful does not justify, in and by itself, coercive interference with the liberty of competent adults. The concern for liberty would certainly support better research and education on the potential benefits as well as the potential harms of steroids. A competent person remains not truly free to make an informed choice if the data essential for such a choice are not available. A beneficent concern for the well-being of athletes would clearly support expenditure of funds for the development of better scientific and clinical data as well as information.

THE "COERCION" CLAIM

12 In one of the few attempts to provide a philosophical rationale for the prohibition of anabolic steroids, Thomas H. Murray has argued that their use creates a coercive environment in which use by one or some athletes "forces" others to use them lest they be disadvantaged. Murray's argument, in my view, rests on a wrong use or a misunderstanding of the *meaning* of coercion, which implies restraint "by force, especially by law or authority." I am not aware of any instance or proposal that athletes be forced to use steroids. I believe what Murray means is that an athlete who *chooses* to compete at the highest levels believes, perhaps correctly, that since his/her opponents are using steroids, he is less likely to win unless he too uses steroids, even though he/she might *prefer* not to use them. But this pressure to "pay the price" comes with the territory in many other ways. Competing and winning at the highest levels requires sacrifices and risks imposed by the activities of competitors. Olympic competition requires years of arduous training, involving many risks and discomforts. The ever-increasing intensity, training and performance of other athletes in some sense "forces" one to also seek higher levels, and endure more risk than one otherwise might have wished. In gymnastics, for example, the new "tricks" which one's opponents develop in some sense "forces" current competitors to match or exceed these tricks. Newer maneuvers are always more difficult than older ones. They require more training, and often more risk, either because of the time of exposure on already hazardous equipment, or because of the complexity of the maneuver and the greater possibility of a dangerous slip. It is certainly the case that a modern gymnast is required to make these sacrifices as a condition of competing at the highest levels. But we could not properly say that the success of the competitors coerces or forces the gymnast into making the choice to compete. At least in the western world, athletes remain free to walk away from the arena or the sport. Yet, such athletes appear to be driven by their own internal desires, not by the threats or physical force of others.

13   It may be that the enormous financial rewards awaiting some winners may constitute a strong part of their motivation. A decision to forego competition, including the risks of preparing for competition, whether it be hours of practice on a balance beam or the use of anabolic steroids, may therefore constitute a decision to forego enormous and most tempting rewards and opportunities. But these rewards are discretionary pursuits. They are not requirements for living. If, in fact, an athlete could not provide for the necessities of life other than by competing and succeeding in international competition, and if steroids were essential for success, then the word coercion might indeed be applicable. But that does not seem to be the case. . . .

14   It may be that athletes who are willing to endure the substantial risks inherent in many sports would prefer not to add to these risks those associated with steroids. That is, if the athletes could make their own rules, a majority might prefer steroid-free competition. Yet it is not clear that such is the case, since professional athletes have the means to negotiate the rules of their employment and they have not heretofore asked for the kind of testing which would be necessary to eliminate the use of such drugs. If they did choose such a system it would not clearly be based on any moral claim, but would appear to be the expression of a preference to endure some kinds of risks—such as those associated with roughing the passer, or more difficult tricks on the balance beam—while foregoing others.

Population Estimates of U.S. Anabolic Steroids Users		
Total	**Ever Used 1,042,000**	**Used Past Year 307,000**
Age, years		
12–17	120,000	64,000
18–25	384,000	103,000
26–34	220,000	31,000
35+	318,000	110,000
Sex		
M	897,000	252,000
F	145,000	55,000
Race		
White	874,000	255,000
Black	100,000	28,000
Hispanic	67,000	28,000
Region		
Northeast	151,000	39,000
North Central	145,000	40,000
South	539,000	175,000
West	208,000	54,000

Source: National Household Survey on Drug Abuse, 1991.

15   In summary, the claim that the use of steroids is coercive seems to constitute the wrong use of the word. Steroid usage does indeed create pressure on
others to conform, but it does not differ in this regard from other pressures
implicit in sports. . . .

THE "UNNATURAL" ARGUMENT

16 The most obscure of the claims that use of steroids is immoral is the one based
on the distaste for *unnatural* means of assisting performance. Like the other
claims, this one lacks internal coherence. Athletes have used unnatural means
of improving performance since the first Greeks started training for athletics.
Today's training approaches and performances are pervaded by unnatural technologies, from greasy swimsuits to computerized exercise machines to scientifically concocted beverages prepared and packaged in laboratories and factories.
To add to the confusion, substances which are completely *natural*, such as testos-
terone or marijuana, are prohibited as *unnatural*. There do not appear to be
coherent principles behind the decisions to allow some performance enhancing chemicals or devices and disallow others. Nor is there an apparent moral
issue involved in the claim that some assists should be banned merely because
they are unnatural. What moral principle would be involved in allowing a shot-
putter to lift rocks as part of his training but not manufactured weights or a Nau-
tilus machine? What moral principle is involved in allowing runners to ingest
some natural substances, such as vitamins or Gatorade, but not others, such as
steroids? Some claim that certain unnatural assists (such as steroids) change the
essential nature of the sport. But has sport an essence? Sports are games, invented
by men and women, with constantly changing rules. Is pole-vaulting *inherently*
something that must be done with a bamboo rather than a fiberglass pole? Has
not the forward pass changed the fundamental nature or essence of football
more than steroid usage? But such comparisons are, I hope, patently irrelevant,
for no sport has an inherent nature or essence. The simplest race requires man-
made rules regarding its distance, the width of the lanes, the number of false
starts allowed, and I suppose, even the diets or drugs the competitors may or
may not use in the hours, days, weeks or years before an event. I certainly do
not dispute the right of the athletes and organizers or of the entire sporting
community to make whatever rules they wish. I simply dispute the claim that
some rules are more "natural" than others, or have an inherent moral basis.

CONCLUSION

17 Something is surely amiss in sports. If amateurism means competing for the "love
of the thing," it seems to have faded as the sole basis of athletics and of Olympic
competition long before the present time. Exploitation, politics, and economic
considerations increasingly dominate sports throughout the world, as the third
millennium draws near. In the face of these complex and seemingly intractable
problems, it is perhaps understandable that scapegoats would be sought as a

distraction. The extent and intensity of the vilification cast on Ben Johnson would lead one to believe he has violated some moral principle that is at the bedrock of society. I fail to see what, if any, purely moral principle he violated. He *broke* a rule and most assuredly risked losing (and indeed lost) his medal as a consequence. But the rule is not based on any coherent moral principle the demonstration of which has been offered by those who had promulgated the rules. And whatever moral principles might be involved, such as gaining unfair advantage, or preventing harm, are most everywhere violated in far more obvious and worrisome ways, with little comment or apparent effort at correction.

MEANING

1. What reasons does Fost present for rejecting the common objections to the use of drugs in sports?
2. How does the difficulty of distinguishing between "restorative" and "performance-enhancing" drugs illustrate the need for clearer guidelines as to when athletes may take drugs?
3. In Fost's view, why is it hypocritical to condemn the use of steroids while allowing improvements in equipment and training practices that increase competitiveness for athletes who have access to them?
4. Why does Fost fault Thomas H. Murray for the way in which Murray defines coercion?

TECHNIQUE

1. How does Fost's argument depend on his endorsement and use of ideas put forward by the eighteenth century philosopher John Stuart Mill (paragraph 8)? Is his use of these ideas appropriate for his argument? Why or why not?
2. What aspects of Fost's argument depend on his assumption that possible dangers of steroids should be seen as part of the overall risk taking that competitive sports involves?
3. Where does Fost downplay correlations between performance-enhancing drugs and disease, heart failure, and early deaths of athletes?
4. **Other Patterns.** How does Fost use **classification and division** to create a framework within which to analyze drug use by athletes?

LANGUAGE

1. How does Fost draw attention to and question the relevance of terms in this debate by italicizing them?
2. If you don't know the meaning of the following words look them up: *anabolic* (1), *anecdotal* (8), *paternalistic* (10), *disingenuous* (10), *ubiquitous* (10), *inherently* (16), *scapegoats* (17).

SUGGESTIONS FOR WRITING

1. **Critical Writing.** Choose one aspect of Fost's argument with which you agree or disagree, and expand on or refute it.

2. In recent years, which athletes have been penalized or barred from their sports because of drug use? Pick one of these controversies, and analyze it through the framework of Fost's analysis.

3. Read Fost's online editorial "Let the Doping Begin" (February 21, 2006) at seedmagazine .com, and analyze how he applies his ideas to current issues.

4. Give **examples** in a short essay that applies Fost's statement that current policies allow an athlete to restore his function to normal or baseline but prohibit the use of performance-enhancing drugs in other areas, such as biotechnology.

5. **Thematic Links.** How might John McMurtry in "Kill 'Em! Crush 'Em! Eat 'Em Raw!" (Chapter 6, "Comparison and Contrast") respond to Fost's argument?

▓▓▓▓ STUDENT ESSAY: ARGUMENT

The following essay by Christopher Denice illustrates several of the techniques of argument. In the course of his essay, Denice rejects the idea that technology, as an end in itself, guarantees students a better education. He was also asked to document his sources in the MLA style and include a list of Works Cited at the end of his paper. Annotations on Christopher's paper and the follow-up commentary ("Strategies") can help you to understand the important principles of argument.

Denice 1

Emphasize Teaching, Not Technology

Christopher Denice

1   Surely it is a step in the right direction to utilize technology in the classroom. It helps educate the students about the "real world" by making it possible for them to do assignments on computers. However, this "progress" is actually becoming a problem. Teachers are focusing so much attention on making projects fun and technologically sound that they are losing focus on their curriculum.

Introduction

2   Such was the case at my high school, and over the course of my four years at East Greenwich High School in East Greenwich, Rhode Island, I noticed this problem becoming more of an issue with the coming of every September. This is a predicament on a number of levels: for students, teachers, and for the future of our nation. The dilemma is not the usage of technology, but rather the ignorance that many teachers have when they decide to assign these projects: they are lessening the standards of education in order to include technology. The

Thesis statement

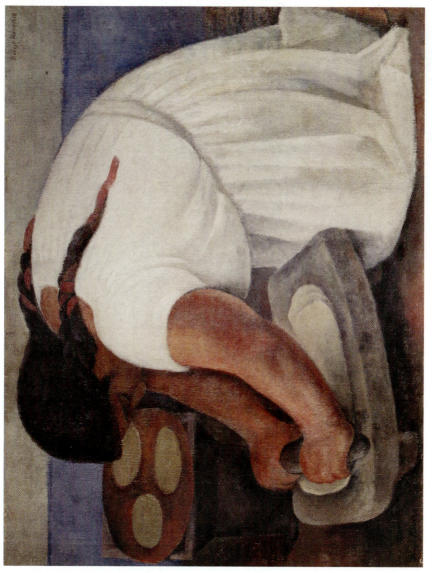

How does this image suggest the integral nature of tortillas in Mexican culture, as discussed by Jose Antonio Burciaga in "Tortillas"?

How does this picture of an Afghan woman showing her face after the defeat of the Taliban in 2001 reveal how traditional veiling has undergone changes of the kind described by Elizabeth W. and Robert A. Fernea in "A Look Behind the Veil"?

What qualities in this picture of the Dalai Lama conducting an initiation rite may also be found in his essay "The Role of Religion in Modern Society"?

How does this picture of a girl herding ducks through a pig pen in a village in China illustrate circumstances in which the influenza virus can spread from ducks to pigs to humans, as Gina Kolata discusses in "An Incident in Hong Kong"?

How does this image of a woman carrying bananas on her head through the market in Papua New Guinea illustrate David R. Counts's analysis of the role bananas play as both a food and a form of currency in "Too Many Bananas"?

How does this non-traditional wedding cake topper illustrate the need for a non-confrontational approach to setting arguments?

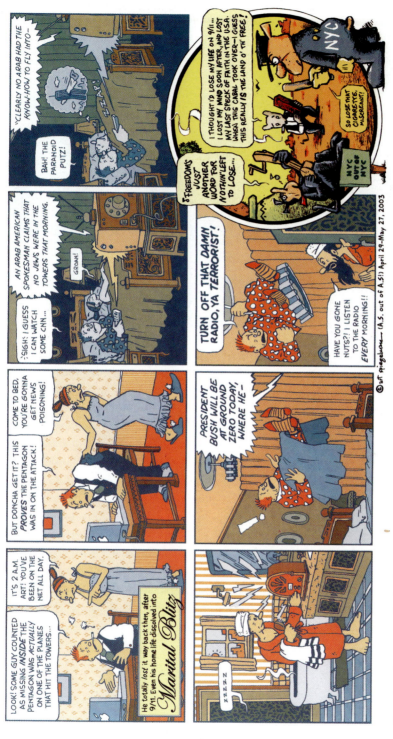

How does this cartoon by Art Spiegelman communicate the social concerns brought about by September 11, 2001, that have led to the present debate on torture (see Michael Levin's "The Case for Torture" and Henry Porter's "Now the Talk Is About Bringing Back Torture")?

Does this picture of the only known adult wholphin (a hybrid between a killer whale and bottle-nosed dolphin) and her calf in Hawaii in 2005 change the basis for the arguments by Carol Grunewald ("Monsters of the Brave New World") and Caroline Murphy ("Genetically Engineered Animals")—and if so, how?

Denice 2

emphasis on utilizing technology in projects throughout high school has, in fact, diminished the focus on the educational aspect of the classes.

3   At the high-school level, projects using technology are assigned too frequently when a more traditional assignment would be more beneficial. Milton Chen, executive director of the George Lucas Education Foundation, recently said "[t]he more we, who see the promise of technology, talk about it just as technology, the more it leads us away from issues of teaching and learning" (Vojtek 1). As we try to incorporate technology just for the sake of incorporating technology, the quality of education will continue to fall. Concurrently, students are becoming less interested in doing these "creative assignments because of the time commitment and sheer volume of technology projects being assigned. Although common sense tells us otherwise, it is surprising that students actually would prefer to write a paper than complete a technology project 71% of the time" (Denice). Education experts and students alike recognize that solely incorporating technology instead of improving education is devastating for our schools. Teachers must realize the same soon.

Evidence in the form of a poll

4   Some people claim that projects are beneficial because they are more creative than regular assignments and incorporate technology into the classroom to prepare students for the world outside. While these points appear to be true, projects still make each class easier for students to pass. Technological projects are often too casual, requiring less thinking about the subject matter, despite the fact that teachers are more ready to give an "A" to a project than to a paper. Too often our teachers are amazed by the creativity and the technological aspects of projects (Tomei 37). They should be looking for the educational value as related to the curriculum, but instead are dazzled by the animation and polish that accompany technological projects. And due to the fact that it would require a great amount of self-discipline for a student to ask for a more challenging assignment, this problem will likely go unaddressed from within the classroom. As teachers

Summary of an opposing viewpoint

Refutation of opposing viewpoint

continue to assign technological projects to simply use technology, they are making their classes easier. This has long-term repercussions; our nation will face serious problems when our schools move backwards as other nations' schools are becoming more rigorous.

5   I can say that projects make school easier because I have gone through public school for thirteen years and have seen the difference in difficulty between technological projects and other assignments. When teachers assign a PowerPoint slideshow, I have found that it is actually more difficult to get lower than a "C" on it than getting an "A" on a paper. My senior-year British literature class was assigned a final project (rather than an exam) that had to "use technology in a practical and useful manner." Our group chose to create a website about British Literature and to summarize what we had learned throughout the year. Another group chose to make a DVD reenacting scenes from various works we had read.

Evidence in the form of personal experience

6   Contrastingly, in my history class junior year, we had to write a three-to-five-page paper every week about a topic we covered in our notes. I can honestly say that I can recall more from that "boring, old-fashioned" history class than any other class from high school. Writing a paper every week was not necessarily fun, but it forced us to learn the material thoroughly. Having to create a webpage earned me an "A" on the project, but I can barely recollect anything from the class (despite creating ten web pages summarizing everything I supposedly learned just four months ago). It is clear from a student's perspective that projects, specifically those that focus on technology, allow mediocrity to be graded as creativity, where more traditional teaching methods prove more productive.

7   Despite teachers' expectations that their projects be completed using the newest technology, often schools are unable to provide the materials needed. While 67% of projects were required to use technology, only 13% of students said the materials and help they needed to complete the project were

Denice 4

provided by their school (Denice). At my high school, the only digital video camera was owned by the Student Council, but since it could not be taken over the weekend, there was often difficulty gaining access. Despite this, I alone had to create at least one video project in ten different classes over the four years of high school. After the first few projects, my family ended up buying a $200 camera to ease the burden of having to schedule around borrowing the school's one camera with everyone else in the class. Often, technology usage comes down to the haves and have-nots, leaving underprivileged students behind because they do not have the same access to technology (Wright 33).

8   However, it is also a problem if the teachers assigning the projects are unable to provide assistance. In fact, a recent report, "Technology Quality: A Report on the Preparation and Qualifications of Public School Teachers," said only 20% of teachers felt very well prepared to employ educational technology in the classroom (Vojtek 2). There is no value in giving work to students that teachers themselves do not confidently know how to use. If the school cannot provide the materials and help for technological projects to students, teachers simply cannot expect the students to use it.

Additional refutation of opposing viewpoint

9   The debate of technological haves and have-nots, known as the "Digital Divide," is a major problem that our educational system faces today (Attewell 251). It has caused great controversy because the "haves" tend to be affluent, suburban, white schools while the "have-nots" are the underprivileged, urban, minority-populated schools. Many have labeled the divide "cyber-segregation" (Attewell 252). All of these new terms signal just how awkward technology is making the educational world feel. Already faced with plentiful troubles, these "have-not" schools now have been criticized for not being able to provide technological access (Wright 34). Putting these schools under the microscope for yet another reason can add no positive impact to an already awkward situation.

Evidence in the form of scholarly studies

Denice 5

10   Now, critics are using racism as the excuse why these   schools do not have computer access. They are saying that politicians and administrators do not put proper emphasis on improving these schools because of the high minority population in the student body. Clearly, this is a very controversial attack. It is damaging because there is a huge need for upgrading the schools' technology and education, but neither is seeing any significant improvements. If this one issue—the issue of adding technology into classrooms—proves so controversial, then it should make us ask just how necessary this over-emphasis on technology really is.

11   Specifically regarding young children, computer usage is rarely linked to success, despite ongoing misconceptions that claim otherwise. In fact, computer usage in children is proven to cause problems ranging from vision problems to bad posture. But the real loss here is that computers are seen to "displace authentic childhood learning experiences" (Attewell 254). This childhood problem transitions to a crisis for high-school   students because it is related to the "cognitive and emotional development" of young adults (Attewell 254). Specifically, many experts believe that it may cause disorders like ADD (Attention-Deficit Disorder) and ADHD (Attention-Deficit Hyperactivity Disorder) in children. Just going room-to-room for the poll I conducted, I learned that 100% of the 45 people I polled in my dormitory found it more difficult to concentrate while using a computer than just sitting at a desk (Denice). As it appears, technology may not only have fewer advantages than planned, but may actually cause more problems than we ever expected for our children.

12   Many projects that are assigned place a burden on the students to get access to numerous devices for their work. And despite the good intention of trying to implement technology into the classroom, assignments designed to use certain materials make busywork out of important lessons.

Denice 6

13   Creating a website should never be substituted for taking a final exam; on no level do the two require the same thought process. And contrary to what many students are expected to say, I was not in that British literature class to learn how to create a website or make a DVD. I was there with the rest of the class to study British literature. While I got an "A" on my final project, I know I would have been lucky with a "C" if I had taken a written exam. I did not learn the material I was responsible for in the curriculum, nor did I need to, apparently. It is alarming that teachers are making such a grand effort to incorporate technology into their classes that they are forgetting that students are in the class to learn about the course material, not to practice using the newest gadgets. With 82% of students saying that doing projects with technology was more work and 67% saying that they actually retained less information doing a project compared to a paper, students feel like these new assignments are wasting their time (Denice).

14   Teachers should be more practical with their expectations of using technology and assigning projects and should realize that their focus should be on their curriculum. Technology should be used for the purpose of creating shortcuts and saving time, not wasting it when students should be learning. Nobody ever asked how to implement the pencil or chalkboard into lessons, so why should we do so now that the medium of technology has changed? This overzealous attitude of teachers to "keep up with technology" is not making education any more profound but rather lowering the quality of what is being taught while simultaneously making the classes easier, as they also make homework more time-consuming (Kent 11). It is one more way we are "dumbing down" our schools, only this time it is a by-product of trying to advance them.

Restatement of thesis

15   If teachers were more practical in their applications of technology, then it would not be a problem. But they should stop worrying about how much technology they make their

Concluding Statement

Denice 7

students use and should instead think about how to improve the quality of education overall. Also, until teachers are masters of the technology themselves, they should not be assigning projects that they themselves could not complete. Technology continues to develop in order to create shortcuts in activities that would normally take more time and effort. Despite the valid goal of society to be more technologically savvy, it is foolish to force a burden on students to use technology while simultaneously reducing the quality of the actual subject material being taught in our schools. Today, while the technological projects teachers assign may be more fun and different from the expected, the reality of the situation is that these projects are more disadvantageous for everyone in the long run.

Works Cited

Attewell, Paul. "The First and Second Digital Divides." Sociology of Education 74 (2001): 252–59.

Denice, Christopher. Poll. Boston College Freshman High School Survey. 25 Sept. 2005.

Kent, Todd W., and Robert F. McNergney. Will Technology Really Change Education?: From Blackboard to Web. Thousand Oaks: Corwin, 1999.

Tomei, Lawrence A. Challenges of Teaching with Technology Across the Curriculum: Issues and Solutions. Hershey: IRM, 2003.

Vojtek, Bob, and Rosie O'Brien Vojtek. "Not a Blunt Instrument: An Interview with Milton Chen." Journal of Staff Development 24 (1999). 25 Sept. 2005 <http://www.nsdc.org/library/publications/jsd/vojtek203.cfm>.

Wright, Cream, ed. Issues in Education & Technology: Policy Guidelines and Strategies. London: Commonwealth, 2000.

In your paper, the works cited would begin on a separate page

Strategies for Argument

1. Providing Evidence

Christopher has supported his thesis with evidence from various sources. He cites his personal experience in high school. He also conducted a survey of freshman college students about their experiences and used the results to back up his own observations. He cites authorities from print and Internet sources. He also uses the example of an assignment in which he had to create a web-site to illustrate his thesis that technology has displaced more conventional and productive written assignments.

2. Refuting Opposing Viewpoints

Christopher devotes several paragraphs to presenting and refuting arguments made by people who believe that technology is the direction education should take. He refutes the supposed benefits of incorporating technology, such as being more creative and preparing students for life after college. He does this by contrasting the work he did and the grades he received in a traditional versus a technology-oriented classroom. He also refutes the claim that using computers leads to success by citing studies that computer use by children is linked to a range of problems, including attention-deficit disorder. Another element in his counterargument is that teachers who themselves are not proficient in the technology are more inclined to give higher grades for projects requiring computers than they would for written work.

3. Considering the Audience

Christopher strengthens his credibility by using a reasonable tone, not using sweeping generalizations, and using clear transitional words to guide his readers from one stage of his analysis to the next.

4. Organizing the Essay

Christopher employs several strategies that were discussed in this chapter. In his introduction, he demonstrates that he is aware that his claim goes against the current trends in education and gains a hearing for his views by fairly stating those of the opposition. This leads to his thesis and the first phase of his argument demonstrating that technology-based projects have begun to displace traditional writing assignments. He draws on deductive assumptions that true education should maintain high standards, require critical thinking, develop reading and writing skills, and reward the quality of work with grades that are merited. He compares and contrasts the work required and the grades received in a class in British literature versus one in history to support his thesis.

The next phase of his argument (beginning with paragraph 7) is designed to show that schools are often ill-equipped to supply the technology that is needed for these projects, nor are teachers well-trained and proficient in using the technology they assign. This leads to Christopher's discussion of unequal access to technology depending on race and social class and the possible detrimental psychological and neurological effects of excessive computer use on children.

Christopher's concluding section (beginning with paragraph 12) returns to his personal experience and what he learned (and did not learn) in his British literature class, in which, instead of taking a final exam, he created a website. He then restates his thesis and pulls his argument together in a way that highlights the paradox of increasingly requiring students to use technology while ignoring the curriculum.

5. Suggestions for Revision

Overall, this is a provocative and effective argument. However, in a review of the essay, some areas for improvement became apparent. Although Christopher appropriately uses quotes from sources, he also puts quotes around other words and phrases for rhetorical emphasis that might be better omitted (as in his first and next-to-last paragraphs). Christopher might also revise some of his overly long sentences and eliminate redundancies.

Guidelines for Writing an Essay in Argument

- If your assignment requires you to put forth and support an opinion, the introduction should clearly state what is at stake in the issue and present your position.
- Present evidence that supports your thesis in a way that your audience will find compelling. Evidence can take a variety of forms, including personal experience, facts, statistics, and expert opinions. Do not suppress conflicting evidence, but integrate it into your overall presentation and refute it. Also, keep a careful record of your sources for when you document your paper (for a discussion of documentation, see Chapter 2).
- Use a clear logical scheme of inductive and/or deductive reasoning to reach your conclusions from the evidence you present. Make sure you do not make sweeping generalizations or develop your argument using other logical fallacies (see the discussion of fallacies on pages 621–23).
- Incorporate previous patterns to organize sections of your essay, including problem solving. End your essay by rephrasing your central thesis, and provide a title that gives the reader an insight into your approach.
- Acknowledge opposing viewpoints in a way that emphasizes an open-minded, objective approach. Adopt a reasonable tone and use clear transitional words and phrases to guide your readers from one section to the next.

Grammar Tips for Argument

The words a writer uses play a vital role in making any argument more effective for a given audience. By adapting the style of an argument to a particular audience, writers can increase their chances of not only getting a fair hearing for their case, but also convincing the audience to share their viewpoint. Tone is a vital element in the audience's perception of the author.

Credibility is created by the audience's perception of the writer as a person of good sense. Good sense might be demonstrated by the writer's knowledge of the subject, adherence to the principles of correct reasoning, and judgment in organizing a persuasive case. The more intangible qualities of the writer's character might be gauged from the writer's respect for commonly accepted values and unwillingness to use deceptive reasoning simply to win a point.

The most appropriate tone is usually a reasonable one. Tone is produced by the combined effect of word choice, sentence structure, and the writer's success in adapting his or her voice to suit the audience and the occasion. Tone indicates the writer's attitude toward both the subject and the audience. For example, which version of the following assertion would be more likely to reach an audience who expected a reasonable appeal?

Indignant:

Why don't people wake up and admit that it is outrageous that although the law allows adopted children to gain access to their birth records and find out who their biological parents are, these natural parents are cruelly denied the same right to learn the identity and whereabouts of their children?

Reasonable:

Since the law allows adopted children to gain access to their birth records and find out who their biological parents are, it would be only fair that the natural parents should have the right to learn the identity and whereabouts of their children.

Of all the characteristics of tone, the first and most important to audiences is clarity. Use a natural rather than an artificial vocabulary. Keep in mind that insight, wit, and sensitivity are always appreciated. Certain kinds of tone are more difficult for beginning writers to manage successfully. A writer who is flippant will run the risk of not having the argument taken seriously by the audience. Arrogance, belligerence, and anger are usually inappropriate in argumentative essays. Even if you are indignant and outraged, make sure that you present evidence to back up your emotional stance; otherwise, you will appear self-righteous and pompous. By the same token, steer away from special pleading, sentimentality, and an apologetic "poor me" tone—you want the audience to agree with your views, not to feel sorry for you.

Keep out buzzwords or question-begging epithets (such as "bleeding-heart liberal" or "arch-conservative") that some writers use as shortcuts to establishing identification with readers instead of arguing logically and supporting their position with facts and evidence.

CHECKLIST for Revising Argument Essays

- What issue is the basis of your argument?
- Is it an issue about which you have a strong opinion?
- Can you express your opinion as a debatable thesis statement?
- What does your audience already know about the issue, and are they in agreement, disagreement, or neutral on it? Have you taken this into account?
- Is your evidence persuasive, representative, and timely?
- Have you provided documentation for evidence drawn from sources?
- Do you fairly summarize and refute the opposing viewpoint?
- Have you adequately and correctly used deductive and/or inductive reasoning in drawing a valid conclusion from the reasons and evidence you present?
- Have you inadvertently used any logical fallacies?
- Do your transitional words and phrases make your case more coherent?

ADDITIONAL WRITING ASSIGNMENTS AND ACTIVITIES

COMMUNICATING WITH DIFFERENT AUDIENCES

1. Should religious institutions be required to pay taxes? Why or why not? Write a letter to a member of Congress or state representative expressing your opinion.

2. Should laws be changed to permit same-sex marriage and the adoption of children by same-sex couples? Write a letter to a member of Congress or state representative expressing your opinion.

3. Is it the state or federal government's responsibility to fund stem cell research? Write a letter to a member of Congress, a state representative, or the governor expressing your views.

4. Should corporations be obligated to allocate a portion of their profits for charities? Write a letter to a CEO of a corporation expressing your opinion.

WRITING FOR A NEWSPAPER

Are public schools the appropriate forum in which to offer sex education for children? If not, why not? If so, at what age should this be started? Write an editorial to a local newspaper with your opinion on this issue.

ARGUMENTATIVE ESSAYS

1. Should intelligent design be taught along with evolution in public schools? Why or why not?

2. Should there be a date-rape crisis center on college campuses?

3. Has the impact of blogging and/or iPods had a positive or negative effect on personal communication? Why?

4. Lawyers are expected to provide *pro bono* legal services. Should physicians have the same obligation? Why or why not?

5. Has granting credentials rather than providing an education become the primary business of American universities?

6. Do you consider having children important in your future? Make a case for having or not having children.

7. Should students attending public schools be required to wear uniforms? Why or why not?

8. Would you use genetic engineering to enhance your child's capabilities? If not, why not? If so, why, and what traits would you want her or him to have?

RESEARCH SUGGESTIONS

1. Does the United States have an effective immigration policy? If not, how should it be modfied? Write a research paper in support of your opinion. Be sure to acknowledge and refute the opposing viewpoint.

2. Does prolonged exposure to violent video games make children more aggressive and violent? Why or why not?

3. Will outsourcing jobs and services ultimately be beneficial or detrimental to America? Why or why not?

4. What impact will there be on individual rights if medical information becomes readily available to employers, insurers, schools, and courts?

5. Investigate the national laws and guidelines that govern research on live animals. On the basis of your findings, argue for or against this practice.

COLLABORATIVE ACTIVITY

Divide into small groups of two to four students, each of which advocates a pro or con position on any of these topics. After your presentation, the rest of the class decides which group made the strongest case. Alternatively, one group may be appointed to formulate a compromise or middle ground position that is acceptable to both sides.

1. Is the practice of racial and/or ethnic profiling a justifiable way to combat terrorism?

2. Is it immoral to keep animals in zoos for entertainment and education? Why or why not?

3. Should sororities and fraternities be abolished? If so, for what reasons? If not, what benefits do they provide for members, the campus, and the community?

USING COMBINED PATTERNS

13

Each of the previous chapters focuses on a specific pattern or strategy, and the selections in these chapters exemplify a specific method of development. But as you have become aware, although one particular pattern may dominate, writers also use other rhetorical modes to achieve an effective result. For example, an essay that primarily uses process analysis might also contain descriptions or introduce examples of the process being discussed. In effect, writers mix and match strategies depending on the purpose, the audience they are writing for, and the occasion that motivated them to write.

The writing assignments in your classes will often require you to use a combination of patterns. For example, your biology professor might assign a paper on a rare or little-known species. Because you have chosen the tree kangaroo, a little-known species that makes its home in the cloud forest of Papua, New Guinea, you could open your essay with a definition of the characteristics of kangaroos; follow with a description of this particular creature and its environment; compare and contrast it with its better-known non-tree-climbing relatives; provide examples of its habits, food requirements, and statistics as to how many tree kangaroos are left in the wild; and close with an argument as to how to help them survive.

Before graduation or after college, you might apply for a summer internship, a job in your field, or graduate school. These would require you to write cover letters focusing on examples that support a claim about your qualifications and a résumé describing your educational background, classifying the different categories of your work experience, and defining your objectives.

Once in the workplace, as a middle-level manager, you might be required to write a report that identifies and gives examples of a problem, analyzes its causes, evaluates and compares possible solutions, and argues for and seeks to persuade higher-ups to adopt your solution. More routine writing tasks in business include instructional memos and quarterly and annual reports that compare year-over-year sales or sales from quarter to quarter, examine causes of a product's strength or weakness, spot market trends, and classify potential consumers demographically for purposes of advertising.

When approaching a writing assignment that requires a mixed pattern format, decide what your overall objective is and which combination of strategies will best serve your purpose. You can use the following list of questions to identify the distinctive requirements of your writing assignment:

1. *Narration*: Can you tell a story about something that happened that would dramatize an idea or event that the reader would need to understand?

2. *Description*: Would sensory details better enable your readers to understand the role a person, place, or object plays in your essay?

3. *Exemplification*: Can you explain your subject by using specific and concrete examples—statistics, facts, case histories, personal experiences—that illustrate its nature and qualities?

4. *Comparison and contrast*: Can you help your readers understand or appreciate your subject by showing how it is similar to or different from another subject?

5. *Process analysis*: Will a detailed step-by-step explanation of how to do something or how something works help your readers to understand your subject?

6. *Classification and division*: Can readers benefit from understanding the categories into which your subject can be arranged or the parts into which it can be divided?

7. *Cause and effect*: Would it be helpful for your readers to understand the reasons for and/or the effects of an object, event, or idea?

8. *Definition*: Can you limit and specify the nature of your subject in a way that would help your readers to better understand it?

9. *Problem solving*: Would it be useful to propose a remedy that would alleviate existing negative effects of or difficulties related to your subject?

10. *Argument*: Does the nature of your subject require you to advance your opinion supported by evidence?

Not every assignment will require you to use more than a few of these questions, but they can help you to decide what writing strategies to use in your essay.

In writing an essay that mixes different rhetorical patterns, look carefully at how your thesis statement is worded, since it will suggest both your primary method of development and the subordinate strategies. Remember that your thesis statement expresses your purpose, the scope of your essay, and the approach you intend to take. For example, suppose your thesis stated:

Celebrities should not be treated preferentially by being allowed to work off drug sentences with community service or time served in rehab.

Notice how the wording of this thesis statement suggests **comparison and contrast** as a primary strategy by showing the way in which ordinary people who have committed the same crimes are treated; the supporting strategies might include **description** (of notable cases) and **exemplification** (typical examples and statistics). In addition, you might include a **process analysis** of how legal and judicial procedures favor celebrities.

In the following five readings, you will be able to observe how writers use a mixture of patterns in their essays. We have annotated Elizabeth Kolbert's "Shishmaref, Alaska" and Lucy Grealy's "Autobiography of a Face" so that you can clearly see the patterns used.

Shishmaref, Alaska

Global warming has become an important issue but, for most people, an entirely theoretical one. For a small Inupiat village, stranded on a thin slip of land in Alaska, the issue is immediate and quite real. Elizabeth Kolbert, a staff writer for *The New Yorker* since 1999, visited this location and reported on her findings in a series of articles titled "The Climate of Man," which appeared in that magazine in April and May 2005. The series was awarded the American Association for the Advancement of Sciences Journalism award and was later developed into *Field Notes from a Catastrophe: Man, Nature and Climate Change* (2006), in which the following selection first appeared. In it, we can observe a convergence of scientific predictions made by scientists with a vivid demonstration of their accuracy in one of the first communities to experience global warming.

BEFORE YOU READ

How is global warming affecting specific locations around the world?

■ ■ ▨

1   The Alaskan village of Shishmaref sits on an island known as Sarichef, five miles off the coast of the Seward Peninsula. Sarichef is a small island—no more than a quarter of a mile across and two and a half miles long—and Shishmaref is basically the only thing on it. To the north is the Chukchi Sea, and in every other direction lies the Bering Land Bridge National Preserve, which probably ranks as one of the least visited national parks in the country. During the last ice age, the land bridge—exposed by a drop in a sea levels of more than three hundred feet—grew to be nearly a thousand miles wide. The preserve occupies that part of it which, after more than ten thousand years of warmth, still remains above water.

> Description: introduces the reader to the location Kolbert analyzes

2   Shishmaref (population 591) is an Inupiat village, and it has been inhabited, at least on a seasonal basis, for several centuries. As in many native villages in Alaska, life there combines—often disconcertingly—the very ancient and the totally modern. Almost everyone in Shishmaref still lives off subsistence hunting, primarily for bearded seals but also for walrus, moose, rabbits, and migrating birds. When I visited the village one day in April, the spring thaw was under way, and the seal-hunting season was about to begin. (Wandering around, I almost tripped over the remnants of the previous year's catch emerging from storage under the snow.) At noon,

> Definition: characterizes the nature of an Inupiat village

> Narration: begins her story with personal experiences

the village's transportation planner, Tony Weyiouanna, invited me to his house for lunch. In the living room, an enormous television set tuned to the local public-access station was playing a rock soundtrack. Messages like "Happy Birthday to the following elders . . ." kept scrolling across the screen.

3   Traditionally, the men in Shishmaref hunted for seals by driving out over the sea ice with dogsleds or, more recently, on snowmobiles. After they hauled the seals back to the village, the women would skin and cure them, a process that takes several weeks. In the early 1990s, the hunters began to notice that the sea ice was changing. (Although the claim that the Eskimos have hundreds of words for snow is an exaggeration, the Inupiat make distinctions among many different types of ice, including *sikuliaq*, "young ice," *sarri*, "pack ice," and *tuvaq*, "land-locked ice.") The ice was starting to form later in the fall, and also to break up earlier in the spring. Once, it had been possible to drive out twenty miles; now, by the time the seals arrived, the ice was mushy half that distance from shore. Weyiouanna described it as having the consistency of a "slush puppy." When you encounter it, he said, "your hair starts sticking up. Your eyes are wide open. You can't even blink." It became too dangerous to hunt using snowmobiles, and the men switched to boats.

> Classification: different kinds of ice

4   Soon, the changes in the sea ice brought other problems. At its highest point, Shishmaref is only twenty-two feet above sea level, and the houses, most of which were built by the U.S. government, are small, boxy, and not particularly sturdy-looking. When the Chukchi Sea froze early, the layer of ice protected the village, the way a tarp prevents a swimming pool from getting roiled by the wind. When the sea started to freeze later, Shishmaref became more vulnerable to storm surges. A storm in October 1997 scoured away a hundred-and-twenty-five-foot-wide strip from the town's northern edge; several houses were destroyed, and more than a dozen had to be relocated. During another storm, in October 2001, the village was threatened by twelve-foot waves. In the summer of 2002, residents of Shishmaref voted, a hundred and sixty-one to twenty, to move the entire village to the mainland. In 2004, the U.S. Army Corps of Engineers completed a survey of possible sites. Most of the spots that are being considered for a new village are in areas nearly as remote as Sarichef, with no roads or nearby cities or even settlements. It is estimated that a full relocation would cost the U.S. government $180 million.

> Cause and effect: delayed freezing of the ice brings problems

5   People I spoke to in Shishmaref expressed divided emotions about the proposed move. Some worried that, by leaving the tiny island, they would give up their connection to the sea and become lost. "It makes me feel lonely," one woman said. Others seemed excited by the prospect of gaining certain conveniences, like running water, that Shishmaref lacks. Everyone seemed to agree, though, that the village's situation, already dire, was only going to get worse.

Narration: the story continues

6   Morris Kiyutelluk, who is sixty-five, has lived in Shishmaref almost all his life. (His last name, he told me, means "without a wooden spoon.") I spoke to him while I was hanging around the basement of the village church, which also serves as the unofficial headquarters for a group called the Shishmaref Erosion and Relocation Coalition. "The first time I heard about global warming, I thought, I don't believe those Japanese," Kiyutelluk told me. "Well, they had some good scientists, and it's become true."

7   The National Academy of Sciences undertook its first major study of global warming in 1979. At that point, climate modeling was still in its infancy, and only a few groups, one led by Syukuro Manabe at the National Oceanic and Atmospheric Administration and another by James Hansen at NASA's Goddard Institute for Space Studies, had considered in any detail the effects of adding carbon dioxide to the atmosphere. Still, the results of their work were alarming enough that President Jimmy Carter called on the academy to investigate. A nine-member panel was appointed. It was led by the distinguished meteorologist Jule Charney, of MIT, who, in the 1940s, had been the first meteorologist to demonstrate that numerical weather forecasting was feasible.

8   The Ad Hoc Study Group on Carbon Dioxide and Climate, or the Charney panel, as it became known, met for five days at the National Academy of Sciences' summer study center, in Woods Hole, Massachusetts. Its conclusions were unequivocal. Panel members had looked for flaws in the modelers' work but had been unable to find any. "If carbon dioxide continues to increase, the study group finds no reason to doubt that climate changes will result and no reason to believe that these changes will be negligible," the scientists wrote. For a doubling of CO_2 from preindustrial levels, they put the likely global temperature rise at between two and a half and eight degrees Fahrenheit. The panel members weren't sure how long it would take for changes already set in motion to become manifest, mainly because the climate

Cause and effect: increased CO_2 alters climate balance

system has a built-in time delay. The effect of adding CO_2 to the atmosphere is to throw the earth out of "energy balance." In order for balance to be restored—as, according to the laws of physics, it eventually must be—the entire planet has to heat up, including the oceans, a process, the Charney panel noted, that could take "several decades." Thus, what might seem like the most conservative approach—waiting for evidence of warming to make sure the models were accurate—actually amounted to the riskiest possible strategy: "We may not be given a warning until the CO_2 loading is such that an appreciable climate change is inevitable."

9　　It is now more than twenty-five years since the Charney panel issued its report, and, in that period, Americans have been alerted to the dangers of global warming so many times that reproducing even a small fraction of these warnings would fill several volumes; indeed, entire books have been written just on the history of efforts to draw attention to the problem. (Since the Charney report, the National Academy of Sciences alone has produced nearly two hundred more studies on the subject, including, to name just a few, "Radiative Forcing of Climate Change," "Understanding Climate Change Feedbacks," and "Policy Implications of Greenhouse Warming.") During this same period, worldwide carbon-dioxide emissions have continued to increase, from five billion to seven billion metric tons a year, and the earth's temperature, much as predicted by Manabe's and Hansen's models, has steadily risen. The year 1990 was the warmest year on record until 1991, which was equally hot. Almost every subsequent year has been warmer still. As of this writing, 1998 ranks as the hottest year since the instrumental temperature record began, but it is closely followed by 2002 and 2003, which are tied for second; 2001, which is third; and 2004, which is fourth. Since climate is innately changeable, it's difficult to say when, exactly, in this sequence natural variation could be ruled out as the sole cause. The American Geophysical Union, one of the nation's largest and most respected scientific organizations, decided in 2003 that the matter had been settled. At the group's annual meeting that year, it issued a consensus statement declaring, "Natural influences cannot explain the rapid increase in global nearsurface temperatures." As best as can be determined, the world is now warmer than it has been at any point in the last two millennia, and, if current trends continue, by the end of the century it will likely be hotter than at any point in the last two million years.

Cause and effect: a trend emerges

Exemplification: examples that illustrate the warming trend

10   In the same way that global warming has gradually ceased to be merely a theory, so, too, its impacts are no longer just hypothetical. Nearly every major glacier in the world is shrinking; those in Glacier National Park are retreating so quickly it has been estimated that they will vanish entirely by 2030. The oceans are becoming not just warmer but more acidic; the difference between daytime and nighttime temperatures is diminishing; animals are shifting their ranges poleward; and plants are blooming days, and in some cases weeks, earlier than they used to. These are the warning signs that the Charney panel cautioned against waiting for, and while in many parts of the globe they are still subtle enough to be overlooked, in others they can no longer be ignored. As it happens, the most dramatic changes are occurring in those places, like Shishmaref, where the fewest people tend to live. This disproportionate effect of global warming in the far north was also predicted by early climate models, which forecast, in column after column of FORTRAN-generated figures, what today can be measured and observed directly: the Arctic is melting.

Exemplification: warning signs

11 Most of the land in the Arctic, and nearly a quarter of all the land in the Northern Hemisphere—some five and a half billion acres—is underlaid by zones of permafrost. A few months after I visited Shishmaref, I went back to Alaska to take a trip through the interior of the state with Vladimir Romanovsky, a geophysicist and permafrost expert. I flew into Fairbanks—Romanovsky teaches at the University of Alaska, which has its main campus there—and when I arrived, the whole city was enveloped in a dense haze that looked like fog but smelled like burning rubber. People kept telling me that I was lucky I hadn't come a couple of weeks earlier, when it had been much worse. "Even the dogs were wearing masks," one woman I met said. I must have smiled. "I am not joking," she told me.

12   Fairbanks, Alaska's second-largest city, is surrounded on all sides by forest, and virtually every summer lightning sets off fires in these forests, which fill the air with smoke for a few days or, in bad years, weeks. In the summer of 2004, the fires started early, in June, and were still burning two and a half months later; by the time of my visit, in late August, a record 6.3 million acres—an area roughly the size of New Hampshire—had been incinerated. The severity of the fires was clearly linked to the weather, which had been exceptionally hot and dry; the average summertime temperature in Fairbanks was the highest on record, and the amount of rainfall was the third lowest.

Description: environmental and sensory details

13   On my second day in Fairbanks, Romanovsky picked me at my hotel for an underground tour of the city. Like most permafrost experts, he is from Russia. (The Soviets more or less invented the study of permafrost when they decided to build their gulags in Siberia.) A broad man with shaggy brown hair and a square jaw, Romanovsky as a student had had to choose between playing professional hockey and becoming a geophysicist. He had opted for the latter, he told me, because "I was little bit better scientist than hockey player." He went on to earn two master's degrees and two Ph.D.s. Romanovsky came to get me at ten A.M.; owing to all the smoke, it looked like dawn.

14   Any piece of ground that has remained frozen for at least two years is, by definition, permafrost. In some places, like eastern Siberia, permafrost runs nearly a mile deep; in Alaska, it varies from a couple of hundred feet to a couple of thousand feet deep. Fairbanks, which is just below the Arctic Circle, is situated in a region of discontinuous permafrost, meaning that the city is pocked with regions of frozen ground. One of the first stops on Romanovsky's tour was a hole that had opened up in patch of permafrost not far from his house. It was about six feet wide and five feet deep. Nearby were the outlines of other, even bigger holes, which, Romanovsky told me, had been filled with gravel by the local public-works department. The holes, known as thermokarsts, had appeared suddenly when the permafrost gave way, like a rotting floorboard. (The technical term for thawed permafrost is "talik," from a Russian word meaning "not frozen.") Across the road, Romanovsky pointed out a long trench running into the woods. The trench, he explained, had been formed when a wedge of underground ice had melted. The spruce trees that had been growing next to it, or perhaps on top of it, were now listing at odd angles, as if in a gale. Locally, such trees are called "drunken." A few of the spruces had fallen over. "These are very drunk," Romanovsky said.

15   In Alaska, the ground is riddled with ice wedges that were created during the last glaciation, when the cold earth cracked and the cracks filled with water. The wedges, which can be dozens or even hundreds of feet deep, tended to form in networks, so when they melt, they leave behind connecting diamond- or hexagon-shaped depressions. A few blocks beyond the drunken forest, we came to a house where the front yard showed clear signs of ice-wedge melt-off. The owner, trying to make the best of things, had turned the yard into a miniature-golf course. Around the corner, Romanovsky

[margin annotations:]

Definition: permafrost and other technical terms

Description: effects of permafrost

Cause and effect: thawing of permafrost and collapse of forests and houses

Description: realistic details bring readers into the scene

pointed out a house—no longer occupied—that basically had split in two; the main part was leaning to the right and the garage toward the left. The house had been built in the sixties or early seventies; it had survived until almost a decade ago, when the permafrost under it started to degrade. Romanovsky's mother-in-law used to own two houses on the same block. He had urged her to sell them both. He pointed out one, now under new ownership; its roof had developed an ominous-looking ripple. (When Romanovsky went to buy his own house, he looked only in permafrost-free areas.)

Problem solving: an attempt to cope with the negative effects of thawing

16   "Ten years ago, nobody cared about permafrost," he told me. "Now everybody wants to know." Measurements that Romanovsky and his colleagues at the University of Alaska have made around Fairbanks show that the temperature of the permafrost in many places has risen to the point where it is now less than one degree below freezing. In places where the permafrost has been disturbed, by roads or houses or lawns, much of it is already thawing. Romanovsky has also been monitoring the permafrost on the North Slope and has found that there, too, are regions where the permafrost is very nearly thirty-two degrees Fahrenheit. While thermokarsts in the roadbeds and talik under the basement are the sort of problems that really only affect the people right near—or above—them, warming permafrost is significant in ways that go far beyond local real estate losses. For one thing, permafrost represents a unique record of long-term temperature trends. For another, it acts, in effect, as a repository for greenhouse gases. As the climate warms, there is a good chance that these gases will be released into the atmosphere, further contributing to global warming. Although the age of permafrost is difficult to determine, Romanovsky estimates that most of it in Alaska probably dates back to the beginning of the last glacial cycle. This means that if it thaws, it will be doing so for the first time in more than a hundred and twenty thousand years. "It's really a very interesting time," Romanovsky told me.

Cause and effect: explanation of the reasons for changes in the environment

Narration: concludes her story by emphasizing that attention should be paid to these dramatic changes

■ ■ ◪

MEANING

1. How has the thinning of the ice pack on which Shishmaref is situated endangered the existence of this native community?

2. What insights does Kolbert offer into scientific awareness of the existence and magnitude of global warming?

How does this cartoon satirize the idea that the debate over global warming has not been resolved?

3. What dramatic climate changes has the increased volume of carbon dioxide in the atmosphere begun to produce?

4. How does the change in the permafrost also indicate dramatic climate shifts?

TECHNIQUE

1. How does Kolbert use a **narrative** structure to frame her analysis and **description** to set the scene?

2. Where does Kolbert give **examples** of warning signs and use **classification** for the different kinds of conditions of ice?

3. How does Kolbert use **causal analysis** to explain the effect of increased carbon dioxide on global warming?

4. Where does Kolbert use **definition** to explain the meaning of permafrost and other technical concepts?

LANGUAGE

1. How do the distinctions the Inupiat make among different kinds of ice reveal how closely attuned they are to their environment?

2. How would you characterize Kolbert's tone and attitude toward the subject on which she is reporting?

3. If you don't know the meaning of the following words, look them up: *disconcertingly* (2), *subsistence* (2), *roiled* (4), *dire* (5), *global warming* (6), *meteorologist* (7), *unequivocal* (8), *carbon dioxide* (CO_2) (8), *disproportionate* (10), *underlaid* (11), *virtually* (12), *gulags* (13), *repository* (16).

SUGGESTIONS FOR WRITING

1. **Critical Writing.** Are public officials now generally in agreement that the science underlying Kolbert's analysis is sound? If so, how is the problem being addressed?

2. How does the 2006 documentary *An Inconvenient Truth* address the same issues that Kolbert discusses? For an opposing viewpoint, read Robert W. Felix's *Not by Fire but by Ice* (2nd ed., 2005). Which thesis do you find more persuasive? Explain your answer.

3. Use **multiple patterns** to analyze the ecological or environmental challenges that your community faces and how they are being solved.

4. **Thematic Links.** Compare the isolated community of Shishmaref, Alaska, that Kolbert discusses with the remote Shetland Island of Lerwick that Ethel G. Hofman describes in "An Island Passover" (Chapter 7, "Process Analysis").

DIANE ACKERMAN

The Social Sense

A nature writer with the soul of a poet, Diane Ackerman writes erudite and enchanting prose that charts the astonishing range of variations in what cultures have found to be edible or inedible. We can accompany her on her journey through different civilizations, from the tribal to the urbane, in the following essay from *A Natural History of the Senses* (1990). The PBS television series *Mystery of the Senses* grew out of this book. Ackerman's seemingly inexhaustible explorations of every aspect of our world have resulted in her popular works such as *The Rarest of the Rare* (1995), *Deep Play* (1999), *Cultivating Delight: A Natural History of My Garden* (2001), and *An Alchemy of Mind: The Marvel and Mystery of the Brain* (2004).

BEFORE YOU READ

Where do you draw the line on what foods you would be willing to eat?

■ ■ ▨

1   The other senses may be enjoyed in all their beauty when one is alone, but taste is largely social. Humans rarely choose to dine in solitude, and food has a powerful social component. The Bantu feel that exchanging food makes a contract between two people who then have a "clanship of porridge." We usually eat with our families, so it's easy to see how "breaking bread" together would symbolically link an outsider to a family group. Throughout the world, the stratagems of business take place over meals; weddings end with a feast; friends reunite at celebratory dinners; children herald their birthdays with ice cream and cake; religious ceremonies offer food in fear, homage, and sacrifice; wayfarers are welcomed with a meal. As Brillat-Savarin says, "every . . . sociability . . . can be found assembled around the same table: love, friendship, business, speculation, power, importunity, patronage, ambition, intrigue . . ." If an event is meant to matter emotionally, symbolically, or mystically, food will be close at hand to sanctify and bind it. Every culture uses food as a sign of approval or commemoration, and some foods are even credited with supernatural powers, others eaten symbolically, still others eaten ritualistically, with ill fortune befalling dullards or skeptics who forget the recipe or get the order of events wrong. Jews attending a Seder eat a horseradish dish to symbolize the tears shed by their ancestors when they were slaves in Egypt. Malays celebrate important events with rice, the inspirational center of their lives. Catholics and Anglicans take a communion of wine and wafer. The ancient Egyptians thought onions symbolized the many-layered universe, and swore oaths on an onion as we might on a Bible. Most cultures embellish eating with fancy plates and glasses, accompany it with parties, music, dinner theater, open-air barbecues, or other forms of revelry. Taste is an intimate sense. We can't taste things at a distance. And how we taste things, as well as the exact makeup of our saliva, may be as individual as our fingerprints.

2   Food gods have ruled the hearts and lives of many people. Hopi Indians, who revere corn, eat blue corn for strength, but all Americans might be worshiping corn if they knew how much of their daily lives depended on it. Margaret Visser, in *Much Depends on Dinner*, gives us a fine history of corn and its uses: livestock and poultry eat corn; the liquid in canned foods contain corn; corn is used in most paper products, plastics, and adhesives; candy, ice cream, and other goodies contain corn syrup; dehydrated and instant foods contain cornstarch; many familiar objects are made from corn products, brooms and corncob pipes to name only two. For the Hopis, eating corn is itself a form of reverence. I'm holding in my hand a beautifully carved Hopi corn kachina doll made from cottonwood; it represents one of the many spiritual essences of their world. Its cob-shaped body is painted ocher, yellow, black, and white, with dozens of squares drawn in a cross-section-of-a-kernel design, and abstract green leaves spearing up from below. The face has a long, black, rootlike nose, rectangular black eyes, a black ruff made of rabbit fur, white string corn-silk-like ears, brown bird-feather bangs, and two green, yellow, and ocher striped horns topped by rawhide tassels. A fine, soulful kachina, the ancient god Maïs stares back at me, tastefully imagined.

3   Throughout history, and in many cultures, *taste* has always had a double meaning. The word comes from the Middle English *tasten*, to examine by touch, test, or sample, and continues back to the Latin *taxare*, to touch sharply. So a taste was always a trial or test. People who have taste are those who have appraised life in an intensely personal way and found some of it sublime, the rest of it lacking. Something in bad taste tends to be obscene or vulgar. And we defer to professional critics of wine, food, art, and so forth, whom we trust to taste things for us because we think their taste more refined or educated than ours. A companion is "one who eats bread with another," and people sharing food as a gesture of peace or hospitality like to sit around and chew the fat.

4   The first thing we taste is milk from our mother's breast,[1] accompanied by love and affection, stroking, a sense of security, warmth, and well-being, our first intense feelings of pleasure. Later on she will feed us solid food from her hands, or even chew food first and press it into our mouths, partially digested. Such powerful associations do not fade easily, as if at all. We say "food" as if it were a simple thing, an absolute like rock or rain to take for granted. But it is a big source of pleasure in most lives, a complex realm of satisfaction both physiological and emotional, much of which involves memories of childhood. Food must taste good, must reward us, or we would not stoke the furnace in each of our cells. We must eat to live, as we must breathe. But breathing is involuntary, finding food is not; it takes energy and planning, so it must tantalize us out of our natural torpor. ft must decoy us out of bed in the morning and prompt us to put on constricting clothes, go to work, and perform tasks we may not enjoy

---

[1] This special milk, called colostrum, is rich in antibodies, the record of the mother's epidemiologic experience.

for eight hours a day, five days a week, just to "earn our daily bread," or be "worth our salt," if you like, where the word *salary* comes from. And, because we are omnivores, many tastes must appeal to us, so that we'll try new foods. As children grow, they meet regularly throughout the day—at mealtimes—to hear grown-up talk, ask questions, learn about customs, language, and the world. If language didn't arise at mealtimes, it certainly evolved and became more fluent there, as it did during group hunts.

5   We tend to see our distant past through a reverse telescope that compresses it: a short time as hunter-gatherers, a long time as "civilized" people. But civilization is a recent stage of human life, and, for all we know, it may not be any great achievement. It may not even be the final stage. We have been alive on this planet as recognizable humans for about two million years, and for all but the last two or three thousand we've been hunter-gatherers. We may sing in choirs and park our rages behind a desk, but we patrol the world with many of a hunter-gatherer's drives, motives, and skills. These aren't knowable truths. Should an alien civilization ever contact us, the greatest gift they could give us would be a set of home movies: films of our species at each stage in our evolution. Consciousness, the great poem of matter, seems so unlikely, so impossible, and yet here we are with our loneliness and our giant dreams. Speaking into the perforations of a telephone receiver as if through the screen of a confessional, we do sometimes share our emotions with a friend, but usually this is too disembodied, too much like yelling into the wind. We prefer to talk *in person*, as if we could temporarily slide into their feelings. Our friend first offers us food, drink. It is a symbolic act, a gesture that says: *This food will nourish your body as I will nourish your soul.* In hard times, or in the wild, it also says *I will endanger my own life by parting with some of what I must consume to survive.* Those desperate times may be ancient history, but the part of us forged in such trials accepts the token drink and piece of cheese and is grateful.

FOOD AND SEX

6 What would the flutterings of courtship be without a meal? As the deliciously sensuous and ribald tavern scene in Fielding's *Tom Jones* reminds us, a meal can be the perfect arena for foreplay. Why is food so sexy? Why does a woman refer to a handsome man as a real dish? Or a French girl call her lover *mon petit chou* (my little cabbage)? Or an American man call his girlfriend cookie? Or a British man describe a sexy woman as a bit of crumpet (a flat, toasted griddlecake well lubricated with butter)? Or a tart? Sexual hunger and physical hunger have always been allies. Rapacious needs, they have coaxed and driven us through famine and war, to bloodshed and serenity, since our earliest days.

7   Looked at in the right light, any food might be thought aphrodisiac. Phallic-shaped foods such as carrots, leeks, cucumbers, pickles, sea cucumbers (which become tumescent when soaked), eels, bananas, and asparagus have all been prized as aphrodisiacs at one time or another, as were oysters and figs because they reminded people of female genitalia; caviar because it was a female's eggs; rhinoceros horn, hyena eyes, hippopotamus snout, alligator tail, camel hump,

swan genitals, dove brains, and goose tongues, on the principle that anything so rare and exotic must have magical powers; prunes (which were offered free in Elizabethan brothels); peaches (because of their callipygous rumps?); tomatoes, called "love apples" and thought to be Eve's temptation in the Garden of Eden; onions and potatoes, which look testicular, as well as "prairie oysters," the cooked testicles of a bull; and mandrake root, which looks like a man's thighs and penis. Spanish fly, the preferred aphrodisiac of the Marquis de Sade, with which he laced the bonbons he fed prostitutes and friends, is made by crushing a southern European beetle. It contains a gastrointestinal irritant and also produces a better blood flow, the combination of which brings on a powerful erection of either the penis or the clitoris, but also damages the kidneys; it can even be fatal. Musk, chocolate, and truffles also have been considered aphrodisiac and, for all we know, they might well be. But, as sages have long said, the sexiest part of the body and the best aphrodisiac in the world is the imagination.

8   Primitive peoples saw creation as a process both personal and universal, the earth's yielding food, humans (often molded from clay or dust) burgeoning with children. Rain falls from the sky and impregnates the ground, which brings forth fruit and grain from the tawny flesh of the earth—an earth whose mountains look like reclining women, and whose springs spurt like healthy men. Fertility rituals, if elaborate and frenzied enough, could encourage Nature's bounty. Cooks baked meats and breads in the shape of genitals, especially penises, and male and female statues with their sexual organs exaggerated presided over orgiastic festivities where sacred couples copulated in public. A mythic Gaia poured milk from her breasts and they became galaxies. The ancient Venus figures with global breasts, swollen bellies, and huge buttocks and thighs symbolized the female life-force, mother to crops and humans. The earth itself was a goddess, curvy and ripe, radiant with fertility, aspill with riches. People have thought the Venus figures imaginative exaggerations, but women of that time may indeed have resembled them, all breasts, belly, and rump. When pregnant, they would have bulged into quite an array of shapes.

9   Food is created by the sex of plants or of animals; and we find it sexy. When we eat an apple or peach, we are eating the fruit's placenta. But, even if that weren't so, and we didn't subconsciously associate food with sex, we would still find it sexy for strictly physical reasons. We use the mouth for many things—to talk and kiss, as well as to eat. The lips, tongue, and genitals all have the same neural receptors, called Krause's end bulbs, which make them ultrasensitive, highly charged. There's a similarity of response.

10   A man and woman sit across from one another in a dimly lit restaurant. A small bouquet of red-and-white spider lilies sweetens the air with the cinnamon-like tingle. A waiter passes with a plate of rabbit sausage in molé sauce. At the next table, a blueberry soufflé oozes scent. Oysters on the half shell, arranged on a large platter of shaved ice, one by one polish the woman's tongue with silken saltiness. A fennel-scented steam rises from thick crabcakes on the man's plate. Small loaves of fresh bread breathe sweetly. Their hands brush as they both reach

for the bread. He stares into her eyes, as if filling them with molten lead. They both know where this delicious prelude will lead. *"I'm so hungry,"* she whispers.

THE OMNIVORE'S PICNIC

11 You have been invited to dinner at the home of extraterrestrials, and asked to bring friends. Being considerate hosts, they first inquire if you have any dietary allergies or prohibitions, and then what sort of food would taste good to you. What do humans eat? they ask. Images cascade through your mind, a cornucopia of plants, animals, minerals, liquids, and solids, in a vast array of cuisines. The Masai enjoy drinking cow's blood. Orientals eat stir-fried puppy. Germans eat rancid cabbage (sauerkraut), Americans eat decaying cucumbers (pickles), Italians eat whole deep-fried songbirds, Vietnamese eat fermented fish dosed with chili peppers, Japanese and others eat fungus (mushrooms), French eat garlic-soaked snails. Upper-class Aztecs ate roasted dog (a hairless variety named *xquintli*, which is still bred in Mexico). Chinese of the Chou dynasty liked rats, which they called "household deer,"[2] and many people still do eat rodents, as well as grasshoppers, snakes, flightless birds, kangaroos, lobsters, snails, and bats. Unlike most other animals, which fill a small yet ample niche in the large web of life on earth, humans are omnivorous. The Earth offers perhaps 20,000 edible plants alone. A poor season for eucalyptus will wipe out a population of koala bears, which have no other food source. But human beings are Nature's great ad libbers and revisers. Diversity is our delight. In a time of drought, we can ankle off to a new locale, or break open a cactus, or dig a well. When plagues of locusts destroy our crops, we can forage on wild plants and roots. If our herds die, we find protein in insects, beans, and nuts. Not that being an omnivore is easy. A koala bear doesn't have to worry about whether or not its next mouthful will be toxic. In fact, eucalyptus is highly poisonous, but a koala has an elaborately protective gut, so it just eats eucalyptus, exactly as its parents did. Cows graze without fear on grass and grain. But omnivores are anxious eaters. They must continually test new foods to see if they're palatable and nutritious, running the risk of inadvertently poisoning themselves. They must take chances on new flavors, and, doing so, they frequently acquire a taste for something offbeat that, though nutritious, isn't the sort of thing that might normally appeal to them—chili peppers (which Columbus introduced to Europe), tobacco, alcohol, coffee, artichokes, or mustard, for instance. When we were hunter-gatherers, we ate a great variety of foods. Some of us still do, but more often we add spices to what we know, or find at hand, *for variety*, as we like to say. Monotony isn't our code. It's safe, in some ways, but in others it's more dangerous. Most of us prefer our foods cooked to the steaminess of freshly killed prey.

---

[2] It was the food-obsessed Chinese who started the first serious restaurants during the time of the T'ang dynasty (A.D. 618–907). By the time the Sung dynasty replaced the T'ang, they were all-purpose buildings, with many private dining rooms, where one went for food, sex, and barroom gab.

We don't have ultrasharp carnivore's teeth, but we don't need them. We've created sharp tools. We do have incisor teeth for slicing fruits, and molars for crushing seeds and nuts, as well as canines for ripping flesh. At times, we eat nasturtiums and pea pods and even the effluvia from the mammary glands of cows, churned until it curdles, or frozen into a solid and attached to pieces of wood.

12   Our hosts propose a picnic, since their backyard is a meadow lit by two suns, and they welcome us and our friends. Our Japanese friend chooses the appetizer: sushi, including shrimp still alive and wriggling. Our French friend suggests a baguette, or better still croissants, which have an unlikely history, which he insists on telling everyone: To celebrate Austria's victory against the invading Ottoman Turks, bakers created pastry in the shape of the crescent on the Turkish flag, so that the Viennese could devour their enemies at the table as they had on the battlefield. Croissants soon spread to France and, during the 1920s, traveled with other French ways to the United States. Our Amazonian friend chooses the main course—nuptial kings and queens of leafcutter ants, which taste like walnut butter, followed by roasted turtle and sweet-fleshed piranha. Our German friend insists that we include some spaetzle and a loaf of darkest pumpernickel bread, which gets its name from the verb *pumpern*, "to break wind," and *Nickel*, "the devil," because it was thought to be so hard to digest that even the devil would fart if he ate it. Our Tasaday friend wants some natek, a startchy paste his people make from the insides of caryota palm trees. The English cousin asks for a small platter of potted ox tongues, very aged blue cheese, and, for dessert, trifle—whipped cream and slivered almonds on top of a jam-and-custard pudding thick with sherry-soaked ladyfingers.

13   To finish our picnic lunch, our Turkish friend proposes coffee in the Turkish style—using a mortar and pestle to break up the beans, rather than milling them. To be helpful, he prepares it for us all, pouring boiling water over coffee grounds through a silver sieve into a pot. He brings this to a light boil, pours it through the sieve again, and offers us some of the clearest, brightest coffee we've ever tasted. According to legend, he explains, coffee was discovered by a ninth-century shepherd, who one day realized that his goats were becoming agitated whenever they browsed on the berries of certain bushes. For four hundred years, people thought only to chew the berries. Raw coffee doesn't brew into anything special, but in the thirteenth century someone decided to roast the berries, which releases the pungent oil and the mossy-bitter aroma now so familiar to us. Our Indian friend passes round cubes of sugar, which we are instructed to let melt on the tongue as we sip our coffee, and our minds roam back to the first recorded instance of sugar, in the Atharvaveda, a sacred Hindu text from 800 B.C., which describes a royal crown made of glittering sugar crystals. Then he circulates a small dish of coriander seeds, and we pinch a few in our fingers, set them on our tongues, and feel our mouths freshen from the aromatic tang. A perfect picnic. We thank our hosts for laying on such a splendid feast, and invite them to our house for dinner next. "What do jujubarians eat?" we ask.

OF CANNIBALISM AND SACRED COWS

14 Even though grass soup was the main food in the Russian gulags, according to Solzhenitsyn's *One Day in the Life of Ivan Denisovich*, humans don't prefer wood, or leaves, or grass—the cellulose is impossible to digest. We also can't manage well eating excrement, although some animals adore it, or chalk or petroleum. On the other hand, cultural taboos make us spurn many foods that are wholesome and nourishing. Jews don't eat pork, Hindus don't eat beef, and Americans in general won't eat dog, rat, horse, grasshopper, grubs, or many other palatable foods prized by peoples elsewhere in the world. Anthropologist Claude Lévi-Strauss found that primitive tribes designated foods "good to think" or "bad to think." Necessity, the mother of invention, fathers many codes of conduct. Consider the "sacred cow," an idea so shocking it has passed into our vocabulary as a thing, event, or person considered sacrosanct. Though India has a population of around 700 million and a constant need for protein, over two hundred million cattle are allowed to roam the streets as deities while many people go hungry. The cow plays a central role in Hinduism. As Marvin Harris explains in *The Sacred Cow and the Abominable Pig*:

> Cow protection and cow worship also symbolize the protection and adoration of human motherhood. I have a collection of colorful Indian pin-up calendars depicting jewel-bedecked cows with swollen udders and the faces of beautiful human madonnas. Hindu cow worshippers say: "The cow is our mother. She gives us milk and butter. Her male calves till the land and give us food." To critics who oppose the custom of feeding cows that are too old to have calves and give milk, Hindus reply: "Will you then send your mother to a slaughter house when she gets old?"

Not only is the cow sacred in India, even the dust in its hoofprints is sacred. And, according to Hindu theology, 330 million gods live inside each cow. There are many reasons why this national tantalism has come about; one factor may be that an overcrowded land such as India can't support the raising of livestock for food, a system that is extremely inefficient. When people eat animals that have been fed grains, "nine out of ten calories and four out of five grams of protein are lost for human consumption." The animal uses up most of the nutrients. So vegetarianism may have evolved as a remedy, and been ritualized through religion. "I feel confident that the rise of Buddhism was related to mass suffering and environmental depletions," Harris writes, "because several similar nonkilling religions . . . arose in India at the same time." Including Jainism, whose priests not only tend stray cats and dogs, but keep a separate room in their shelters just for insects. When they walk down the street, an assistant walks ahead of them to brush away any insects lest they get stepped on, and they wear gauze masks so they don't accidentally inhale a wayward midge or other insect.

15   One taboo stands out as the most fantastic and forbidden. "What's eating you?" a man may ask an annoyed friend. Even though his friend just got fired by a tyrannical boss with a mind as small as a noose, he would never think to

say "*Who's* eating you?" The idea of cannibalism is so far from our ordinary lives that we can safely use the euphemism *eat* in a sexual context, say, and no one will think we mean literally consume. But omnivores can eat anything, even each other,[3] and human flesh is one of the finest sources of protein. Primitive peoples all over the world have indulged in cannibalism, always ritualistically, but sometimes as a key source of protein missing from their diets. For many it's a question of headhunting, displaying the enemy's head with much magic and flourish; and then, so as not to be wasteful, eating the body. In Britain's Iron Age, the Celts consumed large quantities of human flesh. Some American Indian tribes tortured and ate their captives, and the details (reported by Christian missionaries who observed the rites) are hair-raising. During one four-night celebration in 1487, the Aztecs were reported to have sacrificed about eighty thousand prisoners, whose flesh was shared with the gods, but mainly eaten by a huge meat-hungry population. In *The Power of Myth*, the late Joseph Campbell, a wise observer of the beliefs and customs of many cultures, tells of a New Guinea cannibalism ritual that "enacts the planting-society myth of death, resurrection and *cannibalistic* consumption." The tribe enters a sacred field, where they chant and beat drums for four or five days, and break all the rules by engaging in a sexual orgy. In this rite of manhood, young boys are introduced to sex for the first time:

> There is a great shed of enormous logs supported by two uprights. A young woman comes in ornamented as a deity, and she is brought to lie down in this place beneath the great roof. The boys, six or so, with the drums going and chanting going, one after another, have their first experience of intercourse with the girl. And when the last boy is with her in a full embrace, the supports are withdrawn, the logs drop, and the couple is killed. There is the union of male and female . . . as they were in the beginning. . . . There is the union of begetting and death. They are both the same thing.
>
> Then the couple is pulled out and roasted and eaten that very evening. The ritual is the repetition of the original act of the killing of a god followed by the coming of food from the dead savior.

16   When the explorer Dr. Livingstone died in Africa, his organs were apparently eaten by two of his native followers as a way to absorb his strength and courage. Taking communion in the Catholic Church enacts a symbolic eating of the body and blood of Christ. Some forms of cannibalism were more bloodthirsty than others. According to Philippa Pullar, Druid priests "attempted divination by stabbing a man above his midriff, foretelling the future by the convulsions of his limbs and the pouring of his blood. . . . Then . . . they devoured him." Cannibalism doesn't horrify us because we find human life sacred, but because our social taboos happen to forbid it, or, as Harris says: "the real conundrum is why we who

---

[3] In German, humans eat (*essen*), but animals devour or feed (*Fressen*). Cannibals are called *Menschenfresser*—humans who become animals when they eat.

live in a society which is constantly perfecting the art of mass-producing human bodies on the battlefield find humans good to kill but bad to eat."[4]

THE UTIMATE DINNER PARTY

17 Romans adored the voluptuous feel of food: the sting of pepper, the pleasure-pain of sweet-and-sour dishes, the smoldery sexiness of curries, the piquancy of delicate and rare animals, whose exotic lives they could contemplate as they devoured them, sauces that reminded them of the smells and tastes of love-making. It was a time of fabulous, fattening wealth and dangerous, killing poverty. The poor served the wealthy, and could be beaten for a careless word, destroyed for amusement. Among the wealthy, boredom visited like an impossible in-law, whom they devoted most of their lives to entertaining. Orgies and dinner parties were the main diversions, and the Romans amused themselves with the lavishness of a people completely untainted by annoying notions of guilt. In their culture, pleasure glistened as a good in itself, a positive achievement, nothing to repent. Epicurus spoke for a whole society when he asked:

> Is man then meant to spurn the gifts of Nature? Has he been born but to pluck the bitterest fruits? For whom do those flowers grow, that the gods make flourish at mere mortals' feet? . . . It is a way of pleasing Providence to give ourselves up to the various delights which she suggests to us; our very needs spring from her laws, and our desires from her inspirations.

18 Fighting the enemy, boredom, Romans staged all-night dinner parties and vied with one another in the creation of unusual and ingenious dishes. At one dinner a host served progressively smaller members of the food chain stuffed inside each another: Inside a calf, there was a pig, inside the pig a lamb, inside the lamb a chicken, inside the chicken a rabbit, inside the rabbit a dormouse, and so on. Another host served a variety of dishes that looked different but were all made from the same ingredient. Theme parties were popular, and might include a sort of treasure hunt, where guests who located the peacock brains on flamingo tongues received a prize. Mechanical devices might lower acrobats from the ceiling along with the next course, or send in a plate of lamprey milt on an eel-shaped trolley. Slaves brought garlands of flowers to drape over the diners, and rubbed their bodies with perfumed unguents to relax them. The floor might be knee-deep in rose petals. Course after course would appear, some with peppery sauces to spark the taste buds, others in velvety sauces to soothe them. Slaves blew exotic scents through pipes into the room, and sprinkled the diners

---

[4] For an excellent discussion of cannibalism, and the nutritional fiats that have prompted it in a variety of cultures (Aztecs, Fijians, New Guineans, American Indians, and many others), including truly horrible and graphic accounts by eyewitnesses, see Harris's chapter on "People Eating." Marvin Harris, *The Sacred Cow and the Abominable Pig: Riddles of Food and Culture* (New York: Simon and Schuster/Touchstone Books, 1987).

with heavy, musky animal perfumes like civet and ambergris. Sometimes the food itself squirted saffron or rose water or some other delicacy into the diner's face, or birds flew out of it, or it turned out to be inedible (because it was pure gold). The Romans were devotees of what the German call *Schadenfreude*, taking exquisite pleasure in the misfortune of someone else. They loved to surround themselves with midgets, and handicapped and deformed people, who were made to perform sexually or caberet-style at the parties. Caligula used to have gladiators get right up to the dinner table to fight, splashing the diners with blood and gore. Not all Romans were sadists, but numbers of the wealthy class and many of the emperors were, and they could own, torture, maltreat, or murder their slaves as much as they wished. At least one high-society Roman is recorded to have fattened his eels on the flesh of his slaves. Small wonder Christianity arose as a slave-class movement, emphasizing self-denial, restraint, the poor inheriting the earth, a rich and free life after death, and the ultmate punishment of the luxury-loving rich in the eternal tortures of hell. As Philippa Pullar observes in *Consuming Passions*, it was from this "class-conciousness and a pride in poverty and simplicity the hatred of the body was born. . . . All agreeable sensations were damned, all harmonies of taste and smell, sound, sight and feel, the candidate for heaven must resist them all. Pleasure was synonymous with guilt, it was synonymous with Hell. . . . 'Let your companions be women pale and thin with fasting,' instructed Jerome." Or, as Gibbon put it, "every sensation that is offensive to man was thought acceptable to God." So the denial of the senses became part of a Christian creed of salvation. The Shakers would later create their stark wooden benches, chairs, and simple boxes in such a mood, but what would they make now of the voluptuousness with which people enjoy Shaker pieces, not as a simple necessity but extravagantly, as art, as an expensive excess bought for the foyer or country house? The word "vicarious" hinges on "vicar," God's consul in the outlands, who lived like an island in life's racy current, delicate, exempt, and unflappable, while babies grew out of wedlock and bulls died, crops shriveled up like pokers or were flooded, and local duennas held musicales for vicar, matrons, and spicy young women (riper than the saintliest mettle could bear). No wonder they lived vicariously, giving pause, giving aid, and, sometimes, giving in to the embolisms, dietary manias, and sin. Puritanism denounced spices as too sexually arousing; then the Quakers entered the scene, making all luxury taboo, and soon enough there were revolts against these revolts. Food has always been associated with cycles of sexuality, moral abandon, moral restraint, and a return to sexuality once again—but no one did so with as much flagrant gusto as the ancient Romans.

19   Quite possibly the Roman empire fell because of lead poisoning, which can cause miscarriages, infertility, a host of illnesses, and insanity. Lead suffused the Romans' lives—not only did their water pipes, cooking pots, and jars contain it, but also their cosmetics. But before it did poison them, they staged some of the wildest and most extravagant dinner parties ever known, where people dined lying down, two, three, or more to a couch. While saucy Roman poets like Catullus wrote rigorously sexy poems about affairs with either sex, Ovid wrote charming ones

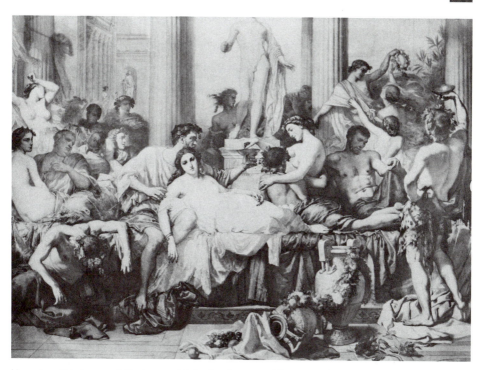

How does this image of the banquet hall of a Roman nobleman perfectly capture the Roman feasts that Ackerman describes?

about his robust love of women, how they tormented his soul, and about the roller coaster of flirtation he observed at dinner parties. "Offered a sexless heaven," he wrote, "I'd say *no thank you*, women are such sweet hell." In one of his poems, he cautions his mistress that, since they've both been invited to the same dinner, he's bound to see her there with her husband. *Don't let him kiss you on the neck*, Ovid tells her, *it will drive me crazy.*

■ ■ ▨

MEANING

1. According to Ackerman, why does food play such an influential role in establishing and confirming group ties? For example, how do rituals involving corn illustrate the way in which food and religious values are interconnected for the Hopi Indians?

2. For primitive peoples, how was food connected with sex, and what vestiges of this connection remain today?

3. How do the dishes served at the omnivores' picnic illustrate the amazing variety of foods that are eaten in different cultures?

4. What inferences about the values of Roman society does Ackerman draw from their elaborate and decadent banquets?

TECHNIQUE

1. How does Ackerman use **description** to depict the range of foods and different circumstances in which they are consumed?

2. Where does Ackerman use **exemplification** to illustrate her thesis that food preferences are culturally conditioned?

3. Evaluate Ackerman's use of **causal analysis** to explore the relationship between "the denial of the senses [that] became part of the Christian creed of salvation" and the lavish indulgences of the Romans.

4. How does Ackerman use **definition** to trace the etymology of food-related terms?

LANGUAGE

1. How effectively does Ackerman use quotations and citations from different fields of study (history, physiology, comparative religions) to illustrate her thesis?

2. In your opinion, does Ackerman sensationalize her subject? If so, does this add to or detract from her essay?

3. If you don't know the meaning of the following words, look them up. *stratagems* (1), *homage* (1), *wayfarers* (1), *importunity* (1), *Seder* (1), *kachina* (2), *ocher* (2), *torpor* (4), *rapacious* (6), *tumescent* (7), *aphrodisiac* (7), *callipygous* (7), *tawny* (8), *cornucopia* (11), *niche* (11), *omnivorous* (11), *nasturtiums* (11), *effluvia* (11), *sacrosanct* (14), *Jainism* (14), *smoldery* (17), *piquancy* (17), *unguents* (18), *duennas* (18).

SUGGESTIONS FOR WRITING

1. **Critical Writing.** Write a short essay about some food-related development that encompasses a social history, such as the emergence of gourmet coffee bars, truth-in-labeling laws, or genetically modified foods.

2. How might early Christian attitudes toward food have been a reaction to the sensuality and indulgences of the Roman civilization Ackerman discusses?

3. Discuss the impact, if any, of exposés such as Eric Schlosser's 2001 book *Fast Food Nation* and the 2005 film *Supersize Me* on Americans' eating habits.

4. Using **multiple patterns**, recreate an event in which food plays an important role, such as a wedding.

5. **Thematic Links.** How does Ethel G. Hofman's "An Island Passover" (Chapter 7, "Process Analysis") support Ackerman's contention that food plays an important part in cultural identity?

LUCY GREALY

Autobiography of a Face

How often do you check your appearance in a mirror? Imagine how you would feel if what you saw caused other people to react with fear or horror. For most of her life, this was the experience of Lucy Grealy (1963–2002). A section of her jaw was removed because of cancer when she was only nine. In the following selection from her 1994 autobiography, Grealy describes the harrowing years of reconstructive surgery and her struggle to move beyond internalizing the intolerance and rejection to which she was subjected. On her way, she discovered the pleasures of reading and found solace in riding horses. Tragically, she died from an accidental drug overdose in 2002 at the age of 39. Grealy also wrote a collection of essays, *As Seen on TV: Provocations* (2000).

BEFORE YOU READ

How do you react to people who are disfigured?

■ ■ ▨

1   It was only when I got home from the hospital that I permitted myself to look more closely at my new face. It was still extremely swollen (it would be months before it went down), and a long thin scar ran the length of it. In the middle of the scar was the island of pale skin from my hip. Placing my hand over the swollen and discolored parts, I tried to imagine how my face might look once it was "better." If I positioned the angle of my face, the angle of my hand, and the angle of the mirror all just right, it looked okay.

Description: begins her essay with how she looks

2   Actually, in my mind, my face looked even better than okay, it looked beautiful. But it was a beauty that existed in the future, a possible future. As it was, I hated my face. I turned my thoughts inward again, and this strange fantasy of beauty became something very private, a wish I would have been ashamed to let anyone in on. Primarily it was a fantasy of relief. When I tried to imagine being beautiful, I could only imagine living without the perpetual fear of being alone, without the great burden of isolation, which is what feeling ugly felt like.

3   The beginning of high school was a couple of months away. Each day I checked my face in private, wondering what I would look like by my first day at a new school. I expected to have a second "revising" operation before school started, but as it turned out I would have to wait at least another three months, a span of time that seemed useless and insurmountable. What

was the point, if I still had to walk into school that first day looking like this?

4   There was only one solution, and that was to stop caring. I became pretentious. I picked out thick books by Russian authors and carried them around with me. Sometimes I even read them. *Anna Karenina, The Brothers Karamazov, Dead Souls.* I read *Jude the Obscure* simply because I liked the title, and anything else that sounded difficult and deep. Often I missed the subtle nuances of these books, but they presented a version of the world in which honor and virtue and dedication to the truth counted. The stories comforted me, though it didn't escape my attention that these qualities were ascribed primarily to men. The women might be virtuous as well, but their physical beauty was crucial to the story.

Cause and effect: explains how she compensated for her appearance

5   On the first day of school I rode the bus, entered my strange homeroom, and went through my day of classes as invisibly as possible. By now my hair was long, past my shoulders, and I walked around with my head bent, my dark blond hair covering half my face. Having decided against seeking anything as inconsequential as social status, I spent the days observing my peers with a perfectly calibrated air of disinterest. I remained the outsider, like so many of the characters I had read about, and in this role I found great comfort. Doubtless I was more keenly aware of the subtleties of the various dramas and social dances of my classmates than they were themselves.

6   For the most part I was left alone. People were a bit more mature, and it was rare that anyone openly made fun of me. But I was still braced for the teasing. Every time I saw someone looking at me, I expected the worst. Usually they just looked the other way and didn't register much interest one way or the other. Then, just as I would start to relax, to let my guard down, some loudmouthed boy would feel a need to point out to his friends how ugly I was.

7   One day when I went to my English class, I found a copy of Hesse's *Siddhartha*, his version of the story of Buddha, lying on my chair. My notions of Buddhism were sketchy at best, but the opening pages immediately reminded me of the messages of grace, dignity, and light that I'd first encountered in those Christian publications, which had long since ceased arriving in the mail. I'd almost forgotten about my quest for enlightenment, imagining my momentous meeting with the great guru. Now, after so much time and so much loss, I took it as a sign that someone had left this book on my chair. Desire and all its painful complications, I decided, was something I should and would be free of.

8 Two months after school started, the long-awaited revision operation was scheduled. I started focusing on the upcoming date, believing that my life would finally get started once I had the face I was "supposed" to have. Logically I knew that this was only one of many operations, but surely it would show promise, offer a hint of how it was all going to turn out.

Narration: continues her story and identifies important turning points

9 When I woke up in recovery the day after the operation, I looked up to see a nurse wearing glasses leaning over me. Cautiously I looked for my reflection in her glasses. There I was, my hair messed and my face pale and, as far as I could tell, looking exactly the same as before. I reached up and felt the suture line. A few hours later, when I was recovered enough to walk unaided to the bathroom, I took each careful step toward the door and geared myself up to look in the mirror. Apart from looking like I'd just gotten over a bad case of flu, I looked just the same. The patch of paler skin was gone, but the overall appearance of my face was no different from before.

10 I blamed myself for the despair I felt creeping in; again it was a result of having expectations. I must guard against having any more. After all, I still had it pretty good by global standards. "I have food," I told myself. "I have a place to sleep." So what if my face was ugly, so what if other people judged me for this. That was their problem, not mine. This line of reasoning offered less consolation than it had in the past, but it distanced me from what was hurting most, and I took this as a sign that I was getting better at detaching myself from my desires.

11 When I returned to school I had resolved that my face was actually an asset. It was true I hated it and saw it as the cause of my isolation, but I interpreted it as some kind of lesson. I had taught myself about reincarnation, how the soul picks its various lives with the intent of learning more and more about itself so that it may eventually break free of the cycle of karma. Why had my soul chosen this particular life, I asked myself; what was there to learn from a face as ugly as mine? At the age of sixteen I decided it was all about desire and love.

12 Over the years my perspective on "what it was all about" has shifted, but the most important point then was that there *was* a reason for this happening to me. No longer feeling that I was being punished, as I had during the chemo, I undertook to see my face as an opportunity to find something that had not yet been revealed. Perhaps my face was a gift to be used toward understanding and enlightenment. This was all noble enough, but by equating my face with ugliness, in

believing that without it I would never experience the deep, bottomless grief I called ugliness, I separated myself even further from other people who I thought never experienced grief of this depth. Not that I did not allow others their own suffering. I tried my best to be empathic because I believed it was a "good" emotion. But in actuality I was judge and hangman, disgusted by peers who avoided their fears by putting their energy into things as insubstantial as fashion and boyfriends and gossip.

13   I tried my best, but for the most part I was as abysmal at seeking enlightenment as I had once been at playing dodge ball. No matter how desperately I wanted to catch that ball, I dropped it anyway. And as much as I wanted to love everybody in school and to waft esoterically into the ether when someone called me ugly, I was plagued with petty desires and secret, evil hates.

14   I hated Danny in my orchestra class because I had a crush on him and knew that he would never have a crush on me. Anger scared me most of all, and I repressed every stirring. Every time I felt hatred, or any other "bad" thought, I shooed it away with a broom of spiritual truisms. But the more I tried to negate my feelings, the more they crowded in. I not only harbored hatred for Danny even while I had a crush on him, I also hated Katherine, the girl in orchestra *he* had a crush on. Trying to repress that feeling, I found myself hating Katherine's cello, of all things, which she played exquisitely well. The cycle eventually ended with me: I hated myself for having even entertained the absurd notion that someone like Danny could like me.

> Description: conveys feelings about a boy on whom she has a crush

15   I didn't begrudge Danny his crush on Katherine. She was pretty and talented, so why shouldn't he want her? I was never going to have anyone want me in that way, so I mustn't desire such a thing; in this way I could be grateful to my face for "helping" me to see the error of earthly desire. This complicated gratitude usually lasted for about five minutes before giving way to depression, plain and simple.

16 When my father's insurance money came, and before we learned of the accumulated tax debt we owed, my mother generously kept her promise and bought me another horse. Her registered name was even more silly than Sure Swinger, so I simply called her Mare. I kept her at Snowcap, a more professional and better-kept stable than Diamond D. There I undertook learning to ride seriously. I fell in love with Mare just as I had with Swinger, and again I had bad luck. Not long

> Narration: continues her story with an incident about her horse, Mare

after I got her, she broke her leg while turned out in a field. As she limped pathetically onto the trailer to be taken away, they told me they could sell her as a brood mare, but I knew she was too old for this and would be put down shortly. Again my heart was broken, but this time I saw it in much more self-pitying terms. I told myself that anything I loved was doomed, and even as I was aware of my own overblown melodrama, just as I had been that night I nearly collapsed on the hospital floor, I took a strange comfort in this romantic, tragic role.

17   Luckily, the owners of Snowcap permitted me to continue on at the barn as their exercise rider. This was ideal. Not only did I get to ride horses for free, sometimes as many as six a day, and gain a great deal of experience in the process, but it also gave my life a center. I withstood school all day, knowing I would go straight to the barn afterward and stay there until eight or nine o'clock at night. The barn became the one place where I felt like myself, and I relished the physicality of riding, performing acts I was good at, feeling a sense of accomplishment. I spent as little time at home as possible.

18   During the tenth grade I had one more operation to work on shaping the free flap, and the results seemed as trivial and ineffectual to me as the last time. The following summer I spent every day with the horses. One day when it was too hot to get very much accomplished, I went along for the ride on an errand with some people from the stable. We got caught in traffic on the main road, and as we crept along at a snail's pace, I looked out the window and got lost in my own world. A bakery storefront, its door set at a very odd angle, caught my attention, reminding me of something I couldn't quite put my finger on. Then I remembered that I had been to this town some ten or twelve years earlier with my father. He loved to go out for a drive on a Sunday and explore the area, and Sarah and I loved to accompany him. We'd stand up in the back seat and sing songs with him, songs from his own distant childhood, so familiar and lovely to him that we could both hear that strange, sad love in his voice as we sang. Unexpectedly, and consciously for the first time since his death, I missed my father.

19   The one time I had visited him in the hospital, I had to wait outside in the hallways briefly. The smells and sounds were so familiar—the sweet disinfectant and wax, always an aroma of overcooked food in the background, the metallic clinks of IV poles as they were pushed along the floor on their stands. Yet I was only visiting, passing through. I had felt alone and without purpose, unidentified, not sure how to act. Now, more than a year after his death, I again didn't

Description: sensory details evoke a visit to her father

know how to act. I didn't want to ignore the grief or even get over it, because that would mean I hadn't loved my father. When my horse died, I had cried almost continuously for days. The loss was pure and uncomplicated. Loving my father had been a different matter. I finally and suddenly found myself consumed with a longing for his presence.

20   I started imagining my father standing next to me in the hospital, visiting me. With all my might I strained to hear the background noises of the hospital, feel the starch of the sheets, and hear my father's footsteps approaching, hear the rustle of his clothes as he stood near me, his cough to see if I was awake. I'd imagine opening my eyes very slowly, very carefully, and try to see him, standing beside my hospital bed. All I could conjure was the vaguest of outlines, a passing detail that only seemed to obscure the rest of him: how his watch fitted on his wrist, how he would trace the edge of his ear with one finger.

21 Spending as much time as I did looking in the mirror, I thought I knew what I looked like. So it came as a shock one afternoon toward the end of that summer when I went shopping with my mother for a new shirt and saw my face in the harsh fluorescent light of the fitting room. Pulling the new shirt on over my head, I caught a glimpse of my reflection that was itself being reflected in a mirror opposite, reversing my face as I usually saw it. I stood there motionless, the shirt only halfway on, my skin extra pale from the lighting, and saw how asymmetrical my face was. How had that happened? Walking up to the mirror, reaching up to touch the right side, where the graft had been put in only a year before, I saw clearly that most of it had disappeared, melted away into nothing. I felt distraught at the sight and even more distraught that it had taken so long to notice. My eyes had been secretly working against me, making up for the asymmetry as it gradually reappeared. This reversed image of myself was the true image, the way other people saw me.

22   I felt like such a fool. I'd been walking around with a secret notion of promised beauty, and here was the reality. When I saw Dr. Baker a few weeks later, I wanted desperately to ask him what had gone wrong, but I found myself speechless. Besides, I knew that the graft had been reabsorbed by my body—the doctor had warned me it might happen. He spoke of waiting a few years before trying any more big operations, of letting me grow some more. We spoke about a series of minor operations that would make readjustments to what was

Comparison and contrast: her real versus imagined appearance

already there, but there was only vague talk of any new grafts, of putting more soft tissue or bone in place. Sitting in his expensively decorated office, I felt utterly powerless. Realizing I was going to have to change my ideals and expectations was one thing, but knowing what to replace them with was another.

23   That unexpected revelation in the store's fitting room mirror marked a turning point in my life. I began having overwhelming attacks of shame at unpredictable intervals. The first one came as I was speaking to Hans, my boss at the stable. He was describing how he wanted me to ride a certain horse. I was looking him in the eye as he spoke, and he was looking me in the eye. Out of nowhere came an intense feeling that he shouldn't be looking at me, that I was too horrible to look at, that I wasn't worthy of being looked at, that my ugliness was equal to a great personal failure. Inside I was churning and shrinking, desperate for a way to get out of this. I took the only course of action I knew I was any good at: I acted as if nothing were wrong. Steadying myself, breathing deeply, I kept looking him in the eye, determined that he should know nothing of what I was thinking.

24   That summer I started riding horses for Hans in local schooling shows. In practice I always wore a helmet with my hair hanging loose beneath it, but etiquette required that during shows my hair be tucked neatly up beneath the helmet, out of sight. I put this off until the very last minute, trying to act casual as I reached for the rubber band and hair net. This simple act of lifting my hair and exposing my face was among the hardest things I ever had to do, as hard as facing Dr. Woolf, harder than facing operations. I gladly would have undergone any amount of physical pain to keep my hair down. No one at the show grounds ever commented to me about it, and certainly no one there was going to make fun of me, but I was beyond that point. By then I was perfectly capable of doing it all to myself.

25   The habits of self-consciousness, of always looking down and hiding my face behind my hair or my hand, were so automatic by now that I was blind to them. When my mother pointed out these habits to me in the hope of making me stop, telling me they directed even more attention to my face, she might as well have been telling me to change the color of my eyes.

26   I fantasized about breakthroughs in reconstructive surgery, about winning the lottery and buying my own private island, about being abducted by space aliens who'd fix me up and plop me back in the midst of a surprised public. And

there were still acts of heroism waiting to be thrust upon me, whole busloads of babies to be saved and at least one, there had to be at least one out there, wise older man who would read about my heroism in the papers, fall in love with my inner beauty, and whisk me away from the annoyance of existence as defined by Spring Valley High School.

27   During the eleventh and twelfth grades I had several small operations. The hospital was the only place on earth where I didn't feel self-conscious. My face was my battle scar, my badge of honor. The people in the plastic surgery ward hated their gorgeously hooked noses, their wise lines, their exquisitely thin lips. Beauty, as defined by society at large, seemed to be only about who was best at looking like everyone else. If *I* had my original face, an undamaged face, *I* would know how to appreciate it, know how to see the beauty of it. Yet each time I was wheeled down to the surgical wing, high on the drugs, I'd think to myself, *Now, now I can start my life, just as soon as I wake up from this operation.* And no matter how disappointed I felt when I woke up and looked in the mirror, I'd simply postpone happiness until the next operation. I knew there would always he another operation, another chance for my life to finally begin.

Cause and effect: charts changes in her ability to cope

28   In the wake of my recurring disappointment I'd often chide myself for thinking I'd ever be beautiful enough, good enough, or worthy enough of someone else's love, let alone my own. Who cared if I loved my own face if no one else was going to? What was beauty for, after all, if not to attract the attention of men, of lovers? When I walked down a street or hallway, sometimes men would whistle at me from a distance, call me *Baby*, yell out and ask me my name. I was thin, I had a good figure, and my long blond hair, when I bothered to brush it, was pretty. I would walk as fast as possible, my head bent down, but sometimes they'd catch up with me, or I'd be forced to pass by them. Their comments would stop instantly when they saw my face, their sudden silence potent and damning.

29   Life in general was cruel and offered only different types of voids and chaos. The only way to tolerate it, to have any hope of escaping it, I reasoned, was to know my own strength, to defy life by surviving it. Sitting in math class, I'd look around and try to gauge who among my classmates could have lived through this trauma, certain that none of them could. I had already read a great deal about the Holocaust, but now we were reading first-person accounts by Elie Wiesel and Primo Levi in social studies. I was completely transported by their work, and the more I absorbed of their message, the

more my everyday life took on a surreal quality. Now everything, *everything*, seemed important. The taste of salt and
peanut butter and tomatoes, the smell of car fumes, the small
ridge of snow on the inside sill of a barely open window.
I thought that this was how to live in the present moment, to
resee the world: continuously imagine a far worse reality. At
these moments, the life I was leading seemed unimportant,
uncomplicated. Sometimes I could truly find refuge in the
world of my private senses, but just as often I disingenuously
affected a posture of repose, using it as a weapon against people I envied and feared, as a way of feeling superior to and
thus safe from them.

30   After the section on the Holocaust, my social studies class
moved on to art history. One day I walked into class late and
found the lights off. My teacher was just about to show slides.
Giacometti's sculptures flashed on the wall, their elongated
arms simultaneously pointing toward and away from the
world, while their long legs held them tall and gracefully but
tenuously. Next were de Chirico's paintings, with the shadows from unseen others falling directly across the paths of
the visible. I had seen Munch's "The Scream" and had identified it with my own occasional desire to let out a howl, but
it was only at that moment, sitting in that darkened classroom, that I understood the figure might not be screaming
himself but shielding his ears from and dropping his mouth
open in shock at the sound of someone, or something else's
loud, loud lament. Matisse's paintings seemed to be about
how simple it was to see the world in a beautiful way. Picasso's
were about how complex, how difficult, beauty was.

> Description: con-
> cludes her essay
> with what she
> learned from art
> and literature

31   The poems we read in English class had similar effects on
me. My taste was not always sophisticated, but I did read poetry
by Keats, Emily Dickinson, and Wallace Stevens, which moved
me in ways I couldn't understand. It was, in part, the very lack
of understanding that was so moving. I would read Keats's
"Ode to a Nightingale" and feel that something important and
necessary was being said here, but the moment I tried to examine the words, dissect the sentences, the meaning receded.

32   Senior year I applied to and was accepted at Sarah
Lawrence College with a generous scholarship. Not sure what
to do with my life, I decided to work toward medical school.
The day senior class yearbook photos were taken, I purposefully cut school, and I threw away all the subsequent
notices warning that unless I attended the makeup shoot, my
photo would not appear in the yearbook.

■ ■ ▨

MEANING

1. What predicament did Grealy confront after undergoing multiple reconstructive surgeries of her face following cancer?

2. How did she react to the operations in terms of how she felt about herself and the way others reacted to her?

3. How did reading provide a refuge for her? How did riding horses help her in her struggle with being ostracized?

4. What does the title "Autobiography of a Face" mean to you as a reader? What do you think it meant to the author?

TECHNIQUE

1. How does Grealy use **narration** to identify important stages and key turning points in her journey to self-acceptance?

2. Where does Grealy use **description** to provide a graphic view of her appearance?

3. Where does Grealy use **comparison and contrast** to juxtapose what she imagined she looked like with the reality she was forced to confront?

4. How does Grealy analyze key moments in her transformation as a series of **causes and effects** that enabled her to move beyond feeling shame at her appearance? What role did art and literature play in this process?

LANGUAGE

1. Where is Grealy unusually honest in revealing the negative emotions of self-pity and anger she felt?

2. In what way is Grealy's style and her decision to write about her experiences a way of gaining perspective on a traumatic experience?

3. If you don't know the meanings of the following words, look them up: *ascribed* (4), *calibrated* (5), *guru* (7), *suture* (9), *karma* (11), *abysmal* (13), *esoterically* (13), *ether* (13), *truisms* (14), *conjure* (20), *distraught* (21), *surreal* (29), *disingenuously* (29), *tenuously* (30), *dissect* (31).

SUGGESTIONS FOR WRITING

1. **Critical Writing.** Compare Grealy's attempt through surgery to appear "normal"—or at least unnoticeable—with the common uses of cosmetic surgery.

2. Even without events as traumatic as those Grealy experienced, high school can be extremely difficult. Describe your own high-school experiences and how you survived.

3. Grealy finds solace in literature, art, and riding horses. Use **multiple patterns** to explore the comparable comforts you have found when faced with a stressful event.

4. **Thematic Links.** How does Paul Barber's analysis in "The Real Vampire" (Chapter 9, "Cause and Effect") and Grealy's account give you insight into the connection between an unnatural appearance and ostracism of the "other"?

The Turbid Ebb and Flow of Misery

Margaret Sanger (1883–1966) was born in a rural community in upstate New York but worked as a public health nurse in New York City, where she witnessed the horrendous circumstances that were caused, in part, by ignorance in sexual matters of poor families in New York's tenement districts. She dedicated her life to giving poor women a choice by distributing information about birth control, and in 1916, she opened the first family-planning clinic in the United States, in Brooklyn. She was repeatedly harrassed and even arrested. Through her efforts, laws were passed legalizing the dissemination of safe birth control methods throughout the country. The following selection is drawn from Chapter 7 of *Margaret Sanger: An Autobiography* (1938). Sanger took her chapter title from a line in Matthew Arnold's poem "Dover Beach."

BEFORE YOU READ

How has legalizing birth control changed modern culture?

■ ■ ▨

> *Every night and every morn*
> *Some to misery are born.*
> *Every morn and every night*
> *Some are born to sweet delight.*
> *Some are born to sweet delight,*
> *Some are born to endless night.*
> *—William Blake*

1 During these years [about 1912] in New York trained nurses were in great demand. Few people wanted to enter hospitals; they were afraid they might be "practiced" upon, and consented to go only in desperate emergencies. Sentiment was especially vehement in the matter of having babies. A woman's own bedroom, no matter how inconveniently arranged, was the usual place for her lying-in. I was not sufficiently free from domestic duties to be a general nurse, but I could ordinarily manage obstetrical cases because I was notified far enough ahead to plan my schedule. And after serving my two weeks I could get home again.

2 Sometimes I was summoned to small apartments occupied by young clerks, insurance salesmen, or lawyers, just starting out, most of them under thirty and whose wives were having their first or second baby. They were always eager to know the best and latest method in infant care and feeding. In particular, Jewish patients, whose lives centered around the family, welcomed advice and followed it implicitly.

3   But more and more my calls began to come from the Lower East Side, as though I were being magnetically drawn there by some force outside my control. I hated the wretchedness and hopelessness of the poor, and never experienced that satisfaction in working among them that so many noble women have found. My concern for my patients was now quite different from my earlier hospital attitude. I could see that much was wrong with them which did not appear in the physiological or medical diagnosis. A woman in childbirth was not merely a woman in childbirth. My expanded outlook included a view of her background, her potentialities as a human being, the kind of children she was bearing, and what was going to happen to them.

4   The wives of small shopkeepers were my most frequent cases, but I had carpenters, truck drivers, dishwashers, and pushcart vendors. I admired intensely the consideration most of these people had for their own. Money to pay doctor and nurse had been carefully saved months in advance—parents-in-law, grandfathers, grandmothers, all contributing.

5   As soon as the neighbors learned that a nurse was in the building they came in a friendly way to visit, often carrying fruit, jellies, or gefüllter fish made after a cherished recipe. It was infinitely pathetic to me that they, so poor themselves, should bring me food. Later they drifted in again with the excuse of getting the plate, and sat down for a nice talk; there was no hurry. Always back of the little gift was the question, "I am pregnant (or my daughter, or my sister is). Tell me something to keep from having another baby. We cannot afford another yet."

6   I tried to explain the only two methods I had ever heard of among the middle classes, both of which were invariably brushed aside as unacceptable. They were of no certain avail to the wife because they placed the burden of responsibility solely upon the husband—a burden which he seldom assumed. What she was seeking was self-protection she could herself use, and there was none.

7   Below this stratum of society was one in truly desperate circumstances. The men were sullen and unskilled, picking up odd jobs now and then, but more often unemployed, lounging in and out of the house at all hours of the day and night. The women seemed to slink on their way to market and were without neighborliness.

8   These submerged, untouched classes were beyond the scope of organized charity or religion. No labor union, no church, not even the Salvation Army reached them. They were apprehensive of everyone and rejected help of any kind, ordering all intruders to keep out; both birth and death they considered their own business. Social agents, who were just beginning to appear, were profoundly mistrusted because they pried into homes and lives, asking questions about wages, how many were in the family, had any of them ever been in jail. Often two or three had been there or were now under suspicion of prostitution, shoplifting, purse snatching, petty thievery, and, in consequence, passed furtively by the big blue uniforms on the corner.

9   The utmost depression came over me as I approached this surreptitious region. Below Fourteenth Street I seemed to be breathing a different air, to be in another world and country where the people had habits and customs alien to anything I had ever heard about.

10   There were then approximately ten thousand apartments in New York into which no sun ray penetrated directly; such windows as they had opened only on a narrow court from which rose fetid odors. It was seldom cleaned, though garbage and refuse often went down into it. All these dwellings were pervaded by the foul breath of poverty, that moldy, indefinable, indescribable smell which cannot be fumigated out, sickening to me but apparently unnoticed by those who lived there. When I set to work with antiseptics, their pungent sting, at least temporarily, obscured the stench.

11   I remember one confinement case to which I was called by the doctor of an insurance company. I climbed up the five flights and entered the airless rooms, but the baby had come with too great speed. A boy of ten had been the only assistant. Five flights was a long way; he had wrapped the placenta in a piece of newspaper and dropped it out the window into the court.

12   Many families took in "boarders," as they were termed, whose small contributions paid the rent. These derelicts, wanderers, alternately working and drinking, were crowded in with the children; a single room sometimes held as many as six sleepers. Little girls were accustomed to dressing and undressing in front of the men, and were often violated, occasionally by their own fathers or brothers, before they reached the age of puberty.

13   Pregnancy was a chronic condition among the women of this class. Suggestions as to what to do for a girl who was "in trouble" or a married woman who was "caught" passed from mouth to mouth—herb teas, turpentine, steaming, rolling downstairs, inserting slippery elm, knitting needles, shoe-hooks. When they had word of a new remedy they hurried to the drugstore, and if the clerk were inclined to be friendly he might say, "Oh, that won't help you, but here's something that may." The younger druggists usually refused to give advice because, if it were to be known, they would come under the law; midwives were even more fearful. The doomed women implored me to reveal the "secret" rich people had, offering to pay me extra to tell them; many really believed I was holding back information for money. They asked everybody and tried anything, but nothing did them any good. On Saturday nights I have seen groups of from fifty to one hundred with their shawls over their heads waiting outside the office of a five-dollar abortionist.

14   Each time I returned to this district, which was becoming a recurrent nightmare, I used to hear that Mrs. Cohen "had been carried to a hospital, but had never come back," or that Mrs. Kelly "had sent the children to a neighbor and had put her head into the gas oven." Day after day such tales were poured into my ears—a baby born dead, great relief—the death of an older child, sorrow but again relief of a sort—the story told a thousand times of death from abortion and children going into institutions. I shuddered with horror as I listened to the details and studied the reasons back of them—destitution linked with excessive childbearing. The waste of life seemed utterly senseless. One by one worried, sad, pensive, and aging faces marshaled themselves before me in my dreams, sometimes appealingly, sometimes accusingly.

15   These were not merely "unfortunate conditions among the poor" such as we read about. I knew the women personally. They were living, breathing, human

beings, with hopes, fears, and aspirations like my own, yet their weary, misshapen bodies, "always ailing, never failing," were destined to be thrown on the scrap heap before they were thirty-five. I could not escape from the facts of their wretchedness; neither was I able to see any way out. My own cozy and comfortable family existence was becoming a reproach to me.

16   Then one stifling mid-July day of 1912 I was summoned to a Grand Street tenement. My patient was a small, slight Russian Jewess, about twenty-eight years old, of the special cast of feature to which suffering lends a madonna-like expression. The cramped three-room apartment was in a sorry state of turmoil. Jake Sachs, a truck driver scarcely older than his wife, had come home to find the three children crying and her unconscious from the effects of a self-induced abortion. He had called the nearest doctor, who in turn had sent for me. Jake's earnings were trifling, and most of them had gone to keep the none-too-strong children clean and properly fed. But his wife's ingenuity had helped them to save a little, and this he was glad to spend on a nurse rather than have her go to a hospital.

17   The doctor and I settled ourselves to the task of fighting the septicemia. Never had I worked so fast, never so concentratedly. The sultry days and nights were melted into a torpid inferno. It did not seem possible there could be such heat, and every bit of food, ice, and drugs had to be carried up three flights of stairs.

18   Jake was more kind and thoughtful than many of the husbands I had encountered. He loved his children, and had always helped his wife wash and dress them. He had brought water up and carried garbage down before he left in the morning, and did as much as he could for me while he anxiously watched her progress.

19   After a fortnight Mrs. Sachs' recovery was in sight. Neighbors, ordinarily fatalistic as to the results of abortion, were genuinely pleased that she had survived. She smiled wanly at all who came to see her and thanked them gently, but she could not respond to their hearty congratulations. She appeared to be more despondent and anxious than she should have been, and spent too much time in meditation.

20   At the end of three weeks, as I was preparing to leave the fragile patient to take up her difficult life once more, she finally voiced her fears, "Another baby will finish me, I suppose?"

21   "It's too early to talk about that," I temporized.

22   But when the doctor came to make his last call, I drew him aside. "Mrs. Sachs is terribly worried about having another baby."

23   "She well may be," replied the doctor, and then he stood before her and said, "Any more such capers, young woman, and there'll be no need to send for me."

24   "I know, doctor," she replied timidly, "but," and she hesitated as though it took all her courage to say it, "what can I do to prevent it?"

25   The doctor was a kindly man, and he had worked hard to save her, but such incidents had become so familiar to him that he had long since lost whatever delicacy he might once have had. He laughed good-naturedly. "You want to have your cake and eat it too, do you? Well, it can't be done."

26   Then picking up his hat and bag to depart he said, "Tell Jake to sleep on the roof."

27   I glanced quickly at Mrs. Sachs. Even through my sudden tears I could see stamped on her face an expression of absolute despair. We simply looked at each other, saying no word until the door had closed behind the doctor. Then she lifted her thin, blue-veined hands and clasped them beseechingly. "He can't understand. He's only a man. But you do, don't you? Please tell me the secret, and I'll never breathe it to a soul. *Please!*"

28   What was I to do? I could not speak the conventionally comforting phrases which would be of no comfort. Instead, I made her as physically easy as I could and promised to come back in a few days to talk with her again. A little later, when she slept, I tiptoed away.

29   Night after night the wistful image of Mrs. Sachs appeared before me. I made all sorts of excuses to myself for not going back. I was busy on other cases; I really did not know what to say to her or how to convince her of my own ignorance; I was helpless to avert such monstrous atrocities. Time rolled by and I did nothing.

30   The telephone rang one evening three months later, and Jake Sachs' agitated voice begged me to come at once; his wife was sick again and from the same cause. For a wild moment I thought of sending someone else, but actually, of course, I hurried into my uniform, caught up my bag, and started out. All the way I longed for a subway wreck, an explosion, anything to keep me from having to enter that home again. But nothing happened, even to delay me. I turned into the dingy doorway and climbed the familiar stairs once more. The children were there, young little things.

31   Mrs. Sachs was in a coma and died within ten minutes. I folded her still hands across her breast, remembering how they had pleaded with me, begging so humbly for the knowledge which was her right. I drew a sheet over her pallid face. Jake was sobbing, running his hands through his hair and pulling it out like an insane person. Over and over again he wailed, "My God! My God! My God!"

32   I left him pacing desperately back and forth, and for hours I myself walked and walked and walked through the hushed streets. When I finally arrived home and let myself quietly in, all the household was sleeping. I looked out my window and down upon the dimly lighted city. Its pains and griefs crowded in upon me, a moving picture rolled before my eyes with photographic clearness: women writhing in travail to bring forth little babies; the babies themselves naked and hungry, wrapped in newspapers to keep them from the cold; six-year-old children with pinched, pale, wrinkled faces, old in concentrated wretchedness, pushed into gray and fetid cellars, crouching on stone floors, their small scrawny hands scuttling through rags, making lamp shades, artificial flowers; white coffins, black coffins, coffins, coffins interminably passing in never-ending succession. The scenes piled one upon another on another. I could bear it no longer.

33   As I stood there the darkness faded. The sun came up and threw its reflection over the house tops. It was the dawn of a new day in my life also. The doubt

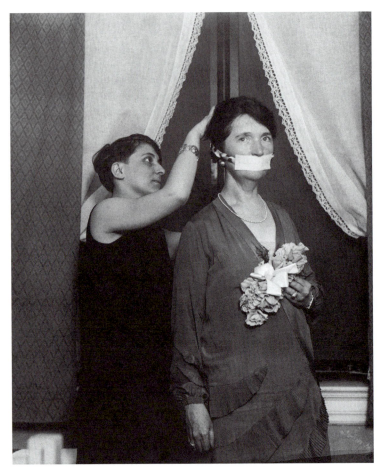

How does this image of Sanger with her mouth covered in protest convey her attitude toward the limitations she had to contend with?

and questioning, the experimenting and trying, were now to be put behind me. I knew I could not go back merely to keeping people alive.

34   I went to bed, knowing that no matter what it might cost, I was finished with palliatives and superficial cures; I was resolved to seek out the root of evil, to do something to change the destiny of mothers whose miseries were vast as the sky.

◼ ◼ ▨

MEANING

1. What kinds of nursing duties brought Sanger into contact with poor families on the Lower East Side of Manhattan in 1912?

2. What seemingly unsolvable problem was dooming these women?

3. Why was the case of Mrs. Sachs a turning point in Sanger's life?

4. How did this turning point result in Sanger's becoming an activist for the dissemination of birth-control information?

TECHNIQUE

1. How does Sanger use **narration** to relate an episode that changed her views on providing information on birth control?

2. Where does she use **exemplification** to provide a case history of one of these women along with examples of others?

3. How does Sanger use **classification** to characterize the conditions of women at different levels in society?

4. How does Sanger use a **problem-solving** format to frame her account of how she became aware of the extent of the problem and the unequal access to information and how she vowed to try to find a solution?

LANGUAGE

1. How does Sanger's use of lines from poems in the title and to preface her essay suggest the level of education and social class of the audience she is trying to reach?

2. Where does Sanger use dialogue to make her patients' crises real to her readers?

3. If you don't know the meaning of the following words, look them up: *vehement* (1), *stratum* (7), *derelicts* (12), *pensive* (14), *septicemia* (17), *torpid* (17), *despondent* (19), *temporized* (21), *beseechingly* (27), *pallid* (31), *palliatives* (34).

SUGGESTIONS FOR WRITING

1. ***Critical Writing.*** If you could be the Margaret Sanger of today, what cause would you champion and what remedies would you propose?

2. Should federally funded family-planning agencies be permitted to suggest abortion as an option for pregnant women? Why or why not?

3. Use **multiple patterns** to explore current social problems that might be remedied by a wider dissemination of correct information.

4. ***Thematic Links.*** In what sense might Sanger be seen as a feminist in the same tradition as Simone de Beauvoir (see "The Married Woman" in Chapter 10, "Definition")?

JONATHAN SWIFT

A Modest Proposal

The noted English satirist Jonathan Swift (1667–1745) was born in Ireland to an impoverished family who were originally from England. He was educated at Trinity College, Dublin, and in 1688, he left for England to become the secretary to Sir William Temple. During this period, Swift wrote *Tale of a Tub* (1704), an ironic history of the Church that revealed his gift for satire. Between 1708 and 1714, Swift lived in London and befriended the literary luminaries of the time: Joseph Addison, Richard Steele, and Alexander Pope, among others. He switched his allegiance from the Whig Party to the Tory Party and wrote pamphlets on its behalf before its collapse. He returned to Dublin in 1713, as Dean of St. Patrick's Cathedral. (He was ordained as an Anglican priest.) In Ireland, Swift used his pen to defend Irish political and economic interests against the English. From 1721 to 1725, he continued to work on his satiric masterpiece, *Gulliver's Travels* (1726). His essay "A Modest Proposal" (1729), which employs an outrageous premise to illustrate England's death grip on the Irish economy, made Swift an Irish national hero.

BEFORE YOU READ

What examples of satire appear in contemporary pop culture?

■ ■ ▨

For Preventing the Children of
Poor People in Ireland from Being a Burden to
Their Parents or Country, and for Making
Them Beneficial to the Public

1   It is a melancholy object to those who walk through this great town,[1] or travel in the country, when they see the streets, the roads, and cabin doors crowded with beggars of the female sex, followed by three, four, or six children, all in rags and importuning every passenger for an alms. These mothers, instead of being able to work for their honest livelihood, are forced to employ all their time in strolling to beg sustenance for their helpless infants; who as they grow up either turn thieves, for want of work, or leave their dear native country to fight for the Pretender[2] in Spain, or sell themselves to the Barbados.[3]

2   I think it is agreed by all parties that this prodigious number of children in the arms, or on the backs, or at the heels of their mothers, and frequently of

---

[1] *this great town*: Dublin.

[2] *the Pretender*: James Stuart (1688–1766), son of King James II, "pretender" or claimant to the throne which his father had lost in the Revolution of 1688. He was Catholic, and Ireland was loyal to him.

[3] *sell . . . Barbados*: Because of extreme poverty, many of the Irish bound or sold themselves to obtain passage to the West Indies or other British possessions in North America. They agreed to work for their new masters, usually planters, for a specified number of years.

their fathers, is, in the present deplorable state of the kingdom, a very great additional grievance; and therefore whoever could find out a fair, cheap, and easy method of making these children sound, useful members of the commonwealth would deserve so well of the public as to have his statue set up for a preserver of the nation.

3   But my intention is very far from being confined to provide only for the children of professed beggars: it is of a much greater extent and shall take in the whole number of infants at a certain age who are born of parents in effect as little able to support them as those who demand our charity in the streets.

4   As to my own part, having turned my thoughts for many years upon this important subject and maturely weighed the several schemes of other projectors, I have always found them grossly mistaken in their computation. It is true, a child just dropped from its dam may be supported by her milk for a solar year, with little other nourishment: at most not above the value of two shillings, which the mother may certainly get, or the value in scraps, by her lawful occupation of begging; and it is exactly at one year old that I propose to provide for them in such a manner, as, instead of being a charge upon their parents or the parish, or wanting food and raiment for the rest of their lives, they shall, on the contrary, contribute to the feeding and partly to the clothing of many thousands.

5   There is likewise another great advantage in my scheme, that it will prevent those voluntary abortions and that horrid practice of women murdering their bastard children, alas! too frequent among us, sacrificing the poor innocent babes, I doubt more to avoid the expense than the shame, which would move tears and pity in the most savage and inhuman breast.

6   The number of souls in this kingdom being usually reckoned one million and a half, of these I calculate there may be about two hundred thousand couple whose wives are breeders; from which number I subtract thirty thousand couple, who are able to maintain their own children (although I apprehend there cannot be so many, under the present distresses of the kingdom), but this being granted, there will remain an hundred and seventy thousand breeders. I again subtract fifty thousand for those women who miscarry, or whose children die by accident or disease within the year. There only remain one hundred and twenty thousand children of poor parents annually born. The question therefore is, How this number shall be reared and provided for? which, as I have already said, under the present situation of affairs, is utterly impossible by all the methods hitherto proposed. For we can neither employ them in handicraft or agriculture; we neither build houses (I mean in the country) nor cultivate land: they can very seldom pick up a livelihood by stealing till they arrive at six years old, except where they are of towardly[4] parts; although I confess they learn the rudiments much earlier; during which time they can, however, be properly looked upon only as probationers; as I have been informed by a principal gentleman in the county of Cavan, who protested

---

[4] *towardly*: dutiful; easily managed.

to me that he never knew above one or two instances under the age of six, even in a part of the kingdom so renowned for the quickest proficiency in that art.

7   I am assured by our merchants that a boy or a girl before twelve years old is no salable commodity and even when they come to this age they will not yield above three pounds, or three pounds and half a crown at most, on the exchange; which cannot turn to account either to the parents or kingdom, the charge of nutriment and rags having been at least four times that value.

8   I shall now therefore humbly propose my own thoughts, which I hope will not be liable to the least objection.

9   I have been assured by a very knowing American of my acquaintance in London that a young healthy child well nursed is at a year old a most delicious, nourishing, and wholesome food, whether stewed, roasted, baked, or boiled; and I make no doubt that it will equally serve in a fricassee or a ragout.[5]

10   I do therefore humbly offer it to public consideration that of the hundred and twenty thousand children already computed, twenty thousand may be reserved for breed, whereof only one-fourth part to be males; which is more than we allow to sheep, black cattle, or swine; and my reason is that these children are seldom the fruits of marriage, a circumstance not much regarded by our savages; therefore one male will be sufficient to serve four females. That the remaining hundred thousand may, at a year old, be offered in sale to the persons of quality and fortune through the kingdom; always advising the mother to let them suck plentifully in the last month, so as to render them plump and fat for a good table. A child will make two dishes at an entertainment for friends; and when the family dines alone, the fore or hind quarter will make a reasonable dish, and seasoned with a little pepper or salt will be very good boiled on the fourth day, especially in winter.

11   I have reckoned upon a medium that a child just born will weigh twelve pounds, and in a solar year, if tolerably nursed, will increase to twenty-eight pounds.

12   I grant this food will be somewhat dear, and therefore very proper for landlords, who, as they have already devoured most of the parents, seem to have the best title to the children.

13   Infant's flesh will be in season throughout the year, but more plentifully in March, and a little before and after: for we are told by a grave author, an eminent French physician,[6] that fish being a prolific diet, there are more children born in Roman Catholic countries about nine months after Lent than at any other season; therefore, reckoning a year after Lent, the markets will be more glutted than usual, because the number of popish infants is at least three to one in this kingdom: and therefore it will have one other collateral advantage, by lessening the number of papists among us.

14   I have already computed the charge of nursing a beggar's child (in which list I reckon all cottagers, laborers, and four-fifths of the farmers) to be about

---

[5] *ragout:* (ra gü´), a highly seasoned meat stew.

[6] *grave author . . . physician:* François Rabelais (c. 1494–1553), who was anything but a "grave author."

two shillings per annum, rags included; and I believe no gentleman would repine to give ten shillings for the carcass of a good fat child, which, as I have said, will make four dishes of excellent nutritive meat, when he has only some particular friend or his own family to dine with him. Thus the squire will learn to be a good landlord and grow popular among his tenants; the mother will have eight shillings net profit and be fit for work till she produces another child.

15   Those who are more thrifty (as I must confess the times require) may flay the carcass; the skin of which artificially[7] dressed will make admirable gloves for ladies and summer boots for fine gentlemen.

16   As to our city of Dublin, shambles[8] may be appointed for this purpose in the most convenient parts of it, and butchers we may be assured will not be wanting; although I rather recommend buying the children alive and dressing them hot from the knife as we do roasting pigs.

17   A very worthy person, a true lover of his country, and whose virtues I highly esteem, was lately pleased, in discoursing on this matter, to offer a refinement upon my scheme. He said that many gentlemen of this kingdom, having of late destroyed their deer, he conceived that the want of venison might be well supplied by the bodies of young lads and maidens, not exceeding fourteen years of age nor under twelve; so great a number of both sexes in every country being now ready to starve for want of work and service; and these to be disposed of by their parents, if alive, or otherwise by their nearest relations. But with due deference to so excellent a friend and so deserving a patriot, I cannot be altogether in his sentiments; for as to the males, my American acquaintance assured me from frequent experience that their flesh was generally tough and lean, like that of our schoolboys, by continual exercise, and their taste disagreeable; and to fatten them would not answer the charge. Then as to the females, it would, I think, with humble submission be a loss to the public, because they soon would become breeders themselves: and besides, it is not improbable that some scrupulous people might be apt to censure such a practice (although indeed very unjustly), as a little bordering upon cruelty; which, I confess, has always been with me the strongest objection against any project, how well soever intended.

18   But in order to justify my friend, he confessed that this expedient was put into his head by the famous Psalmanazar,[9] a native of the island Formosa, who came from thence to London above twenty years ago: and in conversation told my friend that in his country when any young person happened to be put to death, the executioner sold the carcass to persons of quality as a prime dainty; and that in his time the body of a plump girl of fifteen, who was crucified for an attempt to poison the emperor, was sold to his imperial majesty's prime minister of state, and other great mandarins of the court, in joints from the gibbet, at four hundred

---

[7] *artificially*: artfully: skillfully.

[8] *shambles*: slaughterhouses.

[9] *Psalmanazar*: the imposter George Psalmanazar (c. 1679–1763), a Frenchman who passed himself off in England as a Formosan, and wrote a totally fictional "true" account of Formosa, in which he described cannibalism.

crowns. Neither indeed can I deny that if the same use were made of several plump girls in this town, who, without one single groat to their fortunes, cannot stir abroad without a chair, and appear at a playhouse and assemblies in foreign fineries which they never will pay for, the kingdom would not be the worse.

19   Some persons of a desponding spirit are in great concern about that vast number of poor people who are aged, diseased, or maimed; and I have been desired to employ my thoughts, what course may be taken to ease the nation of so grievous an encumbrance. But I am not in the least pain upon that matter, because it is very well known that they are every day dying and rotting, by cold and famine, and filth and vermin, as fast as can be reasonably expected. And as to the young laborers, they are now in almost as hopeful a condition: they cannot get work, and consequently pine away for want of nourishment to a degree that if at any time they are accidentally hired to common labor, they have not strength to perform it; and thus the country and themselves are happily delivered from the evils to come.

20   I have too long digressed and therefore shall return to my subject. I think the advantages, by the proposal which I have made, are obvious and many, as well as of the highest importance.

21   For first, as I have already observed, it would greatly lessen the number of papists, with whom we are yearly overrun, being the principal breeders of the nation, as well as our most dangerous enemies; and who stay at home on purpose to deliver the kingdom to the Pretender, hoping to take their advantage by the absence of so many good Protestants, who have chosen rather to leave their country than stay at home and pay tithes against their conscience to an Episcopal curate.[10]

22   Secondly, the poorer tenants will have something valuable of their own, which by law may be made liable to distress,[11] and help to pay their landlord's rent; their corn and cattle being already seized, and money a thing unknown.

23   Thirdly, whereas the maintenance of a hundred thousand children, from two years old and upwards, cannot be computed at less than ten shillings a piece per annum, the nation's stock will be thereby increased fifty thousand pounds per annum, beside the profit of a new dish introduced to the tables of all gentlemen of fortune in the kingdom who have any refinement in taste. And the money will circulate among ourselves, the goods being entirely of our own growth and manufacture.

24   Fourthly, the constant breeders, besides the gain of eight shillings sterling per annum by the sale of their children, will be rid of the charge of maintaining them after the first year.

25   Fifthly, this food would likewise bring great custom to taverns: where the vintners will certainly be so prudent as to procure the best receipts for dressing it to perfection, and consequently have their houses frequented by all the fine

---

[10] *Protestants . . . curate*: Swift is here attacking the absentee landlords.

[11] *distress*: distraint, the legal seizure of property for payment of debts.

gentlemen, who justly value themselves upon their knowledge in good eating: and a skilful cook, who understands how to oblige his guests, will contrive to make it as expensive as they please.

26   Sixthly, this would be a great inducement to marriage, which all wise nations have either encouraged by rewards or enforced by laws and penalties. It would increase the care and tenderness of mothers toward their children, when they were sure of a settlement for life to the poor babes, provided in some sort by the public, to their annual profit instead of expense. We should see an honest emulation among the married women, which of them could bring the fattest child to the market. Men would become as fond of their wives during the time of their pregnancy as they are now of their mares in foal, their cows in calf, or sows when they are ready to farrow; nor offer to beat or kick them (as is too frequent a practice) for fear of a miscarriage.

27   Many other advantages might be enumerated. For instance, the addition of some thousand carcasses in our exportation of barreled beef, the propagation of swine's flesh, and improvement in the art of making good bacon, so much wanted among us by the great destruction of pigs, too frequent at our tables; which are no way comparable in taste or magnificence to a well-grown, fat, yearling child, which roasted whole will make a considerable figure at a lord mayor's feast, or any other public entertainment. But this and many others I omit, being studious of brevity.

28   Supposing that one thousand families in this city would be constant customers for infants' flesh, besides others who might have it at merry meetings, particularly weddings and christenings, I compute that Dublin would take off annually about twenty thousand carcasses, and the rest of the kingdom (where probably they will be sold somewhat cheaper) the remaining eighty thousand.

29   I can think of no one objection that will possibly be raised against this proposal, unless it should be urged that the number of people will be thereby much lessened in the kingdom. This I freely own, and it was indeed one principal design in offering it to the world. I desire the reader will observe that I calculate my remedy for this one individual kingdom of Ireland, and for no other that ever was, is, or, I think, ever can be upon earth. Therefore let no man talk to me of other expedients: of taxing our absentees at five shillings a pound: of using neither clothes nor household furniture, except what is of our own growth and manufacture: of utterly rejecting the materials and instruments that promote foreign luxury: of curing the expensiveness of pride, vanity, idleness, and gaming in our women: of introducing a vein of parsimony, prudence, and temperance: of learning to love our country, in the want of which we differ even from Laplanders and the inhabitants of Topinamboo:[12] of quitting our animosities and factions, nor acting any longer like the Jews, who were murdering

---

[12] *Topinamboo*: a savage area of Brazil.

one another at the very moment their city was taken[13] of being a little cautious not to sell our country and conscience for nothing: of teaching landlords to have at least one degree of mercy toward their tenants: lastly, of putting a spirit of honesty, industry, and skill into our shopkeepers; who, if a resolution could now be taken to buy only our native goods, would immediately unite to cheat and exact upon us in the price, the measure, and the goodness, nor could ever yet be brought to make one fair proposal of just dealing, though often and earnestly invited to it.[14]

30   Therefore, I repeat, let no man talk to me of these and the like expedients, till he has at least some glimpse of hope that there will ever be some hearty and sincere attempt to put them in practice.

31   But as to myself, having been wearied out for many years with offering vain, idle, visionary thoughts, and at length utterly despairing of success, I fortunately fell upon this proposal; which, as it is wholly new, so it has something solid and real, of no expense and little trouble, full in our own power, and whereby we can incur no danger in disobliging England. For this kind of commodity will not bear exportation, the flesh being of too tender a consistence to admit a long continuance in salt, although perhaps I could name a country which would be glad to eat up our whole nation without it.[15]

32   After all, I am not so violently bent upon my own opinion as to reject any offer proposed by wise men, which shall be found equally innocent, cheap, easy, and effectual. But before something of that kind shall be advanced in contradiction to my scheme, and offering a better, I desire the author or authors will be pleased maturely to consider two points. First, as things now stand, how they will be able to find food and raiment for an hundred thousand useless mouths and backs. And, secondly, there being a round million of creatures in human figure throughout this kingdom, whose whole subsistence put into a common stock would leave them in debt two millions of pounds sterling, adding those who are beggars by profession to the bulk of farmers, cottagers, and laborers, with their wives and children, who are beggars in effect; I desire those politicians, who dislike my overture, and may perhaps be so bold as to attempt an answer, that they will first ask the parents of these mortals, whether they would not at this day think it a great happiness to have been sold for food at a year old in the manner I prescribe, and thereby have avoided such a perpetual scene of misfortunes as they have since gone through by the oppression of landlords, the impossibility of paying rent without money or trade, the want of common sustenance, with neither house nor clothes to cover them from the inclemencies of the weather, and the most inevitable prospect of entailing the like or greater miseries upon their breed for ever.

---

[13] *city was taken*: While the Roman Emperor Titus was besieging Jerusalem, which he took and destroyed in A.D. 70, within the city factions of fanatics were waging bloody warfare.

[14] *invited to it*: Swift had already made all these proposals in various pamphlets.

[15] *a country . . . without it*: England; this is another way of saying, "The English are devouring the Irish."

33   I profess, in the sincerity of my heart, that I have not the least personal interest in endeavoring to promote this necessary work, having no other motive than the public good of my country, by advancing our trade, providing for infants, relieving the poor, and giving some pleasure to the rich. I have no children by which I can propose to get a single penny; the youngest being nine years old, and my wife past childbearing.

■ ■ ▨

MEANING

1. How would you characterize the narrator, and what does he propose as a solution to overpopulation and poverty in Ireland?

2. Who are the principle targets of this satire? To what extent does Swift criticize the Irish for not doing enough to help themselves?

3. What advantages would this proposal, if accepted, produce?

4. When did you realize that Swift is being ironic and not literal? What purpose is his essay designed to achieve?

TECHNIQUE

1. How does Swift use **description** to establish the nature of the problem?

2. How does Swift use **process analysis** to explain how the narrator's scheme would work?

3. How does Swift use **causal analysis** to emphasize the benefits the scheme would produce?

4. How does the narrator blend both reasons and evidence in his **argument**? For example, where does he use mathematical calculations to enhance his credibility? What function do paragraphs 29–32 serve?

LANGUAGE

1. What effect does Swift achieve by having his narrator present himself as analytical in paragraph 4 and describe his proposal as "modest"?

2. What does Swift seek to accomplish by applying terms to the Irish that are usually applied to breeding, butchering, and serving farm animals for food?

3. What are some of the shocking details about life in Ireland that the narrator casually reveals, and how do these strengthen Swift's satire?

4. If you don't know the meanings of the following words, look them up: *importuning* (1), *alms* (1), *sustenance* (1), *prodigious* (2), *commonwealth* (2), *computation* (4), *raiment* (4), *rudiments* (6), *probationers* (6), *nutriment* (7), *fricassee* (9), *repine* (14), *flay* (15), *scrupulous* (17), *censure* (17), *mandarins* (18), *desponding* (19), *encumbrance* (19), *tithes* (21), *vintners* (25), *emulation* (26), *farrow* (26), *expedients* (29), *parsimony* (29), *temperance* (29), *disobliging* (31), *consistence* (31), *inclemencies* (32).

Suggestions for Writing

1. **Critical Writing.** Create your own ironic and satiric "modest proposal" (using understatement and skewed statistics) for a contemporary problem, such as childhood obesity or overpaid athletes.

2. How do contemporary social satirists such as Jon Stewart or Steven Colbert (*The Colbert Report*) use Swift's tongue-in-cheek approach to address serious social issues?

3. Argue against a proposal offered by the government, a business, or your school that seems to you as preposterous as Swift's solution.

4. **Thematic Links:** How do Swift and Jessica Mitford in "Mortuary Solaces" (Chapter 7, "Process Analysis") use irony and satire in their respective works?

GLOSSARY

abstract/concrete language   Describes ideas, concepts, or qualities rather than specific people, places, or things.

allusion   A brief reference in a literary work to a real or fictional person, place, thing, or event that the reader might be expected to recognize.

analogy   A comparison drawn between two basically different things that have some points in common, often used to explain a more complex idea in terms of a simpler and more familiar one. (See *metaphor* and *symbol.*)

analysis   A method of exposition that separates the subject into its component parts and explains their function and relationship within the framework of a particular subject.

argumentation   A process of reasoning and putting forth evidence to support an interpretation.

assumption   An idea or belief that is taken for granted. (See *warrant.*)

audience   The group of spectators, listeners, viewers, or readers that a performance or written work reaches.

cause and effect   A method of analysis that seeks to discover why something happened or will happen.

chronological   The arrangement of events in the order in which they occurred.

claim   The assertion that a writer wishes the audience to discover as the logical outcome of the case being presented.

classification and division   A method of sorting, grouping, collecting, and analyzing things by categories based on features shared by all members of a class or group. Division is a method of breaking down an entire whole into separate parts or sorting a group of items into nonoverlapping categories; arguments can use classification as part of the writer's analysis in making a case.

cliché   A timeworn expression that, through overuse, has lost its power to evoke concrete images, as in the phrase "cool as a cucumber."

coherence   The quality in writing that results from clear connections of the parts so that readers can understand the relationship of each part to the overall flow of ideas, achieved chiefly through transitions. (See *transitions.*)

comparison and contrast   A rhetorical technique for pointing out similarities or differences; writers may use a point-by-point or subject-by-subject approach.

conclusion   The end or closing; the last main division of a discourse, usually containing a summation and a statement of opinion or decisions reached.

concrete   Pertaining to actual things, instances, or experiences. (See *abstract.*)

connotation   The emotional implications that a word suggests, as opposed to its literal meaning. The word *fireplace*, for example, might connote feelings of warmth, hospitality, and comfort, whereas it denotes the portion of a chimney in which fuel is burned. (See *denotation*.)

critical thinking, reading, and writing   Interrelated skills that identify and question assumptions and evaluate the strategies the writer uses.

culture   The totality of practices and institutions and the entire way of life of the people who produce them. In a narrow sense, specific aesthetic productions of literature, art, and music.

deductive reasoning   A form of argument that applies a set of principles to specific cases and draws logical conclusions.

definition   A method for specifying the basic nature of any phenomenon, idea, or thing. Dictionaries place the subject to be defined in the context of the general class to which it belongs and give distinguishing features that differentiate it from other things in its class.

denotation   The explicit, primary, or literal meaning of a word as found in the dictionary, as distinct from its associative meanings. (See *connotation*.)

description   Writing that reports how a person, place, or thing is perceived by the senses. *Objective* description recreates the appearance of objects, events, scenes, or people. *Subjective* description emphasizes the writer's feelings and reactions to a subject.

diction   The choice of words in a written work or spoken statement. An element of style that is important to the work's effectiveness. (See *style, tone, connotation,* and *denotation*.)

dominant impression   The main idea or central focus that the writer communicates by using description.

drafting   A preliminary phase of the writing process in which the writer formulates ideas in sentences and connects them through a pattern of organization.

essay   A relatively brief prose discussion on a particular theme or subject.

euphemism   From the Greek phrase meaning "to speak well of" or "to use words of good omen"; the substitution of an inoffensive indirect or agreeable expression for a word or phrase that would be perceived as socially unacceptable or unnecessarily harsh. For example, in Victorian times, undergarments were called "unmentionables," and the birth of a baby was referred to as the "arrival of the little stranger."

evidence   All material, including testimony of experts, statistics, cases (whether real, hypothetical, or analogical), and reasons brought forward to support a claim.

examples   Specific incidents that clarify, illustrate, or support a writer's thesis or claim.

fallacies   Errors of pseudo-reasoning caused by incorrect interpretations of evidence and incorrectly drawn inferences.

figurative language   The use of words outside their literal or usual meanings, used to add freshness and to suggest associations and comparisons that create effective images; includes figures of speech such as hyperbole, irony, metaphor, personification, simile, and synechdoche.

flashback   An interruption in the major action of a story or essay to show an episode that happened at an earlier time, used to shed light on characters and events in the present by providing background information.

hyperbole A figure of speech involving great exaggeration, used to emphasize strong feeling and to create a satiric or comic effect, not intended to be taken literally ("to wait an eternity").

image The use of a word or phrase to convey sensory experience that may be literal ("he ate many sardines") or figurative ("the passengers were packed together like many sardines").

inductive reasoning A form of argument that draws inferences from particular cases to support a generalization.

inference The term used to refer to a conclusion that is reached through inductive reasoning that is speculative rather than logically certain.

introduction A preliminary part (as of a book) leading to the main part. The function of the introduction is to engage the reader in the central issue and present the thesis regarding the question at hand.

irony, ironic (from the Greek *eiron*, a stock comic character who misled his listeners) A contrast between appearance and reality, what is and what ought to be. *Situational irony* is produced by incongruous circumstances in which what occurs is the opposite of what would be expected. *Verbal irony* is the contrast between what is said and what is actually meant, frequently used as a device in satire.

jargon The specialized language used by particular academic fields, trades, or professions (for example, medical jargon) that provides a shorthand method of quick communication that is not readily understood by the general public.

journal writing A method of recording ideas based on readings and writing about them.

metaphor A figure of speech that implies comparison between two fundamentally different things without the use of "like" or "as." It works by ascribing the qualities of one to the other, linking different meanings together, such as abstract and concrete and literal and figurative. (See *figurative language.*)

narration A true or made-up story that relates events and/or experiences. Narrations tell what happened, when it happened, and to whom; relate events from a consistent point of view; organize a story with a clear beginning, middle, and end; and use events and incidents to dramatize important moments in the action.

narrator Refers to the ostensible teller of a story, who may be a character in the story or an anonymous voice outside the story who relates events in the third person. (See *point of view.*)

organization The order of presentation that best fulfills the writer's purpose; may be chronological, least familiar to most familiar, simple to complex, or arranged according to some other rhetorical principle (such as comparison and contrast, classification, definition, cause and effect, process analysis, and problem solution).

outlining Creating an organized idea map before writing a first draft. May be formal or informal.

paradox A seemingly self-contradictory statement that may nevertheless be true.

parallelism The expression of similar or related ideas in similar grammatical form in order to highlight these ideas and give them greater force.

paraphrase The process of rewriting an original sentence or paragraph using your own words to convey an idea and supporting details that you use as evidence in your essay.

personification   A figure of speech that endows abstractions, ideas, animals, or inanimate objects with human characteristics.

persuasion   The winning of the acceptance of a claim achieved through the combined effects of the audience's confidence in the speaker's character, appeals to reason, and the audience's emotional needs and values.

plagiarism   Using someone's words or ideas without giving proper credit.

point of view   The perspective from which the events in a story are related; a story may be related in either the first person ("I") or the third person ("he," "she," or "they"). A first-person *narrator* is a character who tells the story that he or she participated in or directly observed. The observations and inferences of such a narrator may be reliable, as far as they go, or unreliable. A third-person *omniscient narrator* stands outside the events of the story but allows the reader unlimited access to the characters' thoughts and feelings and may comment on the story or characters.

premise   An assumption from which deductive reasoning proceeds in an argument.

problem solving   A process that writers use to identify problems, search for solutions, and verify them; an indispensable part of all academic and professional research. An argument that proposes a solution will often incorporate problem solving.

process analysis   A method of clarifying the nature of something by explaining how it works in separate, easy-to-understand steps.

proofreading   The final stage in the writing process in order to catch errors in spelling, grammar, and punctuation, or typographical errors.

purpose   The writer's objective; also, the goals of the four types of prose writing: narration (to tell or relate), description (to represent or delineate), exposition (to explain or clarify), and argument (to persuade).

quotation   Reproducing the exact words of a source enclosed in quotation marks as evidence in an essay or research paper.

revision   A phase of the writing process in which one first corrects major problems that require redrafting, reorganization, and adding or deleting material and then correcting errors within paragraphs, transitions between paragraphs, and errors at the sentence level.

rhetoric   In ancient Greece and Rome, the art of using language to influence or persuade others. Today, the term also refers to the specialized literary uses of language to express oneself effectively and the study of elements of visual persuasion as well.

rhetorical question   A question that is asked solely to produce an effect and not to elicit a reply.

satire   A technique that ridicules both people and societal institutions, often in an effort to bring about social reform. Exaggeration, wit, and irony are devices frequently used by satirists.

simile   A figure of speech involving a direct comparison between two unlike things and using the words "like" or "as." For example, "passengers crammed *like* sardines in a can." (See *metaphor*.)

slang   Very informal usage in vocabulary and idiom that is characteristically more metaphorical, playful, elliptical, vivid, and ephemeral than ordinary language.

style   The author's characteristic manner of expression. Style includes the types of words used, their placement, as well as the distinctive features of tone, imagery, figurative language, sound, and rhythm.

summary   An abstract or condensed version of the original that preserves the ideas of the original but reduces it to its essential points with evaluations or commentaries.

support   In argument, all the evidence the writer brings forward to enhance the probability of a claim being accepted; can include evidence in the form of summary, paraphrases, quotes drawn from the text, examples from personal experience, hypothetical cases, the testimony of experts, appeals to the audience's emotions and values, and the writer's own character or personality.

suspense   The feeling of psychological tension experienced by the reader or spectator in anticipation of learning the outcome of a developing sequence of events.

syllogism   A classic form of deductive reasoning illustrating the relationship between a major and minor premise and a conclusion in which the validity of a particular case is drawn from statements that are assumed to be true or self-evident.

symbol   Something concrete, such as an object, person, place, or event, that stands for or represents something abstract, such as an idea, quality, concept, or condition.

thesis   The position taken by a writer, often expressed in a single sentence, that an essay develops or supports. (See *claim.*)

tone   The writer's attitude toward the subject, expressed in style and word choice; the voice the writer chooses to project—for example, serious, lighthearted, concerned—to relate to readers.

topic sentence   The sentence often beginning a paragraph that conveys the main idea that the paragraph develops.

transitions   A signal word or phrase that connects two sentences, paragraphs, or sections of an essay to produce coherence. Can include pronoun references, parallel clauses, conjunctions, restatements of key ideas, and terms such as "furthermore," "moreover," "by contrast," "therefore," "consequently," "accordingly," and "thus."

understatement   A form of verbal irony, often used for humorous effect, in which an opinion is expressed less emphatically than it might be. (See *irony.*)

voice   (See *tone.*)

warrant   According to Stephen Toulmin, a general statement that expresses implicit or explicit assumptions about how the agreed-upon facts of a particular case are connected to the claim or conclusion being offered.

CREDITS

Text Credits

Accawi, Anwar F., "The Telephone," first published in *The Sun*, English Language Institute, Knoxville, TN. Reprinted by permission of the author.

Ackerman, Diane, "The Social Sense," copyright © 1990 by Diane Ackerman, from *A Natural History of the Senses* by Diane Ackerman. Used by permission of Random House, Inc.

al-Shaykh, Hanan, "The Persian Carpet" from *Modern Arabic Short Stories*, trans. Denys Johnson-Davies, Three Continents Press, 1988. Reprinted by permission of Denys Johnson-Davies

Angelou, Maya, "Champion of the World," copyright © 1969 and renewed 1997 by Maya Angelou, from *I Know Why the Caged Bird Sings* by Maya Angelou. Used by permission of Random House, Inc.

Anzaldúa, Gloria, "How to Tame a Wild Tongue," from *Borderlands/La Frontera: The New Mestiza.* Copyright © 1987, 1999 by Gloria Anzaldúa. Reprinted by permission of Aunt Lute Books.

Baquero, Edison, "True Life: Life as a Gamer" by Edison Baquero, *New Comm Ave*, Boston College. Reprinted by permission of New Comm Ave.

Barber, Paul, "The Real Vampire" reprinted from *Natural History*, October 1990; copyright © Natural History Magazine, Inc. 1990

Britt, Suzanne, "That Lean and Hungry Look," *Newsweek*, October 9, 1978. Reprinted by permission of the author.

Bryant, Jr., Vaughn M. and Sylvia Grider, "To Kiss: Why We Kiss Under the Mistletoe at Christmas," WorldandIJournal.com. Reprinted by permission.

Bunn, Austin, "The Bittersweet Science" from *New York Times Magazine*, March 16, 2003. © 2003 by Austin Bunn. Reprinted by permission.

Burciaga, Jose Antonio, "Tortillas" (originally titled, "I Remember Masa") from *Weede Peepo*, Pan American University Press, Edinburgh, Texas. With permission from Cecilia P. Burciaga.

Cao, Guanlong, "Chopsticks" from *The Attic: A Memoir of a Chinese Landlord's Son* by Guanlong Cao, © 1996 by The Regents of the University of California. Published by the University of California Press.

Carroll, Raymonde, "Minor Accidents" from *Cultural Misunderstandings: The French-American Experience*, University of Chicago Press. Copyright © 1988 University of Chicago Press. Reprinted with permission.

Chapman, Stephen M., "The Prisoner's Dilemma," *The New Republic*, March 8, 1980. Reprinted by permission of The New Republic.

Chernin, Kim, pages 20–28 from *The Obsession: Reflections on the Tyranny of Slenderness* by Kim Chernin. Copyright © 1981 by Kim Chernin. Reprinted by permission of HarperCollins Publishers.

Cofer, Judith Ortiz, "The Myth of the Latin Woman: I Just Met a Girl Named Maria" from *The Latin Deli.* Reprinted by permission of The University of Georgia Press.

Counts, David R., "Too Many Bananas, Not Enough Pineapples, and No Watermelon at All: Three Object Lessons in Living with Reciprocity," from *The Humbled Anthropologist*, Wadsworth, 1990, pp. 18–24. Reprinted by permission of the author.

Dalai Lama, "The Role of Religion in Modern Society," from *Ethics for the New Millennium* by Dalai Lama and Alexander Norman, copyright © 1999 by His Holiness The Dalai Lama. Used by permission of Riverhead Books, an imprint of Penguin Group (USA) Inc.

de Assis, Joaquim Maria Machado, "A Canary's Ideas" from *The Devil's Church and Other Stories* by Joaquim Maria Machado de Assis, translated by Jack Schmitt and Lori Ishimatsu, Copyright © 1977. By permission of the University of Texas Press.

de Beauvoir, Simone, "The Married Woman" from *The Second Sex* by Simone de Beauvoir, translated by H. M. Parshley, copyright 1952 and renewed 1980 by Alfred A. Knopf, a division of Random House, Inc. Used by permission of Alfred A. Knopf, a division of Random House, Inc.

Deane, Daniela, "The Little Emperors," from the *Los Angeles Times Magazine*, July 26, 1993. Reprinted by permission of the author.

Denice, Christopher, "Emphasize Teaching, Not Technology" by Christopher Denice, *New Comm Ave*, Boston College. Reprinted by permission of New Comm Ave.

Durning, Alan Thein, "Asking How Much Is Enough" by Alan Durning, from *State of the World 1991: A Worldwatch Institute Report on Progress Toward a Sustainable Society* by Lester R. Brown, et al. Copyright © 1991 by the Worldwatch Institute. Used by permission of W.W. Norton & Company, Inc.

El Saadawi, Nawal, "Circumcision of Girls" from *The Hidden Face of Eve: Women in the Arab World*, trans. & ed by Sherif Hetata, pp. 33–43. Reprinted by permission of Zed Books, London & New York.

Ellis, C. P., "Why I Quit the Klan," from *American Dreams Lost and Found* by Studs Terkel, Pantheon. Reprinted by permission of Donadio & Olson, Inc. Copyright © 1980 Studs Terkel.

Evans, Keith, "An Academic Deficiency" by Keith Evans, *New Comm Ave*, Boston College. Reprinted by permission of New Comm Ave.

Fernea, Elizabeth W. and Robert A. Fernea, "A Look Behind the Veil," *Human Nature Magazine*, January 1978, Volume 2, Number 1, pp. 164–68. Used with permission of the authors.

Fost, Norman C., "Ethical and Social Issues in Antidoping Strategies in Sports," in F. Landry, M. Yerles (eds.), *Sport . . . The Third Millennium*, Québec, Les Presses de l'Université Laval, 1991, pp. 479–85. Reprinted by permission.

Frost, Robert, "The Road Not Taken" from *The Poetry of Robert Frost* edited by Edward Connery Lathem. Copyright 1969 by Henry Holt and Company. Reprinted by permission of Henry Holt and Company, LLC.

Ghinsberg, Yossi, "Jungle" from *Jungle*, Greenleaf Book Group LP, pp. 140–42. Reprinted by permission of Yossi Ghinsberg.

Granderson, Peter, "Iwakuni: Truly Unique" from *The Atu Writer*. Reprinted by permission of the author.

Grealy, Lucy, "The Habits of Self-Consciousness" from *Autobiography of a Face* by Lucy Grealy. Copyright © 1994 by Lucy Grealy. Reprinted by permission of Houghton Mifflin Company. All rights reserved.

Grunewald, Carol, "Monsters of the Brave New World," *The New Internationalist Ltd.*, Jan. 1991, Issue #215. Reprinted by kind permission of the New Internationalist. Copyright New Internationalist.

Hanel, Megan, "Mediocre Media" by Megan Hanel from *New Comm Ave*, Boston College. Reprinted by permission of New Comm Ave.

Sheraton, Mimi, excerpt from pp. 199–203 from *Eating My Words* by Mimi Sheraton. Copyright © 2004 by Mimi Sheraton. Reprinted by permission of HarperCollins Publishers.

Skinner, Joseph K., "Big Mac and the Tropical Forests," *Monthly Review Press*, December 1, 1985. Copyright © 1985 by Monthly Review Press. Reprinted by permission of Monthly Review Foundation.

Soseki, Natsume, "I Am A Cat" from *I Am A Cat*, Putnam, 1982. Trans. by Katsue Shibata & Motonari Kai, pp. 1–15. Reprinted by permission of Peter Owen Publishers, London.

Tan, Amy, "Mother Tongue." Copyright © 1990 by Amy Tan. First appeared in *The Three Penny Review*. Reprinted by permission of the author and the Sandra Dijkstra Literary Agency.

Turnbull, Colin, from *The Mbuti Pygmies: Change and Adaptation*, 1st ed., by Colin Turnbull, 1983. Reprinted with permission of Wadsworth, a division of Thomson Learning: www.thomsonrights.com. Fax 800-730-2215.

Urrea, Luis Alberto, "Nobody's Son" from *Across the Wire: Life & Hard Times* by Luis Alberto Urrea, copyright © 1993 by Luis Alberto Urrea. Photographs © 1993 by John Lueders-Booth. Used by permission of Doubleday, a division of Random House, Inc.

Valenzuela, Luisa, "The Censors," trans. David Unger. Copyright 1982 by David Unger. Reprinted by permission of David Unger and Luisa Valenzuela.

Visser, Margaret, "Fingers" from *The Rituals of Dinner*. Copyright © 1991 by Margaret Visser. Used by permission of Grove/Atlantic, Inc.

Yalom, Marilyn, pages 386–400 from *A History of the Wife* by Marilyn Yalom. Copyright © 2001 by Marilyn Yalom. Reprinted by permission of HarperCollins Publishers.

Zamyatin, Evgeny, "The Lion" from *The Penguin Book of Russian Short Stories*, 1988. Trans. David Richards, 1989. Reprinted by permission of David Richards.

Photo Credits

10 © Danny Lehman/Corbis; 71 © Bettmann/Corbis; 78 © Eva-Lotta Jansson/Corbis; 109 © Hilary B. Price. King Features Syndicate; 137 © Reinhard Krause/Reuters/Corbis; 144 © Paul Almasy/Corbis; 184 © David Gray/Reuters/Corbis; 216 © Sean Justice/Corbis; 255 © Bettmann/Corbis; 335 © Wendy Stone/Corbis; 349 © Catherine Karnow/Corbis; 376 © Bettmann/Corbis; 382 © Lucien Aigner/Corbis; 397 © Hulton-Deutsch Collection/Corbis; 414 © Contemporary African Art Collection Limited/Corbis; 440 © Bettmann/Corbis; 460 © William Campbell/Sygma/Corbis; 504 © Bloomimage/Corbis; 568 © Bettmann/Corbis; 645 © Daniele LaMonaca/Reuters/Corbis; 716 Courtesy of Chris Britt and Copley News Service; 729 © Bettmann/Corbis; 746 © Bettmann/Corbis; A-1 © Fayaz Kabli/Reuters/Corbis; A-2 © Noshir Desai/Corbis; A-3 © Giuseppe Dall'Arche/Grand Tour/Corbis; A-4 © Ric Ergenbright/Corbis; A-5 © Nik Wheeler/Corbis; A-6 http://commons.wikimedia.org; A-7 © Bil Keane, Inc. King Features Syndicate; A-8 © Bettmann/Corbis; B-1 © Francois Duhamel/Universal Studios/Bureau L.A. Collection/Corbis; B-2 © Philip Gould/Corbis; B-3 © Ted Spiegel/Corbis; B-4 © Anna Clopet/Corbis; B-5 © Scott Speakes/Corbis; B-6 © Karen Kasmauski/Corbis; B-7 © Royalty-Free/Corbis; B-8 © Strauss/Curtis/Corbis; C-1 © Archivo Iconografico, S.A./Corbis; C-2 © Reuters/Corbis; C-3 © Kazuyoshi Nomachi/Corbis; C-4 © Karen Kasmauski/Corbis; C-5 © Wolfgang Kaehler/Corbis; C-6 © Peter Dazeley/zefa/Corbis; C-7 Courtesy of In the Shadow of No Towers, Art Spiegelman, Viking, 2004, Random House.; C-8 © Lucy Pemoni/Reuters/Corbis

Index